MCSE Exam Objectives
Exam 70-227: Installing, Configuring, and Administering Microsoft Internet Security and Acceleration (ISA) Server

Installing ISA Server	
Preconfigure network interfaces	
• Verify Internet connectivity before installing ISA Server and verify	
Install ISA Server. Installation modes include Integrated, Firewall, and	
• Construct and modify the local address table (LAT), calculate the size of the cache and configure it, and install an ISA Server computer as a member of an array.	3
Upgrade a Microsoft Proxy Server 2.0 computer to ISA Server.	4
• Back up the Proxy Server 2.0 configuration.	4
Troubleshoot problems that occur during setup.	3

Configuring and Troubleshooting ISA Server Services	Chapter
Configure and troubleshoot outbound Internet access.	15
Configure ISA Server hosting roles.	15
• Configure ISA Server for Web publishing, for server proxy, and for server publishing.	15
Configure H.323 Gatekeeper for audio and video conferencing.	11
• Configure gatekeeper rules. Rules include telephone, email, and Internet Protocol (IP).	11
• Configure gatekeeper destinations by using the Add Destination Wizard.	11
Set up and troubleshoot dial-up connections and Routing And Remote Access dial-on-demand connections.	15
• Set up and verify routing rules for static IP routes in Routing And Remote Access.	15
Configure and troubleshoot virtual private network (VPN) access.	16
• Configure the ISA Server computer as a VPN endpoint without using the VPN Wizard.	16
• Configure the ISA Server computer for VPN pass-through.	16
Configure multiple ISA Server computers for scalability. Configurations include network load balancing (NLB) and Cache Array Routing Protocol (CARP).	8

Configuring, Managing, and Troubleshooting Policies and Rules	Chapter
Configure and secure the firewall in accordance with corporate standards.	10
• Configure the packet filters for different levels of security, including system hardening.	6
Create and configure access control and bandwidth policies.	6
• Create and configure site and content rules to restrict Internet access, protocol rules to manage Internet access, routing rules to restrict Internet access, and bandwidth rules to control bandwidth usage.	6
Troubleshoot user-based and packet-based access problems.	15
Create new policy elements. Elements include schedules, bandwidth priorities, destination sets, client address sets, protocol definitions, and content groups.	6
Manage ISA Server arrays in an enterprise	14
• Create an array of proxy servers, and assign an enterprise policy to an array.	14

Deploying, Configuring, and Troubleshooting the Client Computer	Chapter
Plan the deployment of client computers to use ISA Server services. Considerations include client authentication, client operating system, network topology, cost, complexity, and client function.	15
Configure and troubleshoot the client computer for secure network address translation (SecureNAT).	15
Install the Firewall client software. Considerations include the cost and complexity of deployment.	15
• Troubleshoot AutoDetection.	5
Configure the client computer's Web browser to use ISA Server as an HTTP proxy.	9

Monitoring, Managing, and Analyzing ISA Server Use	Chapter
Monitor security and network usage by using logging and alerting.	15
• Configure intrusion detection and alert to send an email message to an administrator.	15
• Automate alert configuration and monitor alert status.	15
Troubleshoot problems with security and network usage.	15
• Detect connections by using Netstat and test the status of external ports by using Telnet or Network Monitor.	15
Analyze the performance of ISA Server by using reports. Report types include summary, Web usage, application usage, traffic and utilization, and security.	15
Optimize the performance of the ISA Server computer. Considerations include capacity planning, allocation priorities, and trend analysis.	15
• Analyze the performance of the ISA Server computer by using Performance Monitor, reporting, and logging, and control the total RAM used by ISA Server for caching.	8

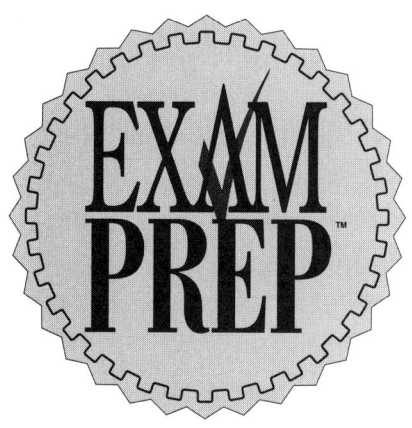

MCSE™
ISA Server 2000

Kim Simmons
Masaru Ryumae

MCSE™ ISA Server 2000 Exam Prep

© 2001 The Coriolis Group. All rights reserved.

This book may not be duplicated in any way without the express written consent of the publisher, except in the form of brief excerpts or quotations for the purposes of review. The information contained herein is for the personal use of the reader and may not be incorporated in any commercial programs, other books, databases, or any kind of software without written consent of the publisher. Making copies of this book or any portion for any purpose other than your own is a violation of United States copyright laws.

Limits of Liability and Disclaimer of Warranty

The author and publisher of this book have used their best efforts in preparing the book and the programs contained in it. These efforts include the development, research, and testing of the theories and programs to determine their effectiveness. The author and publisher make no warranty of any kind, expressed or implied, with regard to these programs or the documentation contained in this book.

The author and publisher shall not be liable in the event of incidental or consequential damages in connection with, or arising out of, the furnishing, performance, or use of the programs, associated instructions, and/or claims of productivity gains.

Trademarks

Trademarked names appear throughout this book. Rather than list the names and entities that own the trademarks or insert a trademark symbol with each mention of the trademarked name, the publisher states that it is using the names for editorial purposes only and to the benefit of the trademark owner, with no intention of infringing upon that trademark.

The Coriolis Group, LLC
14455 N. Hayden Road, Suite 220
Scottsdale, Arizona 85260

(480)483-0192
FAX (480)483-0193
www.coriolis.com

Library of Congress Cataloging-in-Publication Data
Simmons, Kim
    MCSE ISA server 2000/by Kimberly Simmons and Masaru Ryumae.
      p. cm. -- (Exam Prep)
    ISBN 1-57610-957-7
    1. Electronic data processing personnel--Certification. 2. Microsoft software--Examinations--Study guides. 3. Client/server computing--Examinations--Study guides. 4. Microsoft ISA server. I. Ryumae, Masaru. II. Title. III. Series.
    QA76.3.S475 2001
    005.7'13769--dc21   2001028458

Printed in the United States of America
10 9 8 7 6 5 4 3 2 1

President and CEO
Keith Weiskamp

Publisher
Steve Sayre

Acquisitions Editor
Lee Anderson

Product Marketing Manager
Brett Woolley

Project Editor
Karen Swartz

Technical Reviewer
Deniss Suhanovs

Production Coordinator
Carla J. Schuder

Cover Designer
Jesse Dunn

Layout Designer
April Nielsen

CD-ROM Developer
Chris Nusbaum

The Coriolis Group, LLC • 14455 North Hayden Road, Suite 720 • Scottsdale, Arizona 85260

ExamCram.com Connects You to the Ultimate Study Center!

Our goal has always been to provide you with the best study tools on the planet to help you achieve your certification in record time. Time is so valuable these days that none of us can afford to waste a second of it, especially when it comes to exam preparation.

Over the past few years, we've created an extensive line of *Exam Cram* and *Exam Prep* study guides, practice exams, and interactive training. To help you study even better, we have now created an e-learning and certification destination called **ExamCram.com**. (You can access the site at **www.examcram.com**.) Now, with every study product you purchase from us, you'll be connected to a large community of people like yourself who are actively studying for their certifications, developing their careers, seeking advice, and sharing their insights and stories.

I believe that the future is all about collaborative learning. Our **ExamCram.com** destination is our approach to creating a highly interactive, easily accessible collaborative environment, where you can take practice exams and discuss your experiences with others, sign up for features like "Questions of the Day," plan your certifications using our interactive planners, create your own personal study pages, and keep up with all of the latest study tips and techniques.

I hope that whatever study products you purchase from us—*Exam Cram* or *Exam Prep* study guides, *Personal Trainers*, *Personal Test Centers*, or one of our interactive Web courses—will make your studying fun and productive. Our commitment is to build the kind of learning tools that will allow you to study the way you want to, whenever you want to.

Visit ExamCram.com now to enhance your study program.

Help us continue to provide the very best certification study materials possible. Write us or email us at **learn@examcram.com** and let us know how our study products have helped you study. Tell us about new features that you'd like us to add. Send us a story about how we've helped you. We're listening!

Good luck with your certification exam and your career. Thank you for allowing us to help you achieve your goals.

Keith Weiskamp
President and CEO

Look for these other products from The Coriolis Group:

MCSE Exchange 2000 Administration Exam Prep
by Phillip Schein and Evan Benjamin

MCSE Exchange 2000 Design Exam Prep
by Michael Shannon

MCSE Migrating from NT4 to Windows 2000 Exam Prep
by Glen Bergen, Graham Leach and David Baldwin

MCSE Windows 2000 Directory Services Design Exam Prep
by J. Peter Bruzzese and Wayne Dipchan

MCSE Windows 2000 Network Design Exam Prep
by Geoffrey Alexander, Anoop Jalan and Joseph Alexander

MCSE Windows 2000 Security Design Exam Prep
by Richard McMahon and Glen Bicking

To Eddie, thanks for putting up with me.
—*Kim Simmons*

*This book is dedicated to my wife Kyong and my children, Rena and Ken,
in gratitude for all their love and support.*
—*Masaru Ryumae*

About the Authors

Kim Simmons earned MCSE, MCP+Internet, and MCT status in 1997. Some of her 13 certifications include development exams in support of her emphasis in Internet technologies. She is currently working at Microsoft developing materials for the Windows XP Resource Kit. She is also developing a postgraduate E-commerce IT Professional program for Alta Colleges. Kim has worked for MCI Systemhouse and EDS performing network architecture analysis and upgrade recommendations on a per project basis for outside companies. As a technical trainer teaching MCSE certification courses, she received corporate awards for being one of the top 15 and 50 trainers in the ExecuTrain Corporation national system. Before moving into technical training, Kim served in Saudi Arabia in support of the Gulf war doing engagement control using the PATRIOT missile system to search for SCUD missiles.

Kim doesn't have any spare time, but she spends her off teaching time with her 3 children and husband. Her goal is to develop a non-computer hobby someday.

Masaru Ryumae currently works at Agilent Technologies in Colorado Springs as a system administrator/system integrator. He was the main technical lead for deploying Windows 2000 domain controllers and WINS infrastructures worldwide for Agilent Technologies. He also heavily contributed to the Japan data center closure project, which included transitioning support of 100+ NT/HP-UX systems. He has worked at Lucent Technologies and MCI Systemhouse as an Internet application developer and NT network consultant. He serves as an adjunct professor at Colorado Technical University and National American University and is responsible for a Windows 2000 MCSE track. He also provides Internet consulting services to Fountain Valley School.

Masaru is a Windows 2000 Microsoft Certified Systems Engineer (MCSE), NT 4 Microsoft Certified Systems Engineer + Internet (MCSE+I), and Microsoft Certified Trainer (MCT). He received his double undergraduate degrees in Computer Science and Business Administration with an International Business and Marketing emphasis, and he holds a Master's degree in Telecommunications from the University of Colorado at Boulder. Masaru likes to spend his spare time with his wife and two children and tries to play an electric guitar so that he can stay away from computers. It has, however, been hard for him to find such time. Masaru was born in Yokohama, Japan. He spent most of his years in Yokosuka, Japan, and he has lived with his family in Colorado Springs for the last 8 years.

Acknowledgments

There are many people who helped make this book possible. As it turns out, a 600+ page book is a whole lot more work than a 300+ page book (who would have thought!) and I needed a lot of help to get it all done in time. Thanks so much to Masaru Ryumae for agreeing to coauthor the book with me. You are always positive and so easy to work with. Also, thanks to Gregory Smith for the sample test and answers as well as John Crockett for his work on Chapter 16 of the book. I never could have finished this book on time without your help. And most importantly thanks to my family for their patience during the worst of it. Now it's time for a vacation for all of us!
—*Kim Simmons*

It was just about six months ago when my coauthor, Kim Simmons, called and asked me if I would be interested in writing an ISA book. I was not sure how much time I could spend, but after all I was able to get my part done somehow. I have known Kim for the last three years or so, and we worked together for a time teaching at a local college. Kim is very knowledgeable in Internet-related technologies, and I am glad I was able to work with her to complete this book. Thanks! I also would like to show my appreciation to Karen Swartz at Coriolis for guidance when I was stuck. Finally, I cannot afford to ignore my family's support. Thank you, Kyong, Rena, and Ken for supporting me in this busy time. I would not have been able to complete the book without you guys!
—*Masaru Ryumae*

Contents at a Glance

Chapter 1   ISA Server 2000 Overview   1
Chapter 2   Preparing for ISA Server Installation   27
Chapter 3   Installing ISA Server 2000   55
Chapter 4   Upgrading from Proxy Server 2.0   87
Chapter 5   Planning and Deploying Clients   111
Chapter 6   Policies and Rules   141
Chapter 7   Authentication   179
Chapter 8   Caching and Acceleration   203
Chapter 9   Understanding the Web Proxy Service   241
Chapter 10   Securing the Internal Network   265
Chapter 11   Supporting Media Services   289
Chapter 12   Publishing Services   319
Chapter 13   Managing Multiple ISA Servers   353
Chapter 14   Integrating Services with ISA Server   385
Chapter 15   Troubleshooting and Reporting   411
Chapter 16   Setting Up External Client Connections   451
Chapter 17   Scenarios   487
Chapter 18   Sample Test   511
Chapter 19   Answer Key   535
Appendix A   Answers to Review Questions   549
Appendix B   Objectives for Exam [70-227]   575
Appendix C   TCP and UDP Port Assignments   577

Table of Contents

Exam Insights xxv

Self-Assessment liii

Chapter 1
ISA Server 2000 Overview 1

    Microsoft Proxy Server   2
        Not Just an Upgrade   3
    The .NET Platform   3
    Internet Connections   4
        The OSI Model   4
        TCP/IP Protocols   6
        Uniform Resource Locator   6
    Ports and Sockets   8
    Internet Security Basics   9
        When Is It a Firewall?   10
        When Is It a Proxy Server?   10
        If They Are So Different, Why Can't You Tell Them Apart?   12
    Connection Types   13
        Packet Level   13
        Circuit Level   13
        Application Level   14
    New Capabilities and Features   14
        Installation   14
        Administration   15
    ISA Server As a Firewall   15
    ISA Server As a Proxy   17
        Extensibility   18

xi

Chapter Summary 18
Review Questions 19
Real-World Projects 23

Chapter 2
Preparing for ISA Server Installation 27

Hardware Requirements 28
    Firewall Requirements 29
    Caching Requirements 29
Software Requirements 30
Clean Install or Upgrade (Migrate) from Proxy Server 2.0 31
ISA Server Mode 31
ISA Server Array 32
ISA Server Client Support 33
Final System Preparation before ISA Server Installation 36
    Hardware Configuration 36
    Software Configuration 37
Chapter Summary 42
Review Questions 43
Real-World Projects 47

Chapter 3
Installing ISA Server 2000 55

ISA Server Editions 56
    Hardware Support 56
Before the Installation 57
    Gathering the Necessary Information 57
    Setting Up a Network Installation Point 57
    Recent Software Updates 58
Installing ISA Server Enterprise Edition 59
    Installation Types 59
    Standalone or Array? 62
    Installation Mode 65
    Setting Up Disk Space for Caching 66
    Constructing the Local Address Table (LAT) 67

The ISA Server Getting Started Wizard 69
Unattended Installation 69
    Understanding Each Section 70
    Running the Unattended Installation File 72
Creating or Joining an Array During Installation 73
    Creating the First Array 73
    Joining an Array 74
    Upgrading a Standalone Enterprise Edition ISA Server to an Array Member 74
Installing the Standard Edition of ISA Server 75
Removing ISA Server 75
Chapter Summary 75
Review Questions 76
Real-World Projects 80

Chapter 4
Upgrading from Proxy Server 2.0 87

Proxy Server vs. ISA Server 88
Preparing for the Upgrade 88
    Protocol Configuration 88
    The Local Address Table 89
    Backing up a Proxy Server Configuration 89
Proxy on NT 4 90
    Stopping Services 90
    Performing the First Upgrade 92
    Upgrading to ISA Server 92
Upgrading from Proxy Server on Windows 2000 95
Upgrading a Proxy Server Array 95
Configuration Settings from Proxy Server to ISA Server 96
    Settings That You Don't Have to Reconfigure 96
    Settings That You Need to Reconfigure 97
Making the Administrative Change 98
Uninstalling ISA Server 99
Chapter Summary 100
Review Questions 101
Real-World Projects 105

Chapter 5
Planning and Deploying Clients 111

Client Types   112
    What Are You Trying to Do?   113
    The Web Proxy Client   113
    The Firewall Client   114
    The SecureNAT Client   116
    Socks   116
Client Differences   118
    Client Combinations   118
Web Proxy Client Setup   119
Firewall Client Setup   122
    Changes Made During the Installation of the Firewall Client   123
    Removing the Firewall Client   123
Configuring Firewall Client Files   123
    Configuring the Msplat.txt File   124
    Configuring the Mspclnt.ini File   124
    The Local Domain Table   126
Setup Needed for SecureNAT Clients   126
Socks Client Setup   127
    AutoDiscovery Setup   128
Assessing Client Needs   130
    Client Connection Needs   130
    Client Operating System Differences   131
    Security and Setup Needs   131
Chapter Summary   131
Review Questions   132
Real-World Projects   136

Chapter 6
Policies and Rules 141

Controlling Access with ISA Server   142
What Is a Policy?   143
    Enterprise vs. Array Policies   143

Do You Need a Policy?   144
    What Kind of Policy Can You Support?   144
How Rules Apply   144
Policy Elements   145
    Protocol Definitions   146
    Destination Sets   147
    Content Groups   149
    Client Address Sets   150
    Schedules   152
Using Protocol Rules   153
    Creating Protocol Rules   153
    Protocol Rule Order   155
Site and Content Rules   155
    How Site and Content Rules Are Applied   155
    Creating Site and Content Rules   156
Packet Filters   159
    Packet Filters Before   159
    Packet Filters Now   159
Bandwidth Rules   160
    Bandwidth Priorities   161
    Creating and Configuring Bandwidth Rules   162
    Ordering Rules   163
    Disabling or Deleting Rules   163
Planning Policies for a Network   164
    The Need for Paper Policies   164
    Will You Implement a Policy at the Enterprise, Array, or Standalone Level?   165
    Which Settings Do You Want to Control?   165
    Do You Need to Create Policy Elements?   165
    Creating and Testing Rules   166
Creating Enterprise Policies with Enterprise-Level Rules   166
Backing Up and Restoring Policy Settings   167
Chapter Summary   168
Review Questions   169
Real-World Projects   173

Chapter 7
Authentication 179

    Why Use Authentication?   180
    Types of Authentication   180
        Basic Authentication   180
        Digest Authentication   182
        Integrated Windows Authentication   183
        Certificates   184
    Authentication Pros and Cons   185
    Setting Up Authentication   186
        Listeners   186
        Configuring Authentication   186
        Editing Listeners to Change Authentication Requirements   189
    Passing Around Authentication Requests   189
        Using Pass-through Authentication   190
        Chained Authentication   190
    Combining Rules and Authentication   191
    Chapter Summary   191
    Review Questions   192
    Real-World Projects   197

Chapter 8
Caching and Acceleration 203

    Potential Issues   204
    What Is Caching?   205
    Understanding the Caching Process   207
    What Is CARP?   210
        CARP Benefits   211
        CARP Configuration   211
    Scheduled Cache Content Download   213
    Cache Chaining   214
    Web Proxy Routing   216
    Cache Filtering   218
    Tuning and Monitoring Cache Performance   219
        Tuning ISA Server   219
        Monitoring ISA Server   219

Chapter Summary 221
Review Questions 222
Real-World Projects 226

Chapter 9
Understanding the Web Proxy Service 241

What Is the Web Proxy Service? 242
Protocols Used by the Web Proxy Service 243
    HTTP and HTTP-S 243
    FTP 244
    Gopher 244
Clients for the Web Proxy Service 244
    CERN-Compliant Web Browsers 244
    HTTP Redirector Filter 244
How Does the Web Proxy Service Work? 245
    Extensions to the Web Proxy Service 246
Accessing Secured Web Pages through the Web Proxy Service 246
    SSL Components 247
    Establishing an Identity with Certificates 248
    Ports and Protocols 249
    The SSL Process 250
The Effect of ISA Server on Secure Web Pages 250
    SSL Tunneling 250
    SSL Bridging 251
    SSL and Performance 253
Configuring the Web Proxy Service 253
    Port Settings 253
    Listeners 254
    SSL Listeners 255
    Configuring the HTTP Redirector Filter 255
    Connection Settings 256
    Cache Settings 257
Chapter Summary 257
Review Questions 258
Real-World Projects 262

Chapter 10
Securing the Internal Network 265

Employing Windows 2000 Security   266
    ISA Server Security Configuration Wizard   266
    Using the Security Configuration Wizard   269
Guidelines for ISA Server Security   269
Intrusion Detection   271
Configuring Intrusion Detection   273
Configuring Alerts   274
Chapter Summary   275
Review Questions   276
Real-World Projects   279

Chapter 11
Supporting Media Services 289

What Is Multimedia?   290
What Is the H.323 Gatekeeper Service?   291
    H.323 Components   291
    H.323-compliant Applications   292
An H.323 Connection   293
    H.323 Gatekeeper Roles and Functions   294
    A Different Kind of RAS   294
H.323 Components and Settings   295
    Configuring the H.323 Protocol Filter   295
    Creating the H.323 Protocol Rule   296
Installing the H.323 Gatekeeper Service   297
    Adding a Gatekeeper Server   298
Configuring Connections   298
    Active Terminals   298
    Active Calls   299
    Call Routing   299
Configuring the H.323 Gatekeeper   303
Additional Configurations for
    Incoming Connections   304
Streaming Media Filter   306
    Windows Media Server   306
    Media Protocol Definitions   307

Chapter Summary   308
Review Questions   309
Real-World Projects   314

Chapter 12
Publishing Services 319

How ISA Server Protects Internal Servers   320
Publishing Policies   320
    Configuring the LAT   321
    Listeners   322
Web Publishing Rules   323
    Destination Sets for Web Publishing   323
    Client Type   324
    The Rule Action   324
    Safety Precautions   326
SSL Bridging   326
Reverse Caching   328
Server Publishing Rules   328
    Address Mapping   329
    Protocol Settings   330
    Client Types   330
    Server Publishing Setup   330
Setting Up a Mail Server   331
Special Publishing Configurations   331
Publishing a Mail Server   331
    The Mail Server Security Wizard   332
    The SMTP Filter   332
Using Packet Filters When Publishing   337
Configuring Publishing Rules   339
    Configuring a Web Publishing Rule   339
    Configuring a Server Publishing Rule   340
Setup for Internal Servers   341
Chapter Summary   341
Review Questions   342
Real-World Projects   347

Chapter 13
Managing Multiple ISA Servers 353

What Is an Array?   354
What Is Chaining?   356
Installing ISA Server in an Array   357
    Installing the First ISA Server Computer in an Array   358
    Installing Additional Array Members   359
    Promoting a Standalone Server to an Array Member   359
    Creating Arrays in ISA Management   360
    Deleting Arrays in ISA Management   362
    Setting Up Chaining   362
    Backup/Restore Enterprise Configurations   364
    Backup and Restore Array Configurations   364
    Using Enterprise Policies and Array Policies   365
    Configuring an Enterprise Policy   365
    Configuring an Array Policy   366
    Combining Enterprise Policies and Array Policies   368
Chapter Summary   369
Review Questions   370
Real-World Projects   374

Chapter 14
Integrating Services with ISA Server 385

Why Do Some Services Require Special Configurations?   386
Integrating Services on a Local ISA Server   386
Exchange and ISA Server   387
    Proxy Server 2.0 and Exchange Server   387
The Mail Server Security Wizard   388
The SMTP Filter   389
    Configuring the ISA Server and Other Applications for the SMTP Filter   390
    Configuring the SMTP Filter Property Pages   392
    The RPC Filter   394
    DNS Setup   395
Exchange and ISA on the Same Server   396
ISA Server and NLB   396

Installing NLB   398
Configuring NLB for Use with ISA Server   399
An Alternative to NLB   400
ISA Server and Terminal Services   401
Integrating ISA Server with a Web Server   401
Chapter Summary   402
Review Questions   403
Real-World Projects   408

Chapter 15
Troubleshooting and Reporting 411

Troubleshooting Guidelines   412
Windows 2000 Basic Troubleshooting   413
IE5 Configuration   418
Troubleshooting Resources   419
ISA Server Troubleshooting   421
Resolving Issues with Access Policies   421
Resolving Issues with Authentication   422
Resolving Issues with Caching   423
Resolving Issues with Client Connections   424
Resolving Dial-up Entries Issues   425
Resolving Issues with Logging   426
Resolving Issues with Services   427
Reporting   427
Creating Reports   428
Viewing Predefined Reports   431
Configuring Reports   432
Report Database   432
Scheduling Reports   432
Credentials   433
Specifying User Credentials for a Report Job   433
Other Functionalities   433
Chapter Summary   435
Review Questions   436
Real-World Projects   439

Chapter 16
Setting Up External Client Connections 451

Remote Connections and Clients   452
Dial-up Networking and the Routing And Remote Access Service   453
Dialing Out to the Internet   454
Dial-up Entries   455
    Configuring Dial-Up Access   455
    Setting Active Dial-up Entries   457
    Skipping a Connection to ISA Server   458
Virtual Private Networks   462
Integrating a VPN and ISA Server   463
    Local or Remote?   464
    Changes Made by the VPN Wizards   465
    PPTP or L2TP?   465
Configuring the Wizards   466
    Local ISA VPN Wizard   466
    Remote ISA VPN Wizard   468
    Clients To ISA Server VPN Wizard   469
    Making Changes to the VPN   470
Bandwidth Issues   472
    Identifying Bandwidth Issues   472
    Setting Effective Bandwidth   475
Chapter Summary   476
Review Questions   477
Real-World Projects   481

Chapter 17
Scenarios 487

Small Network Scenario   488
    Physical Network Description   488
    Issues   489
    Solution   489
    Steps for Installing the New ISA Server   490
    Configuring the New ISA Server   491
    Configuring Clients   493

Network with Remote Locations   493
   Physical Network Description   494
   Issues   495
   Solution   495
   Configuring the Three-Homed Perimeter Network   496
   Configuring the ISA Server   497
   Configurations for SecureNAT Connections   499
Upgrade a Network That Has Outgrown Its Settings   500
   Physical Network Description   500
   Issues   500
   Solutions   501
   Decisions   501
   Configuring the Back-to-Back Perimeter Network   502
   Upgrading the ISA Server to Enterprise Edition and Creating an Array   503
Chapter Summary   505
Review Questions   506

Chapter 18
Sample Test 511

Chapter 19
Answer Key 535

Appendix A
Answers to Review Questions 549

Appendix B
Objectives for Exam [70-227] 575

Appendix C
TCP and UDP Port Assignments 577

Glossary 581

Index 591

Exam Insights

Welcome to *MCSE Windows 2000 ISA Server Exam Prep*! This comprehensive study guide aims to help you get ready to take—and pass—Microsoft certification Exam 70-227, titled "Installing, Configuring, and Administering Microsoft Internet Security and Acceleration (ISA) Server 2000, Enterprise Edition." This Exam Insights section discusses exam preparation resources, the testing situation, Microsoft's certification programs in general, and how this book can help you prepare for Microsoft's Windows 2000 certification exams.

Exam Prep study guides help you understand and appreciate the subjects and materials you need to pass Microsoft certification exams. We've worked from Microsoft's curriculum objectives to ensure that all key topics are clearly explained. Our aim is to bring together as much information as possible about Microsoft certification exams.

Nevertheless, to completely prepare yourself for any Microsoft test, we recommend that you begin by taking the Self-Assessment included in this book immediately following this Exam Insights section. This tool will help you evaluate your knowledge base against the requirements for an MCSE under both ideal and real circumstances.

Based on what you learn from that exercise, you might decide to begin your studies with some classroom training or some background reading. You might decide to read The Coriolis Group's *Exam Prep* book that you have in hand first, or you might decide to start with another study approach. You may also want to refer to one of a number of study guides available from Microsoft or third-party vendors. We also recommend that you supplement your study program with visits to **ExamCram.com** to receive additional practice questions, get advice, and track the Windows 2000 MCSE program.

We also strongly recommend that you install, configure, and fool around with the software that you'll be tested on, because nothing beats hands-on experience and familiarity when it comes to understanding the questions you're likely to encounter on a certification test. Book learning is essential, but hands-on experience is the best teacher of all!

How to Prepare for an Exam

Preparing for any Windows 2000 related test (including "Installing, Configuring, and Administering Microsoft Internet Security and Acceleration (ISA) Server 2000 Enterprise Edition") requires that you obtain and study materials designed to provide comprehensive information about the product and its capabilities that will appear on the specific exam for which you are preparing. The following list of materials will help you study and prepare:

➤ The Windows 2000 ISA Server Standard or Enterprise product CD includes comprehensive online documentation and related materials; it should be a primary resource when you are preparing for the test.

➤ The exam preparation materials, practice tests, and self-assessment exams on the Microsoft Training & Services page at **www.microsoft.com/ trainingandservices/default.asp?PageID=mcp**. The Testing Innovations link offers samples of the new question types found on the Windows 2000 MCSE exams. Find the materials, download them, and use them!

➤ The exam preparation advice, practice tests, questions of the day, and discussion groups on the **ExamCram.com** e-learning and certification destination Web site (**www.examcram.com**).

In addition, you'll probably find any or all of the following materials useful in your quest for ISA Server expertise:

➤ *Microsoft TechNet CD*—This monthly CD-based publication delivers numerous electronic titles that include coverage of Directory Services Design and related topics on the Technical Information (TechNet) CD. Its offerings include product facts, technical notes, tools and utilities, and information on how to access the Seminars Online training materials for ISA Server. A subscription to TechNet costs $299 per year, but it is well worth the price. Visit **www.microsoft.com/technet/** and check out the information under the "TechNet Subscription" menu entry for more details.

➤ *Study guides*—Several publishers—including The Coriolis Group—offer Windows 2000 titles. The Coriolis Group series includes the following:

  ➤ *The Exam Cram series*—These books give you information about the material you need to know to pass the tests.

  ➤ *The Exam Prep series*—These books provide a greater level of detail than the *Exam Cram* books and are designed to teach you everything you need to know from an exam perspective. Each book comes with a CD that contains interactive practice exams in a variety of testing formats.

  Together, the two series make a perfect pair.

- *Multimedia*—These Coriolis Group materials are designed to support learners of all types—whether you learn best by reading or doing:
  - *The Exam Cram Personal Trainer*—Offers a unique, personalized self-paced training course based on the exam.
  - *The Exam Cram Personal Test Center*—Features multiple test options that simulate the actual exam, including Fixed-Length, Random, Review, and Test All. Explanations of correct and incorrect answers reinforce concepts learned.
- *Classroom training*—CTECs, online partners, and third-party training companies (like Wave Technologies, Learning Tree, Data-Tech, and others) all offer classroom training on ISA Server. These companies aim to help you prepare to pass the ISA Server test. Although such training runs upwards of $350 per day in class, most of the individuals lucky enough to partake (including your humble authors, who've even taught such courses) find them to be quite worthwhile.

By far, this set of required and recommended materials represents a nonpareil collection of sources and resources for ISA Server and related topics. We anticipate that you'll find that this book belongs in this company.

Taking a Certification Exam

Once you've prepared for your exam, you need to register with a testing center. Each computer-based MCP exam costs $100, and if you don't pass, you may retest for an additional $100 for each additional try. In the United States and Canada, tests are administered by Prometric (formerly Sylvan Prometric), and by Virtual University Enterprises (VUE). Here's how you can contact them:

- *Prometric*—You can sign up for a test through the company's Web site at **www.prometric.com**. Within the United States and Canada, you can register by phone at 800-755-3926. If you live outside this region, check the company's Web site for the appropriate phone number.
- *Virtual University Enterprises*—You can sign up for a test or get the phone numbers for local testing centers through the Web page at **www.vue.com/ms/**.

To sign up for a test, you must possess a valid credit card, or contact either company for mailing instructions to send them a check (in the U.S.). Only when payment is verified, or a check has cleared, can you actually register for a test.

To schedule an exam, call the number or visit either of the Web pages at least one day in advance. To cancel or reschedule an exam, you must call before 7 P.M. pacific standard time the day before the scheduled test time (or you may be charged, even if you don't appear to take the test). When you want to schedule a test, have the following information ready:

➤ Your name, organization, and mailing address.

➤ Your Microsoft Test ID. (Inside the United States, this means your Social Security number; citizens of other nations should call ahead to find out what type of identification number is required to register for a test.)

➤ The name and number of the exam you wish to take.

➤ A method of payment. (As we've already mentioned, a credit card is the most convenient method, but alternate means can be arranged in advance, if necessary.)

Once you sign up for a test, you'll be informed as to when and where the test is scheduled. Try to arrive at least 15 minutes early.

The Exam Situation

When you arrive at the testing center where you scheduled your exam, you'll need to sign in with an exam coordinator. He or she will ask you to show two forms of identification, one of which must be a photo ID. After you've signed in and your time slot arrives, you'll be asked to deposit any books, bags, or other items you brought with you. Then, you'll be escorted into a closed room.

All exams are completely closed book. In fact, you will not be permitted to take anything with you into the testing area, but you will be furnished with a blank sheet of paper and a pen or, in some cases, an erasable plastic sheet and an erasable pen. Before the exam, you should memorize as much of the important material as you can, so you can write that information on the blank sheet as soon as you are seated in front of the computer. You can refer to this piece of paper anytime you like during the test, but you'll have to surrender the sheet when you leave the room.

You will have some time to compose yourself, to record this information, and to take a sample orientation exam before you begin the real thing. We suggest you take the orientation test before taking your first exam, but because they're all more or less identical in layout, behavior, and controls, you probably won't need to do this more than once.

Typically, the room will be furnished with anywhere from one to half a dozen computers, and each workstation will be separated from the others by dividers designed to keep you from seeing what's happening on someone else's computer. Most test rooms feature a wall with a large picture window. This permits the exam coordinator to monitor the room, to prevent exam-takers from talking to one another, and to observe anything out of the ordinary that might go on. The exam coordinator will have preloaded the appropriate Microsoft certification exam—for this book, that's Exam 70-227—and you'll be permitted to start as soon as you're seated in front of the computer.

All Microsoft certification exams allow a certain maximum amount of time in which to complete your work (this time is indicated on the exam by an on-screen counter/clock, so you can check the time remaining whenever you like). All Microsoft certification exams are computer generated. In addition to multiple choice, you'll encounter select and place (drag and drop), create a tree (categorization and prioritization), drag and connect, and build list and reorder (list prioritization) on most exams. Although this may sound quite simple, the questions are constructed not only to check your mastery of basic facts and figures about ISA Server, but they also require you to evaluate one or more sets of circumstances or requirements. Often, you'll be asked to give more than one answer to a question. Likewise, you might be asked to select the best or most effective solution to a problem from a range of choices, all of which technically are correct. Taking the exam is quite an adventure, and it involves real thinking. This book shows you what to expect and how to deal with the potential problems, puzzles, and predicaments.

When you complete a Microsoft certification exam, the software will tell you whether you've passed or failed. If you need to retake an exam, you'll have to schedule a new test with Prometric or VUE and pay another $100.

Note: *The first time you fail a test, you can retake the test the next day. However, if you fail a second time, you must wait 14 days before retaking that test. The 14-day waiting period remains in effect for all retakes after the second failure.*

In the next section, you'll learn more about how Microsoft test questions look and how they must be answered.

Exam Layout and Design

The format of Microsoft's Windows 2000 exams is different from that of its previous exams. For the design exams (70-219, 70-220, 70-221), each exam consists entirely of a series of case studies, and the questions can be of six types. For the Core Four exams (70-210, 70-215, 70-216, 70-217) and the ISA Server exam (70-227), the same six types of questions can appear, but you are not likely to encounter complex multiquestion case studies.

For design exams, each case study or "testlet" presents a detailed problem that you must read and analyze. Figure 1 shows an example of what a case study looks like. You must select the different tabs in the case study to view the entire case.

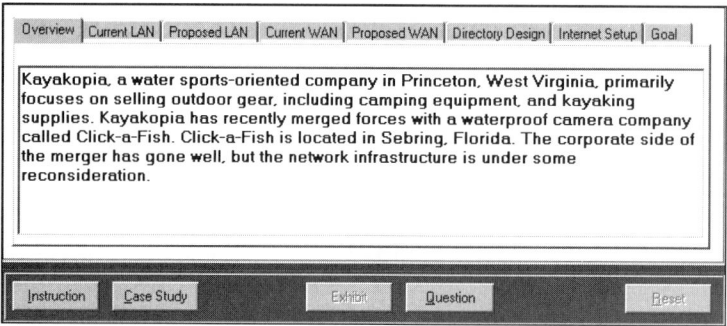

Figure 1 This is how case studies appear.

Following each case study is a set of questions related to the case study; these questions can be one of six types (which are discussed next). Careful attention to details provided in the case study is the key to success. Be prepared to toggle frequently between the case study and the questions as you work. Some of the case studies also include diagrams, which are called *exhibits,* that you'll need to examine closely to understand how to answer the questions.

Once you complete a case study, you can review all the questions and your answers. However, once you move on to the next case study, you may not be able to return to the previous case study and make any changes.

The six types of question formats are:

➤ Multiple choice, single answer

➤ Multiple choice, multiple answers

➤ Build list and reorder (list prioritization)

➤ Create a tree

➤ Drag and connect

➤ Select and place (drag and drop)

Note: *Exam formats may vary by test center location. You may want to call the test center or visit* **ExamCram.com** *to see if you can find out which type of test you'll encounter.*

Multiple-Choice Question Format

Some exam questions require you to select a single answer, whereas others ask you to select multiple correct answers. The following multiple-choice question requires you to select a single correct answer. Following the question is a brief summary of each potential answer and why it is either right or wrong.

Question 1

You are planning on installing ISA Server Enterprise in a Windows 2000 Active Directory domain. What do you need on a server before installing ISA Server?

○ a. Windows NT 4 Domain

○ b. Windows 2000 Service Pack 1

○ c. Windows NT 4 Workstation Operating System

○ d. Windows NT 4 Server Operating System

The correct answer is b, because ISA Server requires either a Windows 2000 Server/Advanced Server with the Windows 2000 Service Pack 1 installed or a Datacenter Server. The other answers (a, c, d) are misleading because you do not need Windows NT 4 Domain, and you cannot install ISA Server on either NT4 Workstation or Server.

> This sample question format corresponds closely to the Microsoft certification exam format—the only difference on the exam is that questions are not followed by answer keys. To select an answer, you would position the cursor over the radio button next to the answer. Then, click the mouse button to select the answer.
>
> Let's examine a question where one or more answers are possible. This type of question provides checkboxes rather than radio buttons for marking all appropriate selections.

Question 2

Scheduled cache content download can download web related information at what level? [Check all correct answers]

❏ a. Single URL

❏ b. Multiple URLs

❏ c. Single IP address

❏ d. Entire Web site

Answers a, b and d are correct. Scheduled cache content download can download Web related information at the level of a single URL, multiple URLs, and an entire Web site. You cannot, however, use the single IP address for scheduled cache content downloads; therefore answer c is incorrect. For this particular question, three answers are required. Microsoft sometimes gives partial credit for partially correct answers. For Question 2, you have to check the boxes next to items a, b and d to obtain credit for a correct answer. Notice that picking the right answers also means knowing why the other answers are wrong!

Build-List-and-Reorder Question Format

Questions in the build-list-and-reorder format present two lists of items—one on the left and one on the right. To answer the question, you must move items from the list on the right to the list on the left. The final list must then be reordered into a specific order.

These questions can best be characterized as "From the following list of choices, pick the choices that answer the question. Arrange the list in a certain order." To give you practice with this type of question, some questions of this type are included in this study guide. Here's an example of how they appear in this book; for a sample of how they appear on the test, see Figure 2.

Question 3

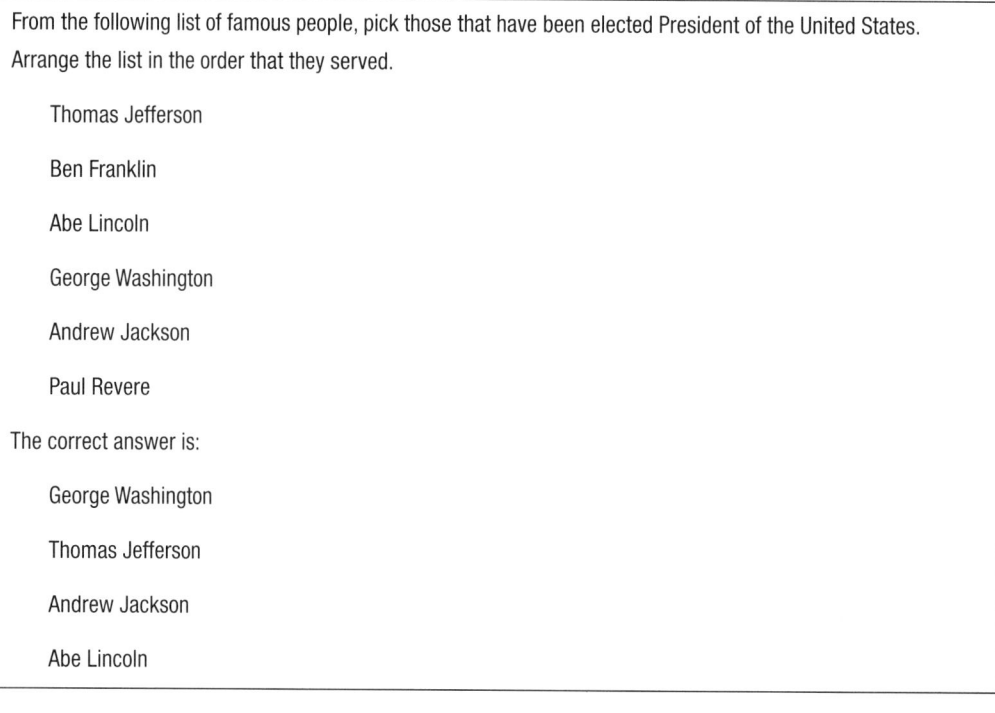

On an actual exam, the entire list of famous people would initially appear in the list on the right. You would move the four correct answers to the list on the left, and then reorder the list on the left. Notice that the answer to the question did not include all items from the initial list. However, this may not always be the case.

To move an item from the right list to the left list, first select the item by clicking on it, and then click on the Add button (left arrow). Once you move an item from one list to the other, you can move the item back by first selecting the item and then clicking on the appropriate button (either the Add button or the Remove button). Once items have been moved to the left list, you can reorder an item by selecting the item and clicking on the up or down button.

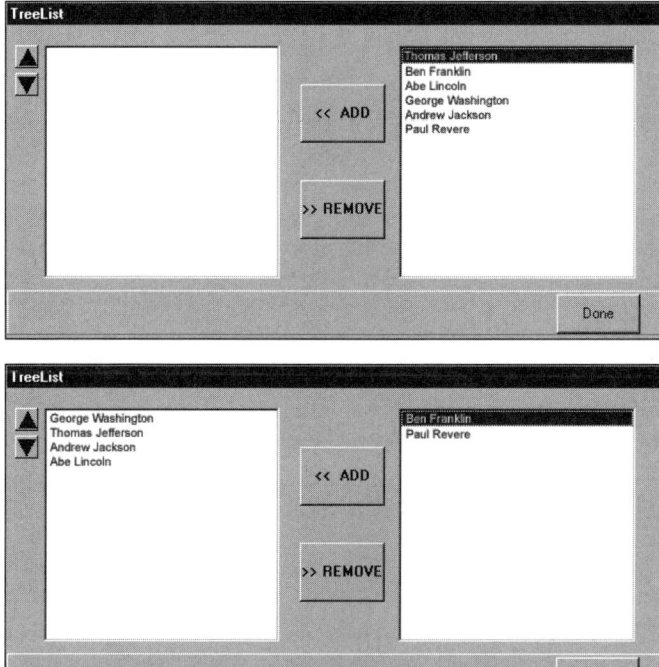

Figure 2 This is how build-list-and-reorder questions appear.

Create-a-Tree Question Format

Questions in the create-a-tree format also present two lists—one on the left side of the screen and one on the right side of the screen. The list on the right consists of individual items, and the list on the left consists of nodes in a tree. To answer the question, you must move items from the list on the right to the appropriate node in the tree.

These questions can best be characterized as simply a matching exercise. Items from the list on the right are placed under the appropriate category in the list on the left. Here's an example of how they appear in this book; for a sample of how they appear on the test, see Figure 3.

Question 4

> The calendar year is divided into four seasons:
>
> Winter
>
> Spring
>
> Summer
>
> Fall
>
> Identify the season when each of the following holidays occurs:
>
> Christmas
>
> Fourth of July
>
> Labor Day
>
> Flag Day
>
> Memorial Day
>
> Washington's Birthday
>
> Thanksgiving
>
> Easter

The correct answer is:

Winter

Christmas

Washington's Birthday

Spring

Flag Day

Memorial Day

Easter

Summer

> Fourth of July
>
> Labor Day

Fall

> Thanksgiving

In this case, all the items in the list were used. However, this may not always be the case.

To move an item from the right list to its appropriate location in the tree, you must first select the appropriate tree node by clicking on it. Then, you select the item to be moved and click on the Add button. If one or more items have been added to a tree node, the node will be displayed with a "+" icon to the left of the node name. You can click on this icon to expand the node and view the item(s) that have been added. If any item has been added to the wrong tree node, you can remove it by selecting it and clicking on the Remove button.

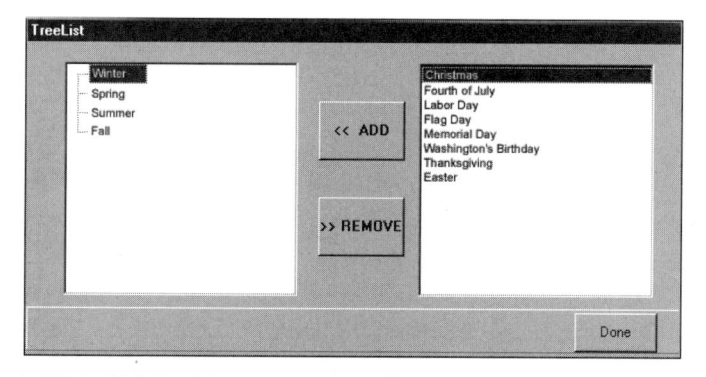

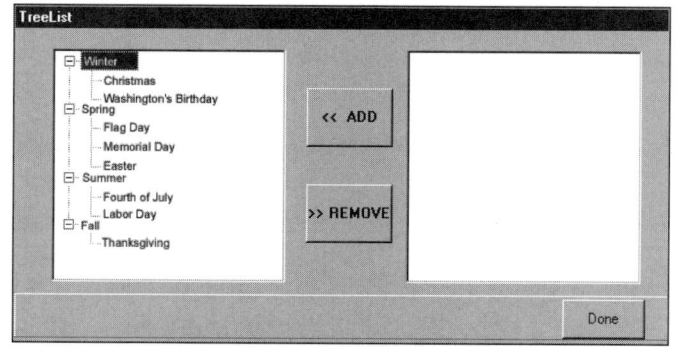

Figure 3   This is how create-a-tree questions appear.

Drag-and-Connect Question Format

Questions in the drag-and-connect format present a group of objects and a list of "connections." To answer the question, you must move the appropriate connections between the objects.

This type of question is best described using graphics. Here's an example.

Question 5

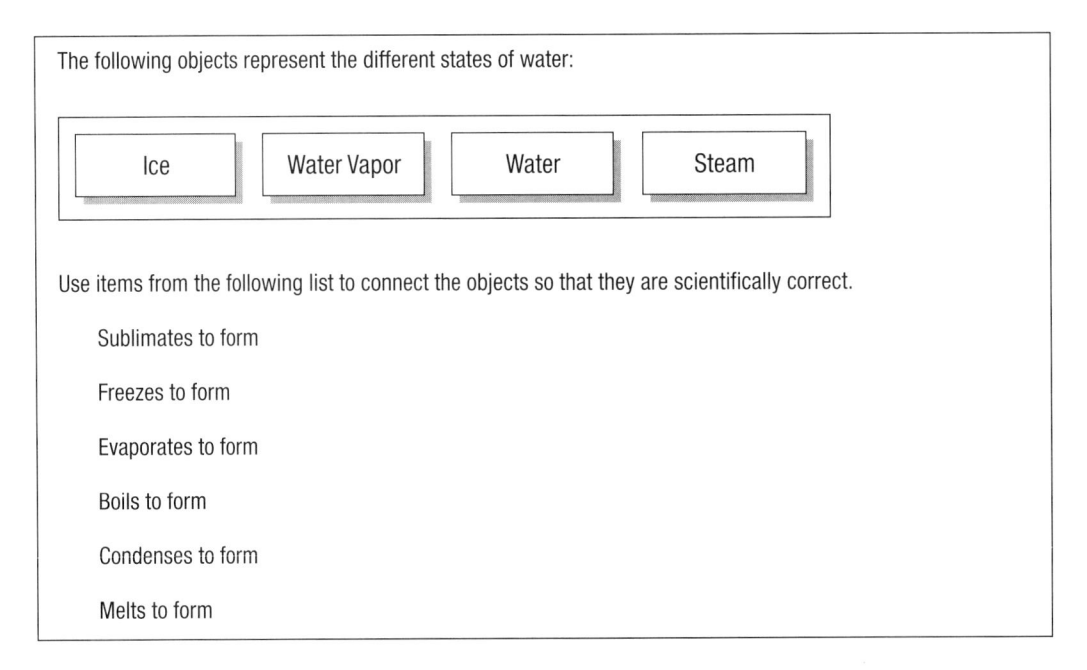

The following objects represent the different states of water:

- Ice
- Water Vapor
- Water
- Steam

Use items from the following list to connect the objects so that they are scientifically correct.

Sublimates to form

Freezes to form

Evaporates to form

Boils to form

Condenses to form

Melts to form

The correct answer is:

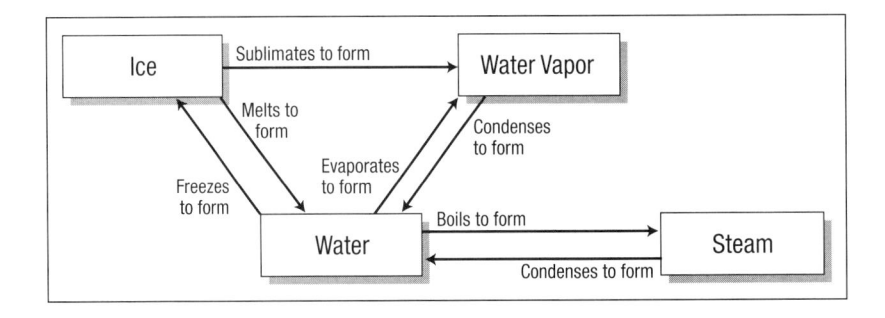

- Ice — Sublimates to form → Water Vapor
- Ice — Melts to form → Water
- Water — Freezes to form → Ice
- Water — Evaporates to form → Water Vapor
- Water Vapor — Condenses to form → Water
- Water — Boils to form → Steam
- Steam — Condenses to form → Water

For this type of question, it's not necessary to use every object, and each connection can be used multiple times.

Select-and-Place Question Format

Questions in the select-and-place (drag-and-drop) format present a diagram with blank boxes, and a list of labels that need to be dragged to correctly fill in the blank boxes. To answer the question, you must move the labels to their appropriate positions on the diagram.

This type of question is best described using graphics. Here's an example.

Question 6

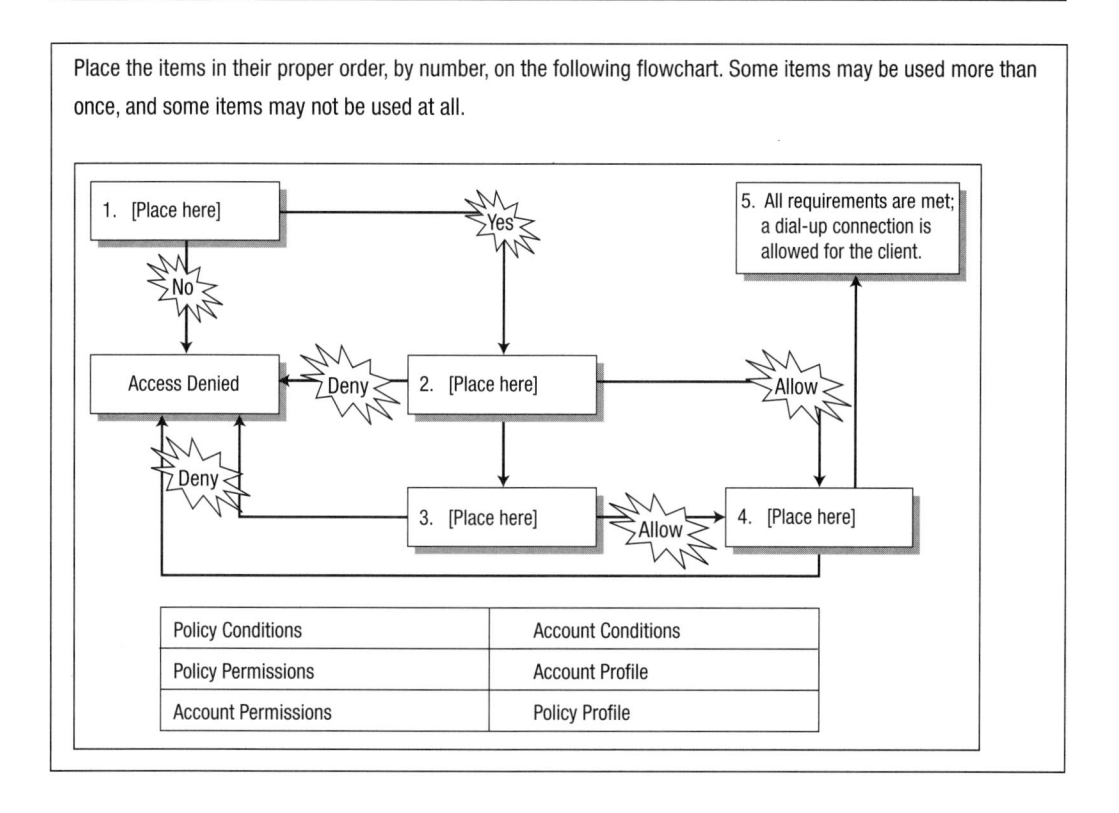

Place the items in their proper order, by number, on the following flowchart. Some items may be used more than once, and some items may not be used at all.

1. [Place here]
2. [Place here]
3. [Place here]
4. [Place here]
5. All requirements are met; a dial-up connection is allowed for the client.

Access Denied

Policy Conditions	Account Conditions
Policy Permissions	Account Profile
Account Permissions	Policy Profile

The correct answer is:

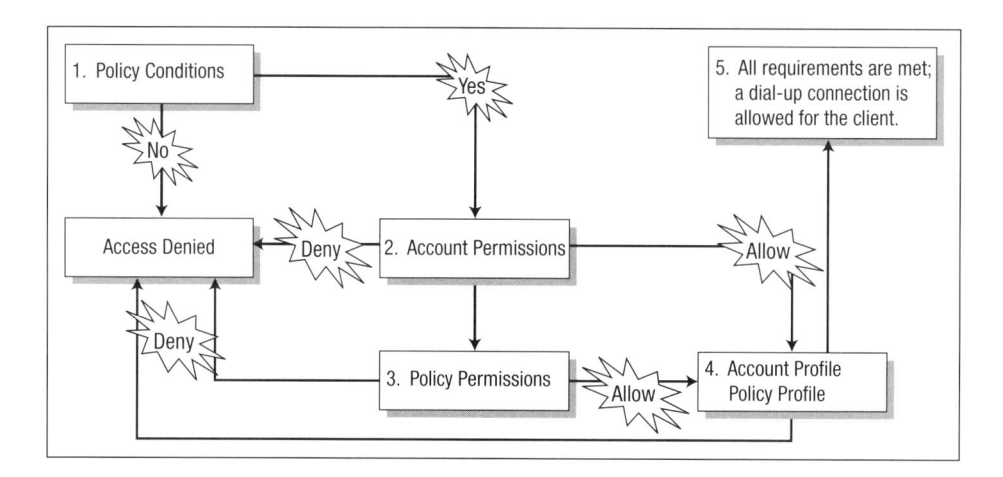

```
┌─────────────────────────────────────────────────────────────────┐
│  1. Policy Conditions ──Yes──┐        5. All requirements are met; │
│         │                     │           a dial-up connection is  │
│        No                     ▼           allowed for the client.  │
│         ▼                                      ▲                   │
│   Access Denied ◄──Deny── 2. Account Permissions ──Allow──┐        │
│         ▲                     │                            │        │
│        Deny                   ▼                            │        │
│         └──── 3. Policy Permissions ──Allow──► 4. Account Profile  │
│                                                   Policy Profile   │
└─────────────────────────────────────────────────────────────────┘
```

Microsoft's Testing Formats

Currently, Microsoft uses four different testing formats:

➤ Case study

➤ Fixed length

➤ Adaptive

➤ Short form

As we mentioned earlier, the case study approach is used with Microsoft's design exams. These exams consist of a set of case studies that you must analyze to enable you to answer questions related to the case studies. Such exams include one or more case studies (tabbed topic areas), each of which is followed by 4 to 10 questions. The question types for design exams and for Core Four Windows 2000 exams are multiple choice, build list and reorder, create a tree, drag and connect, and select and place. Depending on the test topic, some exams are totally case-based, whereas others are not.

Other Microsoft exams employ advanced testing capabilities that might not be immediately apparent. Although the questions that appear are primarily multiple choice, the logic that drives them is more complex than older Microsoft tests, which use a fixed sequence of questions, called a *fixed-length test*. Some questions employ a sophisticated user interface, which Microsoft calls a *simulation*, to test your knowledge of the software and systems under consideration in a more or less "live" environment that behaves just like the original. The Testing Innovations link at **www.microsoft.com/trainingandservices/default.asp?PageID=mcp** includes a downloadable practice simulation.

For some exams, Microsoft has turned to a well-known technique, called *adaptive testing*, to establish a test-taker's level of knowledge and product competence. Adaptive exams look the same as fixed-length exams, but they discover the level of difficulty at which an individual test-taker can correctly answer questions. Test-takers with differing levels of knowledge or ability therefore see different sets of questions; individuals with high levels of knowledge or ability are presented with a smaller set of more difficult questions, whereas individuals with lower levels of knowledge are presented with a larger set of easier questions. Two individuals may answer the same percentage of questions correctly, but the test-taker with a higher knowledge or ability level will score higher because his or her questions are worth more.

Also, the lower-level test-taker will probably answer more questions than his or her more-knowledgeable colleague. This explains why adaptive tests use ranges of values to define the number of questions and the amount of time it takes to complete the test.

Adaptive tests work by evaluating the test-taker's most recent answer. A correct answer leads to a more difficult question (and the test software's estimate of the test-taker's knowledge and ability level is raised). An incorrect answer leads to a less difficult question (and the test software's estimate of the test-taker's knowledge and ability level is lowered). This process continues until the test targets the test-taker's true ability level. The exam ends when the test-taker's level of accuracy meets a statistically acceptable value (in other words, when his or her performance demonstrates an acceptable level of knowledge and ability), or when the maximum number of items has been presented (in which case, the test-taker is almost certain to fail).

Microsoft also introduced a short-form test for its most popular tests. This test delivers 25 to 30 questions to its takers, giving them exactly 60 minutes to complete the exam. This type of exam is similar to a fixed-length test, in that it allows readers to jump ahead or return to earlier questions, and to cycle through the questions until the test is done. Microsoft does not use adaptive logic in this test, but claims that statistical analysis of the question pool is such that the 25 to 30 questions delivered during a short-form exam conclusively measure a test-taker's knowledge of the subject matter in much the same way as an adaptive test. You can think of the short-form test as a kind of "greatest hits exam" (that is, the most important questions are covered) version of an adaptive exam on the same topic.

Note: *Several test-takers have reported that some of the Microsoft exams can appear as a combination of adaptive and fixed-length questions.*

Microsoft tests can come in any one of these forms. Whatever you encounter, you must take the test in whichever form it appears; you can't choose one form over another. If anything, it pays more to prepare thoroughly for an adaptive exam than for a fixed-length or a short-form exam: The penalties for answering incorrectly are built into the test itself on an adaptive exam, whereas the layout remains the same for a fixed-length or short-form test, no matter how many questions you answer incorrectly.

> **Tip:** The biggest difference between an adaptive test and a fixed-length or short-form test is that on a fixed-length or short-form test, you can revisit questions after you've read them over one or more times. On an adaptive test, you must answer the question when it's presented and will have no opportunities to revisit that question thereafter.

Strategies for Different Testing Formats

Before you choose a test-taking strategy, you must know if your test is case study based, fixed length, short form, or adaptive. When you begin your exam, you'll know right away if the test is based on case studies. The interface will consist of a tabbed Window that allows you to easily navigate through the sections of the case.

If you are taking a test that is not based on case studies, the software will tell you that the test is adaptive, if in fact the version you're taking is an adaptive test. If your introductory materials fail to mention this, you're probably taking a fixed-length test (50 to 70 questions). If the total number of questions involved is 25 to 30, you're taking a short-form test. Some tests announce themselves by indicating that they will start with a set of adaptive questions, followed by fixed-length questions.

> **Tip:** You'll be able to tell for sure if you are taking an adaptive, fixed-length, or short-form test by the first question. If it includes a checkbox that lets you mark the question for later review, you're taking a fixed-length or short-form test. If the total number of questions is 25 to 30, it's a short-form test; if more than 30, it's a fixed-length test. Adaptive test questions can be visited (and answered) only once, and they include no such checkbox.

The Case Study Exam Strategy

Most test-takers find that the case study type of test used for the design exams (70-219, 70-220, and 70-221) is the most difficult to master. When it comes to studying for a case study test, your best bet is to approach each case study as a standalone test. The biggest challenge you'll encounter is that you'll feel that you won't have enough time to get through all of the cases that are presented.

> **Tip:** Each case provides a lot of material that you'll need to read and study before you can effectively answer the questions that follow. The trick to taking a case study exam is to first scan the case study to get the highlights. Make sure you read the overview section of the case so that you understand the context of the problem at hand. Then, quickly move on and scan the questions.

As you are scanning the questions, make mental notes to yourself so that you'll remember which sections of the case study you should focus on. Some case studies may provide a fair amount of extra information that you don't really need to answer the questions. The goal with this scanning approach is to avoid having to study and analyze material that is not completely relevant.

When studying a case, carefully read the tabbed information. It is important to answer each and every question. You will be able to toggle back and forth from case to questions, and from question to question within a case testlet. However, once you leave the case and move on, you may not be able to return to it. You may want to take notes while reading useful information so you can refer to them when you tackle the test questions. It's hard to go wrong with this strategy when taking any kind of Microsoft certification test.

The Fixed-Length and Short-Form Exam Strategy

A well-known principle when taking fixed-length or short-form exams is to first read over the entire exam from start to finish while answering only those questions you feel absolutely sure of. On subsequent passes, you can dive into more complex questions more deeply, knowing how many such questions you have left.

Fortunately, the Microsoft exam software for fixed-length and short-form tests makes the multiple-visit approach easy to implement. At the top-left corner of each question is a checkbox that permits you to mark that question for a later visit.

Note: Marking questions makes review easier, but you can return to any question by clicking the Forward or Back button repeatedly.

As you read each question, if you answer only those you're sure of and mark for review those that you're not sure of, you can keep working through a decreasing list of questions as you answer the trickier ones in order.

Tip: There's at least one potential benefit to reading the exam over completely before answering the trickier questions: Sometimes, information supplied in later questions sheds more light on earlier questions. At other times, information you read in later questions might jog your memory about ISA Serverfacts, figures, or behavior that helps you answer earlier questions. Either way, you'll come out ahead if you defer those questions about which you're not absolutely sure.

Here are some question-handling strategies that apply to fixed-length and short-form tests. Use them if you have the chance:

➤ When returning to a question after your initial read-through, read every word again—otherwise, your mind can fall quickly into a rut. Sometimes, revisiting a question after turning your attention elsewhere lets you see something you missed, but the strong tendency is to see what you've seen before. Try to avoid that tendency at all costs.

➤ If you return to a question more than twice, try to articulate to yourself what you don't understand about the question, why answers don't appear to make sense, or what appears to be missing. If you chew on the subject awhile, your subconscious might provide the details you lack, or you might notice a "trick" that points to the right answer.

As you work your way through the exam, another counter that Microsoft provides will come in handy—the number of questions completed and questions outstanding. For fixed-length and short-form tests, it's wise to budget your time by making sure that you've completed one-quarter of the questions one-quarter of the way through the exam period, and three-quarters of the questions three-quarters of the way through.

If you're not finished when only five minutes remain, use that time to guess your way through any remaining questions. Remember, guessing is potentially more valuable than not answering, because blank answers are always wrong, but a guess may turn out to be right. If you don't have a clue about any of the remaining questions, pick answers at random, or choose all a's, b's, and so on. The important thing is to submit an exam for scoring that has an answer for every question.

Tip: At the very end of your exam period, you're better off guessing than leaving questions unanswered.

The Adaptive Exam Strategy

If there's one principle that applies to taking an adaptive test, it could be summed up as "Get it right the first time." You cannot elect to skip a question and move on to the next one when taking an adaptive test, because the testing software uses your answer to the current question to select whatever question it plans to present next. Nor can you return to a question once you've moved on, because the software gives you only one chance to answer the question. You can, however, take notes, because sometimes information supplied in earlier questions will shed more light on later questions.

Also, when you answer a question correctly, you are presented with a more difficult question next, to help the software gauge your level of skill and ability. When you answer a question incorrectly, you are presented with a less difficult question, and the software lowers its current estimate of your skill and ability. This continues until the program settles into a reasonably accurate estimate of what you know and can do, and takes you on average through somewhere between 15 and 30 questions as you complete the test.

The good news is that if you know your stuff, you'll probably finish most adaptive tests in 30 minutes or so. The bad news is that you must really, really know your stuff to do your best on an adaptive test. That's because some questions are so convoluted, complex, or hard to follow that you're bound to miss one or two, at a minimum, even if you do know your stuff. So the more you know, the better you'll do on an adaptive test, even accounting for the occasionally weird or unfathomable questions that appear on these exams.

> **Tip:** Because you can't always tell in advance if a test is fixed length, short form, or adaptive, you will be best served by preparing for the exam as if it were adaptive. That way, you should be prepared to pass no matter what kind of test you take. But if you do take a fixed-length or short-form test, remember the tips from the preceding section. They should help you improve on what you could do on an adaptive test.

If you encounter a question on an adaptive test that you can't answer, you must guess an answer immediately. Because of how the software works, you may suffer for your guess on the next question if you guess right, because you'll get a more difficult question next!

Question-Handling Strategies

Based on exams we have taken, some interesting trends have become apparent. For those questions that take only a single answer, usually two or three of the answers will be obviously incorrect, and two of the answers will be plausible—of course, only one can be correct. Unless the answer leaps out at you (if it does, reread the question to look for a trick; sometimes those are the ones you're most likely to get wrong), begin the process of answering by eliminating those answers that are most obviously wrong.

Almost always, at least one answer out of the possible choices for a question can be eliminated immediately because it matches one of these conditions:

➤ The answer does not apply to the situation.

➤ The answer describes a nonexistent issue, an invalid option, or an imaginary state.

After you eliminate all answers that are obviously wrong, you can apply your retained knowledge to eliminate further answers. Look for items that sound correct but refer to actions, commands, or features that are not present or not available in the situation that the question describes.

If you're still faced with a blind guess among two or more potentially correct answers, reread the question. Try to picture how each of the possible remaining answers would alter the situation. Be especially sensitive to terminology; sometimes the choice of words ("remove" instead of "disable") can make the difference between a right answer and a wrong one.

Only when you've exhausted your ability to eliminate answers, but remain unclear about which of the remaining possibilities is correct, should you guess at an answer. An unanswered question offers you no points, but guessing gives you at least some chance of getting a question right; just don't be too hasty when making a blind guess.

Note: *If you're taking a fixed-length or a short-form test, you can wait until the last round of reviewing marked questions (just as you're about to run out of time, or out of unanswered questions) before you start making guesses. You will have the same option within each case study testlet (but once you leave a testlet, you may not be allowed to return to it). If you're taking an adaptive test, you'll have to guess to move on to the next question if you can't figure out an answer some other way. Either way, guessing should be your technique of last resort!*

Numerous questions assume that the default behavior of a particular utility is in effect. If you know the defaults and understand what they mean, this knowledge will help you cut through many Gordian knots.

Mastering the Inner Game

In the final analysis, knowledge breeds confidence, and confidence breeds success. If you study the materials in this book carefully and review all the practice questions at the end of each chapter, you should become aware of those areas where additional learning and study are required.

After you've worked your way through the book, take the practice exam in the back of the book and the practice exams on the CD-ROM. Be sure to click on the Update button in our CD-ROM's testing engine to download additional free questions from **ExamCram.com**! Taking tests will provide a reality check and help you identify areas to study further. Make sure you follow up and review materials related to the questions you miss on the practice exams before scheduling a real exam. Only when you've covered that ground and feel comfortable with the whole scope of the practice exams should you set an exam appointment. Only if you score 85 percent or better should you proceed to the real thing (otherwise, obtain some additional practice tests so you can keep trying until you hit this magic number).

Tip: If you take a practice exam and don't score at least 85 percent correct, you'll want to practice further. Microsoft provides links to practice exam providers and also offers self-assessment exams at **www.microsoft.com/trainingandservices/**). You should also check out **ExamCram.com** for downloadable practice questions.

Armed with the information in this book and with the determination to augment your knowledge, you should be able to pass the certification exam. However, you need to work at it, or you'll spend the exam fee more than once before you finally pass. If you prepare seriously, you should do well. We are confident that you can do it!

The next section covers the exam requirements for the various Microsoft certifications.

The Microsoft Certified Professional (MCP) Program

The MCP Program currently includes the following separate tracks, each of which boasts its own special acronym (as a certification candidate, you need to have a high tolerance for alphabet soup of all kinds):

➤ *MCP (Microsoft Certified Professional)*—This is the least prestigious of all the certification tracks from Microsoft. Passing one of the major Microsoft exams qualifies an individual for the MCP credential. Individuals can demonstrate proficiency with additional Microsoft products by passing additional certification exams.

➤ *MCP+SB (Microsoft Certified Professional + Site Building)*—This certification program is designed for individuals who are planning, building, managing, and maintaining Web sites. Individuals with the MCP+SB credential will have demonstrated the ability to develop Web sites that include multimedia and searchable content and Web sites that connect to and communicate with a back-end database. It requires one MCP exam, plus two of these three exams: "70-055: Designing and Implementing Web Sites with Microsoft FrontPage 98," "70-057: Designing and Implementing Commerce Solutions with Microsoft Site Server 3.0, Commerce Edition," and "70-152: Designing and Implementing Web Solutions with Microsoft Visual InterDev 6.0." Microsoft will retire Exam 70-055 on June 30, 2001 and the MCP+SB certification on June 30, 2002.

➤ *MCSE (Microsoft Certified Systems Engineer)*—Anyone who has a current MCSE is warranted to possess a high level of networking expertise with Microsoft operating systems and products. This credential is designed to prepare individuals to plan, implement, maintain, and support information systems, networks, and internetworks built around Microsoft Windows 2000 and its BackOffice family of products.

To obtain an MCSE, an individual must pass four core operating system exams, one core option exam, and two elective exams. The operating system exams require individuals to prove their competence with desktop and server operating systems and networking/internetworking components.

For Windows NT 4 MCSEs, the Accelerated exam, "70-240: Microsoft Windows 2000 Accelerated Exam for MCPs Certified on Microsoft Windows NT 4.0," is an option. This free exam covers all of the material tested in the Core Four exams. The hitch in this plan is that you can take the test only once. If you fail, you must take all four core exams to recertify. The Core Four exams are: "70-210: Installing, Configuring and Administering Microsoft Windows 2000 Professional," "70-215: Installing, Configuring and Administering Microsoft Windows 2000 Server," "70-216: Implementing and Administering a Microsoft Windows 2000 Network Infrastructure," and "70-217: Implementing and Administering a Microsoft Windows 2000 Directory Services Infrastructure."

To fulfill the fifth core exam requirement, you can choose from four design exams: "70-219: Designing a Microsoft Windows 2000 Directory Services Infrastructure," "70-220: Designing Security for a Microsoft Windows 2000 Network," "70-221: Designing a Microsoft Windows 2000 Network Infrastructure, or "70-226: Designing Highly Available Web Solutions with Microsoft Windows 2000 Server Technologies." You are also required to take two elective exams. An elective exam can fall in any number of subject or product areas, primarily BackOffice Server 2000 components. The three design exams that you don't select as your fifth core exam also qualify as electives. If you are on your way to becoming an MCSE and have already taken some exams, visit **www.microsoft.com/trainingandservices/** for information about how to complete your MCSE certification.

The ISA Server exam: "70-227: Installing, Configuring, and Administering Microsoft Internet Security and Acceleration (ISA) Server 2000, Enterprise Edition" fulfills requirements for an elective.

Individuals who wish to remain certified MCSEs after 12/31/2001 must "upgrade" their certifications on or before 12/31/2001. For more detailed information than is included here, visit **www.microsoft.com/trainingandservices/**.

New MCSE candidates must pass seven tests to meet the MCSE requirements. It's not uncommon for the entire process to take a year or so, and many individuals find that they must take a test more than once to pass. The primary goal of *Exam Prep* and *Exam Cram* test preparation books is to make it possible, given proper study and preparation, to pass all Microsoft certification tests on the first try. Table 1 shows the required and elective exams for the Windows 2000 MCSE certification.

➤ *MCSD (Microsoft Certified Solution Developer)*—The MCSD credential reflects the skills required to create multitier, distributed, and COM-based solutions, in addition to desktop and Internet applications, using new technologies. To obtain an MCSD, an individual must demonstrate the ability to analyze and interpret user requirements; select and integrate products, platforms, tools, and technologies; design and implement code, and customize applications; and perform necessary software tests and quality assurance operations.

Table 1 MCSE Windows 2000 Requirements

Core

If you have not passed these 3 Windows NT 4 exams	
Exam 70-067	Implementing and Supporting Microsoft Windows NT Server 4.0
Exam 70-068	Implementing and Supporting Microsoft Windows NT Server 4.0 in the Enterprise
Exam 70-073	Microsoft Windows NT Workstation 4.0
then you must take these 4 exams	
Exam 70-210	Installing, Configuring, and Administering Microsoft Windows 2000 Professional
Exam 70-215	Installing, Configuring, and Administering Microsoft Windows 2000 Server
Exam 70-216	Implementing and Administering a Microsoft Windows 2000 Network Infrastructure
Exam 70-217	Implementing and Administering a Microsoft Windows 2000 Directory Services Infrastructure
If you have already passed exams 70-067, 70-068, and 70-073, you may take this exam	
Exam 70-240	Microsoft Windows 2000 Accelerated Exam for MCPs Certified on Microsoft Windows NT 4.0

5th Core Option

Choose 1 from this group	
Exam 70-219	Designing a Microsoft Windows 2000 Directory Services Infrastructure
Exam 70-220	Designing Security for a Microsoft Windows 2000 Network
Exam 70-221	Designing a Microsoft Windows 2000 Network Infrastructure
Exam 70-226	Designing Highly Available Web Solutions with Microsoft Windows 2000 Server Technologies

Elective*

Choose 2 from this group	
Exam 70-019	Designing and Implementing Data Warehouse with Microsoft SQL Server 7.0
Exam 70-056	Implementing and Supporting Web Sites Using Microsoft Site Server 3.0
Exam 70-080	Implementing and Supporting Microsoft Internet Explorer 5.0 by Using the Internet Explorer Administration Kit
Exam 70-085	Implementing and Supporting Microsoft SNA Server 4.0
Exam 70-086	Implementing and Supporting Microsoft Systems Management Server 2.0
Exam 70-222	Migrating from Microsoft Windows NT 4.0 to Microsoft Windows 2000
Exam 70-223	Installing, Configuring, and Administering Microsoft Clustering Services by Using Microsoft Windows 2000 Advanced Server
Exam 70-224	Installing, Configuring, and Administering Microsoft Exchange 2000 Server
Exam 70-225	Designing and Deploying a Messaging Infrastructure with Microsoft Exchange 2000 Server
▶ Exam 70-227	Installing, Configuring, and Administering Microsoft Internet Security and Acceleration (ISA) Server 2000 Enterprise Edition
Exam 70-228	Installing, Configuring, and Administering Microsoft SQL Server 2000 Enterprise Edition
Exam 70-229	Designing and Implementing Databases with Microsoft SQL Server 2000 Enterprise Edition
Exam 70-244	Supporting and Maintaining a Microsoft Windows NT Server 4.0 Network

This is not a complete listing—you can still be tested on some earlier versions of these products. However, we have included mainly the most recent versions so that you may test on these versions and thus be certified longer. We have not included any tests that are scheduled to be retired.

* 5th Core Option exams may also be used as electives, but can only be counted once toward a certification. You cannot receive credit for an exam as both a core and an elective in the same track.

To become an MCSD, you must pass a total of four exams: three core exams and one elective exam. Each candidate must choose one of these three desktop application exams—"70-016: Designing and Implementing Desktop Applications with Microsoft Visual C++ 6.0," "70-156: Designing and Implementing Desktop Applications with Microsoft Visual FoxPro 6.0," or "70-176: Designing and Implementing Desktop Applications with Microsoft Visual Basic 6.0"—*plus* one of these three distributed application exams—"70-015: Designing and Implementing Distributed Applications with Microsoft Visual C++ 6.0," "70-155: Designing and Implementing Distributed Applications with Microsoft Visual FoxPro 6.0," or "70-175: Designing and Implementing Distributed Applications with Microsoft Visual Basic 6.0." The third core exam is "70-100: Analyzing Requirements and Defining Solution Architectures." Elective exams cover specific Microsoft applications and languages, including Visual Basic, C++, the Microsoft Foundation Classes, Access, SQL Server, Excel, and more.

▶ *MCDBA (Microsoft Certified Database Administrator)*—The MCDBA credential reflects the skills required to implement and administer Microsoft SQL Server databases. To obtain an MCDBA, an individual must demonstrate the ability to derive physical database designs, develop logical data models, create physical databases, create data services by using Transact-SQL, manage and maintain databases, configure and manage security, monitor and optimize databases, and install and configure Microsoft SQL Server.

To become an MCDBA, you must pass a total of three core exams and one elective exam. The required core exams are "70-028: Administering Microsoft SQL Server 7.0" or "70-228: Installing, Configuring, and Administering Microsoft SQL Server 2000 Enterprise Edition," "70-029: Designing and Implementing Databases with Microsoft SQL Server 7.0" or "70-229: Designing and Implementing Databases with Microsoft SQL Server 2000 Enterprise Edition", and "70-215: Installing, Configuring and Administering Microsoft Windows 2000 Server" or "70-240: Microsoft Windows 2000 Accelerated Exam for MCPs Certified on Microsoft Windows NT." The elective exams that you can choose from cover specific uses of SQL Server and include "70-015: Designing and Implementing Distributed Applications with Microsoft Visual C++ 6.0," "70-019: Designing and Implementing Data Warehouses with Microsoft SQL Server 7.0," "70-155: Designing and Implementing Distributed Applications with Microsoft Visual FoxPro 6.0," "70-175: Designing and Implementing Distributed Applications with Microsoft Visual Basic 6.0," and two exams that relate to Windows 2000: "70-216: Implementing and Administering a Microsoft Windows 2000 Network Infrastructure," and "70-087: Implementing and Supporting Microsoft Internet Information Server 4.0."

If you have taken the three core Windows NT 4 exams on your path to becoming an MCSE, you qualify for the Accelerated exam (it replaces the Network Infrastructure exam requirement). The Accelerated exam covers the objectives of all four of the Windows 2000 core exams. In addition to taking the Accelerated exam, you must take only the two SQL exams—Administering and Database Design.

> *MCT (Microsoft Certified Trainer)*—Microsoft Certified Trainers are deemed able to deliver elements of the official Microsoft curriculum, based on technical knowledge and instructional ability. Thus, it is necessary for an individual seeking MCT credentials (which are granted on a course-by-course basis) to pass the related certification exam for a course and complete the official Microsoft training in the subject area, and to demonstrate an ability to teach.

> This teaching skill criterion may be satisfied by proving that one has already attained training certification from Novell, Banyan, Lotus, the Santa Cruz Operation, or Cisco, or by taking a Microsoft-sanctioned workshop on instruction. Microsoft makes it clear that MCTs are important cogs in the Microsoft training channels. Instructors must be MCTs before Microsoft will allow them to teach in any of its official training channels, including Microsoft's affiliated Certified Technical Education Centers (CTECs) and its online training partner network. As of January 1, 2001, MCT candidates must also possess a current MCSE.

Microsoft has announced that the MCP+I and MCSE+I credentials will be discontinued on 2/28/2001 when the MCSE exams for Windows 2000 are in full swing because the skill set for the Internet portion of the program has been included in the new MCSE program. Therefore, details on these tracks are not provided here; go to **www.microsoft.com/trainingandservices/** if you need more information.

Once a Microsoft product becomes obsolete, MCPs typically have to recertify on current versions. (If individuals do not recertify, their certifications become invalid.) Because technology keeps changing and new products continually supplant old ones, this should come as no surprise. This explains why Microsoft has announced that MCSEs have 12 months past the scheduled retirement date for the Windows NT 4 exams to recertify on Windows 2000 topics. (Note that this means taking at least two exams, if not more.)

The best place to keep tabs on the MCP Program and its related certifications is on the Web. The URL for the MCP program is **www.microsoft.com/mcp/**. But Microsoft's Web site changes often, so if this URL doesn't work, try using the Search tool on Microsoft's site with either "MCP" or the quoted phrase "Microsoft Certified Professional Program" as a search string. This will help you find the latest and most accurate information about Microsoft's certification programs.

Tracking MCP Status

As soon as you pass any Microsoft exam (except Networking Essentials), you'll attain Microsoft Certified Professional (MCP) status. Microsoft also generates transcripts that indicate which exams you have passed. You can view a copy of your transcript at any time by going to the MCP secured site and selecting Transcript Tool. This tool will allow you to print a copy of your current transcript and confirm your certification status.

Once you pass the necessary set of exams, you'll be certified. Official certification normally takes anywhere from six to eight weeks, so don't expect to get your credentials overnight. When the package for a qualified certification arrives, it includes a Welcome Kit that contains a number of elements (see Microsoft's Web site for other benefits of specific certifications):

➤ A certificate suitable for framing, along with a wallet card and a lapel pin.

➤ A license to use the MCP logo, thereby allowing you to use the logo in advertisements, promotions, and documents, and on letterhead, business cards, and so on. Along with the license comes an MCP logo sheet, which includes camera-ready artwork. (Note: Before using any of the artwork, individuals must sign and return a licensing agreement that indicates they'll abide by its terms and conditions.)

➤ A subscription to *Microsoft Certified Professional Magazine*, which provides ongoing data about testing and certification activities, requirements, and changes to the program.

Many people believe that the benefits of MCP certification go well beyond the perks that Microsoft provides to newly anointed members of this elite group. We're starting to see more job listings that request or require applicants to have an MCP, MCSE, and so on, and many individuals who complete the program can qualify for increases in pay and/or responsibility. As an official recognition of hard work and broad knowledge, one of the MCP credentials is a badge of honor in many IT organizations.

About the Book

Career opportunities abound for well-prepared Web Server/Proxy Server administrators. This book is designed as your doorway into ISA Server implementation. If you are new to Internet caching and firewall, this is your ticket to an exciting future. Others who have prior experience with Proxy Server will find that the book adds depth and breadth to that experience. Also, the book provides the knowledge you need to prepare for Microsoft's certification exam 70-227 "Installing, Configuring, and Administering Microsoft Internet Security and Acceleration

(ISA) Server 2000 Enterprise Edition. The exam is one of the available electives, and it is a crucial step in becoming a Microsoft Certified Systems Engineer. The exam has been active since February 27, 2001.

When you complete this book, you will be at the threshold of a ISA Server design career that can be very fulfilling and challenging. This is a rapidly advancing field that offers ample opportunity for personal growth and for making a contribution to your business or organization. The book is intended to provide you with knowledge that you can apply right away and a sound basis for understanding the changes that you will encounter in the future. It also is intended to give you the hands-on skills you need to be a valued professional in your organization.

The book is filled with real-world projects that cover every aspect of installing, managing, and designing ISA Server. The projects are designed to make what you learn come alive through actually performing the tasks. Also, every chapter includes a range of practice questions to help prepare you for the Microsoft certification exam. All of these features are offered to reinforce your learning, so you'll feel confident in the knowledge you have gained from each chapter.

Features

To aid you in fully understanding ISA Server concepts, there are many features in this book designed to improve its value:

- *Chapter objectives*—Each chapter in this book begins with a detailed list of the topics to be mastered within that chapter. This list provides you with a quick reference to the contents of that chapter, as well as a useful study aid.

- *Illustrations and tables*—Numerous illustrations of screenshots and components aid you in the visualization of common setup steps, theories, and concepts. In addition, many tables provide details and comparisons of both practical and theoretical information.

- *Notes, tips, and warnings*—Notes present additional helpful material related to the subject being described. Tips from the author's experience provide extra information about how to attack a problem, how to set up an ISA Server for a particular need, or what to do in certain real-world situations. Warnings are included to help you anticipate potential mistakes or problems so you can prevent them from happening.

- *Chapter summaries*—Each chapter's text is followed by a summary of the concepts it has introduced. These summaries provide a helpful way to recap and revisit the ideas covered in each chapter.

- *Review questions*—End-of-chapter assessment begins with a set of review questions that reinforce the ideas introduced in each chapter. These questions not only ensure that you have mastered the concepts, but are written to help prepare you for the Microsoft certification examination. Answers to these questions are found in Appendix A.

➤ *Real-world projects*—Although it is important to understand the theory behind server and networking technology, nothing can improve upon real-world experience. To this end, along with theoretical explanations, each chapter provides numerous hands-on projects aimed at providing you with real-world implementation experience.

➤ *Sample tests*—Use the sample test and answer key in Chapters 18 and 19 to test yourself. Then, move on to the interactive practice exams found on the CD-ROM. The testing engine offers a variety of testing formats to choose from.

Where Should You Start?

This book is intended to be read in sequence, from beginning to end. Each chapter builds upon those that precede it, to provide a solid understanding of ISA Server. After completing the chapters, you may find it useful to go back through the book and use the review questions and projects to prepare for the Microsoft certification test for "Installing, Configuring, and Administering Microsoft Internet Security and Acceleration (ISA) Server 2000 Enterprise Edition (Exam 70-227). Readers are also encouraged to investigate the many pointers to online and printed sources of additional information that are cited throughout this book.

Please share your feedback on the book with us, especially if you have ideas about how we can improve it for future readers. We'll consider everything you say carefully, and we'll respond to all suggestions. Send your questions or comments to us at **learn@examcram.com**. Please remember to include the title of the book in your message; otherwise, we'll be forced to guess which book you're writing about. And we don't like to guess—we want to *know*! Also, be sure to check out the Web pages at **www.examcram.com**, where you'll find information updates, commentary, and certification information. Thanks, and enjoy the book!

Self-Assessment

The reason we included a Self-Assessment in this *Exam Prep* book is to help you evaluate your readiness to tackle MCSE certification. It should also help you understand what you need to know to master the topic of this book—namely, Exam 70-227, "Installing, Configuring, and Administering Microsoft Internet Security and Acceleration (ISA) Server 2000 Enterprise Edition." But before you tackle this Self-Assessment, let's talk about concerns you may face when pursuing an MCSE for Windows 2000, and what an ideal MCSE candidate might look like.

MCSEs in the Real World

In the next section, we describe an ideal MCSE candidate, knowing full well that only a few real candidates will meet this ideal. In fact, our description of that ideal candidate might seem downright scary, especially with the changes that have been made to the program to support Windows 2000. But take heart: Although the requirements to obtain an MCSE may seem formidable, they are by no means impossible to meet. However, be keenly aware that it does take time, involves some expense, and requires real effort to get through the process.

Increasing numbers of people are attaining Microsoft certifications, so the goal is within reach. You can get all the real-world motivation you need from knowing that many others have gone before, so you will be able to follow in their footsteps. If you're willing to tackle the process seriously and do what it takes to obtain the necessary experience and knowledge, you can take—and pass—all the certification tests involved in obtaining an MCSE. In fact, we've designed *Exam Preps*, the companion *Exam Crams*, *Exam Cram Personal Trainers*, and *Exam Cram Personal Test Centers* to make it as easy on you as possible to prepare for these exams. We've also greatly expanded our Web site, **www.examcram.com**, to provide a host of resources to help you prepare for the complexities of Windows 2000.

Besides MCSE, other Microsoft certifications include:

➤ MCSD, which is aimed at software developers and requires one specific exam, two more exams on client and distributed topics, plus a fourth elective exam drawn from a different, but limited, pool of options.

- Other Microsoft certifications, whose requirements range from one test (MCP) to several tests (MCDBA).

The Ideal Windows 2000 MCSE Candidate

Just to give you some idea of what an ideal MCSE candidate is like, here are some relevant statistics about the background and experience such an individual might have. Don't worry if you don't meet these qualifications, or don't come that close—this is a far from ideal world, and where you fall short is simply where you'll have more work to do.

- Academic or professional training in network theory, concepts, and operations. This includes everything from networking media and transmission techniques through network operating systems, services, and applications.

- Three-plus years of professional networking experience, including experience with Ethernet, token ring, modems, and other networking media. This must include installation, configuration, upgrade, and troubleshooting experience.

Note: *The Windows 2000 MCSE program is much more rigorous than the previous NT MCSE program; therefore, you'll really need some hands-on experience. Some of the exams require you to solve real-world case studies and network design issues, so the more hands-on experience you have, the better.*

- Two-plus years in a networked environment that includes hands-on experience with Windows 2000 Server, Windows 2000 Professional, Windows NT Server, Windows NT Workstation, and Windows 95 or Windows 98. A solid understanding of each system's architecture, installation, configuration, maintenance, and troubleshooting is also essential.

- Knowledge of the various methods for installing Windows 2000, including manual and unattended installations.

- A thorough understanding of key networking protocols, addressing, and name resolution, including TCP/IP, IPX/SPX, and NetBEUI.

- A thorough understanding of NetBIOS naming, browsing, and file and print services.

- Familiarity with key Windows 2000-based TCP/IP-based services, including HTTP (Web servers), DHCP, WINS, DNS, plus familiarity with one or more of the following: Internet Information Server (IIS), Index Server, and Proxy Server.

- An understanding of how to implement security for key network data in a Windows 2000 environment.

➤ Working knowledge of NetWare 3.x and 4.x, including IPX/SPX frame formats, NetWare file, print, and directory services, and both Novell and Microsoft client software. Working knowledge of Microsoft's Client Service For NetWare (CSNW), Gateway Service For NetWare (GSNW), the NetWare Migration Tool (NWCONV), and the NetWare Client For Windows (NT, 95, and 98) is essential.

➤ A good working understanding of Active Directory. The more you work with Windows 2000, the more you'll realize that this new operating system is quite different than Windows NT. New technologies like Active Directory have really changed the way that Windows is configured and used. We recommend that you find out as much as you can about Active Directory and acquire as much experience using this technology as possible. The time you take learning about Active Directory will be time very well spent!

Fundamentally, this boils down to a bachelor's degree in computer science, plus three years' experience working in a position involving network design, installation, configuration, and maintenance. We believe that well under half of all certification candidates meet these requirements, and that, in fact, most meet less than half of these requirements—at least, when they begin the certification process. But because all the people who already have been certified have survived this ordeal, you can survive it too—especially if you heed what our Self-Assessment can tell you about what you already know and what you need to learn.

Put Yourself to the Test

The following series of questions and observations is designed to help you figure out how much work you must do to pursue Microsoft certification and what kinds of resources you may consult on your quest. Be absolutely honest in your answers, or you'll end up wasting money on exams you're not yet ready to take. There are no right or wrong answers, only steps along the path to certification. Only you can decide where you really belong in the broad spectrum of aspiring candidates.

Two things should be clear from the outset, however:

➤ Even a modest background in computer science will be helpful.

➤ Hands-on experience with Microsoft products and technologies is an essential ingredient to certification success.

Educational Background

1. Have you ever taken any computer-related classes? [Yes or No]

    If Yes, proceed to question 2; if No, proceed to question 4.

2. Have you taken any classes on computer operating systems? [Yes or No]

    If Yes, you will probably be able to handle Microsoft's architecture and system component discussions. If you're rusty, brush up on basic operating system concepts, especially virtual memory, multitasking regimes, user mode versus kernel mode operation, and general computer security topics.

    If No, consider some basic reading in this area. We strongly recommend a good general operating systems book, such as *Operating System Concepts, 5th Edition*, by Abraham Silberschatz and Peter Baer Galvin (John Wiley & Sons, 1998, ISBN 0-471-36414-2). If this title doesn't appeal to you, check out reviews for other, similar titles at your favorite online bookstore.

3. Have you taken any networking concepts or technologies classes? [Yes or No]

    If Yes, you will probably be able to handle Microsoft's networking terminology, concepts, and technologies (brace yourself for frequent departures from normal usage). If you're rusty, brush up on basic networking concepts and terminology, especially networking media, transmission types, the OSI Reference Model, and networking technologies such as Ethernet, token ring, FDDI, and WAN links.

    If No, you might want to read one or two books in this topic area. The two best books that we know of are *Computer Networks, 3rd Edition*, by Andrew S. Tanenbaum (Prentice-Hall, 1996, ISBN 0-13-349945-6) and *Computer Networks and Internets, 2nd Edition*, by Douglas E. Comer and Ralph E. Droms (Prentice-Hall, 1998, ISBN 0-130-83617-6).

    Skip to the next section, "Hands-on Experience."

4. Have you done any reading on operating systems or networks? [Yes or No]

    If Yes, review the requirements stated in the first paragraphs after questions 2 and 3. If you meet those requirements, move on to the next section. If No, consult the recommended reading for both topics. A strong background will help you prepare for the Microsoft exams better than just about anything else.

Hands-on Experience

The most important key to success on all of the Microsoft tests is hands-on experience, especially with Windows 2000 Server and Professional, plus the many add-on services and BackOffice components around which so many of the Microsoft certification exams revolve. If we leave you with only one realization after taking this Self-Assessment, it should be that there's no substitute for time spent installing, configuring, and using the various Microsoft products upon which you'll be tested repeatedly and in depth.

5. Have you installed, configured, and worked with:

    ➤ Windows 2000 Server? [Yes or No]

    If Yes, make sure you understand basic concepts as covered in Exam 70-215. You should also study the TCP/IP interfaces, utilities, and services for Exam 70-216, plus implementing security features for Exam 70-220.

Tip: You can download objectives, practice exams, and other data about Microsoft exams from the Training and Certification page at **www.microsoft.com/trainingandservices/default.asp?PageID=mcp**. Use the "Exams" link to obtain specific exam information.

If you haven't worked with Windows 2000 Server, you must obtain one or two machines and a copy of Windows 2000 Server. Then, learn the operating system and whatever other software components on which you'll also be tested.

In fact, we recommend that you obtain two computers, each with a network interface, and set up a two-node network on which to practice. With decent Windows 2000-capable computers selling for about $500 to $600 apiece these days, this shouldn't be too much of a financial hardship. You may have to scrounge to come up with the necessary software, but if you scour the Microsoft Web site you can usually find low-cost options to obtain evaluation copies of most of the software that you'll need.

➤ Windows 2000 Professional? [Yes or No]

If Yes, make sure you understand the concepts covered in Exam 70-210.

If No, you will want to obtain a copy of Windows 2000 Professional and learn how to install, configure, and maintain it. You can use *MCSE Windows 2000 Professional Exam Cram* to guide your activities and studies, or work straight from Microsoft's test objectives if you prefer.

Tip: For any and all of these Microsoft exams, the Resource Kits for the topics involved are a good study resource. You can purchase softcover Resource Kits from Microsoft Press (search for them at **http://mspress.microsoft.com/**), but they also appear on the TechNet CDs (**www.microsoft.com/technet**). Along with *Exam Crams* and *Exam Preps*, we believe that Resource Kits are among the best tools you can use to prepare for Microsoft exams.

---

6. For any specific Microsoft product that is not itself an operating system (for example, SQL Server), have you installed, configured, used, and upgraded this software? [Yes or No]

    If the answer is Yes, skip to the next section. If it's No, you must get some experience. Read on for suggestions on how to do this.

Experience is a must with any Microsoft product exam, be it something as simple as FrontPage 2000 or as challenging as SQL Server 7.0. For trial copies of other software, search Microsoft's Web site using the name of the product as your search term. Also, search for bundles like "BackOffice" or "Small Business Server."

Tip: If you have the funds, or your employer will pay your way, consider taking a class at a Certified Training and Education Center (CTEC) or at an Authorized Academic Training Partner (AATP). In addition to classroom exposure to the topic of your choice, you get a copy of the software that is the focus of your course, along with a trial version of whatever operating system it needs, with the training materials for that class.

Before you even think about taking any Microsoft exam, make sure you've spent enough time with the related software to understand how it may be installed and configured, how to maintain such an installation, and how to troubleshoot that software when things go wrong. This will help you in the exam, and in real life!

Testing Your Exam-Readiness

Whether you attend a formal class on a specific topic to get ready for an exam or use written materials to study on your own, some preparation for the Microsoft certification exams is essential. At $100 a try, pass or fail, you want to do everything you can to pass on your first try. That's where studying comes in.

We have included a practice exam in this book, so if you don't score that well on the test, you can study more and then tackle the test again. We also have exams that you can take online through the **ExamCram.com** Web site at **www.examcram.com**. If you still don't hit a score of at least 70 percent after these tests, you'll want to investigate the other practice test resources we mention in this section.

For any given subject, consider taking a class if you've tackled self-study materials, taken the test, and failed anyway. The opportunity to interact with an instructor and fellow students can make all the difference in the world, if you can afford that privilege. For information about Microsoft classes, visit the Training and Certification page at **www.microsoft.com/education/partners/ctec.asp** for Microsoft Certified Education Centers or **www.microsoft.com/aatp/default.htm** for Microsoft Authorized Training Providers.

If you can't afford to take a class, visit the Training and Certification page anyway, because it also includes pointers to free practice exams and to Microsoft Certified Professional Approved Study Guides and other self-study tools. And even if you can't afford to spend much at all, you should still invest in some low-cost practice exams from commercial vendors.

7. Have you taken a practice exam on your chosen test subject? [Yes or No]

    If Yes, and you scored 70 percent or better, you're probably ready to tackle the real thing. If your score isn't above that threshold, keep at it until you break that barrier.

    If No, obtain all the free and low-budget practice tests you can find and get to work. Keep at it until you can break the passing threshold comfortably.

Tip: When it comes to assessing your test readiness, there is no better way than to take a good-quality practice exam and pass with a score of 70 percent or better. When we're preparing ourselves, we shoot for 80-plus percent, just to leave room for the "weirdness factor" that sometimes shows up on Microsoft exams.

Assessing Readiness for Exam 70-227

In addition to the general exam-readiness information in the previous section, there are several things you can do to prepare for the Installing, Configuring, and Administering Microsoft Internet Security and Acceleration (ISA) Server 2000, Enterprise Edition exam. As you're getting ready for Exam 70-227, visit the Exam Cram Windows 2000 Resource Center at **www.examcram.com/studyresource/w2kresource/**. Another valuable resource is the Exam Cram Insider newsletter. Sign up at **www.examcram.com** or send a blank email message to **subscribe-ec@mars.coriolis.com**. We also suggest that you join an active MCSE mailing list. One of the better ones is managed by Sunbelt Software. Sign up at **www.sunbelt-software.com** (look for the Subscribe button).

You can also cruise the Web looking for "braindumps" (recollections of test topics and experiences recorded by others) to help you anticipate topics you're likely to encounter on the test. The MCSE mailing list is a good place to ask where the useful braindumps are.

Tip: You can't be sure that a braindump's author can provide correct answers. Thus, use the questions to guide your studies, but don't rely on the answers in a braindump to lead you to the truth. Double-check everything you find in any braindump.

Microsoft exam mavens also recommend checking the Microsoft Knowledge Base (available on its own CD as part of the TechNet collection, or on the Microsoft Web site at **http://support.microsoft.com/support/**) for "meaningful technical support issues" that relate to your exam's topics. Although we're not sure exactly what the quoted phrase means, we have also noticed some overlap between technical support questions on particular products and troubleshooting questions on the exams for those products.

Onward, through the Fog!

Once you've assessed your readiness, undertaken the right background studies, obtained the hands-on experience that will help you understand the products and technologies at work, and reviewed the many sources of information to help you prepare for a test, you'll be ready to take a round of practice tests. When your scores come back positive enough to get you through the exam, you're ready to go after the real thing. If you follow our assessment regime, you'll not only know what you need to study, but when you're ready to make a test date at Prometric or VUE. Good luck!

CHAPTER ONE

ISA Server 2000 Overview

After completing this chapter, you will be able to:

✓ Identify the different Microsoft Internet security servers

✓ Identify the operating systems on which ISA Server can be installed

✓ Describe ISA Server's role in Microsoft's .NET platform

✓ Distinguish among types of Internet connections

✓ Describe the formation of a socket

✓ Identify the need for ISA Server on a network

✓ Identify the parts of a URL

✓ Differentiate between a proxy server and a firewall

✓ Identify categories of traffic that ISA Server needs to control

✓ Describe the concept of transparency in proxy servers

✓ Recognize new proxy services included in ISA Server

✓ Recognize new firewall services included in ISA Server

✓ Identify the intrusion-detection capabilities of ISA Server

Imagine that you are given a valuable item and you're responsible for protecting this item. Because the item is large and immovable, you put a box around it and weld it shut so that you can be assured no one can easily get to this valuable item. How safe would you feel if a hole were cut in that box? Would you be able to keep a watch over the box to make sure that the valuable item was always protected? Now make the valuable item your company's network and all of the information that it holds. Placing it in a box is ensuring that the network is secure in a building with no external connections. Someone would have to be physically inside the company's building (the box) to get to the network. Now let's say the company wants a connection to the Internet. That's the hole in the box. Connecting a company to the Internet is opening a hole that—unless carefully monitored—provides an entryway to anyone connected to the Internet. And that's a lot of people.

Microsoft's Internet Security and Acceleration Server 2000 (ISA Server) acts as a guard to watch over the hole. You can leave simple or complicated instructions for the guard, describing what traffic is allowed into the box. This explains the "Security" part of the name for ISA Server, but what about the "Acceleration" part? Inside your network, users will want to use the Internet connection to download information, such as Web pages. Acceleration refers to ISA Server's ability to speed up the response time for connections from inside your network out to the Internet.

ISA Server protects and controls Internet connections by interfering with them. To understand exactly how it does this, you must have a complete understanding of how these connections work. The Internet doesn't just provide Web pages. You will need to understand many types of services and applications that your users will want to access. First, let's start with an overview of the background of Microsoft's Internet security servers and its future plans for ISA Server.

Microsoft Proxy Server

ISA Server is not the first product from Microsoft designed to protect Internet connections. Microsoft's Proxy Server, in versions 1.0 and 2.0, was the first. Version 1.0 started out as a service that provided protection to outbound client connections only. Version 2.0 added protections for the internal network from requests that originated from the external connection. Proxy Server 2.0 also extended the protocols that the previous version supported.

Proxy Server does not have the reputation of providing the best Internet security, but it does have something that no other one has. As long as a company is using a Microsoft operating system, Proxy Server holds a distinct advantage over Internet security servers that are created by other vendors. For user authentication, Proxy Server uses the database of accounts from Windows NT. Microsoft included Proxy

Server in the BackOffice suite of applications, which all integrate directly with Microsoft operating systems' user accounts and security procedures. Products from different companies can use different sets of user accounts and permissions, and require the administrator to duplicate security settings. This additional set of user accounts or permissions make it a more complicated system of communication between Windows operating systems and the Internet security server. Also, it opens up the possibility that gaps can exist in the security. It is important that any security solution integrate well with existing operating systems and clients. Unfortunately for Microsoft's Proxy Server, this advantage was the best feature of the product. Without it, Proxy Server fell far below other Internet security products in supported protocols and services, and its security was not as strong as that of other products.

Not Just an Upgrade

Although ISA Server is the next version of an Internet security server from Microsoft, calling it an upgrade to Microsoft's Proxy Server 2.0 is oversimplifying the changes. First, of course, the name had to change to more accurately reflect the services it provides to the network. Calling a product a proxy server implies that it is designed to protect and speed up response times for outgoing connections. Microsoft wants to make it clear that its product provides security and services to both inbound and outbound connections. Also, many of the major changes can be attributed to the long span of time between releases of an Internet security server by Microsoft. Version 2.0 of Proxy Server was released four years before ISA Server—a change was long overdue.

As connectivity to the Internet grows, so does the need for a secure solution for those connections. Microsoft is creating a whole platform of products that will make it easy to create custom applications that can be deployed over the Internet. ISA Server's job is to protect these new custom solutions.

The .NET Platform

Windows for the PC revolutionized the way we use computers. Windows allowed computer novices to access the power of a PC. Because many PCs now have some form of Windows already loaded on them, Microsoft has taken on a new market. Windows allowed PCs to become interlaced in the structure of everyday life. For its next big revolution, Microsoft wants to unleash the potential of the Internet the way it unleashed the potential of PCs to change the lives of people who use them. According to Microsoft, browsers are most often used to download and view information over the Internet. Microsoft's goal is make the Internet a vehicle for integrating all the devices that people use, such as cell phones, laptops, handheld PCs, pagers, and so on and personalizing the information that they retrieve for you. Microsoft's goal with the .NET platform is to provide a set of technologies that allow a company to create applications specifically designed for use over the Internet. These applications can enable you to access or change information from any location at any time. You will be able to access information you need from the company using your cell phone as well as your desktop at home or work. Although each of the servers in the .NET platform runs on Windows 2000, together they give you the resources needed to create a solution for use on the Internet or provide you with a secure and robust connection to the Internet. The list of servers that comprise the .NET platform is like the platform itself—new and evolving. Each is just a tool that will help a business create custom solutions for use over the Internet or with Internet technologies. Much of the .NET platform, including ISA Server, can also be helpful in more traditional Internet uses.

The .NET platform is designed to give developers all the tools needed to create applications that run over the Internet. ISA Server's role, of course, is to provide security for the solutions and services that are created using .NET platform servers. Here is a list of products included in the .NET platform besides ISA Server 2000:

- Application Center 2000
- BizTalk Server 2000
- Commerce Server 2000
- Exchange Server 2000
- SQL Server 2000
- Host Integration Server 2000
- Mobile Information Server 2000

It may sound different and a bit far-fetched, but who would have thought even 15 years ago that nearly every desktop would end up with a computer on it. Or even 10 years ago that you could log on to the Internet and download any kind of information on any subject you wanted.

Internet Connections

Configuring ISA Server requires a good understanding of a basic Internet connection and the different types of connections used on the Internet. For a quick review, we will cover basic network and Internet connections, which involves reviewing the OSI model and the client/server nature of the Internet.

The OSI Model

Yes, it's back. Oftentimes when the subject of networking and TCP/IP is described, the OSI model is used to help illustrate the use of a product or service. Since

Table 1.1 The OSI model layers and a description of each.

Layer	Description
Application	Directly communicates with the application
Presentation	Translates data into intermediary form
Session	Makes a connection between computers
Transport	Delivers packets
Network	Addresses and routes packets
Data Link	Controls the flow of traffic
Physical	Defines components that physically connect the computers

Internet security servers interfere with Internet connections, it is a good idea to use the OSI model to see exactly where this interference takes place. This understanding will allow you to better administer ISA Server. Table 1.1 gives a quick review of the seven layers of the OSI model and an overview of the responsibilities that a protocol should have if it works at that layer.

Instead of creating just one protocol, vendors have created sets of them that work in conjunction with one another. Because the Internet and TCP/IP have grown so popular, most of the other suites of protocols are ignored now. Also, TCP/IP is often shown in a four-layer model instead of a seven-layer one. The four-layer model is just a simplified version of the seven-layer model. Figure 1.1 shows a comparison of the seven- and four-layer models so that you can easily see the similarities. In the four-layer model, the top three layers of the seven-layer model are combined into one, as are the bottom two. Also, in Figure 1.1 notice that the Network layer is referred to as the Internetworking layer in the four-layer model.

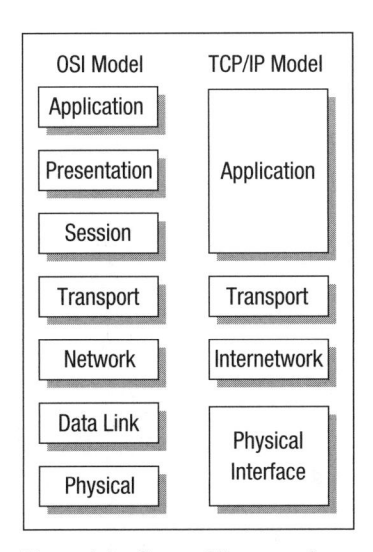

Figure 1.1 Some of the seven layers of the OSI model are joined for a simplified four-layer model.

TCP/IP Protocols

Different protocols and services included in the TCP/IP suite will need different settings when you're administering ISA Server. Protocols that work at the Application layer of the OSI model are more sophisticated and specific to a purpose, while protocols that work at the lower layers are more generic and not application specific. This creates an upside-down pyramid effect when listing TCP/IP and other protocols. The two main protocols at the Transport layer, TCP and UDP, both use IP at the Internetworking layer. In the TCP/IP suite, all Application-layer protocols will be designed to use TCP or UDP for delivery of packets. TCP and UDP both deliver packets, as Transport-layer protocols should, but TCP guarantees delivery of packets and UDP does not. While guaranteed delivery is a good thing, the process of guaranteeing delivery can slow things down. So, TCP gives a guarantee while UDP provides speedier delivery.

Knowing whether a service uses TCP or UDP can be important when you're taking the exam and when you're administering ISA Server. For example, HTTP is the Application-layer protocol used to download Web pages over the Internet. HTTP uses TCP at the Transport layer. RealAudio is a streaming protocol that transmits high-quality audio over the Internet. RealAudio uses UDP as its Transport-layer protocol. Users cannot select which protocol they would like to use. This difference can have implications when you're configuring rules that allow or disallow client connections through ISA Server. When a user selects a service, the protocols that the service uses are determined when the service is created.

Uniform Resource Locator

To find a file on the Internet, a user must have the correct Uniform Resource Locator (URL) for that resource. Most users enter only a partial URL and are able to find their resource through hyperlinks, but to control Internet security you must be aware of all the parts of a full URL:

- Protocol
- IP address
- Port number
- Directory
- Filename

A URL is like a street address for a resource. It begins with the generic information on the left side and works its way to the name of a specific resource on the right. The format looks like this:

```
Protocol://IP address:port number/directory/filename
```

Working from left to right we will look at each of the five parts of the URL and discuss the importance of each one:

1. The Application-level protocol is the first part of the URL. Only the Application-level protocol is listed. A URL is mostly used on the Web, but it can be used with other services that retrieve files, such as FTP. A protocol will change based on the service that is being performed. For example, a URL used to retrieve a Web page will use HTTP as the protocol. A URL used to transfer a file using the FTP service will use FTP as the protocol. A URL connecting to newsgroups or downloading an article will use NNTP as the protocol. Therefore, all requests for Web pages will start in a generic manner, with HTTP as the protocol.

2. The second part of the URL is often the name of the server instead of the IP address. People just aren't good at remembering the up to 12 digits needed for an IP address, such as 192.168.250.100. But people can remember a computer name, such as **www.microsoft.com** or **www.coriolis.com**. If a server name is used, a Domain Name System (DNS) server will immediately translate the name into an IP address. Every computer on the Internet must have a unique IP address. The IP address identifies specifically which computer you are trying to reach on the Internet.

3. Ports are a required part of the URL, but most people stop typing after the second part of the URL. Every service has a default port number that it uses if the port number is not specified in the URL. If the IP address gets you to the computer, think of the port as the doorway into the computer. Since each service provided by the computer has a different doorway, entering the correct one is important. Understanding ports is critical to securing a network from Internet connections. We discuss ports later in this chapter.

4. Once a request enters the computer through the port, it will immediately need to know which directory on the computer's hard disk will give it the requested information. If the directory is left out of the URL—as it often is—the computer will assume that the directory it is currently in is the correct one. When loaded onto a server, each service creates a default directory. Microsoft's Web server, Internet Information Server (IIS), creates an **Inetpub\wwwroot** directory for Web services by default. Any directory listed in the URL will start from the default directory for the service. If a URL starts with **http:// www.examprep.com/books** and the server **www.examprep.com** is using IIS for its Web services, **Inetpub\wwwroot\books** is the path on the hard disk of the Web server this URL is looking for. **Inetpub\wwwroot** is the path used by IIS Server by default. This default can be changed during installation, but the concept is the same. This part of the URL lists any directories that are located under the directory that is being used by the Web site.

5. Finally, the URL specifies which file it is requesting. A Web browser needs to display a specific Web page to show something to the user. Even error messages are Web pages. If a page is not specified, a Web server usually provides a default page. The default page is often the home page of the Web site, which displays links to other pages on the site.

Here is a full URL that illustrates how a client would find a Web page using that URL:

http://www.examprep.com:80/new_releases/ISA_Server.htm

A Web page is being requested, so HTTP is the protocol. The second part of the URL is the name of the server, **www.examprep.com**. This server name is sent to DNS, which converts it to the IP address **192.168.0.5**. After the server name you see port 80—the default port for HTTP and the Web. The directory is **new_releases**. Because the server is an IIS server, the default directory for the Web server is **Inetpub\wwwroot**, and it is loaded on the C: drive. The full path is **C:\Inetpub\wwwroot\new_releases**. In that directory, the requested Web page is **ISA_Server.htm**.

It is easy to practice recognizing full URLs by logging on to any Web site. Click a few hyperlinks to work your way into the site. You most likely won't see the port number because you will probably be using the default port of 80, but you should see directories and file names after the server name.

Ports and Sockets

Every computer in a network using TCP/IP must have a unique IP address. When you have the IP address of a computer on the Internet, you know exactly which computer you are trying to find. Even though you can find a computer with just one IP address, you still need more information to get into that computer. An IP address—like an address for a house—gets you to the computer, but if you want to communicate or get information from that computer, you need to get inside. Imagine reaching a house and seeing over 65,000 doors. Every computer using TCP/IP has more than 65,000 ports. Like doorways, ports can be opened to allow passage inside, or they can be closed and allow nothing in or out. To make a connection to a computer and exchange information with it, you must have the correct IP address and an open port. The combination of IP address and open port forms what is called a socket. A socket works just above the Transport layer in the four-layer version of the OSI model, below the Application-layer protocol. A socket is the connection between the client computer and the server computer.

Figure 1.2 shows how a socket is formed with the IP address and port number. A socket must be formed to make a connection to a computer using TCP/IP. One way to block a connection is to close the port—it's like closing the door. An open port can accept a connection and form the socket, but a closed port cannot.

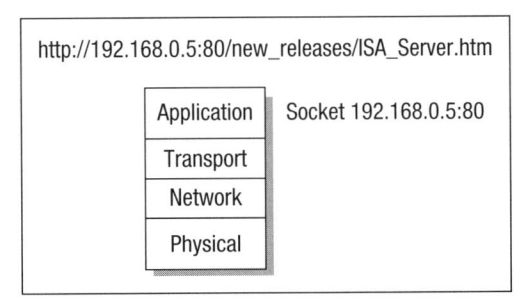

```
http://192.168.0.5:80/new_releases/ISA_Server.htm

    ┌─────────────┐
    │ Application │── Socket 192.168.0.5:80
    ├─────────────┤
    │  Transport  │
    ├─────────────┤
    │   Network   │
    ├─────────────┤
    │   Physical  │
    └─────────────┘
```

Figure 1.2 An IP address and port number form a socket. A connection is made to an open port. If the port is closed, the connection is not made.

With more than 65,000 doors to choose from, which one should you select? That depends on what you are trying to do. The first 1,023 ports have been designated as well-known ports and are reserved as default ports for defined services. That means they can be assigned to certain services. For example, when a user wants to download a Web page, the connection to the Web server is made through port 80 (unless otherwise specified). The client computer will attempt to make a connection to port 80 when trying to access a Web page, and the server will know to leave that port open when providing Web services. Ports are important to understand because Internet security at its most basic level simply closes ports to prevent connections. As an administrator of Internet security, you can open, close, or even change the default ports of the services you are providing.

Internet Security Basics

How do Internet security servers meddle in Internet connections? The process can vary according to the service the security server is interrupting and the sophistication of that server. They can interfere at different levels of the OSI model. It makes a difference whether the interference is needed for a connection coming in from the Internet or for a connection coming from the internal network going out to the Internet. Generic terms exist for the types of services that Internet security servers offer. This section describes basic Internet security terms and components. Once you understand these basic terms, you can move on to the specific way in which ISA Server implements these components.

The main purpose of Internet security is to keep a company's internal network separate and protected from a connection to the Internet. To do this, ISA Server provides so many security services that sometimes it can be difficult to keep them sorted out. The easiest way to keep track of the different services is by placing them in one of three categories. The ISA Server service controls or accelerates one of three types of connections:

1. Inbound from the Internet to the company's internal network
2. Outbound from the company's network to the Internet
3. Inbound from the Internet to the company's Web server or other server

Protection from the first type of connection is referred to collectively as a *firewall*. Protection for the second type is referred to as *proxy services*. Providing protection from the third type is referred to as *reverse proxying* or *publishing*. You might think the third type should be placed in the first category, but a company's Web server that is supposed to be open to the public through the Internet presents a new kind of risk to the company's internal network. A company's internal network must be protected from all public connections—especially the Internet—but if the company is providing Web services, it must allow this type of traffic in—which explains why these two types of connections have separate services. We will discuss the services provided by ISA Server throughout the book, but as you are introduced to each one, you should be able to keep it separate from all others by placing it into one of these three categories.

When Is It a Firewall?

One difficulty in understanding Internet security components is that the terms firewall and proxy are used interchangeably when they are actually two different types of services. Inbound connections are initiated by users that are physically located outside the company's network. This means these connections are coming in from the Internet and trying to connect to the company's network or Web server. Networking components that provide protection from inbound connections are referred to collectively as a firewall. Figure 1.3 shows a firewall protecting a network from inbound Internet connections. The firewall blocks all incoming connections except those specifically allowed by the network administrator.

When Is It a Proxy Server?

An outbound connection is one that is initiated from inside the company's network and is trying to get out to the Internet. A component that protects this outbound connection is referred to as a proxy server. A generic definition of the word proxy

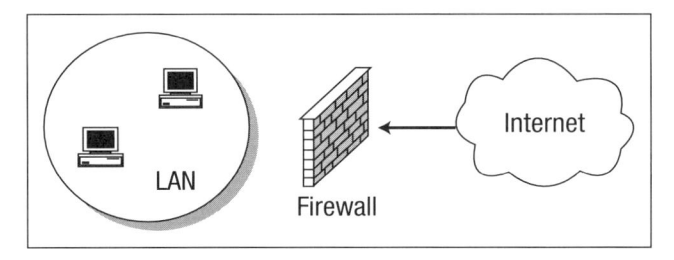

Figure 1.3 A firewall protecting a network from inbound connections from the Internet.

is a substitute or replacement for something else. When making an Internet connection, a user must leave sensitive information, such as IP address and username, with the Internet server. An Internet user is not even specifically asked for this information, but the user's computer gives this information when it makes a connection to a Web site.

A proxy server avoids this exchange of information by making the Internet connections for your internal company users. A user from the internal network will send a request that needs to go out to the Internet to the proxy server. The proxy server, acting as a substitute, will retrieve the needed information from the Internet for the internal user. A proxy server performing this service for a network will need to be dual-homed. This means it has at least two network adapters—one connected to the outside network (the Internet) and one connected to the internal network. The only computer on the network making a connection to the Internet is the proxy server. Therefore, all internal company computers are protected from making these connections. Figure 1.4 shows an internal client making an Internet request to the proxy server and the proxy server fulfilling that request for the internal user. The proxy server does not simply pass a Web request on to the Internet. Instead, it formulates a separate request of its own. This way, the original requesting client computer is completely anonymous to the Web server.

As long as the proxy server is filling Internet requests on behalf of clients, it tries to optimize the response time of these requests. If two internal clients ask for the same Web page within a short span of time, a proxy server will try to fill the second request from the cache instead of making another trip to the Internet to retrieve the same Web page. A generic definition of cache is just a quicker method of retrieving data than going back to the original source. Internet cache generally uses hard disk space to store Web pages. Retrieving a page off the local hard disk of the proxy server is quicker than going back out to the Internet to get the page. The second client should get a quicker response and never know that the page was

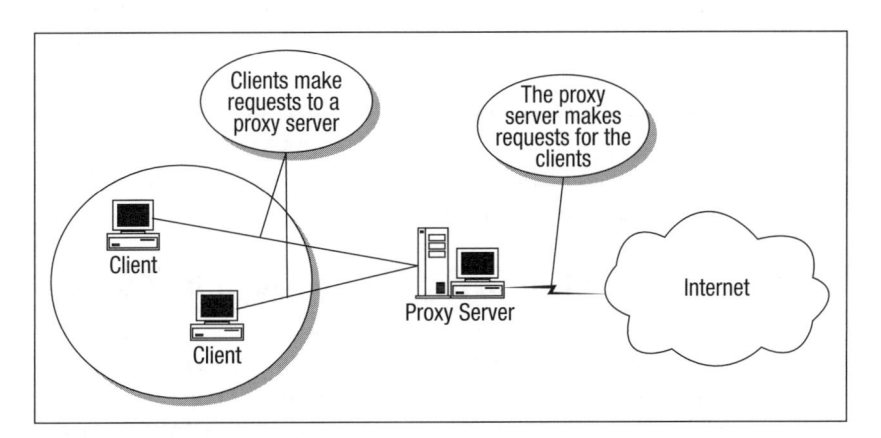

Figure 1.4 A proxy server makes outbound Internet requests on behalf of internal clients.

sitting in the cache for a few minutes. A firewall doesn't need to try to speed up connections since its main job is to block connections anyway. But a proxy's job is to make connections and retrieve information. The proxy server usually comes with features that allow it to do its job in as speedy a fashion as possible. Cache is used only for Web pages, but users connect to the Internet to do more than just retrieve Web pages. Caching is covered in depth in Chapter 8 of this book.

Reverse Proxy

A reverse proxy is different from both a firewall and a regular proxy server. A firewall and a reverse proxy are checking inbound connections. Instead of simply blocking or allowing connections, a reverse proxy accepts incoming connections bound for a Web server located on the internal network. The client component of the inbound connection believes that it has reached the Web server when in reality it has reached the reverse proxy server. Web and other Internet-related services can be fulfilled by a number of servers on a network, but the client will be led to believe that all services are coming from the reverse proxy server. The reverse proxy server's job is to protect the servers providing services to Internet clients by checking and controlling all incoming requests.

Transparency

A transparent proxy connection is one in which users or computers are unaware that a proxy server is interfering in the connection to the Internet. Setting up proxy services on a network is more complicated when the user wants to do more than just download Web pages over the Internet. A client trying to connect to an Internet application over the Internet usually needs to have proxy client software installed. This software allows the client computer to connect to the proxy server instead of trying to make a direct connection over the Internet. It also allows the proxy server to create a connection to the Internet server and pass the information between the internal client and the Internet server. When client software is loaded on a proxy client, the connection is not transparent. The client machine is aware that a proxy server is intervening in the connection. Proxy servers are transparent only from the user's point of view—the URL they are connecting to does not change when connecting through a proxy server. ISA Server introduces a new proxy client that is truly transparent. The client computers as well as the users are not aware that they are using a proxy server to connect to the Internet. No software needs to be loaded on the clients at all.

If They Are So Different, Why Can't You Tell Them Apart?

When firewalls and proxy servers first became popular, they were separate entities on a network. Now, things are getting a bit fuzzy. A firewall can be as simple as a router that closes certain ports. In this case, if users are making a request through the Internet, they will not be able to make a connection if the port is closed.

Of course, with over 65,000 ports, if you leave just one open that could be enough for a malicious user to cause damage. So, most people like to have a router as the first of many layers of security.

A router works only at the Network layer of the OSI model. This makes the router a pretty simple piece of equipment. A port is either open or closed. But what if you want the port open to some users, but not to others? A level of control beyond simply opening or closing the port will take a more sophisticated firewall, one that needs to work up to the Application layer of the OSI model.

Proxy servers started out at the Application level because they needed to be able to formulate requests for Web pages that went up to the Application layer. As firewalls became more sophisticated and were given Application-layer abilities, often proxy services were thrown in with the firewall capabilities. At the same time, the makers of proxy servers were adding firewall capabilities to their products. As long as each was sitting on the edge of the network, it was thought that they would need both capabilities. The fuzziness of the line between firewalls and proxies makes it difficult to understand the services they provide. The creators of each type of product wanted to provide all-in-one solutions as part of their products.

Connection Types

Firewalls and proxies make certain types of connections based on the services they are providing. These connections work at different layers of the OSI model. The higher they work in the OSI model, the more sophisticated the service is. These connections are called Packet level, Circuit level, and Application level.

Packet Level

This type of connection works at the Network layer of the OSI model. It is a Packet-level connection because the individual packets are examined for such information as source and destination IP address as well as the port number to which they are trying to connect. Components that allow Packet-level connections are not complex ones. They cannot block or allow packets based on more sophisticated criteria, such as user authentication or service type. They block or forward packets based on IP or port information.

Circuit Level

When users want to connect to Internet applications, a proxy server can interfere with the connection. This type of connection is usually made for proxy services, because a user on the internal network will want to connect to a server on the Internet and run an application. Since proxy servers are designed to make requests for a Web page for internal users, they are essentially interrupting the process before the user reaches the Internet. This interruption can cause problems when an

Internet application needs to make a connection between an internal client and a server on the Internet. The proxy server needs to pass the information between the internal client and the Internet server without disturbing the connection between the two. This kind of connection works at the Circuit level. No Circuit layer appears in the OSI model, but one layer is responsible for connections between computers—the Session layer. The Session layer is the layer at which connections between computers occur and the layer at which Circuit-level services work.

Application Level

Components that provide Application-level connections are the most sophisticated type. Application-level proxies and firewalls can distinguish between services and even disallow packets based on the contents contained in them. Instead of just blocking access to certain sites on the Web that could contain questionable material, some components that provide Application-level connections can scan the material that passes through the connection and disallow certain material based on specified guidelines. Application-level firewalls and proxies can vary on how specific you can get when placing constraints. When integrated with Active Directory, ISA Server can distinguish between users and groups when allowing connections on the Internet. It can also allow incoming connections to only certain servers on the internal network. Components that provide Application-level connections can vary in level of sophistication, much like Application-layer protocols vary.

New Capabilities and Features

As the name Internet Security and Acceleration implies, ISA Server includes two main concentrations of services. The "Internet Security" portion of the name refers to the protective firewall services provided by ISA Server. The "Acceleration" part of the name refers to the caching and performance-enhancing services.

Installation

When designing an Internet connectivity solution, you can install ISA servers to work as standalone or together. For an enterprise environment, you might want to emphasize the security aspects on some ISA servers and the performance-enhancing abilities on others. You can choose between three different modes when installing ISA Server:

➤ *Firewall*—To focus on security services

➤ *Cache*—To focus on performance-enhancing services

➤ *Integrated*—If you need both types of services on the same server

Integrated mode can be used in a smaller environment where the servers are not as specialized in the services they provide to the network.

ISA Server installs only on Windows 2000 Server—all versions of Windows 2000 Server, including Advanced Server and Datacenter Server. ISA Server does not install on Windows NT 4. Although ISA Server can participate in a Windows 2000 Active Directory domain, it does not have to belong to one. However, as with many services in Windows 2000, without a domain environment you get only the basic services of the product. Many of the enhancements that come along with domain membership are for large-scale environments. Without Active Directory in the network, ISA Server will allow only a smaller scale installation. Large-scale installations include multiple ISA servers acting as if they are one. This configuration is referred to as an array. An installation into a domain environment also requires more planning. We will cover installation into standalone and domain environments in Chapter 3 of this book.

ISA Server supports the TCP/IP protocol suite, just as the Internet does. Proxy Server 2.0 supported IPX/SPX on the internal network only. This means you could use IPX/SPX on your internal network, and Proxy Server would accept incoming requests from internal computers that used the IPX/SPX protocol suite. Proxy Server would then make the request on the Internet using TCP/IP. ISA Server drops support for IPX/SPX on the internal network because TCP/IP is now the standard protocol suite. Even Novell, the creator of the IPX/SPX protocol, can use TCP/IP as its primary protocol.

Administration

Like all products running on Windows 2000 Server, ISA Server is administered through Microsoft Management Console (MMC). MMC gives a tree view of objects that you can administer and allows you to right-click on anything in the tree to open a menu of commands just for that object. Figure 1.5 shows the ISA Server console in MMC. ISA Server lets you set up policies, rules, filters, and other types of control. ISA Server also includes a tool called the Taskpad that assists you with the administrative tasks. The Taskpad enables you to personalize the console with additional views and shortcuts to commands. Figure 1.6 shows the Taskpad in the ISA console.

ISA Server As a Firewall

Inbound requests coming in from the Internet can take many different forms. In general, firewalls tend to deny all services except those that are specifically allowed. The administrator of ISA Server needs to specify which connections are allowed. So many services are legitimate for inbound requests that it can be difficult for the administrator to establish control over them. A company can have a Web server that allows public access or one that allows only authenticated users to access it. Other servers on the internal network can provide services that are needed by outside

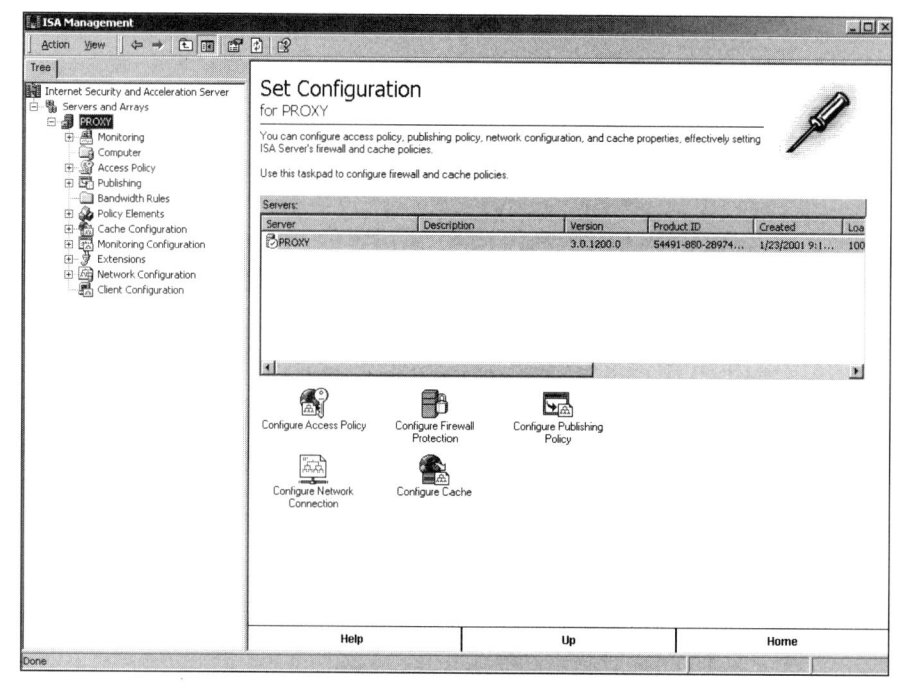

Figure 1.5 The ISA Management console.

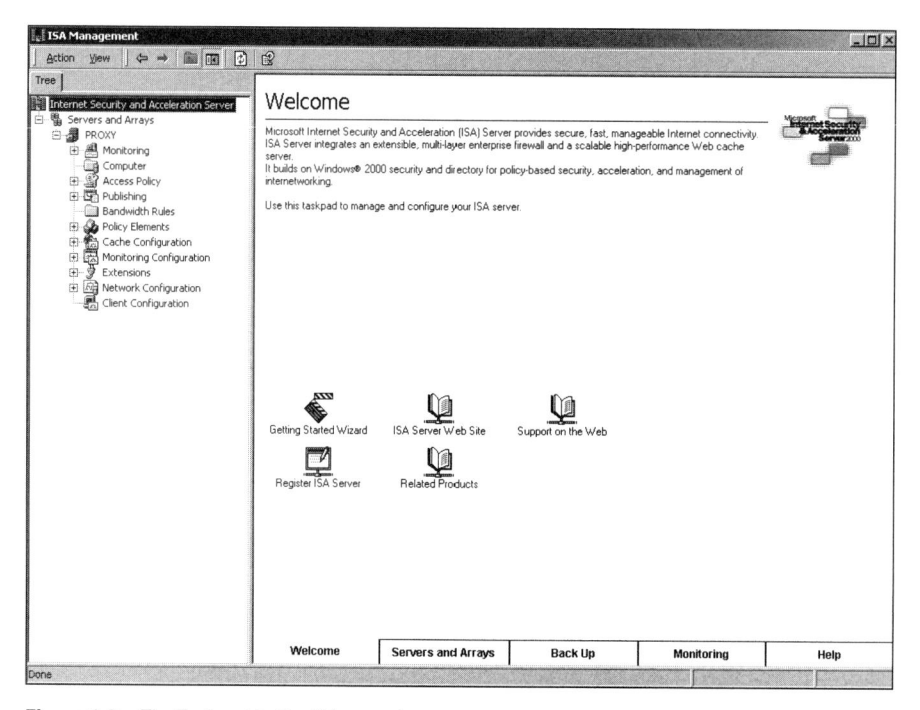

Figure 1.6 The Taskpad in the ISA console.

users. A company employee working from home who needs to get to private company documents is a good example. Internet applications can also allow users to connect to meetings through the Internet or stream audio and video. Each of these scenarios requires a different service to secure it.

You can set up Web publishing rules to control the inflow of requests to a Web site. Server publishing rules control inbound requests attempting to access servers on the internal network. Internal clients wanting to participate in a meeting over the Internet with software such as NetMeeting will need to have the H.323 Gatekeeper service configured on ISA Server. ISA Server includes a Getting Started Wizard and other wizards to help you create settings.

The security services provided by ISA Server include detection of attacks that can come through an Internet connection. Instead of just trying to break into a site, a hacker can attempt to disable a Web site by overloading it with so many packets that the server either crashes or does not allow other legitimate users to get to the site. A hacker can also capture outgoing packets from the network and reconfigure them so that they are destructive and designed to crash the server. You can set up ISA Server to detect a possible attack and even take steps to thwart it. When ISA Server detects potential attacks, it notifies you.

ISA Server As a Proxy

As a proxy server, ISA Server gives you a fine level of control over connections allowed for the internal network's users. You can establish rules that control which protocols are permitted for outgoing connections as well as what sites, what time of day, and even what type of content users can connect to. Also, part of the services that a proxy provides is the caching of Web pages. A Web page retrieved from the cache comes up faster for a user than one that must be retrieved from the Internet. ISA Server can route requests through other ISA servers to try to find the item in their cache before sending the request to the Internet. Rules and filters for ISA Server users can be combined into access policies. You can copy these policies to other ISA servers for easy administrative overhead or modify them for different ISA servers throughout the enterprise.

Traditionally, you don't have to load any software onto the client to use a proxy server to retrieve Web pages. However, this is not the case if users need to access Internet applications. You must load proxy client software on each client. The need for proxy client software causes an administrative headache that only gets worse if a network contains different types of client operating systems.

With ISA Server, you don't need proxy client software. SecureNAT allows the use of Internet applications through ISA Server without loading software on the client.

This option is available for all types of client operating systems. Client software is also available; installing the software creates what is called a firewall client. If you're willing to go to the trouble of installing this client software, you'll be rewarded with extra features, such as Active Directory integration. Also, the Firewall client is the only client that allows ISA Server to require user authentication. The Firewall client can be loaded only on recent versions of Microsoft operating systems: Windows 95/98 and Millennium, Windows NT 4, or Windows 2000.

Extensibility

Like most new Microsoft products, ISA Server is extensible. This means you can add to the product the features you feel you need. New features include new filters for blocking packets, administrative tools, or even alerts for new types of attacks developed by hackers. ISA Server comes with its own Software Development Kit (SDK), which contains sample code so that you can develop your own custom features. You can also purchase solutions from third-party vendors.

Chapter Summary

Microsoft's first release of an Internet security server, called Proxy Server, was never very well received in the Internet community. Proxy Server was improved with the release of version 2, but its greatest strength has always been its close integration with other Microsoft products. With Microsoft's release of a new Internet security server the name, as well as the performance, is vastly different.

Internet security servers like ISA Server are necessary due to the public nature of the Internet. These servers protect internal networks by intercepting all incoming requests and making all outgoing requests for internal computers. Different Internet security servers use different methods to provide this security, but all must work with the basic way that connections are made over the Internet. A comprehensive understanding of TCP/IP, URLs, ports, and sockets is needed before you can understand how Internet security servers work.

Internet security servers used to be classified as either firewalls or proxies, but now they are generally packaged in one server. Firewalls were designed to protect an internal network from incoming packets from a public network whereas proxy servers were designed to protect the computers on an internal network when making outgoing connections to a public network. ISA Server provides both types of connections, including the ability to publish internal servers to the Internet.

Review Questions

1. Why would you choose the firewall client as a proxy client option? [Check the two best answers]
   a. To avoid loading client proxy software.
   b. To give proxy protection to a variety of client operating systems.
   c. All your client operating systems are Microsoft Windows 98 and 2000.
   d. You have a need for user-based security.

2. Which of the following are true? [Check the two best answers]
   a. A proxy server protects outbound Internet traffic.
   b. A proxy server protects inbound Internet traffic.
   c. A firewall protects a network from outbound Internet traffic.
   d. A firewall protects a network from inbound Internet traffic.

3. Which of the following is true of TCP/IP Transport-layer protocols? [Check the two best answers]
   a. UDP guarantees delivery of a message.
   b. UDP does not guarantee delivery of a message.
   c. TCP guarantees delivery of a message.
   d. TCP does not guarantee delivery of a message.

4. Which of the following forms a socket? [Check the two best answers]
   a. Computer name
   b. IP address
   c. The URL
   d. Protocol
   e. Port number

5. Which ports are designated as well known?
   a. The first 1,023
   b. The last 1,023
   c. Over 65,000
   d. Up to 65,000

6. ISA Server must be installed in an Active Directory environment.
   a. True
   b. False

7. If ISA Server is protecting an internal network from Internet connections, what service is needed to allow internal users to use NetMeeting through the Internet?
   a. Web publishing
   b. Server publishing
   c. Web proxy
   d. H.323 Gatekeeper

8. In the four-layer model, which OSI layer is responsible for addressing?
   a. Application
   b. Transport
   c. Internetworking
   d. Physical

9. Why would a developer of a new Internet service use UDP instead of TCP as the Transport-layer protocol?
   a. To speed up the service
   b. To form a socket
   c. To guarantee delivery
   d. To follow the OSI model

10. Why would you choose SecureNAT as a proxy client option? [Check the two best answers]
    a. To avoid loading client proxy software.
    b. To give proxy protection to a variety of client operating systems.
    c. All your client operating systems are Microsoft Windows 98 and 2000.
    d. You have a need for user-based security.

11. A firewall protects a network from packets coming from which direction?
    a. Inbound
    b. Outbound

12. A proxy server protects a network from packets coming from which direction?
    a. Inbound
    b. Outbound

13. What is another name for a Network-layer firewall?
    a. Proxy server
    b. Cable
    c. Network adapter card
    d. Router

14. When is a Circuit-level proxy needed?
    a. When downloading Web pages
    b. When you don't have enough memory
    c. When you're using Internet applications
    d. Always

15. What is cache?
    a. A router that closes ports
    b. A mechanism that provides a quicker method for accessing data than going back to the original source
    c. A proxy server that protects users from Internet connections
    d. An Application-layer firewall

16. Where does ISA Server store most of its Internet cache?
    a. In memory
    b. In the network adapter card
    c. In the disk controller
    d. On the hard disk
    e. On the Internet

17. If a client machine is unaware that a proxy server is connecting it to the Internet, the proxy server is said to be what?
    a. Working
    b. In the wrong port
    c. A firewall
    d. Transparent

18. Which is not a protocol?
    a. OSI
    b. HTTP
    c. FTP
    d. UDP
    e. IP
    f. TCP

19. What type of request could be filled from cache?
    a. Inbound
    b. Outbound

20. Why is there a differentiation between inbound requests coming to the internal network and inbound requests coming into a company Web server?

    a. A Web server and the internal network must be on separate networks.

    b. Inbound requests to the Web server must be allowed.

    c. To protect each from outbound requests.

    d. There is no good reason.

21. ISA Server is a part of the .NET platform and works only as a part of this platform.

    a. True

    b. False

22. At the release of ISA Server 2000, how many years had it been since Proxy Server, in its latest version, was released?

    a. 1 year

    b. 2 years

    c. 3 years

    d. 4 years

    e. 5 years

23. In comparison to other Internet security servers what is Proxy Server 2.0's strongest feature?

    a. Firewall packet filters

    b. Caching abilities

    c. Integration with BackOffice

    d. Integration with Windows NT operating system

24. On how many operating systems can ISA Server's firewall client be installed?

    a. 2

    b. 3

    c. 4

    d. 5

    e. 6

25. On which of the following operating systems can ISA Server be loaded?

    a. Windows NT 4

    b. Windows NT 4 with Service Pack 6 applied

    c. Windows 2000 Professional

    d. Windows 2000 Server

    e. Windows 2000 Advanced Server

26. Which protocol suites can ISA Server work with?
    a. TCP/IP
    b. DecNET
    c. IPX/SPX
    d. Appletalk

27. Which of the following can be included in an access policy?
    a. Protocol rules
    b. Site and content rules
    c. Packet filter
    d. All of the above
    e. None of the above

28. To access Internet applications through ISA Server client proxy, software must be loaded.
    a. True
    b. False

Real-World Projects

"The Web site has been broken into... again." Joe looked up to see the Chief Operations Officer at his office door. "We are having an emergency meeting in 15 minutes to discuss a solution." Joe looked past the COO to see the IT manager also standing in the doorway. Why were they telling him this? "We have decided to create a new position at the company to deal with these security issues," the COO continued. "The position will be Internet Security Specialist. What do you think?"

"That's a great idea," said Joe, thinking that finally the company was going to get serious about the issues of Internet security. He meant it: this was a great idea. He had been saying all along that not enough attention had been focused on this important issue. He had even brought up the subject at some recent meetings. Joe knew that Internet security was something that required planning and...wait a minute.

"Great, then we'll announce it at the meeting. Congratulations, Joe!"

Congratulations? "Wait...I, uh..."

"Jot down a few ideas and bring them to the meeting. We're looking forward to a resolution on this problem."

Joe had started with the company just three months earlier. The company, Training4U, provides soft skills training for companies on such subjects as project and time management, team building, and sales techniques. Six months earlier, the company managers had hired a Web design company to build a Web site for them. After the site had been up for a few months, the managers realized that they needed some technical expertise to administer and update the site. Because the managers hadn't budgeted for a Web development position, they looked within the company for someone with Web development expertise. Joe wasn't exactly an expert Web developer. He knew some HTML and could read the Web page code with a pretty good understanding of what it was doing. Because he was only updating the information in the Web pages and not changing their functionality, the new duties had not been too overwhelming.

Joe's real expertise was in IIS administration and networking. The company had nearly finished an upgrade to Windows 2000. With all of the planning and work that went into the upgrade, Joe was ready to take a break. Updating the Web site gave him a chance to do something different.

Joe knew exactly why the managers had selected him for this new Internet Security Specialist position. Besides bringing up the subject often to anyone who would listen, he had been talking with the IT manager about getting certified in Windows 2000 and maybe getting his MCSE. He was also thinking of gaining expertise in Internet technologies. He knew a number of Microsoft products and exams were Internet related.

Because the company was just finishing an upgrade to Windows 2000, Joe decided to try **www.microsoft.com** to see if the Web site would give him any ideas.

Project 1.1

To search the Microsoft Site for Internet Security ideas:

1. Open Internet Explorer.

2. Type "www.microsoft.com" in the Address bar near the top of the window.

3. Type "Internet Security" including the quotation marks so that the search only finds documents with both words side by side.

4. Click the Go button.

After performing these steps, Joe received a search results page. Nearly all of the documents listed in the search results page had something to do with a product named Internet Security and Acceleration Server. Joe realized that this product might be the answer he needed.

Because his Internet connection was slow, just those steps had taken five minutes of the 15 minutes that Joe had before the meeting. He selected a few documents that looked like they would provide some quick answers, taking note of the full URL of each document so he could reference them later. The home page for ISA Server (with a URL of **www.microsoft.com/isaserver**) was the first Joe selected. Because it was the home page, Joe found links to a variety of information on ISA Server. To try to get a feel for the services that ISA Server provides to a network, Joe selected a link to a page on features. Its URL was **www.microsoft.com/isaserver/productinfo/features.htm**.

Project 1.2
To locate Internet Security and Acceleration Server documents:

1. With Internet Explorer open, type the following URL in the Address bar: **www.microsoft.com/isaserver**. This brings up the default product page for ISA Server.

2. In the Address bar of Internet Explorer, start with the URL **www.microsoft.com/isaserver, add /productinfo/features.htm**. The result is **www.microsoft.com/isaserver/productinfo/features.htm**.

While skimming the features page, Joe got a good feel for the services that ISA Server provided to the network. ISA Server is a firewall that has the ability to connect at the Packet, Circuit, and Application levels. It also has Web caching abilities that can speed up a Web user's response time. Joe had been around Web sites enough to know that all of these terms were good buzzwords to use at the meeting. Five more minutes had passed. Joe would use the last five minutes to prepare what he would say at the meeting when he was introduced as the new Internet Security Specialist.

CHAPTER TWO

Preparing for ISA Server Installation

After completing this chapter, you will be able to:

✓ Identify hardware requirements

✓ Identify software requirements

✓ Decide whether to do a clean install or upgrade

✓ Decide which ISA Server mode to use

✓ Describe the ISA Server array

✓ Decide which ISA Server client to use

✓ Complete the final system preparation before the ISA Server installation

Now that you have a basic idea of what Internet Security and Acceleration Server 2000 (ISA Server) does, it is time to talk more about how to install it and start playing with it. You pop the ISA Server installation CD into your system, and you are ready to rock and roll. But wait! Just as Microsoft recommends for a Windows 2000 Active Directory implementation, careful planning before installing the ISA Server components to your system certainly helps. In this chapter, we will go through all the pre-installation components you need to achieve a smooth and successful installation of ISA Server.

Hardware Requirements

To install ISA Server without any problems, you will need to know the hardware requirements. Table 2.1 shows the minimum as well as the recommended hardware requirements. You can obtain the latest hardware requirements for the ISA Server at **www.microsoft.com/isaserver/productinfo/sysreq.htm**. Use only the hardware listed in the Windows 2000 Hardware Compatibility List (HCL) to avoid any hardware-related installation problems. The Windows 2000 HCL is a list of hardware that Microsoft maintains, and it lists all the hardware that Windows 2000 officially supports. As of this writing, the recommended hardware requirements for both ISA Server Standard and Enterprise editions are the same, although you should change them depending on various factors, such as network load and cache activities.

To use ISA Server's caching feature, which stores Internet content locally, you will need to allocate extra hard disk space for that content.

Microsoft recommends the following hardware configurations, depending on how the ISA server will be used in a network environment. We will explain Firewall mode and Cache mode in detail in the "ISA Server Mode" section in this chapter. At this point, however, just keep in mind that the hardware requirements for Firewall mode and Cache mode may vary.

Table 2.1 Hardware requirements.

Hardware Component	Minimum Requirements	Recommended Requirements
Processor	Pentium 133MHz or higher	Pentium II 300MHz or higher Pentium II compatible processors
Memory	128MB	256MB
Hard Disk Space	20MB	20MB with 2GB + cache space
Network Card	Two: One for the internal network, another for the external network (Internet)	Two: One for the internal network, another for the external network (Internet)

Firewall Requirements

You can deploy an ISA server as a dedicated firewall that acts as the secure gateway to the Internet for internal clients. Depending on how much throughput is needed for your internal clients when accessing the Internet, the hardware requirements for the ISA server change.

Table 2.2 shows ISA Server's hardware configurations and network connections for Firewall and SecureNAT clients accessing objects on the Internet. (These clients will be discussed in the "ISA Server Client Support" section of this chapter.)

Caching Requirements

You can deploy an ISA server as a caching server that maintains a centralized cache of frequently accessed Internet objects. Clients' Web browsers, such as Internet Explorer and Netscape, access these Internet objects. Depending on how many Web browser clients are accessing the Internet, the hardware requirements for ISA Server vary.

Table 2.3 shows ISA Server's hardware configurations, random access memory (RAM) and the disk space allocated for caching, which will be stored on an NT File System (NTFS) volume.

If you do not have any NTFS volumes, you must create one using convert.exe. Its Help file shows the following syntax:

```
Convert volume /FS:NTFS [/V]
```

Table 2.2 ISA Server hardware configurations and network connections for Firewall and SecureNAT clients.

Throughput Requirements	Hardware Configurations	Internet Connection
1-25Mbps	Pentium II, 300MHz	ISDN (128Kbps+), cable modem, or xDSL (256Kbps+)
25-50Mbps	Pentium III, 550MHz	T3 (45Mbps) or better
More than 50Mbps	Pentium III, 550MHz, for each 50 Mbps needed	T3 or better

Table 2.3 ISA Server hardware configurations, memory, and disk space allocated for caching.

Number of Users	Hardware Configurations	RAM (MB)	Disk Space Allocated for Caching
Up to 500	Single ISA server with Pentium II, 300MHz	256	2-4GB
500-1000	Single ISA server with Pentium III, 550MHz	256	10GB
1,000+	ISA server with Pentium III, 550 MHz, for each 2,000 users. Using System Monitor can determine bottlenecks, which may tell you whether you should add more servers to an array.	256 for each server	10GB

For example, if you want to convert your C: drive, the command would be

```
Convert C: /FS:NTFS /V
```

The **convert** command itself and any arguments such as **C:** and **/FS** are not case sensitive.

A reboot is needed only if the partition is currently active. For example if you are converting an OS system or boot partition, the system will ask if you want to convert the file system the next time the system restarts. You can answer in the affirmative by typing "y". When the system restarts, the file system will be converted. **/V** is an optional switch for the verbose mode. Unlike with the formatting process, executing the **convert** command does not result in a loss of data.

Software Requirements

As you probably have figured out by now, the ISA Server must be installed on top of the Windows 2000 Server, the Windows 2000 Advanced Server, or the Windows 2000 Datacenter Server. To run the ISA Server successfully, you have to meet the following software requirements:

➤ *Windows 2000 Server with Service Pack 1 (SP1), Windows 2000 Advanced Server with SP1, or Windows 2000 Data Center Server*—To check whether your system has the SP1 installed, run winver.exe from a command prompt. It will show you a Graphical User Interface (GUI) displaying which build version of Windows 2000 you have and whether SP1 has been installed. If your system does not have the SP1 installed, you can download it from Microsoft's Web site or order a CD from Microsoft. Windows 2000 Data Center Server includes all the bug fixes that are included in the Service Pack 1 for Windows 2000 Server and Advanced Server, and therefore it does not require the Service Pack 1 installation.

➤ *At least one NTFS partition*—You need this to implement the caching feature.

➤ *Windows 2000 Active Directory*—You must have AD in your network to implement the array feature and advanced policies configuration.

To remotely administer an ISA server, you will need to install the ISA Management. You can run the ISA Management on Windows 2000 Professional or higher systems. If you do not want to install the ISA Management for your remote administration, you can use the Windows 2000 Terminal Services, which requires a Terminal Services Client software installed on NT 4 Workstation or Server, or Windows 2000 Professional and higher systems.

The hardware and software requirements listed here will vary depending on the ISA Server features you want to install and the expected system load.

Clean Install or Upgrade (Migrate) from Proxy Server 2.0

After making sure your system meets the minimum hardware and software requirements, you will need to decide whether you want to do a clean ISA Server installation or upgrade an existing Proxy Server 2.0 system. Why Proxy Server 2.0? This is because the ISA Server's Web Proxy service has a more improved version of caching functionality than that of Proxy Server 2.0, and there is a full migration path from a Proxy Server 2.0 system. If you are upgrading from the existing Proxy Server 2.0 system, you need to perform some steps before the actual migration, and we will cover those steps in Chapter 4.

A clean installation is just as it sounds. You are installing the ISA Server on a Windows 2000 Server or higher system from scratch. You will have to specify some information to complete the installation process. This method is necessary if your network environment does not currently use an ISA server and you would like to install it, or you want to use a new ISA server configuration instead of using an existing ISA Server.

ISA Server Mode

ISA Server can be installed in three different modes: Firewall mode, Cache mode, or Integrated mode. The Firewall mode lets the ISA server act solely as a secure firewall between your internal network—your Local Area Network (LAN)—and the external network—the Internet. A LAN is a network that is usually connected with a high bandwidth network connection (10Mbps+). An example of a LAN is an office network on one floor or one building. You will have an opportunity to configure rules that allow or deny the flow of data packets to keep hackers from attacking your internal network. In addition, Firewall mode allows you to publish your internal servers, and Internet users will be able to access shared data. Of course, Internet users will not be able to access the internal servers directly. All the communications among Internet users and the internal servers will have go to through the ISA server, where packets are routed according to the Network Address Translation (NAT). The NAT is a Windows 2000 service that allows multiple LAN clients to share only one public IP address and an Internet connection. The NAT takes care of translating and modifying packets so that correct addressing information is used. Keep in mind, however, that you should not rely solely on the security mechanism of ISA Server. In many organizations, security is also dependent on the hardware security such as firewall routers and physical access to the systems.

Cache mode lets the ISA server store frequently accessed objects on the Internet on its local hard drive, and this will allow internal network users to get the information from the ISA server instead of going out to the Internet. Because most corporations have local LANs with 10Mbps or higher bandwidths, keeping needed data closed to the internal users will increase the network performance. ISA Server uses a sophisticated algorithm of getting frequently accessed objects on the Internet. In addition, packets to access internal Web servers from the Internet users can be routed by the ISA server to a corresponding Web server.

Integrated mode lets the ISA server use the benefits of both Firewall and Cache modes. Although this mode employs the full power of ISA Server, you must select the server mode carefully to meet the objectives of your network environment.

Table 2.4 shows the features available according to the ISA Server mode you choose to use. Integrated mode has all the features available.

ISA Server Array

After thinking about the ISA server implementation planning, you may decide to deploy more than one ISA Server in your organization. Why would you have more than one ISA server? You learned about three different modes—Firewall, Cache, or Integrated—that an ISA server can play. You might want to deploy more than one ISA server for several reasons. For instance, you may decide to use Firewall mode on one ISA server and use Cache mode on another ISA server. Or you might like to implement load balancing on two or more ISA servers configured as Cache mode. Whatever your reason, implementing more than one ISA server will require a bit more discussion. In addition, implementing an ISA Server array has a lot of advantages, and it is worth spending some time talking about it.

The basic idea behind the ISA Server array is to group more than one ISA server into a single, logical entity that you can manage at the same time. Instead of configuring each separate ISA server, which is called a standalone configuration,

Table 2.4   Features and modes available.

Feature	Firewall Mode	Cache Mode
Access Policy	Yes	Yes, only HTTP protocol supported
Alerts	Yes	Yes
Application Filters	Yes	No
Cache Configuration	No	Yes
Enterprise Policy	Yes	Yes
Packet Filtering	Yes	No
Real-time Monitoring	Yes	Yes
Reports	Yes	Yes
Server Publishing	Yes	No
Web Publishing	Yes	Yes

ISA servers in an array use a common configuration. You set up only one configuration, and it will be effective for all the ISA servers in the array. To utilize the ISA Server array, all the computers in the array have to be members of a Windows 2000 domain and in the same site. A site is a LAN, which is connected with high bandwidth (512Kbps+). In addition, the Windows 2000 Active Directory schema must be modified before an ISA server can be configured as a member of the array. It is generally a good idea to create an array even though you currently have only one ISA server in your network. This is because it allows you to have scalability in case you decide to add more ISA servers in your network, and the array configuration can be replicated to other domain controllers, as it will be stored in the Active Directory. You will also be able to apply enterprise policy to the array.

There are two main advantages of using the ISA server array. One is that you can apply a unique array policy to each array in the enterprise. If you have more than one array in your organization, and if each array is supposed to provide different functionalities, then ISA Server will allow you to apply a separate policy to each array so that arrays can function in a different manner. Another advantage is that you can distribute the network load to each member of the array, and it will improve the network performance for client computers.

If you decide not to install the ISA server as an array member, you can install it as a standalone ISA server. The standalone ISA server does not have to be a member of a Windows 2000 domain. In the standalone configuration, each ISA server uses a unique configuration that needs to be maintained separately by the ISA server administrator.

Table 2.5 shows the differences between the array and standalone ISA server.

ISA Server Client Support

Depending on the applications and services your users need, you must determine what kind of client software to install on the client computers, if any. In Proxy Server 2.0, you had a choice to install the Winsock Proxy client either by using a client setup program or by using a Web browser. You could also install Web Proxy and Socks Proxy under the Proxy Server 2.0. The Winsock Proxy is used to provide secure and transparent connectivity to Internet resources to client applications. These applications use the Windows Sockets API, including IRC clients for

Table 2.5 Array and standalone ISA Server differences.

Features	Array	Standalone ISA Server
Active Directory	Required. It can be installed only on a Windows 2000 domain.	Not Required.
Enterprise Policy	Yes. You can apply a single policy to all the arrays available.	No.
Scalability	More than one ISA member servers.	Only one ISA member server.

Internet chat and RealPlayer for streaming audio and video. The Web Proxy is used to provide an intermediary step between clients' Web browsers and the Internet to improve Web performance by storing frequently accessed Web objects on the Proxy Server 2.0. The Socks Proxy is used to provide Socks connections between Socks client and Socks server, mainly for Macintosh and Unix clients. If you installed the Winsock Proxy client by using the client setup program, then it would try to configure the Web Proxy client in addition to configuring it to be a Winsock Proxy client. The idea here is basically the same. To employ ISA Server's full functionality, you may be required to install a client software onto all the clients. However, the good thing is that you are required to install the client software onto clients only if they are using ISA Server's Firewall service! If they are just trying to be SecureNAT clients or Web Proxy clients (which we will explain in Table 2.6), they do not have to have any client software installed. Furthermore, the communication among all clients on your network is secured, and all clients can take advantage of the benefits of the ISA Server cache for HTTP and FTP objects. ISA Server transparently does HTTP and FTP object caching, and you do not have to even worry about them! So what are these clients we are talking about?

ISA Server supports three kinds of clients:

➤ SecureNAT clients

➤ Firewall clients

➤ Web Proxy clients

Table 2.6 compares various features supported by these clients.

Table 2.6 Various features supported by ISA Server clients.

Features	SecureNAT client	Firewall client	Web Proxy client
Installation necessary	No.	Yes.	No.
OS support	Any OS with TCP/IP support.	Only Windows platform.	Any platform using browser or other Web applications.
Protocol support	All protocol definitions installed with ISA Server. For multiconnection protocols, application filters are needed.	All Winsock protocols.	HTTP, HTTPS, FTP, and Gopher.
Network configuration change necessary	Yes. Default gateway, DNS server addresses and others need to be changed.	No.	No.
Server applications	No installation or configuration needed.	Configuration file needed.	N/A
User-level Authentication	By IP address.	By IP address or user name.	A Web browser passes authentication information.

One thing to note here is that SecureNAT clients and Firewall clients are mutually exclusive, meaning if a client is a SecureNAT client, it cannot be a Firewall client at the same time, and vice versa. This is not true, however, with Web Proxy clients. Both SecureNAT clients and Firewall clients can also be Web Proxy clients at the same time. The Firewall service first tries to take care of all the requests from clients except for the Web requests (HTTP, HTTPS, FTP, and Gopher), which are sent directly to the ISA server's Web Proxy service if the Web application, such as a browser on clients, is configured to use the ISA server.

Now let's discuss all the supported clients in a little more detail:

➤ *SecureNAT clients*—Secure Network Address Translation (SecureNAT) clients do not have the Firewall client software installed. As we mentioned earlier, SecureNAT clients cannot be Firewall clients at the same time. You do not have to install any special software for clients to become SecureNAT clients. You can configure SecureNAT clients either manually or by using a Dynamic Host Configuration Protocol (DHCP) server. A DHCP server assigns IP addresses and other information, including the subnet mask, default gateway, and Domain Name Service (DNS) IP addresses, to DHCP clients. Clients configured as DHCP clients get the IP address and other information from a DHCP server when they boot up. DNS, a naming service that the Internet depends on, provides a hostname-to-IP-address translation. (If you need more information about DHCP and DNS, refer to the *MCSE TCP/IP Exam Cram, third edition*.)

➤ *Firewall clients*—Firewall clients have the Firewall client software installed and enabled. You can currently install the Firewall clients onto Windows 98/95, Windows NT 4, Windows 2000, and Windows ME operating systems. The Firewall client software is not supported by any other operating systems. The Firewall clients run Winsock applications, and these applications use the Firewall service of ISA Server.

➤ *Web Proxy clients*—Web Proxy clients have a Web application, such as a Web browser configured to use a CERN (Conseil European pour la Recherche Nucleair, or The European Laboratory for Particle Research) compliant HTTP proxy server. CERN is an organization in Switzerland that has established industry standards for Internet-compliant client and server applications. All Web browsers' requests that are configured to use a proxy server to access the Internet will go through ISA Server's Web Proxy service. You can configure clients' Web browsers at any time. Depending on the browser used, you may need to go into different menus, such as Internet Options (as in Internet Explorer) and Preferences (as in Netscape). If you decide to install the Firewall client software onto a client, you can configure the Web browser automatically. If you have to, you can reconfigure the Web browser at a later time.

Now you know what these clients do; the next question is which one to pick for your environment. In many cases, using the SecureNAT clients is recommended. The following list shows some examples:

- *You are using the ISA server only for forward caching of Web objects*—Using SecureNAT clients is recommended because you do not have to install any software or configure the clients' systems, and by default client requests are routed in the background to the ISA server's Firewall service and then to the Web Proxy server for caching.

- *You are publishing servers that are located on your internal network*—Although you can configure publishing servers as Firewall clients—which require a complicated configuration—using SecureNAT clients is recommended. You can simply create a server-publishing rule on the ISA Server without any configuration files.

- *You do not want to configure the client systems or install client software*—SecureNAT clients are also recommended in this case. You do not have to install any software or perform additional configuration for the SecureNAT clients. On the other hand, Firewall clients require the installation of the client software, and Web Proxy clients require configuration on the Web applications on clients' systems.

Using Firewall clients is recommended if you want to allow access only for authenticated clients. This is because you can deploy user-based access policy rules for Firewall clients. It is also possible to deploy user-based policy rules for Web Proxy clients, but you are limited in that the policy rules can be supported only if the Web application can send the user authentication information. SecureNAT clients, unfortunately, are not capable of supporting the user-based authentication.

Final System Preparation before ISA Server Installation

You are almost ready for the actual ISA Server installation. In this section, we will describe the final system preparation setup before the ISA Server installation. First, we must mention some important hardware and software configuration issues. Some of these settings may already have been configured, but let's make sure that's really the case. If not, follow the items in this section, and you are all set for the ISA Server installation.

Hardware Configuration

As we stated earlier in this chapter, you must make sure that your system has two connections: one for the internal network (LAN) and another for the external network (the Internet). The internal network connection is usually based on Ethernet or Token Ring, although Ethernet is the most popular network topology in use today. Therefore, if you have an ISA server in a large organization with a lot of Web traffic, you might set up an ISA server with two Network Interface Cards (NICs) in it, one NIC connecting to the local LAN with a 100Mbps Ethernet and another NIC connecting to the Internet through an Internet Service Provider (ISP) with a T3 line backbone. Whatever you use—NIC or modem—make sure the hardware is also set up correctly in the system BIOS level, including the IRQ, memory range, I/O range, and so on. The external network connection can be based on the direct connection using T1 (1.5Mbps), T3 (45Mbps), DSL (256Kbps+), cable modem, or a dial-up connection. With a direct connection, you normally have an NIC on your system. Depending on the network topology you have in your network, you may have an Ethernet NIC (10Mbps, 100Mbps, and 1000Mbps), Token Ring NIC (4Mbps and 16Mbps), and others. If you have a dial-up connection, you need to make sure that you have a Network and Dial-up Connection already set up in your system and that it actually works.

Software Configuration

Next, we will look at TCP/IP configuration. In many cases, network clients should be configured as DHCP clients. It may not be reasonable, however, to do the same for servers. For instance, if you have a server with a DHCP IP address and the server goes down for a while, then gets a different DHCP IP address when it comes back on line, you can probably guess that users will be widely affected. This is because if your network is fully or partly based on the DNS, unless you are using the Dynamic Domain Name Server (DDNS), the host entry will not be pointing to a correct IP address. You should assign a specific IP address for any server. Any NICs on the ISA server that you are going to install should also have unique IP addresses on them. If your ISP assigns a DHCP IP address for the external network connection, it may be a special case that is acceptable, but for your internal connection, always use a unique IP address.

In some cases, the gateway address is modified if you use a DHCP server to get an IP address, and all the connections to the Internet might be dropped. When configuring the TCP/IP setting for the external connection, obtain all the necessary information from your ISP. This information includes the IP address, subnet mask, default gateway, and DNS server IP addresses to be used for DNS name search orders, such as **ftp.coriolis.com** and **coriolis.com**. If your ISP uses a DHCP server to assign IP addresses and other information to clients—which your server will be—then the TCP/IP setting for the external connection is a piece of cake as you normally do not have to configure anything on the client server! In most cases, the ISA server will have only one default gateway IP address, which is configured on the NIC for the external connection. This is because all the clients will be talking to the ISA server first, and the ISA server will route packets to the

Internet through the ISP. In addition, the ISA server will prevent any hackers on the Internet from directly accessing the NIC for the internal network. Leave the default gateway IP address blank for the NIC on the internal network. Things can be a bit confusing if you have more than one NIC on your system (multi-homed system), and you are trying to figure out if a particular card has the correct setting. Windows 2000 comes with a command-line utility (called ipconfig.exe) that lets you see all the necessary information. If you run this command on your system with the **/all** option, you will see an output similar to that in Figure 2.1. (This example shows that the second NIC is still not configured correctly.)

The Physical Address (also referred to as a MAC address) for a NIC is not shown if you look at the Local Area Connection property in Network And Dial-up Connections in Windows 2000. To make sure you are configuring the correct NIC, you may need to use the ipconfig.exe output. If you are still not sure which NIC you are configuring, you can go into Network And Dial-up Connections and disable the Local Area Connection by right-clicking on it. Because you have two NICs on your system, you will see the Local Area Connection 2 in Network And Dial-up Connections. By disabling one of the Local Area Connections and running the **ipconfig /all** command again, you can make sure the card you are disabling does not show up in the result output from running the ipconfig.exe command-line utility.

The last thing to note in the TCP/IP configuration is to make sure you are on the network! Use the **ping** command—which comes with Windows 2000—or any

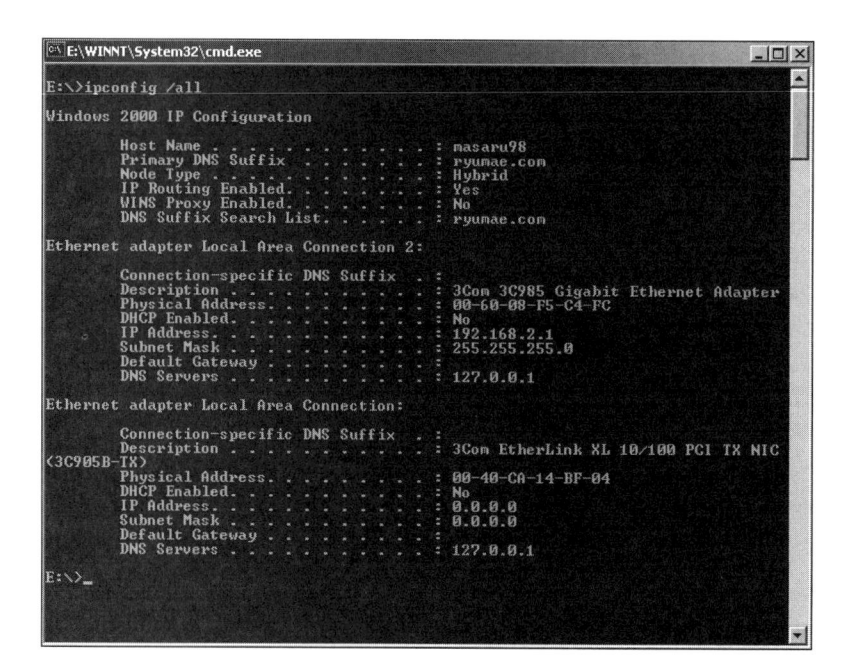

Figure 2.1 **ipconfig /all** output.

```
E:\WINNT\System32\cmd.exe

E:\>ping 192.168.2.1

Pinging 192.168.2.1 with 32 bytes of data:

Reply from 192.168.2.1: bytes=32 time<10ms TTL=128
Reply from 192.168.2.1: bytes=32 time<10ms TTL=128
Reply from 192.168.2.1: bytes=32 time<10ms TTL=128
Reply from 192.168.2.1: bytes=32 time<10ms TTL=128

Ping statistics for 192.168.2.1:
    Packets: Sent = 4, Received = 4, Lost = 0 (0% loss),
Approximate round trip times in milli-seconds:
    Minimum = 0ms, Maximum =  0ms, Average =  0ms

E:\>
```

Figure 2.2 **ping** output.

other similar utility to determine you have network connectivity to and from other systems. If you run this command on your system without options, you will see an output similar to that shown in Figure 2.2

By default, Windows 2000 sends a 32-byte packet four times to the host you are trying to reach. (In some Unix systems, the number of bytes and how many times to send vary.) You can use many options with **ping**, such as changing the size of the packet and the number of times to ping. Try **ping /?** to see all the switch options. (Issuing **ping /?** only works under Windows 2000 systems; use **ping -?** under NT 4 and Windows 98 systems.)

Other settings you need to check include the following:

➤ *Modem or ISDN adapter configuration*—If you do not have a direct connection to the Internet (T1, T3, and others) and you need to use a dial-up link, you will have to use a modem or an ISDN adapter with your ISA server. If you have multiple phone lines for the dial-up connection for a multilink functionality, make sure that both the ISA server and the ISP are set up to use the multilink functionality. This configuration requires that you have more than one modem installed on your system. In some cases, Windows 2000 does not recognize two 64K ISDN channels, depending on the ISDN adapter. You normally configure the bandwidth on the second channel through the ISDN adapter's driver. You must ensure that the ISDN adapter's driver is properly set up so that both channels are functional. In addition, your ISP must be able to support two channels at the same time, which is usually the case.

➤ *Windows 2000 Routing Table*—ISA Server employs the Windows 2000 routing table when initially creating the Local Address Table (LAT). You can use the Windows 2000 route.exe utility to configure the routing table or use the Routing and Remote Access Server's (RRAS) static routes section to define static routes to various connected interfaces (NICs). You can also modify the LAT at a later time. The LAT defines all the internal IP addresses and excludes all the external IP addresses. The ISA server refers to this table when routing packets to internal clients. If the table is not defined correctly, therefore, you may have problems routing packets from the Internet to the internal network, and vice versa. The LAT needs to include at least one IP address assigned to the ISA Server's NIC. This ensures that the ISA server knows which NIC to use to route packets to your internal network. In many cases, you can assign an IP address from a private address space for the internal NIC, which is to be included in the LAT. The private IP address ranges are 10.0.0.0 to 10.255.255.255 (Class A), 172.16.0.0 to 172.31.255.255 (Class B), and 192.168.0.0 to 192.168.255.255 (Class C). Depending on the number of clients, you can use any one of these private IP address ranges. (RFC 1918 at **www.cis.ohio-state.edu/rfc/rfc1918.txt** describes more about the private IP address ranges.) It is a good idea to include all the internal networks across internal routers in the LAT so that the ISA server and its clients can determine when to use the ISA server to get to a resource or to get to the resource directly without going through the ISA server.

➤ *ISA Server schema installation*—As we stated earlier, you can install the ISA server as a member of an array. (This section is relevant only if you plan to use the ISA server array, not the standalone ISA server.) Before you install the ISA server as a member of the array, the Windows 2000 Active Directory schema must be modified on a domain controller in the domain in which you are adding the ISA server. If the ISA Server schema has not been installed in the Active Directory, you will have an opportunity to install it when you run the Setup program or run the ISA Server Enterprise Initialization program. You need to install the ISA Server schema only once in the beginning. When you add ISA servers to your network, they can use the already-installed ISA Server schema. The Active Directory schema modification is not reversible—which means if you do it once, there is no way to go back to the original Active Directory schema. Ignore the resulting warning message—Microsoft has tested the ISA Server schema extensively with the Active Directory schema, and it is supposed to work! You need to keep a few things in mind regarding permissions, though. To be able to install the ISA Server schema onto the Active Directory, you must have the following permissions:

➤ You have to be a member of both the Enterprise Admins and Schema Admins groups.

➤ You have to be logged on as a user with the permission to write to Active Directory.

Refer to the Windows 2000 Active Directory online help for further information about permissions.

Once the installation of the ISA Server schema completes, you will be able to install the ISA server as a member of an array, which is created at the same time as the ISA server installation. If you have more than one domain controller in your domain, it will take some time to replicate the schema information to all the domain controllers. If your domain controllers exist in the same site, defined to have a high bandwidth network connectivity (512Kbps+), then the replication should go through within five minutes. In many cases, however, domain controllers are in different sites, and they replicate in three hours by default. As the array information is processed in the first member of the array, it is a good idea to create another array, if needed, after the Active Directory replication completes for the first time.

Here is a checklist of what we have discussed in this section:

1. Make sure your system has two connections (two NICs)—one for the internal network (LAN) and one for the Internet. Figure 2.3 shows what this means visually.

2. Make sure your system BIOS is set up correctly to reflect all the hardware installed. Figure 2.4 shows one example of what the system BIOS looks like.

3. If you use a dial-up connection, make sure it is properly configured; test it to be sure.

4. Make sure all NICs have static IP addresses assigned. (The only exception is when your ISP assigns a DCHP IP address to your ISA server's external connection to the Internet.)

5. Make sure the default gateway address is entered only for the external connection.

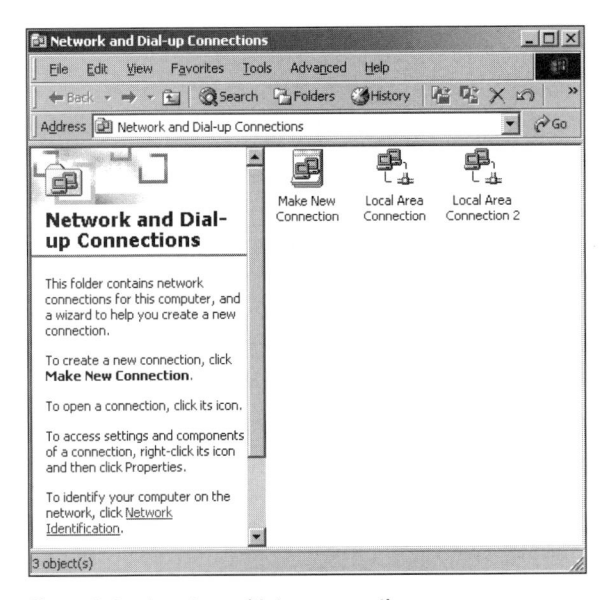

Figure 2.3 A system with two connections.

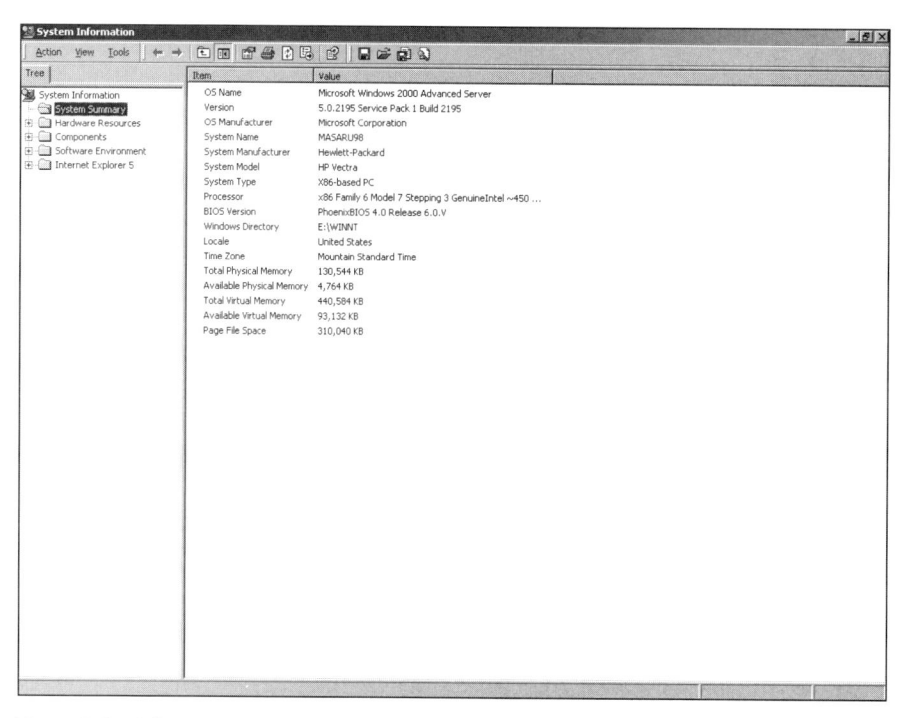

Figure 2.4 A System BIOS output.

6. Make sure that you are on the network by pinging other systems on the LAN.

7. Make sure that the modem or ISDN adapter is properly configured.

8. Make sure the routing table is constructed properly on the server where the ISA server is to be installed.

9. Ensure that the ISA Server schema is installed prior to utilizing the ISA Server Array.

Chapter Summary

In this chapter, we covered important steps to prepare for the ISA Server installation. To install ISA Server without any problems, you will need to be aware of the hardware requirements. It is also important to know the software requirements. You learned that the minimum hardware requirements for the ISA Server installation are the same as the ones for Windows 2000 Server for processor and memory. Remember that the ISA Server installation will fail without Service Pack 1 for Windows 2000 Server and Windows 2000 Advanced Server, and you will be asked to install it before you can continue. To use the caching feature, make sure you have at least one NTFS partition. To use the array feature and advanced policies configuration, you must have the Windows 2000 Active Directory available in your network.

If you decide to upgrade a Proxy Server 2.0 system, a full migration path is available. A clean install is for a start-from-scratch environment where you do not have any ISA Server installed in your network.

ISA Server can be installed in three different modes: Firewall mode, Cache mode, or Integrated mode. Firewall mode lets the ISA server act solely as a secure firewall between your internal network and the external network, the Internet. Cache mode lets the ISA server store frequently accessed objects on the Internet on its local hard drive—that way, internal network users can get the information from the ISA server instead of going out to the Internet. Integrated mode lets the ISA server use the benefits of both Firewall and Cache modes.

The basic idea behind the ISA server array is to group more than one ISA Server into a single, logical entity that you can manage at the same time. Instead of you having to configure each separate ISA server in the standalone configuration, ISA servers in an array use a common configuration.

ISA Server supports three kinds of clients: SecureNAT clients, Firewall clients, and Web Proxy clients. SecureNAT clients do not have the Firewall client software installed. Firewall clients have the Firewall client software installed and enabled. Web Proxy clients have a Web application, such as a Web browser, configured to use a CERN-compliant HTTP proxy server.

Final preparation includes checking the entire hardware and software configuration that are currently set up on the system. Network adapter configurations, TCP/IP configurations, a modem or ISDN adapter configuration, the Windows 2000 routing table, and ISA Server schema installations are settings you need to check before the ISA Server installation.

Review Questions

1. What is the minimum processor requirement to install and run ISA Server?
    a. 80486/33MHz
    b. Pentium 100MHz or higher processor
    c. Pentium 133MHz or higher processor
    d. Pentium II 233MHz or higher processor
    e. Pentium II 300MHz or higher processor

2. What is the recommended memory requirement to install and run ISA Server?
    a. 32MB
    b. 64MB
    c. 128MB
    d. 192MB
    e. 256MB

3. What is the minimum free hard disk space requirement to install and run ISA Server?
    a. 5MB
    b. 10MB
    c. 15MB
    d. 20MB

4. What is the minimum number of network interfaces, including NICs and modems, required to install and run ISA Server?
    a. One Network Interface
    b. Two Network Interfaces
    c. Three Network Interfaces
    d. Four Network Interfaces

5. What is the minimum software requirement to install and run ISA Server?
    a. Windows NT 4 Server with Service Pack 4
    b. Windows NT 4 Server with Service Pack 6
    c. Windows 2000 Server with Service Pack 1
    d. Windows 2000 Advanced Server build 2195

6. To use ISA Server's caching feature, what kind of file system do you need?
    a. FAT 16
    b. FAT 32
    c. NTFS version 4
    d. NTFS version 5

7. To use ISA Server's array feature and advanced policies configuration, what do you need?
    a. Windows NT 4 Workgroup
    b. Windows NT 4 Domain
    c. Windows 2000 Workgroup
    d. Windows 2000 Active Directory Domain

8. What full migration path does ISA Server support?
   a. From Proxy Server 1.0
   b. From Proxy Server 2.0
   c. From Site Server 3.0
   d. From Small Business Server 4.5

9. Which ISA Server modes does ISA Server support? [Check all correct answers]
   a. Firewall mode
   b. Cache mode
   c. Mixed mode
   d. Integrated mode

10. What features does Firewall mode support? [Check all correct answers]
    a. Application filters
    b. Cache configuration
    c. Packet filtering
    d. Server publishing

11. What features does Cache mode support? [Check all correct answers]
    a. Alerts
    b. Application filters
    c. Packet filtering
    d. Web publishing

12. Under what conditions is it recommended you have an ISA server array? [Check all correct answers]
    a. When you have only one ISA server without Active Directory.
    b. When you have only one ISA server with Active Directory.
    c. When you have more than one ISA server without Active Directory.
    d. When you have more than one ISA server with Active Directory.

13. What kind of clients does ISA Server support? [Check all correct answers]
    a. SecureNAT clients
    b. Secure LAT clients
    c. Firewall clients
    d. Web Proxy clients

14. Which client software is recommended when you are using the ISA server only for forward caching Web objects?
    a. SecureNAT clients
    b. Secure LAT clients
    c. Firewall clients
    d. Web Proxy clients

15. Which client software is recommended when you want to allow access only for authenticated clients?
    a. SecureNAT clients
    b. Secure LAT clients
    c. Firewall clients
    d. Web Proxy clients

16. How would you configure two NICs on your ISA server?
    a. One for the internal network, another for the internal network
    b. One for the internal network, another for the external network
    c. One for the external network, another for the external network
    d. One for the internal network, another for the local network

17. What command would you use to check the MAC address on a NIC?
    a. **nslookup**
    b. **ipconfig /all**
    c. **ping**
    d. **route**

18. What command would you use to check if you can reach a remote host system?
    a. **nslookup**
    b. **ipconfig /all**
    c. **ping**
    d. **route**

19. If you need to configure 1,000 clients to use the ISA server, what reserved IP address range would you use? [Check all correct answers]
    a. 10.0.0.0 to 10.255.255.255
    b. 172.16.0.0 to 172.31.255.255
    c. 192.168.0.0 to 192.168.255.255
    d. 224.0.0.0 to 239.255.255.255

20. To install the ISA Server schema, what permissions do you need?
    a. You have to be a member of Power Users group.
    b. You have to be a member of both Enterprise Admins and Schema Admins groups.
    c. You have to be logged on as a user with the permission to write to Active Directory.
    d. You have to be a member of the Server Operators group.

Real-World Projects

Note: This exercise assumes a test Windows 2000 Server, Windows 2000 Advanced Server with Service Pack 1, or Windows 2000 Data Center Server and two Network Interface cards (NICs): one for the internal network and another for the external network installed. Read the instructions carefully and do not perform this installation on your production machine unless you understand the options presented.

Joe is now the Internet Security Specialist for his company, Training4U. He has been raising a flag about Internet security for a while now, and it looks like the company is getting serious about it. He has been seeing news almost every day about some large companies being attacked by hackers. Training4U has not been the exception. The Chief Operations Officer told Joe that Training4U's Web site was broken into again. Joe thinks that it is now time for him to take action to prevent these incidents from happening again. He is getting excited, but at the same time, he is also nervous. Hackers use very sophisticated methods to break into networks, and in some cases, it is difficult to trace who initiated the action in the first place.

In any case, however, it looks like the COO and others liked the idea of using the Internet Security and Acceleration Server when Joe presented it in the meeting. Joe now has a couple of test servers that he can use to test some ISA Server configurations. It will be a start-from-scratch type approach, because he has not installed ISA Server.

Joe has started to get some ideas about Internet Security and is learning what ISA Server can do to help keep hackers out of Training4U's internal network. Joe has learned that before he can install ISA Server on the test systems, he must perform several steps.

Joe is now ready to perform those initial steps on his test systems. He logs onto the system as a local administrator.

Project 2.1

To check hardware requirements:

1. Click once on the Start menu.

2. Select Run.

3. Type "winmsd" in the Run dialog box, and then click OK. Figure 2.5 shows the System Information output.

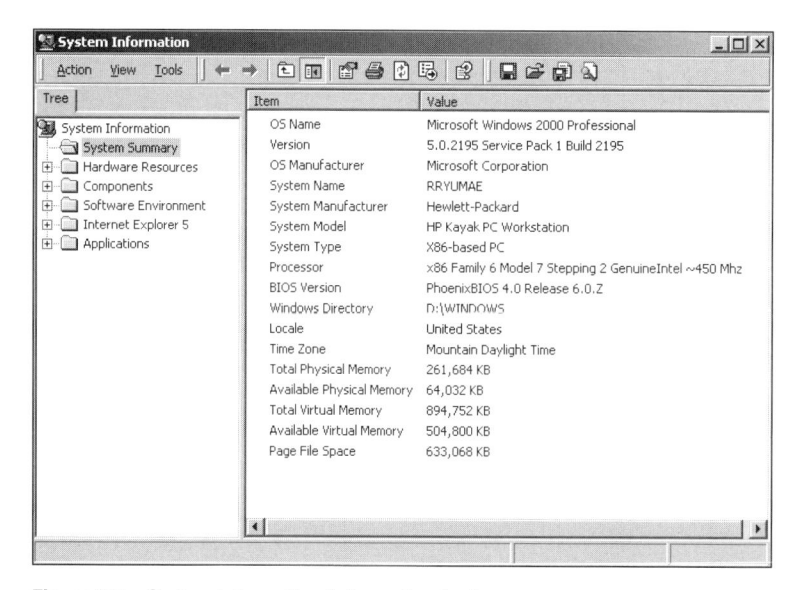

Figure 2.5 System Information (**winmsd**) output.

Joe makes sure that his test systems' processor and total physical memory meet the minimum hardware requirements before continuing.

4. Select Action from the menu at the top of the System Information screen.

5. Select Print.

6. Select Export List, name the file winmsd1.out.txt, and save it in a convenient location.

Joe prints the system information page and saves it to a text file so that he can add this information to the internal Internet Security documentation. Joe has learned that keeping careful documentation is good practice.

Joe wants to use one test server as the Web caching server and tries to see whether an NTFS partition for the caching has been set up.

Project 2.2

To check whether you have an NTFS partition for caching:

1. Right-click on My Computer on the desktop.

2. Select Manage.

3. Expand the storage tree if necessary.

4. Click on Disk Management. Figure 2.6 shows the output from Disk Management.

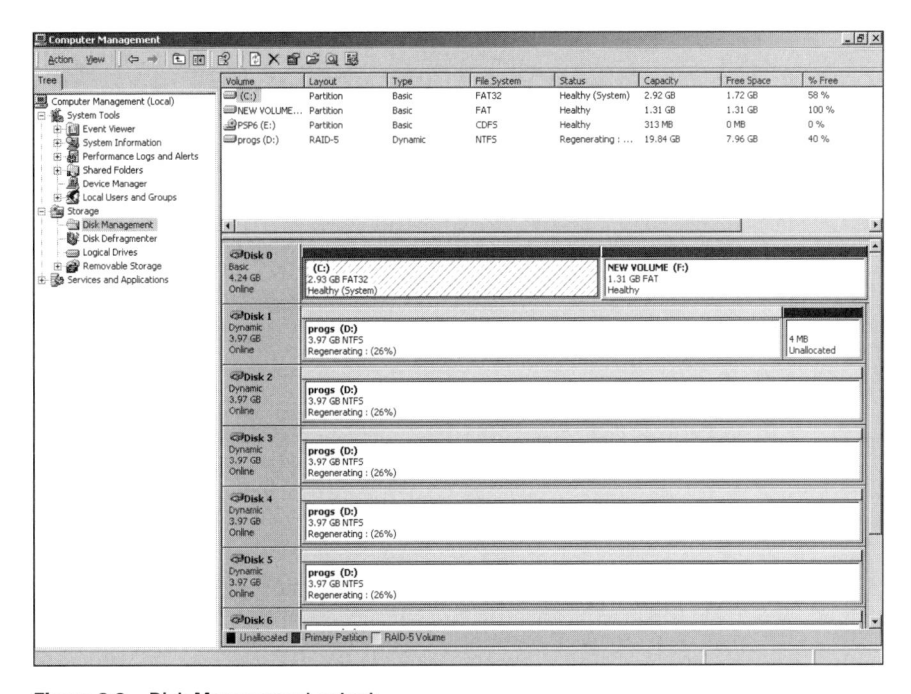

Figure 2.6 Disk Management output.

Joe finds that all the partitions on the system are formatted as FAT32, which are not used to keep the cached files. Now he needs to perform a FAT-to-NTFS partition conversion. Unfortunately, he does not know how to convert, although he knows how to format, which does not help at this point. Joe searches Microsoft Technet and finds that there is a **convert** command available to use. The help file for the **convert** command displays the following format:

```
CONVERT volume /FS:NTFS [/V]
```

After reading more about this command, Joe learns he can run **convert** from either the command prompt or the Run dialog box. He plans to convert his E partition from FAT32 to NTFS, so he types the following command:

```
CONVERT E: /FS:NTFS /V
```

After a while, it looks like the conversion is done; no reboot was necessary. Joe discovers that a reboot is needed only if the partition is currently active. For example if you are converting an OS system or boot partition, the system will ask if you want to convert the file system the next time the system restarts. You can answer in the affirmative by typing "y". When the system restarts, the file system will be converted. /V is an optional switch for the verbose mode. Unlike with the formatting process, executing the **convert** command does not result in a loss of data.

Joe has now set up the NTFS partition for caching Web objects. He remembers that test systems also must meet software requirements. One of those requirements was having the latest service pack installed. By checking Microsoft's Web site, Joe finds that the latest service pack for Windows 2000 is Service Pack 1, and Microsoft is scheduled to release Service Pack 2 in April or May 2001. He tries to verify whether his test systems are compliant.

Project 2.3
To check if Service Pack 1 is installed:

1. Click once on the Start menu.

2. Select Run.

3. Type "winver" in the Run dialog box, and then click OK. Figure 2.7 shows what the winver.exe output looks like.

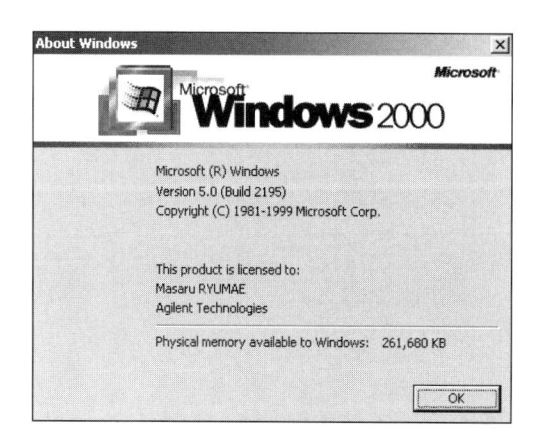

Figure 2.7 Windows (**winver**) output.

Unfortunately, Joe's test systems do not appear to have Service Pack 1 installed—only the build version 2195. Joe knows this build version is the latest version; he still remembers that the final production code (Gold code) for the version Windows 2000 released on February 17, 2000, was in fact version 2195. Joe is now looking for a CD that might have the Windows 2000 Service Pack 1. Because he can't locate it, Joe visits the Microsoft Web site to read about Service Pack 1.

Joe learns that he can download Service Pack 1 from **www.microsoft.com/windows2000/downloads/recommended/sp1/x86Lang.asp**.

The Service Pack is over 83MB, and Joe anticipates that downloading it would take at least half an hour. He sees that you can order a CD from Microsoft at **www.microsoft.com/windows2000/downloads/recommended/sp1/ordercd.asp**.

Ordering the CD would take too much time, Joe says to himself. He looks up the clock; it is 11:45 A.M., and he is getting hungry. He starts the download and then leaves for lunch.

When Joe comes back from lunch, the download has completed. He then follows the steps for installing the SP1.

Project 2.4
To install Service Pack 1:

1. Double-click on W2Ksp1.exe (the file just downloaded). W2Ksp1.exe will start extracting files to your temp folder.

2. In the Windows 2000 Service Pack Setup dialog box, select the Accept The License Agreement check box. The Windows 2000 Service Pack 1 has proved to be stable; you do not necessarily need to keep the backup files. If you do not want to keep the backup files, deselect the second check box. Finally, click Install (see Figure 2.8).

3. When the Service Pack installation completes, the system must be rebooted for the changes to take effect. Click Restart, and let the system reboot.

The system boots back to Windows 2000, and Joe logs onto the system. He runs the **winver** command again (see Project 2.1) to make sure Service Pack 1 is now displayed. He is happy to see that Service Pack 1 now appears. Next, he needs to check the network connectivity. Joe has used the commands **ipconfig** and **ping** before, and he knows these commands are useful for testing network configurations and connectivity. He tries these commands next.

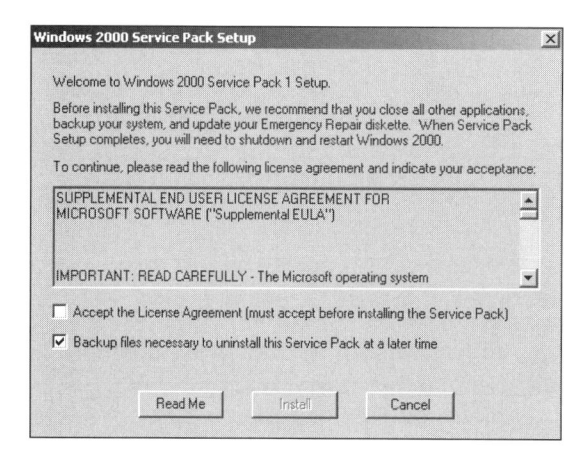

Figure 2.8 Windows 2000 Service Pack Setup dialog box.

Project 2.5

To use ipconfig for network configurations:

1. Open a command prompt.

2. Type "ipconfig /all". Figure 2.9 shows the **ipconfig /all** output.

Figure 2.9 **ipconfig /all** output.

Joe sees the output in the command prompt, and as far as he can tell, it looks good. Then, he tries the next command, **PING**.

Project 2.6
To use ping for network connectivity:

1. Open a command prompt.

2. Type "ping host", where host is your local LAN's client IP address. For instance, typing

   ```
   ping 192.168.1.2
   ```

   would work. You can also specify the name of the host you are trying to reach, such as

   ```
   ping coriolis
   ```

   if a DNS server or any other naming resolution system exists in your network. Figure 2.10 shows an example **PING** output.

Figure 2.10 **ping** output.

From his previous experiences, Joe knows that if you get a reply from the host, that means the host is reachable from your system. If you get a request time-out, then the host is not reachable from your system. It may be the case that the host system is down or a network connection issue is preventing your system from reaching the host. Joe makes sure that he can ping the other test system, and everything looks good so far.

CHAPTER THREE

Installing ISA Server 2000

After completing this chapter, you will be able to:

✓ Differentiate between the versions of ISA Server

✓ Gather information for ISA Server installation

✓ Set up a network installation point for ISA Server

✓ Identify different ISA Server installation types

✓ Select the correct installation options

✓ Distinguish between modes of ISA Server installation

✓ Configure caching during installation

✓ Construct a Local Address Table (LAT)

✓ Plan and write an unattended installation file

✓ Recognize the prerequisites for installing an array

✓ Install ISA Server into an array

Installing ISA Server requires planning and preparation. Chapter 2 of this book shows how to obtain the prerequisite hardware and software information needed for planning the installation. After obtaining this information, you are ready to start performing the installation. There are two different versions of ISA Server that you can choose to install: Standard Edition and Enterprise Edition. Although the Microsoft exam focuses only on the installation and running of the Enterprise Edition of ISA Server, this chapter will show the installation of both versions as well as highlight the differences between the two.

ISA Server Editions

Why are two editions of ISA Server needed? The main reason has to do with the number of users that ISA Server can handle. ISA Server is capable of supporting very large environments. If configured correctly, groups of ISA servers can handle a high volume of requests. These servers can also be specialized, with some providing caching services while others accept connections for services published from the internal network. Of course, some companies do not have this large an environment and do not need a chain of ISA servers to protect their internal clients. Instead they may need only one ISA server. Microsoft had to choose between offering one product at one price with the ability to scale to all sizes of networks or to offer the most powerful and scalable version of ISA Server at one price and another more limited version at a lower price. They chose to offer two versions of their product. ISA Server Standard Edition is designed to protect a network as a standalone single Internet security server. It cannot participate in arrays or work with Active Directory. It works only in a local fashion. Beyond the size of the network that each can support there are not many differences between the two editions of ISA Server. Each has the same administrative interface and each uses rules and policies to check inbound and outbound traffic. The installation for each is also very similar, except that the Enterprise Edition supports the installation of an array, which is not possible in the Standard Edition. All of the add-ins included in a Full installation as well as each of the three modes of installation are supported on both editions.

Hardware Support

The Enterprise Edition of ISA Server supports a much larger environment and a larger number of clients than the Standard Edition. The Standard Edition of ISA Server can only support up to four Central Processing Units (CPUs) whereas Enterprise Edition puts no limit on the number of processors that it can support. The Standard Edition of ISA Server assumes that it will be a standalone Internet security server that will not depend on or share the burden of handling requests with other servers. The policies and rules set in the Standard Edition are designed not to be copied or shared with any other ISA server.

Before the Installation

Regardless of how much you have prepared for the installation of ISA Server, some of the information must be immediately handy when actually performing the installation. To save yourself time and frustration, it is good to know ahead of time what questions you will be asked during the installation. Since you can perform the install from a local CD or over a network, we will also discuss the creation of a network installation point.

Gathering the Necessary Information

As with any installation, the Setup program will ask some questions during the installation. Table 3.1 shows the information needed in the order that the installation program will ask for it. This information needs to be checked ahead of time and some decisions need to be made before the installation begins.

Setting Up a Network Installation Point

Setting up an installation of ISA Server over the network requires just a little extra information than an installation from a local CD. The ISA Server CD contains an ISA directory under the root. This is the location of the setup.exe file that begins the ISA Server Setup Wizard. You also can start the installation through an autorun program on the root of the ISA CD. This autorun file, called ISAAutorun.exe, will create a dialog box that allows the user to choose from installation options. Figure 3.1 shows the dialog box created by ISAAutorun.exe from the Enterprise Edition of ISA Server. While in this dialog box, you can rest the mouse on an option to learn its purpose. An explanation of what each option does pops up in the on the left side of the dialog box. Some of the options bring up documentation, while others change configuration settings on the machine. However, while you can run this program over the network, none of the documentation options work over a network connection. The only options that work are the options that change configurations on the local machine. To launch any of the options, a single mouse click is all that is needed. To begin the installation of ISA Server from this dialog box, click the Install ISA Server option.

Table 3.1 Information needed to complete the installation of ISA Server.

Required installation information	Basis for decision
CD Key	Back of CD-ROM jewel case
Installation mode	Design of the environment and role of the individual ISA Server
Disk configuration and format	Enough NTFS disk space for caching
Cache configuration	Number of available NTFS disks and performance
IP address configuration	Network diagram of internal vs. external IP addresses

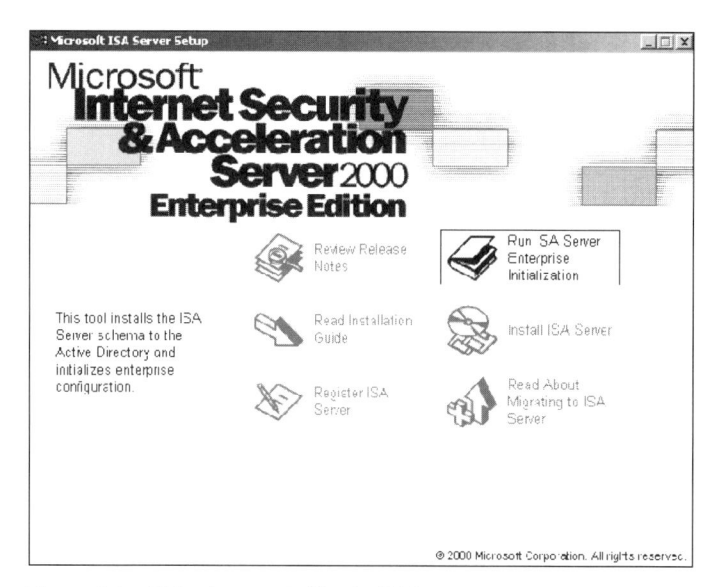

Figure 3.1 Dialog box created by the ISAAutorun.exe program.

By now, you should have made sure that the computer meets the basic hardware requirements for installing ISA Server. If the software requirement of Windows 2000 is not met, the installation will begin and end with a dialog box stating, "This Setup program is not intended to be used with your version of Windows". Windows 2000 Service Pack 1 or higher is also required before the installation of ISA Server can begin. Figure 3.2 shows the dialog box that will appear if Windows 2000 Server Service Pack 1 has not been applied before beginning the installation of ISA Server.

Recent Software Updates

Before starting the installation, check the readme.htm file that is in the root of the ISA Server CD. This file contains last-minute changes or issues that do not make it into official product documentation. You may find software updates or hot fixes. As issues arise or bugs are discovered, Microsoft publishes these hot fixes to provide immediate solutions. These hot fixes are often assembled into a service pack release. The latest fixes are placed on the ISA Server CD in the Support\hotfixes

Figure 3.2 Setup error when Windows 2000 Server Service Pack 1 is not present on the system.

folder. Until Windows 2000 Service Pack 2 is available, check the Support\hotfixes\Win2000 folder for hot fixes that deal with issues between Windows 2000 and ISA Server. In that folder, run Q275286_W2K_SP2_x86_en.EXE after installing Windows 2000 Service Pack 1.

Installing ISA Server Enterprise Edition

After all the preparation and prerequisites are out of the way, it is finally time to start the installation of ISA Server. We will cover the installation of ISA Server Enterprise Edition first because this is the focus of exam 70-227. We will cover installation of the Standard Edition and the differences between the two later in this chapter. The first couple of dialog boxes in the install do not check the system or hardware components for the target computer of the installation. If the computer does not meet the basic system or hardware requirements, you won't find out until after you have entered the product CD key and accepted the licensing agreement.

The first dialog box will welcome you to the installation of ISA Server. All you need to do is click the Continue button to dismiss this dialog box and continue the installation. The next dialog box will ask you for the CD key. You will find this key on the back of the CD jewel case for the ISA Server product. After entering the CD key, click the OK button. Another dialog box will appear that gives you the product ID for this installation of ISA Server. If you plan on calling Microsoft for technical support with ISA Server, you should write down that number and keep it with the product CD and documentation so you can have it handy when you make the call to Microsoft support. Click OK to dismiss the Product ID dialog box and continue with the installation.

Installation Types

The next dialog box in the installation asks for two decisions. The first is whether you would like a Typical, Full, or Custom installation and the second is what local path you would like ISA Server to install onto. Figure 3.3 shows this dialog box. You don't need to spend too much time wondering about these choices because you won't have many options to choose from at this point in the ISA Server installation. Table 3.2 shows the differences that each choice presents. The table displays the options that are chosen for you when you pick Typical, Full, or Custom as an installation option. Typical and Full will install their options without asking again; the Custom option will display the dialog box in Figure 3.4. The Typical installation choices are selected, and the user can select or deselect options before proceeding with the rest of the installation.

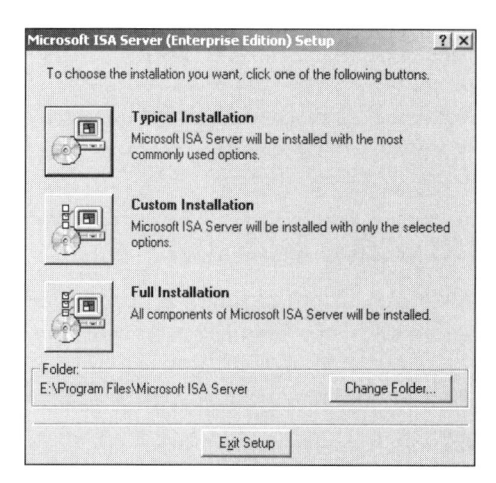

Figure 3.3 The installation type dialog box.

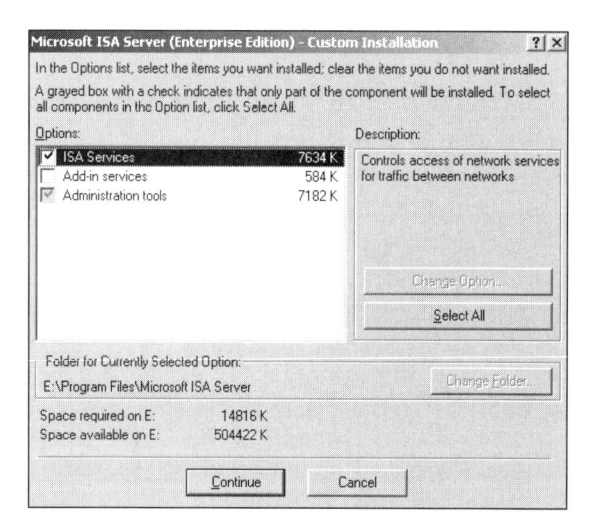

Figure 3.4 Choices in the Custom dialog box.

Table 3.2 Installation options for each choice.

Options	Typical	Full	Custom
ISA Services	✓	✓	✓
Add-in Services		✓	
Install H.323 Gatekeeper Service	✓	✓	✓
Message Screener		✓	
Administration Tools	✓	✓	✓
Administration Tools	✓	✓	✓
H.323 Gatekeeper Administration Tool		✓	

Because the ISA Services option is not broken down into suboptions, so different ISA Services are not listed. It is an all-or-nothing choice. Add-in services include installing the H.323 Gatekeeper service or the Message Screener. None of these offer any options from which to select. Administration Tools are broken down into basic administration tools for ISA Server or an extra tool for H.323 Gatekeeper. The administration tool for the Gatekeeper service is not automatically installed when the H.323 Gatekeeper service is selected.

Surprisingly, none of these options, even the basic ISA Services, are required. If you remove the ISA Services checkmark, the ISA server will be for management and remote administration of other ISA servers only. It will provide no Internet security or caching services. The only selection that must be made is for the ISA Server Administrative Tools. If you choose to deselect the suboption of Administrative Tools under the Administrative Tools option, a dialog box warning you that you will need the component will appear. Figure 3.5 shows this dialog box. Removing other options results in no complaints from the ISA Server Setup Wizard.

In many installations, the path that the server will be installing on is included in the dialog box that lists the options. The reason usually is disk space. Different options can use up different amounts of disk space. But a Typical installation for ISA Server uses just over 12.4MB of disk space while a full installation uses just over 13.5MB. Since the difference between these installations could fit on a floppy disk, this is not where disk space is used in an ISA Server installation. The most significant use of disk space will come when configuring cache settings for the ISA server, and we will do that later in the installation process.

At this point in the installation, the calculations for the amount of disk space used by cache should already be completed. Chapter 2 reviewed the basics for the amount of hard disk space that should be allotted for cache. The recommended size of cache is based on the number of users. If you have fewer than 250 users, only 2 to 4GB of disk space is recommended, but if you need to support close to 2,000 users, move that amount up to 10GB. To make more precise estimates, you should start with 100MB and add one-half of a megabyte per cache user. That means 200 cache users should be allowed 200MB of disk space for cache and 2,000 users should be allowed 1100MB of disk space for cache. You do not need to ensure that the drive on which you are installing ISA Server has enough space for cache.

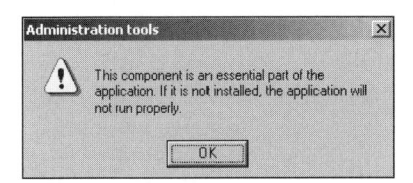

Figure 3.5 You will see this dialog box if the Administration Tools option is removed during the installation of ISA Server.

A code for ISA Server can be created on any drive on the server. If the ISA Server you are installing will provide caching services, you will be asked to allot disk space for caching later in the installation.

Click OK to continue the installation of ISA Server.

Standalone or Array?

At this point, the ISA Server Setup Wizard hasn't yet given you the choice to install this ISA server as standalone or in an array. The assumption is that if you have gone to the extra expense of buying the Enterprise Edition of ISA Server, you have a large environment to support and want an array. However, you do have the choice to install the Enterprise Edition as a standalone ISA server or array member. Microsoft recommends that you install the Enterprise Edition as an array member even if you only need one ISA server on a network. Microsoft refers to this as leaving room to grow. If you install ISA Server, even the Enterprise Edition, as a standalone ISA server and then decide at a later date to install another ISA server, the original ISA server can be upgraded to an array member. During the upgrade a new array will be created. The steps for upgrading a standalone Enterprise Edition ISA server to an array member will be covered later in this chapter.

If instead you want to install the second ISA server as a standalone server, you can do that, but you will need to individually set all the configurations for each ISA server. Making the two servers members of the same array will simplify their administration. When you configure one of the servers, the other will automatically be configured also. If you install the original ISA server as an array member at the start even though it is the only member, you will be able to add more ISA servers in the future. Additional ISA servers can easily be added to the array.

While installing ISA servers into an array provides many advantages, an array requires a Windows 2000 domain environment and a few more decisions about the application of policies. A network that is still in a Windows NT 4 domain or a non-Microsoft environment will need to be installed as a standalone ISA server. You must install ISA on Windows 2000, but in a standalone configuration, you do not need to be in a Windows 2000 Active Directory environment. Also, the Enterprise Edition allows the installation of a standalone server if you decide that you don't want an array.

Because array members need to belong to the same Windows 2000 domain and the same Windows 2000 site, they are designed to include only ISA servers connected by high-speed links. Sites in Windows 2000 are one or more subnets connected by high-speed links. Networks separated by slow—usually Wide Area Network (WAN)—links are often installed as separate sites in Windows 2000 and consequently separate arrays in ISA Server. So ten ISA servers supporting a large company location in Seattle would be one array, whereas two ISA servers at a smaller location in Wichita need to be installed into a separate array if Seattle and Wichita belong to different Windows 2000 Active Directory Sites.

We have not yet covered policies, but after the installation is complete, you will need to focus on them. An ISA server allows no connections into or out of the internal network when it is first installed. Rules contained in policies need to be configured to allow any access at all. Policies can be implemented at an enterprise (entire network, including all arrays), individual array, or local level. Standalone ISA servers can only use a local policy, and this policy cannot be applied to any other ISA server. Enterprise policy and individual array policies differ in the centralization of settings and the amount of flexibility given to individual network locations. Enterprise policies centralize the administration, but this centralization can also take away all administration at the array level.

Array members can have the enterprise policy, the array policy, or a combination of both applied to it. When an enterprise policy is applied, you can decide to disallow all array-level policies, which means that no rules can be created at the array level. This may not work in a large diversified environment. An alternative is to apply an enterprise policy but also allow array-level policies. It is important to remember in this situation that if an enterprise policy is applied to an array, any connection denied at the enterprise policy level cannot be overridden by the array policy. A combination of enterprise and array-level policies creates a situation in which the enterprise policy sets the boundaries for what can be done. Array-level rules can only move within the boundaries set by the enterprise-level policy. The third choice is to set no policy at the enterprise level and instead allow individual locations to set their own array-level policies.

Regardless of how you have decided to install ISA Server, its Setup Wizard will start looking for ISA Server schema in Active Directory as soon as you click OK in the installation type dialog box. Even though the Enterprise Edition is being installed if the wizard doesn't find the ISA Server schema—either because you haven't run the ISA Server Enterprise Initialization or because a Windows 2000 Active Directory domain is not currently found on the network due to network problems or the computer being disconnected from the network—a dialog box informing you that you must install this ISA server as a standalone server will appear, as shown in Figure 3.6. If you click No, Setup will end and ISA Server will not be installed. ISA Server Enterprise Initialization adds the ISA Server schema to Active Directory and must be run before the start of the ISA Server installation. We discussed ISA Server Enterprise Initialization in Chapter 2. If you want to install ISA Server Enterprise Edition as an array member and this message pops up, you will be able to install ISA Server as a standalone server only. You will need to stop the installation and check the network connections of the computer you want to install ISA Server on and check the state of the network.

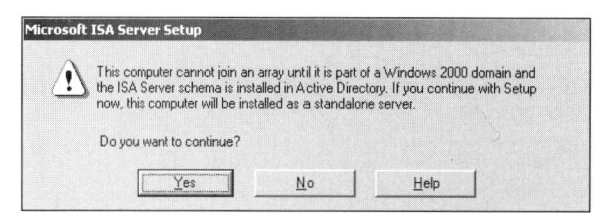

Figure 3.6 A dialog box informing you that you must install ISA Server as standalone because the prerequisites for an array were not found by the ISA Server Setup Wizard.

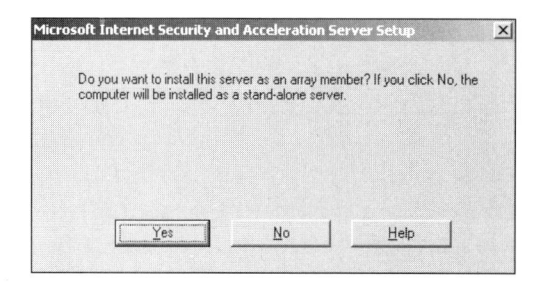

Figure 3.7 A dialog box asking if you want to install ISA Server as a standalone server or as a member of an array is shown when the prerequisites for creating an array are fulfilled.

If the ISA Server schema is found, you will be asked if you want to install the ISA server as a standalone server or as a member of an array. This dialog box is shown in Figure 3.7.

Next, you will be asked if you want to join an existing array. Type in the name of an existing array, or create an array by entering a new name. If you create a new array, you will need to configure how you want to apply it and configure rules for it.

The dialog box Configure Enterprise Policy Settings appears next (see Figure 3.8). If you select Use Default Enterprise Policy Settings, the array policy that you are creating will inherit settings from the enterprise policy. Rules set in the enterprise policy will be implemented in the array. If you select Use Custom Enterprise Policy Settings, you can select Use Array Policy Only if you want to create a separate array policy or Use Enterprise Policy Only if you want to use only the enterprise policy rules and do not want to configure or use any array rules. If you choose the latter option you will also be able to choose the enterprise policy that you want to use. Only enterprise policies that are already created will be listed. Once you select an enterprise policy, you also have the choice of checking Allow Array Level Access Policy Rules That Restrict Enterprise Policy, which will allow you to work within the rules set by the enterprise policy that you selected. You will not be able to allow any actions that the enterprise policy denies, but you will be able to place further restrictions on what the enterprise policy allows. It is not much freedom for an array administrator, but if you do not place a checkmark in this dialog box, you will not be able to create any rules at the array level. The last

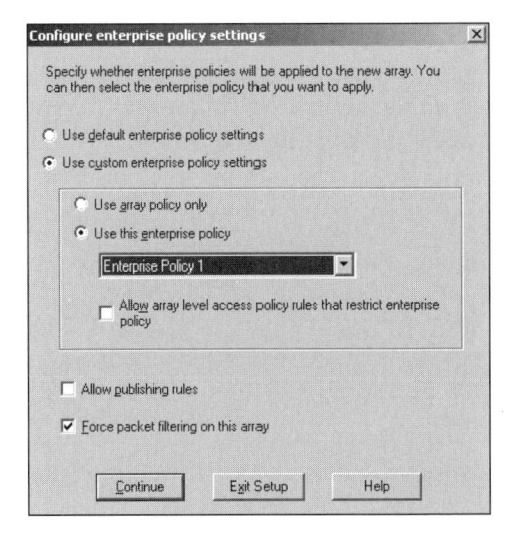

Figure 3.8 The Configure Enterprise Policy Settings dialog box allows you to choose the policies and rules that will apply to a new array.

two checkboxes in this dialog box allow you to create array-level publishing rules or packet filters.

Installation Mode

The next dialog box that appears requires you to select a mode for the ISA server. ISA Server mode establishes how an ISA server should allocate its resources. Figure 3.9 shows the installation mode dialog box and the choices it contains.

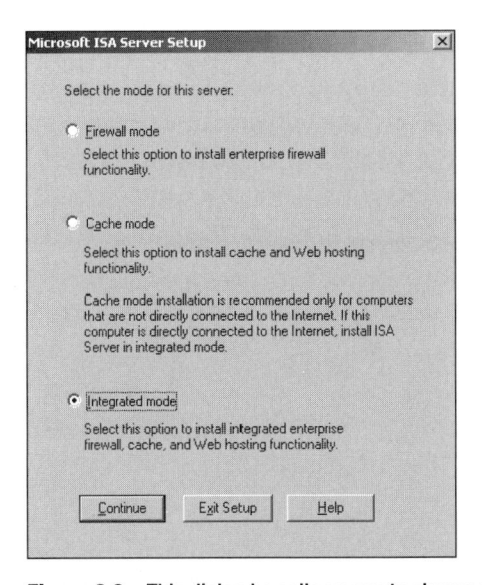

Figure 3.9 This dialog box allows you to choose a mode for installing ISA Server.

ISA Server can provide security services through Firewall mode, acceleration services through Cache mode, or security and acceleration through Integrated mode. Which mode you select depends on the complexity of your network. If you have a large network, you would not want to set up a single ISA server in Integrated mode. Because it is a single gateway to the Internet, the one ISA server could end up being a bottleneck for users trying to get out to the Internet.

In a large network, you can set up groups of ISA servers to help one another handle the load. Connections for incoming users can be separate from those being used by internal users trying to get out to the Internet. In addition, groups of servers installed in Cache mode can devote all of their resources to speeding up Internet responses rather than having to divert resources to firewall tasks. A server that has specialized tasks can handle a large load better. However, in a small environment specialization may not be necessary. One ISA server installed in Integrated mode can provide all of the necessary services for the network. This is the reason why Integrated mode is also a possibility. The size of the network is not the only factor. Other factors include the services provided by the internal network that Internet users want to get to and traffic over the Internet connection.

If you choose Cache mode, the installation moves to setting up disk space for caching. If you choose Firewall mode, the installation moves to the construction of the Local Address Table (LAT). If you choose Integrated mode, the Setup Wizard begins with setting up disk space for cache and then sets up the LAT.

Setting Up Disk Space for Caching

Because caching requires a disk drive formatted with NTFS the ISA Server Setup Wizard searches for an NTFS partition before it brings up the dialog box that sets up the cache. The wizard will find the largest NTFS partition to set a default cache size of 100MB if at least 150MB are available. You can set a cache size as small as 5MB, but as we discussed earlier in the chapter, the minimum recommended is 100MB plus one-half of a megabyte per cache user. If you need more cache, you can reset sizes later in the ISA Server snap-in.

Note: You can't convert a FAT drive to NTFS during the installation of ISA Server. You have to use the Windows 2000 Convert command at the command prompt. If the drive you are converting does not contain system files, it will convert immediately with no reboot needed. But if the drive you are converting contains system files, you'll need to reboot to perform the conversion.

If an NTFS drive does not have a drive letter assigned to it, the ISA Server Setup Wizard will not recognize the drive and will not be able to set up cache on it.

Figure 3.10 shows the dialog box that allows you to set up cache in the ISA Server Setup Wizard. It resembles the dialog box that allows you to set up the pagefile size in Windows 2000. Even though the Setup Wizard automatically selects the largest

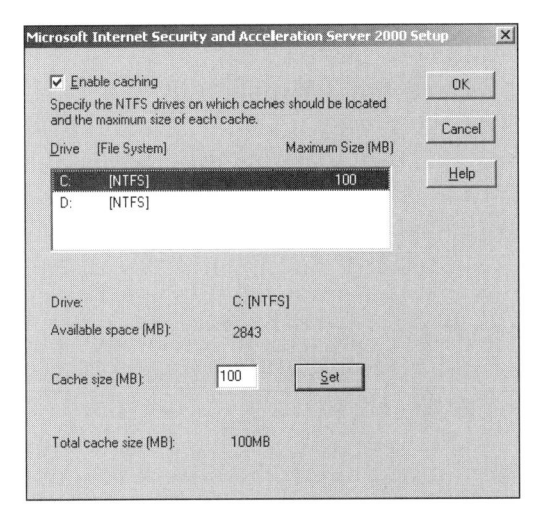

Figure 3.10 If you have enough NTFS disk space the Setup Wizard enters 100MB for a minimum cache setting, but it also allows you to adjust the settings.

NTFS drive, it is recommended that the ISA Server files and cache actually reside on different physical drives for better performance. To change the selected drive, just click on another drive, type in the size that you would like the cache to be, and click the Set button. As with the pagefile in Windows 2000, you can set a cache file on more than one drive.

Once you set the cache size and location, click OK to open the next dialog box. If you are installing ISA Server in Cache mode, you will not need to fill in anymore dialog boxes. You have given the Setup Wizard all of the information it needs to complete the installation. If you are setting up an ISA server in Firewall or Integrated mode, you will need to construct the LAT to complete the installation process.

Constructing the Local Address Table (LAT)

ISA Server needs a LAT only if it is installed in Firewall or Integrated mode. These modes allow it to act as a proxy server for internal clients, and the LAT specifies who the internal clients are. This portion of the installation is skipped if you choose Cache mode. Figure 3.11 shows the dialog box that allows you to construct the LAT.

The purpose of the LAT is to give ISA Server a list of IP addresses that belong to the internal network. If the ISA server receives a packet that is destined for an address inside the internal network, it does not need to send that request out to the Internet. Any packet containing an IP address that is not on the LAT needs to have a request sent out the ISA's external adapter. It is very important that the LAT be accurate. Otherwise, packets meant for the internal network will be sent out to the Internet and possibly never reach their destination on the internal network. Also,

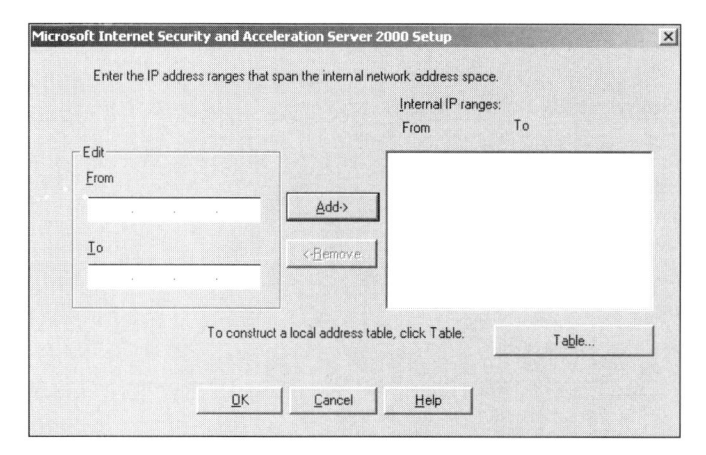

Figure 3.11 The Setup Wizard LAT dialog box.

packets that should be sent out the external interface on the ISA server will never be allowed out and will not reach their destination.

In the Setup Wizard LAT dialog box, you can enter the range of IPs on the left side and click the Add button to include the range in the LAT. It is a good idea to use the Table button to construct the LAT. Figure 3.12 shows the dialog box that appears when you click the Table button. It will use the computer's internal routing table to add IP address ranges to the LAT. You can add ranges of IPs to the list or remove them. Constructing the LAT from the internal routing table will make it less likely that some ranges of IPs will be forgotten. Think of the list as a good place to start. You still need to check the address ranges to make sure that they contain all of the internal ranges of IPs and *only* the internal ranges of IP addresses. Remember to connect the ISA server to the internal network before constructing the LAT; otherwise you will never be able to finish constructing it. ISA Server must be able to detect that the ISA server's internal adapter is listed on the LAT or you will get an error message and not be able to continue with the installation.

Once you have selected a choice or choices in the Local Address Table dialog box, click OK to return to the LAT construction dialog box. Add or remove IP address ranges so that all internal IP address ranges are included. Click OK to dismiss the dialog box.

You have now completed the choices for installing ISA Server. Now the installation program will copy files and set up what you have told it you need for your configuration of ISA Server. Before you see the dialog box that tells you that the installation is complete, a dialog box will announce that you can open a Getting Started Wizard for ISA Server. If you clear the checkmark before clicking the OK button, you will see a dialog box telling you that the installation is complete, as shown in Figure 3.13. If you do not clear the checkmark, you'll still see this dialog box, but the Getting Started Wizard will open after you dismiss it.

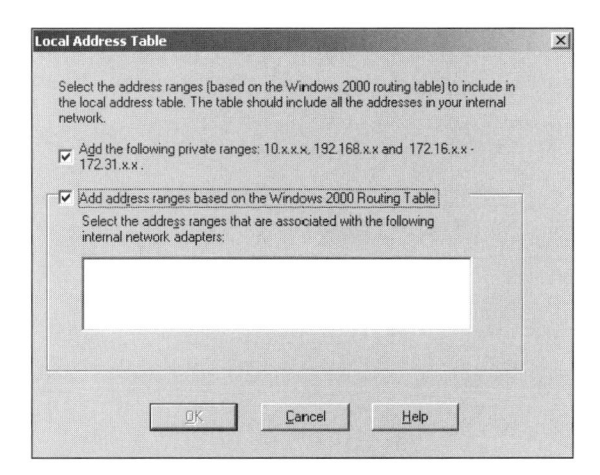

Figure 3.12 The LAT construction dialog box.

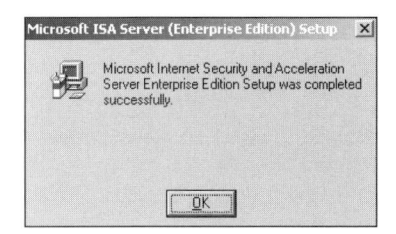

Figure 3.13 This dialog box informs you that the installation is complete.

The ISA Server Getting Started Wizard

The Getting Started Wizard is for administrators who need to get started immediately with ISA Server and who are new to the product. It will help you configure security, client, and cache settings that you can set up manually in the ISA Server snap-in. The wizard will step you through needed configurations while displaying the ISA Server snap-in so that you can see where these settings are configured. It explains the different views of the ISA Server snap-in as well as the options that are available. If you dismiss the dialog box that asks if you want to use the Getting Started Wizard during the installation, you can call it up at any time from within the ISA console. In the ISA Server snap-in, select the View menu and click the Taskpad option. From the Welcome section of the Taskpad, you can launch the Getting Started Wizard.

Unattended Installation

ISA Server allows an unattended installation. As with any unattended installation, some setup is required ahead of time. You must create a file that answers all the questions asked during the install. Call this file msiaund.ini and place it in the root

Table 3.3 Required sections in the unattended installation file for ISA Server.

Section Name	Possible Settings	Default Value
Install	Install directory	First drive with enough space
	Override existing configuration	0 (program retains any settings that are present and upgrades)
Array Membership	Join an existing array	Installs ISA Server as standalone
	Create a new array and join	Installs ISA Server as standalone
Features	Firewall_And_Cache	Firewall_And_Cache
	Firewall	
	Cache	
Proxy Setup LAT Config	Include Ranges from all cards	Places all detected IP address ranges and puts them in the LAT
	Include Private Ranges	Places all detected IP address ranges and puts them in the LAT
	Range1, Range2, RangeX	No default value
Proxy Setup Cache Config	drive=*drive*	First NTFS drive with enough space
	Size_min=	100MB
	Size_max	100MB

directory of the server on which ISA Server will be installed. The file should contain five sections, as explained in Table 3.3. At first glance, this seems like a lot of settings. Actually, many of the settings have default values that are used if they are not specified in the unattended installation file. The file can turn out to be pretty short if you are willing to accept the default settings.

Note: Unattended installation does not include settings for Typical, Full, or Custom installations. An unattended installation always installs a Full installation of ISA Server.

Understanding Each Section

The Install section has two possible settings. The first setting selects the drive on which ISA Server will install. The syntax of this setting is ***drive:\folder***. An example of this would be **C:\ISA Server**. If you leave out this setting, the default drive will be the root and the default folder will be \Program Files\Microsoft ISA Server. The second setting under the install section is Override Existing Settings, which requires a 0 (no) or 1 (yes) response. An example of this setting is Override Existing Settings=1. The default setting is 0, which means if any setting from previous installations exist, such as cache or Proxy Server settings, they will not be upgraded or used in ISA Server.

The Array Membership section has two possible settings: Join An Existing Array or Create A New Array And Join. These settings specify whether the ISA server will install as a standalone server or as part of an array. You can specify either of these settings, but not both. If neither setting is specified, the ISA server will install as a standalone server. Arrays require Active Directory on the network and the ISA

Server schema must be installed into Active Directory. We cover installing the ISA Server schema into Active Directory in Chapter 2 of this book.

The Features section specifies the mode in which ISA Server will install. In the GUI install, the choices are Cache, Firewall, or Integrated. Cache and Firewall are still called these names in the unattended installation file. Choose Cache_And_Firewall if you want an Integrated setup. You do not need to create the Proxy Setup LAT Config section if Cache is the only feature that you select. If Firewall is the only selected feature, the section titled Proxy Setup Cache Config is not necessary. If Firewall_And_Cache is the selected feature, you can use both of these sections. Firewall_And_Cache is the default if the Features section is not specified.

The Proxy Setup LAT Config section constructs the LAT during the installation. This section has three possible settings, just as the dialog box does. Figure 3.11 (shown earlier) shows the LAT construction dialog box used during the installation. The first checkbox, if selected, includes the listed private address ranges. You can select this setting in the unattended installation if you use the Include Private Ranges setting. In the dialog box, the second checkbox, if selected, will use the internal routing table in the computer on which ISA Server is being loaded. You can use this setting by selecting the Include Ranges From All Cards setting. This setting will take the IP network addresses listed on the internal routing table and include them in the LAT. The IP address of the external connection must not be included in the LAT. If the IP address of the external connection is persistent it will be included in the internal routing table.

Both the Include Private Ranges and the Include Ranges From All Cards settings exclude no IP range, which means that neither of these settings should be used if the external connection to the Internet is a persistent one. They can be used if the external connection is dial-up. If the external connection is persistent, you should use the RangeX setting. Each range can be specified using the syntax of **RangeX** *www.xxx.yyy.zzz*. An example would be **Range1 192.168.000.000 192.168.255.255**.

The Proxy Setup Cache Config section configures the cache settings for ISA Server. The possible settings are Drive, Size_min, and Size_max. The Drive setting tells ISA Server on which drive it should create a cache. The syntax is **drive=***driveletter*. The Size_min and Size_max settings specify the minimum and maximum size of the cache. The syntax for each is **Size_min** or **max=150MB**. If this section is left out of the unattended installation file, the cache will be set to 100MB on the first NTFS drive that ISA Server finds. Cache settings are not needed if you use the Firewall setting in the Features section.

Remember to name the file msiuand.ini and place it in the root drive or ISA Server installation won't use it. Below is a sample msiuand.ini file:

```
[Install]
C:\ISA Server
Override existing configuration = 0

[Array Membership]
Join an existing array = "Array1"

[Features]
Firewall

[Proxy Setup LAT Config]
Range1 192.168.000.000 192.168.255.255
Range2 10.0.0.0 10.255.255.255
```

Running the Unattended Installation File

Before the installation can begin, you must provide the location of the installation files for ISA Server as well as the product ID number. The syntax required to run the unattended installation file is **path\isa\setup /q/k PID_Number**. The *path* is the drive on which the ISA Server installation files reside and **PID_Number** is the CD key. The **Q** parameter is required to specify that an unattended installation will occur, but other parameters can be set in conjunction with the **/Q** parameter. Other unattended installation options are also possible. Table 3.4 displays a list of possible settings for the installation path used by ISA Server. The **/U** parameter in this table also triggers an unattended installation, but does not have the subparameter options that the **/Q** parameter has.

The subparameters listed for **/Q** are **0**, **1**, and **T**. These subparameters should be listed next to the **/Q** parameter with no spaces and no forward slashes. For example, if the ISA Server installation files reside on a CD-ROM drive D, the path can be **D:\isa\setup /qt /k ##########**. This sample path starts an unattended installation and specifies that the dialog boxes should not be displayed during the installation.

Table 3.4 Parameters that can be used when running an unattended installation for ISA Server.

Parameter	Use
/Q	Performs an unattended installation of ISA Server.
0	A setting for the **/Q** parameter. Specifies that the Finish dialog box should appear at the end of the installation.
1	A setting for the **/Q** parameter. Specifies that the Finish dialog box should not appear at the end of the installation.
T	A setting for the **/Q** parameter. Specifies that no dialog boxes should appear during the installation of ISA Server.
/R	Performs an unattended reinstallation of ISA Server.
/U	Performs an unattended uninstallation of ISA Server.

Creating or Joining an Array During Installation

To install an array, not only must you have initialized the enterprise, but the computer must be a domain member and belong to the same site within the domain as well. Computers that belong to the same site need to have a persistent, high-speed IP connection between them. Installing into an array is similar to installing a standalone ISA server. The exception is that a few extra dialog boxes are added during the beginning of the installation process.

Creating the First Array

If you will need more than one ISA server on a network, Microsoft recommends that you consider using an array. An array is created when the first member of it is installed. When creating an array, you will start the installation wizard and go through the first few steps:

1. The installation will begin and you will confirm that you want to install ISA Server.

2. The installation will ask for the CD key and will not continue until you provide a valid one.

3. The licensing agreement will appear and you will need to click I Agree to continue the installation.

4. The installation type dialog box will appear, asking if you want a Typical, Full, or Custom installation.

5. At this point, if the prerequisites have been met you will be asked if you want this ISA server to join an array. If you click Yes, you'll see another dialog box asking you to name the array (see Step 6). If you click No, this step will be skipped and the rest of the installation will continue in the same manner as a standalone installation.

6. This step is time consuming if an array has not yet been created. This step allows you to name the array you will be joining. Since this is the first member, you will need to type the name of the array. You may have to wait while the array is created.

7. The installation will continue with the choosing of a mode for the ISA server. The rest of the installation involves setting up cache and the LAT with the same dialog boxes used in the standalone installation.

Choosing to create an array adds the step of naming that array—so it does lengthen the installation, but not by much. The time-consuming part is waiting for the installation wizard to create the array. Naming the array is all that is required from the administrator.

Joining an Array

Although you still need to install a server into an existing array, joining the array during the install will complete much of the new array member's configuration settings. Settings for policies and rules are saved as part of an enterprise or array policy and are automatically set for new members. The process of joining an array is accomplished during an installation of ISA Server. Once an array is created, other ISA servers may join. During the installation, you will be able to select the name of the array you want the ISA server to join instead of typing the name of a new one. You can supply this name after selecting Yes when asked if you want to join an array. After joining an array, the installation will select the mode for the ISA server. When joining members to an array, make sure that Active Directory has the chance to replicate that information out across the domain before joining other members. In a large domain this replication can take some time.

Upgrading a Standalone Enterprise Edition ISA Server to an Array Member

If an Enterprise Edition ISA Server can be installed as a standalone server, it cannot participate in an array, but it can be upgraded to an array member. When you upgrade the standalone ISA server, you can select what policies and rules will apply to the array that you are creating. Follow these steps:

1. Open ISA Management.

2. Expand Internet Security And Acceleration Server and then expand Servers And Arrays.

3. Right click the name or the server that you need to upgrade to an array and select Properties.

4. Select Promote, then click Yes.

5. In the Set Global Policy dialog box you will have the same choices that you have when you create a new array. Select between Use Default Enterprise Policy Settings and Use Custom Enterprise Policy Settings. If you select Default Enterprise Policy Settings, any existing server rules that are in conflict with the default enterprise policy will be deleted. If you select Custom Enterprise Policy Settings, choose between Use Array Policy Only if you want to create your own array policy and Use This Enterprise Policy if you want to select a different Enterprise policy besides the default one. Also, you can check Allow Array Level Access Policy Rules That Restrict Enterprise Policy if you want the enterprise policy to allow you to set access policy rules that work within the boundaries of the enterprise policy that you selected.

6. Check Allow Publishing Rules if you want to keep any publishing rules that you have already created on the server.

7. Check Force Packet Filtering On This Array if you want to create packet filters at the array level.

8. Click OK.

Installing the Standard Edition of ISA Server

As discussed earlier in this chapter, the Standard Edition of ISA Server is simply a version of ISA Server that is not scalable to large networking environments. The ISA Server snap-in used to administer ISA Server works the same way with both editions. This means that the administration of the Standard Edition works the same way and with the same dialog boxes as the administration of the Enterprise Edition. The main difference you'll find between the two is the installation dialog boxes. During the installation of the Standard Edition, Active Directory is not searched for the ISA schema and the dialog boxes asking you to create or join an array do not appear. Because the choice of a Custom, Full, or Typical installation is still available, as well as the three modes of installation, the rest of the installation is the same as it is in the Enterprise Edition. Project 3 at the end of the chapter covers the installation of the Standard Edition of ISA Server.

Removing ISA Server

ISA Server can be uninstalled and completely removed from a server. To remove ISA Server, open Add/Remove Programs in Control Panel. Select the Change Or Remove Programs option and then click Microsoft Internet And Acceleration Server 2000. The Change and Remove buttons will become available. Click the Remove button, and click Yes when you're asked to confirm the removal of ISA Server. Another dialog box will ask if you want to remove all settings, including the Web pages in cache, logs, and any backup configuration information you may have saved. Click Yes if you want to remove everything. Uninstalling ISA Server does not remove the ISA Server schema information from Active Directory.

Chapter Summary

ISA Server can be installed from the local CD or over the network. Before installing ISA Server, make sure you have checked the computer for compliance with hardware and software requirements. Gather all necessary information you will need to enter during the installation before the process actually begins.

An installation wizard leads you through the process of installing ISA Server. It takes you through the steps of the installation and displays dialog boxes to gather the information needed to complete the installation.

You can install ISA Server in one of several ways. A Typical, Full, or Custom installation enables you to install different components. The ISA Administration Tool is the only component that must be installed with all installation types. In a large environment, you may want your ISA servers to specialize in either security or acceleration, so you must specify a mode of installation. Integrated mode uses both security and acceleration settings and is best suited for smaller environments. Depending on the mode chosen, the LAT or cache or even both the LAT and cache settings will need to be set.

The Enterprise Edition of ISA Server can be installed as a standalone server or into an array. The standalone server can be more complex than the array installation. If the enterprise has not been initialized or Active Directory is not on the network, all ISA servers will be standalone. Both of these conditions must be created before the ISA Server installation begins. If both conditions are met, the ISA server can be installed as either a standalone or into an array. You can create an array during the installation of the array's first member. The Standard Edition of ISA Server installs as a standalone ISA server only and cannot participate in arrays.

You can perform an unattended installation of ISA Server, but doing so requires prior setup. You must create a file called msiuand.ini in a text editor and save the file to the root directory on the server. The file must contain up to five sections; each section specifies settings that otherwise would be answered by an administrator during the installation process. Different installation modes make some sections of the answer file unnecessary. Each section of the answer file has a default answer. If settings in the section are left blank or if the whole section is not included in the answer file, the default settings will apply to the installation.

Review Questions

1. Which are required for the installation of ISA Server? [Check all correct answers]
    a. An NTFS-formatted partition
    b. Active Directory
    c. Windows 2000 Server
    d. Windows 2000 Service Pack 1
    e. None of the above

2. What is the minimum recommended cache size?

   a. .5MB
   b. 5MB
   c. 100MB
   d. 2GB
   e. 10GB

3. What is the minimum required cache size when cache setup is required?

   a. .5MB
   b. 5MB
   c. 100MB
   d. 2GB
   e. 10GB

4. Which installation option is considered essential to the running of ISA Server? [Check all correct answers]

   a. ISA Services
   b. Add-In Services
   c. Administration Tools
   d. All are essential
   e. None are essential

5. Which installation mode requires the setup of cache? [Check all correct answers]

   a. Firewall mode
   b. Cache mode
   c. Integrated mode
   d. None require the setup of cache

6. Active Directory is required for what purpose when installing ISA Server?

   a. The installation of ISA Server
   b. The use of cache
   c. The installation of a standalone server
   d. The installation of an array

7. What should be included on the LAT?
   a. Internal IP address ranges
   b. External IP address ranges
   c. Cache settings
   d. All IP address ranges

8. Which file runs the installation for ISA Server?
   a. ISAAutorun.exe
   b. Setup.exe
   c. Install.exe
   d. ISA.exe

9. What can happen if the LAT is inaccurate? [Check all correct answers]
   a. Packets meant for the internal network could be sent out the external interface.
   b. Packets meant for the external network could be restricted to the internal network only.
   c. Packets meant for the internal network will stay on the internal network.
   d. Packets meant for the external network will be sent out the external interface.

10. What is the name of the unattended installation file?
    a. You can name the file whatever you want
    b. msp.ini
    c. isauatd.ini
    d. msiaund.ini

11. Where must the unattended installation file for ISA be stored?
    a. In the root drive
    b. In any drive
    c. On the C: drive
    d. On the CD-ROM drive

12. What happens if a setting is left out of the unattended installation file?
    a. The installation fails and ends.
    b. The dialog box asking the question pops up and waits for an answer.
    c. The default value for that setting is used.
    d. The computer crashes.

13. How many sections are in the unattended installation file for ISA Server?
    a. 3
    b. 5
    c. 7
    d. 9

14. Which of the following is required when typing the path for an unattended installation? [Check all correct answers]
    a. The path to the installation files
    b. The name of the unattended installation file
    c. The path to the unattended installation file
    d. The product ID number
    e. The **/Q** parameter
    f. The **/U** parameter
    g. All of the above

15. When should ranges for IP network addresses be specified during an unattended installation?
    a. If the external network connection is not persistent
    b. If the external network connection is persistent
    c. If the internal network connection is persistent
    d. If the internal network connection is not persistent

16. How is the Getting Started Wizard launched? [Check all correct answers]
    a. At the end of the installation
    b. Only during the installation
    c. From the Taskpad
    d. Only from the Taskpad

17. How do you remove ISA Server schema information from Active Directory?
    a. By using Add/Remove Programs in Control Panel
    b. By using the ISA uninstall program
    c. By uninstalling the original ISA server
    d. By uninstalling the last ISA server on the network
    e. You can't

18. How is an array created?

    a. During the installation of the first member

    b. Through the array creation tool in ISA console

    c. Through a separate wizard after the installation of the first member

    d. Through a separate wizard before the installation of the first member

19. Joining an array does what to the installation of ISA Server?

    a. Shortens the time of the installation process

    b. Lengthens the time of the installation process, but not by much

    c. Greatly lengthens the time of the installation process

    d. Has no effect on the time of the installation process

20. How often must you initialize the enterprise for ISA Server?

    a. Only once

    b. Every time an ISA server is removed from the network

    c. Every time a member is added to an array

    d. Once a month

    e. Never

Real-World Projects

Note: This exercise assumes a test Windows 2000 server with Service Pack 1 installed. Read the instructions carefully and do not perform this install on your production machine unless you understand the options presented. If you are unsure about an option, cancel the installation and read the ISA Help about the option to be installed.

Joe had recently been given a newly created position at work. His company, Train4U, created the position of Internet Security Specialist to try to protect its Web site from being broken into. Because the company was nearly finished with its upgrade to Windows 2000, Joe was looking into Microsoft's Internet and Acceleration Server (ISA) as a product that could solve the problem. From his research into the product, Joe discovered that the Web site was not all that needed protection. All computers in the company's network needed to be protected from an Internet connection.

During a meeting, Joe presented his research and recommended that he build a test lab to try out some of the settings. It was agreed that he would get two test servers and two client computers to create a simulated network with an ISA server. Joe gathered the network diagram that contained all of the IP network addresses and information about the connection that the company had to the Internet.

Joe decided to install ISA Server onto one of his test servers. This way, he could better see the options that were available and plan an approach for the entire network. He could see what the default options were and get a better hands-on feel for the changes he would need to implement for different settings.

He knew the prerequisites and had even installed two network adapters on the computer to get a real simulation out of it. Windows 2000 Server was already installed, and Windows 2000 Service Pack 1 was applied.

Joe also knew that last-minute software updates or updates to the ISA Server documentation would be on the ISA Server CD. He decided to make sure that he really did have all of the prerequisites before beginning the installation of ISA Server by checking the resources on the CD.

Project 3.1
To check the ISA Server CD for software updates and new documentation:

1. Insert the ISA Server CD.
2. An autorun file will appear called ISA Server Setup.
3. Select Read Installation Guide. The Installation Guide is a Web-based document that provides details on installation procedures and the ISA Server Installation Wizard.
4. Close the Installation Guide.
5. Select Review Release Notes. The release notes can contain special instructions and guidelines that are not included in regular help and are contained in a file called readme.htm.
6. Close the release notes.
7. Open Windows Explorer.
8. Expand the CD-ROM drive to explore the contents of the ISA Server CD.
9. Explore the path **CD root\ISA\chmbook** and find the file isa.chm.
10. Open the isa.chm file to launch ISA Server help.
11. Explore help topics.
12. Close ISA Server help.

Joe found from the release notes that he did not have all of the necessary prerequisites to install ISA Server. According to the release notes, problems between Windows 2000 and ISA Server had recently been discovered. The ISA Server CD contained these hot fixes in the Support\hotfixes\Win2000 folder. Relieved that he had averted future problems by stopping to check out the ISA Server CD before installing, Joe was more confident now. After he applied the hot fixes to the server that would be his ISA server, he felt ready to try installing ISA Server.

Because Joe did not have Active Directory on his network, he could not initialize the enterprise to get the ISA Server schema into it. He knew that the ISA installation could be removed, so he decided to try a standalone installation first. Later, he would remove this installation of ISA Server and then create an array.

Project 3.2

To install the Enterprise Edition of ISA Server 2000 as a standalone server:

1. Insert the ISA Server CD.
2. From ISA Server Setup, select Install ISA Server.
3. A dialog box will welcome you to the installation of ISA Server. Click Continue.
4. The next screen will ask for the CD key. Enter the key from the back of the ISA Server jewel case.
5. Click OK to continue the install.
6. Write down the Product ID number in the next screen for future reference.
7. Click OK to continue the install.
8. Setup will search for components of ISA Server and then display the licensing agreement.
9. Read through the licensing agreement and then click I Agree to continue the install.
10. Check that the installation directory is correct and then click Typical Installation to continue the install.
11. Setup will search for the ISA Schema. When it does not find the ISA Server schema, Setup will warn you that only a standalone server can be installed. Click Yes to continue with a standalone installation of ISA Server.
12. Next, select the mode for ISA Server. Then, click Continue.
13. Setup will stop all related services. Cache settings will appear if you selected Cache or Integrated mode. If necessary, type a different cache size and click the Set button.
14. Click OK to continue.

15. If you selected Firewall or Integrated mode, the LAT dialog box will appear. Click the Table button to build the LAT. Select the appropriate choices and click OK to return to the LAT dialog box. Check the IP addresses to make sure all internal addresses are included. Click OK to proceed with the install.

16. Setup will copy the necessary files and restart the needed services to complete the installation of ISA Server.

17. A message screen will appear asking if you want to start the Getting Started Wizard. Click OK to continue the install.

18. A dialog box will appear informing you that the installation is complete. Click OK to end the installation of ISA Server.

The Getting Started Wizard started. Joe closed it and then decided he did want to review what options were available on it.

To open the Getting Started Wizard manually:

1. Click once on the Start menu.
2. Select Programs|Administrative Tools|ISA Server.
3. The ISA console will start.
4. In the ISA console, select the View menu.
5. Click Taskpad. The Taskpad appears in the right side of the console.
6. Select the Welcome option in the Taskpad.
7. The Getting Started Wizard will appear.

Joe navigated around in the Getting Started Wizard and saw many of the terms he had been reading about. He had just installed a standalone ISA server, but he wanted more practice.

Joe decided that he needed to try an installation into an array. After studying the network, he determined he might need more than one ISA server. He wanted to practice both types of installations.

Joe decided to remove the standalone installation of ISA Server he just completed and go through the prerequisites for installing ISA Server into an array.

Project 3.3

To remove ISA Server:

1. Click once on the Start menu.
2. Select Settings|Control Panel.

3. In Control Panel, double-click Add/Remove Programs.

4. Select Change Or Remove Programs and click Internet Security And Acceleration Server 2000.

5. Click the Remove button.

6. A confirmation dialog box will appear asking if you are sure you want to remove ISA Server from the computer. Click Yes to continue.

7. A dialog box will appear asking if you want to remove all settings, including the Web pages in cache, logs, and any backup configuration information you may have saved. Clicking Yes will remove the items; clicking No will not. After you make a selection, the removal process will continue.

8. Setup will update the system and present a dialog box informing you that the uninstall is complete. Click OK to complete the removal of ISA Server.

Joe was now ready to start the prerequisites for installing an array. First, he promoted his Windows 2000 Server to a domain controller. Then, he initialized the enterprise to add the ISA Server schema to Active Directory. After these steps were completed successfully, he was ready to install his ISA server into an array.

Project 3.4

To install ISA Server 2000 into an array:

1. Insert the ISA Server CD.

2. From ISA Server Setup, select Install ISA Server.

3. A dialog box will welcome you to the installation of ISA Server. Click Continue.

4. The next screen will ask for the CD key. Enter the key from the back of the ISA Server jewel case.

5. Click OK to continue the install.

6. Write down the Product ID number in the next screen for future reference.

7. Click OK to continue the install.

8. Setup will search for components of ISA Server and then display the licensing agreement.

9. Read through the licensing agreement and click I Agree to continue the install.

10. Check that the installation directory is correct and then click Typical Installation to continue the install.

11. Setup will search for the ISA schema. When it finds the Schema, Setup will ask if you want to join an array. Click Yes to continue the installation of ISA Server into an array.

12. Since no array exists on the network, type a name for an array. This will create a new array and the ISA server being installed will be the only member.

13. Select the policy that will apply to this ISA server. Click OK.

14. Next, select the mode for ISA Server and click Continue.

15. Setup will stop all related services. Cache settings will appear if you chose Cache or Integrated mode. If necessary, type a different cache size and click the Set button.

16. Click OK to continue.

17. If you chose Firewall or Integrated mode, the LAT dialog box will appear. Click the Table button to build the LAT. Select the appropriate choices. Click OK to return to the LAT dialog box. Check the IP addresses to make sure all internal addresses are included. Click OK to continue the install.

18. Setup will copy the necessary files and restart the needed services to complete the installation of ISA Server.

19. A message screen will appear asking if you want to start the Getting Started Wizard. Click OK to continue the install.

20. The dialog box stating that the installation is complete will appear. Click OK to end the installation of ISA Server.

CHAPTER FOUR

Upgrading from Proxy Server 2.0

After completing this chapter, you will be able to:

✓ Determine requirements for an upgrade

✓ Compare ISA Server services to those provided by Proxy Server 2.0

✓ Identify different types of upgrades possible

✓ Back up Proxy Server 2.0 settings

✓ Stop Proxy 2.0 services

✓ Restore Proxy Server 2.0 settings

✓ Upgrade from Proxy Server 2.0 on Windows NT 4

✓ Upgrade from Proxy Server 2.0 on Windows 2000

✓ Distinguish between settings that do and do not need to be reconfigured

✓ Compare an upgrade to a new install of ISA Server 2000

✓ Compare ISA Server and Proxy Server 2.0 administrative interfaces

✓ Return an ISA Server installation to Proxy Server 2.0

Compared with Proxy Server, ISA Server provides a higher level of control, better security options, and improved integration with new services. Therefore, if your network is using Proxy Server, you will probably want to upgrade. Microsoft released Proxy Server 2.0 before Windows 2000. This means that you could be running a Proxy Server on Windows NT 4 or Windows 2000. Once you complete the upgrade, you'll find that administration is the main area of change. For example, you'll have to learn to configure the new settings in ISA Server.

Proxy Server vs. ISA Server

Why should you upgrade to ISA Server? The most important reason is that the nature of the Internet calls for it. This is especially true for security services. Internet technologies are constantly being enhanced. To keep up with this improvement, upgrades are necessary. As Internet technologies improve, so do malicious attacks from hackers. ISA Server offers you better security and a higher level of control over the security settings. One reason for the improved control is the fact that ISA Server can integrate with Active Directory in a Windows 2000 environment. Proxy Server was designed to run on Windows NT, and although it can be upgraded to run on Windows 2000, Proxy Server itself should be upgraded to take advantage of the latest improvements in Internet technologies.

Preparing for the Upgrade

Before you can perform an upgrade, you must study your network. How many Internet security servers does your network currently have? How many will you need after the upgrade? We will cover setting up and configuring multiple ISA Servers later in this book, but when planning for an upgrade, keep in mind that a mix of Proxy Server 2.0 and ISA Server is allowed in some configurations. We will cover this topic more thoroughly later in this chapter.

Protocol Configuration

ISA Server supports only TCP/IP on both the external and internal connections. However, in case Novell NetWare exists on the internal network, Proxy Server also supports IPX/SPX. If you load only IPX/SPX on the internal network clients, they cannot make a direct connection to the Internet. This is because TCP/IP is required on the Internet. A client with IPX/SPX as its only protocol suite needs to go through the Proxy Server to get to the Internet.

Proxy Server can support IPX/SPX on the connection to the internal network and TCP/IP on the external connection. All major vendors of operating systems now support TCP/IP as a protocol suite, so support for IPX/SPX has been dropped in ISA Server. Therefore, before installing ISA Server, you must change all clients on the internal network and any network adapters in the Proxy Server to TCP/IP.

The Local Address Table

ISA Server and Proxy Server both use the Local Address Table (LAT) to distinguish internal from external IP addresses. Be prepared to check the LAT and make sure it contains all internal IP address ranges even if the Proxy Server LAT was complete and accurate. Check a network diagram and develop a complete list of internal IP address ranges before performing the upgrade to ISA Server.

Backing up a Proxy Server Configuration

Regardless of whether Proxy Server is running on Windows NT 4 or Windows 2000, you should back up its configuration settings before performing an upgrade to ISA Server. By default, Proxy Server files are saved in a folder called \Msp. In this folder, Proxy Server creates a subfolder called \Config. When you back up the configuration settings, Proxy Server creates a text file and saves the file in this folder. If something goes wrong during the upgrade and you need to return to Proxy Server 2.0, you can use this file to restore the Proxy Server settings.

You administer Proxy Server from within Internet Information Server's administrative console, Internet Services Manager. To back up the Proxy Server 2.0 settings, follow these steps:

1. From Internet Services Manager, click the plus (+) sign to view the Internet and Proxy Server services installed on the computer you want to back up.

2. Right-click on any Proxy Server service and select Properties. This will bring up the Service Properties dialog box.

3. In the Service Properties dialog box, click the Server Backup button in the Configuration section.

4. A Backup dialog box will show that a backup file will be created with the name MSP★.mpc. The ★ will be replaced with the date that the file was made according to the computer. This date will have the format of yyyymmdd, with yyyy representing a four-digit year, mm representing the month, and dd representing the day. A backup file created on July 1, 2001, would be named MSP20010701.mpc. This file will be saved by default in the \MSP\Config folder.

5. Click OK to save the file.

6. You will be returned to the Service Properties dialog box. Click OK to dismiss the dialog box and return to Internet Services Manager.

7. Open Windows Explorer and check the \MSP\Config folder for the backup file you just created. You can open the file with Notepad and see that it is a lengthy configuration file with all of your Proxy Server settings.

If the install of ISA Server is not successful, you can reinstall Proxy Server 2.0 and restore its configuration settings from the backup file. To restore Proxy Server 2.0 settings from the MSPyyyymmdd.mpc backup file, follow these steps:

1. From Internet Services Manager, click the plus (+) sign to view the Internet and Proxy Server services installed on the computer you want to restore.

2. Right-click on any Proxy Server service and select Properties. This will bring up the Service Properties dialog box.

3. In the Service Properties dialog box, click the Server Restore button in the Configuration section. It is located right below the Server Backup button used to create the backup file.

4. A Restore Configuration dialog box will appear that offers you the choice of a partial or a full restore. Select Full Restore and type in the name of the server backup file that you created. At the bottom of the dialog box, type the full path to the server backup file. If you click the Browse button, it will default to the \MSP\Config folder.

5. Click OK to perform the restore. This will return you to the Service Properties dialog box.

6. Click OK to dismiss this dialog box and return to Internet Services Manager. Close Internet Services Manager.

Backing up Proxy Server information is just a precaution. Like other types of backups, you perform it just in case something goes wrong.

Proxy on NT 4

Because ISA Server requires Windows 2000 Server as its operating system, if you're running Proxy Server 2.0 on Windows NT 4 you have to perform two upgrades. You have to upgrade Windows NT 4 to Windows 2000 before you can upgrade Proxy Server to ISA Server. Before performing either upgrade, you must stop Proxy Server's services. You can do this in a couple of ways.

Note: No upgrade to ISA Server from Proxy Server 1.0 is available. Before you upgrade the operating system to Windows 2000, you can either upgrade Proxy Server 1.0 to Proxy Server 2.0 or remove it. To check the version of Proxy Server, open Control Panel and double-click Add/Remove Programs. If you are running IIS 4.0 to support Proxy Server, this indicates that you are running Proxy Server 2.0. Proxy Server 1.0 is not supported with IIS 4.0.

Stopping Services

For a Proxy Server running on Windows NT 4, your first step is to upgrade that server to Windows 2000. Before performing this upgrade, you have to stop the services used by Proxy Server 2.0. You can accomplish this at the command prompt or by using the Services application in Control Panel. You must stop a total of four services. Three of these are Proxy Server services, and one is an IIS service. It is important that you disconnect from the external Internet connection before you stop these services. Remember that these are the proxy services that protect your internal network from the Internet connection; if you don't disconnect, then your network will be vulnerable.

Table 4.1 lists the services that you must stop at the command prompt. The syntax for the command used to stop the services is as follows:

```
Net stop service
```

An example is

```
Net stop wspsrv
```

You need to type each command at the command prompt on the computer running Proxy Server. The w3svc service is actually a service from Microsoft's Web server, IIS. Proxy Server runs from within IIS and requires that IIS be loaded on the same computer. Figure 4.1 shows the command prompt with the commands successfully being executed. If you try to stop the services out of order, you might receive some error messages. Here's an example: The mailalrt service is dependent on the mspadmin service. Stopping the mspadmin service before stopping the mailalrt service will result in a message that the Proxy Alert Notification Service (mailalrt) will also have to be stopped, as shown in Figure 4.2. As Figure 4.2 also shows, typing "y" results in both services being stopped.

You can also stop the services by using the Services application in Control Panel in Windows NT4. In Table 4.1, we list the Proxy service names as they appear in the Services application next to the respective name used at the command prompt. After opening the Services application, select the service by clicking on its name. Simply click the Stop button to stop the service. Click Yes when asked to confirm the action, and you'll see a message box telling you that the service has been stopped.

Table 4.1 Proxy 2.0 services as they appear in the Services application.

Proxy service name	Shortened name	Purpose of the service
Microsoft WinSock Proxy Service	wspsrv	Connects Internet applications to internal clients
Proxy Alert Notification Service	mailalrt	Provides notification of possible attempts to break into the network
Microsoft Proxy Server Administration	mspadmin	Proxy Server administration tool
World Wide Web Publishing	w3svc	The World Wide Web publishing service that is Microsoft's IIS Web server component (actually an IIS service)

Figure 4.1 Stopping services on which Proxy Server is dependent at the command prompt.

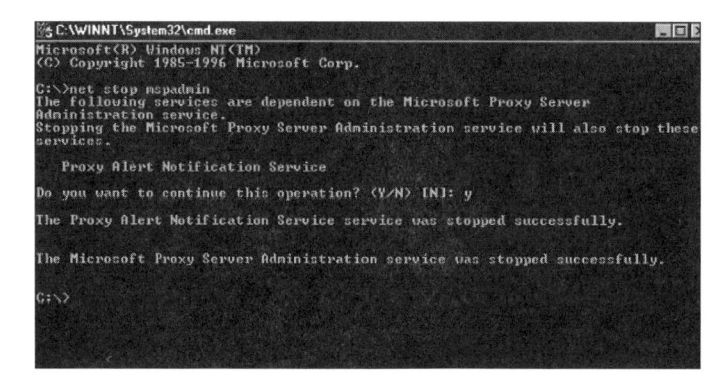

Figure 4.2 Command prompt error message.

Performing the First Upgrade

At this point, you are ready to upgrade Windows NT 4 to Windows 2000. Insert the Windows 2000 CD and follow the directions to complete the upgrade. Don't forget to also apply Windows 2000 Service Pack 1, which is required for any ISA Server installation.

Once you complete the install to Windows 2000, the system will reboot. During this reboot, the Proxy Server and IIS service that you stopped prior to the upgrade from Windows NT 4 will be started. During the upgrade from Proxy Server 2.0 to ISA Server, ISA Server will detect these services and settings so that they can be upgraded.

Upgrading to ISA Server

The second upgrade you need to perform when starting from a Proxy Server running on Windows NT 4 is the upgrade from Proxy Server to ISA Server. Begin the upgrade to ISA Server from Proxy Server by starting the ISA Installation

Wizard. You do so by running Setup.exe from the ISA directory on the ISA Server CD or by selecting Install ISA Server from the application that runs automatically when you insert the ISA Server CD in the CD-ROM drive. The process is similar to that for a new installation of ISA Server, with a few new steps. The steps for upgrading are as follows:

1. A Welcome screen appears that introduces the installation of ISA Server. Click Continue to move to the next step.

2. A dialog box will appear asking for the CD key. Enter the key from the back of the ISA Server jewel case and click OK to continue the installation.

3. The next screen will give the Product ID number for this installation of ISA Server. Microsoft product support personnel will ask for this number if you call them, so it's a good idea to write it down. Click OK to continue.

4. The ISA Server Installation Wizard will look for files on the hard disk(s) that indicate you have Proxy Server installed. If you have loaded Proxy Server on the computer, the wizard displays a dialog box asking if you want the previous version upgraded. This dialog box also displays the root folder for the previous installation. Figure 4.3 shows this dialog box. If you click OK, the wizard will install ISA Server into Proxy Server's folder and will overwrite the previous version. If you change the folder to a different one for ISA, the Proxy Server installation will not be overwritten. Later in the installation process, you will be able to decide if you want to upgrade the Proxy Sever settings. For now, click OK to perform the upgrade.

5. The End User License Agreement (EULA) will appear. Click I Agree to continue the upgrade.

Figure 4.3 This dialog box shows that the ISA Server Installation Wizard has detected Proxy Server files.

6. Next, you will need to select the installation type. The choices are Typical, Full, or Custom. We discuss these choices thoroughly in Chapter 3 of this book. Before selecting an installation type, you get another chance to change the folder in which ISA Server will install. If you did not change the folder in Step 4, the Installation Wizard will list the Proxy Server folder. Click on an installation type to continue with the ISA Server upgrade.

7. If you are installing the Enterprise Edition of ISA Server then the ISA Server Installation Wizard will now search for the ISA Server Schema in Active Directory. If it does not find the Schema in Active Directory, it will warn you that you can install ISA Server only as a standalone server. If it does find the Schema, you will have the choice of installing ISA Server as an array member or standalone. If you are installing the Standard Edition of ISA Server, skip to Step 9.

8. If you chose to install ISA Server as an array member, you will now have the choice of joining or creating an array.

9. The Proxy 2.0 Migration dialog box, shown in Figure 4.4, allows you to choose to migrate Proxy Server 2.0 settings to ISA Server. Click Yes to continue the upgrade.

10. Next, the wizard will warn you that it has detected IIS. IIS was required in order for Proxy Server to run, but it is not required for ISA Server. For security reasons, it is best to uninstall IIS on a computer that is running ISA Server. Microsoft designed ISA Server to protect users and services running behind it, and the product cannot protect services running on the same computer. If you don't remove IIS, you'll need to change the port numbers for Web services because ISA Server uses these port numbers. Click the Help button to see an explanation of the port issue. Click OK to continue the upgrade.

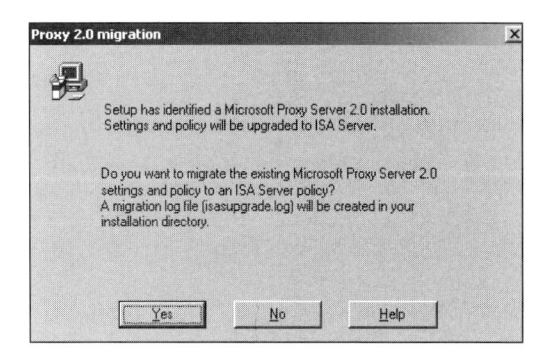

Figure 4.4 This dialog box allows you to choose whether you want to migrate detected Proxy Server settings to ISA Server.

11. Unlike with a new installation, you will not pick the mode of installation during an upgrade. Instead, you will see the LAT setup dialog box, which will let you confirm the settings that Setup will upgrade to ISA Server. Setup will upgrade cache settings without displaying any confirmation dialog boxes.

12. Setup will upgrade services and remove unnecessary Proxy Server files. You will have the choice of launching the Getting Started Wizard before you see the final dialog box for the installation. Click OK if you want to launch this wizard, and then click OK to end the upgrade.

Upgrading from Proxy Server on Windows 2000

Microsoft released Proxy Server before Windows 2000; therefore, Proxy Server was not designed to run on Windows 2000. However, Microsoft developed an upgrade to Proxy Server that allows Proxy Server to run on Windows 2000. This upgrade is available at **www.microsoft.com/proxy**. To run Proxy Server 2.0 on Windows 2000, you should have already loaded this upgrade. Although the installation starts the same way as a new installation of ISA Server, Setup will detect the Proxy Server settings during the installation of ISA Server and will retain those settings. As with the upgrade discussed in the previous section, the ISA Server installation looks for already installed Internet security and acceleration features, such as packet filters and cache settings.

*Note: You can run Proxy Server 2.0 on Windows 2000, but it requires a special installation wizard that will apply all of the needed patches along with the Proxy Server Service Pack. Go to **www.microsoft.com/proxy** to find a link to this installation wizard. For more information, refer to the Knowledge Base article Q253131.*

As we mentioned, the upgrade from Proxy Server 2.0 on Windows NT 4 occurs in two stages. The second part involves upgrading Proxy Server 2.0 to ISA Server on Windows 2000. The steps are identical to those for upgrading from Proxy Server 2.0 on Windows 2000. Follow the steps in the previous section for this upgrade.

Upgrading a Proxy Server Array

If you set up Proxy Server 2.0 in a large enterprise environment, you may have also set up an array. Although you still need to upgrade the individual Proxy Servers, you must take additional steps before you do this. Before upgrading an array of Proxy Servers to ISA Server, it is best to dismantle the array by removing all members. In Proxy Server, you can accomplish this in the following way:

1. From Internet Services Manager, click the plus (+) sign to view the Internet and Proxy Server services installed on the computer you want to upgrade.

2. Right-click on any Proxy Server service and select Properties. This will bring up the Service Properties dialog box.

3. In the Service Properties dialog box, click the Array button in the Shared Services section.

4. Select a member of the array and click the Remove From Array button.

5. Repeat the previous step until all members of the array are removed.

6. Click the OK button to return to the Service Properties dialog box.

7. Click OK to close the Service Properties dialog box and close the Internet Services Manager.

After removing each member from the array, upgrade each Proxy Server individually to ISA Server. If you want to create a new ISA server array with the same members, simply create an array during the upgrade of the first ISA server. Each Proxy Server can join this new array during its upgrade. Setup will detect the Proxy Server settings on each former array member and upgrade those settings. Since array settings are different in ISA Server, you'll need to make some adjustments to the array policy or the enterprise policy once the upgrade is complete. Array creation is covered thoroughly in Chapter 3.

Configuration Settings from Proxy Server to ISA Server

While some configurations settings will be retained during the upgrade to ISA Server from Proxy Server, you'll have to reconfigure a few settings once the upgrade is complete. ISA Server has many more capabilities than Proxy Server, especially when it comes to control over security services. ISA Server provides a much finer degree of control over who is allowed access and what users are allowed to access. Since Proxy Server did not use the distinctions that ISA Server uses, you'll have to redefine many of the firewall security settings after an upgrade from Proxy Server. Many acceleration services work in much the same way and will upgrade to ISA Server without reconfiguration.

Settings That You Don't Have to Reconfigure

Services that work the same way in Proxy Server as they do in ISA Server will not require any reconfiguration. The settings that you'll need to reconfigure are the ones for services that have changed significantly from Proxy Server to ISA Server.

For example, configuring the LAT has not changed. During the installation of Proxy Server, you can use the internal routing table of the server to add IP network addresses. This works the same way in ISA Server. Because the contents of the LAT affect which connections go to the ISA server and which stay internal, it is important that its settings be correct. You should check the addition of IP addresses during the upgrade when the LAT from Proxy Server is transferred to the LAT for ISA Server. Table 4.2 shows a summary of settings that will be preserved during the upgrade.

Settings That You Need to Reconfigure

Because many of the control features have been greatly expanded, you'll have to reconfigure some settings in ISA Server to take advantage of the improvements. ISA Server will upgrade the settings, but you might find them in a different place. Some of these features do not go by the same name in ISA Server. Internet security has changed more dramatically than acceleration settings. Examples include security settings, such as domain filters and proxy software for clients.

Domain Filters

Proxy Server uses the term domain filter for settings that block users from accessing certain IP addresses, IP networks, or domain names. This setting is for outbound connections. Packet filters are set to test and possibly block incoming packets. Because both of these different types of settings are called filters in ISA Server, it can be confusing for a Proxy Server administrator. In ISA Server, the term filter can refer to a number of different filters, but they are all for inbound requests. Outbound requests are still checked, but they are controlled with rules. The term *rule* replaces the term *filter* for outbound protection in ISA Server.

Client Software

To run Internet applications between an Internet server and an internal client, you need certain software loaded that allows Proxy Server to intercede in the connection and provide protection for the internal client. Proxy Server provides two types of client software: one for Windows clients, called Winsock Proxy, and one for non-Windows clients, called Socks Proxy. If your clients want to run Internet applications and Proxy Server is protecting the Internet connection, you must load the appropriate software on each client computer.

Table 4.2 Settings that will be preserved during the upgrade.

Setting	How the setting upgrades
Cache settings	Cache location and size are upgraded; however, the contents residing in Proxy Server's cache are removed.
LAT	The ranges of addresses transfer to the new LAT. You can check the LAT settings during the upgrade.
Alerts	The number of alerts in Proxy 2.0 is limited compared to those available in ISA Server, but any that are configured will upgrade.
Log settings	The type of logging, as well as the name and location of the log, is upgraded.

Microsoft has changed the client software in ISA Server. You now have a choice when you want to provide a truly transparent connection for Internet applications. SecureNAT allows connections for Internet applications, but you don't have to load any software on the client. You can load a firewall client onto recent Windows operating systems. The Firewall client is an upgrade to the Winsock client from Proxy Server 2.0. Although Socks clients can still make connections through ISA Server, a full-fledged Socks client is not supported in ISA Server. Non-Windows clients can now get a Socks connection through an application filter that is an extension to ISA Server. When you migrate the Socks proxy client in Proxy Server 2.0 to ISA Server, any configured Socks rules are not migrated to ISA Server. You will need to reconfigure them.

Domain filters and client software are only two examples of settings that you need to reconfigure in a migration from Proxy Server to ISA Server. Table 4.3 provides a summary of settings that you'll have to reconfigure in ISA Server.

Making the Administrative Change

Although you administer Proxy Server 2.0 in a console, this administration takes place inside the Internet Services Manager console—the console for IIS administration. Proxy services run inside the main process for IIS called the inetinfo process and require the presence of IIS on the same computer. Proxy Server is dependent on IIS, but ISA Server is not. ISA Server has its own console, called ISA Management. This console runs through Microsoft Management Console (MMC) and follows the same rules as the rest of the consoles in Windows 2000. Figure 4.5 shows the administrative interface of Proxy Server in Internet Services Manager; Figure 4.6 shows ISA Management. In Internet Services Manager, if you open any of the three proxy services properties you'd see that they all share the same property sheets. In ISA Server, you can expand the choices under each array to get to the settings of an ISA Server. Standalone and array members are listed under Servers And Arrays.

Table 4.3 Settings that must be reconfigured.

Setting	Why a change is needed
Domain Filters	A domain filter in Proxy Server 2.0 is now referred to differently in ISA Server. Site and content rules in ISA Server include the functionality of a domain filter in Proxy Server.
Web Proxy Port	ISA Server uses port 8080 to listen for Web requests from internal clients. Proxy Server uses port 80 to do this. This affects client settings.
Reverse proxy	You'll have to reconfigure an internal Web server that must be set up to publish to the Internet. This service has a different architecture in ISA Server.
Socks rules	The handling of Socks requests from the internal network has a new architecture in ISA Server. Socks requests are now handled by an application filter called Socks V4 Filter.
Client Setup	The client software choices have changed from Proxy Server to ISA Server, so the setup has changed as well.

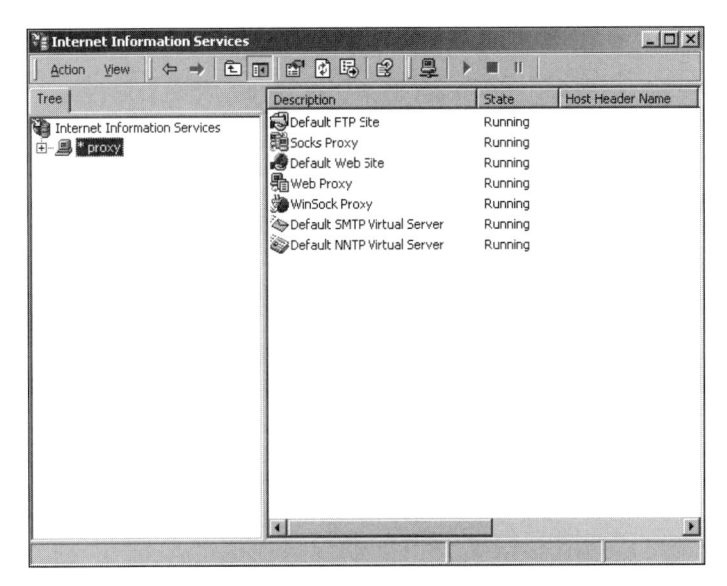

Figure 4.5 The Proxy Server administrative interface in Internet Services Manager.

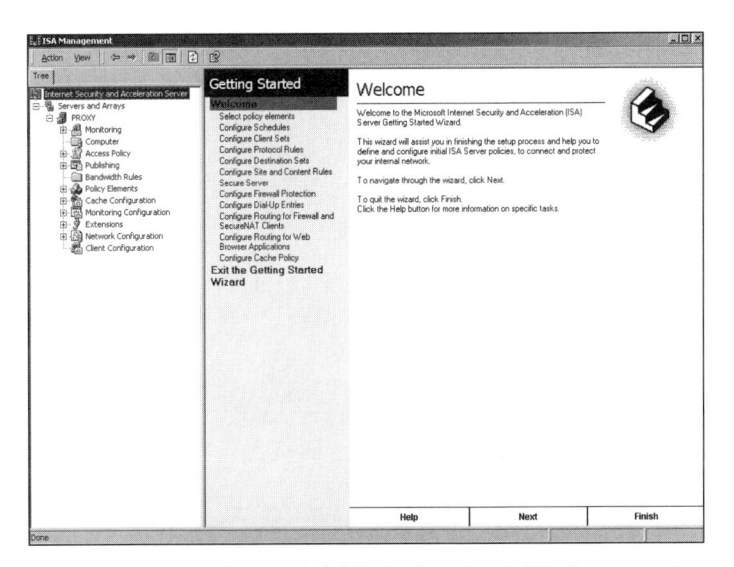

Figure 4.6 The ISA Server administrative interface in ISA Management.

Uninstalling ISA Server

You can uninstall ISA Server from a computer, but an uninstall only removes the components of ISA Server—it will not restore the Proxy Server settings. When you install ISA Server, it does not retain the settings from the Proxy Server. No uninstall option exists for ISA Server that allows the Proxy Server settings to be restored.

The only way to retain Proxy Server settings is to use the Server Backup option to back up Proxy Server settings. Then, you can install Proxy Server and, using the Restore Server option, restore the Proxy configuration.

Chapter Summary

Upgrading from Proxy Server to ISA Server provides you with much greater control over how an Internet connection is accessed from an internal network. Upgrading technologies that are Internet related is an important part of keeping up with the rapid changes in this important arena.

Before you start an upgrade, you must be prepared. First, you should check the Proxy Server settings to see if you need to make any changes. Internal protocols and IP address ranges might have to be changed or verified. Also, be aware that you have no way to back out of an upgrade without losing settings. Therefore, ensure that you have a backup of the Proxy Server configuration before beginning the upgrade. If something goes wrong, you can reinstall Proxy Server and restore the original settings. Planning ahead might save a lot of time during the upgrade.

The complexity of upgrading the software from Proxy Server to ISA Server depends on where the upgrade starts. Because Proxy Server can run on Windows NT 4 or Windows 2000 and ISA Server runs only on Windows 2000, you might have to upgrade the operating system on which the Proxy Server is currently running. Once you've upgraded the underlying operating system, you can proceed with the upgrade of Proxy Server 2.0 to ISA Server.

If a Proxy Server array exists on a network, keep in mind that no direct array upgrade exists. This means that you'll have to remove the members from the array before you upgrade their software. You'll have to upgrade each former member separately. However, the first upgraded server can create a new array during the upgrade, and the former members can then join the new ISA server array during their own upgrade.

During the upgrade, ISA Server will migrate settings that it detects during the installation process. Some of the settings will upgrade directly and you won't need to reconfigure them. However, some configurations have changed dramatically from Proxy Server 2.0 to ISA Server. Settings that have not changed are more likely to be in the acceleration services that ISA Server provides. Security service settings are more likely to have changed significantly. Some settings, such as domain filters in Proxy Server 2.0, are not even named the same. You may also need to install client software because ISA Server's client software can now integrate with the directory services provided by Windows 2000.

The administrative interfaces for Proxy Server 2.0 and ISA Server are not alike. Proxy Server ran in the administrative interface for IIS, and its services were listed with the IIS services. ISA Server's administrative interface is separate from IIS's administrative tool. ISA Management also has dialog boxes and settings that look different from Proxy Server's choices. You'll need to make an adjustment to perform similar administrative tasks in ISA Server. We will cover the ISA Management extensively throughout the rest of this book.

You can remove ISA Server from a server once the upgrade is complete. You accomplish this task by using Add/Remove Programs in Control Panel. However, the uninstall process will remove ISA Server from the computer and will not retain the old Proxy Server settings. The only way to retain Proxy Server settings is to use the Server Backup option in Proxy Server 2.0 before the upgrade. Then, after the removal of ISA Server you need to reinstall Proxy Server and use the Server Restore option to gain back the lost settings.

Review Questions

1. On which operating systems can ISA Server be upgraded from Proxy Server? [Check all correct answers]
    a. Windows NT 3.51 Server
    b. Windows NT 4 Server
    c. Windows 2000 Professional
    d. Windows 2000 Server

2. Windows 2000 Service Pack 1 is not required if you're performing an upgrade from Proxy Server 2.0 on Windows NT 4.0.
    a. True
    b. False

3. Within which IIS service does Proxy Server run?
    a. inetinfo
    b. wspsrv
    c. mailalrt
    d. mspadmin
    e. w3srv

4. Within which IIS process does Proxy Server run?
    a. inetinfo
    b. wspsrv
    c. mailalrt
    d. mspadmin
    e. w3srv

5. The LAT is constructed differently in Proxy Server than it is in ISA Server.
    a. True
    b. False

6. ISA Server can be upgraded from which versions of Proxy Server?
    a. Proxy Server 1.0
    b. Proxy Server 2.0
    c. Any version of Proxy Server
    d. None

7. IIS and Proxy Server are administered from the same console.
    a. True
    b. False

8. Which protocols suites can you run on the internal network when running Proxy Server? [Check all correct answers]
    a. TCP/IP
    b. IPX/SPX
    c. DecNet
    d. Any protocol suite

9. Which protocol suites can you run on the internal network when running ISA Server?
    a. TCP/IP
    b. IPX/SPX
    c. DecNet
    d. Any protocol suite

10. What default directory does the Proxy Server installation create to store server backup files?
    a. \MSP
    b. \MSP\Backup
    c. \MSP\Config
    d. \MSP\Restore

11. What is the file extension of the server backup file for Proxy Server 2.0?

    a. .msp

    b. .mpc

    c. .msc

    d. .bak

12. The Domain Filter feature in Proxy Server 2.0 does not exist in ISA Server. Which feature(s) can you set to have the same effect in ISA Server? [Check all correct answers]

    a. Site and Content rule

    b. Domain rule

    c. Publishing rule

    d. Policy

13. Which command do you use to stop the Microsoft Winsock Proxy Service at the command prompt?

    a. Net stop wspsvc

    b. Net stop mailalrt

    c. Net stop mspadmin

    d. Net stop w3svc

    e. Net stop Microsoft Winsock Proxy Service

14. You can use the command prompt to stop Proxy services before upgrading the operating system to Windows 2000. What is another application in which this can be done?

    a. Proxy Services Console

    b. ISA Console

    c. Services in Control Panel

    d. Proxy Services in Control Panel

15. Why don't you have to reconfigure cache services after upgrading from Proxy Server 2.0 to ISA Server?

    a. Cache is not used in ISA Server.

    b. No services need to be reconfigured in ISA Server.

    c. Their setup has not changed.

    d. Their setup has changed.

16. What is the recommended way to upgrade a Proxy Server array to ISA Server?
    a. Use the Upgrade Array option during the installation of the first array member.
    b. Remove all members, then upgrade each one individually.
    c. Keep all members in the array, then upgrade the members individually.
    d. There is no recommended method.

17. What is the administrative interface for Proxy Server 2.0?
    a. Internet Services Manager
    b. Internet Services Administrator
    c. Proxy Server console
    d. Proxy Server Administrator
    e. MSP console

18. What is the administrative interface for ISA Server?
    a. Internet Services Manager
    b. Internet Services Administrator
    c. ISA Management
    d. Proxy console
    e. MSP console

19. What installation program do you use to upgrade Proxy Server 2.0 to ISA Server?
    a. Upgrade.exe
    b. Install.exe
    c. Setup.exe
    d. ISAAutorun.exe

20. During the removal of ISA Server, which option allows you to restore Proxy Server settings?
    a. Return To Original State
    b. Uninstall To Proxy Server
    c. Option 1
    d. None

Real-World Projects

Note: This exercise assumes a test Windows NT 4 server with Proxy Server 2.0 installed. Read the instructions carefully and do not perform this install on your production machine unless you understand the options presented. If you are unsure about an option, cancel the installation and read the help files provided with Proxy Server and ISA Server about the option to be installed.

Tim approached the Proxy Server confidently. The network at his company was being upgraded to Windows 2000 and the Proxy Server was currently on Windows NT 4. He had researched all of the steps needed to upgrade the server without losing any Proxy Server settings. He felt confident this would go off without a hitch. All he had to do was upgrade the underlying operating system on the Proxy Server and he would be done with this part of the upgrade.

Tim's company is a dessert-delivery company called ChocolatesToGo. The company has a Web site that accepts orders and then delivers the desserts by mail. ChocolatesToGo has been in business for two years. The company has Proxy Server to protect outgoing connections and a separate firewall from a different vendor.

Just when Tim was ready to start the upgrade, the IS manager ran up and started talking excitedly. After listening and trying to understand what he was saying, Tim realized something.

"Are you telling me not to upgrade the operating system on this Proxy Server?" he asked.

"Yes... well, no," the IS manager replied. "There is a new version of Proxy Server called ISA Server. I want you to upgrade to that instead, or also... whatever is needed. I already bought the software so everything is set."

"Back to the drawing board," thought Tim.

"Oh, and could you complete the upgrade today?" added the IS manager. "Thanks."

Tim headed back to his office and did some quick research on upgrading to ISA Server. It turned out that it wouldn't be a lot different from upgrading Proxy Server. At least the first step wouldn't be much different. The upgrade involved two stages. ISA Server requires Windows 2000, so first Tim had to upgrade Windows NT to Windows 2000.

The best thing about upgrading to ISA Server was that Tim would no longer need a separate firewall from a different vendor. The firewall capabilities of ISA Server were much improved over those provided in Proxy Server. It would be a good solution to set up the firewall and proxy services in one product that was integrated with the Windows 2000 operating system.

To begin, Tim physically disconnected the cable to the external Internet connection. This way, no Internet connection could be made while he upgraded the Proxy services.

Tim then continued by stopping the Proxy services on the Proxy Server.

Project 4.1

To stop Proxy services:

1. Open the command prompt.

2. Type the following commands, pressing the Enter key after each command:

   ➤ Net stop wspsvc

   ➤ Net stop mailalrt

   ➤ Net stop mspadmin

   ➤ Net stop w3svc

3. You should receive a message stating that each service was stopped after entering the command.

4. Close the command prompt.

With one prerequisite down, Tim moved on to the important step of backing up the Proxy Server configuration.

To back up the Proxy Server configuration:

1. From Internet Services Manager, click the plus (+) sign to view the Internet and Proxy Server services installed on the computer you want to back up.

2. Right-click on any Proxy Server service and select Properties. This will bring up the Service Properties dialog box.

3. In the Service Properties dialog box, click the Server Backup button in the Configuration section.

4. A Backup dialog box will show that a backup file will be created with the name MSP★.mpc. The ★ will be replaced with the date that the file was made according to the computer. This date will have the format of yyyymmdd, with yyyy representing a four-digit year, mm representing the month, and dd representing the day. A backup file created on July 1, 2001, would be named MSP20010701.mpc. This file will be saved by default in the \MSP\Config folder.

5. Click OK to save the file.

6. You will be returned to the Service Properties dialog box. Click OK to dismiss the dialog box and return to Internet Services Manager.

7. Open Windows Explorer and check the \MSP\Config folder for the backup file you just created. You can open the file with Notepad and see that it is a lengthy configuration file with all of your Proxy Server settings.

With the preliminary work done, Tim was ready to start stage one of the upgrade.

Project 4.2
To upgrade Windows NT to Windows 2000:

1. Insert the Windows 2000 CD.

2. The system will automatically display a message stating that this version of Windows can be upgraded. Select Yes.

3. Follow the steps to complete the upgrade to Windows 2000.

4. Restart the server when prompted. The Proxy Server services will restart when the server reboots.

5. Apply Windows 2000 Service Pack 1 to the new installation of Windows 2000.

Now that that stage of the upgrade was complete, the most complicated step of upgrading Proxy Server to ISA Server was still left to do. Tim reviewed a few details before starting stage two. First, he checked a network diagram to make sure that all internal IP address ranges would be included on the LAT. Also, he checked to make sure that no internal computers were still using IPX/SPX.

Now he was ready to perform the actual upgrade to ISA Server. Tim inserted the ISA Server CD into the CD-ROM drive.

Project 4.3
To upgrade to ISA Server:

1. The ISA Server Standard Edition Setup screen appears automatically. Select Install ISA Server. A Welcome screen appears that introduces the installation of ISA Server. Click Continue to move to the next step.

2. A dialog box appears asking for the CD key. Enter the key from the back of the ISA Server jewel case and click OK to continue the installation.

3. The next screen gives the Product ID number for this installation of ISA Server. Microsoft product support personnel will ask you for this number if you call them, so write it down. Click OK to continue.

4. The ISA Server Installation Wizard will look for files on the hard disk(s) that indicate an installation of Proxy Server. If Proxy Server is loaded on the computer, then you'll see a dialog box asking if you want the previous version upgraded. This dialog box also displays the root folder for the previous installation. Figure 4.3 shows this upgrade dialog box. If you click OK in this dialog box, ISA Server will be installed into Proxy Server's folder and will overwrite the previous version. If you change the folder to a different one for ISA, the Proxy Server installation will not be overwritten. Later in the installation, you will be able to decide if you want to upgrade the Proxy Sever settings. Click OK to perform the upgrade.

5. The End User License Agreement (EULA) will appear. Click I Agree to continue the upgrade.

6. Next, you will need to select the installation type. The choices are Typical, Full, or Custom. We cover these choices thoroughly in Chapter 3 of this book. Before selecting an installation type, you get another chance to change the folder in which ISA Server will install. If you did not change the folder in Step 4, the Installation Wizard will list the Proxy Server folder. Click on an installation type to continue with the ISA Server upgrade.

7. If you chose to install as an array member, you will now have the choice of joining or creating an array.

8. This step allows you to choose to migrate Proxy Server 2.0 settings to ISA Server. Figure 4.4 shows this dialog box. Click Yes to continue the upgrade.

9. The next dialog box will warn you that IIS has been detected. IIS was required in order for Proxy Server to run, but it is not required for ISA Server. Figure 4.7 shows this dialog box.

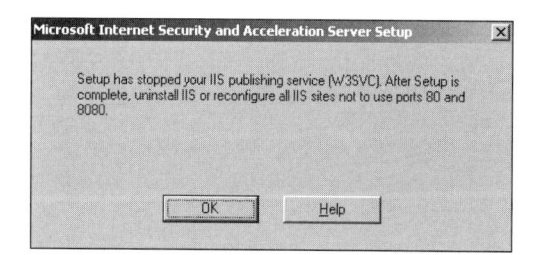

Figure 4.7 If IIS is detected on the server a warning dialog box appears during the installation of ISA Server.

Tim stopped when he saw the warning dialog box. The last thing he needed was a problem to slow him down. He clicked the Help button for more information and found that unlike Proxy Server, ISA Server did not require IIS to be loaded on the same server. Now he would need to uninstall IIS Sever after completing the installation of ISA Server. Tim quickly opened Internet Services Manager to check to see if there were any Web sites located on the local Web server. There weren't supposed to be any, but he thought he would check just in case. He could not see any separate sites, so he checked the Default Web Site and found nothing. This looked like an easy problem to solve. All he had to do was remove IIS after he was done installing ISA Server. He switched back to the ISA installation dialog box. Luckily, this problem would not require him to stop the installation of ISA Server. He clicked the OK button and continued.

10. Unlike with a new installation, you will not pick the mode of installation during an upgrade. Instead, you will see the LAT setup dialog box, which will allow you to confirm the settings that will be upgraded to ISA Server. Cache settings will be upgraded without any confirmation dialog boxes being displayed.

Tim finished the rest of the settings and clicked what he hoped was the last OK button. Suddenly he got an error message stating that a file could not be deleted. Perhaps a file that should have been removed was still on the hard disk. He clicked the Ignore button, but the same error message appeared. Tim clicked Ignore again and another appeared. It looked like a failed installation, and Tim was about to give up when he remembered that he had not closed Internet Services Manager. What a stupid mistake. How could it delete or update files when the files were open? Tim ended the upgrade and closed all programs and files. He started the upgrade again and made it all the way up to the same step. This time, all the necessary files were upgraded by the ISA Installation Wizard. He knew the upgrade had worked when the next dialog box appeared.

11. You will have the choice of launching the Getting Started Wizard before seeing the final dialog box for the installation. Click OK if you want to launch this wizard, and then click OK to end the upgrade.

With the upgrade completed, Tim was ready to check the settings in ISA Server. He knew that he would need to reconfigure some settings and that he still needed to delete IIS from the server. He could worry about those things later.

CHAPTER FIVE

Planning and Deploying Clients

After completing this chapter, you will be able to:

✓ Explain how ISA Server handles client requests

✓ Categorize client requests

✓ Describe the differences between the types of clients available

✓ Describe the architectural differences between the clients

✓ Choose between the Firewall and SecureNAT client

✓ Choose between the SecureNAT and Socks client

✓ Determine the ISA client needs for your network

✓ Set up the different client types

✓ Configure the mspclnt.ini file

✓ Describe the combinations of clients that can be used

✓ Select correct port settings for client access

Now that you have set up ISA Server, you will need to plan and configure the setup of your clients. The internal architecture of ISA Server includes two services that handle client requests from the internal network. They act as proxy services designed to protect the internal clients from the public nature of the Internet. The two services split the duties of retrieving objects and making connections for the clients. An often-needed service is retrieving Web pages. One service, the *Web Proxy service*, is designed to retrieve Web pages and a few other types of objects from the Internet. The other service, known as the *Firewall* service, handles all other types of connections. These connections are usually needed for internal users to connect to and use Internet applications. Both services handle client requests for the network.

Although only two services are available to handle client requests, more than two client types can be configured or installed on internal client computers. The setup for each client is different, as are the reasons for using them. In this chapter, you will learn how to assess the needs of the clients so that you can choose the right client type. We will then discuss how each client can be configured or installed.

Client Types

The three major client types for ISA Server are the Web Proxy client, the Firewall client, and the SecureNAT client. Many internal network clients can end up needing more than one client type, depending on what kind of Internet connections they call for. Some client types can be used together. Knowing the purpose and requirements for each type of client will help you choose the right client for your internal clients.

Why do you need to install a client to connect to ISA Server? The answer to that question is complex because of the nature of the Internet and the types of connections it can provide. The first reason that special settings or software are needed for clients in an environment using ISA Server is that ISA Server interferes with Internet connections. This interference is necessary if ISA Server is going to control and protect Internet connections. The internal client computers need to know about the interference ISA Server is creating. They need to know where to send and how to handle requests destined for external networks. The software or special settings gives the clients of ISA Server the information they need to make successful connections.

Also, the Internet is a medium on which many different kinds of connections are made. Clients will probably want to do a lot more than just download Web pages. Users can download different types of files with different protocols or can connect to any number of applications that run over the Internet. ISA Server provides a choice of Internet clients because the needs of the clients can vary.

What Are You Trying to Do?

Even though the Internet offers a large number of choices, ISA Server client types can be placed into two categories. Clients will either want to retrieve an object over the Internet or connect to an application. Objects can be Web pages, news articles, or files retrieved by HTTP or FTP. The difficulty in selecting a client type is that the Web Proxy client will retrieve the most often used objects while the Firewall or SecureNAT client will retrieve the others. The Web Proxy retrieves only those objects that use the Hypertext Transfer Protocol (HTTP), Secure Hypertext Transfer Protocol (HTTP-S), File Transfer Protocol (FTP), or Gopher protocols. If clients want objects other than from these protocols, or they want to make a connection to an Internet application, they will use the Firewall client or the SecureNAT client. This means the client can be both a Firewall and Web Proxy client, or it can be both a SecureNAT and a Web Proxy client. Both types of ISA clients are needed if clients want both types of connections.

An internal client does not request to use one of the client services provided by ISA Server. When the client makes a request, it is handled based on the architecture of ISA Server. How an internal client request is handled depends on what type of request it is making.

The Web Proxy Client

The Web Proxy client retrieves objects for users on the internal network. However, it retrieves only specific types of often-requested objects. The Web Proxy service retrieves objects that are requested using the HTTP, HTTP-S, FTP, or Gopher protocols. Web pages are the type of object most often retrieved using the HTTP protocol, although in the latest version of HTTP, documents of any format can be retrieved using HTTP. The protocol FTP also retrieves documents for internal users. Web pages that are encrypted and sent over a secure channel using Secure Sockets Layer use HTTP-S. Gopher sites give the user a list of the folder structure and pages that are available on a site. Gopher was at its highest popularity before the Web and its use of hyperlinks became popular. A gopher URL looks like **gopher://cwis.unomaha.edu**, and you can connect to it using most browsers or Telnet.

Web Proxy client requests are sent to the Web Proxy service in ISA Server to be handled. By default, Web Proxy clients send their requests to port 8080 on the ISA server. This port is different than the port normally used for Web requests. Without ISA Server, a normal Web HTTP request uses port 80. Figure 5.1 shows a Web Proxy client connecting to the Web Proxy service in the ISA Service with the client port setting changed to port 8080.

Once the client makes a connection to the Web Proxy service, cache is checked for the object. If the object is in cache and is not expired, then it can be returned to

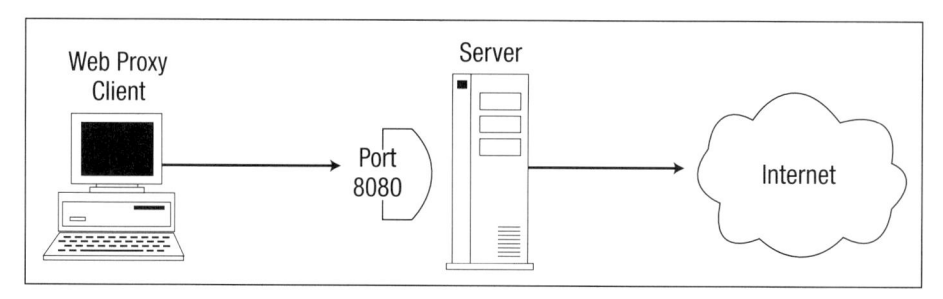

Figure 5.1 A Web Proxy client connects to port 8080 on the ISA Server.

the requesting client from cache. A trip to the Internet is not needed in this case, giving the requesting client a quicker response time. If the object is not in cache or the object in cache has expired, then the ISA server will make its own connection to the Internet server to retrieve the object. If the object is "cacheable," it will be placed in cache and then returned to the requesting internal client. This process is more complicated if more ISA servers and array caches are involved. Caching is covered in detail in Chapter 8 of this book.

Keep in mind that the Web Proxy client is not software that you have to load on internal clients. Web browsers can directly connect to the Web Proxy service in ISA Server without any extra software. Because the Web Proxy service communicates with the Web browser, any client operating system can be used with the Web Proxy service. The only requirements are that the Web browser be CERN (Conseil Europeen pour la Recherche Nucleaire, or The European Laboratory for Particle Research)compliant and configured to use the ISA Server instead of making a direct request to the Internet. Because the CERN lab created the first Web browser and the standards for it, it is difficult to find a Web browser that is not CERN compliant. If your clients have Web browsers such as Netscape Navigator or Communicator or Microsoft Internet Explorer, the only thing left to do is configure the browser to use ISA Server. Later in this chapter we will discuss configuring internal network clients to act as Web Proxy clients.

Web Proxy clients are the only client type that benefits from cache, because the other services are mainly for connecting users and not for retrieving objects. Often there's nothing to cache when using the other services. Later in this chapter, you will see how Firewall and SecureNAT clients can also be Web Proxy clients so that they can also benefit from cache when they need it.

The Firewall Client

The Firewall client connects users to Winsock applications. When a Firewall client wants to access an application, it first checks its internal Local Address Table (LAT) to see if the IP address it needs to connect to is in the internal network. If the address is found within one of the ranges listed in the LAT, it is in the internal network. The Firewall client can then make a direct connection to that computer. If the address is not in the LAT, it is in an external network and the request is sent to the Firewall service in ISA Server. The Firewall service will check the policies and rules in ISA Server to make sure that the user is allowed to connect to the requested site. If the user is allowed, the Firewall client will forward the request on to the Internet server. ISA Server will refer to its rules and polices to approve or deny the request from the client.

Firewall client software is more specialized than Web Proxy, so it works on the most recent Windows operating systems only.

Operating systems that support the Firewall client include:

- Windows 2000
- Windows 95
- Windows 98
- Windows Millennium
- Windows NT 4

The Firewall client simplifies setup of the ISA Server by allowing all Winsock applications to use the Firewall service in the same way. The Firewall service works with all Winsock applications using Winsock versions 1.1 and 2.0. A setup for each application is not necessary. However, the Firewall client setup is the most complicated of the three major clients. You must install software on the individual clients that you want to be Firewall clients. In return, you get a great deal of flexibility in the level of security you can impose on your internal clients. We will discuss loading and configuring Firewall client software later in this chapter.

Winsock

Winsock is a version of sockets designed for use with Windows operating systems. Winsock stands for Windows Sockets. A socket is designed as the session-layer connection between TCP/IP and applications. As covered in Chapter 1, a socket is formed by combining the IP address and port number. It is an Application Programming Interface (API) that developers can build application specifications to. An application built to the sockets API should work with any operating system that understands the sockets API. The Winsock designers adhered closely to the sockets standards so that socket developers would be able to make the change easily. Winsock is implemented as a Dynamic Link Library (DLL) called Winsock.dll. This file handles the translation between the application and TCP/IP. Winsock comes in two versions—1.1 and 2.0. Each version of Winsock has its own DLL file. Both versions of the DLL files are included in Windows products so that applications that use Winsock 1.1 still work even when Winsock 2.0 is the latest supported version.

The SecureNAT Client

SecureNAT, or Secure Network Address Translation, is a client that is completely different from Firewall client. In fact, a client set up as a Firewall client cannot also be a SecureNAT client. Both the Firewall and SecureNAT clients connect internal computers in a secure manner to applications on the Internet. But SecureNAT differs from the Firewall client in that it does not require software to be loaded on the client. In addition, SecureNAT can be used with any client operating system. Although SecureNAT is more flexible in that respect, it does not afford the same flexibility with policy and rule setup. The Firewall client can be set up to differentiate between separate users when configuring settings that allow or disallow access to sites. The SecureNAT client cannot do that. However, the architecture that determines how SecureNAT requests are handled in ISA Server allows many of the security policies to be applied.

Is SecureNAT a Part of Network Address Translation (NAT)?

In a small to medium network, you can protect the internal network from an external connection to the Internet with a NAT server. A NAT server sits between the private and public network just like ISA Server. The internal network is given a private range of IP addresses not intended for use on the Internet, while the NAT server is given a few public IP addresses intended for use on the Internet. NAT doesn't provide the performance enhancements or complexity of security that ISA Server does; instead, it does exactly what it's named for—translates internal private IP addresses to a public IP address. This IP address translation protects the internal network's IP addressing scheme from the Internet. It is a transparent service in that the internal computers use the NAT server as their default gateway. Therefore, any request bound for an external network is automatically sent to the NAT server.

SecureNAT in ISA Server continues where NAT leaves off and extends its capabilities. You do not need a NAT server on a network to use SecureNAT as a client for ISA Server. Also, SecureNAT, like NAT, does not have any built-in security policies. However, SecureNAT clients have ISA Server's policies and rules applied to them just as the other client types are.

SecureNAT client requests are first directed to the NAT driver, which translates the internal IP address into one that can be used on the Internet. From there, the requests are passed on to the Firewall service to be handled by ISA Server. Figure 5.2 shows the architecture of how SecureNAT requests are handled by ISA Server.

Socks

Microsoft Proxy Server 2.0 also included three client types. One was the Web Proxy client, which in an improved form is in ISA Server. Another was a Winsock Proxy client, which in its improved form is the Firewall client. The other client was the Socks Proxy client, which is no longer a major client type in ISA Server.

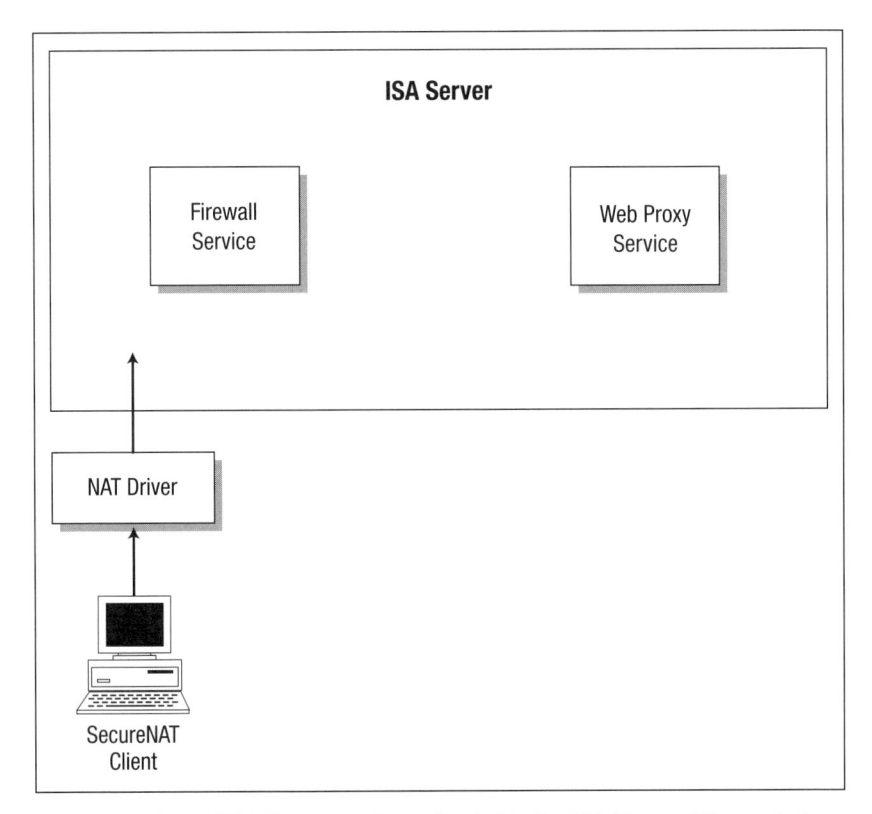

Figure 5.2 SecureNAT client requests are directed to the NAT driver and then on to the Firewall service in ISA Server.

But even though it is not listed as a major client type, the need for Socks has not gone away, and the ability to use Socks as a client in ISA Server is still there. Socks connections are handled by an extension to ISA Server called the Socks V4 Filter.

In Proxy Server 2.0, the Winsock proxy client handles Winsock application connections, while the Socks Proxy client handles socket application connections. The difference between the two is that Windows operating systems use Winsock while non-Windows operating systems such as Unix and Macintosh use sockets. The Socks protocol was created by NEC Computers to allow applications using sockets over the Internet to connect when a proxy server was interfering with the connection.

Normally, these applications expect a direct connection between the client and server, but a proxy server turns that direct connection into a two-step process. Any connection to an application that is not from a Firewall client is assumed to be a SecureNAT connection, including connections from Socks clients. The Firewall service accepts these connections and then passes them on to the Socks application filter.

Currently, Socks is most widely implemented in versions 4 and 5. ISA Server's Socks filter supports Socks protocol version 4. Because of known security issues in Socks V4, it is recommended that administrators configure clients to use Socks on an individual basis and allow only these IP addresses to make Socks connections. Also, the network interface connected to the external network should not accept any Socks connections. Socks connections should be allowed only from the internal network out to the external network.

Client Differences

The client that you choose from among these three—Web Proxy, Firewall, SecureNAT—depends on your network users' needs. Some clients can be used together whereas others cannot. Differentiating between the purposes of each of the clients is important. If the clients have the same purpose, they can't be used together.

Client Combinations

The SecureNAT and Firewall clients cannot be used together because they have the same purpose—to connect internal network users to Internet applications. The Firewall client requires that software be loaded on a client, and it can be installed only on recent Windows operating systems. SecureNAT does not require any client software to be loaded on the client, and it can work with any client operating system. However, it cannot provide user-level authentication. The Web Proxy client does something different than the SecureNAT or the Firewall client does, so it can be combined with either. This means that an internal client can be a SecureNAT and Web Proxy client or a Firewall and Web Proxy client, which are the only client combinations allowed.

Retrieving Objects

The Web Proxy client retrieves objects for users from the Internet instead of making connections to Internet applications. The Firewall and SecureNAT clients do not retrieve Web pages so if internal network clients want to use the Web they will need the Web Proxy client.

HTTP Redirector

SecureNAT client requests end up at the Firewall service to be handled by ISA Server. Firewall client requests are also sent to the Firewall service to be handled. If either of these clients is making a request for an HTTP object, then the Firewall service will send the request to the HTTP redirector. The HTTP redirector is an application filter that can pass HTTP object requests on to the Web Proxy service. These requests are then processed through caching services and, if needed, sent out on the Internet just like any Web Proxy request. This way, SecureNAT and Firewall

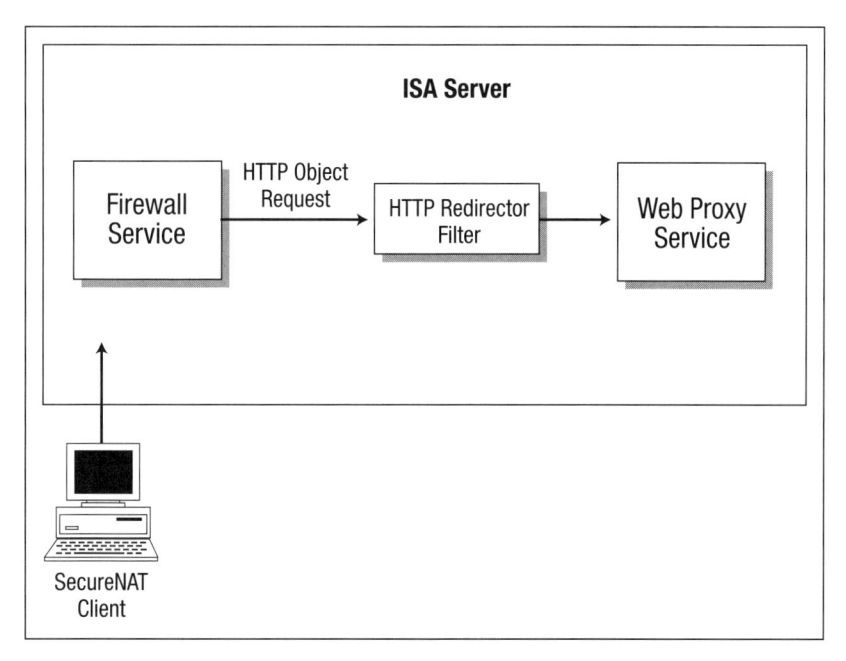

Figure 5.3 The HTTP redirector passes HTTP object requests from SecureNAT and Firewall clients to the Web Proxy service.

client requests can benefit from cache when requesting HTTP objects. Figure 5.3 shows the architecture of how SecureNAT and Firewall client requests are redirected through the HTTP redirector to the Web Proxy service. Configuring the HTTP Redirector Filter is covered in Chapter 9 of this book.

Web Proxy Client Setup

A Web Proxy client does not require any special software beyond a CERN-compliant Web browser. However, the Web browser does have to be configured to use ISA Server instead of trying to make its own direct request to the Internet. ISA Server allows a choice in how the Web Proxy client is configured. You can select from four methods, as shown in Table 5.1.

Table 5.1 Web Proxy client configuration methods.

Method	Use this configuration when you have...
Client configuration script	A complex network configuration with multiple subnets and ISA servers and your Web browsers are Internet Explorer 3.02 or Netscape Navigator 2.0, or a higher version of each.
Manual configuration	A small network or very few clients that need access to objects on the Internet.
Automatic Discovery	Roaming clients.
Firewall client setup	Firewall clients. (They can be automatically configured as Web Proxy clients when they are configured as Firewall clients.)

Each method requires a different setup, but none is very complicated. The client configuration script is created by default when ISA Server is installed. The ISA Server gathers the information that a Web Proxy client would need, based on default and configured settings, and creates a script with these settings. It then creates a Web connection at a URL that Web Proxy clients can connect to and download: **http://*ISAServerName*/array.dll?Get.Routing.Script**. (ISAServerName is the name of the ISA Server to which the internal clients will connect to download the script.) You still need to configure the Web browser to download the script. You can do this on the property pages of the Web browser. Follow these steps in Internet Explorer:

1. Right-click on the Internet Explorer icon on the desktop and select Properties.
2. Select the Connections tab.
3. On the Connections tab, click the LAN Settings button.
4. Select the option Use Automatic Configuration Script.
5. In the Address box, type "http://*ISAServerName*/array.dll?Get.Routing.Script" where *ISAServerName* is the name of the ISA Server that contains the script.
6. Deselect the Automatic Discovery option.
7. Click OK to accept the changes.
8. Close the Internet Explorer Properties dialog box.

Automatic Discovery for Web Proxy settings is supported only by Internet Explorer 5.0 and later. The configuration for AutoDiscovery involves many different services. We will discuss AutoDiscovery configuration near the end of this chapter.

You can manually set up a Web Proxy client on the Internet Explorer property pages. Figure 5.4 shows the dialog box that accepts the settings needed for the browser to connect to a proxy server, including ISA Server. To open this dialog box, right-click on the Internet Explorer icon on your desktop and select Properties. Next, select the Connections tab. At the bottom of the Connections dialog box, click the LAN Settings button. Select the Use A Proxy Server checkbox, and then fill in the IP address and port number that the client should connect to when trying to make a connection. Figure 5.5 shows the dialog box that will appear if you click the Advanced button. Use this dialog box if separate settings are needed for different services provided by ISA Server.

One configuration setting ensures that a Firewall client will also be set up as a Web Proxy client. This setting is turned on by default, but you can disable it if you don't need it. Check the following setting:

1. Open ISA Management.
2. Expand Servers And Arrays.
3. Expand the array for which you will be configuring Firewall clients.
4. Click on Client Configuration.
5. In the details pane of the right side of the window, right-click on Web Browser and select Properties.
6. Make sure the General tab is selected and that the Configure Web Browser During Firewall Client Setup option is enabled.

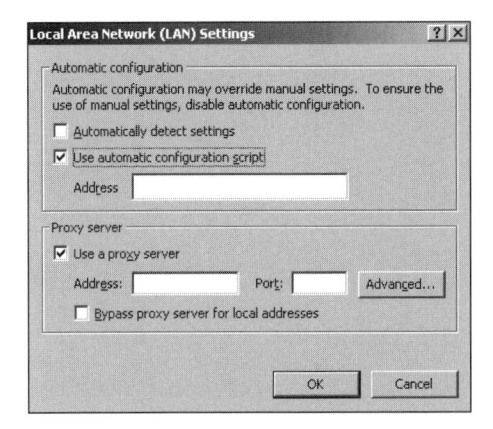

Figure 5.4 The LAN Settings dialog box accessed from the Connections tab in Internet Explorer can be used for a manual configuration of a Web Proxy client.

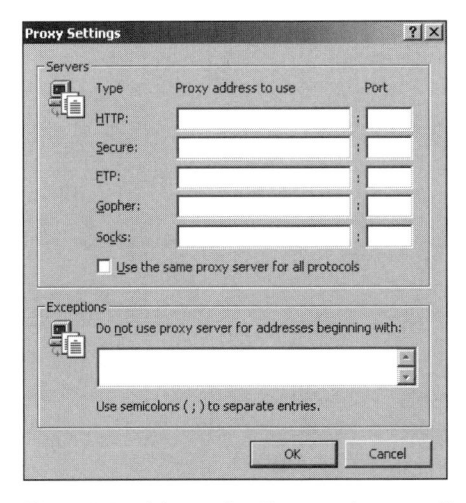

Figure 5.5 Advanced settings can be manually set in Internet Explorer.

7. The Firewall client can be set to obtain the configuration information from Automatic Discovery or Configuration Script.

8. Click OK to accept the changes.

Firewall Client Setup

To install Firewall client software, you can run the installation path from the computer that will be a Firewall client. The path is *ISAServerName*\mspclnt\setup, where *ISAServerName* is the name of the ISA server. The mspclnt share is created on the ISA server when the ISA Server software is installed.

After starting the installation, follow these steps:

1. Click OK.

2. Click Next at the Welcome message.

3. Click Next to accept the default installation folder of C:\Mspclnt.

4. Click the Install button.

5. Files will copy to the hard disk.

6. Click Finish.

7. Click Yes to restart the computer.

Note: The Firewall client software should never be installed on the ISA server. The two applications are not designed to work together on the same computer and will interfere with each other.

There is also a Web version of the Firewall client installation. Basically, it is a Web page that Microsoft created for ISA Server that includes a link to the setup.exe file for the Firewall client. This Web page and a setup.exe file are placed in a subfolder called \WEBINST, also located in the \Clients folder. You make this subfolder a virtual directory in an intranet Web site. (See *MCSE IIS 4 Exam Cram*, third edition, for more information.)

Installing the Firewall client on each desktop in an enterprise environment could prove to be a daunting and time-consuming task. Using the Windows 2000 Software Installation extension is a more efficient way to perform a mass install of software. This extension is part of the group policy snap-in in the Windows 2000 administration tools. An administrator can assign the Firewall client to computers or groups of computers. The next time the assigned computer is started, it will automatically install the Firewall client. Using the Windows 2000 Software Installation extension with the Firewall client is an easy setup because the files are already configured and a network share is created, all by default. The only step left is to assign the Firewall client to the client computers.

Changes Made During the Installation of the Firewall Client

During the installation of the Firewall client, folders and files are added to the hard disk and connections are established to the Firewall service on the ISA server. The Firewall client installation application will create a Firewall client folder called Mspclnt. It then copies two files—Msplat.txt and Mspclnt.ini—from the ISA server to the local hard disk of the Firewall client. Msplat.txt is the LAT. It allows the Firewall client to differentiate between a local and external IP address. Mspclnt.ini is the configuration file for the Firewall client. These files will automatically refresh from the ISA server mspclnt share every six hours, which means that an administrator can make a change to the files and the changes will automatically be sent to the clients in the next refresh.

Removing the Firewall Client

You can remove the Firewall client from a client machine. To uninstall the Firewall client and remove it from a client computer, complete the following steps:

1. Open Control Panel.

2. Open Add/Remove Programs.

3. In the Change Or Remove Programs dialog box, click on Microsoft Firewall Client.

4. Click the Remove button.

5. When asked if you are sure you want to remove Microsoft Firewall client from your computer, click Yes.

6. Click Yes to restart your computer.

Configuring Firewall Client Files

The most complex part of setting up a Firewall client involves loading the Firewall client on the internal computers. After the software is loaded, you can easily make a configuration change at the ISA server and download it to each client so that they all receive the change. Also, once the Firewall client is loaded, all Winsock applications from the internal client can use it to make a connection to the Internet through ISA Server. Differentiating between the various configuration files and learning how to configure them gives you more control over Firewall clients.

Configuring the Msplat.txt File

As we discussed in Chapter 3 a LAT file is created so that ISA Server knows which IP addresses are on the local network and which IP addresses are external. It calls this file msplat.txt and puts it in a \Clients folder in the ISA folder structure. The full path for this folder is Rootdrive\Program Files\Microsoft ISA Server\Clients\Msplat.txt. If ISA Server is upgraded from Proxy Server 2.0, the path is Rootdrive\Msp\Clients. It is more efficient if the clients of ISA Server also have a copy of the LAT. This way, they can perform the check to see whether the IP addresses to which they want to connect are local or need to be sent to ISA Server. With a local copy of the LAT, the clients can make the decision of where to send a request without having to contact the ISA Server.

Because the client's copy of the LAT is updated from the ISA server, any changes made at a single client will be overwritten when the client's LAT is updated. If you want to make a change to a single client that won't be overwritten, use a file called Locallat.txt. Format this file by giving it two entries that define the IP address range. The entries should be formatted like this:

```
192.168.0.0     192.168.255.255
```

The preceding example in a Locallat.txt file would include all IP addresses 192.168.0.0 through 192.168.255.255. Save the Locallat.txt file to the local \Clients directory on the client.

Configuring the Mspclnt.ini File

The configuration information for the Firewall client is contained in the Mspclnt.ini file. Like Msplat.txt, this file has a master version at the ISA server and an updated version is sent to the client at regular intervals. This means that once the Firewall client is loaded on each client, a configuration change can be implemented at the ISA server and sent automatically to the clients at the next scheduled interval. The administrator only needs to know what information is contained in the Mspclnt.ini file and how it can be changed.

Table 5.2 includes settings that can be included in the Mspclnt.ini file. You can adjust these entries if you want different settings from the default ones set by ISA Server.

Not all settings that can be in the Mspclnt.ini file need to be included. Here's a sample Mspclnt.ini file:

```
[Common]
WWW-Proxy=Server1
Set Browsers to use Proxy=1
Set Browsers to use Auto Config=0
WebProxyPort=8080
```

```
Configuration Url=http://Server1:80/array.dll?Get.Routing.Script
Port=1745
Configuration Refresh Time (Hours)=6
Re-check Inaccessible Server Time (Minutes)=10
Refresh Give Up Time (Minutes)=15
Inaccessible Servers Give Up Time (Minutes)=2
Setup=setup.exe
AutoDetect ISA Servers=0
ServerVersion=11
[Servers Ip Addresses]
Name=Server1
[Master Config]
Path1=\\Server1\mspclnt\
[w3proxy]
Disable=1
```

Table 5.2 Settings that can be included in the Mspclnt.ini file.

Section Name	Entry and purpose of setting
[Master Config]	Path1= Path in the form of a UNC to share that updates the mspclnt.ini file.
[Server IP addresses]	IP= or Name= The IP address of a standalone ISA Server or a list of IP addresses of the members of an array. (The name of the ISA Server can be in this section if the IP addresses are not included.)
[Common]	Port= The number of the port used as a control channel for ISA Server.
[Common]	Configuration Refresh Time (Hours=) The number of hours between download requests for updates on the mspclnt.ini file from the Firewall client.
[Common]	Re-check Inaccessible Server Time Cache (Minutes)= The number of minutes a Firewall client will give to a server marked as inaccessible to respond.
[Common]	Refresh Give Up Time (Minutes)= The number of minutes a Firewall client will wait before again attempting a refresh.
[Common]	Inaccessible Servers Give Up Time (Minutes=) The number of minutes a Firewall client will wait before trying another server.
[Common]	Set Browsers to Use Proxy= Turning this setting on tells the client computer to use a Proxy server. It refers the client to the WWW-Proxy configuration to find the name of the proxy server.
[Common]	WWW-Proxy= Names the proxy server that a client will use.
[Common]	Configuration URL= The URL of the script that tells the client how to handle routing to particular arrays.
[Common]	Local Domains= Gives a list of DNS domain names that can be resolved locally.
[Common]	WebProxyPort= The port number that the proxy client needs to use to connect to the proxy server.

Making a change to the file is considered a manual change. If a manual change is made to the Mspclnt.ini file, then the Firewall service must be stopped and restarted for the change to take effect. This can be accomplished one of two ways. You can open the Services application in Administrative Tools, right-click on Microsoft Firewall Service, and select Stop. Repeat this step and select Start to restart the service. Or you can use the Net Stop wspsrv and Net Start wspsrv commands at the command prompt.

The Mspclnt.ini file is updated and overwritten and a local version called the Wspcfg.ini can be saved on the client. To create a Wspcfg.ini file make any changes to the MSpclnt.ini file that you want to apply to just one client. Save the new version of the file in the client's local \Clients folder as Wspcfg.ini. These changes will apply only to that client and will not be overwritten on the next refresh.

The Local Domain Table

In previous versions of Windows operating systems, clients could easily distinguish by name format the difference between a local computer and one outside the local network. This was because the local network used NetBIOS computer names while external computers used domain names from the Domain Name System (DNS). Starting with Windows 2000, Microsoft names all of its computers using the DNS system. This means that a destination computer with a DNS name can no longer be assumed to be remote.

This causes a problem for the client computer when it is deciding where to send the computer name for name resolution to an IP address. Local computer names should be sent to the DNS server in the local network, whereas names for remote computers should be sent to the ISA server for resolution to occur on the Internet. The solution to this problem is to create a Local Domain Table (LDT) on each Firewall client. Just as the LAT is updated from the ISA server, so is the LDT. The Firewall checks the LDT to decide where the name resolution query should be sent. After receiving the IP address of the destination computer, the Firewall client checks its LAT to see whether the request should be sent to a local computer or to the ISA server. The LDT can be configured from the ISA administration tool. Select the array and then choose Network Configuration. Right-click on the Local Domain Table folder to add a new entry to the LDT.

Setup Needed for SecureNAT Clients

SecureNAT client is the most transparent of all the clients in that it requires the least amount of setup at the client. You don't need to install any software. In fact, ISA Server considers every client that does not have the Firewall client installed on it to be a SecureNAT client. The only configuration needed on a SecureNAT client involves configuring the default gateway of the SecureNAT client as the ISA Server. In a large environment, you can configure the default gateway of some SecureNAT clients as a router that forwards requests to the ISA Server. Either way, the requests that have to be fulfilled on the Internet need to end up at the ISA Server. You can set a SecureNAT client's TCP/IP settings either manually or with DHCP.

Of course, it is not as simple as it sounds to use the SecureNAT client. You need to perform other network configurations besides routing in order for the SecureNAT clients to have everything they require. SecureNAT clients do not have local versions of ISA Server's LDT or LAT files. With no local LDT, the SecureNAT client also has no way of differentiating between the local and remote computer names. To make up for this, you'll have to set up DNS servers on the internal network so that they can handle external name-resolution requests.

With no local version of the LAT, the SecureNAT client will send all requests to the ISA Server, even internal ones. This will put an additional burden on the ISA Server to process all SecureNAT requests instead of just the ones that are meant for external networks. Both of these situations require extra planning on a network that uses SecureNAT clients instead of Firewall clients.

Firewall clients work automatically with all Winsock applications; allowing access to SecureNAT clients may involve extra settings. SecureNAT clients require that any protocol they want to use have a configured protocol definition. We will cover setting up protocol definitions in Chapter 6 of this book.

Socks Client Setup

Essentially, no setup is needed for the Socks client. Socks clients by definition use sockets instead of Winsock, so they can't be a Firewall client. Because Socks clients cannot be Firewall clients, they are treated as SecureNAT clients. As long as the network has been set up to handle SecureNAT client requests, the ISA server will receive the Socks request, process it through the Firewall service, and send it to the Socks application filter to be handled. The Socks application filter is responsible for sending the request out to the Internet and making a connection with an Internet server.

Although Microsoft Proxy Server allowed the setup of Socks rules, these rules are not migrated to ISA Server. This is because all clients must follow the same set of policies and rules setup in ISA Server. ISA Server has an order of applying these policies and rules, and every client type has them applied in the same way.

By default, Socks clients connect to port 1080 on the ISA server. You can change the port used by the Socks filter in ISA Management:

1. In ISA Management, expand Servers And Arrays.

2. Expand the array on which you would like to change the Socks port by clicking on the plus (+) sign.

3. Expand Extensions and then select Application Filters.
4. In the details pane on the right side of the window, right-click the Socks V4 Filter and then click Properties.
5. Select the Options tab.
6. On the Options tab, change the port number to your choice.
7. Click the OK button to close the Socks V4 Filter Properties.
8. Close ISA Management.

AutoDiscovery Setup

Both the Firewall and Web Proxy clients support Automatic Discovery of their settings. Automatic Discovery of client settings is especially useful for roaming clients that may need to connect to a different ISA server. ISA servers that are on different subnets may belong to the same array, which would allow the client to find their closest ISA server when they change locations. This will save a user or administrator from having to reconfigure the client each time this happens. Setting up AutoDiscovery of ISA Server settings requires many steps. Not only do the ISA Server and the client need to be configured, but also the DNS and/or DHCP server.

When a Firewall or Web Proxy client has moved to a new location because they are a roaming user, they will try to make a request to their configured ISA server. When this request fails, the client will either ask the DNS for the IP address of their ISA server array or ask the DHCP server if it needs a new IP address. The Firewall client that is loaded from ISA Server supports AutoDiscovery, but Web Proxy clients need at least Internet Explorer version 5.0 to support AutoDiscovery.

Configuration on the DNS Server

You must configure the DNS server to handle the requests from the Firewall or Web Proxy clients. To configure the DNS server, you add a Web Proxy AutoDiscovery (WPAD) entry to the DNS database. To configure this entry, complete the following steps:

1. Open the DNS management console in Administrative Tools.
2. In the DNS console, expand DNS and then expand the applicable DNS server.
3. Expand the Forward Lookup Zones folder.
4. Right-click the zone that the client will use and select New Alias.
5. In the Alias Name box, type "WPAD".
6. In the Fully Qualified Name For Target Host box, type the name of the ISA server or array that the client should be using.

7. Click the OK button to close the Alias dialog box.

8. Close the DNS console.

The WPAD entry is for Web Proxy clients. For Firewall clients you need to create a WSPAD entry in DNS. Repeat the previous steps with only one change: enter WSPAD instead of WPAD in Step 5. DNS will use this entry to return the correct IP address for the closest ISA Server to the Firewall client.

Configuration on the DHCP Server

To configure the DHCP server to support AutoDiscovery, complete these steps:

1. Open the DHCP management console in Administrative Tools.

2. In the DHCP console, right-click the DHCP server and select Set Predefined Options.

3. In the Name box, type "WPAD".

4. In the Code box, type "252".

5. Click the Data Type drop-down box and select String.

6. In the Value box, type one of the following:

    If the DNS server is configured for AutoDiscovery, type "http://WPAD/WPAD.dat".

    If the DNS server is not configured for AutoDiscovery, type "http://ISAServerName/WPAD.dat", where *ISAServerName* is the name of the ISA server or array to which the client needs to connect.

7. Click the OK button to close the Predefined Options dialog box.

8. Close the DHCP console.

You also need to configure Automatic Discovery of ISA Server settings on the ISA server and the client. The ISA server will publish the Automatic Discovery information when configured to do so. To publish the Automatic Discovery information, complete the following steps:

1. Open ISA Management.

2. Expand Servers And Arrays.

3. Right-click the array that will be using Automatic Discovery and select Properties.

4. Select the Auto Discovery tab.

5. Select the Publish Automatic Discovery Information checkbox.

6. Leave the default port of 80 or enter another port.

7. Click OK to accept the changes.

8. Close ISA Management.

Finally, you need to configure AutoDiscovery on the clients. You can configure the settings on individual clients or for all clients. It depends on how many clients in your network roam and need to change ISA Server settings. To configure AutoDiscovery on individual clients, begin by opening Control Panel and opening the Firewall client icon. Then, select the Automatically Detect ISA Server checkbox. To configure all Web Proxy and Firewall clients to use AutoDiscovery, complete the following steps:

1. Open ISA Management.

2. Expand Servers And Arrays.

3. Expand the array for which you will be configuring Firewall clients.

4. Click on Client Configuration.

5. In the details pane on the right side of the window, right-click on Web Browser or the Firewall client and select Properties.

6. In the Web Browser General tab, select the Automatically Discover Settings option. In the Firewall client in the General tab, select the Enable ISA Firewall Automatic Discovery In Firewall Client.

7. Click OK to accept the changes.

8. Close ISA Management.

Assessing Client Needs

So which client type should you configure or install for your internal network users? If you do not assess the needs of your client and network before making this decision, you may end up doing a lot more work than is necessary. First, start with the easy differences, such as type of client operating system. Then, determine the types of connections your users will need. Will they need access to Web pages or files, or will they need to make connections to Internet applications? The answers to these questions will allow you to decide which client type or combination is best for your users.

Client Connection Needs

For your internal network clients, you first have to determine what kind of connections they need to make. If they do not have to connect to Web pages or download documents, the Web Proxy client is not needed. If these objects are needed but no Internet applications will be used, then SecureNAT and Firewall client are not needed. If both of these connections are required on a network, you have to address such issues as client operating systems and security needs.

Client Operating System Differences

On the surface it seems easy to decide between the Firewall and SecureNAT clients simply by the client operating systems that are loaded on the client. But it is not that simple when dealing with Internet connections. Just because you have the most recent Windows operating systems does not automatically mean that you should choose Firewall client. Also, SecureNAT and Web Proxy client are operating system independent, so although the operating systems can eliminate the Firewall client, you must ask more questions before making a decision. You may not want the overhead of loading software on each client and may not need the fine level of control that it provides over Internet connections. Security and setup requirements need to be assessed before making a final decision.

Security and Setup Needs

When choosing between SecureNAT and Firewall client, the need for user-level authentication is important. SecureNAT cannot give user-level authentication while the Firewall client can. However, the Firewall client has a more complex setup because you need to load software on each client. Also, user-level authentication requires that each user authenticate himself when connecting to the ISA server, which causes overhead on the network and ISA Server. However, SecureNAT can be complicated to support because of routing and DNS requirements. If these are difficult to reconfigure, Firewall client may be best. Each client has advantages and disadvantages that when weighed should make the decision less complicated.

Chapter Summary

ISA Server includes three major client types: the Web Proxy client, the Firewall client, and the SecureNAT client. Each one has a different method of setup and reasons why it should be used.

Web browsers can directly connect to the Web Proxy service in ISA Server without any extra software, and the service can work with any operating system. However, you have to use a CERN-compliant browser. The Web Proxy client retrieves objects based on client requests. These requests can use HTTP, HTTP-S, FTP, or Gopher as their protocol. A Web Proxy client has its request fulfilled by the Web Proxy service. This is the only service that can fulfill requests from cache.

The Firewall and SecureNAT clients each make connections to Internet applications. Because they do the same task, a single client cannot be both a Firewall and a

SecureNAT client. The Firewall client requires the installation of client software from the ISA server and can be loaded only on recent versions of Microsoft Windows. SecureNAT does not require the installation of client software. For the extra trouble of loading client software, you can get user-level security with the Firewall client. It is also easier to make mass configuration changes with the Firewall client.

Two configuration files hold the changes for all Firewall clients by default. These files, Mspclnt.ini and Msplat.txt, reside on the ISA server and are periodically copied to the client. Any change made on these files at the server will be copied to all Firewall clients after the next download interval. If a change is made on an individual client, that change will be overwritten after the next download interval. To make a change on an individual client and not have it overwritten, you must create a local copy of each file. For the Mspclnt.ini file, the local copy is called Wspcfg.ini; for Msplat.txt, the local copy is called Locallat.txt.

Although the SecureNAT client does not require the installation of client software, it still will need some network configuration changes to get its requests to the ISA server. First, you need to set the default gateway in the TCP/IP settings to the IP address of the ISA server. In a complex network with subnets, this may require more planning with the routers to direct these requests to the ISA server. Also, the SecureNAT client does not use the LDT file, so the DNS servers in the network must be able to handle internal as well as external name-resolution requests.

Automatic Discovery allows remote clients to be reconfigured without intervention from a user or administrator. However, the setup for AutoDiscovery requires changes at the DNS and/or DHCP server, the client, and the ISA server. Each of these changes is minor. You can configure clients to use AutoDiscovery individually or all at once.

Review Questions

1. What are the major client types for ISA Server? [Check all correct answers]
    a. Socks Proxy client
    b. Web Proxy client
    c. Firewall client
    d. SecureNAT client

2. What versions of Winsock are supported by the Firewall service? [Check all correct answers]
    a. 1.0
    b. 1.1
    c. 2.0

d. 2.1

e. 2.2

3. What port does the ISA server allow internal clients making outbound requests to connect on by default?

    a. 1000

    b. 1010

    c. 80

    d. 8080

4. The Firewall client can be loaded onto what operating systems? [Check all correct answers]

    a. Macintosh

    b. Unix

    c. Windows 2000 Professional

    d. Windows 2000 Server

    e. Windows 95

    f. Windows NT 4

    g. All of the above

5. What client Web browsers work with the Web Proxy service? [Check the best answer]

    a. Internet Explorer

    b. Netscape Navigator

    c. Netscape Communicator

    d. Mosaic

    e. All CERN-compliant browsers

6. What version of Socks client does ISA Server support?

    a. 4.0

    b. 5.0

    c. 5.5

    d. 6.0

7. Which client(s) require(s) the installation of client software?

    a. Socks client

    b. Web Proxy client

    c. Firewall client

    d. SecureNAT client

8. Which clients require configuration at the client level? [Check all correct answers]
   a. Socks client
   b. Web Proxy client
   c. Firewall client
   d. SecureNAT client

9. Which of the following are extensions to ISA Server? [Check all correct answers]
   a. CERN
   b. SecureNAT
   c. HTTP redirector filter
   d. Socks filter

10. The Firewall client should be loaded on the ISA server.
    a. True
    b. False

11. Where should the Locallat.txt file be saved?
    a. On the ISA server in the \Mspclnt folder
    b. On the ISA server in the \Clients folder
    c. On the client in the \Mspclnt folder
    d. On the client in the \Clients folder

12. Which are methods that can be used to configure the Firewall client? [Check all correct answers]
    a. AutoDiscovery
    b. Client configuration script
    c. Manually
    d. Locally
    e. All of the above

13. What is an LDT?
    a. Local Daily Table
    b. Local Domain Table
    c. Local Domain Tab
    d. Local Daily Tab

14. Which client uses the LAT?
    a. Socks client
    b. Web Proxy client
    c. Firewall client
    d. SecureNAT client

15. How is the Socks client set up?
    a. By loading software on the client
    b. By setting up a Firewall client
    c. By setting up a Web proxy client
    d. By default

16. Using SecureNAT as a client can cause a need to configure what other services?
    a. DNS
    b. Routers
    c. Default gateways on clients
    d. All of the above

17. What does WPAD stand for?
    a. Web Proxy AutoDiscovery
    b. Winsock Proxy AutoDiscovery
    c. Web Post AutoDiscovery
    d. Web Page After Destination

18. What version of Internet Explorer supports AutoDiscovery?
    a. 2.0
    b. 3.0
    c. 3.2
    d. 4.1
    e. 5.0
    f. All of the above

19. What needs to be configured for AutoDiscovery?
    a. The ISA server
    b. The individual client
    c. DNS
    d. DHCP
    e. All of the above

20. How are clients configured to use AutoDiscovery? [Check all correct answers]
    a. Individually
    b. In groups
    c. All at once
    d. All of the above

21. Which clients can use AutoDiscovery? [Check all correct answers]
    a. Socks client
    b. Web Proxy client
    c. Firewall client
    d. SecureNAT client

22. What is AutoDiscovery used for?
    a. Configuring clients
    b. Configuring ISA Server
    c. Loading client software
    d. Uninstalling client software

Real-World Projects

Note: This exercise assumes a test Windows 2000 Server with Service Pack 1 installed. Read the instructions carefully and do not change the settings on your production machine unless you understand the options presented. If you are unsure about an option, do not make a change and instead read the ISA Server help files about the option to be installed.

Joe had just installed the new ISA servers and was ready to move on to installing the clients. Joe works for a company that manufactures and sells Widgets. The company has a corporate office and manufacturing plant in Oklahoma and sales offices in 10 towns throughout the state.

He had finished setting up the ISA servers, so it was now time to plan and configure the clients. The network has a mix of clients, so Joe has to do some planning. When he first started looking into upgrading the Internet security server to ISA, he did not realize that he would have to look at network settings and client software. After reviewing the documentation for the client types that can be used with ISA Server, he reviewed the operating systems and Internet usage of the clients on the network.

Most of the network had recently been upgraded to Windows 2000 Professional desktops, though not all of the computers were Windows operating systems. The graphics department has 40 Macintosh computers for graphics programs that the artists refuse to give up. These computers had been Socks clients to the proxy server that had protected the network until it was decided to switch to ISA Server. The Socks service in the proxy server had a text file that stored the settings. He wants to find a way to migrate these settings to ISA Server.

This is not the only client issue that Joe has to deal with. The sales department needs many of their clients to be able to travel around to different branch offices before returning to the corporate office. This means that the settings connecting them to the Internet have to keep changing. Joe needs to make the change as easy as possible so that the often nontechnical sales department members will be able to connect to the Internet without the help of a network administrator.

Joe decided to do some research to see what he could do to handle these problems. In ISA Server Help, Joe discovers that ISA Server does not migrate this Socks file and that Socks clients will have the policies and rules of ISA Server applied to them as if they were any other ISA Server client. He still needs to set up the rules and policies on the ISA server, so he will deal with this later. Joe also finds out that he needs to set up AutoDiscovery for the sales force to automatically change their settings when they change locations. For the rest of his clients, he decides to install the Firewall client. Joe wants to do a test install on one client computer first.

Project 5.1
To install the Firewall client on a client computer:

1. Connect to the share created on the ISA server that contains the Firewall client installation files. By default the path is *ISAServerName*\mspclnt\setup, where *ISAServerName* is the name of the ISA server. This will start the installation.

2. At the Welcome dialog box click OK.

3. Click Next at the Welcome message.

4. Click Next to accept the default installation folder of C:\Mspclnt.

5. Click the Install button.

6. Files will copy to the hard disk.

7. Click Finish.

8. Click Yes to restart the computer.

Joe next needs to change the Socks port number. The company has a policy of using a different port number than the default of 1080. Before connecting the clients, he must check the port setting. He also needs to look into why the company is using a different port number just to make sure the reason makes sense.

Project 5.2

To change the port number for Socks clients:

1. In ISA Management, expand Servers And Arrays.
2. Expand the array on which you would like to change the Socks port by clicking on the plus (+) sign.
3. Expand Extensions and then select Application Filters.
4. In the details pane on the right side of the window, right-click the Socks V4 Filter and then click Properties.
5. Select the Options tab.
6. On the Options tab, change the port number to your choice.
7. Click the OK button to close the Socks V4 Filter Properties.
8. Close ISA Management.

Joe finds that he needs to make more than one configuration change to set up AutoDiscovery for the sales department. He has to configure the DNS server and the individual clients to participate in the AutoDiscovery process.

Project 5.3

To configure AutoDiscovery on the DNS server:

1. Open the DNS management console in Administrative Tools.
2. In the DNS console, expand DNS and then expand the applicable DNS server.
3. Expand the Forward Lookup Zones folder.
4. Right-click the zone that the client will use and select New Alias.
5. In the Alias Name box, type "WPAD".
6. In the Fully Qualified Name For Target Host box, type the name of the ISA server or array that the client should be using.
7. Click the OK button to close the Alias dialog box.
8. Close the DNS console.

Joe created the first record for the Web Proxy clients. He repeated the steps and created a WSPAD record on the DNS Server for the Firewall clients.

To configure AutoDiscovery on the individual clients:

1. Open ISA Management.
2. Expand Servers And Arrays.
3. Expand the array for which you will be configuring Firewall clients.
4. Click on Client Configuration.
5. In the details pane of the right side of the window, right-click on Web Browser or the Firewall client and select Properties.
6. On the Web Browser General tab, select the Automatically Discover Settings option. In the Firewall client on the General tab, select the Enable ISA Firewall Automatic Discovery In Firewall Client.
7. Click OK to accept changes.
8. Close ISA Management.

With the clients set up and ready to go, Joe is ready to connect the ISA server to the network and start using it. The next task will be to set up policies and rules that will allow clients to access what they need over the Internet. Setup of polices and rules are explained in Chapter 6.

CHAPTER SIX

Policies and Rules

After completing this chapter, you will be able to:

✓ Differentiate between array and enterprise policies

✓ Use enterprise and array policies together

✓ Describe how policies and rules are applied

✓ Describe the use of protocol definitions

✓ Define protocol rules

✓ Define site and content rules

✓ Modify content types

✓ Create and use destination sets

✓ Use bandwidth rules

✓ Describe changes in the use of packet filters

✓ Plan for the use of policies in a network

✓ Create access policies

ISA Server can be installed into a number of configurations. Whether an ISA server exists as standalone or as part of an enterprise, you have many ways to plan and execute its configuration. ISA Server allows a fine degree of control over Internet connections. In fact, this degree of control is so fine that it may seem you have too many rules to configure. For this reason, policies were created. Policies combine rules and allow them to be applied to arrays or even to the entire enterprise.

Policies allow a top-down approach to configuring rules. With policies, an administrator can plan how external connections should be used for the enterprise environment. This plan can include setting up rules at the top level for how and when Internet connections are used with the choice of allowing little or no room for individual sites to set their own rules. An administrator can also leave an open policy at the top level that gives control over outgoing connections to individual sites. Policies allow a company to plan and establish patterns of Internet use. In this chapter, you will learn the different elements that can be included in a policy and how to put them together. We will focus on allowing internal clients access to the Internet. Rules that govern access for incoming connections and Web publishing will be covered in Chapter 12 of this book. You will also learn how policies can simplify the creation of rules and their application to an environment.

Controlling Access with ISA Server

Because ISA Server's purpose is to secure and control connections, it offers a variety of types of control over these connections. ISA Server can control access using different types of rules, elements, and policies. Rules are individual settings that control different aspects of ISA Server settings. Rules and other elements can be combined into policies that allow administrators to organize their application to a network. Different types of policies are available that apply to different types of network environments. To make things more complicated, each rule has elements that may have to be defined before the rule can be created. Think of elements as settings organized ahead of time. Elements allow you to group users, computers, protocols, and types of Internet traffic. The rule then needs to control the behavior of these groups only. Elements can be reused in different rules. Table 6.1 describes the different rules that can be configured in ISA Server. We will cover elements later in this chapter.

Table 6.1 Rules that control access in ISA Server.

Rule name	What it does
Site and content rule	Controls who can access what sites on the Internet and the kind of content that can be accessed.
Protocol rule	Controls what protocol requests will be allowed or denied.
Packet filter	Statically opens or closes a port for specified connections.
Bandwidth rule	Allows specified network connections to have priority over others.

What Is a Policy?

Creating and configuring all of the possible rules that can control Internet access through ISA Server is a complex task. You can set up a number of rules as well as elements that are used in each rule. A policy can consist of a number of elements and rules. The purpose of the policy is to implement these elements and rules in an organized manner. By setting up policies, an administrator can set up rules just once or a few times instead of individually on every ISA server or array. Before a rule can be completed, any custom elements need to be configured. Many of the customized elements can be reused in different types of rules. Before you set up rules, you need to make sure you plan how they will be implemented through policies. The two different types of policies that can be applied to a network are enterprise and array, and each has a different role.

Enterprise vs. Array Policies

The enterprise policy is designed to be the base policy for the entire network, whether that is a multilocation forest or a single-site domain. It allows an administrator to set up rules that apply to the whole environment, and the settings in an enterprise policy need to be configured only one time. If you use an enterprise policy, the settings apply to all ISA servers in the enterprise automatically. This means by default the enterprise policy is applied to the array members when they are installed into the array. When setting up an enterprise policy, remember that the rules that deny access in the enterprise policy override any rules that conflict in the array policy. This means that if the enterprise policy denies access to all Web sites between midnight and 8:00 A.M. and the array policy allows access to all Web sites during this time period, access to Web sites during this time of night would be denied. To work with this rule, think of the enterprise policy as a foundation for the array policies. It is important to remember that as you create enterprise policy rules that deny access, the phrase "no exceptions allowed" applies to every rule contained in it. If an enterprise policy is too restrictive for your network, you do not have to use one. Refer to Chapter 3 to see how to establish an array with only array-level policies.

When used in conjunction with enterprise policies, array policies should be used to refine what is allowed by the enterprise policy. Array policies can be used to restrict access allowed by the enterprise policy but cannot be used to allow what is denied by the enterprise policy. If access to some sites is never allowed according to company policy, it is a good idea to put this setting in the enterprise policy. But if access is sometimes allowed, or allowed for select groups of users, then it should not be denied in the enterprise policy. The enterprise policy should allow access, and the array policy can refine that access through rules so that only specified users have access. The enterprise policy sets boundaries that cannot be moved. Array policies cannot allow users to go outside the boundaries, but they can further restrict movement inside the boundaries.

Do You Need a Policy?

Policies are used to simplify an administrator's job, but are they actually necessary or just nice to have? In other words, do you really need to configure a policy at all? In a word, yes. By default, a policy has already been set up for you—but only partially. The policy that is created by default does not allow access to external connections. This means that no one can use the external connection you are trying to protect—which means no one can get out to the Internet (unless you modify the default policy). This makes your network very safe because no one can connect to or from your network, but it is probably more protection than you wanted. The point of having a security server is to protect a connection, not eliminate it. So an administrator needs to go into this default policy and modify it to allow users to access and use the Internet connection.

What Kind of Policy Can You Support?

Before you start planning a policy, you need to know what your network can support. The type of policy that you can use depends on the edition and installation of ISA Server. An enterprise policy is designed to support a large environment, so you must set up many prerequisites first. Enterprise policies can be implemented only with the Enterprise Edition of ISA Server. If you want an enterprise policy, you must have a Windows 2000 domain environment with the ISA schema installed in Active Directory. Even though installing the ISA schema is an irreversible action, you can still choose whether you will use an enterprise-level policy or an array-level policy. Also, ISA servers must be members of an array to have an enterprise policy applied to them. To install the ISA Server schema into Active Directory, refer to Chapter 2.

In an environment without a Windows 2000 domain or without the ISA schema installed in Active Directory, you can have a standalone ISA server with a server-level policy only. It is important to make a distinction between server policies for standalone ISA servers and array policies for ISA servers that are members of an array. The policy that is created on a standalone ISA server applies only to that local server and cannot apply to any other ISA server. All members of the array will have the array policy settings applied to them automatically.

How Rules Apply

Though policies organize and simplify the creation of rules, ISA Server still refers to rules when processing client requests. ISA Server is particular in the way it applies rules, so you need to know how ISA Server processes these requests so that you can create rules that work within ISA Server's application of these rules. ISA

Server applies rules that deny access before rules that allow access. Because rules either allow or deny access, an administrator can create one rule that allows access for specified users or sites and another rule that denies access to those same users or sites. If this conflict happens, the particular type of access specified in those rules will be denied.

But the condition of a request not being denied is not the only condition that must be met in order for access to be allowed. Access must also be specifically allowed in a rule. So it is not enough to not be denied access by a rule—access must also be explicitly allowed.

Policy Elements

Understanding policy elements is an important part of setting up rules in ISA Server. You can set up rules without defining policy elements, but you must be willing to accept default settings. Policy elements allow you to customize which users, groups, or computers the rule will apply to. Groups defined by policy elements can be reused in other rules. Destination sets are a policy element that can be used in defining protocol rules and bandwidth rules. Client address sets and schedules are policy elements that are used in defining protocol rules, site and content rules, and bandwidth rules. Once policy elements are defined, they can be used multiple times in different rules and different types of rules. Table 6.2 shows elements and the rules they can be used in. This does not list rules used for inbound access from the Internet, which are covered in Chapter 12.

Policy elements are relatively simple to set up. Most policy elements have just a few settings and can be created by filling out just one dialog box in the ISA Server snap-in. Only a protocol definition policy element uses a wizard for setup. Policy Elements is a separate container in the ISA Server snap-in listed under each array and under Enterprise for enterprise-level policy elements. If you right-click any Policy Element subfolder and select New, the dialog box to create a new policy element will appear.

Table 6.2 Policy elements that can be used in rules.

Policy element	Rules
Protocol definition	Protocol rules, bandwidth rules
Destination set	Site and content rules, bandwidth rules
Content group	Site and content rules, bandwidth rules
Client address set	Protocol rules, site and content rules, bandwidth rules
Schedule	Protocol rules, site and content rules, bandwidth rules
Bandwidth priorities	Bandwidth rules

Protocol Definitions

Protocol definitions define settings for protocols, such as part number and the underlying transport used by the protocol. Rules that control inbound access from the Internet and protocol rules all can use protocol definitions. When ISA Server is installed, a number of protocol definitions are created, but administrators can also configure their own customized protocol definitions. The protocol definitions created by ISA Server during the installation cannot be changed or even deleted. You can create new protocol definitions at any time, and you can modify or delete these custom protocol definitions.

The predefined protocol definitions that are created during the installation of ISA Server are too numerous to mention. They include all the protocols used by popular services such as FTP, Web pages, secure Web pages, Archie, Finger, Newsgroups, Telnet, SMTP, POP3, Exchange, SQL Server, Internet Relay Chat (IRC), RealAudio, LDAP, and Kerberos. You should be aware of the protocol definitions that are on an ISA server before implementing rules on it. To view a full list of protocol definitions on your ISA server, complete the following steps:

1. Open ISA Management.
2. Expand Internet Security And Acceleration Server for enterprise-level protocol definitions or an array for array-level protocol definitions.
3. Expand Policy Elements.
4. Select Protocol Definitions.
5. On the right side of the window in the Details pane, a list of protocol definitions will appear.
6. Scroll to view the entire list or look for a particular protocol definition in the list. They are listed in alphabetical order.

Secondary Connections

Some services make an initial connection on a certain port and use a different port for the actual download of information. HTTP is an example of a protocol that does this. When you request a Web page, an initial connection is made from the client to the server on port 80. Each object in a Web page, such as an image, is downloaded using randomly selected ports. This means that the first image can be downloaded using port 1077, and the second can be downloaded over a connection using port 1078.

SecureNAT and Firewall clients handle secondary connections differently. SecureNAT clients cannot use protocols that use secondary connections by default while Firewall clients can. One way to work with this restriction is to create a protocol definition to handle protocols that use secondary connections. You can create a setting for a secondary connection in a protocol definition. This setting is needed only when your clients are using SecureNAT and the protocol they are connecting with uses secondary connections.

Creating Your Own Protocol Definitions

Because the Internet is always changing, you may want to use a new Internet service that does not have a predefined protocol definition. That's why you may need to create your own protocol definition. All you need to know is the port number that the service uses, whether it uses TCP or UDP as its transport protocol, and whether you want to use it for inbound or outbound connections. These are the settings that are in a protocol definition.

To create an enterprise- or array-level protocol definition, complete the following steps:

1. Open ISA Management.
2. Expand Internet Security And Acceleration Server for enterprise-level protocol definitions or an array for array-level protocol definitions.
3. Expand Policy Elements.
4. Right-click Protocol Definitions.
5. Point to New and select Definition. The New Protocol Definition Wizard will start.
6. In the first dialog box, type the name of the new protocol definition. Like the other protocol definitions, this one should be named after the service or protocol it will define. Click Next.
7. Type the port number and select whether it uses TCP or UDP and whether it is being defined for inbound or outbound use. Click Next.
8. Set a port range for a secondary connection if that is required. If it is not, leave the default selection of No and click Next.
9. Review the summary of information and click Finish. You can use the Back button to change incorrect information.

Destination Sets

A destination set allows a group of computers to be defined as a set so that they can be referred to in a rule. Because rules are applied to destination sets, they must be created before a rule that refers to it. Destination sets allow administrators to control exactly which computers the rule will apply to. No destination sets are created by default. If you don't create a customized destination set, then you can still pick from other choices when creating a new rule. To create them, you use a dialog box in the ISA Server snap-in. If you want to use a customized destination set in a site and content rule, you need to create the destination set before creating the site and content rule.

A destination set specifies certain computers, but if you want to specify only a certain folder or file in a computer, that level of detail is also possible. Paths allow you to specify what folder or folder/file combination you want to include in the destination set. If you specify a path in a destination set, then only that path is referred to instead of the whole computer. Paths apply only when the protocol used is HTTP or FTP so they are meant to specify a certain Web or FTP site. This is because one server can support more than one Web and/or FTP site. If the destination set is used in a rule for protocols other than these, the path portion of the destination set will be ignored.

To create a destination set, complete the following steps:

1. Open ISA Management.
2. Expand Internet Security And Acceleration Server for enterprise-level destination sets or an array for array-level destination sets.
3. Expand Policy Elements.
4. Right-click Destination Sets.
5. Point to New and select Set. The New Destination Set dialog box will appear.
6. In the Name box, type the name of the destination set.
7. In the Description box, describe the new destination set.
8. Click the Add button to add computer names, a block of IP addresses, or a path to a specific folder or folder/file combination that you want to include in the destination set.
9. Keep using the Add button to create a list of names or add a range of IP addresses. Figure 6.1 shows the dialog box that appears when you click the Add button. Click OK.
10. Once the list is complete, click OK to create the destination set.

Once created, a destination set can be modified. In the ISA Server snap-in in the Policy Elements folder where destination sets are created, you will find a list of existing destination sets by clicking on the Destination Sets folder. If you double-click on the individual destination set that you want to modify, you will see a dialog box with two tabs. The General tab will let you rename the destination set, and the Destinations tab will allow you to redefine the IP address range or computers defined in the destination set. Figure 6.1 shows the dialog box that will appear if you select a defined range and click the Edit button in the Destinations tab.

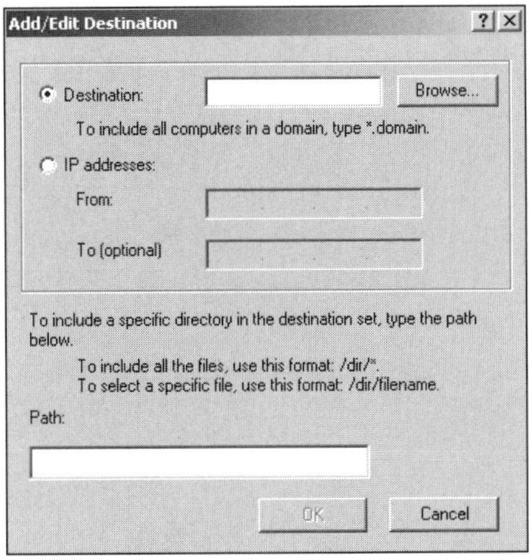

Figure 6.1 The Add/Edit Computer dialog box allows you to modify a destination set after it is created.

Content Groups

Some rules, such as site and content rules, allow a particular type of content to be controlled. When you specify a content type, you are controlling the kind of material that users are allowed to connect to. Content types such as documents, video, or audio are already defined as content groups, but you can create your own content groups. ISA Server identifies content types by the extension of the file in the requested URL and the corresponding Multipurpose Internet Media Extension (MIME) type. You cannot configure content types from a rule wizard; you need to configure them ahead of time in the Policy Elements container in the ISA Server snap-in. In the ISA Server snap-in, expand an array. Then expand Policy Elements and select Content Groups. Figure 6.2 shows the details pane in the ISA Server snap-in when the Content Groups folder is selected. The Content Type section shows the file extensions or MIME types that ISA Server would be searching for when applying a site and content rule that specifies a content type. In Figure 6.2, an HTML document has seven different MIME types or file extensions that are accepted. If you want to add to or remove from this list, right-click on HTML documents and select Properties; then, select the Content Types tab to view or change the list.

Multipurpose Internet Media Extensions (MIME) Types

The documents and messages that were first sent over the Internet contained only text. As email systems became more sophisticated, the ability to send attachments to email became necessary. To add this capability without making major changes to email servers, a specification was developed that expanded the capabilities of email systems so that they could understand more than just email messages. This specification is

Multipurpose Internet Mail Extensions (MIME). MIME types are specified in Requests for Comment (RFCs) from the Internet Engineering Task Force (IETF).

MIME types allow systems to format files so that receiving systems will know how to handle them. Although MIME types were first created for email systems, they are now used also for Web browsers. When the specification was extended, its name was changed to Multipurpose Internet Media Extensions. As HTTP was expanded to download more than just HTML documents, Web browsers and servers were improved to include the use of MIME extensions. With defined MIME types, browsers know how to handle file types such as scripts, video, audio, and images.

Client Address Sets

One way to group computers together so that one rule can be applied to all of them at once is to configure a client address set. Client address sets allow sets of IP addresses to be grouped together. Unlike most policy elements, client address sets do not need to be created before the creation of the rule in which they will be used. Client address sets can be defined during a rule wizard. Figures 6.3 and 6.4 show the dialog boxes that are used to define client address sets. You can access these dialog boxes when you're using a rule wizard, such as the New Site And Content Rule Wizard. In the Client Type dialog box, select Specific Computers (Clients Address Sets) and then click Next. The Client Sets dialog box will appear.

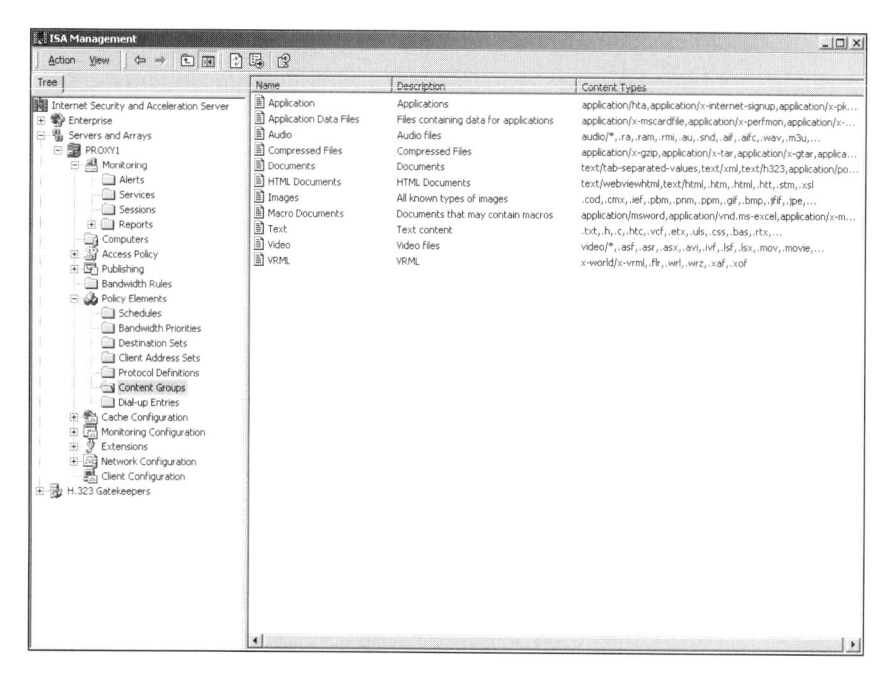

Figure 6.2 The details pane in the ISA Server snap-in when you select Content Groups under Policy Elements.

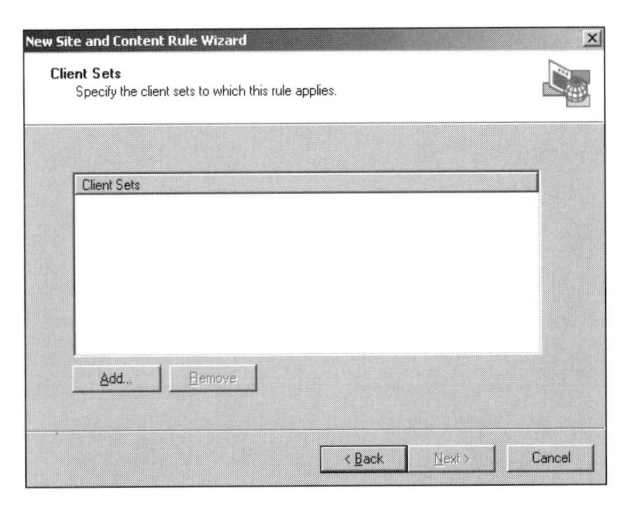

Figure 6.3 The Client Sets dialog box, which shows the defined client sets.

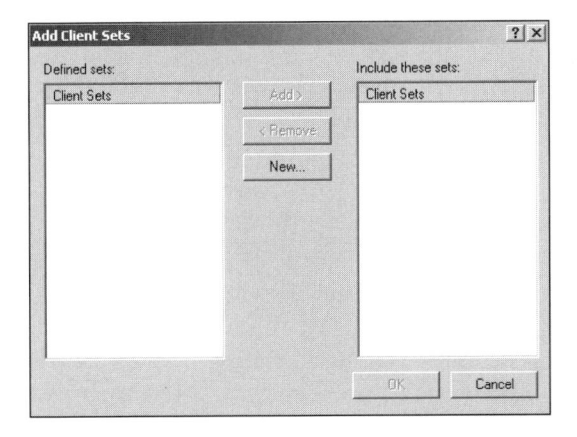

Figure 6.4 The Add Client Sets dialog box is needed to define ranges of IP addresses for client sets.

Figure 6.3 shows this dialog box with no Client Sets defined. To add Client Sets, click the Add button and you'll see the dialog box shown in Figure 6.4. The New button will allow you to define ranges of IP addresses. These ranges become Client Sets that are added to the Clients Sets and the Add Client Sets dialog boxes.

Client address sets are defined so that they can be used multiple times when defining other rules. You can also access the dialog boxes shown in Figures 6.3 and 6.4 from the Policy Elements folder and the Client Address Sets subfolder in the ISA Server snap-in. Right-click on the Client Address Sets subfolder, point to New, and then, after you add the IP address set, select Set.

Once you have the policy elements you need, you can start creating rules. In this chapter, we will discuss the creation of protocol rules, site and content rules, packet filters, and bandwidth rules.

Schedules

Schedules are policy elements that determine what times during the days of the week that the schedule should apply. By default, schedules exist for Weekends and Work Hours. When creating a rule, you can also specify a schedule as Always. These are the only three options available to choose for a schedule when you are creating a rule. Weekends are defined as all day Saturday and Sunday while Work Hours are defined as 9 A.M. to 5 P.M. Monday through Friday. If you want any other options, you will need to create a customized schedule.

Defined schedules can be viewed in the ISA Server snap-in under Policy Elements. Figure 6.5 shows what the hours look like when they are active. When a cell representing the hour is blue, that hour is active and applies to the schedule. When the hour is white, it is inactive and does not apply to the schedule.

To create new schedule, complete the following steps:

1. Open ISA Management.

2. Expand Internet Security And Acceleration Server for an enterprise-level schedule or an array for an array-level schedule.

3. Expand Policy Elements.

4. Right-click Schedules, point to New, and then click Schedule.

5. In the New Schedule dialog box, type the name of the new schedule.

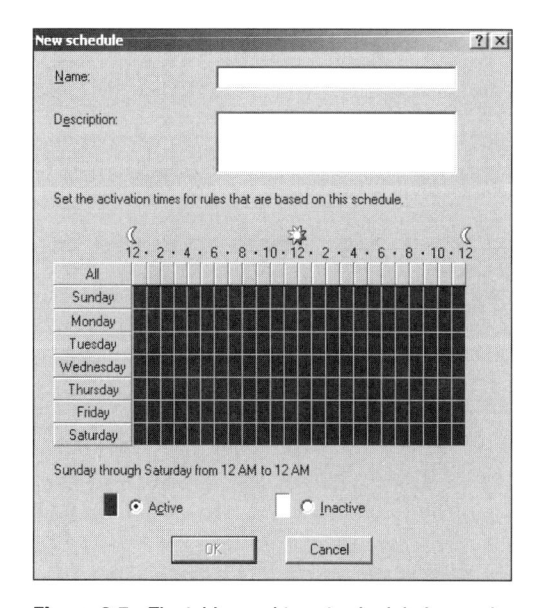

Figure 6.5 The table used to set schedule hours shows blue active cells that apply to the selected schedule or white inactive cells that do not apply to the selected schedule.

6. In the Description box, type a description for the new schedule.

7. In the table in the dialog box, all of the hours will be blue by default. Select hours during which the schedule should not be active.

8. Click the Inactive radio button to turn the cells white—which means they will not apply to the schedule.

9. Click OK to accept the new schedule.

Unlike many other default policy elements and rules, the default Work Hours and Weekends schedules can be modified. In the ISA Server snap-in, open Policy Elements and select the schedule that you would like to modify. A table of hours in the week will be displayed so that you can select and make active or inactive any of the hours.

Using Protocol Rules

Protocol rules allow or deny the use of protocol definitions. As discussed earlier in this chapter, protocol definitions are policy elements that can be defined in the ISA Server snap-in. Protocol rules apply to Firewall, Cache, and Integrated modes. In Cache mode, only the Web Proxy service is being used, which means only HTTP, HTTP-S, FTP, and Gopher protocols are being used. In Cache mode, protocol rules can be applied only to these four protocols.

By default, ISA Server creates an open site and content rule that allows access to all contents on all sites. No access is allowed to external sites because protocol rules are processed first and there is no default protocol rule. In fact, no protocol rules are created during the installation of ISA Server. In order for any access to be allowed, a protocol rule must be defined that specifically allows that access.

Creating Protocol Rules

A wizard in the ISA Server snap-in creates protocol rules. To create a protocol rule, complete the following steps:

1. Open ISA Management.

2. Expand Internet Security And Acceleration Server for enterprise-level protocol rules or an array for array-level protocol rules.

3. Expand Enterprise Policy for enterprise-level protocol rules and Access Policy for array-level protocol rules.

4. Right-click Protocol Rules.

5. Point to New and select Rule. The New Protocol Rule Wizard will start.

6. In the first dialog box, type the name of the new protocol rule. Click Next.

7. In the Rule Action dialog box, select whether the rule will allow or deny clients the use of a protocol. Click Next.

8. In the Protocols dialog box, select the type of traffic or protocol definition to which this rule will apply. Click Next.

9. In the Schedule dialog box, select when the protocol rule will apply. Click Next.

10. In the Client Type dialog box, select the client types that the protocol rule will apply to. You may need to select and/or define client IP address sets or users and/or groups. Click Next.

11. Review the summary of information and click Finish. You can use the Back button to change incorrect information.

Even though the wizard leads you through the steps of creating a protocol rule, it is still important to understand what each step does and how it should be handled to enter the right settings. The first step of the wizard allows an administrator to name the protocol rule. This name should be descriptive so that it is easy to remember what you intended to use it for, and you can pick it out when looking at a list of protocol rules.

The next two steps keep the use of protocol rules very flexible. The second step of the New Protocol Rule Wizard will let you choose whether the protocol rule will accept or deny the use of a protocol. Before reaching this step, you should do some careful planning as to how this protocol rule will work and how it will fit into the larger picture of the policy. Protocol rules allow a flexible combination of settings by letting you to allow or deny access to groups defined by protocol definitions. A protocol rule permits the rule to not only allow or deny a protocol definition, but also to allow or deny all requests except those defined by a specified protocol definition. This gives a great degree of flexibility to an administrator. By permitting you to create your own protocol definitions and choose how those protocol definitions will be applied, the ISA Server snap-in gives you the ability to make the protocol rule exactly what is needed.

The next step in the New Protocol Rule Wizard is the Schedule dialog box. This step allows an administrator to choose whether the rule will be applied Always, Weekends, or Work Hours. This allows you to apply different rules during different parts of the week. A predefined customized schedule can be selected instead of the default ones during this step.

The next step is the Client Type dialog box. This dialog box specifies users and/or computers to which this protocol rule will apply. You can choose from three different possibilities: Any User, Group, Or Client Computer is the first choice, followed by Specific Computers (Client Address Sets), and Specific Users And

Groups. If Specific Computers (Client Address Sets) is selected, you must define the client address sets.

If you select Specific Users And Groups, you will be able to select from user and group accounts that are on the local computer for standalone ISA servers or in Active Directory for an array. These user or group accounts must be created ahead of time and cannot be created using the wizard.

After selecting the client types and clicking Next, you can review the choices made during the wizard. When you click the Finish button, the protocol rule is created.

Protocol Rule Order

Protocol rules cannot be put into any kind of order. Like the rest of the rules in ISA Server, protocol rules that deny are applied before those that allow. For example, if a protocol rule denies the use of HTTP by all computers, then another rule that allows the use of HTTP for a certain group of computers will be denied. This is the only order of application that protocol rules use. Individual protocol rules are independent from the rest and are applied in no order.

Site and Content Rules

Site and content rules can specify the times that sites can be accessed, groups of users or computers that can use a connection, and/or a specified group of Web sites. Basically, they decide who can connect to what and when they can or cannot make these connections. Because they have a lot of possible settings, some site and content rules need elements to be configured ahead of time. These elements include client address sets, groups, and destination sets. Client address sets are the only elements that you can configure while creating a site and content rule. If you need to specify a destination set or a group or user account, you must create these ahead of time before starting the Site And Content Rule Wizard.

How Site and Content Rules Are Applied

When a request comes into ISA Server, first the protocol rule is applied. Then, just as with other rules, ISA Server checks the site and protocol rules to see if the site is specifically denied. It next checks to see if the site is specifically allowed. A site must not be denied and must be explicitly allowed in order for the request to be allowed. Site and content rules apply to Firewall, Cache, and Integrated modes.

Site and content rules contained in an enterprise policy that deny access to a site cannot be overridden in an array-level site and content rule. Like all other rules, site and content rules at the array level can allow only what has not been explicitly denied at the enterprise level. By default, an array-level site and content rule is created that allows access to all sites.

Creating Site and Content Rules

A wizard that is very similar to the New Protocol Rule Wizard creates site and content rules. Some of the same configurations, such as actions, client address sets, and schedules, are used in both protocol rules and site and content rules. The Rule Action dialog box lets the administrator decide whether the rule will allow or deny access.

Because site and content rules are part of policies at the enterprise and array levels, they can be configured in two separate places in the ISA Server snap-in. But once started, the wizard looks the same for enterprise- and array-level site and content rules. The Site And Content Rule Wizard is different from the New Protocol Rule Wizard in that it assumes that an administrator usually wants to set only one type of configuration of the site and content rule and will accept the defaults for the rest.

To create a new site and content rule, complete the following steps:

1. Open ISA Management.

2. Expand Internet Security And Acceleration Server for enterprise-level site and content rules or an array for array-level site and content rules.

3. Expand Enterprise Policy for enterprise-level site and content rules and an array name for array-level site and content rules.

4. Right-click Site And Content Rules.

5. Point to New and select Rule. The New Site And Content Rule Wizard will start.

6. In the first dialog box, type in the name of the new site and content rule. Click Next.

7. In the Rule Action dialog box, select whether the rule will allow or deny clients access to sites. If Deny is selected, you can also specify a URL that users should be redirected to when they are not allowed to connect to their requested URL. This redirected URL should specify a Web page on an internal Web server that explains what has happened to the user. Once you make your selection, click Next.

8. In the Rule Configuration dialog box, select the set of sites, users, or schedule to which this rule will apply. This choice will determine the rest of the dialog boxes that will appear during the wizard. The Custom choice in the Rule configuration dialog box runs you through all of the choices. If Custom is not selected, then you need to choose whether you want the rule to control the Schedule, Client Type, or Destination Sets that the user can or cannot connect to. Click Next.

9. In the Schedule dialog box, select when the site and content rule will apply. Click Next.

10. In the Client Type dialog box, select the client types that the protocol rule will apply to. You may need to select and/or define client IP address sets or users and/or groups. Click Next.

11. Review the summary of information and click Finish. You can use the Back button to change incorrect information.

The first two dialog boxes of the New Site And Content Rule Wizard look just like the New Protocol Rule Wizard. The first dialog box welcomes you to the New Site And Content Rule Wizard and allows you to name the new rule you are creating. The next dialog box, the Action dialog box, lets you specify whether the rule will allow or deny access. A site and content rule that denies access can also specify that users will be redirected to another Web page. Figure 6.6 shows this dialog box and the place where you can enter a URL for the Web page. The point of redirecting users is to give them a Web page that will explain that they have been denied access because of the policies that are set in ISA Server. You will need to create this customized Web page and place it on an internal Web server.

After you click Next in the Action dialog box in the New Site And Content Rule Wizard, the next step allows you to choose which criteria you will use to control access to Web sites. The choice that you make in this dialog box determines the behavior of the wizard during the rest of the creation of the site and content rule. This dialog box in the wizard is called the Rule Configuration dialog box. Figure 6.7 shows the Rule Configuration dialog box if you select Deny in the Action dialog box. If you select Allow, each selection would start with Allow

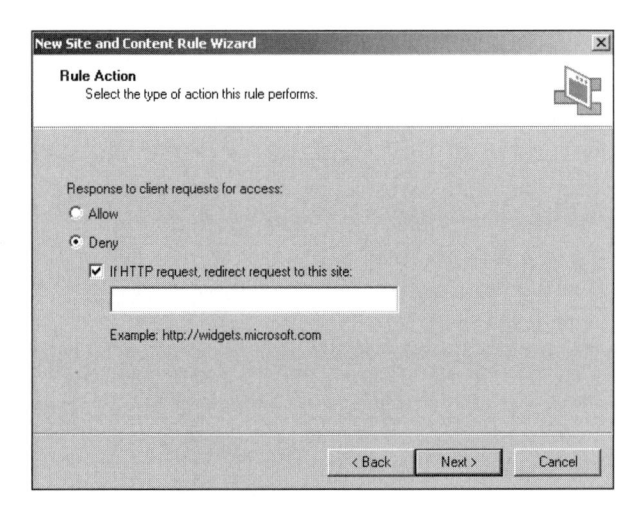

Figure 6.6 The Action dialog box allows you to specify a URL that users will be redirected to when they are denied access to a Web site.

[Figure 6.7 screenshot: New Site and Content Rule Wizard — Rule Configuration dialog with options: Deny access based on destination (selected); Deny access only at certain times; Deny selected clients access to all external sites; Custom.]

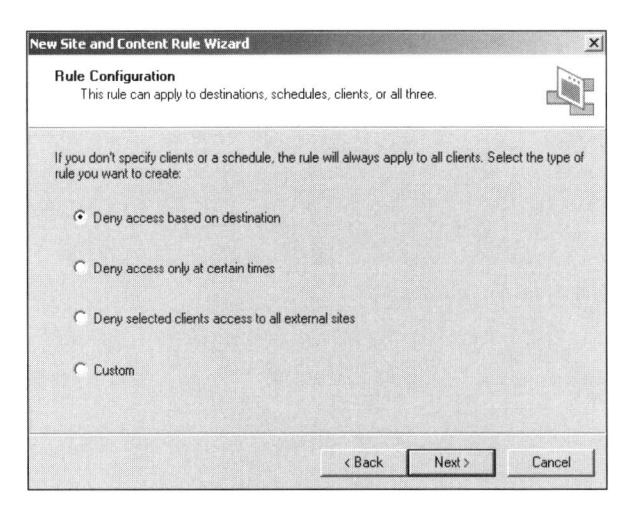

Figure 6.7 The Rule Configuration dialog box in the New Site And Content Rule Wizard allows you to decide which criteria will be applied to internal clients' requests for access to Web sites.

instead of Deny. This dialog box is where the site and content rule and protocol rule wizards differ. The New Protocol Rule Wizard gives an administrator a chance to configure all of the settings that the protocol rule can control while the New Site And Content Rule Wizard (for all except the Custom choice) allows only one possible setting to be configured. If you select the first choice, the next dialog boxes in the wizard will allow you to select destination sets that the rule will use. If you select the second choice, the next dialog boxes will allow you to configure a schedule for the rule. The default choices for a schedule are Always, Weekends, and Work Hours, just like they are in the New Protocol Rule Wizard.

Selecting the third choice will open a series of dialog boxes starting with the Client Type dialog box. These dialog boxes allow you to choose users or groups to which the rule will apply. They work just like the Client Type dialog boxes in the New Protocol Rule Wizard. Because each choice can lead to different dialog boxes and allow you to configure different settings, the wizard needs a method for configuring settings that do not get set during the wizard. Because a site and content rule uses all of the settings, the wizard will accept the default configurations for the rest of the settings in the rule. Table 6.3 shows the default settings that will be set for a

Table 6.3 Default settings for site and content rules.

Dialog box	Default setting
Destination Sets	All Destination Sets
Schedule	Always
Client Type	Any User, Group, Or Computer
Content Type	Any Content Type

for a site and content rule for each configuration that is not set during the wizard. The only way you can set more than one of these choices is to select the fourth choice, Custom, in the Rule Configuration dialog box.

Packet Filters

Array-level access policies include site and content rules, protocol rules, and packet filters. Packet filters do not hold the same importance in ISA Server that they held in Microsoft's Proxy Server. Packet filters were the main method of controlling access for both incoming and outgoing connections, but now you have many other ways to control access for connections. Because ISA Server uses site and content as well as protocol rules and denies access to connections that have not been specifically allowed in these rules, packet filters just do not have the same importance they had before.

Packet Filters Before

ISA Server does not implement packet filters in the same way that Proxy Server does. In Proxy Server, packet filters could be dynamic or static. Dynamic packet filters kept a port closed until it was needed. For example, an outgoing HTTP request from the internal network would use port 80, but with a dynamic outgoing packet filter, port 80 would be closed until the request was received from the internal client. The port would be opened only to allow the request out. A static filter leaves a port open at all times. Because closed ports do not accept connections, a dynamic port is considered to be safer for a proxy or firewall server. In ISA Server, packet filters are only static. This is because site and content and protocol rules provide more flexibility than packet filters and should be used when possible.

Packet Filters Now

By default, packet filters are not enabled in ISA Server. They are not required or needed in many network configurations using ISA Server. The static packet filters that ISA Server implements are less flexible and secure than the dynamic filtering abilities of site and content rules and protocol rules. Also, packet filters can be implemented in ISA Server only when it is installed in Firewall or Integrated mode, whereas rules can be implemented on all installation modes available in ISA Server. Packet filter setup is found in the Array Policy container in ISA Server, but not at the enterprise level in the Enterprise Policy container. This means IP filters, if used, can be implemented at the array level or in a standalone ISA server only.

Packet filters need to be implemented only for certain services running either on or behind the ISA server, such as Web publishing or BackOffice products. Configuring packet filters for services in these situations are covered more thoroughly in Chapters 14 and 16.

Bandwidth Rules

Bandwidth on a network can be thought of as a piping system that carries water. One person can get water by tapping into the main pipe carrying the water. If more people put taps on that pipe, less water is available for each person. The pipe is a fixed diameter and can carry only a certain amount of water. More demand does not make the water flow any faster. Network bandwidth works in much the same way. Like a small pipe tapping into the main one, each connection feeds off the main and only a fixed amount of bandwidth can be divided up. Normally, each connection is treated equally. As traffic becomes heavy, each computer gets a smaller share of the available bandwidth. But not all traffic is equal. Some connections that are realtime and involve video or audio traffic need a consistent stream of bandwidth that will not be squeezed out by a busy network.

QoS

A TCP/IP network transfers packets using a "best effort" delivery system. Each packet is treated equally. Traffic on a network can fluctuate throughout the day, resulting in periods of low and high traffic. During high traffic times, this "best effort" delivery system starts to degrade. Some packets may be dropped, but the system has safeguards for this. Eventually, the packets will be re-sent and the message is completed. This system works well with file transfers, such as email messages and Web pages. But realtime applications, such as audio or video, are adversely affected by sudden changes in bandwidth. A sudden increase in traffic causes video to become jittery and audio to sound like it is skipping. Two-way conferencing applications are even more susceptible to these traffic fluxes. The idea behind Quality of Service (QoS) is to stop treating all connections equally and give priority to connections that need it. QoS allows an administrator to have control over the quality of service that connections are given.

Understanding the reasons why QoS was created is a lot easier than understanding the mechanics of how it is done. When implementing QoS, every connection is still treated equally unless the administrator assigns one a priority. A connection that has priority must use protocols to set a reservation for bandwidth from the receiving to the destination computer. If the connectivity devices (such as routers) on the network do not support QoS protocols, the reservation won't work.

Windows 2000 uses the Integrated Resource Reservation Protocol (RSVP) to make these reservations in QoS. Windows 2000 has a QoS Admission Control service and console that is the central control for QoS on a Windows 2000 network. Every computer that either sends or receives QoS packets on the network needs to have the Packet Scheduler installed on it.

QoS manages available bandwidth by prioritizing connections. The downside to using QoS is that a connection can take longer to establish. The upside is that once the connection is made, the bandwidth will remain constant. It is important to note that QoS cannot create bandwidth where it does not exist. If a connection is only 4Mbps, QoS can't increase that. What it will do is make sure that the bandwidth requested is not squeezed out by other services as the network becomes more active.

Bandwidth rules prioritize network connections. Using bandwidth rules, an administrator can allow some connections to receive a minimum of consistent bandwidth that will not be reduced even if the network becomes busy. Bandwidth rules work by giving priority and guaranteeing a minimum amount of bandwidth per connection. Bandwidth rules work with the Quality of Service (QoS) Scheduling service to provide information on which connections should get preference. The administrator has the flexibility to assign any number of criteria that qualify a connection to receive priority. Any service not assigned a bandwidth rule gets the default rule. An assigned bandwidth rule will always have priority over a service using the default rule.

When ISA Server is installed, it creates a default bandwidth rule. The default rule applies to all traffic passing through ISA Server. To create and order rules, you must understand the default rule. The default rule gives you a base rule on which you can build. The base rule applies to all traffic and gives no special priority to any connections. Any other rule you create will have priority over this base rule. This way, you can choose which connections will have priority. You can specify how a bandwidth rule will apply in several ways. Bandwidth rules can be assigned to any one of the following:

- Protocol
- IP address
- User
- Destination set
- Content type
- Schedule

Bandwidth Priorities

Bandwidth rules are complicated enough to include nearly all of the policy elements. Protocol definitions, content groups, client address sets, schedules, and destination sets can all be used in a bandwidth rule. One policy element that is included only in a bandwidth rule is a bandwidth priority. If a bandwidth policy will be used in the creation of a bandwidth rule, it, like other policy elements, needs to be created before starting the New Bandwidth Rule Wizard. Inbound and outbound connections can have different priorities assigned.

Bandwidth priorities policy elements allow an administrator to prioritize bandwidth rules. Like many policy elements, bandwidth priorities are set up in just one dialog box. The dialog box for creating a new bandwidth priority is shown in Figure 6.8. In this dialog box, you need to fill in a name for the bandwidth priority and enter a number from 1 to 200—the higher the number, the better the priority.

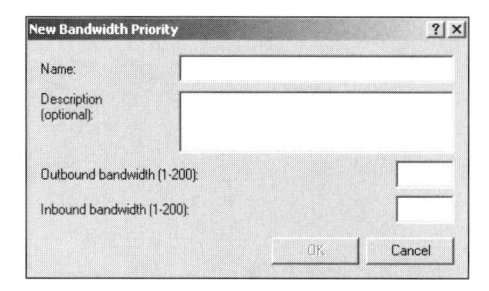

Figure 6.8 Fill in this dialog box to create a new bandwidth priority.

Priorities apply separately to inbound and outbound connections, so you can set a different priority for each. To create a new bandwidth priority, you need to expand an array in the ISA Server snap-in and expand Policy Elements. Right-click on Bandwidth Priority and select New, and then select Bandwidth Priority.

Creating and Configuring Bandwidth Rules

Bandwidth rules are created through a wizard. Because they have so much flexibility in the type of traffic that can apply to them, bandwidth rules have a long and detailed wizard. Protocol definitions, client address sets, and destination sets can all be used to specify traffic that will apply to the bandwidth rule. To create a new bandwidth rule, complete the following steps:

1. Open ISA Management.

2. Expand Servers And Arrays and then expand the array in which you want the bandwidth rule used.

3. Right-click on Bandwidth Rules. Point to New and then select Rule. This will start the New Bandwidth Rule Wizard.

4. In the first dialog box, type the name of the new bandwidth rule you are creating. Click Next.

5. In the Protocols step of the wizard, select the protocols this rule will apply to. If you do not select All IP Traffic, the next step will be to select the protocol definitions that should be used by this rule. If none of the protocol definitions work, stop the bandwidth rule wizard and create a new protocol definition first.

6. In the Schedule step, select whether the rule will apply Always or during Work Hours or Weekends.

7. In the Client Type step, select the clients the rule will apply to. If you select Specific Computers (Client Address Sets), the next step will be to specify the client address set that will apply. You can create the client address set in the

Bandwidth Rule Wizard. If you select Specific Users And Groups, you will need to specify which users and groups in the next step.

8. In the Destination Set step of the wizard, you have five choices. If you choose Specified Destination Set or All Destinations Except Selected Set, you will have to specify at least one destination set. Destination sets must be created before you start the Bandwidth Rule Wizard.

9. The Content Groups step of the wizard also uses preconfigured content groups. If a content group that you want to specify is not listed, you must create it before using the Bandwidth Rule Wizard.

10. The last selection that you need to make in the New Bandwidth Rule Wizard is priority. You can select the default priority or choose a previously created bandwidth priority.

11. The last dialog box of the wizard allows you to review your choices and use the Back button to make any changes. When you are ready to end the wizard and create the bandwidth rule, click the Finish button.

Now that you know how to create all of these rules, it is a good idea to organize the rules into a policy. This requires planning at the enterprise and array levels and then ordering the rules so that their desired effect is achieved.

Ordering Rules

Some rules in ISA Server can be ordered and some cannot. Besides setting priority for bandwidth rules, you can also order the rules to control how they are applied. Bandwidth rules are ordered based on their position in the list of bandwidth rules. Those listed at the top are processed before those listed at the bottom of the list. The first rule that applies to the connection is processed. So a connection that has more than one bandwidth rule that can apply will actually receive the priority of the first bandwidth rule that applies to it. This first rule will be applied and the connection that is needed will be made. Protocol rules as well as site and content rules cannot be ordered and are applied separately.

Disabling or Deleting Rules

Rules can also be deleted or disabled. If you delete a rule, it is gone forever and you will need to re-create it and its settings if you need it again. Disabling a rule allows it to be inactive and not apply to connections until you enable it again. By default, rules are enabled when you create them. If you need to do testing or don't need a rule for a period of time, disabling prevents you from having to re-create the rule later. If you look at the properties of any rule in the ISA Server snap-in, the General tab has an option that if checked enables the rule.

Planning Policies for a Network

Planning policies for a network involves using the structure of how policies work to your advantage. If you plan from the highest level of control down to the lowest, the process will be much easier. What is your highest level? If you have Active Directory with the ISA Server schema installed into it, you can have an enterprise-level policy. In a large environment, an enterprise policy is necessary for controlling Internet access without creating too much overhead. Without an enterprise-level policy, you must create an array-level policy for each array. An enterprise-level policy allows for more centralized control of security settings and less work on your part.

It helps to ask some specific questions when formulating a policy for use with ISA Server. We will discuss the need and purpose of each question over the next few pages.

- What is the corporate Internet use policy?
- What is the corporate Internet security policy?
- Will you implement a policy at the enterprise, array, or standalone level?
- Which settings do you want to control?
- Do you need to create policy elements?
- Do you need to create rules?
- Do you need to create test rules?

The Need for Paper Policies

If the answers to the first and second questions are no, then you need to stop and develop a policy. Some companies do not have policies on Internet use or how Internet security should be handled. Of course, some companies do have these policies, but no one knows about them or refers to them. If you are in charge of Internet security settings, it is a good idea to find out which of these situations applies to your company. If your company has these policies, you must follow them carefully while setting up rules and policies. If your company does not have these policies, you should start asking about creating some. With ISA Server, you can control who has access to the Internet, at what time, which sites they can access, and which applications they can use. If the policies are being developed, you may want to give a quick lesson on security and overhead. More rules on ISA Server means more overhead while it processes all of these rules. The overhead associated with extra security is acceptable if the added security is necessary. With the question of policies out of the way, more questions that help to refine a policy can be asked.

Will You Implement a Policy at the Enterprise, Array, or Standalone Level?

The answer to the third question depends on the size of the network you are working with. The larger the environment, the higher the level of control needed to simplify the administrator's job. A large multilocation or multisubnet network would be best suited to an enterprise policy. Policies and rules can be implemented at a high level and are automatically applied at the lower levels. A network that wants to allow each site to decide its own Internet usage can implement array policies. Because standalone servers have a local array policy they cannot share settings with other servers. A network without Windows 2000 Active Directory or that is still using Windows NT 4 or another type of directory services will have to install its ISA servers as standalone. Also, only the Enterprise Edition of ISA Server can be installed into an array. Arrays and enterprise-level policies make a large environment easier to handle and allow for growth. But if a network is not fully upgraded to Windows 2000 and using its directory services, a standalone ISA server may be necessary.

Which Settings Do You Want to Control?

Now, based on your research of corporate policies and needs of the users, you are ready to decide what type of access to allow. Whether you are planning a policy at the enterprise or array level, you must decide what will be allowed and denied so you can create these settings. Allow your enterprise and array policies to work together to create as few rules as possible. Another way to keep rules from canceling each other out is to use the order that rules are applied in. Although protocol rules and site and content rules have no order of application within each type of rule, there is an order to how rule types apply. Rules are applied in the following order:

1. Protocol rules
2. Site and content rules
3. Packet filters
4. Routing rules

Do You Need to Create Policy Elements?

Most policy elements that are customized need to be created before the rules they are used in. Find out what policy elements can be used in a rule before creating the rule. Often, policy elements simplify the creation of a rule by allowing you to group entities together. Then you can apply one rule to the group instead of having to create more than one rule. When planning and creating policy elements, remember that you will be able to reuse them in different types of rules.

Creating and Testing Rules

These last questions ensure that the rules are working the way you intended. ISA Server rules are applied in a very regimented way: Deny rules are applied before allow rules; an action denied at the enterprise level cannot later be allowed at the array level; and protocol rules can't be ordered, because all protocol rules will apply before a single site and content rule is applied. These are just a few examples of the regimented way that rules apply. If you miscalculate or forget any of the tenets, the rule may not have the desired effect.

Once your planning is complete, the only thing left to do is to modify or create a new policy. At the array level, only one policy is allowed per array. However, at the enterprise level, multiple policies can be created. Multiple enterprise policies can allow an administrator to apply different enterprise policies to different arrays. One enterprise-level policy will be selected as the default policy that will apply to all arrays unless changed by the administrator.

Creating Enterprise Policies with Enterprise-Level Rules

Before creating an enterprise-level policy, you need to define any custom enterprise-level policy elements. Also, enterprise-level policies contain only protocol rules and site and content rules. Bandwidth and other Web publishing rules that you will learn about later in this book are defined at the array level only. You can make changes to the default enterprise policy or create and apply a different enterprise policy. If one base enterprise policy does not work for a large network, different enterprise policies can be created and applied to different arrays.

At both the enterprise and array levels, policies are created the same way. Enterprise-level policies consist of site and content rules and protocol rules. Each enterprise-level policy has subfolders labeled Site And Content Rules and Protocol Rules. Because you can create more than one enterprise-level policy, the wizard allows you to copy the settings of another enterprise-level policy. This will allow you to use previously configured enterprise-level site and content rules and protocol rules. After you copy these settings, you can modify them to fit the new policy you want to create. To create a new enterprise-level policy, complete the following steps:

1. Open ISA Management.
2. Expand Internet Security And Acceleration Server.
3. Expand Policies.
4. Right-click Policies. Point to New and select Rule. The New Enterprise Policy Wizard Rule will start.

5. In the first dialog box, type the name of the new enterprise policy. Click Next.

6. In the Create Or Copy A Policy dialog box, select Create A New Policy or Copy This Policy. Then, type the name of another policy that you want to create. Copy This Policy is not available if you have only the default enterprise policy and have not created any others. Once you make your selection, click Next.

7. Review the summary of information and click Finish. You can use the Back button to change incorrect information.

Creating a new enterprise policy creates a container that contains Site And Content Rules and Protocol Rules folders. If you create a new policy, you will now need to set up both of these types of rules for users to have access to any sites.

Backing Up and Restoring Policy Settings

Once all of the elements, rules, and policies have been configured, enterprise and array policy settings can be backed up so that they do not have to be reconfigured. Policy settings can be saved into a file that can be used later to restore them. Using the Back Up utility in the ISA Server snap-in, both enterprise and array policy settings can be saved to files. Configuration information is saved into a .bif file. Separate files are created for enterprise- and array-level configurations. Using the Restore utility, the configuration settings can be read from the files and restored.

To back up enterprise or array settings, complete the following steps:

1. Open ISA Management.

2. Expand Internet Security And Acceleration Server to back up enterprise policies and Servers And Arrays for an array-level policy.

3. Right-click the policy that you want to back up for an enterprise-level policy or on the array for an array-level policy and select Back Up.

4. The dialog box that appears will allow you to enter a path that the file will be saved to and a description of the backup. Be sure to include the name of the file in the path; a .bif extension will be added to it.

5. Click on the OK button to create the backup file. A dialog box will appear stating that the configuration settings have been backed up.

To restore policy settings, complete the following steps:

1. Open ISA Management.

2. Expand Internet Security And Acceleration Server to restore an enterprise policy or expand Servers And Arrays to restore an array-level policy.

3. Right-click the policy that you want to restore and select Restore.

4. In the Restore dialog box, enter the path, including the filename of the backup file.

5. Click OK to restore the configuration settings from the file.

Chapter Summary

A large part of ISA Server administration is establishing control over the traffic coming into and out of the internal network. ISA Server provides such a range of options and settings for control that they can seem overwhelming when you are trying to get a grasp on them. The easiest method to use when reviewing the options is to break them down into rules, policies, and policy elements.

Policy elements allow you to organize just about anything related to security into manageable groups. Policy elements exist for destinations on the Web, groups of computers, times of day, bandwidth priorities, and even protocols. The purpose of organizing groups is to use that group in a rule. The rule will define the behavior that the group will be allowed or restricted from doing. Before you can create a rule, you must first decide what or who the rule will apply to. These groups that you will apply the rules to are organized into policy elements.

Rules are not difficult to understand. The purpose of a rule is to define specifically what behavior is allowed and what behavior is denied. ISA Server searches and follows rules automatically. It searches for two conditions when a request for access comes in. First, it looks to see if the action is specifically denied. If it is, then it looks no further. Note that if an action is not denied, ISA Server will continue to search for a rule that specifically allows the action. Two conditions must be met before the request for the action is approved and allowed past ISA Server: There cannot be a rule that specifically denies the action, and there must be a rule that allows the action.

Policies simplify the organization and application of rules by grouping rules together and organizing a hierarchy. Of the rules discussed in this chapter, only bandwidth rules may be given an order. Policies bring order to the way rules are applied. There are two levels of policies: enterprise and array.

Enterprise-level policies allow an administrator to create settings that apply to the entire enterprise network. Array policies cannot allow what an enterprise policy has denied. This rule means that careful planning for an enterprise policy is very important. In order to implement an enterprise policy, many prerequisites must be met, including having the proper version of ISA Server installed and having a Windows 2000 Active Directory installed on the network. If there is no enterprise-level policy, array policies can be created. The rules in the policy will automatically apply to each member of an array.

Once policies have been created and applied, the configuration information contained in them should be backed up so that they are not lost. ISA Server comes with the ability to back up configuration information, including policy information, in .bif files. These files can be used to restore the configuration information on a new install of ISA Server if the original is not retrievable.

Not all rule types are covered in this chapter. The focus of the chapter is on rules that are part of a policy and rules that mainly apply to outbound connections. Rules that apply to publishing are covered in Chapter 12.

Review Questions

1. What is a policy?
    a. A collection of rules and elements
    b. A collection of ISA servers
    c. A collection of ISA clients
    d. Individual settings to control access to ISA Server

2. What types of policies are available for use with ISA Server? [Check all correct answers]
    a. Server policy
    b. Domain policy
    c. Array policy
    d. Network policy
    e. Enterprise policy

3. An action denied in what type of policy will override an action allowed in any other type of policy?
    a. Server policy
    b. Domain policy
    c. Array policy
    d. Network policy
    e. Enterprise policy

4. No policies are created by default in ISA Server.
   a. True
   b. False

5. By default, ISA Server allows all connections to the Internet.
   a. True
   b. False

6. What are the preconditions that must be met before an enterprise policy can be used? [Check all correct answers]
   a. Enterprise Edition of ISA Server
   b. NT 4 Domain environment
   c. Windows 2000 domain environment
   d. ISA Server schema installed in Active Directory
   e. Standalone ISA servers
   f. ISA servers installed in an array

7. When a policy is applied, which rules apply first?
   a. Rules that deny access
   b. Rules that allow access
   c. Site and content rules
   d. Protocol rules

8. Which rules are not a part of an enterprise policy? [Check all correct answers]
   a. Packet filters
   b. Site and content rules
   c. Bandwidth rules
   d. Protocol rules

9. A protocol definition is a policy element that is used in which rules? [Check all correct answers]
   a. Packet filters
   b. Site and content rules
   c. Bandwidth rules
   d. Protocol rules

10. A bandwidth priority is a policy element that is used in which rules?

    a. Packet filters

    b. Site and content rules

    c. Bandwidth rules

    d. Protocol rules

11. A content group is a policy element that is used in which rules? [Check all correct answers]

    a. Packet filters

    b. Site and content rules

    c. Bandwidth rules

    d. Protocol rules

12. A destination set is a policy element that is used in which rules? [Check all correct answers]

    a. Packet filters

    b. Site and content rules

    c. Bandwidth rules

    d. Protocol rules

13. Which settings are included in a protocol definition?

    a. Transport Layer protocol

    b. Port number

    c. Direction of connection

    d. Protocol name

14. Client address sets allow an administrator to group what together?

    a. Computer names

    b. Usernames

    c. IP addresses

    d. Protocols

15. When you want to define a group of users to be used in a rule for an enterprise policy, what application do you need to use?

    a. Active Directory Users And Groups

    b. ISA Administrator–Content Group policy element

    c. Computer Management–Local Users And Groups

    d. ISA Administrator–Client Address Sets policy element

16. Bandwidth priority can be set between which numbers?
    a. 1 and 100
    b. 0 and 100
    c. 1 and 200
    d. 0 and 200

17. What does MIME stand for?
    a. Multipurpose Internet Microsoft Elements
    b. Multipurpose Internet Modification Elements
    c. Multipurpose Internet Mail Extensions
    d. Multipurpose Internet Media Extensions

18. Which QoS component do bandwidth rules work with?
    a. Integrated Resource Reservation Protocol
    b. QoS Scheduling service
    c. QoS Admission Control
    d. QoS Bandwidth Manager

19. Internet applications that provide what types of services are best served by using bandwidth rules? [Check all correct answers]
    a. Audio
    b. File
    c. Video
    d. Conferencing
    e. All services need a bandwidth rule.

20. Which kind of packet filters are provided by ISA Server?
    a. Static
    b. Dynamic

21. Packet filters have what role in ISA Server compared with Proxy Server 2.0?
    a. More important
    b. Less important
    c. More complicated
    d. Less complicated

22. Which types of rules can be ordered?
    a. Site and content rules
    b. Protocol rules
    c. Packet filters
    d. Bandwidth rules

23. What file extension is used for a file that backs up policy settings?
    a. .bak
    b. .doc
    c. .bku
    d. .bif
    e. .bfi

24. Which type of policy can be backed up? [Check all correct answers]
    a. Server
    b. Domain
    c. Array
    d. Network
    e. Enterprise

Real-World Projects

Note: This exercise assumes a test Windows 2000 Server with Service Pack 1 installed and a new install of the ISA Server. Read the instructions carefully and do not change the settings on your production machine unless you understand the options presented. If you are unsure about an option, do not make a change and instead read the ISA Server help files about the option to be installed.

Finally Rachel was ready to start allowing access to external Internet sites for the clients in the network. Rachel had just installed the new ISA servers and was ready to plan and create new rules and policies that would allow users to access external sites on the Internet.

Rachel's company was a direct mail marketing company that set up mass-mail advertising campaigns for other businesses. Mailbox Stuffers had been in business for 10 years and had waited about that long to upgrade their computer equipment. It had been a long, arduous upgrade from a few DOS-based PCs to a fully integrated Windows 2000 network. A Windows 2000 domain environment had been established with 1,250 client machines.

The company was divided into teams of people who sold and implemented direct mail campaigns for businesses. These employees needed quick access to business sites so that they could research an approach for the salespeople. After a sale was made, a direct mail campaign needed to be planned and implemented on schedule. A lot of information had to travel between Mailbox Stuffers and the companies they did business with. Currently, these documents traveled back and forth by way of an express mail carrier. The hope was to set up Web sites from which information could be shared between the companies. But for now, plain-old Internet access would be very helpful to the employees.

The first thing that Rachel needed to do was plan how she wanted security to work. Instead of working in a vacuum making up rules, Rachel looked for direction from company policies. Based on her recommendations, the company had recently established security policies for paper and electronic documents. The company had also recently defined a new policy outlining the do's and don'ts of Internet usage during work hours. Rachel had sent out a survey for users to describe their need for Internet connectivity and how much they expected to use it during the day. Armed with this information, Rachel was able to create a grid (shown in Table 6.4) that allowed her to plan the rules and policies she would need to create to meet the demand of her users.

Based on Rachel's findings, users did research at all times of the day and needed access to any site at all times to complete their work. Also, bandwidth was still a bit limited at the company, so salespeople needed priority to provide the quickest responses to their clients. This quick response time was needed only during work hours, so a schedule had to be included in the bandwidth rule. Because salespeople could work odd hours, Rachel decided to extend the default Work Hours schedule to 6:00 a.m. through 7:00 p.m. on weekdays.

Rachel had already installed the ISA Server schema in Active Directory, but she did not need an enterprise-level policy at this time. She also had installed three ISA servers into the same array. She needed to set up an array-level policy. Rachel began by setting up the policy elements first, then the array-level rules.

Table 6.4 Rules needed to meet user demand.

Need	Applicable rule
Access to all sites	Default site and content rule
Access using HTTP only	Customized protocol rule
Bandwidth priority for salespeople	Bandwidth priority in a bandwidth rule

Project 6.1

To modify the default Work Hours schedule:

1. Open ISA Management.

2. Expand an array for an array-level schedule.

3. Expand Policy Elements.

4. Select Schedules.

5. In the details pane, right-click the Work Hours schedule and select Properties.

6. Click on the Schedules tab to view the hours for the Work Hours Schedule.

7. In the table in the dialog box, select the hours from 6:00 A.M. to 9:00 A.M and click Active. The hours will turn blue.

8. In the table in the dialog box, select the hours from 5:00 P.M. to 7:00 P.M. and click Active. The hours will turn blue.

9. Click OK to accept the changes to the Work Hours Schedule.

Next, Rachel needed to create a bandwidth priority for salespeople.

Project 6.2

To create a new bandwidth priority:

1. Open ISA Management.

2. Expand an array for array-level bandwidth priorities.

3. Expand Policy Elements.

4. Right-click Bandwidth Priorities. Then, point to New and click on Bandwidth Priority.

5. Give the bandwidth priority a descriptive name.

6. Fill in a description that describes why the bandwidth priority needs to be created.

7. To give priority to outbound connections, type a number from 1 to 200.

8. To give priority to inbound connections, type a number from 1 to 200.

9. Click OK to create the new bandwidth priority.

Rachel named her new bandwidth priority Sales and gave it a priority of 10 for only outbound connections. Currently, no other bandwidth priorities were being used, so a little bump should be enough for the salespeople to get priority over other connections. Now she needed to use this new bandwidth priority in a new bandwidth rule.

Project 6.3

To create a new bandwidth rule:

1. Open ISA Management.

2. Expand the Arrays and then expand the array in which you want the bandwidth rule used.

3. Right-click on Bandwidth Rules. Point to New and then select Rule. This will start the New Bandwidth Rule Wizard.

4. In the first dialog box, type the name of the new bandwidth rule you are creating. Click Next.

5. In the Protocols step of the wizard, select the protocols this rule will apply to. If you do not select All IP Traffic, the next step will be to select the protocol definitions that should be used by this rule. If none of the protocol definitions work, you need to stop the Bandwidth Rule Wizard and create a new protocol definition first.

6. In the Schedule step, select the schedule that the rule will apply to. Click Next.

7. In the Client Type step, select the clients the rule will apply to. Click Next.

8. In the Destination Set step of the wizard, you have five choices. After you make your choice, click Next.

9. The Content Groups step of the wizard also uses preconfigured content groups. Select the appropriate group and click Next.

10. Select either the default bandwidth priority or a specific bandwidth priority that you created. Click Next.

11. The last dialog box of the wizard allows you to review your choices and use the Back button to make any changes. When you are ready to end the wizard and create the bandwidth rule, click the Finish button.

Rachel was able to use the default settings for the bandwidth rules for all except three of the dialog boxes. In the Schedule dialog box, she selected Work Hours to use the schedule that she had modified for this rule. In the Client Type dialog box, she selected Specific Users And Groups and then selected the Sales group from the groups defined in Active Directory Users And Groups. In addition, in the Bandwidth Priority dialog box, she selected the Sales bandwidth priority that she had created before.

Now Rachel was ready to create an HTTP protocol rule that would allow the users in her internal network to access Web sites with HTTP requests. An HTTP protocol definition already existed, so she was ready to start.

Project 6.4
To create an HTTP protocol rule:

1. Open ISA Management.
2. Expand an array for array-level protocol rules.
3. Expand Access Policy for array-level protocol rules.
4. Right-click Protocol Rules.
5. Point to New and select Rule. The New Protocol Rule Wizard will start.
6. In the first dialog box, type the name of the new protocol rule. Click Next.
7. In the Rule Action dialog box, select whether the rule will allow or deny clients use of a protocol. Click Next.
8. In the Protocols dialog box, select the type of traffic or protocol definition to which this rule will apply. Click Next.
9. In the Schedule dialog box, select when the protocol rule will apply. Click Next.
10. In the Client Type dialog box, select the client types that the protocol rule will apply to. You may need to select and/or define client IP address sets or users and/or groups. Click Next.
11. Review the summary of information and click Finish. You can use the Back button to change incorrect information.

Rachel named the protocol rule HTTP and made it an Allow rule. Next, she selected the predefined HTTP protocol definition and then accepted the defaults for the rest of the wizard.

CHAPTER SEVEN

Authentication

After completing this chapter, you will be able to:

✓ Describe authentication

✓ Discuss the pros and cons of authentication

✓ Explain the use of Basic Authentication

✓ Differentiate other authentication types from Digest Authentication

✓ Discuss Windows Integrated Authentication

✓ Set up authentication with certificates

✓ Set up the different types of authentication supported by ISA Server

✓ Add SSL to the authentication process

✓ Use pass-through authentication

✓ Describe chained authentication

✓ Combine rules and authentication

Authentication requires users to provide credentials before they can connect to a destination server on the Internet. Although authentication is not used on most sites on the Internet, sometimes it is necessary for security reasons. ISA Server provides four different methods by which authentication can be done. Some have higher security while others are more compatible with clients. Authentication standards are not as advanced as some other types of standards so many methods are still proprietary. Because of this, compatibility is often an issue when deciding which authentication method to use. In this chapter, we will cover the authentication methods available in ISA Server and the uses and setup for each.

Why Use Authentication?

HTTP and FTP require authentication as part of their protocol design. However, most Web sites and FTP sites are for public use, so users are allowed to authenticate with an anonymous user account. They do not have to give their actual user account or password information. User account information is extremely sensitive, and most companies that issue this information want it to be protected. Some Internet sites do require authentication if they have sensitive information that should be distributed to a select group of users only. Because user account information is so sensitive, most authentication methods are designed to encrypt and protect this information. You should use authentication only if the risk of unauthorized users accessing the information outweighs the risk of usernames and passwords being transmitted over the Internet.

Types of Authentication

ISA Server uses the same authentication methods as Microsoft's Web server, Internet Information Server (IIS). Although authentication methods have changed recently in IIS, the most current versions of 5.0 and 6.0 (IIS 6.0 is a component of Windows XP Server) use the same four authentication methods as ISA Server, because an ISA server is placed between a client making a request and a Web server receiving the request. ISA Server must understand and work with the authentication methods that the clients and servers may pass between them over the Internet. The four methods used by Microsoft Internet connection products are Basic Authentication, Digest Authentication, Integrated Windows Authentication, and authentication with certificates.

Basic Authentication

Usernames and passwords sent with Basic Authentication are not encrypted, which means that they can be captured and read by another person. If you want to be really picky about it, the messages aren't actually sent in a manner that makes them easily human readable because they are encoded.

Encryption vs. Encoding

Do not confuse encryption and encoding, because there is a huge difference between them. Encryption renders a message that cannot easily be read by another person who does not have the key; encoding makes the messages easily computer readable. Encoding is not done to provide security, but to make sure the message is universally readable by all computers. Simply put, encoding takes data that may contain special characters and converts it to a language all computers understand, American Standard Code for Information Interchange (ASCII). Many of the applications used on the Internet were first designed to send only text. Encoding was created so that all universally understood characters in a message would be converted to characters before transmission.

There are different methods used to encode text. Basic Authentication uses the Base64 method, which was first used to encode MIME attachments to email. Any MIME-compliant application, including Internet Explorer and Netscape browsers, can convert encoded messages. You can buy encoders separately so that you can run encoded messages through them and easily decode the message.

When you attempt to set up Basic Authentication as your authentication method in ISA Server, you will receive a message stating that it is not safe. Figure 7.1 shows this message. After reading the descriptions and inevitable warnings about Basic Authentication, you may wonder why it is even included as an option. There is one main reason: Basic Authentication is part of the specification for HTTP. Basic Authentication is described in Request For Comment (RFC) 1945, which describes the HTTP protocol in version 1.0.

Even the original designers of HTTP Basic Authentication know that it is not very useful for security and describe it as a "non-secure method" of authentication. In RFC 1945, the author suggests that other methods be used to provide security to connections using Basic Authentication. If you need to use Basic Authentication for compatibility reasons, you should encrypt the entire connection using Secure Sockets Layer (SSL) or other methods of establishing a secure channel, like a Virtual Private Network. Even though Basic Authentication is part of the HTTP 1.0 standard, a new standard is proposed for the current version of HTTP, which is 1.1. The new standard is called Digest Authentication, but the HTTP 1.1 standard for Digest Authentication is not the same as the Digest Authentication used by ISA Server.

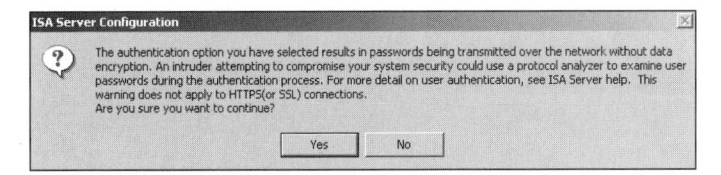

Figure 7.1 Information message from ISA Server warning that Basic Authentication can allow others to capture and read password information.

Digest Authentication

Digest Authentication gets its name because it uses hashing to secure the authentication process. The username is sent from the client to the server, but the client does not send the password. Instead, the client will perform a calculation on the password using a hash function. The calculation results in a string of text and is called a *message digest*, or *hash*. Instead of sending the password along with the username, the client will send the message digest. The server will receive the username and message digest. Using the same hashing algorithm, the server will perform the hash function calculation on the password that belongs to the username it received. If the password at the client is the same as the password on the server, then the message digest that the server calculates will be identical to the message digest sent by the client.

Digest Authentication in ISA Server uses Windows 2000 Active Directory to get its username and password information. This means that ISA Server's Digest Authentication requires a Windows 2000 domain environment.

Hashing

Encryption of a document makes it very safe, but it also places a large amount of overhead on the connection to it. Extra packets must be passed between two computers establishing an encrypted connection—and this is just to begin. Also, encrypting and decrypting documents is costly in terms of time and processing power. For the purpose of authentication, one alternative is digital hashing. A method of checking a small amount of fixed, yet sensitive, data was needed to authenticate the identity of a user. When a one-way hash is performed, the resulting output created is known as a *message digest*. Instead of sending the password over the network, the sending computer will send the message digest. The receiving computer will perform the calculation on the data and should come up with an identical message digest of the data.

Step by step, here is how hashing works:

1. The computer performs a calculation on the original text or document. This calculation is done with a hashing algorithm. The result of the calculation is called a message digest, or hash.
2. The message digest is sent to the receiving computer.
3. The receiving computer performs the same calculation on its copy of the data.
4. If the message digest matches, then the authentication is confirmed.

But what if someone is capturing the packets between these two computers. Can't that person simply steal the message digest and break into a network even if they don't actually know the password? To make sure no one else can capture and send the message digest, a hashing algorithm will include some random numbers and a timestamp in its calculation. Just the small change of the timestamp will result in an entirely different message digest. So a message digest is unique for every connection. It is important to realize that the original message, such as a password, is not contained in the message digest, so it is not possible to extract the original message from the message digest. Hashing is best used for authentication because it allows a user's identity to be confirmed without compromising the sensitive data used to confirm that identity.

Integrated Windows Authentication

Integrated Windows Authentication is an upgraded version of Windows NT Challenge/Response authentication. Windows NT Challenge/Response uses NT LAN Manager (NTLM) as its security protocol. Starting with Windows 2000, Kerberos v5 is also available. The authentication protocol is negotiated between the client and server when setting up an Integrated Windows Authentication connection. Part of this negotiation will be deciding what is the highest authentication protocol understood by the ends establishing the communication channel. NTLM is still a choice for down-level clients, such as browsers running on Windows NT 4. Kerberos also requires a Windows 2000 domain environment, so a Windows 2000 ISA server that does not belong to a domain will also need to use NTLM as its authentication protocol when using Integrated Windows Authentication.

Kerberos

The Kerberos protocol is named after a character in Greek mythology, the three-headed dog who guarded the gates of Hades, the underworld. The developers likened the protocol to the three-headed dog because the system run by the Kerberos protocol requires three pieces: a client, a server, and a Key Distribution Center (KDC). (Actually, more than three components are needed, but making this point ruins the great name that Kerberos has and the story behind it!) The client is the sender of the message, the server is the receiver, and the KDC is the go-between.

The KDC does what it is named for: It distributes keys used for encrypting and decrypting messages. The most secure methods of encryption use a different encryption key for every connection. This kind of key is called a *session key* because it is used for one session only and then discarded. The KDC hands out session keys for the clients and servers to use to encrypt messages they send to each other. The KDC is a needed component to control the distribution of new keys because new keys are constantly required to keep the system secure.

Kerberos is secure because it uses a fairly complicated system to ensure that the right keys are distributed only to those that need them. Remember the point of this complicated-sounding system is so the client and server receive a different session key every time they want to communicate. If a key falls into the wrong hands, then the security of the system is blown. So the system seems like an endless loop of different keys and encrypted messages sealed in other encrypted messages.

Step by step, here is how Kerberos key distribution works:

1. The client and the KDC share a key that they use to encrypt messages to each other.

2. The server and KDC share a key that they use to encrypt messages to each other.

3. To avoid confusion over which session key goes with which client, the server is not given a session key directly. Instead, the client is given its copy of the session key and also the server's copy of the session key to hold. When it wants to initiate a session with a server, the client sends the server its copy of the session key.

4. When the KDC gives the client both session keys, it encrypts the client's copy with the key it shares with the client. It encrypts the server's session key with the key it shares with the server. The client will not be able to decrypt the server's copy of the session key. It can only pass the encrypted message, containing the server's session key, to the server when it is ready to start an encrypted session.

5. Once the client and the server both have their copies of the session keys, they can start their encrypted session.

Why is it so complicated? To make it secure. Security is never efficient, and it always causes overhead. That is just the nature of it. Kerberos was first developed in the late 1980s, but the first version available for public use was version 4. A lot of time was spent on making Kerberos safe, and that requires an intricate system.

Integrated Windows Authentication requires Internet Explorer as a client. The reason for this is that Windows NT uses NTLM as its encryption protocol, which is proprietary to Microsoft. And even though Kerberos v5 is an open standard, Microsoft's implementation of it still requires a Windows 2000 environment because of its use of Active Directory. Because it allows the use of both protocols, Integrated Windows Authentication is supported by Internet Explorer starting at version 2. If you have clients using version 5 of Internet Explorer, then it will be using Kerberos as its authentication protocol.

Certificates

ISA Server supports both client- and server-side certificates. Authentication with certificates is used to set up a Secure Sockets Layer (SSL) connection. Although it is a slow connection, SSL encrypts all the communication between the client and the server. A certificate's role in SSL is to prove the identity of those participating in the SSL connection. Certificates are used to prove an identity of a computer the way a driver's license proves the identity of a person. Just like the Department of Motor Vehicles verifies the identity of a person wanting a driver's license, a trusted third party verifies the identity of a person wanting to obtain a certificate for a computer. If you trust the maker of the certificate, you can trust that the identity designated on the certificate is correct. This trusted third party is called a *certificate authority*.

Before certificates can be used, they must be installed on the server at a minimum and on each client if client-side certificates are required. Client-side certificates are needed only if an internal Web server is giving out sensitive information. If you require an inbound client to present a certificate and one is not installed on that client, then it will be rejected and never get past your ISA server. A certificate must be purchased or obtained from a certificate authority that both the client and the server trust. You can use a certificate server to make your own certificates, but the only way the client and server can both trust these certificates is if they are both from the same company and need to connect and share information over public or networks that are not secure. When SSL sessions are set up between users from different companies, usually the certificate authority is a trusted third-party company, such as VeriSign or Thawte.

To set up the use of certificates, you need to go through many steps in different applications in ISA Server. Table 7.1 shows the steps that must be completed prior to requiring connections to use server-side and client-side certificates. It is important to realize that the use of SSL is required when using certificates so these steps help set this up. The table shows the steps that must be completed as well as the application and specific dialog box required to complete the step.

Once you have a certificate installed on the ISA server and on every client that wants to connect to a protected Web site, you are ready to set up authentication by certificates. The SSL process is covered thoroughly in Chapter 9. SSL bridging for incoming requests using client-side certificates is covered in Chapter 12 of this book.

Authentication Pros and Cons

Authentication is necessary if a site contains sensitive information and access to it must be controlled. However, if this is not necessary, then requiring authentication can cause a number of connectivity and performance problems. Like all security, authentication causes a drag on performance and adds to the overhead on ISA Server. Also, if you require authentication for all connections, you can cause some automated processes—such as scheduled cache content downloads—to fail.

You have four methods of authentication to choose from in ISA Server, but the fundamental problem of security versus compatibility still remains. A more secure version of authentication is not as compatible with differing clients or operating systems, whereas the most compatible version of authentication has no security to it.

It is important to note that the authentication process falls back on supporting services in the operating system and can be helped or hindered not just by the browser and Web server, but also by the operating system that each is running on. Some authentications require a certain browser version while others require a certain operating system or both. For example, Windows Integrated Authentication

Table 7.1 Steps that must be completed prior to requiring certificate authentication.

Required Step	Application and Dialog Box
Access Windows 2000 certificate management program.	Add the Certificates snap-in to a Microsoft Management Console (MMC).
Create a certificate request.	Open the Certificates snap-in. Right-click and create a new certificate request.
Submit the certificate request to a certificate authority (CA).	Contact a certificate authority and follow its instructions.
Install the certificate once you receive it from the CA.	Use the Certificates snap-in and select Install Certificate.

using NTLM cannot support Netscape clients because NTLM is a Microsoft proprietary protocol, but Basic Authentication and Digest Authentication are compatible with Netscape browsers. Also, Integrated Windows Authentication using Kerberos requires a Windows 2000 domain environment. Table 7.2 shows a comparison of authentication methods and the browser or operating system requirements of each.

Setting Up Authentication

Requiring authentication causes all inbound and outbound requests to be checked. Because this is a lot of overhead on a server, you can decide whether you will check inbound or outbound or all connections. These settings should be based on the security needs of the network. For example, a private internal company Web site that allows access by company employees working from home would require inbound authentication. This situation would not require outbound authentication, so you should not set that up. Also, it would be easier on your network if you set up only one IP address on your ISA server to listen for requests for this Web site.

Listeners

A *listener* is an IP address on an adapter that listens for client requests. By default, all IP addresses in an ISA Server listen for client requests. In ISA Server, you can specify authentication type when you set up listeners for incoming or outgoing Web requests. You can configure authentication per listener in ISA Server.

Configuring Authentication

All four methods of authentication are configured in the same dialog box. Any prerequisites that an authentication method requires, such as a domain environment or an installed certificate, are configured in different computers or dialog boxes. This keeps the authentication dialog box easy and simple. By the time you are down to configuring the authentication method, it is simply a matter of clicking a radio button.

Table 7.2 Authentication types and the clients they support.

Authentication Type	Supported Clients
Basic Authentication	All clients are supported.
Digest Authentication	Internet Explorer and Netscape browsers in a Windows 2000 domain.
Windows Integrated Authentication	Internet Explorer in version 2 and higher on Windows NT and Windows 2000 for NTLM or Internet Explorer version 5 for Kerberos.
Certificates	All clients can participate in an SSL connection with server-side certificates. However, Internet Explorer only accepts client side certificates starting in version 4.

Although there are different dialog boxes for setting up inbound and outbound requirements for authentication, each has an identical dialog box that is configured the same way. Figures 7.2 and 7.3 show the Outgoing Web Requests and Incoming Web Requests dialog boxes, respectively.

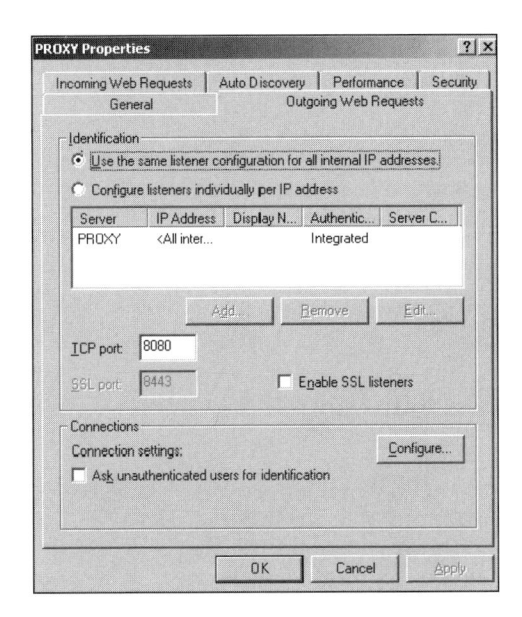

Figure 7.2 The Outgoing Web Requests property page of an ISA array or server.

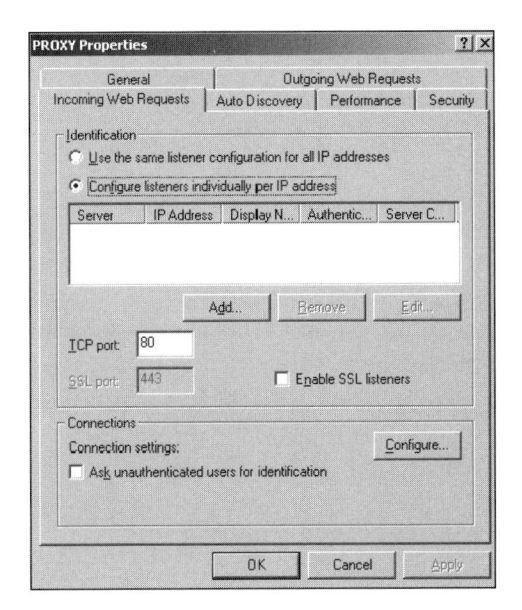

Figure 7.3 The Incoming Web Requests property page of an ISA array or server.

To pull up and configure these dialog boxes, complete the following steps:

1. Open ISA Management.

2. Expand Internet Security And Acceleration Server and then expand Servers And Arrays.

3. Right-click the name of the server or array that you are setting up authentication on and select Properties.

4. Select either the Outgoing Web Requests or Incoming Web Requests property page depending on whether you want to configure authentication for incoming or outgoing requests.

5. At the bottom of the dialog box you'll see the option Ask Unauthenticated Users For Identification. If you check this box, then all requests will be asked to authenticate.

Warning: This setting can cause serious overhead on your site and ISA Server.

---

6. In the Identification Section of the dialog box, select Configure Listeners Individually Per IP Address.

7. Click Add. The dialog box that allows you to configure a type of authentication appears. This dialog box is shown in Figure 7.4.

8. At the top of the dialog box, select the ISA server in the array that has the network adapter and IP address that needs to be configured as a listener.

9. Select the IP address on the adapter that will listen for client addresses.

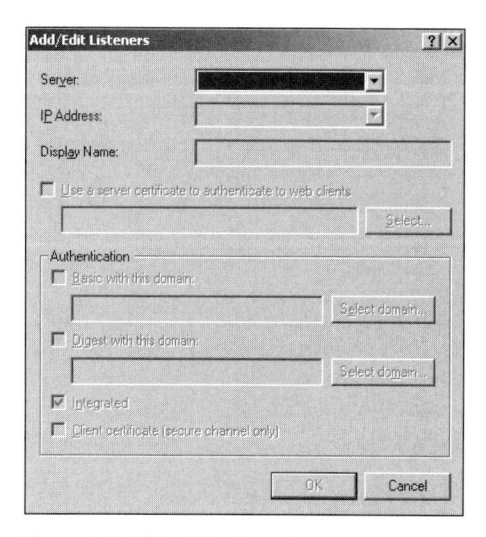

Figure 7.4 This dialog box allows you to select a type of authentication for a configured listener.

10. Type a Display Name that will allow you to recognize and select this listener from a list.

11. Place a checkmark in Use A Server Certificate To Authenticate To Web Clients if you want to use server-side certificates.

12. Click the Select button to choose from a list of certificates loaded on the server.

Note: If no certificates are installed on the server, then you will not be able to make this selection.

13. In the Authentication section, select from the following choices:

    ► Select Basic With This Domain to require Basic Authentication.

    ► Select Digest With This Domain to require Digest Authentication.

    ► Select Integrated to require Integrated Windows Authentication.

Note: You do not select whether Kerberos or NTLM authentication will be used. This is negotiated automatically between ISA Server and the authenticating client.

    ► Select Client Certificate (Secure Channel Only) to require client certificates.

14. Once you make a selection, click OK to apply your change.

15. Click OK to close the Array or Server properties dialog box.

After you configure a listener to use authentication, you can make changes at any time to it.

Editing Listeners to Change Authentication Requirements

To change authentication requirements on a listener, complete the following steps:

1. Open ISA Management.

2. Expand Internet Security And Acceleration Server and then expand Servers And Arrays.

3. Right-click the name of the server or array that you are setting up authentication on and select Properties.

4. Select the listener you want to configure and click the Edit button.

5. In the Edit dialog box, make any desired changes and click OK.

Passing Around Authentication Requests

Authentication requests are designed with the idea that a requesting client and authenticating server have a direct communication between them. But ISA Server is placed on the network so that internal clients and external servers cannot have direct communication. There are different circumstances when outgoing authentication requests can be passed through multiple internal ISA servers or through the external ISA server so that they can reach the destination server on the Internet for which they were intended.

Using Pass-through Authentication

Authentication is supposed to occur between a client making a request and a destination server on the Internet. An outbound request must first go through the ISA server, and by default, the ISA server will reformulate this request and send it to the destination server in the requesting computer's place. Many of the authentication protocols have rules that will not allow another computer to take its place. In order for some methods of authentication to work, pass-through authentication will need to be configured.

Pass-through authentication allows the client and Web server to communicate directly. As usual, the ISA server intercepts the first packets. Pass-through authentication can be configured for outgoing as well as incoming requests:

1. A request is sent from an internal client to the ISA server.
2. ISA Server formulates a request and sends it to the destination server.
3. The destination server rejects the request and specifies the type of authentication needed to complete the request.
4. ISA Server passes this information on to the client.
5. The client resends the request to the ISA server containing the correct authentication information.
6. Instead of reformulating the request, ISA Server passes the client's request on to the destination server.
7. At this point, the ISA server simply passes packets back and forth between the client and the destination server instead of reformulating them.

Pass-through authentication is automatically supported by ISA Server and does not need to be configured. Pass-through authentication is supported by all methods of authentication except Integrated Windows Authentication when Kerberos authentication is being used.

Chained Authentication

When a chain of ISA servers exist in a network, a client's request may need to cross more than one ISA server to get out of the internal network to the destination server. This is called *chained authentication*. Chained authentication can be used with a combination of ISA servers and Proxy servers. To set up chained authentication, you must set up routing rules. Routing rules direct how requests are passed from ISA server to ISA server on their way out of the network. Routing rules are discussed more thoroughly in Chapter 13.

Combining Rules and Authentication

Rules can apply to a number of different policy elements. As described in Chapter 6, you can set up rules to apply to certain times of the day or week, sets of IP addresses, computer names, types of protocols, types of files, or even certain groups or users. When rules are applied to users or groups of users, then the ISA server must know who each user is in order to apply the rule. This is where authentication comes into the process. The ISA server must ask for user account credentials from every request if a rule is based on user account information. This does not happen automatically. As we covered earlier in the chapter, authentication is set up in the properties of an array or server. You can set up a rule that requires ISA Server to check user account information and then not set up authentication, but if you do this, no one will be able to access the content protected by this rule. An authentication method must also be set up for the connections to be successful.

Chapter Summary

Authentication is needed only for some Internet connections. A site that contains sensitive information may require users to identify themselves before they can be allowed access. The first step to setting this up is to configure a rule that allows or denies access based on a user or group of users. This will signal ISA Server that it must authenticate each user so that it can evaluate whether the user is allowed or denied access. However, unless authentication is also set up, all users will be denied access to the protected site.

Four methods of authentication are used by ISA Server. These are the same four methods used by IIS in versions 5 and 6. Regardless of the method used, authentication validates clients when they have the right username and password that is required for access to a site. The four methods of authentication each have different ways to verify the username and password information to the server. Some methods simply pass the username and password to the server, whereas others use various types of encryption processes designed to keep this sensitive information secret.

Basic Authentication has no security and allows usernames and passwords to be easily captured and read by unauthorized users. However, it is the only completed standard for authentication for use with HTTP. This makes Basic Authentication compatible with all clients and servers. However, when using authentication over connections that are not secure, such as the Internet, SSL should also be used to keep others from discovering username and password information.

Digest Authentication verifies the user account information of the client without actually sending a password over a connection between the authenticating client and the destination server. It does this by sending a message digest, or hash, of the password instead. The destination server can perform a hash function on the password that it has for the client. If the message digest that it calculates is the same as the one sent by the client, then the client is authenticated without sending the actual password.

Integrated Windows Authentication is the most proprietary of authentication types. It uses two different protocols that allow it to be compatible with many different Windows clients. One protocol, NTLM, is proprietary to Microsoft and works only with Windows clients. The other protocol is not proprietary but is implemented so that it works only with a Windows 2000 domain environment.

Certificates using SSL is the fourth method of authentication allowed by ISA Server. SSL is very secure because it encrypts the full session and all of the information passed in that session, but it also has a high amount of overhead.

Authentication requests are designed to occur between a requesting client and a destination server. Setting up authentication on ISA Server allows these requests to get past the ISA server so that they can complete the authentication process and allow a connection from the client to the server.

Review Questions

1. Which type(s) of authentication are supported by Internet Explorer in version 5? [Check all correct answers]

    a. Basic Authentication

    b. Digest Authentication

    c. Integrated Windows Authentication using NTLM

    d. Integrated Windows Authentication using Kerberos

    e. Certificates on a client

2. Which type(s) of authentication are supported by Netscape clients? [Check all correct answers]

    a. Basic Authentication

    b. Digest Authentication

    c. Integrated Windows Authentication using NTLM

    d. Integrated Windows Authentication using Kerberos

    e. Certificates

3. Which type(s) of authentication are supported by Internet Explorer version 2? [Check all correct answers]
   a. Basic Authentication
   b. Digest Authentication
   c. Integrated Windows Authentication using NTLM
   d. Integrated Windows Authentication using Kerberos
   e. Certificates

4. Which type(s) of authentication require Windows 2000? [Check all correct answers]
   a. Basic Authentication
   b. Digest Authentication
   c. Integrated Windows Authentication using NTLM
   d. Integrated Windows Authentication using Kerberos
   e. Certificates

5. Encoding and encryption are very similar.
   a. True
   b. False

6. What is encoding? [Check all correct answers]
   a. Encryption of information
   b. Translation of characters
   c. A secure method of transmitting data
   d. A non-secure method of transmitting data
   e. A method of authentication

7. What type of authentication uses encoding?
   a. Basic Authentication
   b. Digest Authentication
   c. Integrated Windows Authentication using NTLM
   d. Integrated Windows Authentication using Kerberos
   e. Certificates

8. Which version of HTTP was Basic Authentication specified for?
   a. .9
   b. 1.0
   c. 1.1
   d. 2.0

9. What is hashing?
    a. A one-way encryption of passwords
    b. A one-way function that checks the validity of a password
    c. A two-way encryption of passwords
    d. A two-way function that checks the validity of a password

10. What is created when a hashing function is performed on a password? [Check all correct answers]
    a. Base64
    b. Message digest
    c. Hash
    d. Certificate
    d. NTLM

11. Why is hashing considered a safe way to validate a user?
    a. The password is encrypted.
    b. The actual password is not sent over the network.
    c. The username is encrypted.
    d. The actual username is not sent over the network.

12. Why does a message box appear when Basic Authentication is selected as an authentication choice?
    a. Basic Authentication provides no backup.
    b. Basic Authentication provides no security.
    c. Basic Authentication works with very few clients.
    d. Basic Authentication works with very few servers.

13. What version of Kerberos is supported in Integrated Windows Authentication?
    a. 4.0
    b. 4.5
    c. 5.0
    d. 5.5

14. What does NTLM stand for?
    a. NT LAN Manager
    b. NT Load Mobility
    c. No Translation Load Method
    d. No More Lost Messages

15. What elements are part of the Kerberos authentication process? [Check all correct answers]
    a. Client
    b. Server
    c. Message digest
    d. KDC
    e. NTLM

16. When does Integrated Windows Authentication require the presence of a Windows 2000 domain?
    a. When NTLM is being used
    b. When Kerberos is being used
    c. When the KDC is being used
    d. Always
    e. Never

17. What does the KDC do in Kerberos?
    a. Controls client connections
    b. Controls server connections
    c. Controls the allocation of keys
    d. Synchronizes the Kerberos connection

18. The use of certificates requires what other services in ISA Server?
    a. IIS
    b. DNS
    c. Kerberos
    d. SSL
    e. Active Directory
    f. ISA Server

19. What does a CA do?
    a. Authenticate users
    b. Encrypts information
    c. Creates a secure channel between a client and a server
    d. Create certificates for distribution
    e. Encodes messages

20. What must a client and server have in common with a certificate authority in order for them to make an SSL connection?

   a. Trust

   b. A network connection

   c. The same level of authentication

   d. The same policy applied to them

21. In what dialog box can authentication be required for Web requests? [Check all correct answers]

   a. An array or server Outgoing Web Requests property page

   b. An array or server Incoming Web Requests property page

   c. In the New Protocol Rule Wizard

   d. In the Add/Edit Listener dialog box

22. What is pass-through authentication?

   a. Authentication is terminated due to a drop in performance.

   b. Internal ISA servers pass authentication requests to external ISA servers.

   c. An ISA server allows a requesting client and destination server to authenticate directly.

   d. ISA servers pass authentication requests to Proxy servers to complete the authentication process.

23. When is chained authentication needed? [Check all correct answers]

   a. When multiple ISA servers are set up to forward requests to one another.

   b. When multiple ISA servers and Proxy servers are set up to forward requests to one another.

   c. When arrays are used.

   d. When certificates are used.

24. How is pass-through authentication set up?

   a. Through the Array or Server properties.

   b. Through the Outgoing Web Requests property page.

   c. Through the Incoming Web Requests property page.

   d. It does not need to be set up.

25. How is chained authentication set up?

   a. Through a routing rule.

   b. Through the Outgoing Web Requests property page.

   c. Through the Incoming Web Requests property page.

   d. It does not need to be set up.

Real-World Projects

Note: This exercise assumes a test Windows 2000 Server with Service Pack 1 as well as ISA Server installed. Read the instructions carefully and do not change the settings on your production machine unless you understand the options presented. If you are unsure about an option, do not make a change and instead read the ISA Server help files about the option to be installed.

"Joe, we have a new Web site," the Vice President of Communications began at the weekly update meeting. Joe was filling in for the IT manager, who was out sick. The update meeting was held every week to make sure all department heads were aware of important milestones or dates that were coming that week.

The Communications VP continued, "It is located in the San Francisco office. This Web site is only for sales personnel. Is there a way we can allow access just for sales personnel and no one else?"

"Sure," said Joe confidently. "Is it already up and running?"

"Yes. How fast can you set that up?"

Somehow, even with the update meeting this was still being done at the last possible minute.

"It can be done today." Joe hated saying those words. They somehow always came back to haunt him.

After the meeting, Joe decided that the best course of action would be to create a site and content rule specifying that only the Sales group had access to the site. Because he did not need to control access to a certain protocol or port, a protocol rule would not be the right choice. Because a site and content rule was created by default in ISA Server that allowed access to all sites for all users, Joe decided that a site and content rule that denied access to all users except for the Sales group was the most secure approach. This approach also kept him from having to redo any existing rules.

First, Joe called the San Francisco office to get the IP address of the Web server that the sales department would need to access. Joe would use this address to create a destination set that would be used in the site and content rule. Then, Joe needed to set up the new site and content rule.

Project 7.1

To create a new destination set:

1. Open ISA Management.

2. Expand Internet Security And Acceleration Server for enterprise-level destination sets.

3. Expand Policy Elements.

4. Right-click Destination Sets.

5. Point to New and select Set. The New Destination Set dialog box will appear.

6. In the Name box, type the name of the destination set. Joe named the new destination set "SF Sales Web Server".

7. In the Description box, describe the new destination set. Joe gave a detailed description of what the destination set defined.

8. Click the Add button to add computer names, a block of IP addresses, or a path to a specific folder or folder/file combination that you want to include in the destination set. Joe specified the IP address of the Web server in San Francisco and added the path to the Web site on the server. Click OK.

9. Click OK once all destinations in this set are defined.

With the destination set ready, Joe could now define a site and content rule that would deny access to all users except those that belonged to the Sales group.

To create a new site and content rule:

1. Open ISA Management.

2. Expand Internet Security And Acceleration Server for enterprise-level site and content rules.

3. Expand Enterprise Policy to define an enterprise-level site and content rule.

4. Right-click Site And Content Rules.

5. Point to New and select Rule. The New Site And Content Rule Wizard will start.

6. In the first dialog box, type the name of the new site and content rule. Joe named the site and content rule "San Francisco Sales Site" so that he could pick it out from a list and immediately know what the rule was for. Click Next.

7. In the Rule Action dialog box, select whether the rule will Allow or Deny clients access to sites. Joe selected Deny. He wrote himself a note to later create a specific error Web page so that users would know this sales site was a restricted site. Maybe that would keep him from getting support calls from users who could not access the site. For now, he did not specify a URL. Click Next.

8. In the Rule Configuration dialog box, select the set of sites, users, or schedule to which this rule will apply. Joe decided to select Custom because he had more than one criterion he needed to specify for this rule. The Custom choice in the Rule configuration dialog box runs you through all of the choices. Click Next.

9. In the Destination Sets dialog box, select the destinations the site and content rule will apply to. Joe selected Specified Destination Set. He then selected the SF Sales Web Server destination set that he had just defined. Click Next.

10. In the Schedule dialog box, select when the protocol rule will apply. Joe selected Always. Click Next.

11. In the Client Type dialog box, select the client types that the protocol rule will apply to. Joe selected Specific Users And Groups. Click Next.

12. In the Users And Groups dialog box, click the Add button. Joe selected the Sales group and clicked the Add button.

13. Click Next.

14. In the Content Type dialog box, specify the type of content that will be affected by this rule. Joe selected Any Content Type. Click Next.

15. Review the summary of information and click Finish. You can use the Back button to change incorrect information.

Project 7.2

Joe was happy to have that done. He had other things that were scheduled to be done that day so he moved on to his other projects, figuring that if there was a problem with what he had set up that he would find out soon enough. Soon enough came quickly when the phone rang less than an hour later.

"Hey Joe." It was John from the sales department. "I was wondering if you had gotten a chance to set up a connection to the sales site yet."

This did not sound good.

"Have you tried to access it this morning?" Joe tried to sound casual.

"Yes, it didn't work."

"All right, I'll take a look at it," said Joe.

Joe checked the site and content rule that he had created earlier. It looked OK, so what was the problem? Joe decided to do some research and found that he was requiring authentication by specifying access to a user group, but he had not set up authentication. No wonder no one could access the site.

To fix the problem, Joe needed to configure authentication. He knew the sales department had laptops with Windows 2000 Professional installed on them. This meant that they had at least Internet Explorer version 5. He also had Windows 2000 domain environment, which meant he had a lot more choices when deciding on an authentication method. Joe decided on Integrated Windows Authentication. He needed it for outbound access only.

To set up Integrated Windows Authentication:

1. Open ISA Management.
2. Expand Internet Security And Acceleration Server and then expand Servers And Arrays.
3. Right-click the name of the server or array that you are setting up authentication on and select Properties.
4. Select either the Outgoing Web Requests or Incoming Web Requests property page depending on whether you want to configure authentication for incoming or outgoing requests. Joe selected Outgoing Web Requests.
5. In the Identification Section of the dialog box, select Configure Listeners Individually Per IP Address.
6. Click Add. The dialog box that allows you to configure a type of authentication appears.
7. At the top of the dialog box, select the ISA server in the array that has the network adapter and IP address that needs to be configured as a listener.
8. Select the IP address on the adapter that will listen for client addresses.
9. Type a Display Name that will allow you to recognize and select this listener from a list.
10. In the Authentication section, select the Integrated option to use Integrated Windows Authentication.
11. Click OK to close the Add/Edit Listeners dialog box.
12. Click OK to close the Array or Server properties dialog box.

Joe called up John and told him to give it another try.

"It still doesn't work," John said.

This is exactly why Joe hated last-minute changes.

"Hold on," Joe said. "I'll call back in 10 minutes."

With more research, Joe discovered that a change in the properties required the Web Proxy service on the ISA server to be restarted. That was easy to fix, and Joe hoped it would be the last detail that was missing.

Project 7.3
To restart the Web Proxy Service:

1. Click the Start button, point to Programs, point to Administrative Tools, and select Services.

2. In the Details pane, right-click Microsoft Web Proxy and select Stop.

3. A dialog box will appear to let you know that the service is being stopped.

4. In the Details pane, right-click Microsoft Web Proxy and select Start.

5. A dialog box will appear to let you know that the service is being started.

6. Close the Services application.

Joe called up John.

"I've set it all up," Joe said. "Do you want to be my tester?"

John tried and connected to the site.

"Great! I'll let everyone know that it's working and ready for us to use," John said. "Thanks, Joe."

CHAPTER EIGHT

Caching and Acceleration

After completing this chapter, you will be able to:

- ✓ Understand potential issues without using caching
- ✓ Understand the purpose of caching
- ✓ Describe how the caching process works
- ✓ Understand Cache Array Routing Protocol (CARP)
- ✓ Describe the benefits of CARP
- ✓ Configure CARP
- ✓ Define a scheduled cache content download
- ✓ Configure a scheduled cache content download
- ✓ Describe cache chaining
- ✓ Define Web Proxy routing
- ✓ Configure Web Proxy routing
- ✓ Define cache filtering
- ✓ Describe tuning and monitoring cache performance
- ✓ Tune the ISA Server cache
- ✓ Monitor ISA Server counters

According to the results of an analysis performed by The Measurement Factory (TMF), ISA Server outperformed other similar enterprise firewall and Web-caching products in key metrics, such as price/performance, hit ratio, and throughput. Corporations expect that they will increasingly incorporate ISA Server into their networks so that they can experience both fast Internet access and lower network infrastructure cost. Monitoring Web caching may be one of the most important functions you perform if you want to provide your clients with easy access to Internet resources. You can read the TMF report at **www.microsoft.com/isaserver/productinfo/TMFcacheoff.htm**.

Potential Issues

Let's suppose you are a system administrator for a company with 100 client systems. You want to allow all 100 clients access to the Internet. At this point, you have several options. First, you could order 100 phone lines for each client, have 100 accounts with an Internet Service Provider (ISP), and let each client dial out to the ISP whenever he or she needs to access Internet resources. Second, you could get a T1 (1.5Mbps) or T3 (45Mbps) line to the company and let all 100 clients share the line. At this time, however, each client goes out to the Internet through the T1 or T3 line whenever necessary. This means that you need to get a pool of public IP addresses for all of your clients, which will be very costly, and because there is no ISA Server type product between internal networks and the Internet, there is no security. Finally, using either a T1 or T3 line to the company, you could use a Web Proxy server to create one central point where all 100 client systems could access Internet resources. In this chapter, we will cover this approach. First, though, we will look at why we don't recommend the other two methods.

The main problem with using the 100 phone lines and 100 ISP accounts is the cost and manageability of these accounts. If you have 1,000 clients, you would need 1,000 phone lines and have to maintain 1,000 ISP accounts. As the number of clients grew, you'd find it harder to maintain the connections for each client. It would be very costly, and managing all the ISP accounts would be time-consuming.

If you're considering using a T1 or T3 line, but letting each client access the Internet resources as necessary, you must take bandwidth into account. If all the clients try to go out to the Internet at the same time, you could congest the T1 or T3 line, and the network performance would be degraded. The degradation would be very noticeable if your clients number 1,000 clients or more.

The best solution is to use a T1 or T3 line along with a Web Proxy server so that each client goes through the Web Proxy server to access Internet resources. Using this approach saves bandwidth. Each client talks with the Web Proxy server first; then, the server accesses the Internet resources requested by the client and provides the Internet resources to the client. In a sense, the Web Proxy server exists as a go-between for the clients and Internet resources. In addition, the Web Proxy server caches, or stores, the Internet resources (HTTP and FTP objects, if they are not using Winsock nor any Secure Socket Layer ([SSL])) on its local hard disk, and if somebody else tries to access the same Internet resources, the Web Proxy server will provide those resources instead of going out to the Internet to get them. The Web Proxy server also protects internal resources.

In this chapter, you will learn about caching and acceleration. The terms *caching* and *acceleration* are interrelated—only successful caching will provide acceleration for the clients. It is not true, however, that acceleration will provide caching. So now you have a basic idea of what this chapter is about. If you are asking, "What in the world is caching anyhow?" the following sections will provide an overview.

What Is Caching?

You may be familiar with the term *caching* in reference to the central processing unit (CPU). CPUs are the brain of computer systems, and they execute the instruction sets so that computer systems can get tasks done. CPUs such as Pentium II have different layers of cache on the chip itself or in another location on the system, and retrieving data from these caches provides better performance than not using cache. Pentium II/III and Celeron chips are different in that Celeron CPUs do not use the cache on the chip. Therefore, although you may have a high-frequency Celeron CPU on your system (such as 733MHz), a system with a Pentium III CPU with 500MHz and 2MB onboard cache may seem to offer better performance than the Celeron system. This is because obtaining data from the cache on the CPU is faster; likewise, it is faster to obtain Internet data from the local cache on the ISA Server than to obtain data by going out to the Internet.

So, what is caching in terms of ISA Server? ISA Server's Web-caching capability lets you retrieve any Web-related data—such as Web pages, graphics, audio and video files—onto its local cache configured on an NTFS partition. This caching automatically occurs when a client system is browsing the Internet using a Web browser such as Internet Explorer. When a client tries to access the Internet, ISA Server captures the request and checks its local cache to see whether the requested objects exist on the local cache. If the requested objects do not exist on the local cache, ISA Server will access the Internet and get the requested objects rather than letting the client obtain them directly.

But watch—the next step is quite sophisticated. Once the requested objects are obtained, ISA Server does not just forward them to the client that requested them. ISA Server caches the retrieved data on its cache before forwarding the data to the client. If this is the first time any client has requested these objects, the process can take some time. If another client requests the same Web objects, ISA Server returns the Web objects to the client from its local cache. Thus, this process saves bandwidth—the client does not have to go out to the Internet to get the requested Web objects. Clients will benefit from the performance gain when the data is obtained locally—which is where the term *acceleration* comes in.

We have just covered a few of the benefits ISA Server's Web caching can provide. Other neat features include the following:

1. *Forward caching*—Forward caching allows internal clients to access the Internet. Figure 8.1 shows how the ISA server responds to the internal clients' request and illustrates the steps it follows to obtain the data for the clients from the Internet. Forward caching is also referred to as "forward proxying."

2. *Reverse caching*—Reverse caching is very similar to forward caching, except that requests come from Internet clients to a network resource on the internal network (such as an internal Web server hosting the Web site for an organization as the Internet presence). In this case, if an Internet client requests a Web page and if that data is on the ISA server's cache, the Web page is returned to the Internet client from the ISA server's cache. If it does not exist on the cache, the ISA server contacts the internal Web server and retrieves the data from it. This action of contacting the internal Web server, retrieving the data from it, and caching the data before it is returned to the Internet user is also referred to as "reverse proxying." Reverse proxying is the same as forward proxying except that the data is flowing in the opposite direction. Figure 8.2 shows how Internet clients would access an internal Web server's data through the ISA server so that Internet clients do not access the internal Web server directly.

3. *Scheduled caching*—If you know which Web or FTP sites are accessed frequently in advance, the ISA server can retrieve the data on a scheduled basis so that it is available on the ISA server's local cache. Clients can retrieve the data from

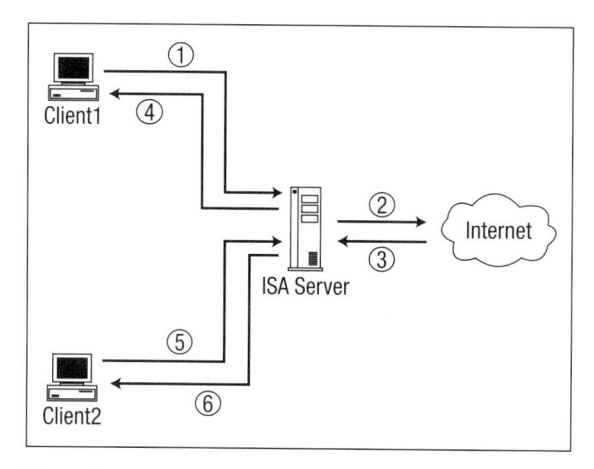

Figure 8.1 How forward caching works.

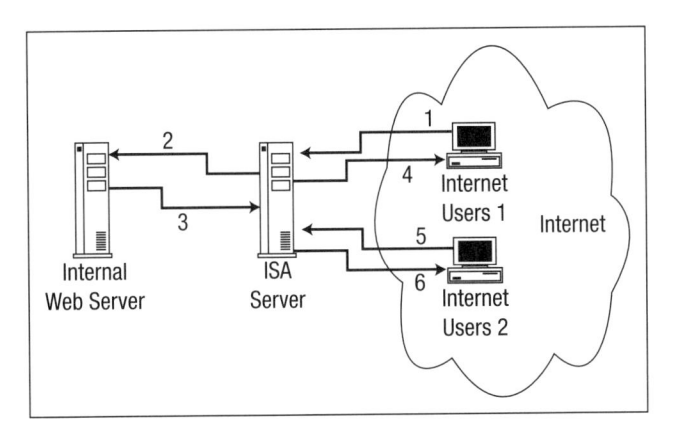

Figure 8.2 How reverse caching works.

   the local cache at any time. In addition, you can schedule the ISA server to retrieve the data during off-business hours so that the process does not affect any network traffic during peak hours.

4. *Distributed caching*—If you have deployed an ISA server array with several ISA servers, you can distribute the load for the ISA servers so that clients can retrieve Web-related objects from different ISA servers. ISA Server uses Cache Array Routing Protocol (CARP) so that you can configure several ISA servers to act as a single logical cache. We will examine CARP later in this chapter.

5. *Hierarchical caching*—ISA Server can combine distributed caching in different geographical regions so that clients obtain data from the ISA server nearest to them. Hierarchical caching can also be useful in a situation where you have several ISA servers in different geographical regions. If a client requests a Web page in one region, it would first contact the ISA server in that region. If the data is on the nearby ISA server, the client can retrieve the data from it. If the data does not exist on that server, the ISA server can contact another ISA server to determine whether it contains the requested data. For the Internet client, obtaining the requested data from a nearby ISA server—instead of an ISA server in another geographical region—is a much faster process. Hierarchical caching is also referred to as "cache chaining," which will be explained later in this chapter.

Understanding the Caching Process

At this point, let's look at what happens when a client requests an Internet resource. Of course, you do not have to worry about what happens in the background—ISA Server takes care of these details for you. As you will recall, in Chapter 3, we talked about the three configuration modes for ISA Server: firewall mode, cache mode, and integrated mode. When you configure the ISA server in firewall mode, it does not keep a local cache; the firewall mode does not include caching features. The caching occurs only if the ISA server is configured in cache or integrated mode, which incorporates both the firewall and caching modes.

As you may also recall, you can configure three kinds of clients to utilize the ISA server's functionalities: SecureNAT clients, Firewall clients, and Web Proxy clients. (Refer to Chapter 5 for details.) Now, don't be confused by the following, which seems to confuse many ISA Server administrators: The HTTP redirector filter allows both SecureNAT and firewall clients to utilize the caching features, assuming the ISA server has been configured in the caching mode. Therefore, from the clients' perspective, with the HTTP redirector filter, SecureNAT and firewall clients can benefit from the ISA server cache for Web-related objects.

The process can get quite complicated, so a diagram can be very useful. Figure 8.3 illustrates the caching process.

Figure 8.3 details how the ISA server decides to provide the information requested from clients using its own cache. According to this algorithm, the worst-case scenario is, of course, the ISA server has to retrieve the data from the Internet to fulfill clients' requests. The following steps describe how the caching decision is made:

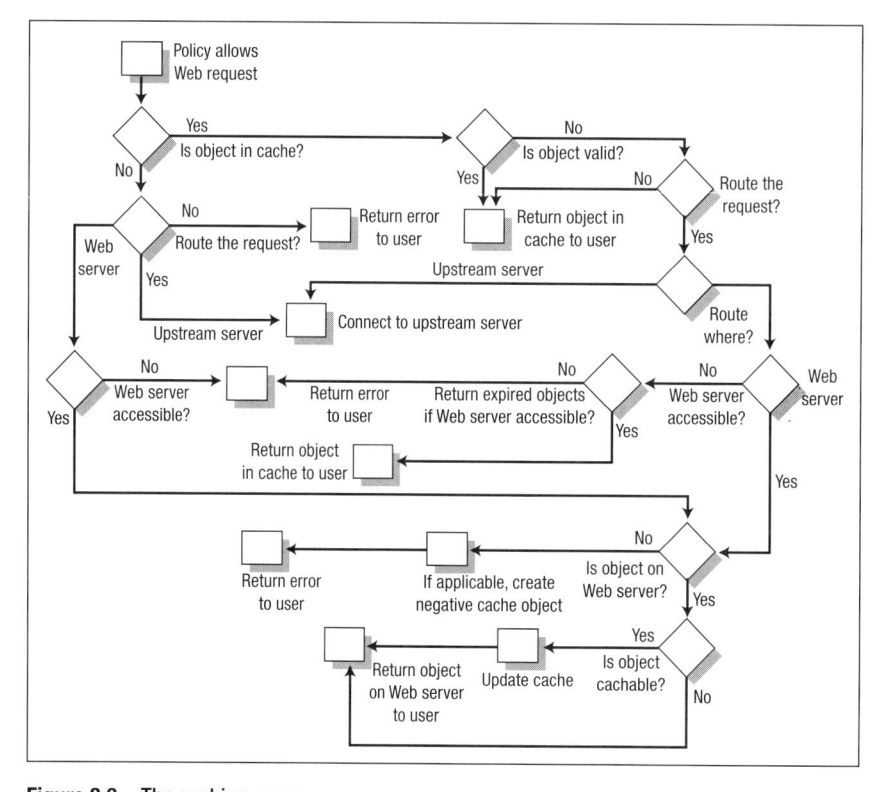

Figure 8.3 The caching process.

1. A client asks for an Internet resource. If the client is allowed to ask for an Internet resource access, the ISA server checks to see whether the requested Web objects exist in its local cache. If the request is for an object that has not been retrieved, the cache will not have the data. If the client contacts the ISA server array, the ISA server uses the CARP algorithm to determine which ISA server's cache to check. We will explain the CARP algorithm later in this chapter.

2. If the object does not exist in the cache, the ISA server decides how to provide the data to the client by checking the routing rule's action.

3. If the object exists in the cache, the ISA server takes the following actions to provide the data to the requesting client in the fastest manner:

    a. The ISA server checks the validity to see whether the object should be provided to the requesting client. The object is not valid if any one of the following conditions is satisfied:

    ➤ The Time to Live (TTL) counter you have configured for the object has expired. The TTL is the amount of time that an object is kept as a valid resource.

    ➤ The TTL that you configured as a scheduled content download job has expired.

    ➤ The TTL specified in the source has expired.

    If the object is valid, it is returned to the requesting client.

    b. If the object is determined to be invalid, the ISA server checks the routing rule. If the routing rule has been configured so that any version of the object can be returned, the object is returned to the client from the cache.

    c. If the routing rule has been configured so that the ISA server routes the client's request, the server decides whether to route it to an upstream server (when hierarchical caching is in place) or to the requested Web server.

    d. If the routing rule has been configured to route the Web server, the ISA server checks to see whether the requested Web server is accessible on the Internet.

    e. If the Web server is accessible, the ISA server checks to see whether the object can be cached. If it can, and if you have configured the cache properties of the routing rule to cache the response, the ISA server caches the object and forwards the object to the client that initially requested the object.

    f. If the Web server is not accessible, the ISA server takes appropriate actions (depending on whether the routing rule specifies that the server should return expired objects from the cache or create a negative cache object). If the routing rule is configured to return expired objects from the cache—and as long as the configured expiration time has not been reached—then the object from the cache is returned. The negative cache object is a response cached by the ISA server for clients requesting the same information; the response states that the requested object could not be retrieved due to the unavailability of the contacted Web server.

It is pretty complicated, isn't it? However, this algorithm ensures that all the clients requesting Internet resource information benefit from the best retrieval performance. And despite all the steps involved, caching is a very fast process. Next, we will take a look at another neat ISA Server feature: CARP.

What Is CARP?

In Chapter 3, we described how ISA Server can incorporate several ISA servers into an array. If you have a Windows 2000 domain with Active Directory, an array may consist of only one ISA server, although the true functionalities come into play only when you combine more than one ISA server into the array.

Microsoft recommends using the ISA server array any time you have an ISA server or ISA servers joining to a Window 2000 domain. You can configure only one ISA server in the Windows 2000 domain as an array member. This is mainly due to the fact that if you later decide to use more than one ISA Server, the ISA servers will be easier to administer. The ISA server array cannot be used if you have only a stand-alone server that does not belong to a Windows 2000 domain. In this case, the ISA server will be configured as the stand-alone ISA server. If you configure more than one ISA server as a stand-alone server, you will have to maintain configurations for each one, which is labor intensive.

Let's think about the following situation. Suppose you are the ISA Server administrator for your company. Because the company is serious about Internet security, you have decided to use the ISA server for both caching and firewall. At this point, you have only one ISA server configured in integrated mode. It has been working fine for a while, and now the company is trying to hire more people. Your manager approves a bigger budget for you so that you can spend additional money. The ISA server seems to be performing a bit slower than before, and you expect that the performance will be worse once your company has hired more people. Therefore, after monitoring performance on the existing ISA server, you determine that you would like to add more ISA servers to your network. After all, you have been very satisfied with the ISA server's functionalities and performance. With the budget increase, you have been able to add another ISA server. Because your network has a Windows 2000 domain, you have configured an ISA server array, which includes the original ISA server and the new ISA server. You have configured the new ISA server in the cache mode, and you've configured the array with these two members to act as a single logical cache. At this point, CARP comes in. CARP will provide efficient caching and scaling if you later decide to add more ISA servers to the array. Let's examine the benefits CARP provides.

CARP Benefits

CARP provides several benefits that you, as the system administrator, cannot afford to ignore. Benefits include the following:

➤ CARP prevents the duplication of contents that could occur using an array of proxy servers. Microsoft Proxy Server 1.0 used Internet Cache Protocol (ICP). With ICP, you had several proxy servers, and each proxy server had duplicate caches of the most frequently requested Internet objects, such as Web pages. CARP creates a true single logical cache, which leads to a faster response for clients and better use of server cache resources. ICP queried the information requested by the client until it found the data on a cache (which could reside on different proxy servers) or until the information requested could be retrieved on the Internet. Unfortunately, ICP also copied the requested information to the client's default proxy server, and it created duplicates of cache information. CARP uses hash-based routing, and no duplicate cache is created. Hash-based routing means that CARP computes a location key to locate a particular data item, and it does not have to query information on other caches. This significantly reduces the network traffic for cache information.

➤ ICP has negative scalability. On the other hand, CARP has positive scalability. In other words, the more servers you have, the harder it is to find the cache information using ICP and the easier it is to find the cache information using CARP. This is because ICP uses queries to find cache information, and CARP becomes faster and more efficient as more ISA servers are added to an array.

➤ Using CARP, you can configure each ISA server to balance how many cache objects are stored in each ISA server.

➤ Every time a new ISA server is added to an array or an existing ISA server is removed from the array, CARP takes care of the change automatically. Because CARP uses hash-based routing, locating cache information is easier even when an ISA server is added to (or removed from) the array.

CARP Configuration

When you create an ISA server array in a Windows 2000 domain, CARP is enabled for all outgoing Web requests and disabled for all incoming Web requests. Therefore, for internal clients accessing Internet resources, all the requested information will be automatically cached on one of the ISA server array members. To enable the incoming Web requests, take the following steps:

1. Open the ISA Management MMC by selecting Start | Programs | Microsoft ISA Server | ISA Management.

2. Right-click the name of the array that you want to enable incoming Web requests, and then click Properties. The array properties appear.

3. On the Incoming Web Requests tab, select Resolve Requests Within Array Before Routing checkbox.

4. If the Resolve Requests Within Array Before Routing checkbox has not been selected before, then you will receive the following message: "When resolving requests within an array, be sure that a listener is configured for the IP address specified for each member server's intra-array address properly." Click OK.

5. Click OK again to close the Array Properties page. ISA Server Warning will appear. The change you just made will not be effective unless some services, such as Web Proxy and Scheduled Content Download, are restarted. Select a proper option, either "Save the changes, but don't restart the services" or "Save the changes and restart the services." Click OK.

You may get into a situation where you have several ISA servers but their hardware configurations are not the same. One ISA server may be more powerful than others, and another ISA server may have more hard disk space allocated for caching. It may be necessary for you to configure CARP so that load balancing takes effect. You configure the load balance by modifying the load factor. Changing the load factor will affect the load on a particular ISA server. To change the load factor, follow these steps:

1. Open the ISA Management MMC by clicking Start | Programs | Microsoft ISA Server | ISA Management. Click on the array that contains the server for which you would like to change the load factor.

2. Double-click the appropriate server in the details pane on the right. The server properties appear.

3. On the Array Membership tab, type the load factor in the Load Factor text box.

4. Click OK to close the server property page.

There may be cases where an ISA server (which is a member of an array) finds that the requested information is not in its own cache. When this happens, the ISA server will contact another ISA server in the array to see if it has the requested information in its cache. It determines which ISA server to contact based on the destination server's intra-array IP address. This value is replicated to all the members in the array, and we do not recommend changing that value unless you have a good reason to do so. The value must be an internal IP address that is included in the

Local Address Table (LAT). See Chapter 3 for a discussion of the LAT. To change the intra-array IP address, follow these steps:

1. Open the ISA Management MMC by clicking Start|Programs|Microsoft ISA Server|ISA Management. Click on the array that contains the server for which you would like to change the load factor.

2. Double-click the appropriate server in the details pane.

3. On the Array Membership tab, type the intra-array IP address in the appropriate text box. Instead of typing the address manually, you can click Find and select one of the internal IP addresses listed.

4. Click OK to close the server properties' page.

Scheduled Cache Content Download

One of the features ISA Server provides is the scheduled cache content download. You can configure ISA Server to download Web-related content, assuming you know what to download in advance. You can download the Web content as a single Universal Resource Locator (URL), such as **http://www.coriolis.com**, as multiple URLs, or as an entire Web site. When creating a scheduled cache content download job, you can limit which content should be downloaded. For instance, you can limit the download to a single domain. Furthermore, you can limit how many links to follow so that the cache does not become overfilled. In some cases, you may just want to download the text content but no graphics or other content. To configure scheduled cache content download, take the following steps:

1. Open the ISA Management MMC by clicking Start|Programs|Microsoft ISA Server|ISA Management.

2. Expand the Servers And Arrays, the name of the array, and Cache Configuration, and then click Scheduled Content Download Jobs.

3. In the details pane, right-click the appropriate scheduled content download job, and then click Properties.

4. On the Frequency tab, in the Date and Time dropdown boxes, type the date and time when the content should be downloaded from the Internet.

5. Under Frequency, configure the appropriate download scheduling:

    ➤ Click Once to download the contents once at a specific time.

    ➤ Click Daily to download the contents daily at a specific time.

    ➤ Click Weekly and then specify which days to download the content.

To configure the location from which to download content, take the following steps:

1. Open the ISA Management MMC by selecting Start | Programs | Microsoft ISA Server | ISA Management.

2. Click Scheduled Content Download Jobs by expanding the Servers and Arrays, name of the array, and Cache Configuration.

3. In the details pane, right-click the appropriate scheduled content download job, and then click Properties.

4. On the Parameters tab, beside Begin Downloading From URL, type the URL from which to download the content.

5. To download only content, click Keep Download Process Inside URL Domain Only.

6. To limit the number of links to follow from a single page when downloading content, click Cache Up To Maximum Links Depth Of and type the number of links to follow.

7. To limit the total number of objects to cache, enter a value in Maximum Number Of Cached Objects.

You can configure both outgoing and incoming Web requests to be downloaded to the cache on a scheduled basis. When outgoing Web requests are scheduled, the Internet site's Web contents are downloaded to the ISA server's cache. On the other hand, when incoming Web requests are scheduled, internal Web servers' contents are cached into the ISA server's cache, which will be available for users on the Internet trying to access the internal Web server's contents. You will need to be careful when scheduling Internet sites that require client authentication to retrieve data. The ISA server cannot schedule automatic downloads for Internet sites that require client authentication. When CARP is enabled, ISA Server uses the CARP algorithm to determine which server will cache the Web objects. When CARP is disabled, all the servers in the array will cache the Web objects, which may waste some cache space.

Cache Chaining

When you have more than one ISA server in the array, the cache load is distributed among them in the array, which results in a performance gain. Another benefit is that fault tolerance is provided in case one ISA server becomes unavailable. The term *fault tolerance* means that if you have more than one ISA server and one of them fails, others can take the responsibility of the failed one. Fault tolerance is important if your clients expect full-time access to the Internet.

The term *chaining* refers to a configuration of ISA servers that are "chained" hierarchically between individual ISA servers or arrays of ISA servers (refer to Chapter 13 for more details on chaining). When a client in the network requests an Internet object, the request goes to the upstream ISA servers to see whether the object is in their cache before ISA server obtains the object from the Internet. Chaining is effective, especially for load balancing, because the data requested does not have to be on one ISA server. In addition, any ISA server in the chain can fulfill a client request.

Let's take a look at the following situation. You have an ISA server array at the main headquarters in California. The ISA servers in the array are directly connected to the Internet. You also have branch offices in Colorado and Washington. Each branch office has an ISA server configured in the cache mode. The ISA Server array in California, along with the ISA servers in both Colorado and Washington, are configured to be in a cache chain, where the ISA server array is upstream. This configuration is depicted in Figure 8.4.

Here is what happens when a client in the network in either Colorado or Washington (or both) requests an Internet object. The closest ISA server in this case is the one located in the local office, either the one in the Colorado or the Washington office. Therefore, the local ISA server is first contacted to see whether the requested Internet object exists in its cache. If the object exists, it is returned to the client. This case provides the best performance for the client.

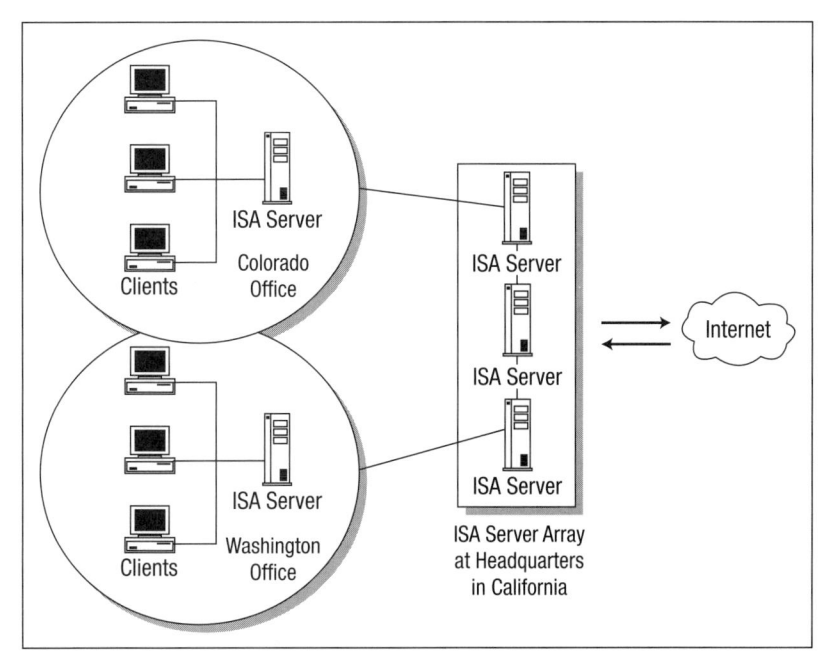

Figure 8.4 An example of cache chaining.

If the object does not exist in the local ISA server's cache, the ISA server contacts the ISA Server array in California to see whether the requested Internet object exists in the array's cache. If the object exists, it is returned to the local ISA server in Colorado or Washington. At the same time, the local ISA server will cache the Internet object returned from the ISA server array so that if the same request comes in the near future, the request can be served locally. The local ISA server then forwards the Internet object to the client that requested it.

The worst-case scenario is that neither the local ISA server nor the remote ISA server array has the Internet object requested. In this case, the remote ISA server array contacts the Internet to retrieve the requested object. It caches the object in its cache and sends the object to the local ISA server. The local ISA Server caches the object in its cache, and finally the client gets the requested information. This method of cascading the Internet object in both the array and the ISA server seems to take a long time before the client finally receives the data. It could be noticeable when the Internet object is requested for the first time. However, the performance gain for clients who request the Internet object *after* that first time is more valuable to the network. If you have a large enterprise, with branch offices in major cities in the world, there may be more ISA servers or ISA server arrays in the upstream location. These servers or arrays are all chained together, and you still have an ISA server or array that all the clients in the country access. How powerful for clients would this concept of ISA server cache chaining be? The answer is limited only to your imagination!

Web Proxy Routing

Web Proxy routing takes the concept of cache chaining and modifies the routing functions of cache information so that the local clients are served in the most efficient manner. Let's say you have an international organization, which has its headquarters in the U.S. and a branch office in Japan. In the U.S., the organization keeps the internal Web servers to store company documents. There is an ISA server array in the U.S. In this case, you can configure the ISA server this way: You have an ISA server array in Japan. When clients in Japan need Internet resource access, the ISA server array in Japan gets the Internet objects from the local ISP to which it is connected. However, when clients in Japan need access to the company documents, all the requests are routed to the ISA server array in the U.S., and the method of hierarchical caching introduced in the previous section is incorporated. Only when the Internet resource is needed does the local ISA server perform what it is originally designed to do. Figure 8.5 illustrates this situation.

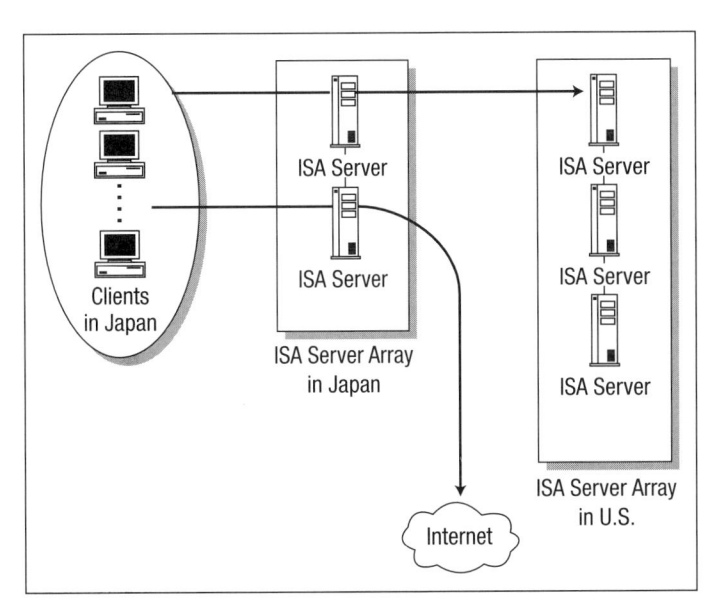

Figure 8.5 An example of Web proxy routing.

The routing specified in this example is accomplished through what is called a *routing rule*. When creating a routing rule, you can define the routing of various client requests in several different ways:

➤ Client requests will be retrieved directly from the specified destination (Internet hosts).

➤ Client requests will be sent to an upstream server, which can be an ISA Server or Proxy Server 2.0.

➤ Client requests will be redirected to an alternate site.

Remember that the routing rules are applicable for both outgoing and incoming Web requests. To configure the specified destination, follow these steps:

1. Open the ISA Management MMC by clicking Start|Programs|Microsoft ISA Server|ISA Management.

2. Expand the Servers and Arrays, the name of the array, and Network Configuration, and then click Routing.

3. In the details pane, right-click the appropriate routing rule, and then click Properties.

4. On the Destination tab, click the destination set to which the routing rule applies. If the destination set that you want to specify does not exist, select

Selected Destination set, and create one by clicking New and then selecting it in the list. You can specify only array-level destination sets for the routing rules, and you cannot select an individual ISA server. You'll see these options:

- All Destinations
- All External Destinations
- All Internal Destinations
- Selected Destination Set
- All Destinations Except Selected Set

5. If you chose Selected Destination Set or All Destinations Except Selected Set, then select a destination set in the Name list.

Let's return to the example introduced earlier in this section. We will assume that the entire HTTP requests for sites in Japan should be routed to the ISA server array at the branch office in Japan. Let's call the ISA array in Japan Array_Japan. You can configure the destination set as follows:

1. Set Destination Set to a set that includes *.jp.
2. Set Action To Route Requests to Upstream Proxy Server, which in this case is the ISA Server array in the U.S.
3. Set the Primary Route to Upstream Proxy Server.
4. Configure the server to Array_Japan.

Cache Filtering

In some cases, you may not want the ISA server or ISA server array to cache Internet objects. For example, suppose the Internet object's information is so sensitive that it should not be cached on the ISA server. Rather, it should be provided from the Internet host. Cache filtering is also configured as the routing rule. For instance, if you want to configure ISA server not to cache any contents from an Internet host, **nottocache.coriolis.com**, you could configure the routing rule as follows:

1. Set Destination Sets to a specific destination set that includes **nottocache.coriolis.com**.
2. Set Request Action to the appropriate routing method.
3. For Cache Configuration, select No Content Will Ever Be Cached so that the contents are never cached on the ISA server's cache.

Tuning and Monitoring Cache Performance

As the system administrator, one of your daily tasks may be ensuring that the ISA server is running in its optimal state and monitoring its performance. Depending on how many clients are accessing the cache—and how the ISA server's physical resources are allocated to different processes running on the system—you want to give your clients the best performance.

Tuning ISA Server

A subtle difference exists between good performance and poor performance on the ISA server. For instance, if you configure the number of connections for the ISA server, and the actual number of connections is slightly less than the number of connections configured on the ISA server, your clients will experience a good performance from the ISA server. If you configure the number of connections for the ISA server to be much higher than the actual number of connections, the clients may not experience fast responses from the ISA server because it is allocating a lot more resources than necessary. Predicting the exact number of connections that will be made in a day is not an easy task, so the ISA server provides a broad range of connection types. To tune performance on the ISA server, take the following steps:

1. Open the ISA Management MMC by clicking Start | Programs | Microsoft ISA Server | ISA Management.

2. Right-click on the array, and click Properties.

3. On the Performance tab, select one of the following:

    ➤ If you expect fewer than 100 users per day to connect to the ISA Server, select Fewer Than 100.

    ➤ If you expect fewer than 1,000 users per day to connect to the ISA Server, select Fewer Than 1000.

    ➤ If you expect more than 1,000 users per day to connect to the ISA Server, select More Than 1000.

Monitoring ISA Server

ISA Server has been working well in your organization. When you come into the office the following morning, clients start calling you saying something is not working properly. They may complain that access to the Internet has become slower. In any case, you have to fix the problem in a timely manner.

When clients experience slow performance on the ISA server, any one of a number of factors could be causing it. The network might be congested due to many users accessing the Internet at the same time. Or perhaps the ISA server is not functioning the way it is supposed to. One of the disks for the cache might have failed, which could cause a degradation of the system performance. Or maybe the CPU on the ISA server is not able to handle all the requests coming from the clients.

Whatever the reason, you should check how the system resources are performing on the ISA server. Windows 2000 offers a system utility called System Monitor. When you install ISA server on a system, it adds many counters specifically designed to monitor ISA server performance (refer to the *MCSE Windows 2000 Foundations Exam Prep* for how to set up the System Monitor).

Note: *Do not become confused about the difference between the System Monitor and the Performance Monitor. In Windows NT 4, the Performance Monitor is used to monitor performance. In Windows 2000, the System Monitor is used. Although the names are different, the functionalities are just about the same.*

In this section, we will describe several important ISA Server counters you can use to monitor the ISA server performance. While not a complete list, Table 8.1 gives you a feel for what to look for when the ISA server performance degrades.

Table 8.1 Important ISA Server counters.

Performance Counter	Description
Total URLs Cached	This counter indicates the cumulative number of URLs that have been stored in the cache. The cache size will limit the counter. If the cache size is too small or if the cache is not configured to be optimal, the counter number may get low, which could indicate a problem with the cache.
Total Memory Bytes Retrieved (KB)	This counter indicates the cumulative number of bytes that have been retrieved from the memory cache compared with client requests to the disk cache. If you consistently have a high number, it indicates that you should allocate more memory to the disk cache. If you consistently have a low number, it indicates that you have too much physical memory allocated and that the memory is not used efficiently.
Total Disk Failures	This counter indicates the number of times that the Web Proxy service could not read from or write to the disk cache. Such a failure is usually the result of an I/O error. A consistent small number indicates that disk I/O is functioning well. A consistent high number indicates that a disk cache may be corrupted so that data cannot be read or written, the disk cache size is too small, or the hard disk itself is too slow to accommodate the requests.
Memory Usage Ratio Percent (%)	This counter (shown as a percentage) indicates the ratio between the number of times that data is taken from the memory cache and the amount of total times that data is taken from the cache. A consistent high number indicates that you may want to allocate more memory to the cache. A consistent low number indicates that the memory is wasted and can be used for other system resources.
Disk URL Retrieve Rate (URL/sec)	This counter indicates how many URLs are forwarded to clients in the network from disk cache in one second. You normally use this counter in the peak and off-peak hours to make sure that the cache performance is able to accommodate maximum and minimum number of requests from the clients.

Chapter Summary

ISA Server's caching provides many features you would not want to miss as the ISA Server administrator. In particular, its caching functionalities make ISA Server one of the best products available.

The idea behind caching is to store data close to the client that requests it. Obtaining Internet data from the local cache on the ISA server is faster than obtaining information by going out to the Internet. The ISA server's Web-caching capability allows you to retrieve any Web-related data (such as Web pages, graphics, and audio and video files) to its local cache configured on an NTFS partition. When a client attempts to access the Internet, the ISA server captures the request and checks its local cache to see whether the requested objects exist on the local cache. If the requested objects do not exist on the local cache, the ISA server will access the Internet and get the requested objects. Once the requested objects are obtained, the ISA server does not simply forward them to the client that requested them. The ISA server caches (stores) the retrieved data on its cache before forwarding the data to the client. For the client requesting the objects, the process is transparent.

Using Active Directory in a Windows 2000 domain, the ISA server could incorporate several ISA Servers into an array. Microsoft recommends using the ISA server array any time you have an ISA server or ISA servers joining to a Window 2000 domain. The ISA server array cannot be used if you have only a stand-alone server that does not belong to a Windows 2000 domain.

The benefits of using CARP include the following: CARP prevents the duplication of content that could occur if you're using an array of proxy servers based on ICP. CARP uses the hash-based routing, and it prevents the creation of duplicate caches. CARP creates a true, single logical cache, which leads to a faster response for clients and better use of server cache resources. CARP uses a deterministic request resolution path created by the hash-based routing. No query is sent to the network to see where the cache information stays, which is normally done with ICP. CARP has positive scalability. The more servers you have, the faster ISA server finds the cache information using CARP. Using CARP, you can configure each ISA server to balance how many cache objects are stored in each ISA server. Every time a new ISA server is added to an array or an existing ISA server is removed from the array, CARP takes care of the change automatically.

You can configure the ISA server to download Web-related content on a scheduled basis. The Web content can be downloaded as a single URL, as multiple URLs, or as an entire Web site. In some cases, you may just want to download the text content but no graphics or other Web content. ISA Sever allows you to configure the cache to download only text content.

When you have more than one ISA server in the array, the cache load is distributed among them in the array, which provides performance gain. In addition, fault tolerance is provided in case one ISA server becomes unavailable. The term *chaining* refers to a configuration of ISA servers that are chained hierarchically between individual ISA server or arrays of ISA servers. Web Proxy routing takes the concept of cache chaining and modifies the routing functions of cache information so that the local clients are served in the most efficient manner. In some cases, you may not want the ISA server or ISA server array to cache Internet objects. Cache filtering is also configured as the routing rule.

Although you have only three options, the ISA server lets you tune the system resources depending on the number of clients requesting resources from the ISA server in a day. The ISA server also adds many system performance counters that you can use to monitor the system resource performance. These counters are useful when you are troubleshooting.

Review Questions

1. Allowing internal clients to access the Internet with caching is called what?
    a. Forward caching
    b. Reverse caching
    c. Scheduled caching
    d. Hierarchical caching

2. Allowing Internet clients to access the internal Web servers with caching is called what?
    a. Forward caching
    b. Reverse caching
    c. Scheduled caching
    d. Hierarchical caching

3. Downloading Internet resources on a scheduled basis is called what?
    a. Forward caching
    b. Reverse caching
    c. Scheduled caching
    d. Hierarchical caching
    e. Distributed caching

4. Obtaining Web-related objects from different ISA servers in an ISA array is best described as what?

   a. Forward caching
   b. Reverse caching
   c. Scheduled caching
   d. Hierarchical caching
   e. Distributed caching

5. The ISA Server configuration in which several ISA servers or ISA server arrays are connected in a cascading manner is best described as what?

   a. Forward caching
   b. Reverse caching
   c. Scheduled caching
   d. Hierarchical caching
   e. Distributed caching

6. To allow both SecureNAT and firewall clients to use the caching features, you will need to use what filter?

   a. HTTP filter
   b. FTP filter
   c. HTTP redirector filter
   d. FTP redirector filter

7. An ISA server array uses what protocol to make sure there are no duplicates of the cached information?

   a. TTL
   b. ICP
   c. CARP
   d. PPTP

8. To use CARP, which of the following do you need?

   a. Windows NT 4 Peer-to-Peer network
   b. Windows 2000 Peer-to-Peer network
   c. Windows NT 4 domain
   d. Windows 2000 domain

9. What is one of CARP's many features?

   a. ICP

   b. The ability to query other servers

   c. The creation of cache duplicates

   d. Deterministic request resolution path

10. Where do you configure CARP?

    a. MMC

    b. ISA Management MMC

    c. ISA Configuration MMC

    d. ISA Wizard

11. An intra-array IP address needs to be which of the following?

    a. External IP address

    b. Internal IP address

    c. External DNS address

    d. External WINS address

12. A scheduled cache content download can download Web-related information at what level? [Check all correct answers]

    a. Single URL

    b. Multiple URLs

    c. Single IP address

    d. Entire Web site

13. Under what condition will the scheduled cache content download fail?

    a. When there is no more memory to allocate.

    b. When there is no more cache space to allocate.

    c. When client authentication is required.

    d. When you have only one ISA server in the network.

    e. When you have only one ISA server array in the network.

14. When you have more than one ISA server on your network and one fails, another one takes over the functions. What is this behavior called?

    a. Replication

    b. Duplication

    c. System copy

    d. Fault tolerance

15. CARP is offered by which Microsoft products? [Check all correct answers]
    a. Proxy Server 1.0
    b. Proxy Server 2.0
    c. ISA Server
    d. Small Business Server 4.5

16. Web Proxy routing can use which of the following options? [Check all correct answers]
    a. Client requests will be retrieved directly from the specified destination.
    b. Client requests will be sent to an upstream server.
    c. Client requests will be redirected to an alternate site.
    d. Client requests will be redirected to an Internet site.

17. When you do not want to cache information on an ISA server, what would you do?
    a. Use CARP
    b. Use cache filtering
    c. Monitor cache performance
    d. Tune ISA Server
    e. Use ICP

18. When you tune the ISA server, what options are available? [Check all correct answers]
    a. Fewer Than 100
    b. Fewer Than 1,000
    c. Fewer Than 10,000
    d. More Than 100
    e. More Than 1,000

19. To check the cumulative number of URLs that have been cached, you would use which ISA Server monitoring counter?
    a. Total URLs Cached
    b. Total Disk Failures
    c. Memory Usage Ratio Percent
    d. Disk URL Retrieve Rate

20. To check the number of times that the Web Proxy Service failed to read from or write to the disk cache, you would use which ISA Server monitoring counter?

   a. Total URLs Cached

   b. Total Disk Failures

   c. Memory Usage Ratio Percent

   d. Disk URL Retrieve Rate

Real-World Projects

Note: This exercise assumes a test Windows 2000 server or Advanced Server with Service Pack 1 or Windows 2000 Datacenter Server installed. Read the instructions carefully and do not perform this install on your production machine unless you understand the options presented. If you are unsure about an option, cancel the installation and read the help files provided with ISA Server about the option to be installed.

Dan works for a medium-sized company, whose employees are located in three geographical regions. He is the main system administrator taking care of Internet related system administration. Each office has about 500 employees, a T1 line, and access to the Internet. If an employee needs to access the Internet, he or she goes out to the Internet through the T1 line. However, there is no Web Proxy server deployed in each office. In the last several months, the IT department has received a lot of calls from clients complaining that the Internet access is too slow. Especially during business hours, the Internet access speed is unacceptable. The IT department manager, Ken, is concerned and talks to Dan about the problem.

"Hey, Dan! How's it going? You know, we are getting a lot of complaints about the Internet access lately."

Dan replies, "Yes, I'm having the same problem at my workstation. Do you have any plans to take care of the problem?"

Ken says, "Well, I wanted to talk to you because you may have the solution. Do you know anything about ISA Server from Microsoft? It may solve our problem."

Dan has been pretty interested in Web technology for a while now, and he does know one thing about ISA Server: It provides some Web-caching capability. Ken has been known to be on top of almost everything relating to IT, and he is a pretty sharp guy. After all, Dan trusts him and that is why Dan is still working for him.

Dan says, "I know a bit about ISA Server. I understand it provides some sort of Web-caching, correct? What do you know about it?"

Ken says, "You know, Web caching is just one of the features that ISA Server provides, and I can spend a whole day talking about its features. We don't have too much time at this point, but we need to implement the Web caching so that the T1 line we have doesn't get too congested. Anyway, would you be interested in implementing a company-wide Web-caching solution using ISA Server?"

Dan is interested. Doing a good job for Ken will not only solve the slow Internet access problem, but will also allow Dan to become familiar with the latest Microsoft technology.

Dan agrees. "Sure. How much time do we have to implement it?"

Ken says, "Let's talk a bit more about it. We need to start planning now. We just have a couple weeks to implement."

"Wait!" Dan thinks he does not have enough time to implement it in just a couple weeks, but Ken is already taking Dan's arm and they are walking toward a meeting room at the corner.

Dan and Ken talk for about an hour, and Dan finds out something very exciting. Ken mentions that he has six servers that are built with Windows 2000 Server in the IT department's test lab. Ken wants Dan to use them to install ISA Server and create several arrays. Now things are getting a bit confusing, because Dan does not understand what arrays are. Ken is a very knowledgeable guy, and he seems to have studied ISA Server for a while now. Ken has ideas about what they should do. Dan's job is to physically execute the implementation. Ken tells Dan to learn as much as he can about ISA Server during the next couple days, and he'll see if Dan can start practicing the ISA server array implementation on the test lab.

A couple days have passed. Dan has spent a lot of time studying—especially for the ISA server array implementation—and he is quite comfortable with the technology now. Dan has already created three ISA server arrays, each consisting of two ISA Servers. One of the requirements for the project is to allow Internet users to access an internal Web server's content, so the first thing Dan has to do is enable the incoming Web requests for the Cache Array Routing Protocol (CARP). Dan takes the following steps to complete it.

Project 8.1
To enable incoming Web requests:

1. Open the ISA Management MMC by selecting Start|Programs|Microsoft ISA Server|ISA Management.

2. Right-click the name of the array that you want to enable incoming Web requests, and then click Properties. The array properties appear. See Figure 8.6.

3. On the Incoming Web Requests tab, select Resolve Requests Within Array Before Routing checkbox. See Figure 8.7.

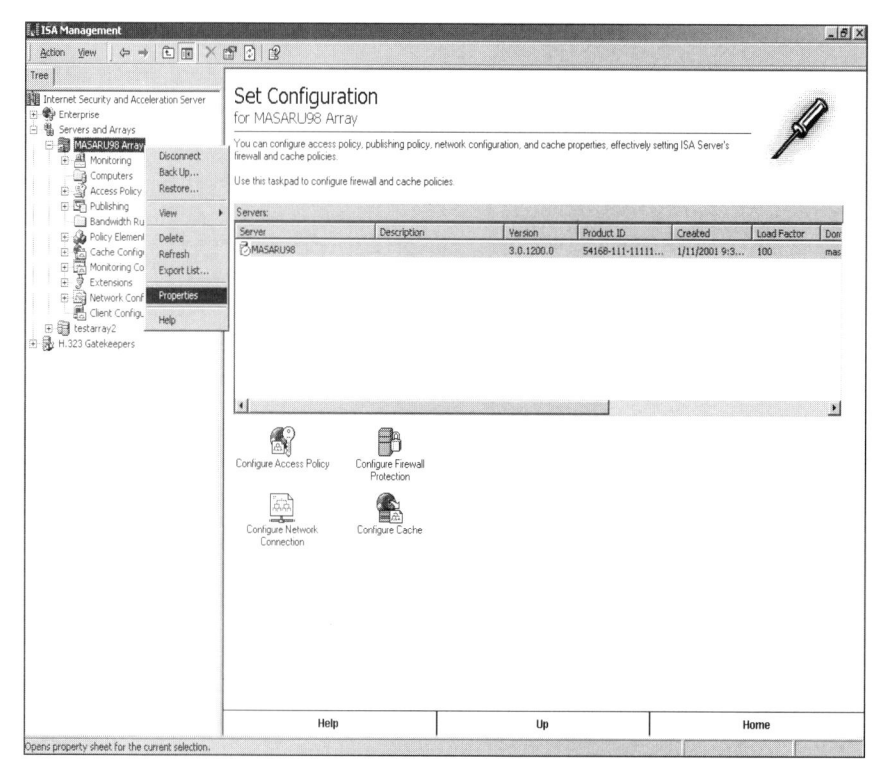

Figure 8.6 Array Properties.

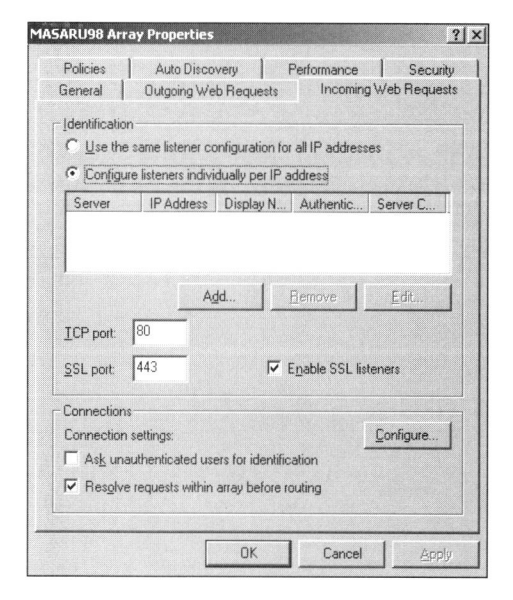

Figure 8.7 Incoming Web Requests tab.

4. If the Resolve Requests Within Array Before Routing checkbox has not been selected before, then you will receive the following message: "When resolving requests within an array, be sure that a listener is configured for the IP address specified for each member server's intra-array address property." Click OK. See Figure 8.8.

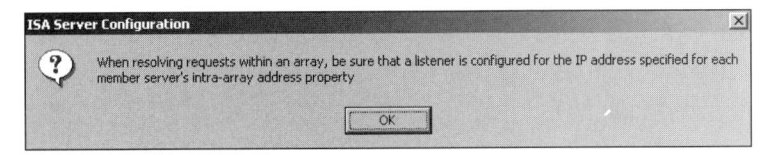

Figure 8.8 ISA Server Configuration dialog box.

5. Click OK again to close the array properties page. The ISA Server Warning will appear. The change you just made will not be effective unless some services, such as Web proxy and Scheduled Content Download, are restarted. Select a proper option, either Save The Changes, But Don't Restart The Service[s] or Save The Changes And Restart The Service[s]. For the sake of this example, select Save The Changes And Restart The Services, and click OK.
See Figure 8.9.

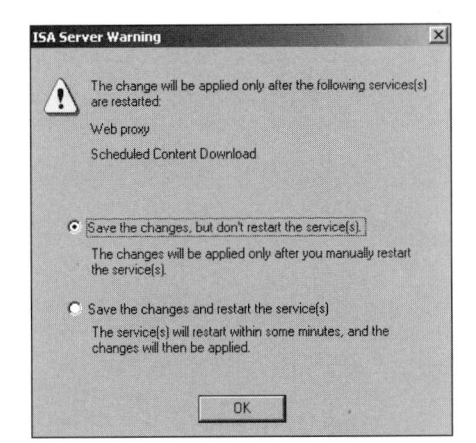

Figure 8.9 ISA Server Warning dialog box.

Now the incoming Web request is configured. One of the things Dan has found is that each of the six servers has a different hardware configuration. Some are more powerful than the others. The ISA server array configured has two ISA servers in it, and one server is more powerful than the other one. Ken has mentioned that Dan needs to change the load factor to ensure that different hardware configurations are taken into account in the array. Dan takes the following steps to modify the load factor.

Project 8.2

To modify the load factor:

1. Open the ISA Management MMC by clicking Start | Programs | Microsoft ISA Server | ISA Management. Click on the array that contains the server for which you would like to change the load factor.

2. Double-click the appropriate server in the details pane on the right. The server properties appear.

3. On the Array Membership tab, type the load factor in the Load Factor text box. For the sake of this example, leave the default load factor of 100. The load factor is a number between 1 and 2147483647. It is recommended that the total load factor of all the ISA member servers in an array be 100 so that you can easily determine how the load factor is distributed among member servers in the array. See Figure 8.10.

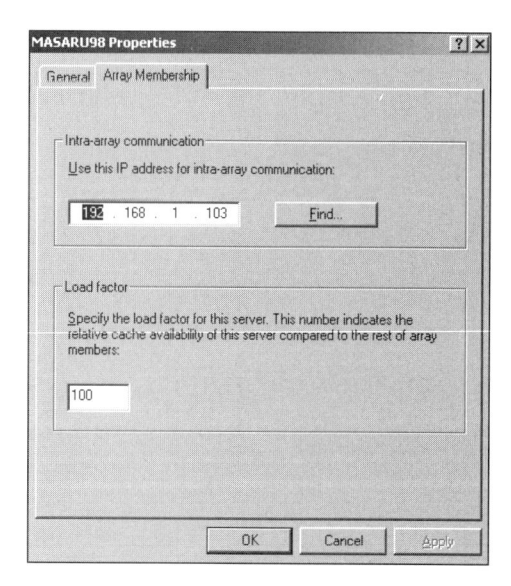

Figure 8.10 Array Membership tab.

4. Click OK to close the server property page.

Ken has a research document showing which Web sites are accessed frequently. Ken gives Dan the document and asks Dan to configure the content of these Web sites to be cached to the ISA server array. Dan knows he can use the scheduled cache content download function on the ISA server.

Project 8.3

To configure the scheduled content download:

1. Open the ISA Management MMC by clicking Start|Programs|Microsoft ISA Server|ISA Management.

2. Expand the Servers And Arrays, the name of the array, and Cache Configuration, and then click Scheduled Content Download Jobs. See Figure 8.11.

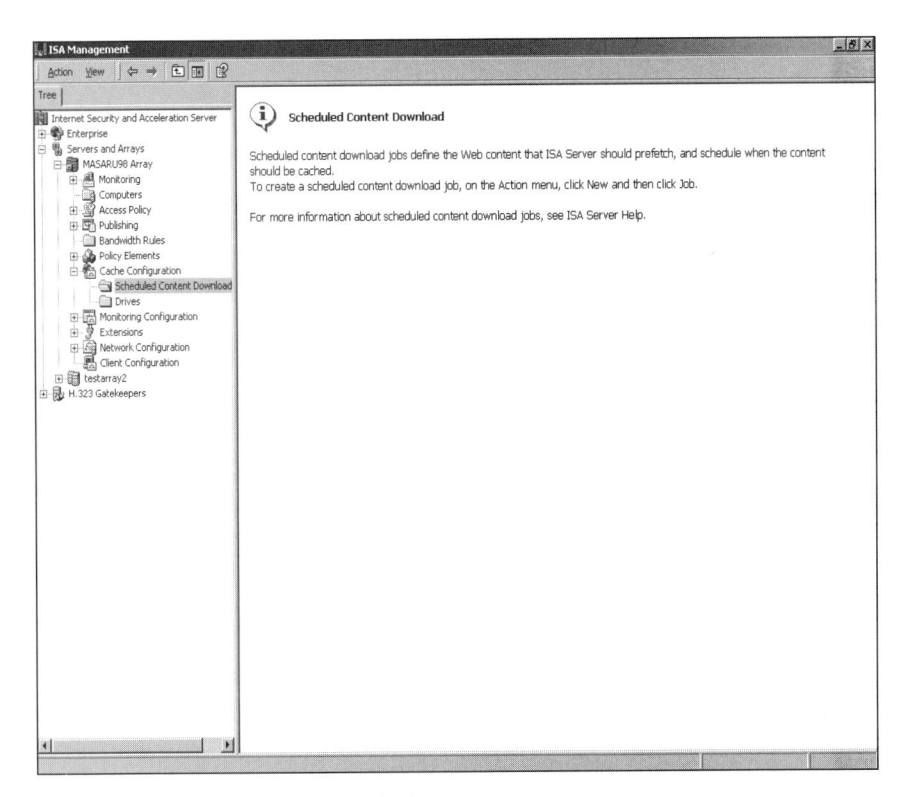

Figure 8.11 Schedule Content Download pane.

3. Right-click on Scheduled Content Download Jobs and select New|Job. The New Scheduled Content Download Job Wizard starts. If there is a job schedule that you would like to change, go to step 10. See Figure 8.12.

4. On the Welcome To The Scheduled Content Download Job Wizard page, type in the job name. For this example, type "job1". Click Next. See Figure 8.13.

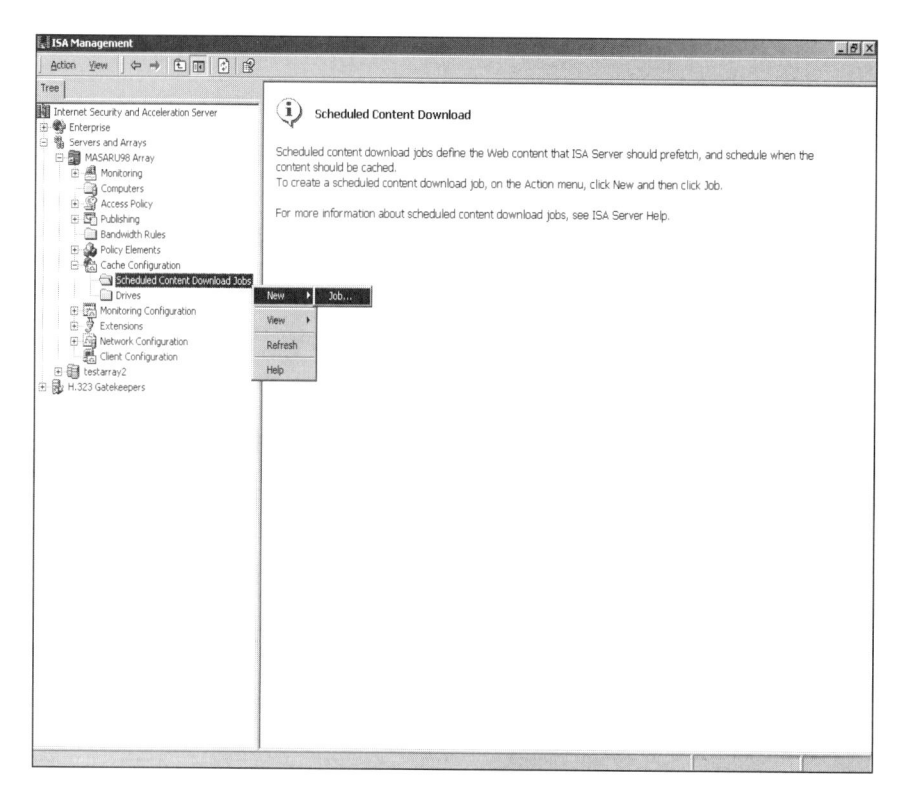

Figure 8.12 Creating a new scheduled content download job.

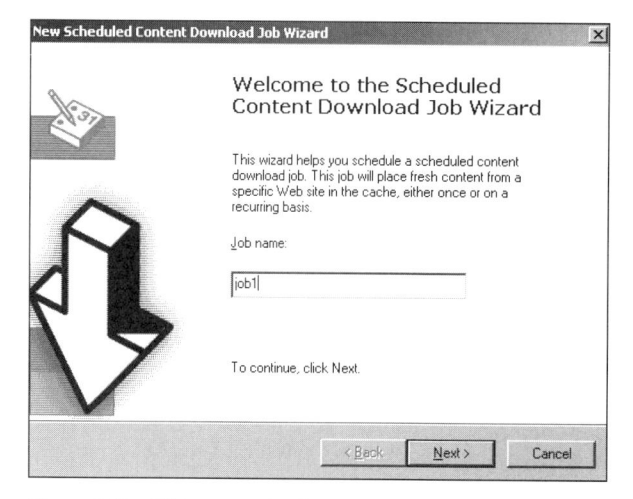

Figure 8.13 Welcome to the Scheduled Content Download Job Wizard page.

5. On the Start Time page, Select the date and time to start downloading if this will be a single download job. If this will be a recurring job, select the date and time for the first job. For this example, just leave the default, which is usually the system time of your system. Click Next. See Figure 8.14.

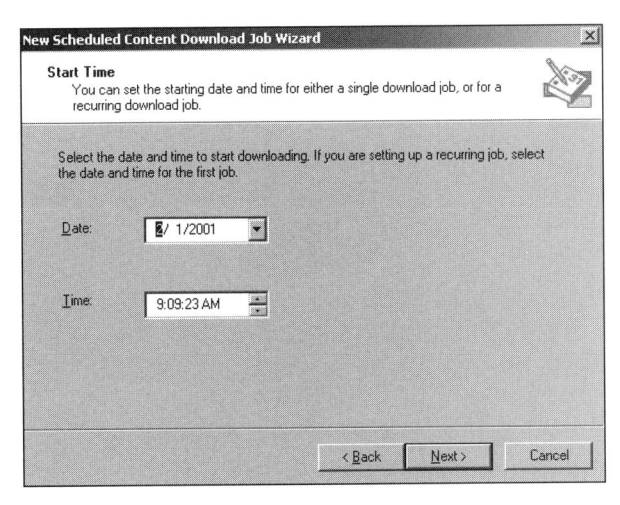

Figure 8.14 Start Time page.

6. On the Frequency page, select Once, Daily, or Weekly. For this example, select Daily, and click Next. See Figure 8.15.

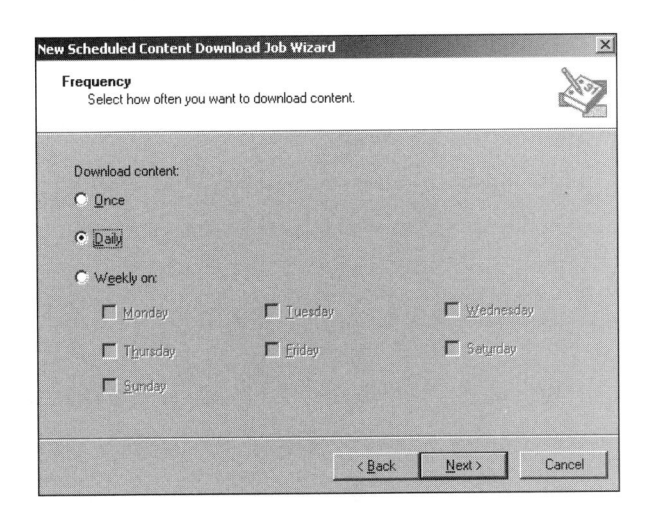

Figure 8.15 Frequency page.

7. On the Content page, type in the download content URL. Use **http://isa.coriolis.com/isalab8** for this example. Leave the two download options unchecked (Content Only From URL Domain and Cache Dynamic Content.) Then, click Next. See Figure 8.16.

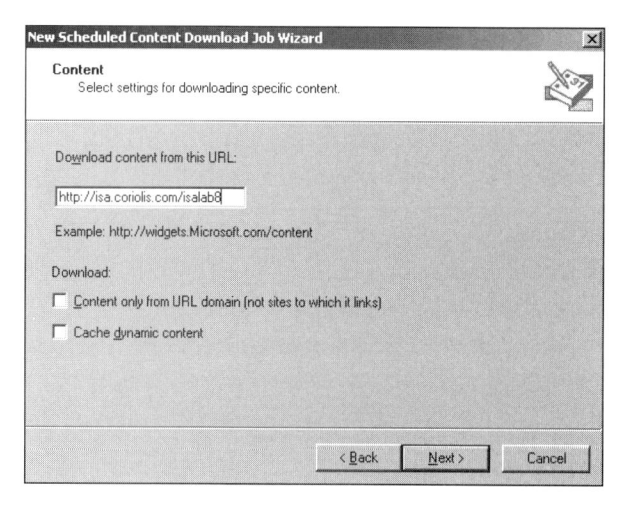

Figure 8.16 Content page.

8. The Links And Downloaded Objects page appears. Leave the default values untouched. Click Next. See Figure 8.17.

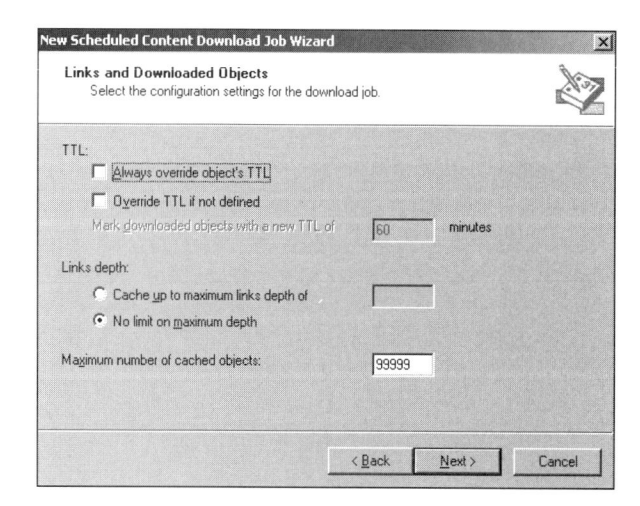

Figure 8.17 Links And Downloaded Objects page.

9. On the Completing The Scheduled Content Download Job Wizard page, confirm all the options selected and click Finish. The job just created, job1, should show up in the Details pane. See Figure 8.18.

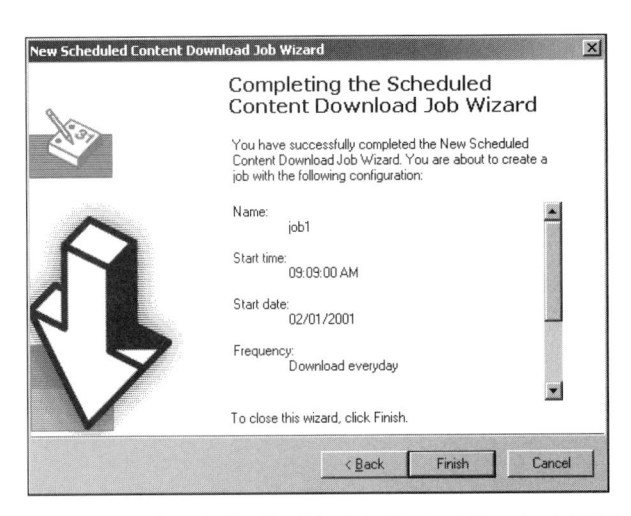

Figure 8.18 Completing the Scheduled Content Download Job Wizard page.

10. In the Details pane, right-click the appropriate Scheduled Content Download Job and then click Properties. See Figure 8.19.

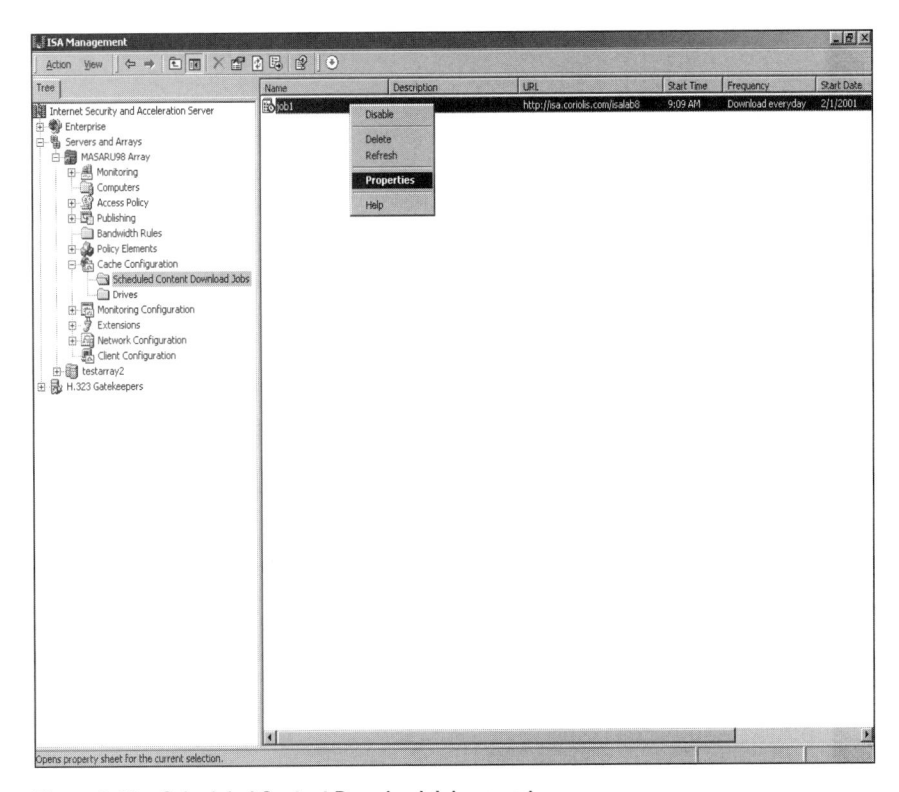

Figure 8.19 Scheduled Content Download Job property.

11. On the Frequency tab, in the Date and Time drop-down menus, type the date and time when the content should be downloaded from the Internet. See Figure 8.20.

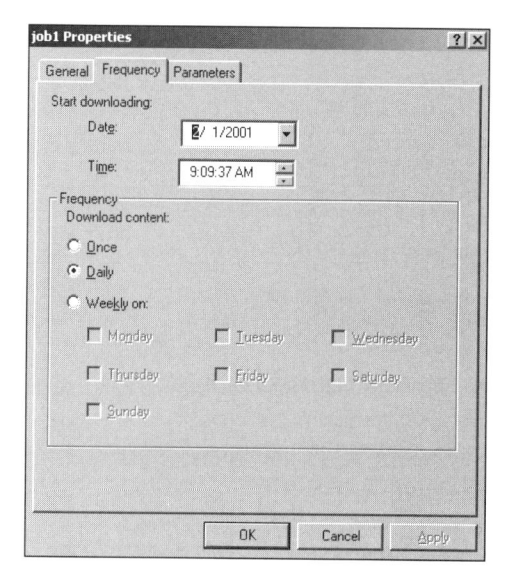

Figure 8.20 Frequency tab.

12. On the Frequency tab from step 11, configure the appropriate download scheduling:

    ➤ Click Once to download the contents once at a specific time.

    ➤ Click Daily to download the contents daily at a specific time.

    ➤ Click Weekly and then specify which days to download the content.

    For this example, confirm that the date and time are the same as the current system and that the frequency to download content is Daily. If not, make the appropriate changes. Click OK to get out of the Job Properties page.

Dan has configured the frequency of the Web sites to download. He now needs to specify which sites to download.

Project 8.4

To configure which sites to download:

1. Open the ISA Management MMC by clicking Start | Programs | Microsoft ISA Server | ISA Management.

2. Expand the Servers And Arrays, the name of the array, and Cache Configuration, and then click Scheduled Content Download Jobs.

3. In the details pane, right-click the appropriate scheduled content download job, and then click Properties.

4. On the Parameters tab, under Begin Downloading From URL, type the URL from which to download the content. For this example, confirm that the URL is **http://isa.coriolis.com/isalab8**. If not, change it. See Figure 8.21.

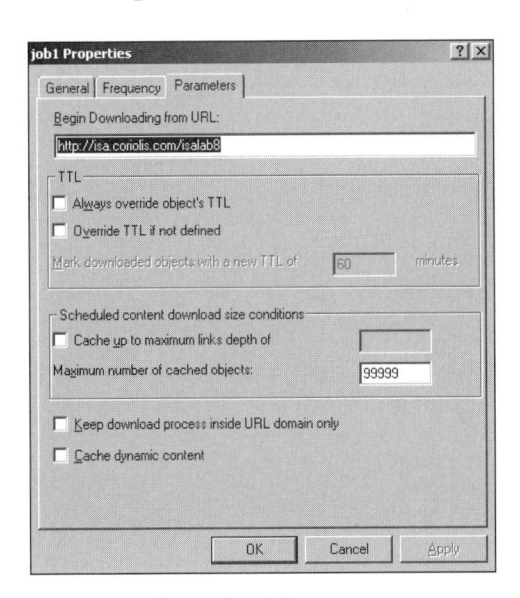

Figure 8.21 Parameters tab.

5. To download only content from the domain, click Keep Download Process Inside URL Domain Only. Select it for this example.

6. To limit the number of links to follow from a single page when downloading content, click Cache Up To Maximum Links Depth Of and type the number of links to follow. Leave blank for this example.

7. To limit the total number of objects to cache, enter a value in Maximum Number Of Cached Objects. Leave the default value of 99999 for this example.

Dan thinks to himself, "The easy part is done. Now what?" The next job is to create Web Proxy routing so that as a result, all the ISA server arrays will be connected to one another and client requests will be forwarded appropriately. Dan takes the following steps to configure Web Proxy routing.

Project 8.5

To configure Web Proxy routing:

1. Open the ISA Management MMC by clicking Start | Programs | Microsoft ISA Server | ISA Management.

2. Expand the Servers And Arrays, the name of the array, and Network Configuration, and then click Routing.

3. In the details pane, right-click the appropriate routing rule (For Dan, because this is the first time he is configuring Web Proxy, only the default rule would be available. In your case, if somebody has created routing rules before, right-click the routing rule that you need to reconfigure.), and then click Properties. For this example, let's create a routing rule as the default rule does not give you too many options to play with. Right-click on Routing | New | Rule. See figure 8.22.

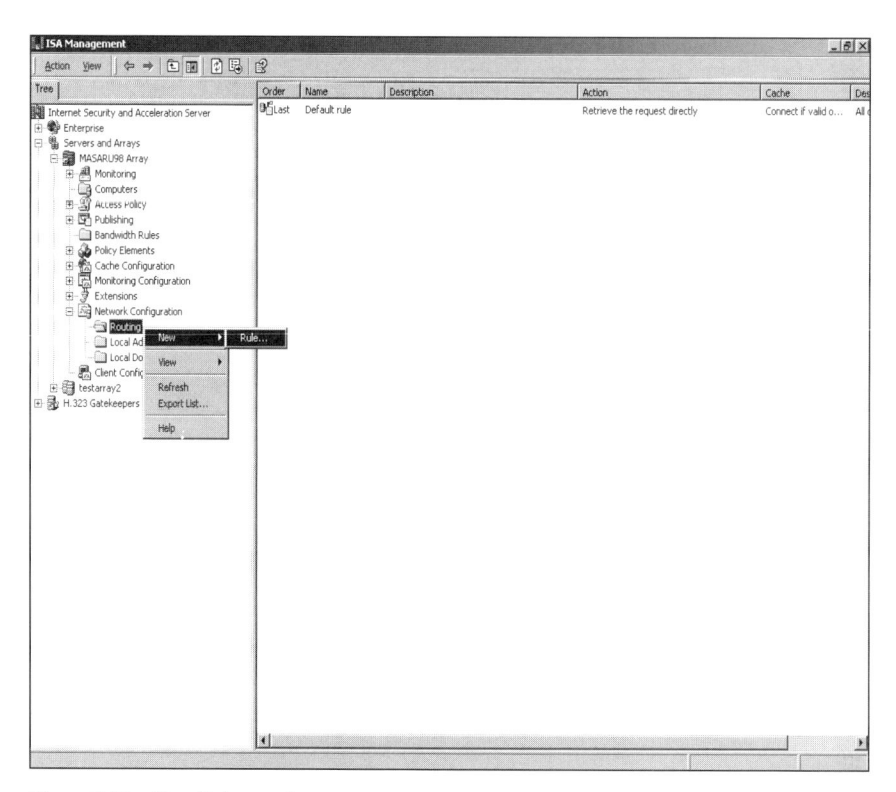

Figure 8.22 New Rule creation.

4. On the Welcome To The New Routing Rule Wizard page, type in "rule1", and take all the default options for the rest of the configuration pages. See figure 8.23.

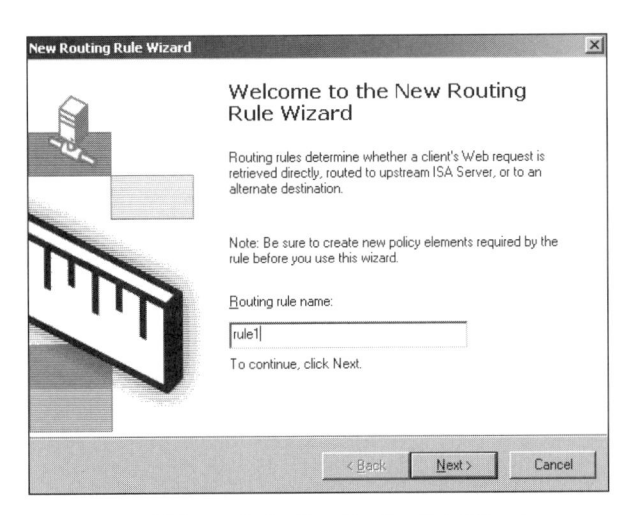

Figure 8.23 Welcome to the New Routing Rule Wizard page.

5. Once rule1 is created, right-click on it and select Properties. See figure 8.24.

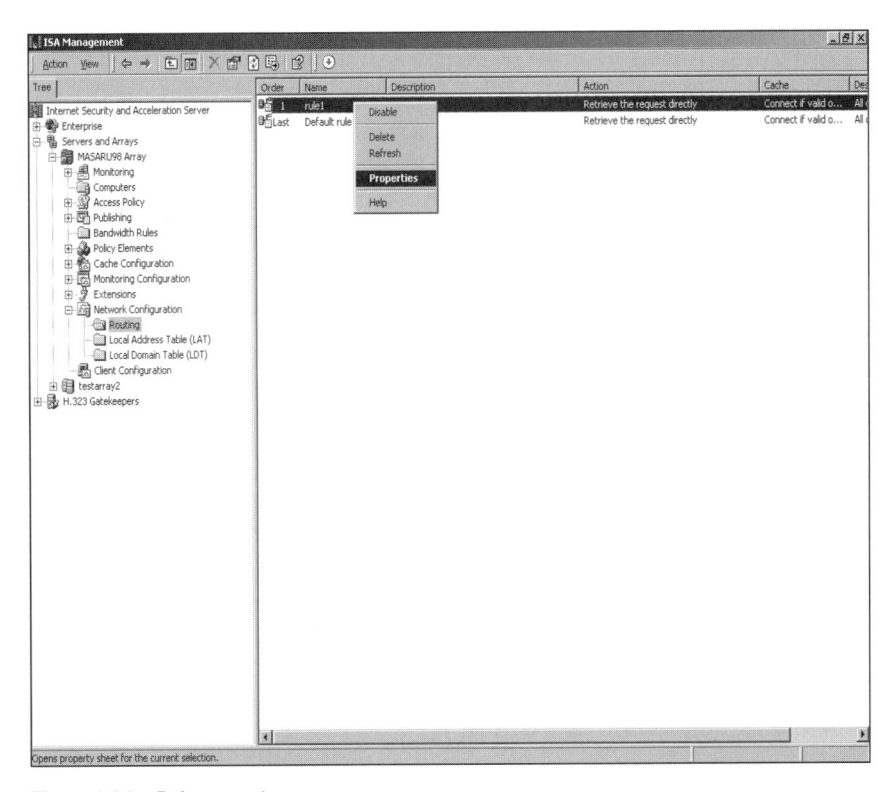

Figure 8.24 Rule property.

6. On the Destinations tab, click the destination set to which the routing rule applies. If the destination set that you want to specify does not exist, select Selected Destination Set and create one by clicking New and then selecting it in the list. You can specify array-level destination sets for the routing rules only, and you cannot select an individual ISA server. The options are as follows:

   ➤ All Destinations

   ➤ All External Destinations

   ➤ All Internal Destinations

   ➤ Selected Destination Set

   ➤ All Destinations Except Selected Set

   For this example, select All Internal Destinations. See Figure 8.25.

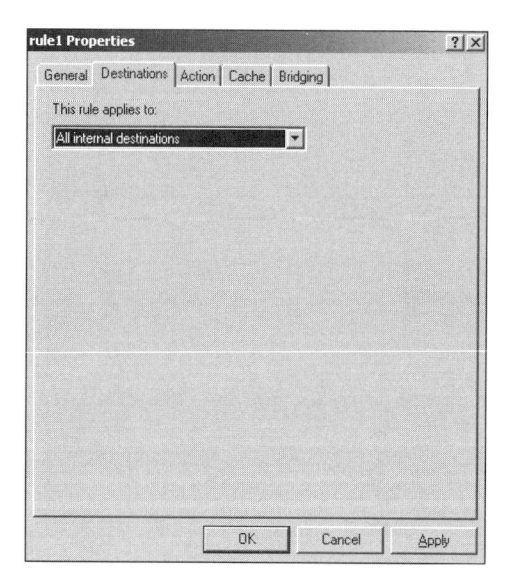

Figure 8.25 Destinations tab.

7. If you chose Selected Destination Set or All Destinations Except Selected Set, then you must select a destination set under Name.

Everything seems to be configured properly now. Dan now will need to talk with Ken to see how they can start testing it. But for now, it has been a long day for Dan, and it is about time for him to go home. Dan has done a lot of things today, and he is excited to start testing the configuration tomorrow.

CHAPTER NINE

Understanding the Web Proxy Service

After completing this chapter, you will be able to:

✓ Define the purpose of the Web Proxy service

✓ Describe the architecture of the Web Proxy service

✓ Explain the Secure Sockets Layer (SSL) process

✓ Explain how SSL affects the Web Proxy service

✓ List the client types that work with the Web Proxy service

✓ List and describe the protocols that work with the Web Proxy service

✓ Configure the Web Proxy service

✓ Describe the role of the HTTP redirector filter in the architecture of ISA Server

✓ Set listeners for the Web Proxy service

✓ Select correct port settings for client access

✓ Explain the addition of Web filters

✓ Configure connection settings

The two main services in ISA Server that make connections for internal clients are the Web Proxy service and the Firewall service. The Web Proxy service is responsible for retrieving objects for internal clients. Using four specific protocols, it can connect to the Internet to retrieve these objects. All other connections through ISA Server not using these protocols use the Firewall service instead. The Firewall service is highlighted in Chapter 10 of this book.

The method for implementing security on sensitive Web pages has not changed significantly with the release of ISA Server. However, the way ISA Server is able to handle these secure connections has changed. Secure Sockets Layer (SSL) uses a process that ensures the identity of the computer and then uses encryption to secure the contents of an object. ISA Server can implement SSL as a circuit- or application-level proxy as well as cache-specified SSL objects. In this chapter, we will discuss the services that the Web Proxy service provides as well as the configuration settings that can affect these services.

What Is the Web Proxy Service?

The Web Proxy service is an application-level proxy service. This means that not only does it retrieve Web pages for internal clients—thereby keeping them anonymous from Internet servers—it also provides application-level extras to its services. These extras can include allowing and disallowing connections based on protocol types, authentication based on user accounts or certificates, caching, logging, and auditing services.

If you are on an internal network that has ISA Server providing proxy services, you will need to go through the Web Proxy service to get your Web pages. The Web Proxy service is one of two main components in ISA Server that handles client requests. The other component is the Firewall service. All outgoing requests to the Internet will be handled by one of these two services, and ISA Server clearly splits the duties between these two services. The Web Proxy service has the specific duty of retrieving objects for internal clients, whereas the Firewall service makes connections for internal clients. Objects available for retrieval from the Internet include Web pages and documents retrieved through protocols such as HTTP and FTP. The Web Proxy service works with four protocols to retrieve these objects, which we'll list in the next section.

Instead of retrieving objects, the Firewall service makes connections by linking internal clients to Internet servers. These connections are for Internet applications. The Web Proxy service intercepts requests from internal clients and handles them based on its settings. The request can be denied (based on security settings), fulfilled from cache, or fulfilled by being sent out to the Internet.

Protocols Used by the Web Proxy Service

The Web Proxy service handles all requests that ask for objects. To do this, it works with four protocols: Hypertext Transfer Protocol (HTTP), File Transfer Protocol (FTP), Gopher, and Secure Hypertext Transfer Protocol (HTTP-S). Services using other protocols will use the Firewall service to connect them.

HTTP and HTTP-S

HTTP is the protocol used to retrieve Web pages and other objects over the Internet. Although HTTP started out very simply, it has gone through version changes that have improved it significantly. As you know, a Web page contains many objects, such as images, sound files, Java applets, and ActiveX objects. When HTTP goes to retrieve a Web page, it has to download each of these as a separate object. This means that a Web page that contains 10 pictures will actually need to download 11 separate objects (including the Web page itself) if each picture is a separate image file. This is why a Web page's text will often download while the pictures remain blank placeholders over a slow WAN link. Also, though many of the documents downloaded by HTTP are HTML documents on the Web, HTTP can download any type of document. You can place Word documents and PowerPoint slides on a Web site, and users can download them in their native file formats without having to convert to HTML. Adobe Acrobat files are another good example of this. As long as you have a reader on the client side, you can download a file in its native file format and read it. HTTP is the protocol used to download all these files. The most current version of HTTP is 1.1.

HTTP is designed as a *stateless* protocol because of the heavy load of work that it needs to do over the Internet. A protocol is *stateless* when it does not retain any information about a user once the user disconnects. If you live in a small town and go to the local grocery store, then the people who own and work at the store will probably remember you. They will remember what kind of customer you are and what kinds of things you like to buy. Computers remembering who you are and whether you have been there before is called *maintaining state*. But if you go into a grocery store in a big city, many people work there and there are too many customers to keep track of. When you come back to the store the next time, no one will remember your individual preferences. Too many people move through the store. The people who own and work at the grocery store cannot maintain state on every customer; instead, they must be stateless and treat every customer the same. They just don't have the resources to remember each customer. On the Internet, HTTP is too busy to remember your individual preferences. It processes requests and retrieves objects, but it can't remember even a little information about each one.

HTTP-S is used in the process of securing Web pages with SSL. A Web page using SSL will be accessed with HTTP-S as the protocol instead of HTTP. The SSL process is described thoroughly later in this chapter.

FTP

FTP is also often used to download files over the Internet, but the files can be a more varied type than Web pages. When FTP was first designed, HTTP was downloading only text files, so there was a need for a separate protocol that could download any type of file. Now that HTTP has been expanded to include any type of file, it is eclipsing the capabilities of FTP. The general consensus of the Internet community is that FTP will decline in use and its functionality replaced by HTTP.

Gopher

The Gopher service was designed to give a user a list of files available on an Internet server. Gopher, like FTP, was created before the Web and its system of using hyperlinks to connect and find documents. Now that users can find documents through hyperlinks, they do not need a list of files on a server. Gopher use is declining but is still supported by the Web Proxy service in ISA Server.

Clients for the Web Proxy Service

Clients do not need additional software to use the Web Proxy service; however, they do need some configuration so that they know to direct their Web page requests to ISA Server and which port to use. Web Proxy client configuration is covered in Chapter 5 of this book.

CERN-Compliant Web Browsers

The Web Proxy service can have a variety of operating systems as clients, including all Windows operating systems, Unix, and Macintosh. The reason the Web Proxy service is so open to operating systems is that it is the Web browser that actually is the client to the Web Proxy service. The Web browser is the component that makes the request to the Web Proxy service. As long as the Web browser is Conseil Européen pour la Recherché Nucléaire (CERN) compliant, it is compatible with the Web Proxy service. CERN, located in Switzerland, created the first Web browser, and nearly all Web browsers are CERN compliant.

HTTP Redirector Filter

Other components within ISA Server can work with the Web Proxy service to make sure that all requests for HTTP objects are redirected to it. All Firewall client and SecureNAT client requests are sent to the Firewall service in ISA Server. The Firewall service then evaluates each request it receives to see how it should fulfill that request. If the request is for an HTTP object, the Firewall Service sends it on to the HTTP Redirector Filter. You can configure the HTTP Redirector Filter to forward these requests to the Web Proxy service. Figure 9.1 shows how this process works.

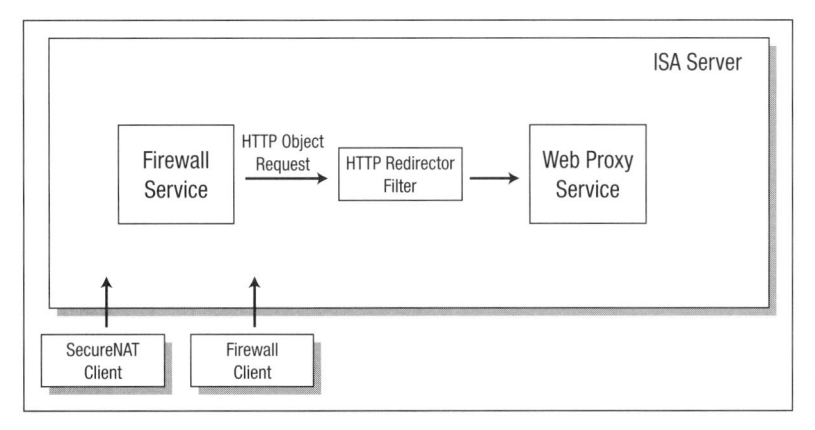

Figure 9.1 Firewall client requests are always sent to the Firewall service. If they are requests for an HTTP object, they are sent to the HTTP Redirector Filter and passed on to the Web Proxy service.

The HTTP Redirector Filter is part of a set of application filters that come with ISA Server. These application filters are considered to be extensions to ISA Server and do not have to be used. You can disable the HTTP Redirector Filter so that it is not a part of the architecture of ISA Server. You can also configure the HTTP Redirector Filter to send these requests out to the Internet and bypass the Web Proxy service or even to discard the requests. By default, the HTTP Redirector Filter is enabled and passes the requests it receives from the Firewall service on to the Web Proxy service.

How Does the Web Proxy Service Work?

Now that you know the purpose of the Web Proxy service, it is important to see how the service works. Figure 9.2 shows the full internal architecture that allows the Web Proxy service to work. An internal client will have its requests passed to either the Firewall service or the Web Proxy service based on what type of client it is. HTTP requests are by default forwarded to the Web Proxy service either directly or through the HTTP Redirector Filter. After that, the request is sent through any Web filters that are added to the ISA Server installation.

The Web Proxy service is dependent on the Microsoft ISA Server Control service. In the Services application, the Microsoft ISA Server Control service starts automatically when the Web Proxy service is started; when the Microsoft ISA Server Control service stops, the Web Proxy service also stops. The Microsoft ISA Server Control service is responsible for coordinating many of the actions of ISA Server, and all of the ISA services—not just the Web Proxy service—are dependent on it.

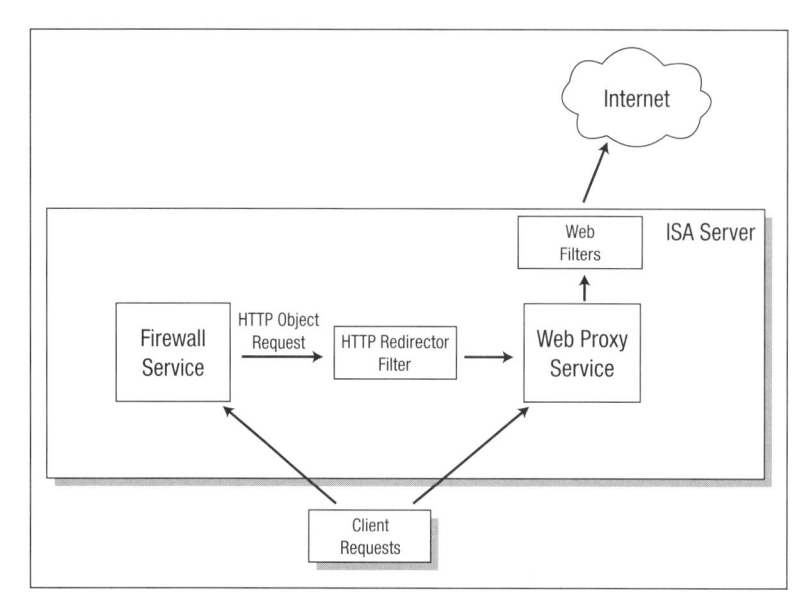

Figure 9.2 The architecture of the Web Proxy service.

Extensions to the Web Proxy Service

As with most Microsoft products, ISA Server capabilities are *extensible*. This means that you can expand those capabilities with add-on components. Your own company, Microsoft, or a third-party vendor can create these components. They can be either Web or application filters. Web filters are different from application filters in that they are Web Proxy service specific. Web filters receive the HTTP object requests from the Web Proxy service before they are sent out to the Internet. They can also process HTTP responses to the requests coming in from the Internet. Application filters can add capabilities to ISA Server and do not have to be Web Proxy specific. Though ISA Server contains several application filters by default, it contains no Web filters when first installed.

Accessing Secured Web Pages through the Web Proxy Service

When Web pages contain sensitive information, security may be needed to protect that information. With SSL, the process of downloading a Web page is changed. A secure channel between the client and the server should be established prior to the downloading of a Web page. The setup for this secure channel can be complicated by the interference of an ISA server between the Internet server and the internal client. To understand this architecture, we will review the process that SSL uses and how an ISA server affects that process.

SSL Components

Cryptography is the process of encrypting information. Cryptography uses algorithms and keys to complete the encryption and decryption process. With this process, information can be read only by computers that have the correct decryption key. One way to accomplish this is to give both parties the same key to perform the encryption and decryption. One user will encrypt the information with the key before sending it. The other will have a matching key that will decrypt the information. Of course, in single-key encryption both parties will need to be known ahead of time so they can each get the key.

Because of the nature of the Internet, single-key cryptography does not work most of the time. Often even though sensitive information is involved, the parties that are transmitting this information to each other are not known ahead of time and are never physically in the same place to each get a copy of a single key. To solve this problem, SSL was designed to encrypt Web pages with a public key cryptography, also known as *asymmetric cryptography*. This means SSL uses a key pair to encrypt the communication between computers. With two keys instead of just one, both the sending and receiving computer do not need to be known ahead of time. Public key cryptography is asymmetric because two keys—one public key and one private key—are used together to complete the encryption/decryption process. When one is used to encrypt, the other is used to decrypt. The public key is given to whomever wants to start a secure channel, while the private key always remains with the owner of the key pair. Figure 9.3 shows the architecture of public key cryptography. The following example assumes that Computer1 is requesting a secure channel and that Computer2 owns the key pair:

1. Computer1 requests a secure channel.

2. Computer2 gives the public key to Computer1.

3. When Computer2, holding the private key, encrypts a packet and Computer1 decrypts the packet, this is called a *digital signature*.

4. When Computer1, holding the public key, encrypts a packet and Computer2 decrypts the packet, this is called a *digital envelope*.

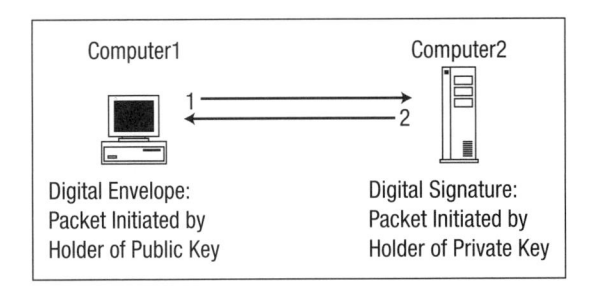

Figure 9.3 Public (asymmetric) key cryptography.

Establishing an Identity with Certificates

How do you know when you establish a secure channel with a computer that it is really the computer you think it is? You can't see the computer over the Internet, so how do you know? The answer: certificates. Certificates prove the identity of a computer before it establishes a secure channel with SSL.

When a secure channel is going to be established, the first step that a computer needs to take is to prove its identity by presenting its certificate. Certificates work like a driver's license. When you are asked to prove your identity, you simply pull out your driver's license—but how does the person looking at your driver's license know that it is proof of who you are? People know because they trust the issuer of the license, the Department of Motor Vehicles. The same works for a certificate. If you trust the maker of the certificate, you trust the identity of the computer that the certificate gives. VeriSign and RSA are two well-established certificate companies.

Where Do the Keys Come From?

Technically speaking, the public and the private key required to establish a secure channel are contained in the certificate. A key pair is generated when a certificate request is created, but it can't be used until a valid certificate is loaded on the machine on which it was created. The certificate request is submitted to a certificate authority, which may ask for more information before creating the certificate. When the certificate authority creates the certificate, the key pair is included in that certificate. The certificate should then be loaded on to the computer that created the certificate request and key pair. Only after this process can SSL be implemented on that computer.

The danger of certificates is that now anyone can make one. Microsoft has its own certificate server that is included with Windows 2000 Server. Anyone can load this server and start making and handing out certificates. A company might want to make its own internally used certificates for many legitimate reasons. However, the availability of this technology means that the acceptor of a certificate needs to make sure it comes from a trusted company.

Note: When a certificate is presented to your Web browser from a company that it does not trust, it will display a message specifically stating this. The message will also ask if you would like the browser to trust the certificate authority issuing the certificate. If you click the OK button, the issuer of the certificate is added to the list of trusted certificate authorities and certificates issued by this certificate authority will not be questioned again. To a user, this message looks physically like any other message. For example, a message warning a user that the connection to the Internet server was suddenly disconnected would look similar to this message, even though it contained different information.

Messages can appear frequently during an Internet connection, and users tend to tire of reading them and simply click OK to dismiss the dialog box with only a cursory look at the message. Because certificates can be created by anyone with the available technologies, it is best to train your users to recognize this dialog box and instruct them to contact their administrator for help when it appears.

Loading the Certificate

So, should the certificate be loaded on the Web server or the client? The answer is either or both. Traditionally, the server had the certificate loaded on it. The reason is that the computer that has something to lose is the one that asks for the certificate. In an e-commerce environment, normally the client has something to lose because the client is giving payment information while the server is receiving that sensitive information. For example, on a Web site when a customer—the client computer—goes to make a purchase, it will want a secure connection to protect the credit card number. In this case, the client will initiate the secure connection and request the certificate for proof of identity. The server will need then to provide the certificate to prove its identity and continue with the SSL process.

It is important to note that although traditionally the server held the certificate and the key pair, you also can load certificates on the client. If a company allows its employees to work from home, the company is the one that has something to lose. In this case, it is not credit cards numbers that need to be secured—it is company information. In this case, when employees connect to the private Web site of the company to retrieve internal company documents, the Web server will ask for the certificate of the client computer. Figure 9.4 shows the process of a client computer connecting to the company's Web server. The client computer is asked for its certificate; after presenting that certificate, it gives its public key to the Web server.

Client-side certificates are a good example of why a company would want to make its own certificates. A company can load a certificate server and make its own certificates so that they can be loaded on employees' laptops. This way, the company doesn't have to pay a third party to provide certificates that are only for use by company employees.

Ports and Protocols

Though the normal port used by ISA Server for Web connections is port 8080, the port number for Web pages using SSL is normally 443. This can affect settings in ISA Server. Also affected is the protocol that is used in URLs for secure Web pages.

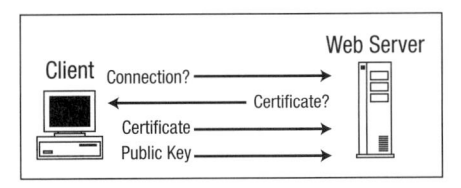

Figure 9.4 An SSL connection with a client certificate.

Instead of HTTP, SSL uses HTTP-S as the protocol. This means the URL **http://www.coriolis.com/default.htm** would change to **https://www.coriolis.com/default.htm** once SSL is implemented for that page. Configuring these settings is covered later in this chapter.

The SSL Process

Now that you know the components of SSL, you can see how they fit together to form the process that SSL follows when setting up a secure channel. ISA Server must interrupt this secure channel without causing it to fail. First, a certificate must be obtained and loaded on to one of the computers. For this example, we will assume we're dealing with a public Web site with the certificate loaded on the Web server. You need to configure the Web page(s) that contain or ask for sensitive information to require a secure channel that SSL has to set up. You perform this configuration on the Web server. The secure channel needs to be set up when one of these pages is accessed. In our example, the client computer links to a registration page called register.htm from a Web page called default.htm. The URL that the computer starts from is **http://www.coriolis.com/default.htm**. The URL for register.htm (since it requires SSL) is **https://www.coriolis.com/register.htm**. The protocol changes from HTTP to HTTP-S.

The Effect of ISA Server on Secure Web Pages

SSL sets up a secure channel between the client and server, but when ISA Server is set up on a network it interferes with this channel. In order for SSL to work with ISA Server, two different configurations are available: SSL tunneling and SSL bridging.

SSL Tunneling

With SSL tunneling, ISA Server acts as a circuit-level proxy server. The first Web request is made from the internal client to ISA Server, as shown in Figure 9.5. ISA Server accepts the request on the default ISA Server Web port, 8080. ISA Server makes a request to the Internet server using HTTPS as the protocol on port 443. Once the connection is established, ISA Server is no longer used. It works as a circuit-level proxy, establishing the communication channel only and then doing nothing else while the client and Internet server continue their secure session.

By default, when an internal client sends an HTTP-S request to ISA Server, SSL tunneling is automatically used. SSL will still need to be configured on the Web server, but no specific configuration settings are needed for ISA Server to perform SSL tunneling.

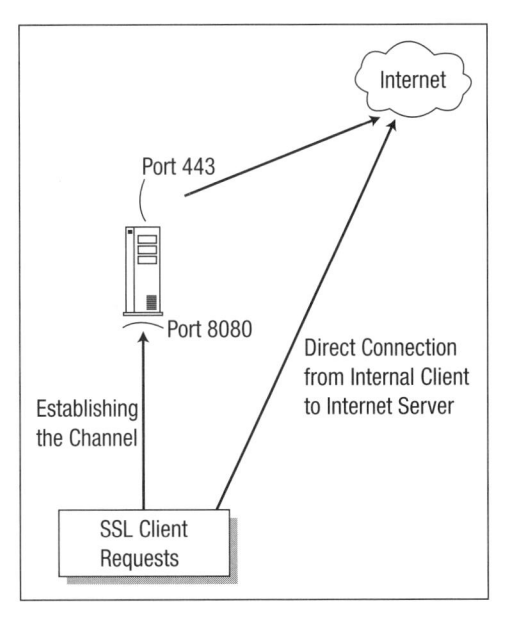

Figure 9.5 ISA Server acting as a circuit-level proxy for SSL tunneling establishes the channel and then allows direct communication between the internal client and the Internet server.

SSL Bridging

Whereas SSL tunneling works at the circuit level and does not have ISA Server interfere with the connection between the client and the Internet server (other than setup of the secure channel), SSL bridging takes a different approach. In SSL bridging, all communication between the internal client and the Internet server is passed to ISA Server. No direct communication occurs between the internal client and the Internet server.

SSL bridging is a feature not often seen on proxy servers. Many proxy servers offer only variations of SSL tunneling. When allowing SSL on your proxy server, your choices were to end the secure channel at the proxy server or allow the internal client to communicate directly with the Internet server. SSL bridging allows you to set a two-hop SSL channel from the client to ISA Server and from ISA Server to the Internet server. Although SSL bridging is slower than SSL tunneling (because two separate channels must be established), bridging gives you a choice. It allows an ISA server to keep the internal clients anonymous. SSL tunneling does not provide this option.

This difference between SSL tunneling and SSL bridging also causes some added changes between the two services. SSL tunneling does not allow the caching of objects passed between the internal client and the Web server, so all secure communications do not benefit from caching services provided by ISA Server when SSL tunneling is used. Since SSL tunneling was the only method of secure communication in Proxy Server 2.0, it could not cache SSL objects. But SSL bridging makes the caching of some SSL objects possible. In addition, it protects the client by taking its place in the secure channel.

To set up SSL bridging, you need to configure the SSL request to be redirected. This will change the default behavior of ISA Server from setting up an SSL tunnel to SSL bridging instead. This setup will require you to change the setting of a routing rule. A default routing rule is automatically created during the setup of ISA Server. You can configure more routing rules, which are covered in Chapter 8 of this book. To configure SSL bridging with the default routing rule, follow these steps:

1. Open ISA Management.
2. Under the Internet Security And Acceleration Server container, expand Servers And Arrays.
3. Expand the array on which you would like to implement SSL bridging.
4. Expand Network Configuration and then select Routing.
5. In the details pane on the right side of the window, right-click the default routing rule and then click Properties.

Tip: If you want SSL bridging to apply only to a specific set of computers, create a rule just for those computers and then apply the settings only to that rule.

6. Select the Bridging tab.
7. On the Bridging tab in the section labeled Redirect SSL Requests As, click SSL Requests (Establish A New Secure Channel To The Site). This will cause ISA Server to establish its own secure channel with the Internet Web server. If you select HTTP Requests (Terminate The Secure Channel At The Proxy), no secure channel will be established from ISA Server to the Internet Web server.
8. Place a checkmark in the Require A Secure Channel check box.

Tip: Do not use 128-bit encryption unless you are sure that connections will be made only within the United States or Canada. Using 128-bit encryption for connections outside these two countries violates US export laws.

9. Place a checkmark in the Use A Certificate To Authenticate To The SSL Web Server if the site requires client-side certificates.
10. Click OK to accept the changes and close the Rule Properties dialog box.

SSL and Performance

The asymmetric, or public, key structure used by SSL is necessary because, with the public nature of the Internet, both parties are not known before the establishment of a secure channel. The implementation of security always slows the exchange of information, but an asymmetric key structure slows things down even more. The good part about this is that the public key structure is used only until a single session key can be established between the two computers. So even though the nature of the Internet requires secure sessions to start out with public key cryptography, it is used only to encrypt packets that establish and communicate the single key that is used just until the session between the two computers is complete. The session key with its single key structure is faster than the public key structure, but still not as fast as using no encryption at all. Encryption and security does slow performance, yet it is necessary when sensitive information is being transmitted.

Configuring the Web Proxy Service

Because the Web Proxy service handles outgoing requests from internal clients for objects on the Web, many configurations set in the ISA Server snap-in have an effect on it. By default, no connections will be accepted or created by ISA Server. No communication will occur, either incoming or outgoing, until you have allowed it.

Port Settings

Unless the client attempts to connect to a port that is accepting connections, the connection will not be made. For internal clients to make a connection to the Web Proxy service, they must know which port to connect to or ISA Server must listen on the port to which the clients are trying to connect. By default, TCP port 80 has been assigned to HTTP connections. This means that Web clients will try to connect to TCP port 80; however, ISA Server is accepting these connections on port 8080. Unless the clients are configured to make their Web requests to ISA Server on port 8080, a connection between the two will not be made. This was not a problem in Proxy Server 2.0 because it listened on port 80 for internal Web requests. This means that some configuration is needed for Web proxy clients whereas in previous versions no such configuration was required.

Tip: Although you had to install IIS on the same server as Proxy Server, that's not necessary for ISA Server. In fact, installing IIS and ISA Server on the same computer can cause port conflicts. If you do install IIS on the same server as ISA Server, special configurations must be made. These configurations are detailed in Chapter 14.

Listeners

The term *listening* is often used when referring to a port that is open and ready for connections. In an environment that has multiple ISA servers, you can set some servers or even a specific network adaptor to listen for and handle certain requests. Figure 9.6 shows an example of two ISA servers on a network. Server1 is set to listen for Web requests from internal clients, whereas Server2 is not set up as a listener for internal Web requests. This means that only Server1 will accept internal Web requests. In this scenario, you can set up Server2 to handle different requests. Server2 can instead be a caching-only server or a server that works as a firewall to evaluate incoming requests. You can split the duties between the ISA servers so that they are specialized.

To configure a listener for outgoing Web requests, complete the following steps:

1. In ISA Management, expand Servers And Arrays.
2. Right-click on the array on which you want to configure a listener and select Properties.
3. In the Array Properties dialog box, select the Outgoing Web Requests tab.
4. By default, a listener will already be configured that allows listening on all IP addresses. To add a listener for a particular server or IP address, click Configure Listeners Individually Per IP Address.
5. Click on the Add button to open the Add/Edit dialog box.
6. Select the server and IP address in the array that you want to configure as a listener. In the Display Name box, type a descriptive name for the listener.
7. If a server certificate is loaded on the server, you can place a checkmark in the Use A Server Certificate To Authenticate Web Clients checkbox. You will need to select a certificate the listener should use if more than one is loaded on the server.

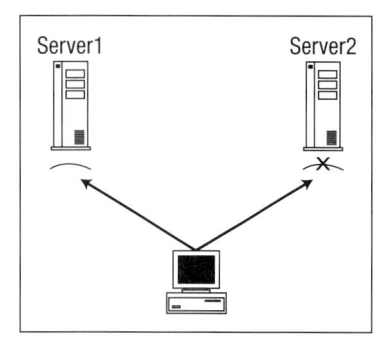

Figure 9.6 An outgoing Web request listener is set on Server1, but not on Server2.

8. Click OK to accept the changes and return to ISA Management. Authentication is covered in Chapter 7 of this book.

After configuring a listener, you will need to stop and restart the Web Proxy service.

SSL Listeners

A listener for SSL requests is already set up and ready in the properties of the ISA server or array. You can add SSL listeners by using the dialog box shown in Figure 9.7. Click the Enable SSL Listeners checkbox and enter a port number for the SSL port to allow a listener for SSL requests. Although no port number is entered by default, SSL does use a default port number of 443. If you choose a different port number, make sure your clients are aware of this change and are set to use the new port number.

Configuring the HTTP Redirector Filter

The Firewall client forwards requests for HTTP objects to the HTTP Redirector Filter. These requests can be handled a few different ways depending on how you've configured the HTTP Redirector Filter. Figure 9.8 shows the dialog box you can use to configure the HTTP redirector.

To configure the HTTP Redirector Filter, perform the following steps:

1. In ISA Management, expand Servers And Arrays.

2. Expand the array you want to configure.

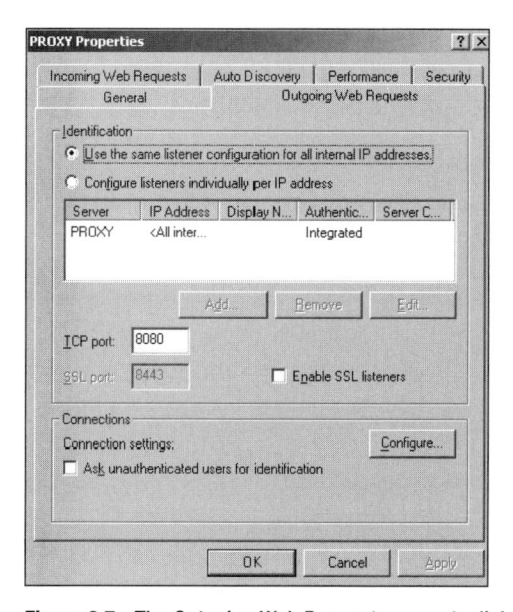

Figure 9.7 The Outgoing Web Requests property dialog box contains an option that enables the SSL listener.

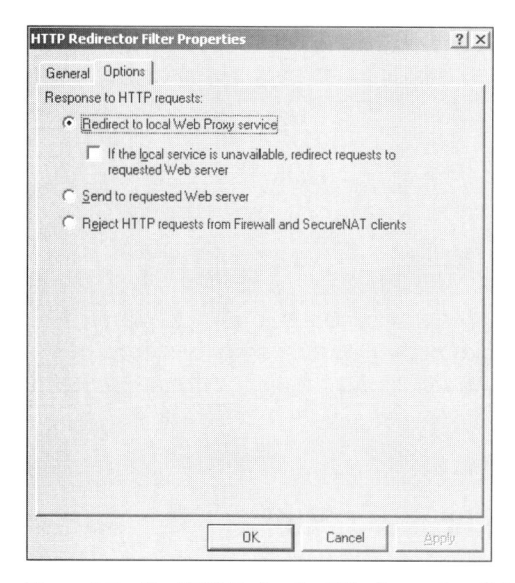

Figure 9.8 The HTTP Redirector Filter Properties dialog box.

3. Expand Application Filters.

4. Right-click on HTTP Redirector Filter and click Properties.

5. Select the Options tab.

6. Select the appropriate option depending on how you want the request handled. The default setting forwards the requests from the Firewall service to the Web Proxy service. The second option allows for the requests to be sent directly to the Internet. The third option sets the HTTP Redirector Filter to reject all requests forwarded to it from the Firewall service.

7. Click OK to accept the changes.

Connection Settings

The Web Proxy service also can control the number of outgoing connections that are allowed from it. By default, the number of connections is unlimited, but you can specify a limit in the Connection Settings dialog box as well as a timeout for the connection. Figure 9.9 shows the Connection Settings dialog box.

To configure the number of outgoing connections, follow these steps:

1. In ISA Management, expand Servers And Arrays.

2. Right-click the array on which you want to configure connection settings and select Properties.

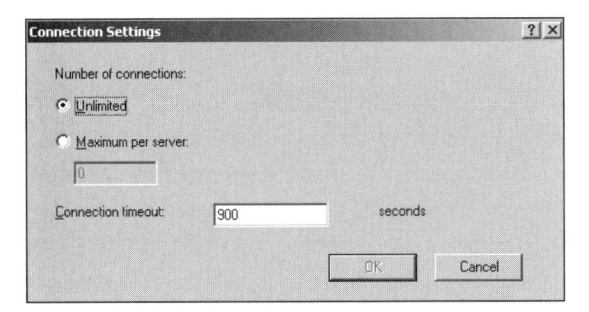

Figure 9.9 The Connection Settings dialog box for the Web Proxy service.

3. In the Array Properties dialog box, select the Outgoing Web Requests tab.
4. Click the Configure button.
5. Specify the number of allowed connections and the connection timeout.

Cache Settings

The Web Proxy service retrieves objects that are cacheable, and it is the service responsible for cache settings. Cache settings are so closely tied to the Web Proxy service that a corrupted cache can keep the Web Proxy service from starting. Setting up and configuring cache is covered in Chapter 8 of this book.

Chapter Summary

The Web Proxy service is one of two main services in ISA Server. It is responsible for fulfilling requests for objects from internal clients. With the default settings in ISA Server, all requests from internal clients for objects end up at the Web Proxy service to be fulfilled.

The Web Proxy service accepts requests from four protocols from internal clients: HTTP, HTTP-S, FTP, or Gopher. Two of these protocols, FTP and Gopher, are still used on the Internet to find and download objects even though their use is declining. HTTP's capabilities are expanding as new versions are released. The most current version is HTTP 1.1. HTTP-S is used when pages are secured with SSL.

A variety of clients can work with the Web Proxy service. All major operating systems work with the Web Proxy service because it is really the Web browser and not the client operating system that communicates with the Web Proxy service. The only requirement for the Web browser is that it be CERN compliant. Since the CERN laboratory created the first Web browser and the first proxy server, nearly all Web browsers are CERN compliant.

The process of handling Web requests by the Web Proxy service is assisted by other components in ISA Server. Requests for HTTP objects that originate from a SecureNAT or Firewall client will automatically be sent to the Firewall service. The Firewall service is responsible for making connections for its clients and not for retrieving objects. Because of this, the Firewall service sends these requests to the HTTP Redirector Filter. By default, these requests are passed to the Web Proxy service for fulfillment.

SSL sets up a secure channel that allows Web pages containing sensitive information to be downloaded over the Internet. Since the Internet is a public network, encryption is a part of this process. Encryption is accomplished between two computers with the use of keys. Keys control how the data is encrypted and decrypted so that only the participating computers—each with a key—can read the encrypted data. Public key cryptography is slow, but it's necessary if the two participants in the process are not known ahead of time. Public key cryptography is used only until a single key can be established. This single-session key is created and used for the duration of one secure session only.

Certificates are an important part of the encryption and SSL process. A certificate works like a driver's license in that the identity of a computer is proven with its use. The SSL process cannot be started or even set up without a certificate.

You configure the Web Proxy service in the ISA Server snap-in. Because security is so important on Internet connections, by default no incoming or outgoing connections are allowed by ISA Server; therefore, configuration is important. In this chapter, we focused on outgoing Web connections that request objects. Ports must be open and accept connections in order for connections to be made between computers. You can set listeners that cause a port to be open and accept connections per server, network adaptor, or IP address. You can also control connections in the Web Proxy service, specifying the number of connections and the timeout period.

Review Questions

1. What are the two main internal services that handle client requests for ISA Server? [Check all correct answers]
    a. Proxy service
    b. Web Proxy service
    c. Firewall service
    d. Cache service

2. Requests using what protocols are handled by the Web Proxy service? [Check all correct answers]
   a. HTTP
   b. HTTP-S
   c. SSL
   d. FTP
   e. Gopher
   f. TCP

3. To what component does the Firewall service hand off requests for HTTP objects?
   a. ISA Server
   b. Web Proxy service
   c. Web Filter
   d. HTTP Redirector Filter

4. What operating systems can be clients to the Web Proxy service? [Check all correct answers]
   a. Macintosh
   b. Unix
   c. Windows 2000 Professional
   d. Windows 2000 Server
   e. Windows 95
   f. Windows NT 4

5. What client Web browsers work with the Web Proxy service? [Check the best answer]
   a. Internet Explorer
   b. Netscape Navigator
   c. Netscape Communicator
   d. Mosaic
   e. All CERN-compliant browsers

6. Which protocol(s) is becoming obsolete due to the expansion of the capabilities of HTTP?
   a. SSL
   b. HTTP-S
   c. FTP
   d. Gopher

7. Which protocol was made obsolete by the popularity of hyperlinks in Web pages?
    a. SSL
    b. HTTP-S
    c. FTP
    d. Gopher

8. The HTTP Redirector Filter is what kind of extension of ISA Server?
    a. Web filter
    b. Application
    c. Application filter
    d. Web extension

9. SSL stands for what?
    a. Secure System Log
    b. Security Socket Log
    c. Safe Socket Layer
    d. Secure Sockets Layer

10. What does SSL do for a Web page?
    a. Caches it
    b. Encrypts it
    c. Does not allow it to transmit
    d. Backs it up

11. What default port is used by HTTP?
    a. 80
    b. 8080
    c. 443
    d. 568

12. What default port does ISA Server use for HTTP?
    a. 80
    b. 8080
    c. 443
    d. 568

13. What is the default port used by SSL?
    a. 80
    b. 8080
    c. 443
    d. 568

14. What is the purpose of a certificate?
    a. To certify a connection
    b. To encrypt a Web page
    c. To prove an identity
    d. To certify a port

15. SSL establishes a session with what kind of cryptography?
    a. Asymmetric key
    b. Single key
    c. 8-bit
    d. Dual-homed

16. Which setup for SSL involves ISA Server only at the beginning of the establishment of a connection?
    a. SSL redirecting
    b. SSL filtering
    c. SSL tunneling
    d. SSL bridging

17. Which setup for SSL involves ISA Server throughout the entire session?
    a. SSL redirecting
    b. SSL filtering
    c. SSL tunneling
    d. SSL bridging

18. What is the default port for an SSL listener?
    a. 80
    b. 8080
    c. 443
    d. 568
    e. There is no default.

19. How does SSL affect performance for a user?

    a. It slows it down.

    b. It speeds it up.

    c. It has no effect.

20. What ports can be used by the ISA server to accept incoming Web requests?

    a. Only the first 1,023

    b. All ports after 1,023

    c. Only port 80

    d. Only ports 80 and 8080

    e. Any port can be used

21. What happens when you disable the HTTP Redirector Filter? [Check all correct answers]

    a. All HTTP Requests are denied.

    b. HTTP requests from Firewall clients are denied.

    c. HTTP requests from SecureNAT clients are denied.

    d. HTTP requests from Web proxy clients are denied.

Real-World Projects

Note: This exercise assumes a test Windows 2000 Server with Service Pack 1 installed. Read the instructions carefully and do not change the settings on your production machine unless you understand the options presented. If you are unsure about an option, do not make a change and instead read the ISA Server help files about the option to be installed.

"Hey Leah, are you busy?" The IS manager poked his head in the door and forced a strained smile on his face.

Leah sighed. She knew that look. It meant that something was wrong and needed to be figured out and fixed immediately.

"I'm ready," she said. "What's up?"

Leah had been working at the Bongo Drum Company for six months. In that time, the company had made several design changes to the Internet security settings. She had just added another ISA server into an existing array. That had brought the total number of ISA servers up to two. She had just installed it and was about to configure the Web Proxy service. After installing ISA Server, Leah decided to unplug it from the network until she could perform the necessary configurations.

Leah did not currently have a need for connections to Internet applications, so she had only configured access to the Web Proxy service. Later, she expected to add support for Internet applications, but that support wasn't needed yet. Because of this, Leah had not yet loaded any client software or changed any configurations on the clients on her network. ISA Server was needed to accept internal connections with the default port used by the clients, TCP port 80. Because ISA Server's default port was 8080 for internal connections, Leah had to change the setting before the new ISA Server could begin accepting internal client requests. Now it looked as though these plans might be interrupted.

"We have a new client that is using a secure Web site to post information that we need. Some users are trying to connect to these secure Web sites and are getting really slow download times. Is there anything we can do to speed up their response times?" the IS manager asked.

"Let me check on that," Leah responded. "Actually, I have another ISA server ready to go. I just need to make some configuration changes before I bring it on line."

"Great! It looks like you're one step ahead of me," the manager said.

"Wouldn't it be better if I knew about changes in client needs before..." Leah was searching for the right words.

"I get you. You want me to tell you when things change so it won't become an emergency." The IT manager nodded. "The next time a user needs support for a connection, you will be included."

"That's exactly what I need." Now he was getting the picture. "Thanks, and I will get right on it."

Leah went to the new ISA server to change the configuration. First, she wanted to change the default port.

Project 9.1

To change the default port for the Web Proxy service:

1. Select Start | Programs | Microsoft ISA Server | ISA Management.

2. Expand Servers And Arrays.

3. Right-click on the array you would like to configure.

4. Select Properties to open the array Properties dialog box.

5. Click the Outgoing Web Requests tab.

6. The default TCP port for ISA Server accepts requests from internal clients on TCP port 8080. Change the port to 80.

7. Click OK to accept the changes and dismiss the array Properties dialog box.

With that out of the way, Leah needed to check the settings for SSL tunneling. Before making any more changes to ISA Server, Leah wanted to determine which SSL options were available and how to configure them. From ISA Help, she learned about SSL tunneling and SSL bridging. SSL tunneling was faster, yet not as secure as SSL bridging. Leah had two reasons for choosing SSL tunneling. First, the users were looking for performance improvements, and SSL tunneling has better performance than SSL bridging. Also, the only secure site that users needed to connect to is the private client's site. Performance seemed more important than extra security at this point. Second, Leah found that SSL tunneling is set up automatically with ISA Server. The users would be able to use the new ISA Server for SSL tunneling as soon as she brought it online by connecting it to the network.

Leah also wanted to enable an SSL listener to listen for SSL requests from the internal clients. To do this, she went back to configure the ISA server.

Project 9.2

To configure the SSL listener:

1. Open ISA Management.

2. Expand Servers And Arrays.

3. Right-click on the array you would like to configure.

4. Select Properties to open the array Properties dialog box.

5. Place a checkmark in the Enable SSL Listeners checkbox. When you do, Enable SSL Listeners the SSL Port box will become available.

6. Enter a port number in the SSL Port box. The port number used by default by clients will be 443.

7. Click OK to accept the property changes.

8. In the ISA Server Warning dialog box, select Save The Changes And Restart The Service(s).

9. Click OK.

CHAPTER TEN

Securing the Internal Network

After completing this chapter, you will be able to:

✓ Employ Windows 2000 security

✓ Understand the ISA Server Security Configuration Wizard

✓ Use the Security Configuration Wizard

✓ Understand the guidelines for ISA Server security

✓ Describe intrusion detection

✓ Configure intrusion detection

✓ Configure alerts

ISA Server provides many different security measures so that internal networks are not compromised by external users who may be malicious. This chapter concentrates on some of the things that you need to consider to protect internal networks and introduces steps you can take to set up ISA Server in a secure way. The main focus will be the ISA Server Security Configuration Wizard, intrusion detection, and alerts.

Employing Windows 2000 Security

ISA Server installs onto the Windows 2000 Server/Advanced Server/Datacenter Server operating system, and therefore, it is based on the Windows 2000 built-in security mechanism. This mechanism is quite extensive, and in this section, we'll cover how ISA Server can employ a part of it. ISA Server includes the Security Configuration Wizard, which you can use to configure the security components of an ISA server or all member servers in an ISA server array. The wizard is based on the built-in Windows 2000 security templates, and you can use one of these predefined templates to secure your ISA server or array at different security levels. In addition, you are not limited to applying the template only; you also can modify some security components so that ISA Server follows your organization's security requirements. Securing a system running ISA Server is very important because usually, the system is connected to the Internet. Although it is difficult to make the internal network 100 percent secure from external networks, you can take action to prevent most undesired activities. Microsoft recommends the network to be set up such that you have an ISA server between your internal network and the Internet. In reality, however, you will likely see other arrangements, such as a Cisco router acting as a firewall between your internal network and the Internet. Deploying ISA Server is just one of the options you can take to secure your internal network.

ISA Server Security Configuration Wizard

The ISA Server Security Configuration Wizard includes the following three built-in Windows 2000 security levels from which you can choose:

▶ *Secure*—Select this option if the system running ISA Server is a multipurpose server that also runs a Web server (Internet Information Server, or IIS), a database server (SQL Server), or a mail server (Exchange Server). This is the least secure option of the three.

▶ *Limited Services*—Select this option if the system running ISA Server runs as both firewall and cache server. The ISA server may be protected by an additional firewall. This is the medium security option.

▶ *Dedicated*—Select this option if the system running an ISA server functions as a dedicated firewall without any other interactive applications running. This is the most secure option of the three. You should not be running any other interactive applications in this mode because some applications do not run under the most secure environment where all the data traffic is being encrypted.

Do you happen to remember a story that Microsoft asked hackers worldwide to hack some of its Windows 2000 systems before it released Windows 2000 to the public? The grand prize was a trip to Redmond, Washington, with all expenses paid, and dinner with Bill Gates to tell him what you thought of Microsoft's latest OS, Windows 2000. Guess what? No break-ins were reported, although five DoS (Denial of Service) attacks—where a server such as a Web server cannot function as it is supposed to after the attack happens—were observed. These servers seemed to have been running security configurations that were listed in hisecdc.inf and hisecws.inf.

These security levels are cumulative, meaning the Limited Services configuration includes the Secure configuration plus a bit more, and the Dedicated configuration includes Limited Services plus a bit more (which includes the Secure configuration).

The Windows 2000 security template differs according to the security level you choose, as shown in Table 10.1.

Notice that server templates for the Limited Services and Dedicated levels are securews.inf and hisecws.inf, respectively. Because you see basicsv.inf, you may have expected to see securesv.inf and hisecsv.inf, but these templates do not exist. Windows 2000 considers a standalone server to be a workstation.

Domain controller templates are shown for your information. While it is possible to install an ISA Server to a domain controller in a Windows 2000 domain, it is highly undesirable. Why? ISA Server will likely be the interface between internal networks and external networks, and you do not want a domain controller—which has all the security information, such as user accounts and groups—to be hacked by external users. These security templates are stored in the *systemroot*\security\templates folder on the system, where *systemroot* is the folder in which Windows 2000 is installed (the default is WINNT). If, for some reason, these templates are not present, you

Table 10.1 Security level reference table.

Security Level	Server Templates	Domain Controller Templates
Secure	basicsv.inf	basicdc.inf
Limited Services	securews.inf	securedc.inf
Dedicated	hisecws.inf	hisecdc.inf

will need to copy templates from the original Windows 2000 installation CD. The ISA Server Security Configuration Wizard uses these security templates to change many operating system settings to preconfigured values. Unfortunately, you have no easy way to return to the previous values, because no automatic method exists for converting the new values to the original values. You can, however, take the snapshot of the current ISA server's security configuration as a template so that you can load it later if needed. (Refer to Chapter 18 of *Microsoft Windows 2000 Server Administrator's Companion* by Charlie Russel and Sharon Crawford [Redmond, WA: Microsoft Press, 2000] for instructions.) You also can fully document all the original values so that you can manually change them back. As the ISA Server Security Configuration Wizard completes its job of reconfiguring security settings, it maintains a log of all the activities in a file called securwiz.log, which is created in the ISA Server installation directory. This is a simple text file that you can open in any text editor, such as Notepad, but the file size is rather large (500KB+). When in doubt, refer to this log file so that you can revert values to whatever necessary. The content of securwiz.log looks like Figure 10.1.

The file securwiz.log shows all the changes made by the ISA Server Security Configuration Wizard. When you first look at it, it appears very detailed and overwhelming. However, when you need to check what changes the wizard made, this log will certainly be the best guide you can count on.

Figure 10.1 securwiz.log content.

Using the Security Configuration Wizard

Now we turn to using the ISA Server Security Configuration Wizard to apply new security settings for a standalone ISA server or all the member servers in an ISA server array. Take the following steps to set system security for an ISA server:

1. In ISA Management, in the left pane, expand Servers And Arrays and the name of the array. Then, click the Computers folder.

2. In the details pane on the right side of the ISA Management MMC, right-click the server you would like to apply the new security settings to, and then click Secure.

3. In the ISA Server Security Configuration Wizard dialog box, read the warning message and click Next.

4. On the Select System Security Level page, select one of these three options:

   - Dedicated
   - Limited Services
   - Secure

   The Secure option is chosen by default. After selecting an option, click Next. The ISA Server Security Configuration Wizard applies the appropriate Windows 2000 security template (see Table 10.1) to configure the security settings on the ISA Server system.

5. On the Congratulations page, make sure you have selected the correct security option to apply, and click Finish.

6. The ISA server applies the security settings. It may take some time to apply all the security settings while it writes all the activities to the securwiz.log file.

7. When the security configuration completes, read the ISA Server pop-up message dialog box and click OK.

Guidelines for ISA Server Security

In general, you should follow several guidelines when setting up a server in any network environment. These guidelines are not only for ISA servers, but also for any servers you may have in your environment. Here are the main points to consider:

- *Physical security*—This is the most important and obvious guide for you. If you do not have a good physical security plan for the server, you are in bad shape. In most of the corporate data center environments, physical security means that you restrict access to the data center to certain people, such as system administrators. You do not want a "normal" user to go into the data center and tinker with the system. If the normal user can touch the system physically, he or she will be able to do pretty much anything to your system; even a simple reboot could possibly affect thousands of users. Therefore, to deploy an ISA server or Windows 2000 domain controller, one requirement is to have a secure data center, which should not be easily accessible to the general workforce.

▶ *Install the latest service pack and security updates*—Although Windows 2000 started to ship in February 2000, as of this writing, its Service Pack 2 is scheduled to come out in April or May 2001. ISA Server requires at least Windows 2000 Service Pack 1 to be installed before the installation can continue. Service packs and security updates tend to have bug fixes that you should have when deploying an ISA server that interfaces with the Internet; these fixes could prevent a security breach.

▶ *Do not run unnecessary services or accept unnecessary packets*—Running unnecessary services or accepting unnecessary packets can be dangerous in some cases. For example, the Windows 2000 Server Service running on an ISA server could possibly expose the internal file system structure to external users. Also, you never know what undesired network packets could do to your system and network. For example, intentionally damaged packets and Internet Control Message Protocol (ICMP) ping packets of certain sizes could crash your system.

▶ *Stay current about security issues*—Security breaches are reported every day. The security measure you are taking today might not work tomorrow.

▶ *Audit security-related events and review the associated log files from time to time*—These actions may detect strange activities on your system or network that could be caused by external user attacks on your internal networks.

▶ *Fully understand the network protocols to use with ISA Server*—This allows you to configure ISA Server properly. For example, you could possibly use IPX/SPX on your internal network and TCP/IP to access the Internet on the ISA server. In this way, the internal network—except for the ISA server's external (TCP/IP) interface—is completely invisible to external users. In addition, you could implement a private IP addressing scheme in your internal network so that packets are not routable. Private IP addresses include 10.0.0.0 through 10.255.255.255 for Class A, 172.16.0.0 through 172.31.255.255 for Class B, and 192.168.0.0 through 192.168.255.255 for Class C. When systems are configured using these IP addresses, they can communicate with each other, but will not be able to communicate with the outside world via the Internet, because packets do not get routed, even though you have a default gateway specified.

▶ *Document all you know about your network configuration*—Microsoft emphasizes the importance of documenting your configuration, which allows you to detect and recover from intrusion.

Intrusion Detection

Your network should be able to deal with a security breach in a timely manner when it actually happens. In many cases, security breach preventative actions should be executed within a matter of milliseconds. Fortunately, ISA Server provides a built-in intrusion detection mechanism so that when a variety of intrusion activities happen, it performs a certain set of preconfigured actions, such as alerts for system administrators. ISA Server's intrusion mechanism is based on the technology from Internet Security Systems (ISS), Inc.

ISA Server considers the following events to be intrusions to the internal network:

- Ping-of-death attack
- UDP bomb attack
- IP half scan attack
- Land attack
- All ports scan attack
- Enumerated port scan attack
- Windows out-of-band attack

These may look like Greek to you, so the following list describes each intrusion event in detail:

- *Ping-of-death attack*—Chapter 2 introduced a command-line tool called **PING** that you can use to see if you can reach a remote system. A ping-of-death attack is based on this tool, and **PING** is used in a malicious way. When you use the **PING** command, it sends several ICMP echo requests to a remote host and receives replies from the remote host. (By default, the size of the packets and the number of times to send packets vary depending on which platform you are working on. You can, however, use different switches to change these values.) When sending the ICMP echo requests, hackers can modify the requests so that they can add a large amount of information (in some cases, the information is just useless). When this is successfully done, a kernel buffer overflows when the remote host tries to respond, and it will ultimately crash the remote host. ISA Server can alert you that you are getting a ping-of-death attack so that the system being attacked does not crash. When you get a ping-of-death attack alert, you should create a protocol rule that specifically denies incoming ICMP echo request packets from the Internet.

- *UDP bomb attack*—You get a UDP bomb attack alert when you get an illegal UDP packet. This may affect systems that are running older operating systems that tend to crash when they receive a UDP packet with illegal values in certain fields. Usually, you would have a hard time determining the cause of the crash.

▶ *IP half scan attack*—You get an IP half scan attack alert when repeated attempts are made by external users (hackers) to reach a destination host and no corresponding acknowledgement (ACK) packets are received. This means that the connection between two hosts is not completely established, so that logging does not take place properly. However, hackers can determine exactly which ports are open without being logged. This could be dangerous because they can do whatever they want while you are unable to detect them. When you get this alert, configure IP packet filters or ISA Server policy rules to prevent traffic from the source of the scans.

▶ *Land attack*—You experience a land attack alert when a TCP Synchronization (SYN) packet is received with a spoofed source IP address and port number that matches those of the destination IP address and port number. This means that it looks like the host being attacked is receiving a packet from itself. When the attack is successful, it could cause some TCP implementations to go into a loop that will ultimately crash the system. When you get a land attack alert, you should configure the IP packet filters or ISA Server policy rules to prevent traffic from the source of the scans.

▶ *All ports scan attack*—You get an all ports scan attack alert when an attempt is made to access more than the preconfigured number of ports. Hackers usually look for ports that are open, so it is not a good idea to leave ports open that are not necessary for daily operations. When this alert happens, you should configure a threshold that indicates the number of ports that can be accessed from the external users.

▶ *Enumerated port scan attack*—You get an enumerated port scan attack alert when an attempt is made to count the services running on a system by probing each port to get a response. When this alert happens, you should try to identify the source of the port scan. Once the scan is done, see if the source is indeed allowed to use the port. If not, check the access log for indications of unauthorized access. If you see indications of unauthorized access, your network is compromised, and you should take appropriate action. Appropriate actions include closing the port being attacked, assuming it does not affect any applications that are using it, or adding another layer of security with a device such as a hardware firewall to block the packets for the port.

▶ *Windows out-of-band attack*—You get a Windows out-of-band attack alert when an out-of-band denial-of-service attack (DoS) is attempted to a system protected by ISA Server. When this is done successfully, the system attacked will ultimately crash, or there will be a loss of network connectivity for the system attacked. Basically, the attacker attaches to port 139 of any Windows 95/NT/2000 computer and sends garbage packets into the port. You will need to block packets addressed for port 139 using a hardware firewall or configure the ISA server to alert you to such an attack.

Configuring Intrusion Detection

Now that you have some idea of what intrusion detection is all about, we will focus on configuring intrusion detection so that it is in effect. Take the following steps to configure intrusion detection:

1. Open the ISA Management MMC by selecting Start | Programs | Microsoft ISA Server | ISA Management.

2. Expand Servers And Arrays, the name of the array, and Access Policy.

3. Right-click IP Packet Filters in the console tree of ISA Management. Then, click Properties.

4. On the General tab, select both the Enable Packet Filtering and Enable Intrusion Detection checkboxes. The Enable Packet Filtering option may be grayed out if the default enterprise policy settings enable Packet Filtering.

5. On the Intrusion Detection tab, select the checkboxes for the types of attacks to generate events:

   - Windows Out-Of-Band (WinNuke)
   - Land
   - Ping Of Death
   - IP Half Scan
   - UDP Bomb
   - Port Scan

6. If you select Port Scan, two options will be available that you will have to configure:

   - In Detect After Attacks On *number* Well-Known Ports, enter the maximum number of well-known ports that can be scanned before generating an event. This is a value between 1 and 2048; the default value is 10.

   - In Detect After Attacks On *number* Ports, enter the total number of ports that can be scanned before generating an event. This is a value between 1 and 65535; the default value is 20.

7. Finally, click OK.

You may notice when configuring intrusion detection that there is currently no way to add additional intrusion detection definitions. You are limited to the six predefined options described in Step 5. We do expect, however, that future service packs or add-on packages for ISA Server will address this issue.

Configuring Alerts

Configuring intrusion detection by itself does not actually generate alerts; you will need to configure alerts separately. There are many predefined alerts that are configured when you install ISA Server. You can, however, create a new alert to meet your security requirements. An alert can attract your attention in the following different ways:

- Send an email message
- Run a program
- Report the event to a Windows 2000 event log
- Stop selected ISA Server services
- Start selected ISA Server services

The alert can be configured easily because ISA Server provides the New Alert Wizard. Take the following steps to create a new alert:

1. Open the ISA Management MMC by selecting Start | Programs | Microsoft ISA Server | ISA Management.

2. Expand Servers And Arrays, the name of the array, and Monitoring Configuration, and then right-click Alerts.

3. Select New | Alert. The New Alert Wizard starts.

4. On the Welcome To The New Alert Wizard page, enter the name of the alert you are creating. Click Next.

5. On the Server page, select either Any Server or This Server. If you select Any Server, all servers in the array will generate an alert. If you select This Server, an alert will be generated only from the particular server you have selected. Then, click Next.

6. On the Events And Conditions page, select the events and conditions that trigger the alert. You can select from many options. Look through all of the lists and familiarize yourself with all the events and conditions and make your selection. Then, click Next.

7. On the Actions page, select all the actions that should be taken when the event configured in Step 6 occurs. Then, click Next.

8. On the Sending E-mail Messages page, enter the system name or IP address of the Simple Mail Transfer Protocol (SMTP) server, such as an Exchange server. If you do not know the system name or the IP address of the SMTP server, you can click the Browse button to look for it in your network. Also, enter the appropriate email address in the From and To fields. Click Next.

9. On the Completing The New Alert Wizard page, confirm that all the information you have entered is correct. Then, click Finish.

10. Confirm that the alert you just created appears in the details pane of the ISA Management MMC. If you need to later change the configuration of the alert, do so by clicking the appropriate alert and modifying the events and actions.

Chapter Summary

When deploying an ISA server or ISA server array, the ISA server administrator must be willing to spend some time learning about security breaches and how to possibly prevent them. Security using ISA Server is an important topic, because the ISA server sits between the internal network and external network, and it is the door that external users open to access internal network resources. As a result, it is the point where malicious hackers will focus their attacks, and therefore, proper security measures must be taken.

ISA Server installs onto the Windows 2000 Server/Advanced Server/Datacenter Server operating system, and therefore, it is based on the Windows 2000 built-in security mechanism. To use Windows 2000's complex built-in security mechanism, ISA Server includes the Security Configuration Wizard, which you can use to configure the security components of an ISA Server or all member servers in an ISA server array. The ISA Server Security Configuration Wizard is based on the built-in Windows 2000 security templates, and you can use one of these predefined templates to secure your ISA server or array at different security levels.

Guidelines that you should follow when setting up a server in any network environment include the following:

➤ Physical security

➤ Installing the latest service pack and security updates

➤ Not running unnecessary services or accepting unnecessary packets

➤ Staying current about security issues

➤ Auditing security-related events and reviewing the associated log files from time to time

➤ Fully understanding the network protocols to use with ISA Server

➤ Documenting all you know about your network configuration

ISA Server provides a built-in intrusion detection mechanism that performs a certain set of preconfigured actions when intrusion activities are detected. The following is a list of intrusions that ISA Server can detect:

- Ping-of-death attack
- UDP bomb attack
- IP half scan attack
- Land attack
- All ports scan attack
- Enumerated port scan attack
- Windows out-of-band attack

Alerts notify you when intrusions are detected. Alerts can attract your attention in several ways—by sending an email message to the system administrator, by running a certain program, by reporting the event to a Windows 2000 event log, or by stopping or starting ISA Server services.

Review Questions

1. Which one of the following is not likely to be a security measure used by ISA Server?
    a. Security Configuration Wizard
    b. Intrusion detection
    c. VPN
    d. SSL

2. The ISA Server Security Configuration Wizard is based on what Windows 2000 built-in security?
    a. NTFS Security
    b. FAT Security
    c. Security templates
    d. Encrypting File System (EFS)

3. Which one of the following is not one of the three security levels available in the ISA Server Security Configuration Wizard?
    a. Secure
    b. More Secure
    c. Limited Services
    d. Dedicated

4. The Security Configuration Wizard's security levels are cumulative. Which one of the following is true?

   a. The Dedicated configuration includes Limited Services.

   b. The Limited Services configuration includes the Dedicated configuration.

   c. The Secure configuration includes the Limited Services configuration.

5. Which one of the following is the correct reference table for the security level and security template?

   a. Level: Secure, Template: basicwk.inf

   b. Level: Limited Services, Template: securesv.inf

   c. Level: Dedicated, Template: hisecsv.inf

   d. Level: Dedicated, Template: hisecws.inf

6. When applying the Security Configuration Wizard, it fails. After investigating, you find that security templates are not present in the systemroot\security templates folder on the system. What must you do to fix it?

   a. Copy security templates from the original Windows 2000 CD.

   b. Create your own security templates.

   c. Quit the Security Configuration Wizard, and do not use the wizard.

   d. Apply security templates manually.

7. When applying the Security Configuration Wizard, ISA Server keeps a log. What is this log file named?

   a. securitylog.log

   b. securwiz.log

   c. securewizard.log

   d. isawizard.log

8. The ISA Server Administrator MMC snap-in needs to know which of the following about the ISA servers that are maintained? [Check all correct answers]

   a. Physical security

   b. The latest service pack and security updates

   c. Security-related events

   d. Network configurations

9. ISA Server considers which of the following as an intrusion? [Check all correct answers]
   a. Ping of death
   b. UDP bomb
   c. Email spam
   d. Physical security breach

10. What is a ping-of-death attack?
    a. Sending ping ICMP echo requests with some extra information
    b. Sending illegal UDP packets
    c. Making TCP/IP implementation go into a loop
    d. Accessing more than the preconfigured number of ports

11. What is a UDP bomb attack?
    a. Sending ping ICMP echo requests with some extra information
    b. Sending illegal UDP packets
    c. Making TCP/IP implementation go into a loop
    d. Accessing more than the preconfigured number of ports

12. What is a land attack?
    a. Sending ping ICMP echo requests with some extra information
    b. Sending illegal UDP packets
    c. Making TCP/IP implementation go into a loop
    d. Accessing more than the preconfigured number of ports

13. What is an all ports scan attack?
    a. Sending ping ICMP echo requests with some extra information
    b. Sending illegal UDP packets
    c. Making TCP/IP implementation go into a loop
    d. Accessing more than the preconfigured number of ports

14. Which of the following are things you can configure with alerts? [Check all correct answers]
    a. Send an email message
    b. Shut down the system
    c. Log off the user currently logged in
    d. Stop selected ISA Server services

15. Where in the ISA Server Administrator MMC snap-in can you configure Alerts?

    a. Monitoring

    b. Monitoring Configuration

    c. Network Configuration

    d. Policy Elements

Real-World Projects

Note: This exercise assumes a test Windows 2000 Server or Advanced Server with Service Pack 1 or Windows 2000 Datacenter Server installed. Read the instructions carefully and do not perform this install on your production machine unless you understand the options presented. If you are unsure about an option, cancel the installation and read the help files provided with ISA Server about the option to be installed.

Mark has just been newly hired as a network administrator for a small elementary school. The school has four Windows 2000 Servers in a Windows 2000 Active Directory domain, and about 150 Windows 2000 workstations. They have a T1 line for Internet access. They have not deployed any software or hardware firewall for security. Recently, teachers have identified a number of security breaches in which hackers have maliciously deleted data on the Windows 2000 Servers. Because the original network administrator did not have much knowledge of Windows 2000 security mechanisms and did not leave any network documents before he left for another job, the upper management at the elementary school decided that Mark would be responsible for all the network related tasks—especially network security. Mark was interviewed a week before he started working at the school.

Today is the first day at school for Mark. The school dean tells him that he has a couple of computers he could use to implement security on the network using ISA Server.

Mark has read the MCSE ISA Server Exam Prep, so he sets up an ISA server array. Now he will implement what he has learned about security. He starts with the Internet Security Wizard.

Project 10.1
To use the ISA Server Security Configuration Wizard:

1. In the ISA Management MMC, in the console tree, expand your server or array. Then, click Computer.

2. In the details pane on the right side of the ISA Management MMC, right-click the server you would like to apply the new security settings to, and then click Secure. See Figure 10.2.

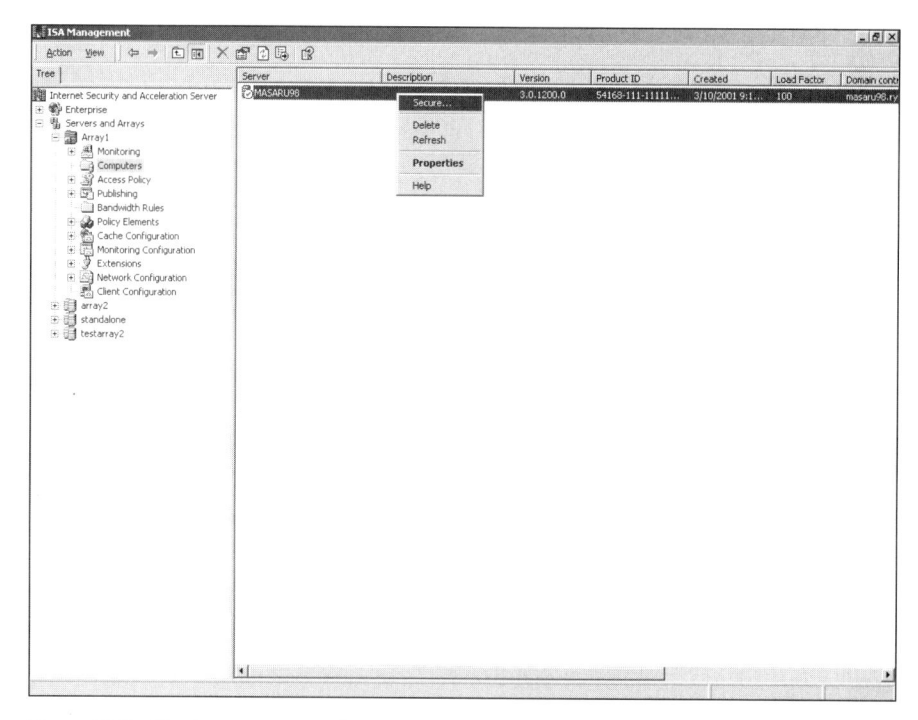

Figure 10.2 The Secure command.

3. In the ISA Server Security Configuration Wizard dialog box, read the warning message and click Next. See Figure 10.3.

Figure 10.3 The ISA Server Security Configuration Wizard dialog box.

4. On the Select System Security Level page, select one of these options:

   ➤ Dedicated

   ➤ Limited Services

   ➤ Secure

   The Secure option is chosen by default. Then, click Next. The ISA Server Security Configuration Wizard applies the appropriate Windows 2000 security template (see Table 10.1) to configure the security settings on the ISA Server system. For this example, select Dedicated. See Figure 10.4.

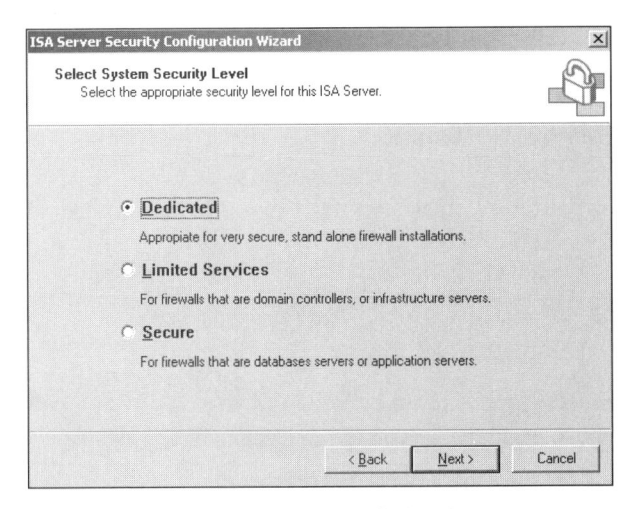

Figure 10.4 The Select System Security Level page.

5. On the Congratulations! page, make sure you have selected the correct security option and click Finish. See Figure 10.5.

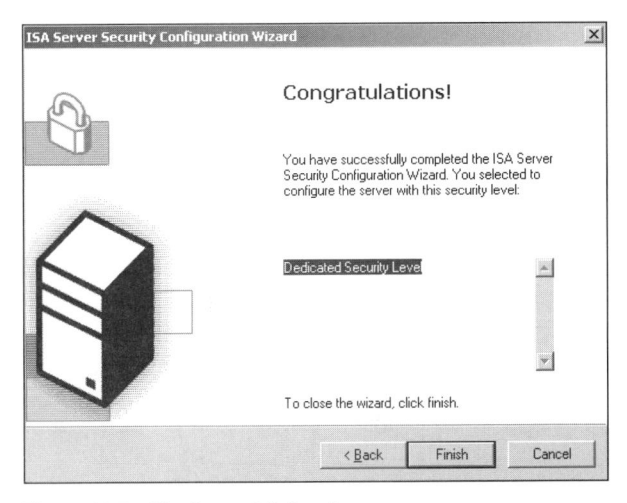

Figure 10.5 The Congratulations! page.

282 Chapter 10

6. ISA Server applies the security settings. It may take some time to apply all the security settings while it writes all the activities to the securwiz.log. See Figure 10.6.

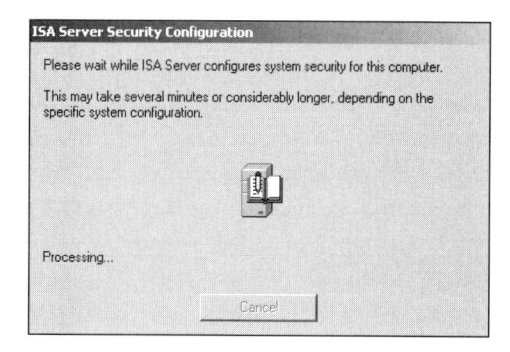

Figure 10.6 The ISA Server Security configuration process.

7. When the security configuration completes, read the information dialog box and click OK. See Figure 10.7.

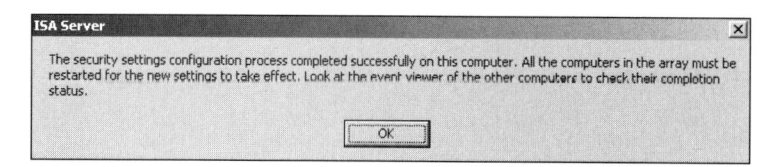

Figure 10.7 The ISA Server Security configuration completion dialog box.

Now that the system is configured securely, Mark configures the intrusion detection and alerts so that he will be notified if there are any indications of break-ins into internal networks using known methods.

Project 10.2

To configure intrusion detection:

1. Open the ISA Management MMC by selecting Start | Programs | Microsoft ISA Server | ISA Management.

2. Expand the Servers And Arrays, the name of the array, and Access Policy.

3. Right-click IP Packet Filters in the console tree of ISA Management. See Figure 10.8. Then, click Properties.

4. On the General tab, select both the Enable Packet Filtering and Enable Intrusion Detection checkboxes. The Enable Packet Filtering option may be grayed out if the default enterprise policy settings enable Packet Filtering. See Figure 10.9.

Securing the Internal Network 283

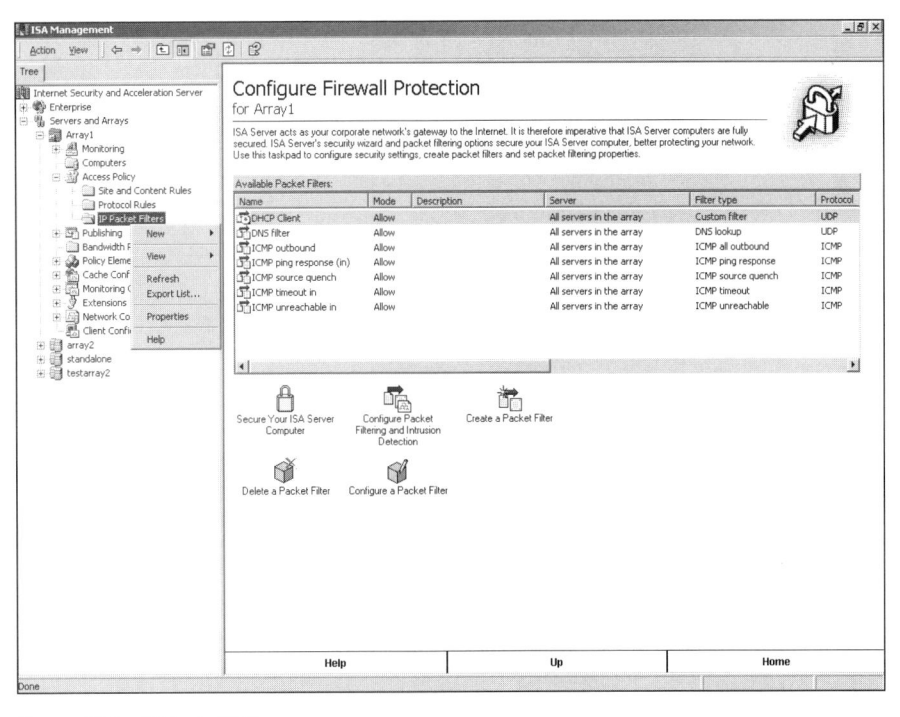

Figure 10.8 IP Packet Filters.

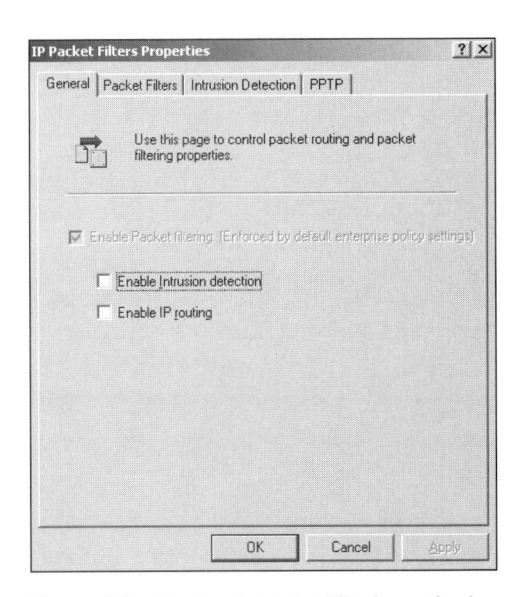

Figure 10.9 The Enable Packet Filtering option is grayed out.

5. On the Intrusion Detection tab, click the checkboxes for the types of attacks to generate events. For this example, select all the checkboxes. The following intrusion detections are listed. See Figure 10.10 (which shows the selection for the port scan).

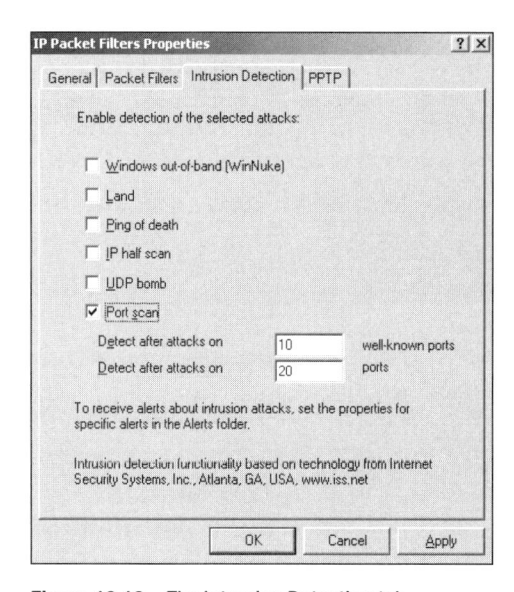

Figure 10.10 The Intrusion Detection tab.

6. Because you are selecting Port Scan, you'll see two options that you will have to configure:

   ➤ In Detect After Attacks On *number* Well-Known Ports, enter the maximum number of well-known ports that can be scanned before generating an event. This is a value between 1 and 2048; the default value is 10.

   ➤ In Detect After Attacks On *number* Ports, enter the total number of ports that can be scanned before generating an event. This is a value between 1 and 65535; the default value is 20.

   For this example, leave the default values.

7. Finally, click OK.

Mark now needs to configure alerts so that he is contacted via email when an intrusion is detected. After all, he has been checking his email every 5 minutes or so since he moved to this position.

Project 10.3

To configure an alert:

1. Open the ISA Management MMC by selecting Start | Programs | Microsoft ISA Server | ISA Management.

2. Expand Servers And Arrays, the name of the array, and Monitoring Configuration.

3. Right-click Alerts. See Figure 10.11.

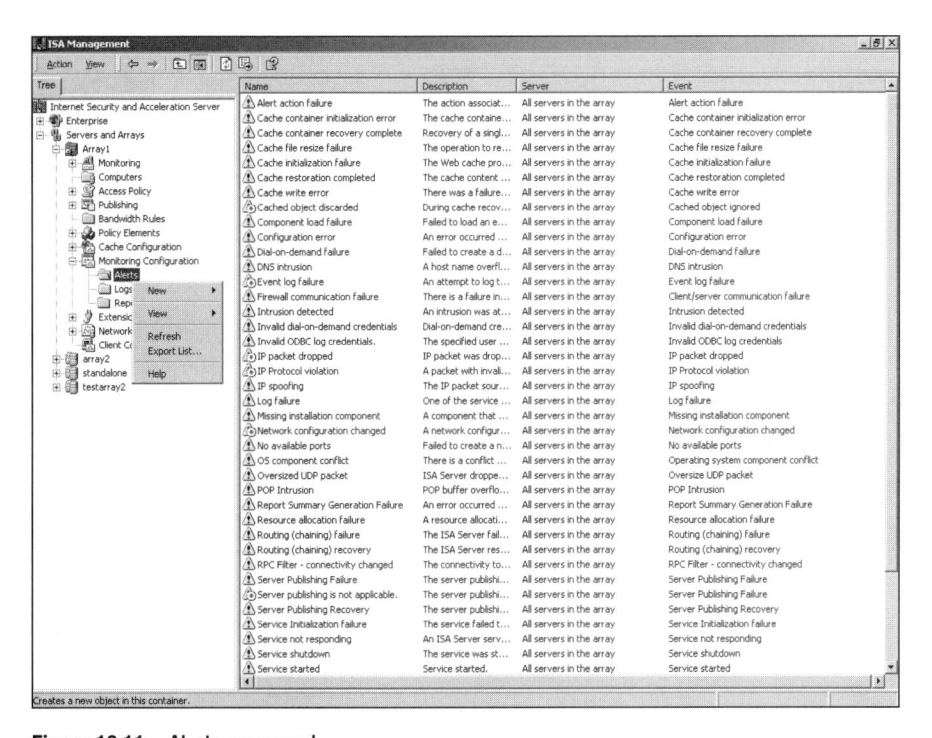

Figure 10.11 Alerts command.

4. Point to New | Alert. The New Alert Wizard starts.

5. On the Welcome To The New Alert Wizard page, enter the name of the alert you are creating. For this example, enter "test1". Click Next.

6. On the Server page, select either Any Server or This Server. If you select Any Server, an alert will be generated by all servers in the array. If you select This Server, an alert will be generated only from the particular server you have selected. See Figure 10.12. Then, click Next.

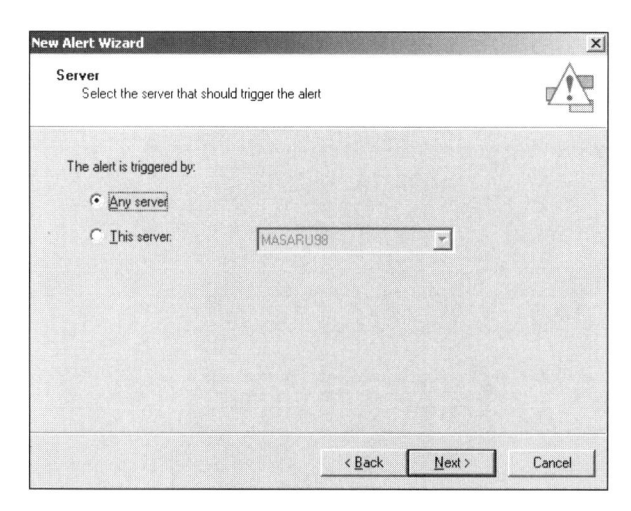

Figure 10.12 The Server page.

7. On the Events And Conditions page, select the events and conditions that trigger the alert. You can select from many options. Look through all of the lists and familiarize yourself with all the events and conditions. For this example, select Intrusion Detected for Event and Any Intrusion for Additional Condition. Then, click Next.

8. On the Actions page, select all the actions that should be taken when the event configured in Step 7 occurs. For this example, select Send An E-mail Message and Report The Event To A Windows 2000 Event Log. See Figure 10.13. Then, click Next.

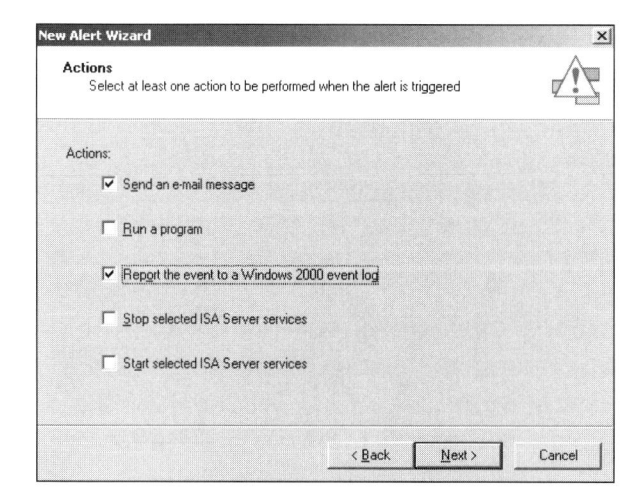

Figure 10.13 Actions page.

9. On the Sending E-mail Messages page, enter the system name or IP address of the Simple Mail Transfer Protocol (SMTP) server, such as an Exchange server. If you do not know the system name or the IP address of the SMTP server, you can click the Browse button to look for it in your network. Also, enter the email address in the From and To fields. For this example, enter the IP address "192.168.1.2" for the SMTP Server; in the From email address field, enter "isa@test-coriolis.com"; and in the To email address field, enter "isaadmin@test-coriolis.com". Click Next. See Figure 10.14.

Figure 10.14 The Sending E-mail Messages page.

10. On the Completing The New Alert Wizard page, confirm that all the information you have entered is correct. Then, click Finish. See Figure 10.15.

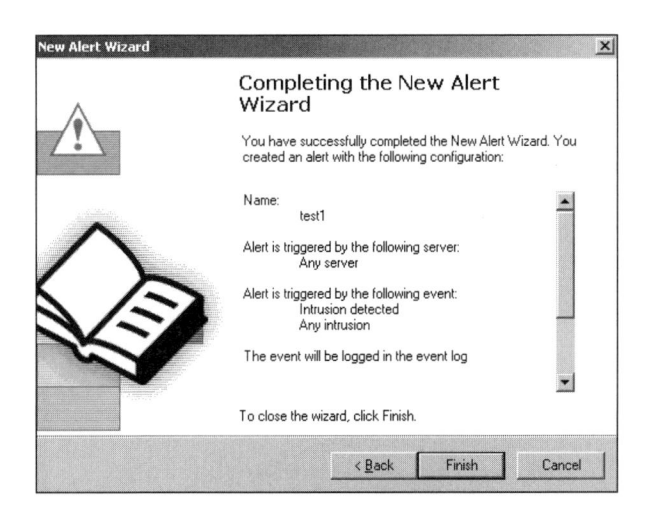

Figure 10.15 The Completing The New Alert Wizard page.

11. Confirm that the alert you just created shows up in the detailed pane of the ISA Management. If you need to later change the configuration of the alert, do so by clicking the appropriate alert and modifying the events and actions.

Believe it or not, Mark completed all these configurations within an hour. An experienced ISA Server administrator might be able to complete the projects in less time. Everything went very smoothly, and Mark is now ready to move on.

CHAPTER ELEVEN

Supporting Media Services

After completing this chapter, you will be able to:

✓ Define what qualifies as media

✓ Explain H.323 services

✓ Configure H.323 components

✓ Set up the H.323 Gatekeeper service

✓ Configure call routing rules

✓ Explain the Registration, Admission, and Status (RAS) protocol

✓ Set up DNS SRV records for the H.323 Gatekeeper

✓ Use protocol definitions needed to support media

✓ Configure the Streaming Media Filter

✓ Allow clients to use live stream splitting

✓ Integrate with Windows Media (WMT) server

Internet connections are not just for downloading documents. Other types of files and connections that allow video and audio, as well as realtime exchanges between users, are available. As these types of connections over the Internet become more popular, companies created their own proprietary methods of making these connections work. This, of course, created a compatibility problem. Unless both ends of the connection use software and hardware from the same vendor, no connection will be made. Also, compatibility is not the only issue when it comes to making these types of connections. Audio and video use a high amount of bandwidth—bandwidth that is often not in large supply over wide area network (WAN) connections. This chapter will cover the setup of H.323 Gatekeeper and streaming media services provided by ISA Server. These services will help your users connect safely using multimedia and conferencing applications.

What Is Multimedia?

When the Internet first came into use, it was a text-only medium. Many early users of the Internet still had command-line-based computers, so they expected just text when they connected to other computers. The fact that you could connect to anywhere else in the world was the important part and not the presentation of the information you received. But as Windows became popular and the use of Graphical User Interfaces (GUI) spread, people began to expect more. They started to think about how nice it would be if you could get more than just text documents over the Internet. Now that you could connect to anyone else, how about sending sound or even video? Then they started thinking really crazy thoughts—for example, about holding realtime conversations with one another using the Internet as the connection. Then they could hold meetings over the Internet. All of these capabilities could be possible with the right applications and bandwidth.

Media vs. Multimedia

Look up *media* in a dictionary and you will find that it is the plural of the word medium. Look up *medium* and you will find that it is something on which information is transmitted or carried. A lot of components in computers transmit or store data, which means that the term medium and its plural, media, are used in a couple of different senses when referring to computers. Media can be the medium over which data is transported from one computer to another—such as networking cable—or it can mean hardware components that store data—such as CD-ROMs, floppy disks, or hard disks. Another sense of the word media is found in the term multimedia: In computers, media can be a format for technology that allows it to be passed from computer to computer. This type of media includes file formats used for sending audio, video, text, and images.

This sense of the word media leads us to the term *multimedia*. Multimedia refers to multiple forms of file formats used simultaneously. A multimedia presentation combines different data formats that work together. A video presentation with accompanying sound is a good example of multimedia, but so is text with still images—though it is definitely not as interesting!

Media and multimedia applications come in different packages and types. It is easiest to categorize multimedia software based on what you want to do with it. Some software allows you to create multimedia files, while other versions of the software allow you to publish multimedia files. Servers with the software that allow it to publish multimedia files to clients are acting as media servers. Other types of software are simply clients that allow you to play media files that are published from a media server.

What Is the H.323 Gatekeeper Service?

If you want to connect to media files or conference over the Internet, all of the information needs to be traded and translated over the entire length of the connection between each endpoint. If a connection originates from outside your company, it can start from a computer using a modem. This signal will travel through the Public Switched Telephone Network (PSTN) to an Internet Service Provider (ISP). From the ISP the signal will be put onto the Internet, which will transport it to the ISA server at your network. The ISA server, if the rules permit, will allow a connection to the internal network. In order for this connection to be successful, it has to travel through different networks with different hardware. Also, the connection will need to pass through protective firewalls and proxies located at each network. The purpose of the H.323 Gatekeeper service is to facilitate connections over different hardware that may even be using different software—at least that is the idea. The standard is still very new and subject to change, so not all vendors comply completely with the H.323 standard.

H.323 is defined as a standard by the International Telecommunication Union (ITU). H.323 is called an umbrella standard because it defines individual standards for audio, video, and data streams as well as standards for setup and control of the connection. The ultimate goal of H.323 is to allow communications between different telephony and conferencing applications. In other words, if a person sets up a conference with NetMeeting, another person would be able to connect even though he or she is using a different application than NetMeeting. H.323 is still being developed and improved, so this level of interoperability is not quite achieved. Also, you can set up successful multimedia connections over different types of hardware. Although H.323 is still being developed, eventually it will allow multimedia connections regardless of the hardware or multimedia application being used.

H.323 Components

The main components that make up an H.323 system include terminals, Multi-point Control Units (MCUs), gateways, and gatekeepers. Terminals are client endpoints that are capable of realtime communications. To qualify as an H.323

terminal, it must support at least voice communication. A terminal can also have video or data capabilities. (Just to get our terminology right, a terminal, MCU, and gateway can each be called an endpoint in an H.323 system.) An example of a terminal is a client multimedia application, such as NetMeeting or RealPlayer, running on a PC.

MCUs coordinate multiple connections. For example, if you were going to hold a videoconference and you wanted 10 individuals—each located in a different physical location and network—to participate, an MCU would coordinate the different connections so that the conference connection is less disjointed for the participants. The MCU makes sure that all of the different types of connections and connection speeds are negotiated and maintained so that all participants can receive transmissions during the conference.

Gateways are not a required component in an H.323 system. Like most gateways, an H.323 Gateway provides translation between different formats. An H.323 Gateway translates between H.323-compliant file formats and protocols and non-H.323-compliant file formats and protocols. If you have all H.323 components on your network and in the networks that you are making multimedia connections to, then you will not need an H.323 Gateway.

H.323 Gatekeepers provide control over H.323 connections. This control ranges from authentication to bandwidth management. Gatekeepers are not required when making multimedia H.323 connections, but without them the connections will not have the optimal level of control. A group of terminals, MCU(s), and, if needed, a gateway is controlled by one H.323 Gatekeeper. This grouping is called a zone. Figure 11.1 shows an example of a zone. The number of terminals, MCUs, and gateways can vary for a zone, but there can be only one gatekeeper per zone.

H.323-compliant Applications

Any multimedia application can be a candidate for H.323 compliance. Besides conferencing applications, multimedia applications can include video games, Internet phones, and players that stream audio and/or video. Compliance with H.323 standards is up to the vendors that create multimedia applications. H.323 compliance is helpful for vendors because it avoids proprietary behavior, allowing an application to make connections using more types of hardware and software. This can open a bigger market base for a vendor's products and multimedia applications.

H.323 applications have to be configured to register users, which is an important role in the H.323 Gatekeeper service. H.323 clients register using the H.323 Registration, Admission, and Status (RAS) protocol. This protocol creates a registration database of addresses used by H.323. We discuss the RAS protocol later in

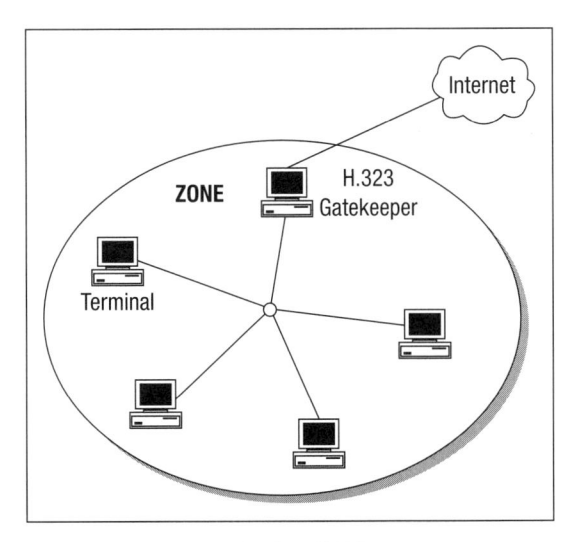

Figure 11.1 An example of an H.323 zone.

this chapter. Most H.323 clients are supposed to register automatically, but they may need to be configured to do so. No standards exist that specify how an application should be set up to register with the registration database, so each one might vary and still complies with H.323 standards.

An H.323 Connection

An H.323 connection has an origination and a destination endpoint. Because an endpoint can be a terminal, MCU, or gateway, the type of connection can vary. The clients on your network may want to hold their own meetings with conferencing applications and so will want to accept incoming calls, or they will want to participate in conferencing or other multimedia connections outside the network, which will involve outbound connections. For the following example, assume a connection between client applications that are attempting to hold a multimedia conference. Also assume for this example that an external client is making an inbound connection to a conference being hosted by an internal client in your network. When the ISA server receives the request on the external interface, it will pass it to the H.323 Gatekeeper for address translation. When the address is confirmed and the type of connection is permissible, the ISA server opens a connection from the originating network through the gatekeeper to the internal client. Figure 11.2 shows this inbound connection. Administrators have control over the type of connection, information, and protocols that are allowed. They can exercise this control by implementing H.323 protocol rules.

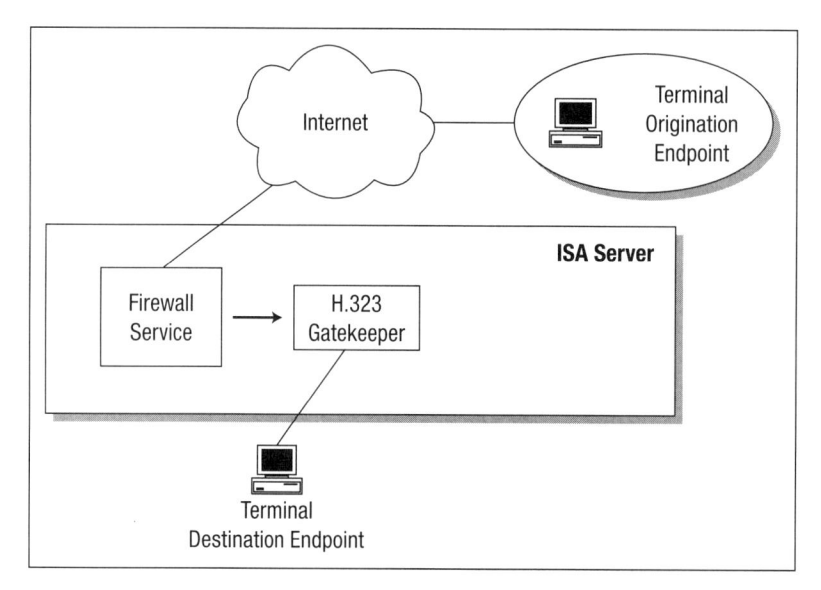

Figure 11.2 A sample H.323 connection that shows an inbound connection from an external client.

H.323 Gatekeeper Roles and Functions

The H.323 Gatekeeper is designed to provide a number of control functions to an H.323 system. These control functions can be grouped into categories. Table 11.1 shows the categories of functions that an H.323 Gatekeeper performs to provide control for an H.323 system. Although an H.323 Gatekeeper is not required when using H.323 terminals, once a gatekeeper is set up on the network, the terminals are forced to make their connections through it.

To set up the H.323 Protocol Filter and H.323 Gatekeeper in ISA Server, you must understand how each component and function works.

A Different Kind of RAS

The RAS protocol in H.323 is used to communicate with the H.323 Gatekeeper. This RAS is completely different from the Remote Access Server (RAS) that

Table 11.1 H.323 Gatekeeper functions.

Function	Purpose
Address Translation	Translates aliases into network addresses using a registration database for a terminal or endpoint.
Admissions Control	Authorizes connections to terminals in the zone.
Bandwidth Control	Controls the amount of bandwidth that is available to multimedia applications using the H.323 service.
Zone Management	Performs required and optional functions for a designated zone of H.323 terminals and components.

provides dial-up communications to and from a network. An H.323 Gatekeeper works with the RAS protocol to set up a database of client registrations that is checked every time a request comes in to be processed by the H.323 Gatekeeper. The purpose of the registration database is to translate aliases that come in with H.323 requests to internal addresses on the network. Oftentimes an H.323 request will come in the form of an email address, such as *person@coriolis.com*. An ISA server receiving this will use a Domain Name System (DNS) server to resolve the domain suffix, but a translation is needed for the email username. The best feature of the registration database is that, with a few exceptions, it is built automatically from client registrations. H.323-compliant applications, such as NetMeeting, register automatically. Static registrations can also be made in the ISA Server snap-in, but they can be used only for outbound and not inbound address translations.

H.323 Components and Settings

Components need to be set up to support the Gatekeeper service and provide information and settings for H.323 connections. Like other connections and components in ISA Server, rules control the behavior of H.323 connections. During its installation, ISA Server creates many of the control features needed for the H.323 Gatekeeper. These features include an H.323 Protocol Definition and the H.323 Protocol Filter. The H.323 Protocol Filter can allow or deny all traffic using H.323, but you will need to configure an H.323 protocol rule to further control access. You must use the H.323 Protocol Definition created by ISA Server to create an H.323 protocol rule that will control traffic coming into and/or out of the H.323 Gatekeeper.

Configuring the H.323 Protocol Filter

The following steps include the use of the T.120 protocol. T.120 enables multimedia conferences to include data transfers (instead of just voice or video) as part of the exchange of information. Data transfers can include file transfers, application sharing, and whiteboards. NetMeeting allows a document to be shared so that some or all meeting participants can take turns editing the same document during the conference.

Note: A problem exists with the H.323 services in ISA Server and the T.120 protocols. When using the T.120 protocol calls through ISA servers, H.323 services may have difficulty disconnecting.

To configure the H.323 Protocol Filter complete the following steps:

1. Open ISA Management.

2. Expand Servers and Arrays, then expand the array that you want to manage.

3. Expand Extensions.

4. Click on the Application Filters container.

5. In the details pane on the right-hand side of the window, right-click H.323 Filter and select Properties.

6. On the General tab, select Enable This Filter.

7. Select the Call Control tab.

8. Select Use This Gatekeeper if you want the H.323 Protocol Filter to use a different Gatekeeper than the local server.

9. Type in the name of the Gatekeeper that you want the H.323 Filter to use.

10. Select Allow Incoming Calls to allow H.323 connections into your network.

11. Select Allow Outgoing Calls if you want to allow H.323 connections out of your internal network.

12. To keep the H.323 Gatekeeper from using DNS for resolution of aliases, select Use DNS Gatekeeper Lookup And LRQs For Alias Resolution.

13. Select Allow Audio to allow audio connections.

14. Select Allow Video to allow video connections.

15. Select Allow T.120 And Application Sharing to allow data connections.

16. Click OK to accept the changes to the H.323 Protocol Filter.

Creating the H.323 Protocol Rule

An H.323 protocol rule is easy to create because the required policy element—the H.323 Protocol Definition—is already created for you. An H.323 protocol rule is needed to allow H.323 clients access in to or out of your internal network.

To create an H.323 protocol rule:

1. Open ISA Management.

2. Expand Internet Security And Acceleration Server for enterprise-level protocol rules or an array for array-level protocol rules.

3. Expand Enterprise Policy for enterprise-level protocol rules and Access Policy for array-level protocol rules.

4. Right-click Protocol Rules.

5. Point to New and select Rule. The New Protocol Rule Wizard will start.

6. In the first dialog box, type "H.323" as the name of the new protocol rule. Click Next.

7. In the Rule Action dialog box, select Allow to allow the use of the H.323 protocol in your network. Click Next.

8. In the Protocols dialog box, choose Selected Protocols to define the type of traffic that this protocol rule will allow. An H.323 Protocol Definition is created by default when ISA Server is installed.

9. Select the H.323 Protocol Definition check box to use it for this protocol rule. Click Next.

10. In the Schedule dialog box, specify when the protocol rule will apply. Click Next.

11. In the Client Type dialog box, select the client types that the protocol rule will apply to. You may need to select and/or define client IP address sets or users and/or groups. Click Next.

12. Review the summary of information and click Finish. You can use the Back button to change incorrect information.

Installing the H.323 Gatekeeper Service

The H.323 Gatekeeper service is automatically installed during a Full Installation of ISA Server. If you chose a Typical installation, it won't be installed. A Custom installation will allow you to select the service during the installation. If the H.323 Gatekeeper service is not installed during the installation of ISA Server, you can install it later.

To install the H.323 Gatekeeper service, complete the following steps:

1. Open Control Panel.

2. Double-click Add/Remove Programs.

3. Select Change/Remove Programs (if necessary).

4. Select Microsoft Internet Security And Acceleration Server 2000.

5. Click the Change button. The Microsoft Security and Acceleration Server 2000 setup will start.

6. In the first dialog box, click the Add/Remove button.

7. Select Add-in Services and click the Change Options button.

8. Select Install H.323 Gatekeeper Service and click OK.

9. Click Continue to begin the installation.

10. Setup will update ISA Server.

11. A dialog box will appear informing you that ISA Server has been updated successfully. Click OK.
12. Click OK to close the Add/Remove application.
13. Close Control Panel.

Adding a Gatekeeper Server

Before you can administer the H.323 Gatekeeper service, you may need to connect to an ISA server that has the H.323 Gatekeeper service installed on it. The local server or a remote server can be added in the ISA Server snap-in.

To add a server to the H.323 Gatekeeper service, complete the following steps:

1. Open ISA Management.
2. Expand Internet Security And Acceleration Server.
3. Right-click H.323 Gatekeeper and select Add Gatekeeper. The Add Gatekeeper dialog box will appear.
4. Click on This Computer or select Another Computer and type in the name of a computer running the Gatekeeper service.
5. Click OK.
6. The server will appear under the H.323 Gatekeeper node.

Configuring Connections

Once you have added a Gatekeeper server, you can view the options and configuration settings available in this service. There are three subfolders under the H.323 Gatekeeper server: Active Terminals, Active Calls, and Call Routing.

Active Terminals

Active Terminals shows you the registration database compiled by the RAS protocol. Every H.323 client that wants to use the H.323 Gatekeeper in your network will need to register first. Two fields displayed in the Active Terminals details pane are the H.323 Type and Q931 Addresses. An H.323 address is usually the email address of the client computer, but it can also be a DNS name. The client application making the registration will choose one of these options. Q931 is a protocol that is part of the H.323 standard and is used for call control and call setup. Q931 addresses are the combination of the IP address of the client and the port number it will use for its connections. H.323 type addresses are not required to be unique, but Q931 addresses must be unique in the registration database of the H.323 Gatekeeper.

Active Calls

The Active Calls folder lists current calls using the H.323 Gatekeeper service. It shows the originating and destination endpoints of the call, as well as how long the call has been connected and its current status. Active Calls is a good place to start when troubleshooting connection difficulties involving the H.323 Gatekeeper service.

Call Routing

ISA Server documentation talks a lot about creating "PBX style" routing plans for your network with H.323 Gatekeeper. These dial plans are just call routing rules. These rules allow you to tell the H.323 Gatekeeper service how it will handle outgoing calls for specified external endpoint addresses. You can route calls to certain defined destinations in H.323 Gatekeeper. It is PBX style because you can define destinations that are internal to the company even if they are external to your local network and handle them differently. Calls to a certain prefix or telephone number can be routed to a specific external H.323 Gatekeeper, or calls destined for a certain range of IP addresses can be routed to a certain proxy server or not allowed to leave the internal network at all. These are just examples; there is a lot of flexibility in the call routing rule setup.

PBX

PBX stands for Private Branch Exchange. Having a PBX system in your company is like having your own private telephone network internally in your company. A PBX system allows a company to have an internal phone line for each telephone that connects to a specified number of outside telephone lines. Companies use PBX systems so that they can have an internal phone line for each employee while having a smaller supply of lines that are for outside use. This way, the company doesn't have to pay for an external phone line for each employee. With a PBX system, all switching occurs internally at the company. Only calls that are outbound from the company need to use an external telephone company's equipment.

Destinations

If you want to route certain calls, then you must specify a destination server to receive these calls by including the destination in the call routing rule. When you are creating call routing rules, destinations work like policy elements in that you must define them before you create the call routing rule. Don't confuse destinations used in a call routing rule with destination sets. They are two distinctly different things. A wizard creates a destination that can subsequently be used when creating a call routing rule. In the wizard, the type of destination and the specific name or address of the destination server are specified. The call routing rule uses this information to find out where to send a routed request and how to communicate with the destination.

Complete the following steps to create a destination that can be used in a call routing rule:

1. Open ISA Management.

2. Expand Internet Security And Acceleration Server.

3. Expand H.323 Gatekeeper and expand one of the H.323 Gatekeeper servers.

4. Expand Call Routing and right-click on Destinations and select Add Destination. The New Destination Wizard will start.

5. The first dialog box welcomes you to the wizard. Click Next.

6. In the Destination Type dialog box, select from four types of destinations: Gateway Or Proxy Server, Internet Locator Service (ILS), Gatekeeper, or Multicast Group. Figure 11.3 shows these choices. Once you make a choice, click Next.

7. In the Destination Name Or Address dialog box, type the DNS name or IP address of the destination. Click Next.

8. In the Destination Description dialog box, type a descriptive name or phrase that will allow you to recognize the destination when you need to select it from a list. You will need to select the appropriate destination when creating a call routing rule. Click Next.

9. Review the summary of information and click Finish. You can use the Back button to change incorrect information.

With a destination defined, you are now ready to create a call routing rule.

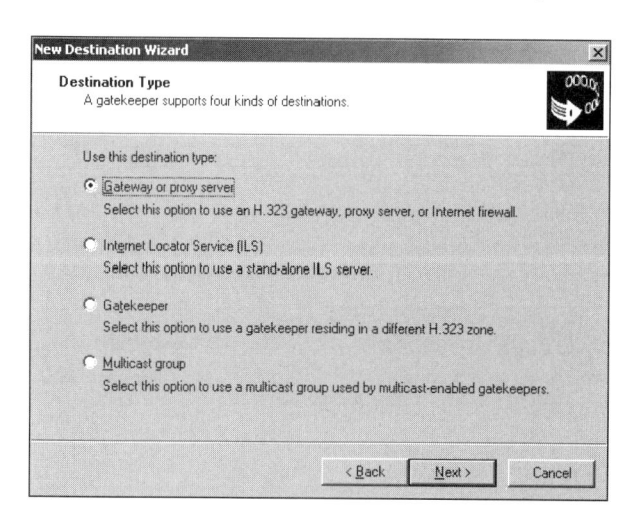

Figure 11.3 These destination types appear in the New Destination Wizard.

Call Routing Rules

Call routing rules are normally used only for outgoing call requests that do not include a unique Q931 address. But call routing rules allow you to specify whether the rule should be invoked any time a certain address or phone number is used. Call routing rules let the H.323 Gatekeeper know exactly what destination type it should send. The choices of destination types are specified prefix or phone numbers, email or DNS addresses, or ranges of IP addresses.

To create a call routing rule, complete the following steps:

1. Open ISA Management.

2. Expand Internet Security And Acceleration Server.

3. Expand H.323 Gatekeeper and expand one of the H.323 Gatekeeper servers.

4. Right-click Call Routing and click Add Routing Rule. The New Routing Rule Wizard will start.

5. The first dialog box welcomes you to the wizard. Click Next.

6. In the Address Type dialog box, select which type of rule you would like to create. Select Prefix Or Phone Number to base the rule on telephone numbers. Select E-mail Address to base the rule on an email address, directory services username, or DNS name. Select IP Address if that is what you want to base your rule on. Figure 11.4 shows this wizard dialog box. Once you make your selection, click Next.

7. In the Name And Description dialog box of the wizard, type the name that you will use to refer to the call routing rule and a description of its use or purpose. Click Next.

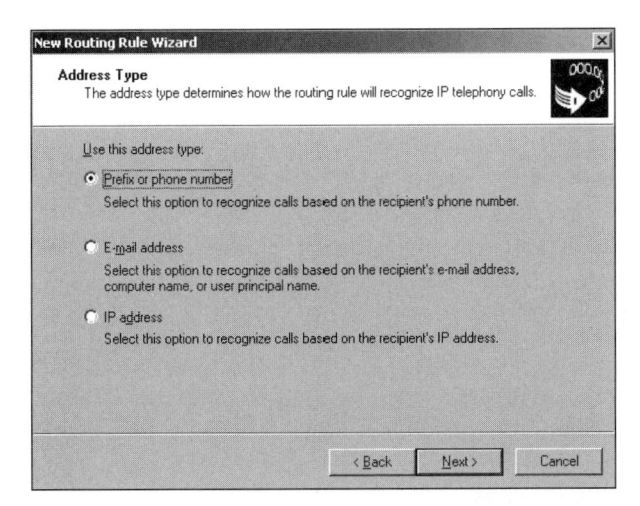

Figure 11.4 Address type choices in the New Routing Rule Wizard.

8. You will now enter the prefix or phone number, DNS domain, or network number and subnet mask, depending on what you specified in Step 6. Click Next.

9. Now, select the type of destination you will be routing this call to. The dialog box offers nine types of destination types, as shown in Figure 11.5. If you select None, then you are specifying that the call be terminated and not allowed to connect to its requested destination.

10. The next dialog box will ask you to select one of the destinations that were created prior to the call routing rule. Only the destinations matching the destination type you selected in Step 9 will be shown. Once you have selected a destination, click Next.

11. You'll then see the Change A Phone Number dialog box. If you selected Prefix Or Phone Number in Step 6, you will be able to specify how the phone number should be handled. For example, if an internal phone network requires users to dial 9 before getting an outside line, a call routing rule can be set up to handle all telephone numbers that start with a 9. In this dialog box, you can specify that 9 be dropped from the phone number so that it can be processed. Figure 11.6 shows the Change A Phone Number dialog box. If you are routing calls based on an email address or IP address, then the wizard will skip this dialog box.

12. In the Routing Rule Metric dialog box, enter a number and click Next. If more than one call routing rule applies to a call, the rule with the lowest metric will take precedence over the others.

13. Review the summary of information and click Finish. You can use the Back button to change incorrect information.

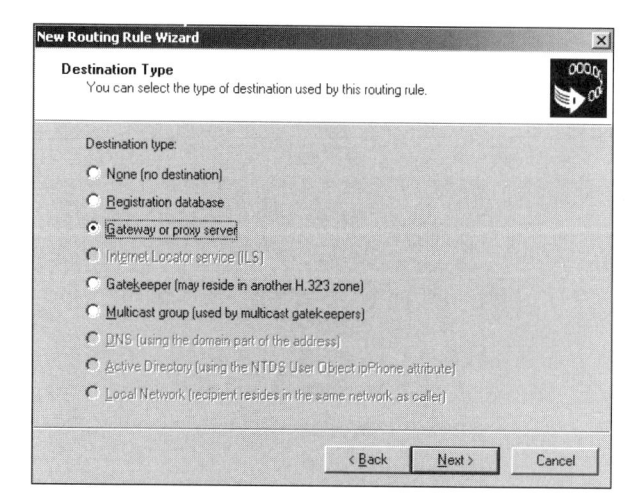

Figure 11.5 Destination types shown in the New Routing Rule Wizard.

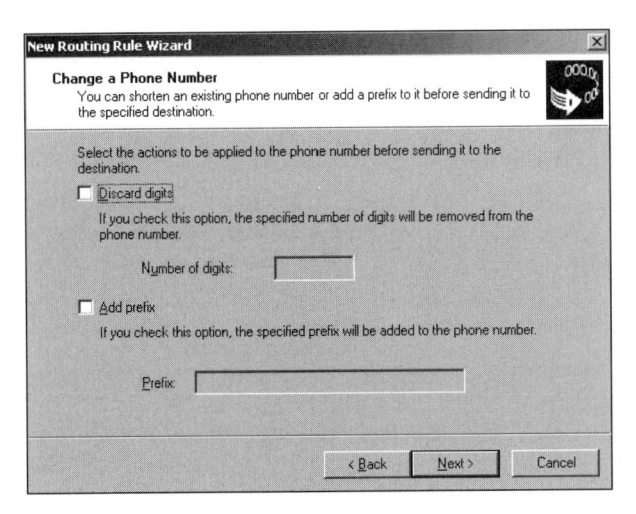

Figure 11.6 The Change A Phone Number dialog box of the Call Routing Rule Wizard.

Some call routing rules are automatically configured during the installation of ISA Server and used when processing outgoing H.323 Gatekeeper requests. A default phone number rule and a default email address rule each specify that all requests should be resolved by the local registration database. These rules can be modified, or more rules can be created. When more than one rule is found that matches the call request, a metric that is assigned to each rule is used to determine which rule will take precedence over the others. Low metric numbers take precedence over high metric numbers.

Configuring the H.323 Gatekeeper

Once H.323 Gatekeeper is set up, you can control its use through its property pages. There are four property pages in H.323 Gatekeeper. Figure 11.7 shows the Advanced property page and the tabs that allow you to access the three other property pages. Right-clicking on a Gatekeeper server in the ISA Server snap-in and selecting Properties accesses these property pages.

The General tab gives the FQDN of the Gateway server as well as information on the status and build of the ISA server. The Network tab allows you to select which network adapter or adapters on the ISA server are used for the H.323 Gatekeeper server. If you use the Network page to change the network adapter of the H.323 Gatekeeper service you will need to restart the H.323 Gatekeeper service for the change to take effect.

The Advanced tab allows you to set an expiration date for a registration in the database maintained on the H.323 Gatekeeper server. By default, the registration expires after 6 minutes. After the expiration period, the Gatekeeper will make

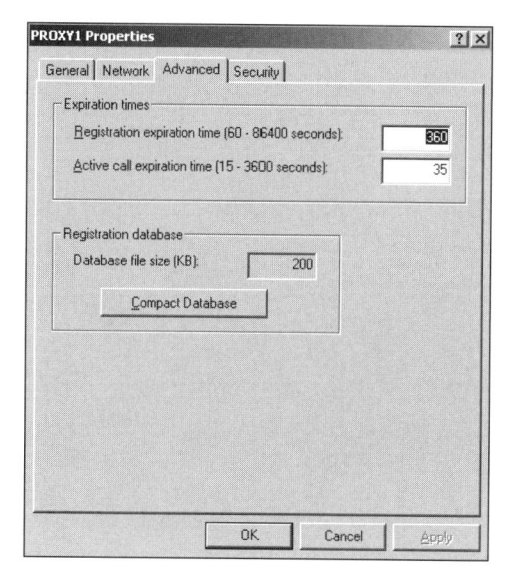

Figure 11.7 The Advanced property page of a Gatekeeper server in ISA Management will display the General property page of a Gatekeeper server.

queries to see if the registration is still needed. You can also set how long the Gatekeeper server will consider a call active when there is no longer activity. By default the server will wait for 35 seconds. The Registration Database section of the dialog box allows you to set the maximum size of the registration database and to perform a manual compact of the database.

Figure 11.8 shows the Security tab, which looks and works like any other Security page in Windows 2000. The Security page allows you to set what groups and users are allowed to use the Gatekeeper server and what level of permission they have when using it. By default, in this Security page, all users have the right to use the Gatekeeper servers. If you want to change this default behavior, you will need to remove the Everyone group and add the specific groups or users that you want to give permission to.

Additional Configurations for Incoming Connections

If you have an H.323 Gatekeeper on your network and you are accepting incoming connections through that gatekeeper, you need to set up an SRV resource record in your DNS server. SRV records are service location records that allow clients to look up the IP address of a server providing a specified type of service on a network.

Note: Although the spelling of SRV suggests that it is an acronym, it is not. According to the Request For Comment that defines the SRV record (RFC 2052), SRV stands for service.

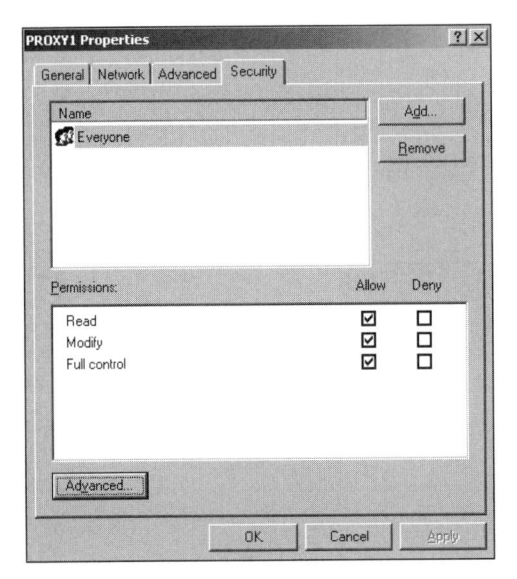

Figure 11.8 The Security page is just like other Security pages in Windows 2000.

To set up an SRV service location record for the Gatekeeper service on a DNS server, complete the following steps:

1. Open the DNS snap-in.
2. Expand the console in the left pane of the window to show the DNS server for your network.
3. Double-click the DNS server and then double-click the Forward Lookup Zones folder to expand it.
4. Right-click the appropriate Forward Lookup Zone and select Other New Records.
5. In the Resource Record Type dialog box, select Service Location.
6. Select Create Record.
7. In the Service box, type "Q931". The Q931 protocol is a specification used by H.323 for call setup and control.
8. In the Protocol box, type "_tcp".
9. In the Port Number box, type "1720".

Note: *The Q.931 protocol uses TCP port 1720.*

10. In the Host Offering This Service box, type the fully qualified domain name of the ISA server running H.323 Gatekeeper.
11. Click OK to create the new record.
12. Close the DNS snap-in.

Streaming Media Filter

Streaming media is used when clients want to download media presentations. Media files are extremely large when compared to documents, and bandwidth over Internet connections is usually extremely scarce. The use of streaming media saves large amounts of bandwidth by compressing the files and then allowing them to be published on your internal network with a media server. Streaming media works with both Firewall and SecureNAT clients. It does not work with Web Proxy clients because it requires a separate application to run, and the Web Proxy service downloads only Web pages and does not make Internet application connections. Windows Media Player, RealPlayer, and QuickTime are applications that can be used with the Streaming Media Filter.

What Does Streaming Mean?

Multimedia connections require a lot of bandwidth. Without a large amount of bandwidth, multimedia connections can skip or become jerky. One solution is to get a lot more bandwidth, but if that is not an option, then using a streaming application might be a solution. Streaming applications control the flow of data so that the user sees a steady stream. Streaming applications do this by using two techniques—buffering and displaying the data before the entire file is transferred. When a client buffers the data, it saves it to memory before showing it, so a slowdown in transfer speed will not be noticed. Of course, an extreme slowdown will cause the buffer to be used up and that will affect the presentation. The other technique used in streaming is to start showing the file before it is completely downloaded. Because multimedia files are extremely large, most modems take longer to download them than a user is willing to wait. This wait is shortened by starting to show the presentation before it is completely downloaded. To benefit from streaming, you need to have an application that uses these techniques. Applications such as RealNetworks' applications RealAudio and RealVideo as well as Microsoft's ActiveMovie and NetShow are examples of streaming media applications.

Windows Media Server

Much of this chapter covers the need to control bandwidth when connecting to multimedia presentations. Multimedia is just extremely bandwidth intensive so the control is needed for two reasons. First, you don't want the rest of the activity on your network to be squeezed out by multimedia transmissions. Second, you want the multimedia presentations to be viewed without transmission problems ruining the presentation. It is necessary to learn about Windows Media Server because the Streaming Media Filter assumes that a WMT server is available on the network.

Note: Although the dialog boxes in ISA Server use the acronym WMT Server, the rest of Microsoft documentation refers to this server as Windows Media Server. WMT is used as an overall acronym referring to Windows Media Technologies, a collection of technologies from Microsoft that allows media to be created, transferred, and played.

Windows Media Server allows files that use stream splitting to be downloaded over external connections and subsequently made available to clients on the local network. One of the most significant features of WMT Server is that it allows media to be significantly compressed and then transferred in non-realtime format, so that media files can be more quickly downloaded over the Internet or slow WAN links. This file is downloaded to the WMT server so that it can then be decompressed and sent out to the clients on the internal network in a realtime stream. This way, the media presentation needs to travel over the internal network only, which usually has a lot more available bandwidth than a WAN connection. Microsoft first released a media server that controlled the use of bandwidth and implemented streaming in 1996 and called it Microsoft NetShow. The current version of Windows Media Services is 4.1. You will need to install Windows Media Server on an internal Web Server that is running Windows NT 4 with Service Pack 4 or higher.

Media Protocol Definitions

ISA Server has six protocol definitions that are specifically for use with the Streaming Media Filter. They actually define only three different media protocols, but there are two protocol definitions for each protocol, one for client access and the other for server publishing. You can open Policy Elements and select Protocol Definitions to view the protocol definitions created for the Streaming Media Filter. Table 11.2 lists each protocol and the applications that can use the protocol definitions defined by ISA Server. Notice that the description for the media protocol definitions state that they work "via streaming filter." This is because they are defined for use with the Streaming Media Filter only. If the Streaming Media Filter is disabled, these protocol definitions will also be disabled.

Like other protocol definitions that are installed with ISA Server, the media protocol definitions cannot be modified or deleted, but the Streaming Media Filter itself can be configured. ISA Server will need to know how to handle client requests for media services.

Table 11.2 Media protocol definitions installed with ISA Server.

Protocol Definition	Name and Purpose
Client PNM	Progressive Networks Protocol for RealPlayer client access.
Server PNM	Progressive Networks Protocol for RealPlayer server publishing.
Client MMS	Microsoft Windows Media Streaming protocol for client access to Windows Media Player.
Server MMS	Microsoft Windows Media Streaming protocol for server publishing with Windows Media Player.
Client RTSP	Real Time Streaming Protocol for RealPlayer and QuickTime client access.
Server RTSP	Real Time Streaming Protocol for server publishing of RealPlayer and QuickTime media presentations.

To configure the Streaming Media Filter, complete the following steps:

1. In ISA Management, expand the array.
2. Expand Extensions, then select Application Filters.
3. In the details pane, right-click Streaming Media Filter, and then click Properties.
4. On the General tab, make sure that the Enable This Filter option is selected.
5. Click the Live Stream Splitting tab.
6. On the Live Stream Splitting tab, leave Disable WMT Live Stream Splitting selected if you do not want your clients to use live stream splitting services. Select Split Live Stream Using A Local WMT Server if the WMT server is local to the ISA server. If you have a WMT Server Pool, select Split Live Stream Using The Following WMT Server Pool.
7. To define a WMT Server Pool, click the Add button. Type the IP address of the WMT Server Pool. A WMT Server Pool is a cluster of Windows Media Servers that provides fault tolerance for media connections.
8. In the User Account box, type the username of the WMT server administrator.
9. In the Password and Confirm Password boxes, type the password to that same user account.
10. Click OK to accept the changes to the Streaming Media Filter.

Application filters take the place of any protocol rules that would normally need to be created for clients to access a service. Configuring the Streaming Media Filter means that no protocol rule needs to be created to allow access to clients requesting streaming media services. However, the Streaming Media Filter implements access to media services on an all or nothing basis. You will need to create a protocol rule to add restrictions to this open access.

Chapter Summary

Although your clients may want to make and receive multimedia connections, it takes some planning and setup to allow these connections through ISA Server. Users generally request two types of connections that you will need to set up: realtime conferencing or multimedia file downloads. The first can use the H.323 Gatekeeper, and the second will need the Streaming Media Filter.

H.323 is a standard created for realtime multimedia and conferencing connections. Realtime connections allow users to talk and interact with one another over a connection. This can be difficult to achieve over the Internet, because the connection has to pass through various hardware and software to connect the endpoints. H.323 standards, though still fairly new, attempt to standardize the format and protocols used for these connections so that hardware and software compatibility is no longer an issue.

Setting up and understanding an H.323 connection requires new vocabulary and at least a basic knowledge of the H.323 standard. H.323 is often called an umbrella standard because it describes standards for all parts of the connection. Within a network, four different components may be needed to make an H.323 connection—terminals, H.323 Gatekeeper, H.323 Gateway, and MCUs. To make a connection from a network, only a terminal (a client computer) is needed.

The H.323 Gatekeeper controls and manages H.323 connections in a network. A collection of H.323 components controlled by a gatekeeper is called a zone. ISA Server has an H.323 Gatekeeper that is part of the software. The H.323 Gatekeeper is not installed as part of a typical installation of ISA Server, but you can add it later.

The Streaming Media Filter provides control over connections that do not need a realtime interaction between connected users. This filter is designed for multimedia presentations that are created ahead of time and downloaded to the internal network. Streaming media is used to compress large media files so that they can be transferred over slow networks and then sent to clients on an internal network. The presentation then appears to happen in realtime, without the jerks and skips that can result from low-bandwidth connections.

Support for both streaming media and H.323 services are setup in ISA Server as application filters. These filters, when configured, remove the need to create protocol rules to allow access for each service. However, because each application filter allows or denies access to the service on an all or nothing basis, protocol rules can still be created in the ISA Server Snap-in to place further restrictions and controls on these connections.

Review Questions

1. How do media differ from multimedia?
    a. Multimedia are multiple hardware devices.
    b. Multimedia are multiple file formats.
    c. Multimedia are multiple network cables presented together.
    d. Multimedia are multiple file formats presented together.

2. What is an example of a multimedia application(s)? [Check all correct answers]
   a. RealPlayer
   b. Excel
   c. NetMeeting
   d. Telephone
   e. Internet

3. What is the PSTN?
   a. Public Site Telephone Network
   b. Public Switched Telephone Network
   c. Private Site Telephone Network
   d. Private Switched Telephone Network

4. What is H.323? [Check all correct answers]
   a. An umbrella standard
   b. Standards for multimedia connections
   c. Standards for all networking
   d. Standards for Microsoft networking

5. What does an H.323 Gateway do?
   a. Controls and manages an H.323 zone.
   b. Connects devices together to form a network.
   c. Translates between H.323 and non-H.323 file formats and protocols.
   d. Originates an H.323 connection.
   e. Connects multiple H.323 terminals so that all can participate in a realtime conferencing connection.

6. What is an endpoint? [Check all correct answers]
   a. Client computer running NetMeeting
   b. Terminal
   c. H.323 Gatekeeper
   d. H.323 Gateway
   e. MCU

7. What is the purpose of an MCU?
    a. Controls and manages an H.323 zone.
    b. Connects devices to form a network.
    c. Translates between H.323 and non-H.323 file formats and protocols.
    d. Originates an H.323 connection.
    e. Connects multiple H.323 terminals so that all can participate in a realtime conferencing connection.

8. What does an H.323 Gatekeeper do?
    a. Controls and manages an H.323 zone.
    b. Connects devices to form a network.
    c. Translates between H.323 and non-H.323 file formats and protocols.
    d. Originates an H.323 connection.
    e. Connects multiple H.323 terminals so that all can participate in a realtime conferencing connection.

9. What does the acronym RAS stand for when referring to H.323 standards?
    a. Remote Access Server
    b. Remote Authentication Server
    c. Registration Access Status
    d. Registration, Admission, and Status

10. A Gatekeeper is a required H.323 component for a network.
    a. True
    b. False

11. What is the maximum number of H.323 Gatekeepers per zone?
    a. 0
    b. 1
    c. 2
    d. 3

12. When an H.323 Gatekeeper is on a zone, the terminals must adhere to its control settings.
    a. True
    b. False

13. H.323 standards were developed by what standards organization?
    a. ITU
    b. CCITU
    c. ITEF
    d. W3C

14. Which tasks are the responsibilities of the H.323 Gatekeeper? [Check all correct answers]
    a. Call Management
    b. Protocol translation
    c. Zone Registration
    d. Zone Management
    e. Call Authorization

15. Which client(s) can be used with the H.323 Gatekeeper service? [Check all correct answers]
    a. None
    b. Firewall client
    c. Web Proxy client
    d. SecureNAT client

16. When creating an SRV record in Windows 2000 DNS, what record type should you select?
    a. Service locator
    b. Service
    c. System
    d. System revelation

17. Why do you need to create an H.323 DNS SRV record?
    a. To send H.323 service requests
    b. To communicate with a publishing server
    c. To resolve H.323 service requests
    d. To connect to a Windows Media Server

18. What is the Q931 protocol used for? [Check all correct answers]
    a. Call signaling
    b. DNS name resolution
    c. Call control
    d. Call routing
    e. Call setup
    f. All of the above

19. What type of media traffic does T.120 specify a format for?
    a. Voice
    b. Video
    c. Data
    d. Voice over IP
    e. Voice and video combined

20. How does Windows Media Technologies save bandwidth when downloading media presentations?
    a. By using non-realtime connections
    b. By using realtime connections
    c. By using a high level of compression
    d. By using a low level of compression

21. How many protocol definitions for the Streaming Media Filter are created with the installation of ISA Server?
    a. 2
    b. 4
    c. 6
    d. 8

22. How many protocol rules must be set up to allow clients to use streaming media on an internal network protected by ISA Server?
    a. 0
    b. 1
    c. 3
    d. 6

23. Which media protocols are supported by ISA Server when first installed? [Check all correct answers]

    a. RAS

    b. RSTU

    c. PNM

    d. MMS

    e. RSTP

    f. RSVP

24. What operating systems can Windows Media Server be installed on? [Check all correct answers]

    a. IIS

    b. Windows NT 4

    c. Windows NT 4 with Service Pack 4

    d. Windows 2000 Server

Real-World Projects

Note: This exercise assumes a test Windows 2000 Server with Service Pack 1 as well as ISA Server installed. Read the instructions carefully and do not change the settings on your production machine unless you understand the options presented. If you are unsure about an option, do not make a change and instead read the ISA Server help files about the option to be installed.

"So today during our kickoff meeting we will present a multimedia presentation to our new client to show them our ideas," said the vice president of communications. "We want them to be fully convinced of our technical knowledge and competence," he continued. "Are there any questions?"

"Just one," said Joe. "How are we going to share a multimedia presentation today when we have no multimedia conferencing abilities?"

The whole room of executives stared at him.

"We have been holding telephone conferences with this client for months," said the VP.

"Yes, but that was over the telephone. Multimedia conferencing is completely different," explained Joe.

"All right, let's not panic," said the president. "Joe, what can be set up in the next five hours?"

"Everything," said Joe. "As long as enough people are working on it," he added.

In the next 15 minutes, Joe laid out a plan. He assigned one IT department person to call the client's IT department to make sure they had NetMeeting set up and ready to use for the conference. It turned out the client's network not only used NetMeeting, but also had video capabilities. The departments coordinated a test connection and scheduled it for two hours before the meeting. Joe sent an IT employee to the nearest computer store to buy video conferencing cameras and set them up.

With the NetMeeting conferencing application being prepared, Joe went to configure the ISA server so that it would accept the NetMeeting connection. Because the company had never needed outside conferencing abilities, he did not even have the H.323 Gatekeeper service installed. He read through help files to make sure he had thought of all the steps; then, he sat down at the server, ready to go.

Project 11.1
To install the H.323 Gatekeeper service:

1. Open Control Panel.
2. Double-click Add/Remove Programs.
3. Select Change/Remove Programs if it is not already selected.
4. Select Microsoft Internet Security And Acceleration Server 2000.
5. Click the Change button. The Microsoft Security And Acceleration Server 2000 setup will start.
6. In the first dialog box, click the Add/Remove button.
7. Select Add-in Services and click the Change Options button.
8. Select Install H.323 Gatekeeper Service and click OK.
9. Click Continue to begin the installation.
10. Setup will update ISA Server.
11. A dialog box will appear informing you that ISA Server has been updated successfully. Click OK.
12. Click OK to close the Add/Remove application.
13. Close Control Panel.

To add an H.323 Gatekeeper server:

1. Open ISA Management.
2. Expand Internet Security And Acceleration Server.
3. Right-click H.323 Gatekeeper and select Add Gatekeeper. The Choose Target Machine dialog box will appear.
4. Click on This Computer or select Another Computer and type the name of a computer running the Gatekeeper service.
5. Click OK.
6. The server will appear under the H.323 Gatekeeper node.

With the Gatekeeper service and a Gatekeeper server loaded, Joe was ready to configure the settings needed to allow the NetMeeting connection. He had a half hour left before the test connection with the other network. It was important that his company look technically competent, so he wanted it to work as quickly as possible. He needed to configure the H.323 Protocol Filter to allow incoming connections.

Project 11.2

To configure the H.323 Protocol Filter:

1. Open ISA Management.
2. Expand Servers And Arrays, then expand the array you want to manage.
3. Expand Extensions.
4. Click on the Application Filters container.
5. In the details pane on the right-hand side of the window, right-click H.323 Filter and select Properties.
6. On the General tab, select Enable This Filter.
7. Click the Call Control tab.
8. Select Use This Gatekeeper if you want the H.323 Protocol Filter to use a different Gatekeeper than the local server.
9. Type the name of the Gatekeeper that you want the H.323 Filter to use.
10. Select Allow Incoming Calls to allow H.323 connections into your network.
11. Select Allow Outgoing Calls if you want to allow H.323 connections out of your internal network.

12. To keep the H.323 Gatekeeper from using DNS for resolution for aliases, select Use DNS Gatekeeper Lookup And LRQs For Alias Resolution.

13. Select Allow Audio to allow audio connections.

14. Select Allow Video to allow video connections.

15. Select Allow T.120 And Application Sharing to allow data connections.

16. Click OK to accept the changes to H.323 Protocol Filter.

Joe knew from his earlier research that he also needed to set up a service location record on the external DNS server. If the client's company tried to make an incoming connection to his network, the DNS server would not be much help unless it knew what they were asking for. He needed to set up a service location record for the H.323 service.

Project 11.3
To add a DNS SRV record for H.323 connections:

1. Open the DNS snap-in.

2. Expand the console in the left pane of the window to show the DNS server for your network.

3. Double-click the DNS server, then double-click the Forward Lookup Zones folder to expand it.

4. Right-click the appropriate Forward Lookup Zone and select Other New Records.

5. In the Resource Record Type dialog box, select Service Location.

6. Select Create Record.

7. In the Service box, type "Q931".

8. In the Protocol box, type "_tcp".

9. In the Port Number box, type "1720".

10. In the Host Offering This Service box, type the fully qualified domain name of the ISA server running H.323 Gatekeeper.

11. Click OK to create the new record.

12. Close the DNS snap-in.

Time was up. It was time for the client to attempt an incoming connection. All of the executives who had been at the meeting started gathering around, staring at the computer that had been set up in the conference room. Joe sat at the terminal and waited for the call to come in …RRRRING. Joe accepted the call and watched the client company's conference room came into view as the video screen popped up. The client company's tester seemed a little puzzled when he heard a collective sigh of relief from Joe's end of the connection. Joe tried to stop the whooping as fast as possible.

"Looks like we've got a good connection," said the client's IT person.

"Yeah, just wanted to double-check," said Joe casually. "How about we reconnect 15 minutes before the meeting so we will be ready to go?"

"Sounds good. See you then."

After they disconnected, the whole room erupted in a chorus of cheers.

"It looks like we're ready, Joe," said the president of the company.

CHAPTER TWELVE

Publishing Services

After completing this chapter, you will be able to:

✓ Define server publishing

✓ Explain how ISA Server protects internal servers

✓ Define the uses of publishing policies

✓ Plan the required access to published services

✓ Use SSL bridging to set up secure channels to and/or from ISA Server

✓ Describe the concept of reverse caching

✓ Set up publishing for a mail server

✓ Set up the SMTP Filter for content filtering

✓ Describe policy elements used in Web publishing rules

✓ Use packet filters instead of rules in certain publishing situations

✓ Create Web publishing rules

✓ Create server publishing rules

Publishing is getting something out on the Internet so that users can access it. Because published services or objects need to be sitting on a server that is accessible to the Internet, a server publishing to the Internet can be in a perilous and vulnerable position. In this chapter, we will show how ISA Server protects your internal servers while allowing them to publish to the Internet. The servers can be located on the internal network or on a perimeter network. Rules or packet filters can protect these servers, but as with many of the safety features in ISA Server, many aspects are involved in setting them up. We will also cover the setup needed to protect and filter the content that can travel to and from internal mail servers.

How ISA Server Protects Internal Servers

When you publish, the servers that provide information to the Internet are vulnerable to attacks from it. The dilemma of publishing to the Internet is that the server needs to be *accessible* to users on the Internet but not be *vulnerable* to them. ISA Server helps solve this dilemma by placing itself between the server and the Internet. A proxy server protects internal users by taking their place when making requests out to the Internet. A reverse proxy accepts the connections on the internal server's behalf and checks them before making a request of its own to the server that is being published. Users on the Internet believe they are directly connected to the internal server, but they are actually connected to the ISA Server. Figure 12.1 shows how ISA Server places itself on the external connection to the Internet and accepts connections for the internal server.

The term reverse proxy was really meant to describe proxy servers that protected internal Web servers. ISA Server uses the term publishing instead because not only does it protect internal Web servers, but it also protects any service that uses TCP/IP as its protocol stack.

Publishing Policies

You can publish services on the Internet by creating a publishing policy on ISA Server. ISA Server supports a number of different types of servers that can be published to the Internet. Publishing policies contain Web publishing rules and

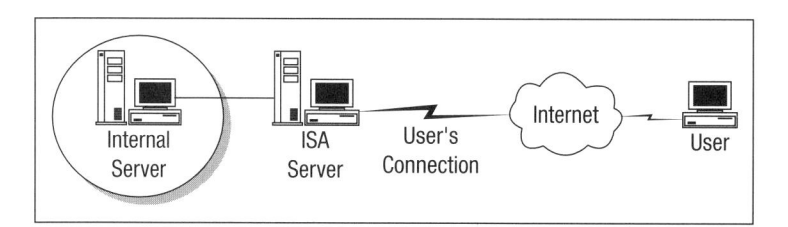

Figure 12.1 ISA Server places itself between the publishing server and the external network.

server publishing rules. To publish Web servers to the Internet from within your internal network, you can configure Web publishing rules. Publishing for any other type of server is set up by server publishing rules. Proxy Server 2.0 used IP filters to control incoming connections, but rules allow a degree of control over connections that IP filters do not. In most situations, rules work better than IP filters, but in some cases, you might have to use IP filters instead of rules. We will discuss IP filters later in this chapter.

Both Web publishing rules and server publishing rules can work in the Standard or Enterprise Editions of ISA Server, but they do not work with every mode of installation on ISA Server. Also, Web publishing and server publishing rules do not work with the same modes. Refer to Table 12.1 for mode requirements for setting up publishing rules.

Configuring the LAT

Servers that you would like to publish to the Internet through ISA Server must have their IP addresses included in the Local Address Table (LAT) on ISA Server. Of course, all internal computers' IP addresses are supposed to be included in the LAT, but it is worth another look to check for the IP addresses of the servers you would like to publish. If for any reason these servers' IP addresses are left out or have been removed from the LAT, internal users will not be able to connect to these servers. Also, ISA Server will not be able to apply the Web publishing and server publishing rules to incoming requests unless these IP addresses are on its LAT. To check the LAT for these IP addresses, complete the following steps:

1. Open ISA Management.
2. Expand Servers And Arrays.
3. Expand the array you would like to check.
4. In the selected array, expand Network Configuration.
5. Select the Local Address Table container.
6. In the details pane, review the IP addresses.
7. If you need to add an IP address to the list, right-click the Local Address Table container, point to New, and select LAT Entry.

Table 12.1 Mode requirements for setting up publishing rules.

Mode	Web Publishing Rule	Server Publishing Rule
Firewall	No	Yes
Cache	Yes	No
Integrated	Yes	Yes

8. After adding the entry or range of IP addresses, click OK to again review the IP addresses contained in the LAT.

9. Close ISA Management.

Listeners

Make sure that a listener is configured for incoming requests so that ISA Server will accept these packets and apply the publishing policy to them. Chapter 7 covers how you can apply authentication to these listeners when you configure them. If you require authentication in a Web publishing rule, you must also configure the listener for incoming Web requests to require authentication. If you do not configure the listener to also require authentication, users will not be able to connect to the published Web server.

To configure a listener for incoming IP addresses, complete the following steps:

1. Open ISA Management.

2. Expand Internet Security And Acceleration Server and then expand Servers And Arrays.

3. Right-click the name of the server or array that you are configuring a listener for, and select Properties.

4. Select the Incoming Web Requests Property tab.

5. You can select Use The Same Configuration For All Listeners or you can select Configure Listeners Individually Per IP Address.

6. If you choose Configure Listeners Individually Per IP Address, click the Add button. If you choose Use The Same Configuration For All Listeners, select the listed listener and click the Edit button.

7. In the Add/Edit Listeners dialog box, select the server that you want to configure.

8. Select an IP address and type a Display Name.

9. Select an authentication method if you are using authentication.

10. Click OK.

11. Click OK in the Array Or Server Properties dialog box.

12. A dialog box will appear asking you to restart the Web Proxy service. You can request that the Web Proxy service be restarted now or later. The changes will not take effect until the Web Proxy service is restarted. This warning dialog box is shown in Figure 12.2. Make a choice in the dialog box, and then click OK.

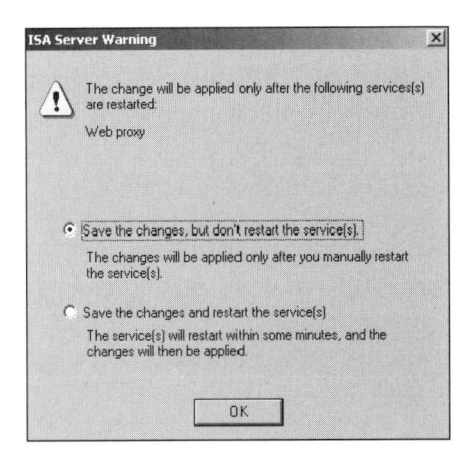

Figure 12.2 ISA Server dispays a warning dialog box when you change the properties of a listener.

Web Publishing Rules

What ISA Server calls Web publishing is also called reverse proxying. Just like a standard proxy, a reverse proxy protects computers internal to your network. Standard proxies protect a computer's identity when it wants to make an outgoing request to the Internet. A reverse proxy protects the identities of internal computers from incoming requests by representing itself as the actual Web server that users are trying to access. Using the same principles as a reverse proxy, when ISA Server receives incoming requests bound for an internal Web server, it does not simply forward the requests on to the internal server. Instead, ISA Server will retrieve the object requested and send it to the requesting user. It will appear to users that they are accessing information from a Web server, when in reality they are connected to ISA Server.

When you install ISA Server, a default Web publishing rule is created. Of course, this rule won't do you much good if you want to publish a Web site on your internal network, because it rejects all incoming packets and allows none through to your network. If you do want to publish a Web site internally, you will need to set up your own Web publishing rules. The default Web publishing rule has the lowest priority, so it will apply last. This means that you can specifically allow certain types of packets through to your Web site with your own rule. All requests that are not specified with the rule or rules you create will end up being handled by the default Web publishing rule, which means they will be rejected.

Destination Sets for Web Publishing

Destination sets created for access policies that are discussed in Chapter 6 need to be set up in a different way than destination sets used in Web publishing rules. In Chapter 6, we discuss the kinds of destination sets that are needed for access policies. Because access policies are used for outgoing requests, these destination sets include groups of computers or IP address ranges that are external to your network. Web publishing rules deal with computers and ranges of IP addresses for incoming requests; consequently, the destination sets used in setting up Web publishing rules most often specify computers that are internal to your network.

Client Type

Just like client types in other types of rules, a client type in a Web publishing rule specifies sets of IP addresses, users, or groups to which the rule should apply. If you are creating a rule for a public Web server, you might want to apply the rule to all requests. This is because a public Web site accepts connections from any user on the Internet. You can specify only one type of access per rule, so for two different types of access by different groups, you will need to create two different rules. You can also use client types to deny access to certain groups of users. Directing what ISA Server should do with the request is the next step: the rule action.

The Rule Action

In Chapter 6, the rule action either denied or allowed access, but in a Web publishing rule, the rule action spells out what ISA Server should do with the request. At this point in the Web publishing rule, you have already specified the destination set and client type the rule will apply to, so once those prerequisites have been met, the rule action can make sure that the request is discarded or that a request is sent to a Web server on the internal network. Figure 12.3 shows the Rule Action setup box that appears when you're creating a Web publishing rule. In this dialog box, you can see that the choices are Discard and Redirect.

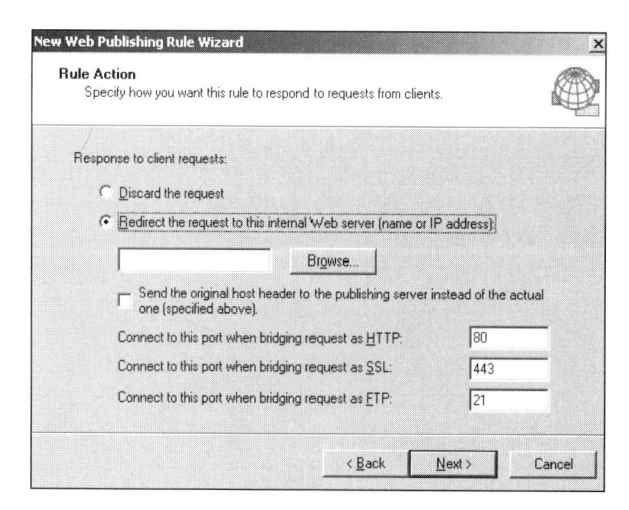

Figure 12.3 The Rule Action setup box in the New Web Publishing Rule Wizard.

As shown in Figure 12.3, HTTP requests are sent by default to port 80 on the internal server, SSL requests are also sent to port 443, and FTP requests are sent using port 21 by default. But Web publishing rules allow these requests to be sent to other ports as well. Before changing a port setting in a Web publishing rule, check to see which ports the internal Web server is accepting connections on. If a request is sent to the wrong port, it will not make a connection to the Web server. Web sites automatically bind to the default port numbers for a service, but you might have reason to change them. Because Web servers can support more than one Web site, sometimes different sites are set up on different ports. This can be done when they are using the same IP address.

Redirection

Although the term redirection is used with rules, it needs to be clear that the ISA Server does not simply pass the original request on to a server located on the internal network. Instead, ISA Server makes its own request to the internal server. With this method, the external user's requests have no direct contact with servers located on your internal network. Instead, ISA Server protects these servers by creating its own requests to send to them.

Because you can redirect incoming requests from ISA Server, you can spread the workload around to different servers on your internal network. For example, a Products directory that contains Web pages about the products the company creates can be located on one Web server while an Employment directory containing Web pages that connect to a database of openings at the company can be located on another Web server. The marketing department can maintain the information about the products while the human resources department can maintain information about the current job openings in the company.

Host Headers

As we discussed earlier, multiple Web sites can be located on one Web server and you have various methods of differentiating between these Web sites. One method is to assign each site a different IP address. However, if the same IP address is used, the sites can each use a different port number. But if the same IP address and the same port number are being used, HTTP in version 1.1 supports the use of host headers to differentiate between the sites. Host headers use only the name of the site to distinguish it from the other Web sites on a server. Because only the name of the Web site differentiates it from other sites on the same server, the name resolution system, Domain Name System (DNS), must be configured correctly. Each site must have a host name record that contains the DNS name of the Web site and the IP address of the Web server. Host headers use the DNS name in the host record to distinguish the sites.

Host headers get their name from a field in the HTTP header called Host. This field identifies by name which Web server the client wants to connect to. With Web publishing, a client connecting to the ISA Server will have the name of the ISA Server listed in the Host field of the HTTP header. By default, ISA Server will replace its own name with the name of the internal Web server when it repackages the client's request. When configuring an Action for a Web publishing rule, you can place a checkmark in the option Send The Original Host Header To The Publishing Server Instead Of The Actual One (Specified Above). This will keep the original name in the host header and prevent the ISA Server from revealing the name of the real Web server.

Safety Precautions

When setting up Web publishing rules, you should take a few precautions to ensure that the internal servers are protected. First, make sure that the Web server does not allow directory browsing. This is a normal security precaution for Web servers. Directory browsing allows a user connected to a Web server to get a list of directories on the Web server and see the files that are contained in them. Second, if you are using client authentication, you should not use Basic or Digest authentication. Because of the design of these authentication methods, the IP address of the internal Web server may be included in the data passed between the ISA server and the external client. This would allow the exposure of the IP address of the internal Web server that you are trying to protect by configuring Web publishing rules in the first place. If you need to implement user authentication, you can use either the Integrated or Certificate method. Refer to Chapter 7 for more information on authentication methods and their setup in ISA Server.

SSL Bridging

One type of port redirection involves SSL connections. ISA Server works with two types of SSL connections: SSL bridging and SSL tunneling. When SSL tunneling is configured for incoming requests, an external client requests a secure channel with a computer on the internal network. ISA Server receives the request and passes it on to the internal computer. Although ISA Server interferes with establishing the connection between the external client and the internal computer, once the connection is established, all information is passed between the two computers without the interference of ISA Server. We explain the architecture of SSL connections and tunneling in detail in Chapter 9.

SSL bridging is different from SSL tunneling in that the ISA server has a more active role during the connection. SSL bridging involves the ISA server maintaining two separate connections between the external and internal computers. Because two separate connections are always maintained, encryption does not have to be used on both sides of the connection. For example, if an external computer requests a secure connection, the ISA server will present a certificate to validate a secure connection. You can then configure whether the ISA server will open a non-secure HTTP connection or a secure SSL connection using HTTP-S with the internal Web server. With SSL bridging, you have a choice. Ending the secure connection at the ISA Server will speed up the connection between the ISA server and the internal Web server, while continuing the SSL connection will keep the connection secure. These two methods show the most common configurations for SSL bridging of incoming connections. Another way to configure SSL bridging is to have an external client make a non-secure HTTP connection to the ISA server and have ISA Server make a secure HTTP-S connection to the internal Web server. This is still SSL bridging, though it is often not practical or useful for incoming connections.

A nice benefit of using SSL bridging is that you can take advantage of caching when using secure connections with SSL. Even if both sides of the connection are using SSL for encryption, the ISA server will decrypt the requests it receives and then check to see whether the requested items are in cache. If they are, the ISA server can retrieve them from cache before re-encrypting the packets to continue the connection. The ISA server can also cache objects from the items returned by the internal server. If for security reasons you do not want an item from a secure Web page cached, you can mark it as not cacheable. You'll find information on designating whether an object is cacheable in the ISA Software Development Kit (SDK).

SSL bridging is configured in the properties of a Web publishing rule. It is not configured during the New Web Publishing Rule Wizard, but after the rule is created. Complete the following steps to configure SSL bridging:

1. Open ISA Management.
2. Expand Internet Security And Acceleration Server and then expand Servers And Arrays.
3. Expand the name of the server or array that you are configuring SSL bridging for.
4. Expand Publishing and select the Web Publishing Rules container.
5. In the details pane, double-click the rule that you want to configure SSL bridging on.
6. On the Rule Properties sheet, select the Bridging tab, as shown in Figure 12.4.
7. You can choose to create a secure channel between the ISA server and the internal Web server or to use HTTP to establish connections between the two.
8. Click OK to accept the changes.

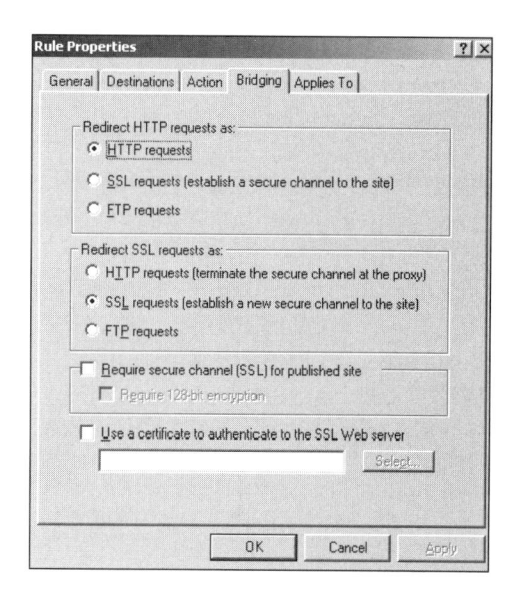

Figure 12.4 The Bridging page of the Rule Properties sheet.

Reverse Caching

Another configuration available for Web publishing is reverse caching. Forward caching is used for internal clients making outbound requests to the Internet. ISA Server saves cacheable Web pages and objects on the hard disk from previous client requests. When another client makes a request, ISA Server checks to see if any of the objects requested can be taken from cache before making a trip to the Internet. Reverse caching uses ISA Server's caching abilities for incoming requests. When ISA Server receives a request from an external user bound for an internal Web server, it can check to see if it has the requested objects in cache. If ISA Server can fill the request from cache, it will never have to bother making a request to the internal Web server. ISA Server will also cache objects from the requested Web pages that it retrieves from the internal Web servers so that it can build the number of objects from internal servers in its cache. Reverse caching allows an ISA server to speed up reaction time for external clients and can lighten the load on internal Web servers by servicing requests from cache. Caching is discussed in detail in Chapter 8.

Server Publishing Rules

So far in this chapter we have discussed publishing Web servers on an internal network. Proxy Server in version 2.0 called this reverse proxying. ISA Server calls this service Web publishing and also provides another service called server publishing. Using server publishing, you can provide services from any other type of server, not just Web servers. The only restriction is that they must use TCP/IP as their protocol suite. No reverse caching is available with server publishing, but most of these servers provide services instead of objects, so their information is not cacheable anyway. Web publishing also allows the redirection of ports, whereas server publishing does not.

ISA Server has a clear-cut way of defining when a Web publishing rule should be used and when a server publishing rule should be used. When ISA Server receives an incoming request using a protocol other than HTTP, HTTP-S, or FTP, a server publishing rule is applied. Requests using these protocols will have a Web publishing rule applied to them.

Address Mapping

One of the dialog boxes that must be configured in the New Server Publishing Rule Wizard is called Address Mapping. This dialog box maps an internal IP address for a server to the external IP address of the ISA server. With address mapping, the ISA Server can have multiple external interfaces mapped individually to different internal servers. Figure 12.5 shows the Address Mapping step of the New Server Publishing Rule Wizard. This step occurs immediately after the Welcome dialog box that allows you to name the rule.

If you don't know the IP address of the internal server, or you forgot to look it up before starting the New Server Publishing Rule Wizard, you can look it up during the wizard. In the Address Mapping step shown in Figure 12.5, simply click the Find button next to the input box labeled IP Address Of Internal Server. The dialog box shown in Figure 12.6 will appear. Enter or browse for the server name, and the IP address will appear in the IP Addresses section. Once you select an IP address, click OK to return to the Address Mapping screen.

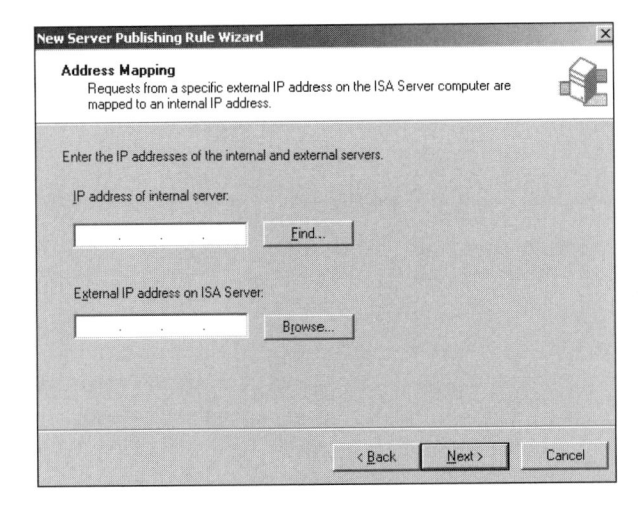

Figure 12.5 The address mapping step of the New Server Publishing Rule Wizard.

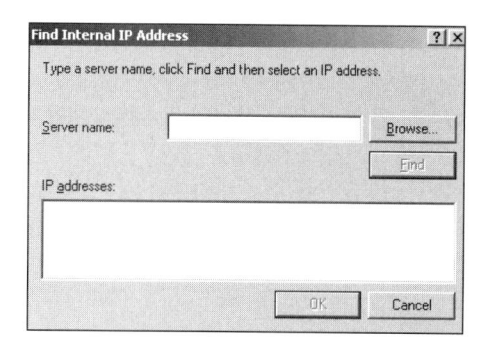

Figure 12.6 The New Server Publishing Rule Wizard will allow you to find an IP address while you are creating a new server publishing rule.

Protocol Settings

The next step of the New Server Publishing Rule Wizard allows you to define the protocols that the internal server supports. ISA Server will intercept the incoming requests and know which rule to apply based on the protocol the inbound request is using. If the protocols that the incoming server supports are not defined in a protocol definition created during the installation of ISA Server, you need to create a protocol definition before you start the New Server Publishing Rule Wizard.

Client Types

Like other rules, server publishing rules allow you to specify which computers or users to apply the rule to. You can apply the rule to all incoming requests, to specific client address sets, or to group and users accounts. Unlike protocol definitions, client address sets do not have to be defined before you start the New Server Publishing Rule Wizard. However, you must define users and groups before creating the rule.

Server Publishing Setup

A server that is published from the internal network is actually a SecureNAT client of ISA Server. This means that it is not necessary to install software on the internal server; however, some configuration is still necessary. Like all SecureNAT clients, the ISA server's IP address needs to be set as the default gateway on the internal server that is the SecureNAT client. Also, if the internal server is separated from the ISA server by one or more routers, the routers might need to be configured to pass the packets from the internal server to the ISA server. Configure the internal server that will be published to the Internet as you would any SecureNAT client on your network.

Note: If you set up an internal server as a Firewall client instead of a SecureNAT client, it will not be able to publish through ISA Server. Firewall clients cannot publish through ISA Server because of a port conflict. All servers that need to publish to the Internet through ISA Server must be SecureNAT and not Firewall clients.

Setting Up a Mail Server

A mail server can be complex to setup, as can an Internet security server, but the complexity of setting them up to work together on the network can get ridiculous. Proxy Server 2.0 could be set up to allow an Exchange server behind it to send mail traffic through the Proxy server, but it was such a complicated setup that it warranted a Knowledge Base (KB) article that detailed the steps required (KB article Q181420 *How to Configure Exchange or Other SMTP with Proxy Server*). If you set this up previously and don't want to mess with it, you can upgrade your Proxy server to ISA and just leave it. However, you won't be able to employ the new server publishing rules that ISA Server can use to protect internal servers such as your Exchange server. To use the new security features on ISA Server, you will need to do some reconfiguration. That's the bad news. The good news is that the reconfiguration is not nearly as complicated as before, because a wizard was created to simplify the procedure. Chapter 14 discusses how to use this wizard to set up the network configuration.

Special Publishing Configurations

Some services that can publish from the internal network are designed to communicate with the client before or while they are providing their services. This means that they will try to send outbound packets to the external client connecting from the Internet. When you set up a Server publishing rule for these services, it will allow only inbound client requests. When the server tries to send outbound packets to the client, the ISA server rejects them by default. This may cause the client-initiated connection to fail, because some services require the outbound connection with the client. If such failures occur, you may need to create a Site and Content rule that allows this outbound traffic. You will need to configure the Site and Content rule to allow all clients using a specified protocol definition for the internal published service.

Publishing a Mail Server

Setting up secure access to an internal mail server through ISA Server is complicated enough to warrant a wizard and an application filter. Instead of just creating another server publishing rule, you need to run the Mail Server Security Wizard to allow incoming connections to an internal mail server. Also, a Simple Mail Transport Protocol (SMTP) filter is installed by default with ISA Server. Although it is not enabled by default, once enabled, it intercepts and filters all SMTP requests that make a connection on the default SMTP port 25. The SMTP Filter allows you to filter messages by the content of the mail messages and their attachments. It affords a greater degree of control over who can send messages to your internal mail server and the type of content that you will allow.

The Mail Server Security Wizard

Use the Mail Server Security Wizard to set up mail servers that are on your internal network. Even if you choose not to filter the content of the mail messages that come into your network—by using the SMTP Filter—you still need to use the Mail Server Security Wizard to allow any messages in at all. You can publish these servers to the Internet and still protect them with ISA Server. When you right-click on the Server Publishing container in ISA Management, your first choice in the list is to start the Mail Server Security Wizard. Following the steps in this wizard, you will need to immediately set the external IP address of the ISA server that will accept connections from external users sending mail. This IP address will appear to the users as the published IP address of your internal mail server. In the same dialog box, you will need to set the IP address of the internal mail server that ISA Server will redirect the mail messages to.

Note: If you do not have the internal mail server installed and connected to the ISA server and a working connection to the external network, you will not be able to get past this step of the wizard.

Next, you will configure which incoming email protocols ISA Server will allow to access the internal mail server. Table 12.2 shows the protocols that can be used by external clients to connect to the internal mail server.

Rules created by the Mail Server Security Wizard are listed with other Server Publishing rules. Their names by default start with the phrase *Mail Wizard rule* so that you can easily identify them. The rest of the name will be created automatically using the protocol specified for mail traffic and the IP address of the internal mail server. The result is a name such as Mail Wizard rule-POP3 (client). Internal IP:*xxx.xxx.xxx.xxx* (where the x's represent the IP address of the internal mail server). In this example, the rule allows external clients to use the POP3 protocol to pass messages through ISA Server to the internal mail server.

The SMTP Filter

The SMTP Filter is much more complicated than many of the other application filters that come with ISA Server. Not only does it have more property pages than most other filters, but it also has a more complicated setup process. Although the

Table 12.2 Protocols that can be used by external clients when accessing an internal mail server configured by the Mail Security Server Wizard.

Supported Protocol	Acronym
Post Office Protocol 3	POP3
Network News Transfer Protocol	NNTP
Secure Network News Transfer Protocol	NNTP-S
Messaging Application Programming Interface	MAPI
Internet Messaging Access Protocol 4	IMAP4

SMTP Filter is installed by default during the ISA Server installation, it is not automatically enabled. Even if you enable the SMTP Filter, it is not ready to use until you complete some configurations that are not a part of the SMTP Filter but instead are services that support, or are supported by, the SMTP Filter. To start with, we will go over the steps of enabling the SMTP Filter; then, we will examine the steps that need to be completed before you can use the SMTP Filter. Finally, we will cover the steps of configuring the SMTP Filter itself.

To enable the SMTP Filter, complete the following steps:

1. Open ISA Management.
2. Expand Internet Security And Acceleration Server and then expand Servers And Arrays.
3. Expand the name of the server or array on which you want to enable the SMTP Filter.
4. Expand Extensions and select the Application Filters container.
5. In the details pane, double-click SMTP Filter.
6. On the Properties sheet of the SMTP Filter, click the General tab if necessary. Then, select the Enable This Filter option.
7. Click the OK button to close the SMTP Filter Properties sheet.

Configuring the ISA Server and Other Applications for the Use of the SMTP Filter

Once the SMTP Filter is enabled, you need to complete steps in different applications that will allow the use of the SMTP Filter. These steps involve installing the necessary ISA Server add-in components, running the Mail Server Security Wizard, and configuring the Internet Information Server (IIS) SMTP Virtual Server.

The Message Screener is an add-in to ISA Server. Installing the Message Screener allows the filtering of mail attachments and the filtering of individual messages for keywords. Because it is an add-in, it is not installed by default when ISA Server installs unless you specify a Full installation. Complete the following steps to install the Message Screener add-in to ISA Server:

1. Open Control Panel.
2. Double-click Add/Remove Programs.
3. Make sure you are in the Change Or Remove Programs dialog box and select Internet Security And Acceleration Server. Click the Change button.
4. In the Welcome To ISA Server Setup dialog box, click the Add/Remove button.
5. Select Add-In Services and click the Change Option button.

6. Place a checkmark next to Message Screener and click OK.

7. Click the Continue button to install this option. Setup will update ISA Server.

8. A dialog box will appear informing you that ISA Server has been updated successfully. Click OK.

9. Click OK to close the Add/Remove application.

10. Close Control Panel.

You also need to use the Mail Server Security Wizard to configure ISA Server to allow content filtering. During the wizard, select Incoming SMTP Mail and Outgoing SMTP Mail, and then select Apply Content Filtering. This allows the SMTP Filter to perform content filtering on attachments and/or email messages. You will still have to configure the SMTP Filter to specify how it will perform this content filtering. These steps are covered later in this chapter.

If you have an internal IIS server with the SMTP service loaded on it, you need to configure it to send all requests to the internal mail server for message handling. Next, you will need to configure the internal IIS Server's SMTP service. In the IIS snap-in on the internal IIS server, complete the following steps:

1. Open the IIS snap-in by selecting Internet Services Manager from the Administrative Tools menu.

2. If necessary, click the plus sign (+) to expand the server and view the available Internet services.

3. Right-click the Default SMTP Virtual Server and select Properties.

4. Select the Access tab.

5. At the bottom of the Access property page, click the Relay button.

6. Select All Except The List Below and click the Add button.

7. Type in the IP address of the internal mail server and click OK twice to return to the Access property page.

8. Click the Delivery tab.

9. At the bottom of the Delivery property page, click the Advanced button.

10. In the Smart Host input box, type the FQDN of the internal mail server. The SMTP Virtual Server will then send all SMTP requests it receives to the internal mail server.

11. Click OK to return to the Delivery property page and click OK again to return to the IIS snap-in.

12. Close the IIS snap-in.

Configuring the SMTP Filter Property Pages

Once the SMTP Filter is enabled and the necessary settings are configured, you can configure several other settings to customize your use of the filter. Including the General tab, the SMTP Filter contains five property pages. As shown in Figure 12.7, the properties allow you to configure how SMTP handles attachments, users/domains, keywords, and SMTP commands.

If you select the Attachment property page, you can configure the SMTP Filter to look for and handle some attachments differently than others. Figure 12.8 shows the Mail Attachment Rule dialog box, which allows you to set attachment rules.

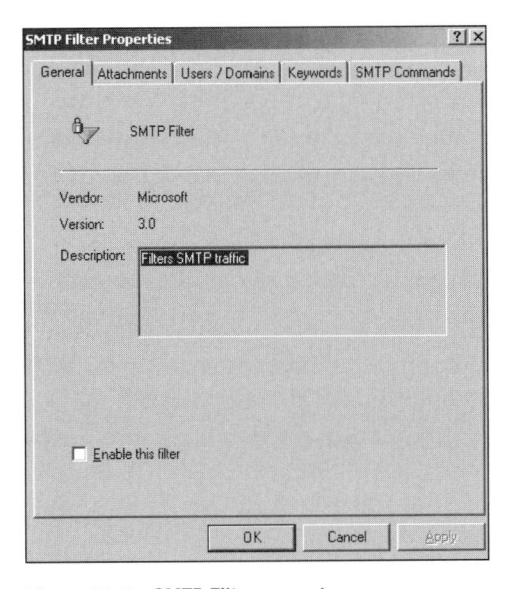

Figure 12.7 SMTP Filter property page names.

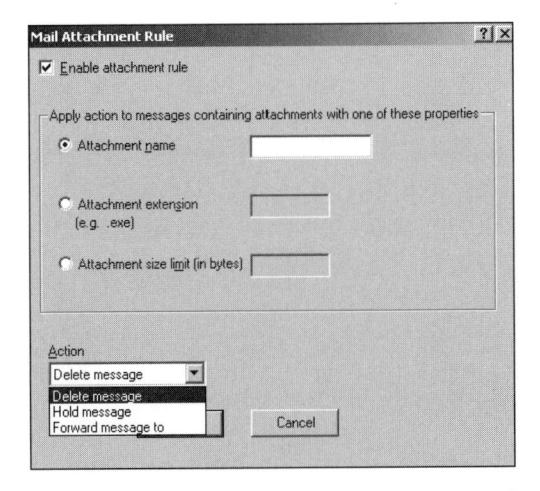

Figure 12.8 The SMTP Filter Mail Attachment Rule dialog box appears when you click the Add button on the Attachment property page.

The Add button on the Attachment property page opens a Mail Attachment Rule dialog box. In this dialog box, you can specify the name, file extension, or size of attachment that SMTP should look for when filtering attachments to mail messages. Each attachment is checked to see if it fits any of the rule requirements. If an attachment meets the requirement of one of the rules, the SMTP Filter performs the action specified by that rule. For example, if you decide not to accept any mail messages with an .exe extension, you can add a rule specifying that all mail attachments with the .exe extension be discarded by choosing Delete Message as the action. Rules are automatically given an order when created, just in case an attachment meets more than one rule's criterion. You can change the order of the rules in the Attachment property page of the SMTP Filter.

The Users/Domains property page allows you to specify whether certain messages should be rejected and not allowed through the ISA server just by who sent them. For example, if you are receiving a lot of junk mail from the WeAreJunkMail.com domain, you can specify that all mail from that domain be rejected. The Users/Domains property page is shown in Figure 12.9, with the WeAreJunkMail.com domain name listed as a domain to reject. Because each user from that domain will be listed as someone@WeAreJunkMail.com, all messages from users in that domain will be rejected.

The Keyword property page works similarly to the Attachments property page. You can add Mail Keyword rules that will cause the SMTP Filter to search the header or contents of a mail message, or even both, for certain keywords. You can use this feature to look for inappropriate types of content that are not allowed by company

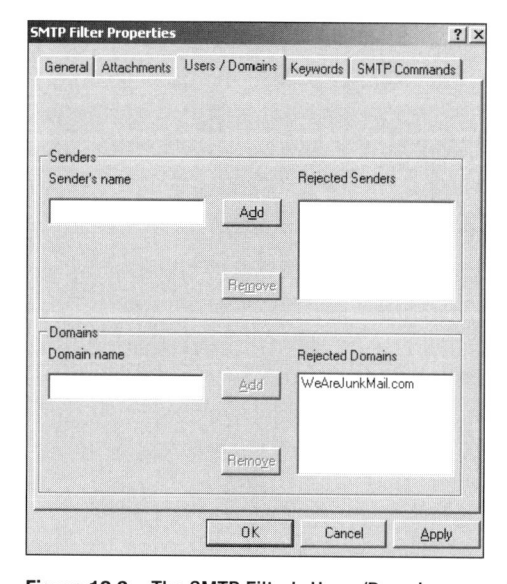

Figure 12.9 The SMTP Filter's Users/Domains property page with a rejected domain listed.

policy. Make sure that any rules you configure match company email policy. Also, even though legally in a business all email is the property of the company and no privacy laws exist for users, it is best to let users know that their email will be filtered for certain types of attachments and words if you are going to set up these rules.

The SMTP Commands property page allows you to guard against attacks that try to overburden the mail server buffers. These messages give the mail server so much information to process that it cannot keep up with regular mail service. The SMTP Commands dialog box does this by checking for messages that are larger than a specified size. If a message using one of the commands exceeds the specified size, you can configure how ISA Server should handle the message. Several commands are listed by default in this property page, and each has its own specified size. Figure 12.10 shows some of the SMTP commands defined by default in the SMTP Filter. You can edit these commands by selecting one and clicking the Edit button, or you can add more to the list by clicking the Add button.

Using Packet Filters When Publishing

Although in this chapter we have discussed only publishing rules, packet filters can also be a part of controlling incoming requests from the Internet. Rules are the recommended method for controlling both incoming and outgoing traffic, because they allow more control over how the requests are processed by ISA Server. However, when a three-homed Demilitarized Zone (DMZ)—also known as a perimeter network or screened subnet—is used to separate the published servers

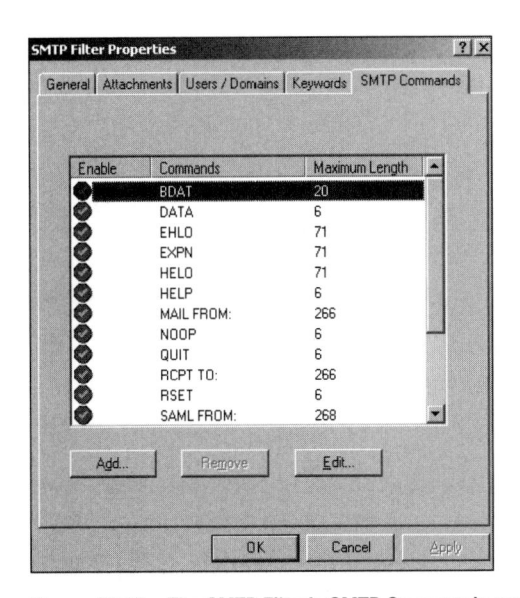

Figure 12.10 The SMTP Filter's SMTP Commands property page.

from the internal network, packet filters must be used. Setup for three-homed and back-to back DMZs is covered thoroughly in Chapter 17. Also, when the service that needs to be published to the Internet is located on the same server as ISA Server, rules will not work and packet filters must be used instead.

Packet filters are implemented differently in ISA Server than in Proxy Server 2.0. In Proxy Server, packet filters could be either dynamic or static, but in ISA Server, only static packet filters are available, because rules allow the dynamic use of ports based on specific settings. Each packet is examined to see whether it fits the requirements set in the rule. If it does not, the packet is rejected. This is a greater degree of control than even dynamic packet filters gave. Because rules allow a greater degree of control than dynamic packet filters, the developers decided that dynamic packet filters were no longer needed. Static packet filters should be used only if rules cannot be used.

You can set up packet filters to either allow or block packets. Packet filters are listed under the Access Policy container in ISA Management because they can be set up for incoming or outgoing packets. By default, packet filtering is not enabled, so before creating a packet filter, you should enable the use of packet filtering on the ISA server.

To enable packet filtering on an ISA server, complete the following steps:

1. Open ISA Management.
2. Expand Internet Security And Acceleration Server and then expand Servers And Arrays.
3. Expand the name of the server or array on which you want to enable IP packet filters.
4. Expand Access Policy, right-click on the IP Packet Filters container, and select Properties.
5. On the General tab, select the Enable Packet Filtering option and click OK. A dialog box will warn you that the Firewall service needs to be restarted. You can choose to restart it then or later. Click OK to restart or schedule the restart of the Firewall service.
6. Click OK to close the IP Packet Filters properties.

Note: *Packet filters cannot be used on an ISA server installed in Cache mode.*

Now that you have enabled packet filtering on the ISA server, you can create packet filters. To create a packet filter for use with publishing either on a perimeter network or for a service that is located on the same server as ISA Server, complete the following steps:

1. Open ISA Management.

2. Expand Internet Security And Acceleration Server and then expand Servers And Arrays.

3. Expand the name of the server or array on which you want to create IP packets filters.

4. Expand Access Policy, right-click the IP Packet Filters container, point to New, and select Filter. The New IP Packet Filter Wizard begins.

5. In the first dialog box, type a name for the new packet filter. Click Next.

6. Select whether the IP packet will Allow Packet Transmissions or Block Packet Transmissions. Click Next.

7. In the Filter Type step of the wizard, select whether you want to create a Custom filter or use a Predefined filter. For email packets, predefined filters are already created for the SMTP and POP3 protocols. Click Next. To create a Custom filter, continue to the next step. To edit a Predefined filter, skip Step 8 and move to Step 9.

8. To create a Custom filter, you need to specify a protocol, port number, and direction that the packet filter will apply to. Selecting ICMP, TCP, or UDP as the protocol will also allow you to specify Local and Remote ports. Click Next.

9. Next, you need to specify the IP address on the ISA server by selecting This ISA Server's External IP Address and typing in that IP address. Click Next.

10. In the Remote Computers step of the wizard, select All Remote Computers and click Next.

11. In the Summary step, review the information that you entered. Click the Back button to fix any incorrect information. Click Finish to end the wizard and create the new rule.

Configuring Publishing Rules

Now that you know all about creating rules, we will cover the steps you have to follow in ISA Management to create rules for a publishing policy. A Web publishing rule created during the installation of ISA Server is called a Default Rule, but no server publishing rules are created by default.

Configuring a Web Publishing Rule

To configure a Web publishing rule, follow these steps:

1. Open ISA Management.

2. Expand Servers And Arrays, then expand the ISA array or server that you want to manage.

3. Expand Publishing.

4. Right-click the Web Publishing Rules container and point to New, then select Rule. The New Web Publishing Rule Wizard will start.

5. In the Welcome dialog box, type a descriptive name for the new Web publishing rule. Click Next.

6. On the Destination Sets tab, select the destinations that will be allowed by this Web publishing rule.

7. In the Client Type dialog box, specify the clients this rule will apply to.

8. In the Rule Action dialog box, specify how ISA Server should handle the incoming requests. The requests can be discarded or redirected to an internal Web server. If the requests are redirected, you can specify a port for HTTP, SSL, or FTP requests.

9. In the Summary step, check the settings. Use the Back button to change settings that are not correct. Click the Finish button to end the wizard and create the new server publishing rule.

Configuring a Server Publishing Rule

To configure a server publishing rule, complete the following steps:

1. Open ISA Management.

2. Expand Servers And Arrays to find the server or array that you need to configure.

3. Expand Publishing.

4. Right-click Server Publishing Rules, point to New, and select Rule. The New Server Publishing Rule Wizard will start.

5. Type a descriptive name for the rule and click Next.

6. In the Address Mapping step of the wizard, enter the IP address of the internal server and the IP address of the external interface on the ISA server. Click Next.

7. In the Protocol Settings dialog box, select a protocol definition. Click Next.

8. In the Client Type dialog box, select the type of client that this rule will apply to. You can specify that the rule apply to all incoming requests or to specific client address sets, or you can select users or group accounts to which the rule will apply. Click Next.

9. In the Summary step, check the settings. Use the Back button to change settings that are not correct. Click the Finish button to end the wizard and create the new server publishing rule.

Setup for Internal Servers

Setting up rules will control how users' requests are handled once ISA Server receives them. But you need to so some setup to direct these incoming requests to ISA Server. First, you must direct requests bound for your Web site to the ISA server. This is done in the DNS server. If your Web site were on the Internet, the host record for your Web server in DNS would contain the IP address of the Web server. But the host record for your Web server must be changed to the IP address of the ISA server. This way, when incoming requests ask for your Web site name to be resolved to an IP address, they receive the IP address of your ISA server.

When you install the Web server or other service—such as SQL Server or a mail server—that you want published to the Internet on the same server that ISA Server is installed on, you cannot set up publishing policies to protect it. ISA Server cannot apply Web publishing rules or server publishing rules unless the services are located on the internal network or a perimeter network. The only way to provide protection for the services that are located on the same server as ISA Server is to use IP packet filters. The use and creation of IP packet filters for publishing are described in Chapter 9 of this book.

Chapter Summary

When you want to publish a service to the Internet, you need to take special precautions to try to protect the server that hosts this service. ISA Server can protect these servers by intercepting all incoming packets bound for them and placing rules on them. ISA Server protects internal servers by not allowing direct connections between external users and internal servers.

Publishing policies contain Web publishing and server publishing rules. A default Web publishing rule is created during the installation of ISA Server, but it rejects all incoming packets. Web publishing rules control incoming packets that are using HTTP, HTTP-S, or FTP as their protocol. Server publishing rules protect all other TCP/IP-based services. Rules that control publishing are in a different container than Access Policies in ISA Management, but they can use some of the same policy elements.

ISA Server allows other types of control over connections that work with publishing policy rules. SSL bridging directs ISA Server to decrypt all incoming SSL packets so that their contents can be processed. ISA Server can then cache objects or fulfill requests from cache. ISA Server can also be configured to re-encrypt the packets or to leave them unencrypted before sending the request to the intended destination.

The setup of an email server contains many steps when securing its use through ISA Server. First, the mail server needs to be installed. Then ISA Server must be configured to allow email messages in. ISA Server has a Mail Server Security Wizard that creates server publishing rules for mail servers. You can even specify the types of email protocols that you will accept in this wizard. Besides allowing email in, you can also filter the mail and its attachments with the SMTP Filter. The Message Screener add-in to ISA Server must be installed to give ISA Server the ability to filter email and attachments, whereas the SMTP Filter controls how the mail will be filtered and what type of action will be taken on filtered mail and attachments.

Publishing rules cannot be used in all publishing scenarios that use ISA Server. Sometimes IP packet filters must be used instead. IP packet filters do not allow the control over connections that rules do, but they must be used to protect internal servers if publishing rules cannot be used. If a published server is placed on a three-homed DMZ, IP packet filters must be used instead of publishing rules. Also, if any service that needs to be published is placed on the same server as ISA Server, you must use IP packet filters rather than rules. If the published server is on the internal network and installed on a computer other than the ISA server, you can use publishing rules to protect it.

Review Questions

1. What protocol suites must a service support to be able to publish through ISA Server?
    a. TCP/IP
    b. IPX/SPX
    c. DECnet
    d. All protocol suites are supported.

2. What rule types are contained in a publishing policy? [Check all correct answers]
    a. Mail publishing rules
    b. IP packet filters
    c. Web publishing rules
    d. Server publishing rules
    e. Protocol publishing rules

3. Web publishing rules are supported in which mode(s) of ISA Server? [Check all correct answers]
    a. Cache
    b. Firewall
    c. Integrated
    d. All modes

4. Server publishing rules are supported in which mode(s) of ISA Server? [Check all correct answers]
   a. Cache
   b. Firewall
   c. Integrated
   d. All modes

5. Why does the LAT need to be checked before publishing a server through ISA Server?
   a. It may be malfunctioning.
   b. If the published server's IP is not on the LAT, ISA Server will apply packet filters to it.
   c. If the published server's IP is on the LAT, ISA Server will apply rules to it.
   d. If the published server's IP is not on the LAT, users will not be able to make a connection to it.
   e. If the published server's IP is on the LAT, users will not be able to make a connection to it.

6. To configure a listener, which dialog box(es) would you use? [Check all correct answers]
   a. The Array properties
   b. An individual ISA Server's properties
   c. The properties of policy elements
   d. The protocol definition properties
   e. The publishing policy properties

7. What rule is created and put in the publishing policy by default when ISA Server is installed?
   a. The reverse proxy rule
   b. The default server publishing rule
   c. The default Web publishing rule
   d. The default publishing rule
   e. The default client address set

8. What does the default publishing policy do?
   a. Rejects all incoming packets
   b. Rejects all outgoing packets
   c. Accepts and processes all incoming packets
   d. Accepts and process all outgoing packets
   e. Accepts but does not process all incoming packets

9. Which policy elements can be used in a Web publishing rule? [Check all correct answers]
    a. Protocol definitions
    b. Schedules
    c. Client address sets
    d. Bandwidth priorities
    e. Destination sets
    f. Content groups

10. Which type(s) of actions can be configured in the Rule Action dialog box for a Web publishing rule? [Check all correct answers]
    a. Allow
    b. Discard
    c. Redirect

11. Ports for which protocol(s) can be configured in the Rule Action dialog box for a Web publishing rule? [Check all correct answers]
    a. HTTP
    b. FTP
    c. SSL
    d. Gopher

12. Which type(s) of authentication should be used on an internal Web server that is publishing through the ISA server? [Check all correct answers]
    a. Basic
    b. Digest
    c. Integrated
    d. Certificate

13. What is the defining characteristic of SSL bridging?
    a. An SSL connection between the client and the Web server through the ISA server
    b. Separate connections between the client and Web server and the ISA server
    c. Separate SSL connections between the client and Web server and the ISA server
    d. A single connection between the client and Web server

14. SSL bridging allows caching to be used with SSL connections.
    a. True
    b. False

15. Where is SSL bridging configured?
    a. The server publishing rule properties
    b. The New Server Publishing Rule Wizard
    c. The Web publishing rule properties
    d. The New Web Publishing Rule Wizard

16. What policy elements can be used in a server publishing rule? [Check all correct answers]
    a. Protocol definitions
    b. Schedules
    c. Client address sets
    d. Bandwidth priorities
    e. Destination sets
    f. Content groups

17. What reconfiguration is needed when you upgrade to ISA Server a Proxy server that is configured to allow an internal Exchange server to publish? [Check all correct answers]
    a. None, if the settings comply with KB article Q181420.
    b. None, if you want to use server publishing rules to protect the internal Exchange server.
    c. None, if you do not want to use server publishing rules to protect the internal Exchange server.
    d. None, if you are using Exchange Server 5 or 5.5.
    e. None, if you are using Exchange Server 2000

18. Which ISA Server component allows email messages to be filtered for content?
    a. Mail Gatekeeper
    b. POP3 packet filter
    c. Message Screener
    d. H.323 Gatekeeper
    e. None are needed

19. When publishing, you should allow only inbound connections to the internal published server.

   a. True

   b. False

20. Why do outbound connections from a server providing published services sometimes need to be allowed inbound client connections in order to successfully connect?

   a. Because the service is not actually publishing.

   b. Some services use different ports for incoming and outgoing connections.

   c. Some services need to establish a separate outbound connection to the connecting client.

   d. ISA Server does not distinguish between inbound and outbound connections.

21. What component of ISA Server replaced dynamic filters?

   a. Policies

   b. Rules

   c. Application filters

   d. They have not been replaced.

22. What is another term for DMZ? [Check all correct answers]

   a. Separate network

   b. Perimeter networks

   c. Screened subnet

   d. New network

23. Packet filters are supported in which mode(s) of ISA Server? [Check all correct answers]

   a. Cache

   b. Firewall

   c. Integrated

   d. All modes

24. A published server needs a DNS host record with which IP address?

   a. Its own IP address

   b. The IP address of the Web server

   c. The IP address of the ISA server's internal interface

   d. The IP address of the ISA server's external interface

Real-World Projects

Note: This exercise assumes a test Windows 2000 Server with Service Pack 1 as well as Enterprise Edition of ISA Server installed. Read the instructions carefully and do not change the settings on your production machine unless you understand the options presented. If you are unsure about an option, do not make a change and instead read the ISA Server help files about the option to be installed.

"… so we should immediately begin providing this service to users" declared the head of the Web development department.

The weekly meeting of the Web Site Enhancement Team was well underway. The purpose of the team was to guide the changes on the company's Web site. Before the team was created, the Web site had been updated in a poorly planned and often disastrous manner. The team's mission was to guide the development and enhancement of the site so that the changes were rolled out in a smooth and controlled manner.

The Web development team often came up with new and sometimes difficult to support ideas for new services on the Web site.

"You want to provide multimedia presentations to users coming in through the Internet?" asked the team leader.

"As we promised in the last meeting, we have tested this internally in the company. We set up a media server, and users from all over the network were able to connect and play the files. And we got the idea from our customers, so we believe we should provide the services they are asking for."

"Are there any technical issues that we need to address?" The team leader looked at Rachel.

"Well…" Rachel began, "some security configurations on the ISA server will need to be changed to allow the external users to access the internal media server."

"How long do you need?" the team leader asked.

"Let's set it up this week and try testing the connection. I will try to have all of the issues resolved by the next meeting."

After the meeting, Rachel made a list of changes that she would need to make to support this new service. The media server was already set up, so that was out of the way. Because no media services were currently being offered through the Web site, she needed to create a server publishing rule. Before she could set that up, she would need to check the application filters that applied to multimedia.

After some research she found that she needed to setup the Streaming Media Filter and then set up a server publishing rule. That didn't seem too bad. She started with the Streaming Media Filter

Project 12.1
To enable the Streaming Media Filter on ISA Server:

1. In ISA Management, expand the array.

2. Expand Extensions, then select Application Filters.

3. In the Details pane, right-click Streaming Media Filter, and then click Properties.

4. On the General tab, make sure that the Enable This Filter is checked.

5. Click on the Live Stream Splitting tab.

6. On the Live Stream Splitting tab, leave Disable WMT Live Stream Splitting selected if you do not want your clients to use live stream splitting services. Select Split Live Stream Using A Local WMT Server if the WMT Server is local to the ISA Server. If you have a WMT Server Pool, select Split Live Stream Using The Following WMT Server Pool.

Rachel decided to leave Live Stream Splitting disabled. This was a service for internal clients, anyway.

7. Click OK to accept the changes to the Streaming Media Filter.

After the filter was enabled, it was time to move on to the creating a server publishing rule. This was all going very smoothly, she thought with a frown. Somehow when it started out smoothly it always ended roughly. She told herself to stop being so pessimistic and moved on to the server publishing rule that would allow external users to access the internal media server and access the media files.

Project 12.2
To configure a server publishing rule for streaming media:

1. Open ISA Management.

2. Expand Servers And Arrays to find the server or array that you need to configure.

3. Expand Publishing.

4. Right-click the Server Publishing Rules, point to New and select Rule. The New Server Publishing Rule Wizard will start.

5. Type in a descriptive name for the rule and click Next.

Rachel called the rule "Media for External Users".

6. In the Address Mapping step of the wizard, enter the IP address of the internal server and the IP address of the external interface on the ISA server. Click Next.

7. In the Protocol Settings dialog box, select a protocol definition. Click Next.

Rachel found that there were several protocol definitions for media protocols. She had forgotten to ask which one the media server needed for client use. She reached for the phone and called the Web development team that had set up the media server. After speaking with them, she selected the MMS-Windows Media Server protocol definition.

8. In the Client Type, select the type of client that this rule will apply to. You can specify that the rule apply to all incoming requests, or specific client address sets, or you can select users or group accounts to which the rule will apply. Click Next.

Rachel applied the rule to all incoming requests.

9. In the Summary step, check the settings. Use the Back button to change settings that are not correct. Click the Finish button to end the wizard and create the new server publishing rule.

Rachel finished configuring the Streaming Media Filter and was ready to head for the test machine. She had configured a computer that was not connected to the internal network and whose IP address was not included in the ISA server's LAT. It had a separate ISP connection that connected it to the Internet. She used the computer to test new configurations on the Web site. It connected to the company's Web site through ISA Server just as if it were a client computer coming in from the Internet.

She checked to make sure a media client was installed on the test computer and then attempted to download the media files from the Web site. She used the test pages that were set up by the Web development team. They worked internally, so now all she had to do was get them to work through the ISA server.

She clicked to play the file. Her computer paused for a few seconds and then she got an error message. She knew it. She tried a few more times and even tried disconnecting and reconnecting to the Web site, but she received the same error every time. ISA Server was denying the connection. What had she done wrong?

After going back to research Rachel found that she needed to restart the Firewall service in the ISA server after configuring an application filter. She tried it, but the connection still failed. She knew it couldn't be that easy. Finally, buried deep in some documentation, she found a small note on publishing. From that note she learned that some services, such as media services, are designed to make an outbound connection to a client as part of the communication between the server and client components. ISA Server was allowing the client inbound access to the media server, but when the media server then tried to make an outbound connection to the external client the connection was denied and both sides of the connection failed as a result. She needed to create a site and content rule that allowed the media server to make an outbound connection to the external clients.

Project 12.3

To create a site and content rule allowing the media server to connect to the client:

1. Open ISA Management.

2. Expand Internet Security And Acceleration Server for enterprise-level site and content rules or an array for array-level site and content rules.

3. Expand Enterprise Policy for enterprise-level site and content rules and an array name for array-level site and content rules.

4. Right-click Site And Content Rules.

5. Point to New and select Rule. The New Site And Content Rule Wizard will start.

6. In the first dialog box, type in the name of the new site and content rule. Click Next.

7. In the Rule Action dialog box, select whether the rule will Allow or Deny client access to sites. If Deny is selected, you can also specify a URL that users should be redirected to when they are not allowed to connect to their requested URL. This redirected URL should specify a Web page on an internal Web server that explains what has happened to the user. Once you make your selection, click Next.

Rachel needed to allow the internal media server to send outbound messages to external clients, so she selected Allow.

8. In the Rule Configuration dialog box, select what set of sites, users, or schedule to which this rule will apply. This choice will determine the rest of the dialog boxes that will appear during the wizard. The Custom choice in the Rule configuration dialog box runs you through all of the choices. If Custom is not selected, then you need to choose whether you want the rule to control the Schedule, Client Type, or Destination Sets that the user can or cannot connect to. Click Next.

Rachel chose Custom because she wanted to make sure she covered all possible settings.

9. In the Destination Sets dialog box, select the when the protocol rule will apply. Click Next.

Rachel chose All External Destinations because she didn't know where the clients might connect from.

10. In the Schedule dialog box, select the when the protocol rule will apply. Click Next.

Rachel chose Always for the schedule. Users might connect to the Web site at any time.

11. In the Client Type dialog box, select what client types that the site and content rule will apply to. You may need to select and/or define client IP address sets or users and/or groups. Click Next.

Here Rachel had a chance to tighten the rule to only the internal media server. She selected Specific Computers (Client Address Sets) and then created a client address set that included only the IP address of the internal media server. This way no other computer could use this rule.

12. Review the summary of information and click Finish. You can use the Back button to change incorrect information.

After creating the site and content rule for the media server, Rachel went back to the test computer. This time she was able to successfully connect. She was glad she had given herself enough time to work out the kinks.

CHAPTER THIRTEEN

Managing Multiple ISA Servers

After completing this chapter, you will be able to:

✓ Describe an array

✓ Describe a chain

✓ Install the first ISA server in an array

✓ Install additional ISA servers in an array

✓ Understand standalone server promotion

✓ Create arrays in ISA Management

✓ Delete arrays in ISA Management

✓ Set up chaining

✓ Back up and restore enterprise and array configurations

✓ Use enterprise policies and array policies

✓ Configure an enterprise policy

✓ Assign a default enterprise policy

✓ Modify default settings for the enterprise policy

✓ Apply an enterprise policy to selected arrays

✓ Configure an array policy

✓ Configure the cache for an array

✓ Force packet filtering for an array

✓ Allow publishing rules in an array

✓ Configure server-specific settings on an ISA server

✓ Combine enterprise policies and array policies

One of the features that you, as an ISA Server administrator, must be familiar with—and something we mentioned several times in previous chapters—is called an array and/or chaining. This chapter concentrates on the actual configuration of the ISA server array, and it walks you through all the steps needed to configure your first ISA server array or chain in an efficient manner. Chaining is very similar to arrays in that we will be employing two or more ISA servers in an enterprise environment in such a way that ISA servers are configured in a cascading manner so that your users get the greatest benefits from ISA Server. We will discuss what array and chaining mean and how you can use them. Keep in mind that the ISA Server final edition has two different versions, Standard and Enterprise. In ISA Server Release Candidate 1 (RC1), these two products were not separated. In order to use the array functionalities, you need the Enterprise edition. If you have a standalone ISA server that you would like to add to a new array, you can promote the standalone ISA server to be a member of the new array.

What Is an Array?

By now, you have come a long way from the day you first installed ISA Server. It is now time for you to think about your network's future. The more Internet traffic that comes into your network and the more people who join your company, the more you need to plan for growth so that users do not experience poor performance on the network. If this planning and implementation is not done in a timely manner, your users may complain that Internet access is unacceptably slow. The standalone ISA server does a good job for a small number of users. However, for a large number of users, you need to move the network infrastructure to multiple ISA servers. This does not mean that you deploy multiple standalone ISA servers. Rather, you deploy multiple ISA servers in a logical set called an *array*. Deploying an ISA server array offers many benefits compared with a standalone ISA server. The main advantages are that you can provide load balancing and fault tolerance, as well as increase your available bandwidth and effective cache size. What does this mean for your network?

Deploying a multiple ISA server array provides load balancing. When you have a standalone ISA server functioning in Cache mode, Firewall mode, or Integrated mode, the ISA server may reach a point where it cannot handle more network traffic, and the users will experience a degradation of network performance. If you have an ISA server array with two more ISA servers in it, each ISA server array can take over some of the work that the whole ISA server array needs to perform. Therefore, you can serve your users better. If the array starts to reach the point where it cannot handle the network traffic effectively, you just need to add another member ISA server to the array for better load balancing. Remember that the more ISA servers you have in an array, the better network performance will be.

There may be situations in which you cannot deploy multiple ISA servers in an array due to some political, technical, or support issues. If that is the case, one option might be to deploy multiple ISA servers separately as standalone servers and use DNS round-robin to handle load balancing. DNS round-robin uses the same host name with several different server IP addresses. Each client hit will pick a different IP address, so that one particular server is not overloaded.

Deploying a multiple ISA server array also provides fault tolerance. If you have only a standalone ISA server in your environment, and it crashes for some reason, the whole network is affected. Users will not be able to employ the ISA server's functionalities until the ISA server is recovered onto the network. When you have multiple ISA servers in an array, if one ISA server crashes, others can take over the loads from the crashed ISA server until it is repaired. Your users may experience a bit of network performance degradation, but they will still be operational.

Deploying a multiple ISA server array also saves more available bandwidth and effective cache size. These two items are interrelated. If you have more ISA servers in an array, as each ISA server contains cache on the disk, you will have more space for the caching. If you can cache more Internet objects on the disks, then many Internet objects will be served to users locally from the cache, and therefore will free up the bandwidth to get out to the Internet.

Figure 13.1 shows how the array looks. This configuration is also called distributed proxying, because all the work is distributed among several ISA server computers.

ISA Servers in an array share configuration information. When you change the array configuration, all the ISA server computers' configurations in the array are also changed, including all the access policies and cache policies. Therefore, the administrator has a central point to control over all the configuration options on the array.

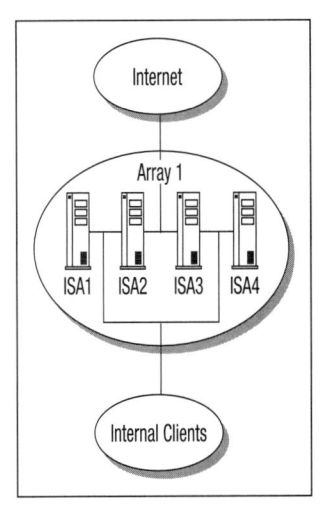

Figure 13.1 A sample array.

Guidelines for creating an array include:

- When creating an array, all the member ISA servers in the array must be located in the same site and the same Windows 2000 domain. A site is defined as a single subnet with high-speed connectivity normally located in one geographical location. A domain is defined as a logical group of systems sharing a common Active Directory.

- All the member ISA servers in the array should be configured using the same mode, namely, Cache mode, Firewall mode, or Integrated mode.

- All the member ISA servers in the array should have the same set of add-ins installed, if necessary. Add-ins such as application filters, Web filters, and other add-ins are not installed automatically on all the member ISA servers in an array if they are installed on only one member ISA server in the array.

- All access policy, publishing, bandwidth rules, and cache are configured only once at the array and are replicated to apply to all the ISA servers in the array. Therefore, do not attempt to configure separate rules among several ISA servers, as it will make the administration more time consuming.

- You can configure alerts for all the servers in an array or for an individual server in an array.

- You can configure reports that display information about all the ISA Server computers in an array so that the report data is stored in a database on a computer and in a specified directory.

- You can configure disk space for caching separately on each ISA server when you install ISA Server, or when you reconfigure the cache after the ISA Server installation. All the cache configuration properties, however, are common to all the ISA servers in an array. These cache configuration properties include HTTP, FTP, and Cache Array Routing Protocol (CARP) protocol properties.

- In order for an administrator to create a new array, he or she needs to be a member of the Domain Admins group for the domain where the array is created or a member of the Enterprise Admins group for the Active Directory forest. Only a member of the Enterprise Admins group creating the array has the required permissions to administer enterprise policies.

What Is Chaining?

Instead of configuring two or more ISA servers in an array, you may choose to configure them in a chain. In this configuration, the ISA server close to the Internet is called the upstream server, and the one close to the end user is called the downstream server. Although ISA servers are not configured in parallel, as in an array, ISA servers in different geographical locations such as the main office and branches can be configured to be upstream and downstream servers.

Chaining is also described as hierarchical proxying. Chaining can provide load balancing and caching along the chain of ISA servers, but configurations are done separately from others in the chain, and therefore, chaining is not fault tolerant. If an ISA server in the chain is not available, users will be affected. One of the ways to provide fault tolerance in chaining is to configure a backup route. That way, if the chain fails to function, you can use a backup route, such as a dial-up to an ISP, so that the network is still functional in some ways. You could also use DNS round-robin, which was described in the section "What is an Array?" earlier in the chapter.

ISA servers in a chain do not share configuration information. Each ISA server in the chain trusts the upstream server to properly route the requests to the Internet when Internet objects are not found in the downstream server's cache. Therefore, a simple scenario for an Internet object request would be that a user requests an Internet object by just accessing certain Web pages, the downstream server checks the cache to see if the Internet object is stored, and if it is, it returns the object. If not, then it will ask an upstream server to see if it has the Internet object in cache. This process is repeated until it gets to the most upstream server. If the cache access fails on the most upstream server, then it will finally request the object from the Internet. When the object is returned from the upstream server, it is cached in every downstream server's cache before it is returned to the user so that any future request for the same object can be satisfied locally.

Installing ISA Server in an Array

Now we will describe how to actually install ISA Server in an array. This section assumes that you have installed the ISA Server schema in Active Directory. Remember that all the member ISA servers in an array need to be in the same Windows 2000 domain, because the ISA Server Enterprise installation modifies Active Directory, and each member ISA server in an array needs to refer to the ISA Server schema to function properly. Refer to Chapters 2 and 3 for the installation of ISA Server schema.

Installing ISA Server in an array involves the following steps:

1. Run Setup.
2. Install ISA Server as an array.
3. Create and name the array.
4. Select Enterprise Policy.
5. Configure custom policy settings.

When you create a new array in your network, you can create a new configuration or you can copy a configuration from an existing array, if available. In addition, you can add a member ISA server to an array at the same time you create the new array.

Installing the First ISA Server Computer in an Array

Let's go through the steps needed to install the first ISA server computer. To install ISA Server on the first computer in an array:

1. Start the Microsoft Internet Security And Acceleration Server Enterprise Edition Setup program. You may start the setup program by inserting the ISA Server installation CD or by running ISAAutorun.exe on the root of the installation CD. Choose which installation to perform: Typical, Full, or Custom.

2. In the Internet Security And Acceleration Server Setup dialog box, click Yes to install ISA Server on an array member.

3. If you are trying to create a new array in a Windows 2000 domain where other arrays already exist, click New.

4. Type the name of the array to be created in the New Array dialog box, and click OK.

5. Select one of the following options in the Select Use Of Enterprise Policy dialog box:

    ▶ *Use Default Enterprise Policy Setting*—When you choose this option, the array will use the default enterprise policy settings. These are usually the policy settings that you configured when you imported the ISA Server schema to Active Directory.

    ▶ *Use Custom Enterprise Policy Setting*—When you choose this option, the array will use the custom enterprise policy settings and will not use the default enterprise policy settings.

6. Select one of the following options if a custom enterprise policy is chosen in Step 5:

    ▶ *Use Array Policy Only*—This option does not apply any enterprise policy, and it applies the array policy only.

    ▶ *Use This Enterprise Policy*—This option applies a specific enterprise policy. You also need to select which enterprise policy to use.

    ▶ *Allow Array Level Access Rules That Restrict Enterprise Policies*—Select this option if you would like the array policy to override an enterprise policy you have specified.

7. Select the Allow Publishing Rules checkbox to allow administrators to create publishing rules.

8. Select the Force Packet Filtering On The Array checkbox to enforce packet filtering on all arrays. Then, click Continue.

9. Select the installation mode in the Microsoft ISA Server Setup dialog box, then configure the cache settings and the Local Address Table (LAT). This step will be the same as what you would do for a standalone ISA server configuration.

Installing Additional Array Members

There will be times that you need to add more ISA servers into an existing array. This is especially true when your network is growing rapidly, and you need to provide better network performance to end users in your environment. To install additional array members into an existing array, take the following steps:

1. Start the Microsoft Internet Security And Acceleration Server Enterprise Edition Setup program. Choose which installation to perform: Typical, Full, or Custom.

2. In the Internet Security And Acceleration Server Setup dialog box, click Yes to install ISA Server on an array member.

3. In the Microsoft ISA Server Setup dialog box, select the array that you would like to add the new ISA server to, and then click OK. Configure the cache settings as you would do for a standalone server.

Promoting a Standalone Server to an Array Member

In some cases, you might have deployed the ISA server as a standalone server in your environment. For whatever the reason you installed it as a standalone—for example, you had political or financial reasons for not deploying an array, you did not have a Windows 2000 Active Directory domain in place, you did not think you would need an array in the future, or you did not read too much about an array in the first place (we hope you did…)—there has to be a way to make it a member ISA Server in an array, right? Fortunately, there is a method you can use. This promotion does not apply to the ISA Server Release Candidate 1 (RC1), because no distinction existed between ISA Server Standard edition and Enterprise edition. So, how do we do that? Before we go through that, keep in mind that you can promote only standalone servers that are members of a Windows 2000 domain. Furthermore, you cannot demote the array member to a standalone server without uninstalling the ISA server from your system. An array requires a name, and in the case of a standalone server promotion to an array member, the name of the array will be the same as the name of the computer name of the ISA server.

Updating Policy Settings

One of the tasks you have to complete when promoting a standalone to an array member involves enterprise policy settings. In the enterprise environment, both the enterprise policy and array policy are effective if you choose, and things can get rather confusing. When promoting a standalone ISA server to an array member, the new array inherits the settings from the default enterprise policy settings. ISA Server will delete some of the existing array policy rules according to the default enterprise policy settings. See Table 13.1.

Now take the following steps to promote a standalone server to an array member:

1. In ISA Management, in the console tree, right-click the ISA server you would like to promote, and then click Promote.

2. Click Yes to confirm that you would like the ISA server to be an array member.

3. If you are not a member of the Enterprise Admins group, click Yes to confirm that the default enterprise policy is to be applied to the new array you are just creating.

If you are a member of the Enterprise Admins group, select one of the options in the Set Global Policy dialog box (see Table 13.2). Then, click OK.

Creating Arrays in ISA Management

ISA Management allows you to create and delete arrays if you have proper permissions to do so. Keep in mind that you have to be a member of the Domain Admins or Enterprise Admins group to create an array in a Windows 2000 domain. You have to be a member of the Enterprise Admins group to configure how the

Table 13.1 Policy settings updating rules.

If default enterprise settings…	Then ISA Server…
Are Enterprise policy only	Deletes all of the array policy rules.
Are Enterprise policy and array policy	Deletes all of the array policy rules that allow access.
Allow publishing	Keeps the publishing rules that are defined for the array.

Table 13.2 Global Policy options.

To specify…	Do the following…
Enterprise policy only	Click Use Default Enterprise Policy Settings.
Enterprise policy and array policy	Click Use Custom Enterprise Policy Settings, and then pick one of the following options: Use Array Policy Only or Use This Enterprise Policy. You will need to select which enterprise policy to apply to the array. If necessary, you can choose to apply the array policy by clicking Also Allow Array Policy.

enterprise policies apply, which applies to the whole Active Directory forest. Take the following steps to create a new array in ISA Management:

1. In ISA Management, in the console tree, right-click Servers And Arrays, then point to New and click Array.

2. In the New Array Wizard, enter a name for the array. Then, click Next.

3. On the Domain Name page, select the site and domain in which to create the new array. Then, click Next.

4. On the Create Or Copy An Array page, choose one of the options shown in Table 13.3.

If you are creating a new configuration array, take the following steps to complete the entire configuration:

1. On the Enterprise Policy Settings page, select one of the following options:

   ➤ *Do Not Use Enterprise Policy*—Select this option when you do not want to use the enterprise policy.

   ➤ *Use Default Enterprise Policy Settings*—Select this option when you want to use the default enterprise policy settings.

   ➤ *Use Custom Enterprise Policy Settings*—By selecting this option, you need to specify an enterprise policy. If you want to also apply the array policy, select the Allow Array Policy check box.

   Then, click Next.

2. On the Array Global Policy Options page, select one or both of the following options:

   ➤ *Allow Publishing Rules To Be Created On The Array*—Use this option to use publishing rules on the array.

   ➤ *Force Packet Filtering On The Array*—Use this option to forcibly use packet filtering on the array so that undesired packets do not access the array.

   Then, click Next.

Table 13.3 Create Or Copy Array options.

If you are...	Then...
Creating a new configuration	Click Create A New Array, and then click Next.
Copying an existing array configuration	Click Copy This Array, select the array to copy from the list, click Next, and then click Finish.

3. On the Array Type page, select one of the following options (these options should be familiar by now; if not, refer to Chapter 3 of this book):

   ➤ Cache Only

   ➤ Firewall Only

   ➤ Integrated

4. On the Completing The New Array Wizard page, be sure to review all of your choices. Then, click Finish.

This step completes the new array creation. If you later need to add an ISA server to this array, it can participate in the new array using the name of the array. You can also promote another standalone ISA server to be a member of this new array.

Deleting Arrays in ISA Management

We will now go through how to delete an array in ISA Management. The steps are rather simple, but you need to remember a couple of things. If you mistakenly delete an array that has members in it, you will be in bad shape. You'll have to re-create the array, uninstall ISA Server from the array member, and then reinstall ISA Server as an array member of the array that was just re-created. Therefore, be very careful when deleting an existing array. Make sure the array is empty before you delete it. In addition, the deletion applies only to arrays. To delete standalone servers, you need to uninstall ISA Server.

To delete an array, in ISA Management in the console tree, right-click the array you want to delete and click Delete.

Setting Up Chaining

As it was introduced in the "What Is Chaining?" section, chaining can be beneficial in cases where you have a branch office in one geographical location and the headquarters in another geographical location. It is important to note that any Internet request that does not have to go to the upstream server but requires the Internet connection should be directed to local ISP from the downstream server site (usually, the branch office) so that Internet objects can be obtained in an efficient manner. In many cases, this particular configuration of pointing to an upstream server for obtaining Internet objects is called Web Proxy routing, and we will go through how to set it up here. The upstream server can be either Microsoft Proxy Server 2.0 or ISA Server. Take the following steps to configure primary Web Proxy routing from a downstream server:

1. In ISA Management, in the console tree, expand Servers And Arrays, the name of the array, and Network Configuration And Routing.

2. In the right pane, right-click the applicable routing rule. Then, click Properties.

3. On the Action tab, click Routing Them To A Specified Upstream Proxy Server. Click Settings. The primary route is preconfigured to be an upstream server, and you cannot change it. The backup route can be Upstream Proxy Server, Direct To Internet or None. The default selection for the backup route is None, which is not a recommended selection, because the ISA server will not function when the primary route fails, and end users will be negatively affected.

4. In the Server Or Array text box, enter the computer name or IP address of the ISA server or array. You can also click on Browse to find the upstream server or array on your network.

5. In the Port text box, enter the port number on which the upstream server or array listens for HTTP requests. By default, the port value is preconfigured as 8080, and this is the default port value that ISA Server uses when it is initially configured.

6. In the SSL Port text box, enter the port number on which the upstream server or array listens for SSL requests. By default, the port value is preconfigured as 8443.

7. If you want to pull the upstream server array configuration information, click Automatically Poll Upstream Server For Array Configuration and enter the URL for the array. It should look something like **http://masaru98.ryumae.com:8080/array.dll**, and if you browsed the ISA server array in Step 4, this option will be automatically filled out.

8. If the upstream server requires server credential information to be accessible, click Use This Account, click Set Account, enter the user account name, password, and click OK. You can click on Browse to select the user account in your network. Then, choose the authentication type, either Basic or Integrated Windows. Basic sends the credentials in clear text over the network whereas Integrated Windows uses NT Challenge/Response, which encrypts credentials sent over the network.

9. If ISA Server should dial out for primary connections and/or backup connections, select Use Dial-up Entry For Primary Route and/or Use Dial-up Entry For Backup Route on the Action tab under Automatic Dial-out. If the dial-up connection is not properly configured on the ISA Server, these options may be greyed out.

Step 9 concludes the Web Proxy routing configuration. Most likely you will need to deal with array configurations more often than the chaining/Web Proxy routing configurations, but these are not mutually exclusive. You may have an array at headquarters, and you may configure Web Proxy routing from the branch office to headquarters. In this case, you can utilize the power of both array and chaining that ISA Server provides.

Backup/Restore Enterprise Configurations

Backing up and restoring enterprise configurations are essential so that you will be prepared when a disaster happens—such as accidental deletion of configurations and a system crash that requires you to rebuild the system from scratch. When you back up the enterprise configurations, you can store the backup locally in a file. This file contains the configurations, such as all the enterprise-specific information, including the enterprise policies and the enterprise policy elements, and information about the enterprise policies used by the arrays in your environment. As you have probably figured out by now, enterprise policies and array policies can sometimes be interrelated if you decide to use both of them. Therefore, when you restore an enterprise configuration, it is possible that the restoration will affect arrays that use enterprise policies. In general you should back up the enterprise configuration and then back up the array's configuration. When you restore the enterprise configuration, it is also possible to restore all the array configurations.

To back up an enterprise configuration, take the following steps:

1. In ISA Management, in the console tree, right-click Enterprise. Then, click Backup.

2. In the Store Backup Configuration In This Location box, enter the name of the file and folder location in which to store the backup data. Then, click OK.

We hope that you will never have to take these steps, but when you have to, you must be able to complete the process successfully. You should test the restore process before a system disaster happens, and document the whole restore process well so that anybody (when you are not available) can get the restore process going without problems.

Now we will cover how to restore the enterprise configuration. To restore the enterprise configuration, take the following steps:

1. In ISA Management, in the console tree, right-click Enterprise, then click Restore. Click Yes to overwrite the existing enterprise configuration with the backup configuration.

2. In the Restore Configuration From The Following Backup (.bef) File box, enter the path of the backup folder and the name of the backup file.

Backup and Restore Array Configurations

Backing up and restoring the array configuration is a very similar process to backing up and restoring the enterprise configurations. To back up an array configuration, take the following steps:

1. In ISA Management, in the console tree, expand Servers And Arrays. Right-click the name of the array you would like to back up and select Backup.

2. In Store Backup Configuration In This Location Box, enter the name of the file and folder location in which to store the backup data. Then, click OK.

To restore an array configuration, take the following steps:

1. In ISA Management, in the console tree, expand Servers And Arrays. Right-click on the array you would like restore and then click Restore. Click Yes to overwrite the existing array configuration with the backup configuration.

2. In the Restore Array Configuration From The Following Backup (.bef) File box, enter the path of the backup folder and the name of the backup file.

Using Enterprise Policies and Array Policies

As we mentioned earlier in this chapter, enterprise policies and array polices are related to each other. What do we mean by that? Also, what are the differences between enterprise policies and array policies? Basically, an enterprise policy is a set of rules applied to all the arrays in the enterprise, whereas an array policy is a set of rules applied to a particular array in the enterprise. Using both enterprise policies and array polices together, you can control how your internal network clients communicate with resources on the Internet. You can apply both enterprise polices and array polices to a particular array so that the array uses the elements from both policies.

Configuring an Enterprise Policy

An enterprise policy includes site and content rules, protocol rules, and policy elements. When you create a new array in a Windows 2000 domain, ISA Server applies a default enterprise policy to the new array. You can assign a specific enterprise policy if you do not want to apply the default enterprise policy to the new array. You can also apply enterprise policies to selected arrays if necessary. By default, only members of the Enterprise Admins group are able to create, configure, and apply enterprise policies. They can also create and configure enterprise-wide policy elements. Refer to Chapter 6 on site and content rules, protocol rules, and policy elements.

Assigning a Default Enterprise Policy

To assign the default enterprise policy, take the following steps:

1. In ISA Management, in the console tree, expand Enterprise, and then expand Policies.

2. Right-click the enterprise policy that you want to make the default enterprise policy, and then click Set As Default Policy.

Modifying Default Settings for the Enterprise Policy

When you create a new array, it tries to apply the default enterprise policy. In some cases you might need to change the default enterprise policy. Take the following steps to change the default policy:

1. In ISA Management, in the console tree, right-click Enterprise. Then, click Set Defaults.

2. In the Set Default Policy dialog box, configure the following options:

   ➤ *Use Array Policy Only, or Use This Enterprise Policy*—If you select Use This Enterprise Policy, you need to select which policy you want to apply to arrays in your environment. Furthermore, you can click on the check box for Allow Array-level Access Policy In Order To Restrict The Enterprise Policy, if needed.

   ➤ *Allow Publishing Rules*—Select this option if you want to allow publishing rules.

   ➤ *Force Packet Filtering*—Select this option if you want to force packet filtering.

Applying an Enterprise Policy to Selected Arrays

This is a sophisticated option that ISA Server provides, and it is a very useful one. Suppose you have implemented several arrays in the enterprise, and you have to apply an enterprise policy to arrays 1, 2, and 3. Then, because of your users' requirement, you have to apply a different enterprise policy to arrays 4 and 5. You can configure them so that arrays 1, 2, and 3 get a different enterprise policy from the one for arrays 4 and 5. But be careful; when you apply an enterprise policy to an array, ISA Server deletes all the previously defined array-level site, content, and protocol rules. Therefore, if any of these rules have to be maintained, you need to take necessary actions. Refer back to Table 13.1 to see how ISA Server behaves. To apply an enterprise policy for selected arrays, take the following steps:

1. In ISA Management, in the console tree, expand Enterprise, and then expand Policies. Right-click the default enterprise policy. Then, click Properties.

2. In the Enterprise Policy Properties dialog box, click the Arrays tab. Select the checkboxes next to the names of the arrays that you want to apply the enterprise policy. Click OK.

Configuring an Array Policy

An array policy includes rules similar to those for enterprise policies, such as site, content, and protocol rules. It also adds IP packet filters and the associated policy elements. ISA Server applies all the rules specified in the array policy to all the members in an array when you configure an array policy. IP packet filtering can also be configured in an enterprise policy at the array level if necessary. This may reduce the administrative overhead so that most of the policy rules are taken care of by the enterprise policy. There are, however, cases where you want to have granular control of policies for your arrays, and that is the time you would use an array policy.

Configuring the Cache for an Array

Caching allows you to store frequently accessed Internet objects into a local hard drive on an ISA server so that requests to the same Internet objects can be served locally without going out to the Internet again to get them. You must remember several things about caching for an array:

➤ All the ISA servers in an array share the same cache configuration properties. Therefore, you cannot assign separate properties to each member of the array.

➤ The cache configurations include HTTP caching properties, FTP caching properties, and the CARP properties.

➤ You allocate certain hard disk space for caching on each ISA server when you install or reconfigure the cache on it. Therefore, cache space is configured separately.

Forcing Packet Filtering for an Array

Packet filtering allows you to filter packets so that undesired packets that access cached Internet objects are prohibited. The following is a list of things to consider:

➤ At the enterprise level, packet filtering cannot be enabled. It can be enabled only at the array level, which an enterprise administrator can configure.

➤ When you're creating a new array, if you are a member of the Enterprise Admins group, ISA Server prompts you to see whether you want to force the packet filtering to be used for the array.

➤ After you create an array, and later you decide to change the packet filtering settings, you can change them at that time.

To force packet filtering for an array, take the following steps:

1. In ISA Management, in the console tree, expand Servers And Arrays. Right-click the array you want to force the packet filtering, and then click Properties.

2. On the Policies tab, confirm that the Use Custom Enterprise Policy Settings option is selected, and select the Force Packet Filtering On The Array checkbox. Then, click OK.

Allowing Publishing Rules in an Array

Publishing allows Internet users to access internal servers such as a Web server, indirectly through the ISA server so that the security is not compromised.

Note: At the array level, you cannot specify whether publishing rules are allowed. An enterprise administrator, however, can specify that publishing packet filtering be allowed at the array level. Remember, publishing packet filtering—not publishing rules—can be specified at the array level.

To allow publishing rules for an array, take the following steps:

1. In ISA Management, in the console tree, expand Servers And Arrays. Right-click the array that you want to allow the publishing rules. Then, click Properties.

2. On the Policies tab, confirm that the Use Custom Enterprise Policy Settings option is selected, and select the Allow Publishing Rules checkbox. Then, click OK.

Configuring Server-Specific Settings on an ISA Server

Some settings are server-specific, meaning each ISA server could have different settings on certain items. However, most of the settings in ISA Server apply to all the members in an array. Here is a list of settings that can be configured for each ISA server:

- *Packet Filters*—You can configure a packet filter on only a single ISA server in an array.

- *Alerts*—You can configure an alert to apply only to a single ISA server in an array.

- *Listeners For Outgoing And Incoming Web Requests*—You have two choices with this setting. You can configure listeners to be active only on a single network interface card, or you can configure a separate listener for each network interface card on each ISA server in an array.

- *Server Publishing Rules*—As the server publishing rules apply to a single external network interface, which most of the ISA servers have, you can configure different server publishing rules for each ISA server member in an array.

Combining Enterprise Policies and Array Policies

Now comes the fun part. Once you define enterprise policies and array policies, you need to apply them. You can pick either enterprise policies or array policies to apply to an array, but in most cases (assuming you know exactly what you need in your environment) you would apply both of them. Yes, this is confusing, but the benefits outweigh the trouble. In a large enterprise environment where you have many ISA server arrays, this is especially beneficial. For instance, say you have a set of rules that you would like to apply to all the arrays in your environment. You use the enterprise policies to take care of that. However, you have some arrays that need more restricted policies, such as for an HR department's array where sensitive information is stored. You would use array policies to restrict the access for this particular array. When you apply an enterprise policy to an array, you cannot create site, content, and protocol rules to allow access for that array, although you can create site, content, and protocol rules that deny access. Keep in mind that only enterprise administrators can specify which enterprise policies allow rules at the array level. To set up an enterprise policy to allow settings at the array level, take the following steps:

1. In ISA Management, in the console tree, right-click the array you want to allow array-level settings, and then click Properties.

2. On the Policies tab, select the Use Custom Enterprise Policy Settings checkbox. Then, click OK.

Chapter Summary

One of the features for using multiple ISA servers is called an array and/or chaining. This chapter emphasized the actual configuration of the ISA server array, and it went through all the steps needed to configure your first ISA server array. The ISA Server final edition has two different versions, the Standard and Enterprise editions. If you have a standalone ISA server that you would like to add to a new array, you can promote the standalone ISA server to be a member of the new array.

The more Internet traffic comes into and goes out of your network, the more you need to plan for growth so that users do not get poor network performance. The standalone ISA server does a good job for a small number of users. However, for a large number of users, you need to move the network infrastructure to multiple ISA servers. You deploy them in either an array or a chain. There are many benefits to deploying an ISA server array compared with using a standalone ISA server. The main advantages are that you can provide load balancing and fault tolerance, as well as increase your available bandwidth and effective cache size.

Deploying a multiple ISA server array provides load balancing. If you have an ISA server array with two or more ISA servers in it, each ISA server array can take some load of the work that the whole ISA server array needs to perform. Therefore, you can serve your users better. If the array starts to reach the point where it cannot handle the network traffic effectively, you just need to add another member ISA server to the array for better load balancing.

Deploying a multiple ISA server array provides fault tolerance. If you have only a standalone ISA server in your environment, and it crashes for some reason, the whole network is affected. Users will not be able to use the ISA server's functionalities until the ISA server is recovered onto the network. If you have multiple ISA servers in an array, if one ISA server crashes, others can take over the loads from the crashed ISA server until it is repaired. Therefore, your users may experience a network performance degradation, but they will still be operational.

Deploying a multiple ISA server array provides more available bandwidth and effective cache size. If you have more ISA servers in an array, as each ISA server contains cache on its disk, you will have more space for caching. If you can cache more Internet objects on the disks, then many Internet objects would be served to users locally from the cache, and therefore, would free up the bandwidth to get out to the Internet.

ISA servers in an array share configuration information. When you change the array configuration, all the ISA server computers' configurations in the array are also changed, including all the access policies and cache policies. Therefore, the administrators have a central point of control for all configuration options on the array.

Instead of configuring two or more ISA servers in an array, you may choose to configure them in a chain. Chaining is also described as hierarchical proxying. Chaining can provide load balancing and caching along the chain of ISA servers, but configurations are done separately from others in the chain, and therefore, chaining is not fault tolerant. If an ISA server in the chain is not available, users will be affected. The only way to provide fault tolerance in chaining is to configure a backup route so that if the chain fails to function, you can use a backup route, such as a dial-up to an ISP, so that the network is still functional to some degree. ISA servers in a chain do not share configuration information.

Review Questions

1. What two concepts are introduced in this chapter to manage multiple ISA servers? [Check the two correct answers]
   a. Array
   b. System duplication
   c. Chaining
   d. CARP

2. What is chaining?
   a. Multiple ISA servers physically connected by a long cable chain
   b. Multiple ISA servers configured in a parallel fashion
   c. Multiple ISA servers configured in a cascading fashion
   d. Multiple ISA servers configured in parallel and cascading fashions

3. You have an ISA server with Release Candidate 1 (RC1) installed, and you cannot promote a standalone server to an array member. Why?

   a. There is no ISA Server product with RC1.
   b. RC1 does not support an array.
   c. RC1 does not run under Windows 2000.
   d. You cannot promote a standalone server to an array member in RC1.
   e. RC1 must be installed on a Windows NT system to work correctly.

4. The ISA Server final product includes which of the following editions? [Check all correct answers]

   a. Single-user edition
   b. Standalone edition
   c. Standard edition
   d. Multiple server edition
   e. Enterprise edition

5. When you add more ISA servers to an array, what one benefit do you get in your network?

   a. Better Internet browsing performance
   b. Longer latency
   c. Higher security
   d. Smaller number of administrators
   e. Smaller number of offices

6. How is fault tolerance achieved?

   a. One ISA server in your network
   b. Multiple ISA servers in a chain
   c. One ISA server in an array
   d. Multiple ISA servers in an array

7. When you're creating an array, what two conditions need to be met? [Check all correct answers]

   a. All the members need to be in the same Organizational Unit.
   b. All the members need to be in the computer container in Active Directory Users and Computers MMC snap-in.
   c. All the members need to be in the same site.
   d. All the members need to be in the same Windows 2000 domain.

8. Your ISA Server consultant says that you can only configure alerts for all the servers in an array. Is this correct?

    a. Yes

    b. No

    c. There is no alerts configuration in ISA Server.

    d. Alerts can be configured only in the standalone ISA server.

9. What protocol properties are included in the cache configuration properties? [Check all correct answers]

    a. HTTP

    b. HTTPS

    c. FTP

    d. CARP

10. To create a new array, what group do you have be a member of? [Check all correct answers]

    a. Local Admins group

    b. Domain Admins group

    c. Enterprise Admins group

    d. Schema Admins group

11. Chaining is also called what?

    a. Connection-less proxying

    b. Hierarchical proxying

    c. Distributed proxying

    d. Connection-oriented proxying

12. Why do all the member ISA servers in an array need to be in the same Windows 2000 domain?

    a. Because it will make administration easier

    b. Because ISA Server cannot change Active Directory

    c. Because the array cannot be configured in a Windows NT domain

    d. Because Active Directory schema is referred by all the members

13. When you create a new array, what two options do you have when configuring the array? [Check all correct answers]

    a. You can create a new configuration.

    b. You can copy a configuration from an existing array.

    c. You can copy a configuration from a Proxy Server 2.0 array.

    d. You can copy a configuration from a Proxy Server 1.0 array.

    e. You can copy a configuration from an array programmed in Visual C++.

14. If default enterprise settings are configured to use enterprise policy only when promoting a standalone server to an array member, then what does ISA Server do?

    a. Deletes all of the array policy rules that allow access.

    b. Deletes all of the array policy rules.

    c. Keeps the publishing rules that are defined for the array.

    d. Nothing.

15. After you create a new array, and if you need to add another ISA server to the array, what do you have to specify?

    a. Windows 2000 domain name

    b. Enterprise Admins group user account name

    c. Array name

    d. Fully Qualified Windows 2000 domain name

16. When you back up the Enterprise configuration, where would you save the file so that you can recover it quickly, assuming the system is currently functioning properly and that you will soon modify the Enterprise configuration?

    a. On a floppy disk

    b. On a local hard disk

    c. On a network share

    d. On a CD-R media

17. The backup configuration file includes mainly which of the following?

    a. Protocol definitions

    b. Array polices

    c. Array cache properties

    d. Enterprise policies

    e. Enterprise user account's permissions

18. What is recommended when you back up enterprise configurations?

    a. Use **NTBACKUP**.

    b. Use system state backup.

    c. Back up enterprise configuration and then back up the array's configuration.

    d. Back up the array's configuration and then back up the enterprise configuration.

    e. Use a third-party backup tool.

19. By default, a member of which group is allowed to create, configure, and apply enterprise policies?

    a. Local Admins group

    b. Domain Admins group

    c. Enterprise Admins group

    d. Schema Admins group

20. Which three of the following can be configured for each ISA server? [Check all correct answers]

    a. Packet filters

    b. Alerts

    c. Server publishing rules

    d. Protocol rules

Real-World Projects

Note: This exercise assumes a test Windows 2000 server or Advanced Server with Service Pack 1 or Windows 2000 Datacenter Server installed. It also requires one or more ISA Servers installed in an array so that you can practice to manage them. Read the instructions carefully and do not perform this install on your production machine unless you understand the options presented. If you are unsure about an option, cancel the installation and read the help files provided with ISA Server about the option to be installed.

Mark is an administrator for a small company with 500 employees located in one office in downtown Chicago. He has been administering various versions of Internet Information Server (IIS) and Proxy Server 2.0. As Microsoft is now producing the ISA Server for caching and security purposes, the CEO of the company has asked Mark to implement an ISA server array in a test environment, see how the array works, and determine how much performance gain they can get. After complete testing, the CEO then wants Mark to deploy it in the production environment to serve all the employees in a timely manner. The reasons they are going with ISA Server are obvious. The company just upgraded all the servers and client systems to Windows 2000 systems. It has a single Windows 2000 domain in the same site where all the 500 employees are being served. More importantly, the company is expecting to double the number of employees in the next three years, and it is time to start preparing for the growth of the network. Mark has already set up an array with the array name of "testarray1". He now has a couple of ISA servers that have been built with Windows 2000 Advanced Server using Service Pack 1. ISA Server has already been installed on these systems, and Mark's intention, first of all, is to add members to the array testarray1.

Project 13.1

To add members to the array:

1. Start the Microsoft Internet Security And Acceleration Server Enterprise Edition Setup program. Choose which installation to perform: Typical, Full, or Custom.

2. In the Internet Security And Acceleration Server Setup dialog box, click Yes to install ISA Server on an array member.

3. In the Microsoft ISA Server Setup dialog box, select the array that you would like to add the new ISA server to, and then click OK. Configure the cache settings as you would do for a standalone server.

Everything seems to be fine. Mark's assistant comes into the computer room and says, "Mark, I found an old server that we could use to test ISA Server's functionality. Do you want to take it?" Mark thinks for a bit and decides to use it. He tells the assistant to install the Windows 2000 Advanced Server with Service Pack 1 and ISA Server with standalone edition. The assistant says, "OK. I will get them loaded right away, but why not with the Enterprise edition?" Mark tells the assistant, "Make sure you install ISA Server as a standalone server, not as a member of an array." The assistant agrees and leaves. Mark's pager goes off and he remembers an important meeting. When the meeting finishes, it is about time for lunch. He finishes his lunch and goes back to the computer room. The assistant has installed the OS and ISA Server. It is ready to go. Mark is convinced, "Gee, I must have hired a pretty good assistant!" One of the things that Mark wanted to try was the promotion of a standalone ISA server to the array member, which seemed pretty cool. He remembers there are certain policy settings that ISA Server manipulates when promoting a standalone to an array member. He reviews the rules, but at this point, as it is in the test environment, he does not worry too much. He completes the following steps to promote the standalone server to the array member for the array "testarray1".

Project 13.2

To promote the stand-alone server to the array member:

1. In ISA Management, in the console tree, right-click the ISA server you would like to promote, and then click Promote. See Figure 13.2.

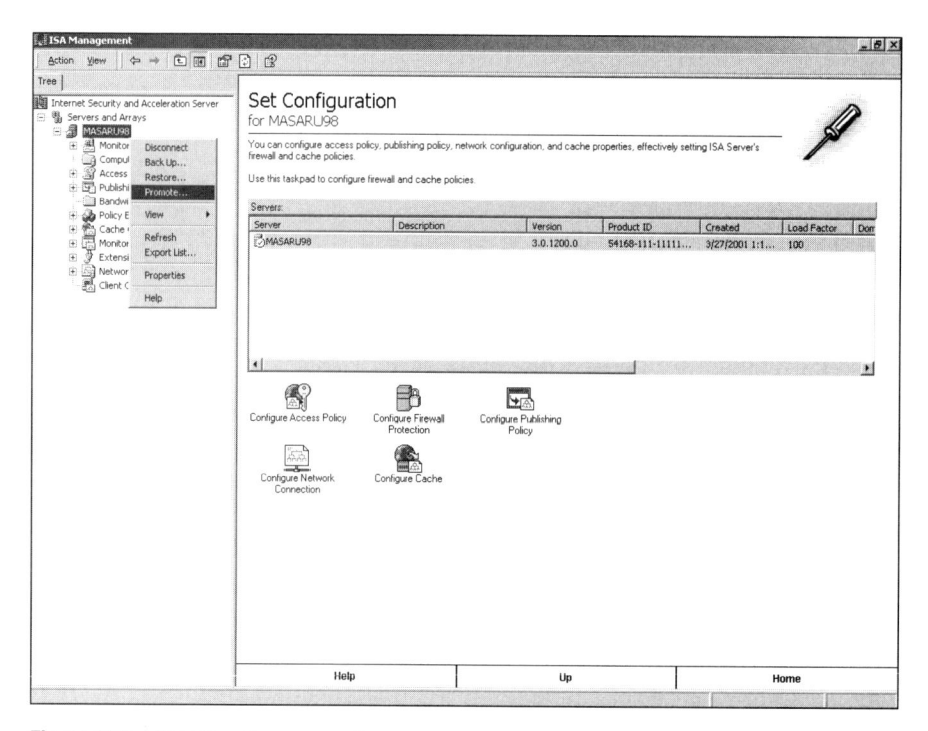

Figure 13.2 The Promote command.

2. Click Yes to confirm that you would like the ISA server to be an array member.

3. If you are not a member of the Enterprise Admins group, click Yes to confirm that the default enterprise policy should be applied to the new array you are just creating. See Figure 13.3. For this example, assuming you have already created "testarray1", you would select it. If you have created an array with a different name, use that instead.

4. Be patient while the promotion completes. It takes some time to complete it.

Mark, surprised, says, "Wow, it worked!" He now tries to do some of the administration tasks for the ISA Server.

Note: Starting in Option Pack 4, Microsoft is adopting the Microsoft Management Console (MMC) as a standard feature in all its software. If you know how to use the MMC in one product, you will know how to use it in any other product. ISA Management is the MMC snap-in for the ISA server where you configure all the settings.

Mark tries to create a new array and then deletes the array to see how it works.

Managing Multiple ISA Servers **377**

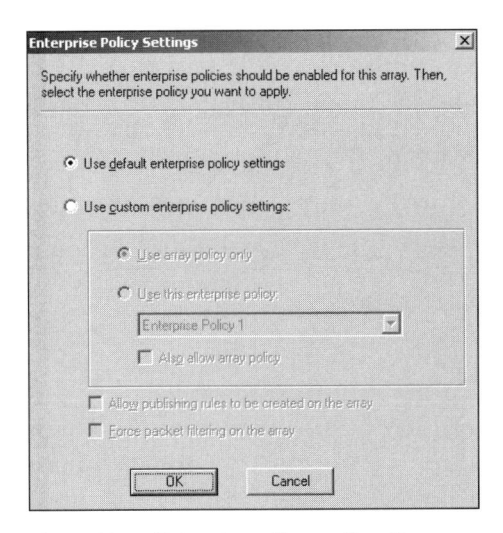

Figure 13.3 Enterprise policy confirmation.

Project 13.3

To create a new array:

1. In ISA Management, in the console tree, right-click Servers And Arrays and point to New. Then, click Array. See Figure 13.4.

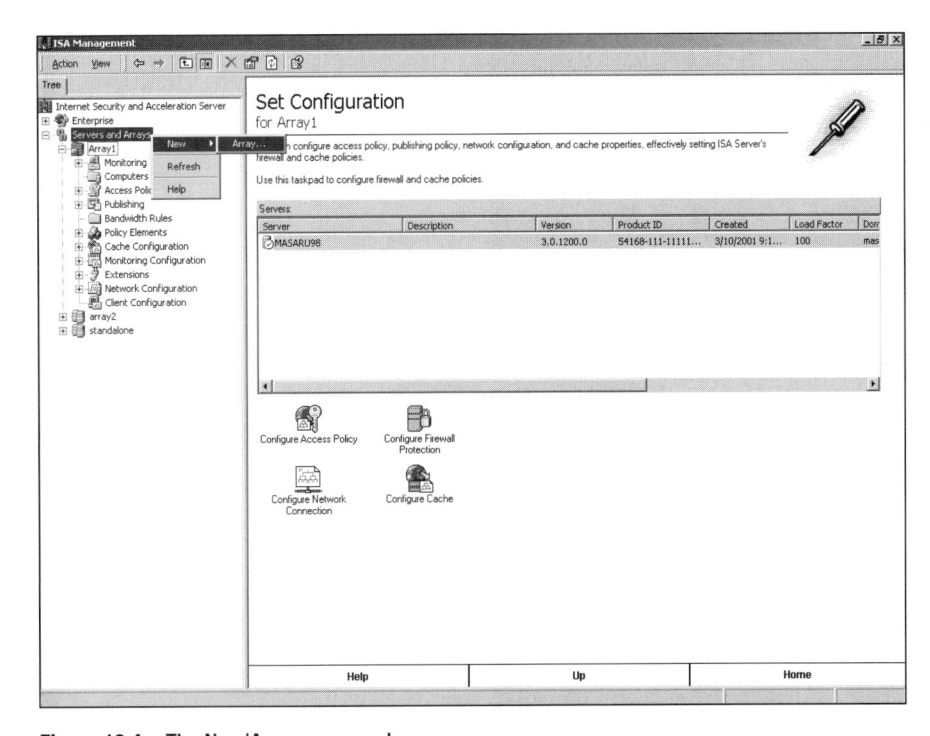

Figure 13.4 The New|Array command.

2. In the New Array Wizard, enter a name for the array: "testarray2". Then, click Next. See Figure 13.5.

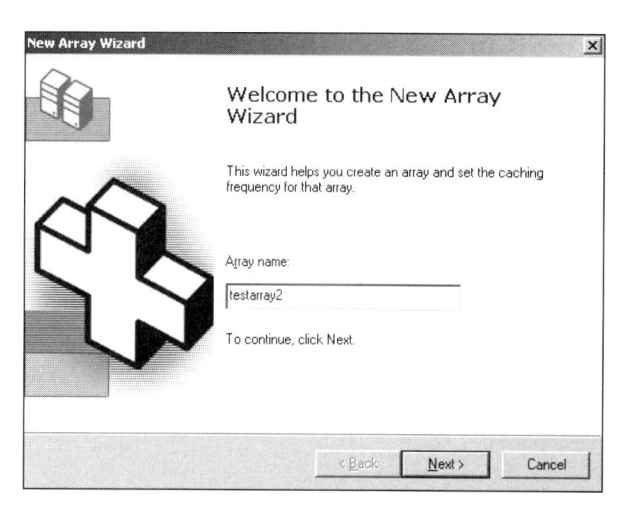

Figure 13.5 The New Array Wizard.

3. On the Domain Name page, select the site and domain in which to create the new array. Then, click Next. See Figure 13.6.

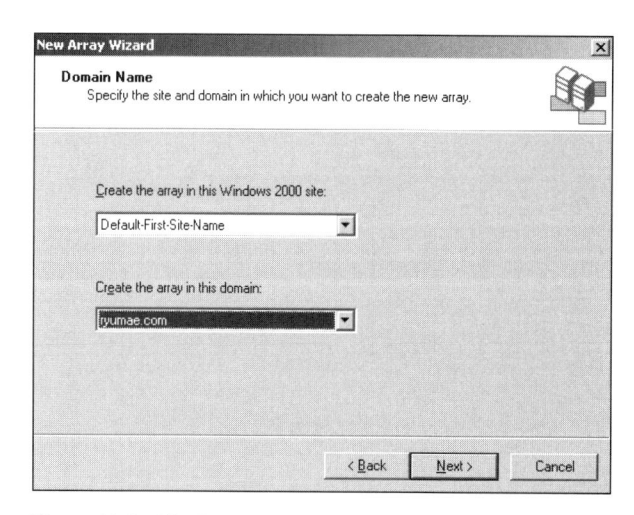

Figure 13.6 The Domain Name page.

4. On the Create Or Copy An Array page, choose the Create option. See Figure 13.7.

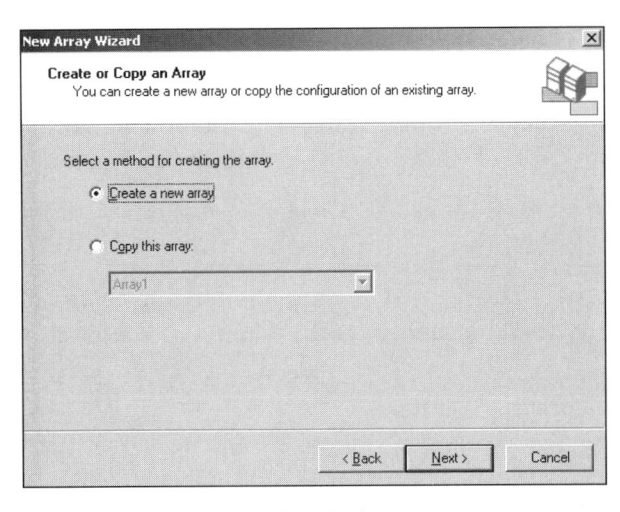

Figure 13.7 The Create Or Copy An Array page.

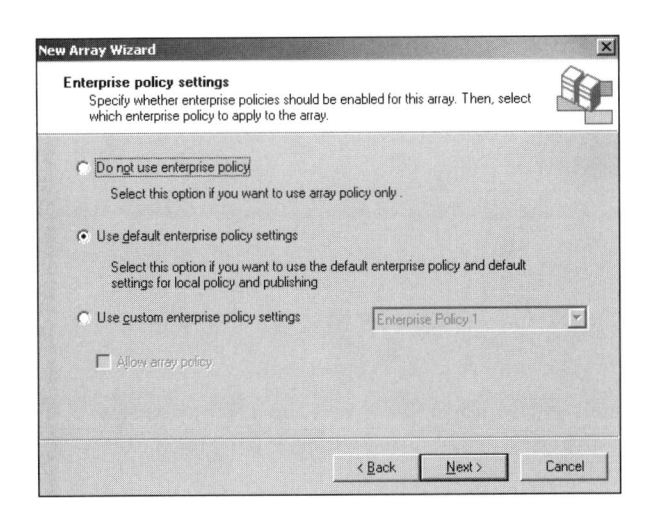

5. On the Enterprise Policy Settings page, select one of the following options (see Figure 13.8):

   ➤ *Do Not Use Enterprise Policy*—Select this option when you do not want to use the enterprise policy.

   ➤ *Use Default Enterprise Policy Settings*—Select this option when you want to use the default enterprise policy settings.

   ➤ *Use Custom Enterprise Policy Settings*—By selecting this option, you need to specify an enterprise policy. If you want to also apply the array policy, select the Allow Array Policy checkbox.

Figure 13.8 The Enterprise Policy Settings page.

For this example, select User Default Enterprise Policy Settings. Then, click Next.

6. This step is necessary only if you have chosen Do Not Use Enterprise Policy or Use Custom Enterprise Policy Settings in Step 5. On the Array Global Policy Options page, select one or both of the following options (see Figure 13.9):

   ➤ *Allow Publishing Rules To Be Created On The Array*—Use this option to use publishing rules on the array.

   ➤ *Force Packet Filtering On The Array*—Use this option to forcibly use packet filtering on the array so that undesired packets do not access the array.

   For this example, select Force Packet Filtering On The Array. Then, click Next.

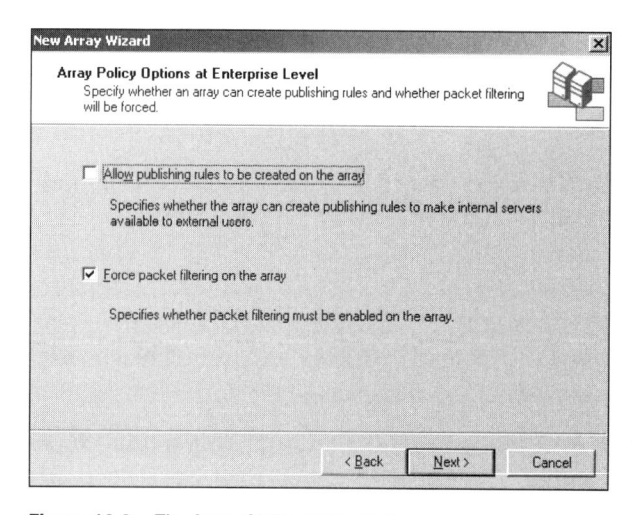

Figure 13.9 The Array Global Policy Options page.

7. On the Array Type page, select one of the following options (see Figure 13.10):

   ➤ Cache Only

   ➤ Firewall Only

   ➤ Integrated

   For this example, select Integrated.

8. On the Completing The New Array Wizard page, be sure to review all of your choices. Then, click Finish. See Figure 13.11.

Mark says to himself, "OK, so far, so good. Now it is time to blow it away!" He tries to delete the array he just created. He does the following:

In ISA Management, in the console tree, right-click the array you want to delete, and click Delete. See Figure 13.12.

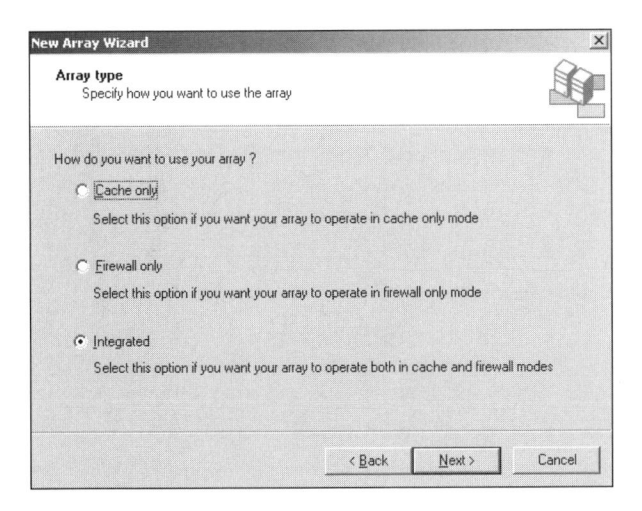

Figure 13.10 The Array Type page.

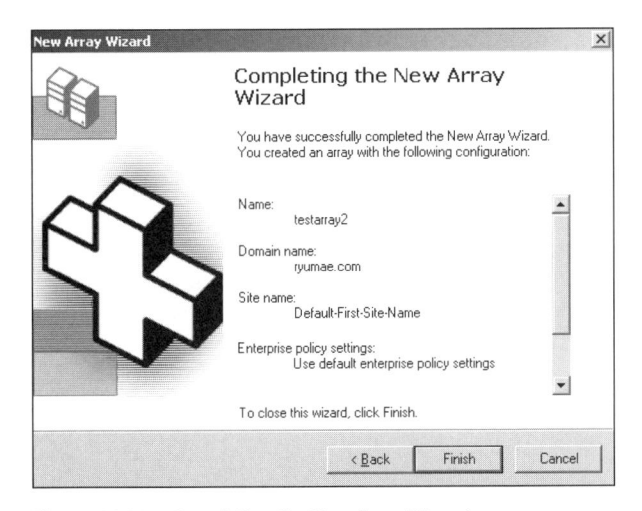

Figure 13.11 Completing the New Array Wizard page.

Mark is now becoming used to getting around in the ISA Management, and he wants to prepare for a disaster. He practices backing up and restoring enterprise configurations, which includes some of the settings for the array. Marks tries to back up the enterprise configurations.

Project 13.4
To back up an enterprise configuration:

1. In ISA Management, in the console tree, right-click Enterprise. Then, click Back Up. See Figure 13.13.

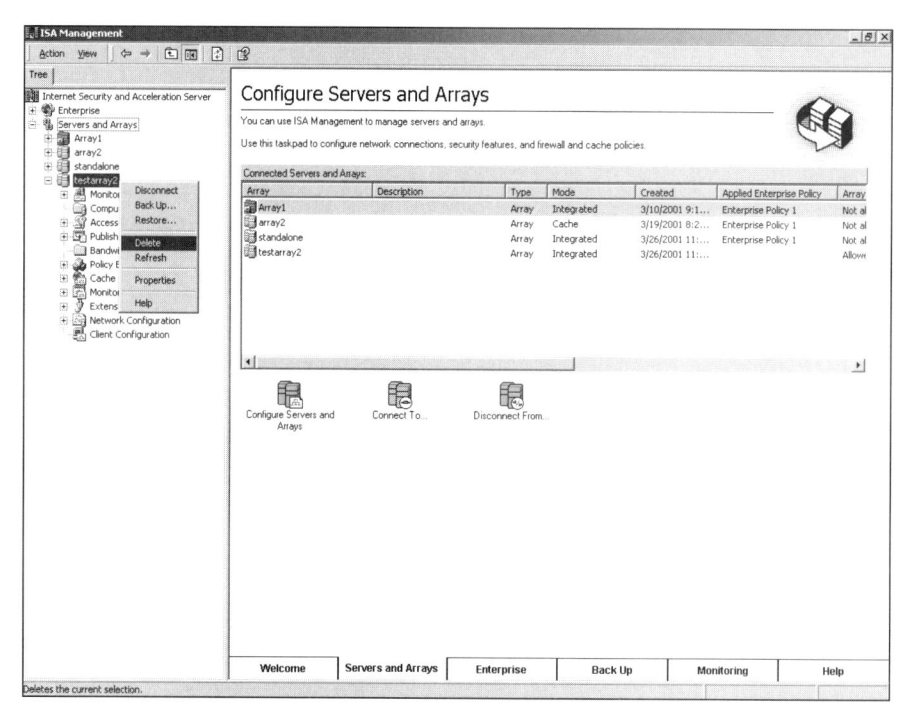

Figure 13.12 The Delete command.

Figure 13.13 The Back Up command.

2. In the Select Location Of Configuration Backup box, enter the name of the folder in which to store the backup data. For this example, use C:\testconfig.bef. Then, click OK. See Figure 13.14.

Now Mark tries to restore the enterprise configurations.

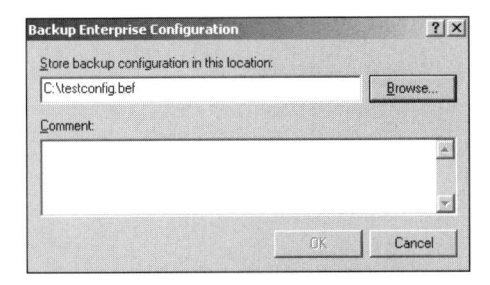

Figure 13.14 The Backup page.

Project 13.5

To restore the enterprise configurations:

1. In ISA Management, in the console tree, right-click Enterprise, then click Restore. Click Yes to overwrite the existing enterprise configuration with the backup configuration. See Figure 13.15.

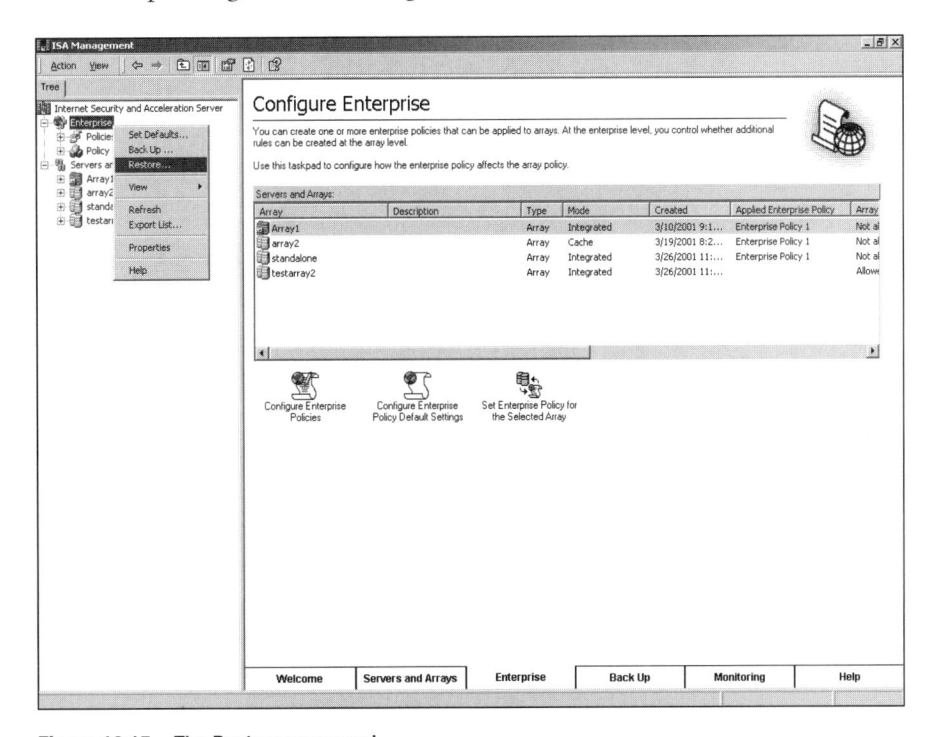

Figure 13.15 The Restore command.

2. In the Restore Configuration From The Following Backup (.bef) File box, enter the path of the backup folder and the name of the backup file. For this exmaple, use c:\testconfig.bef. See Figure 13.16.

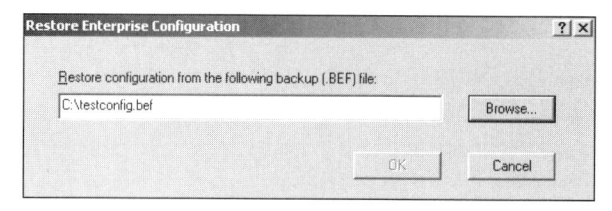

Figure 13.16 The Restore page.

Mark thinks to himself, "It seems the backup and restore are easy and are working. I should probably crash the system or uninstall ISA Server, and see if I can use the backed-up configuration file to restore to the original condition." He plans to finish the full recovery process tomorrow.

CHAPTER FOURTEEN

Integrating Services with ISA Server

After completing this chapter, you will be able to:

✓ Integrate Exchange Server with ISA Server

✓ Set up publishing for a mail server

✓ Use the Mail Server Security Wizard

✓ Set up the SMTP Filter for content filtering

✓ Set up the filters needed for internal mail servers

✓ Provide fault tolerance for ISA servers using Network Load Balancing (NLB)

✓ Provide load balancing with Domain Name Service (DNS)

✓ Use Terminal Services for remote administration of ISA Server

✓ Use packet filters instead of rules in certain publishing situations

✓ Integrate IIS with a local ISA server

When integrating ISA Server with other services on the network, you might need to include some special configurations. Sometimes, the configurations are needed to allow a service to work on the internal network when ISA Server is protecting the network. Special configurations will also be needed if the service is loaded on the same computer as ISA Server. In this chapter, we will discuss the settings that you have to configure in order for ISA Server to be integrated with other services on the same network or even the same server. We will discuss integrating ISA Server with Exchange and other mail servers, as well as load balancing services.

Why Do Some Services Require Special Configurations?

When ISA Server is used to control incoming and outgoing traffic on a network, some services can be implemented on the internal network with no special configurations. Others require special configurations, or client connections to them will fail. By default, ISA Server will not allow any traffic to or from the internal network when it is first installed. You can easily set up rules in an access policy to allow outbound traffic, but when you publish services from inside the internal network to the Internet, the setup can be more involved. Some services need to simply allow inbound access from the Internet. This kind of access is allowed with Web or server publishing rules. But other services also require outbound connections to clients or must work with several protocols. Only specified connections are allowed through ISA Server, so either of these circumstances complicates the setup of ISA Server. More than one rule or the configuration of a filter may be necessary. We will cover services that require special or extra configurations in this chapter.

Integrating Services on a Local ISA Server

In general, it is not a good idea to install services on the same computer that has ISA Server installed on it. The reasons are most often related to security and/or performance. Firewalls are designed to protect what is behind them on the network. A service that is installed on the same server as the firewall services misses out on many of the protections that it offers. Also, an ISA server will often be weighed down with the protection of a network and all the processing it must do to implement its security settings. This can cause a drain in performance that will be exaggerated by the addition of another service.

Even so, administrators might choose to combine ISA Server with other services on the same computer for legitimate reasons. In a medium to large enterprise networking environment, several ISA servers can be spread throughout the network. Some of these servers might be part of a chain of ISA servers, and their job might be to check the cache for requests that they pass downstream or upstream. A network engineer might decide that the load on this internal ISA server is light enough that other services can also be installed. Also, a small network might contain only a few servers, and multiple services can be loaded on each server. This is because the traffic being processed by each server is not a great burden. Whatever the reason, other services might end up being combined with ISA Server.

The chief method of providing security in ISA Server is the implementation of rules, but rules cannot be applied to services loaded on the same computer as ISA Server. Instead, other security measures must be taken, such as the use of static packet filters. You can still install other services on the same server as ISA Server. However, the configurations required to make this situation work are nearly always different from the ones you'd make if the service were located behind the ISA server.

Exchange and ISA Server

Setting up an Internet security server so that email can be passed to and from an internal mail server is a complex task. This was especially true when setting up an Exchange server for use on a network protected by Proxy Server 2.0. In ISA Server, Microsoft attempted to simplify the process. As a result, ISA Server offers a setup wizard and two application filters that control the configurations so that communication between ISA Server and Exchange Server can work. Allowing an internal mail server to communicate through an ISA server falls into the publishing services provided by ISA Server. Publishing rules are described in Chapter 12, but instead of just creating another server publishing rule, you need to run the Mail Server Security Wizard to allow incoming connections to an internal mail server. Also, a Simple Mail Transport Protocol (SMTP) Filter is installed by default with ISA Server as well as a Remote Procedure Call (RPC) Filter.

Proxy Server 2.0 and Exchange Server

Administrators using Proxy Server 2.0 have a difficult task to accomplish when they want to publish mail services from their internal network. The setup for Proxy Server and Exchange Server is intricate enough to warrant a Knowledge Base (KB) article. If you used the steps outlined in this article to set up communication between these two products, you have two choices when it comes time to upgrade your Proxy server to an ISA server. The first is to simply upgrade the Proxy server to ISA server and then just continue your email operations as normal. Of course, although this option is the easiest to configure, it does not allow your Exchange server to benefit from the new security features available in ISA server. The second choice is to undo the configurations made on the Exchange server from the steps outlined in the KB article and use the Mail Server Security Wizard to set up a server publishing rule for the Exchange server. This method requires more configurations, but not nearly as many as required to get your Proxy server and Exchange server to communicate in the first place.

Note: *The KB article Q181420, "How to Configure Exchange or Other SMTP with Proxy Server," is written for Exchange Server versions 5 and 5.5. If you want to upgrade to Exchange 2000 and integrate it with a Microsoft Internet security server, Microsoft recommends using ISA Server along with the Mail Server Security Wizard.*

For the second option, you should delete the wspcfg.ini file from the Exchange server. This file will no longer be needed. Next, follow the setup instructions in this chapter for the Mail Server Security Wizard to create a server publishing rule for the Exchange server on the ISA server.

The Mail Server Security Wizard

Use the Mail Server Security Wizard to set up mail servers that are on your internal network. Even if you choose not to filter the content of the mail messages that come into your network—by using the SMTP Filter—you still have to use the Mail Server Security Wizard to allow any messages in at all. You can publish these servers to the Internet and still protect them with ISA Server.

When you right-click on the Server Publishing container in ISA Management, your first choice in the list is to start the Mail Server Security Wizard. Following the steps in this wizard, you will need to immediately set the external IP address of the ISA server that will accept connections from external users sending mail. This IP address will appear to the users as the published IP address of your internal mail server. In the same dialog box, you set the IP address of the internal mail server that ISA Server will redirect the mail messages to.

Note: *If you do not have the internal mail server installed and connected to the ISA server as well as a working connection to the external network, you will not be able to get past this step of the wizard, because the wizard tests the connection and cannot continue if a connection between the ISA server and the mail server is not made.*

Next, you will configure which incoming email protocols ISA Server will allow to access the internal mail server. Table 14.1 shows the protocols that can be used by external clients to connect to the internal mail server. Each has a predefined protocol definition that is created during the installation of ISA Server. Find out which protocols your clients and Exchange Server support. The version of Exchange Server you're running affects which mail protocols you can use. POP3 is supported in Exchange 5 and 5.5, while IMAP4 is supported only in version 5.5 of Exchange Server.

Table 14.1 Protocols that can be used by external clients when accessing an internal mail server configured by the Mail Security Server Wizard.

Supported Protocol	Acronym
Post Office Protocol 3	POP3
Network News Transfer Protocol	NNTP
Secure Network News Transfer Protocol	NNTP-S
Messaging Application Programming Interface	MAPI
Internet Messaging Access Protocol 4	IMAP4

Rules created for inbound mail traffic by the Mail Server Security Wizard are listed with other Server Publishing rules. To differentiate them, their names by default start with the phrase "Mail Wizard rule." The rest of the name will automatically be created using the protocol specified for mail traffic and the IP address of the internal mail server. The result is a name like Mail Wizard rule-POP3 (client).Internal IP:*xxx.xxx.xxx.xxx* (where the x's represent the IP address of the internal mail server). In this example, the rule allows external clients to use the POP3 protocol to pass messages through ISA Server to the internal mail server. If you specify that outbound mail traffic be allowed, the wizard will also create a protocol rule allowing this access.

The SMTP Filter

The SMTP Filter allows you to filter messages by the actual content of the mail messages and their attachments. Once enabled, it intercepts and filters all SMTP requests that make a connection on the default SMTP port 25. The SMTP Filter is much more complicated than many of the other application filters that come with ISA Server. Not only does it have more property pages than many of the others, but also it has a more complicated setup process. It gives you a greater degree of control over who can send messages to your internal mail server and the type of content you will allow.

Although the SMTP Filter is installed by default during the ISA Server installation, it is not automatically enabled. Even if you enable the SMTP Filter, it is not ready to use until you complete some configurations that are not a part of the SMTP Filter setup but instead are services that support or are supported by the SMTP Filter. To start with, we will go over the steps of enabling the SMTP Filter, and then we will examine the steps you must complete before using the SMTP Filter. Finally, we will cover the steps of configuring the SMTP Filter itself.

To enable the SMTP Filter, complete the following steps:

1. Open ISA Management.

2. Expand Internet Security And Acceleration Server and then expand Servers And Arrays.

3. Expand the name of the server or array on which you want to enable the SMTP Filter.

4. Expand Extensions and select the Application Filters container.

5. In the details pane, double-click the SMTP Filter.

6. On the property sheet of the SMTP Filter, select the General tab, if necessary. Then, select the Enable This Filter option.

7. Click the OK button to close the SMTP Filter property sheet.

Configuring the ISA Server and Other Applications for the SMTP Filter

Once the SMTP Filter is enabled, you need to complete steps in different applications that will allow you to use the SMTP Filter. These steps involve installing the necessary ISA Server add-in components, running the Mail Server Security Wizard, and configuring the Internet Information Server (IIS) SMTP Virtual Server.

The Message Screener

The Message Screener is an add-in to ISA Server. Installing the Message Screener lets you filter mail attachments and individual messages for keywords. Because it is an add-in, it is not installed by default when ISA Server installs unless you choose a Full installation. Complete the following steps to install the Message Screener add-in to ISA Server:

1. Open Control Panel.

2. Double-click Add/Remove Programs.

3. In the Change Or Remove Programs dialog box, select Internet Security And Acceleration Server. Click the Change button.

4. In the Welcome To ISA Server Setup dialog box, click the Add/Remove button.

5. Select Add-In Services and click the Change Option button.

6. Place a checkmark next to Message Screener and click OK.

7. Click the Continue button to install this option. Setup will update ISA Server.

8. A dialog box will appear informing you that ISA Server has been updated successfully. Click OK.

9. Click OK to close the Add/Remove Programs application.

10. Close Control Panel.

You also need to use the Mail Security Server Wizard to configure ISA Server to allow content filtering. During the wizard, select Incoming SMTP Mail and Outgoing SMTP Mail, and then select Apply Content Filtering. This allows the SMTP Filter to perform content filtering on attachments and/or email messages. You will still have to configure the SMTP Filter to specify how it should perform this content filtering. We will cover these steps later in this chapter.

The SMTPCred.exe Tool

If you install the Message Screener on a computer other than the ISA server, you must run a tool that allows the remote Message Screener and the SMTP Filter to communicate with each other. You will find this tool, which is called SMTPCred.exe, in the \ISA\I386 directory of the ISA Server CD. It comes with both the Standard Edition and the Enterprise Edition of ISA Server. You might find a reference to the Setregs.vbs script in the ISA Server documentation; however, this script is no longer used and has been replaced by the SMTPCred.exe tool. Run this tool on the remote computer that has the Message Screener and not ISA Server installed on it.

Configurations for IIS's SMTP Virtual Server

If you have an internal IIS server with the SMTP service loaded on it, you need to configure it to send all requests to the internal mail server for message handling. Next, you must configure the internal IIS server's SMTP service. In the IIS snap-in on the internal IIS server, complete the following steps:

1. Open the IIS snap-in by selecting Internet Services Manager in the Administrative Tools menu.

2. If necessary, click on the plus sign (+) to expand the server and view the available Internet services.

3. Right-click on the Default SMTP Virtual Server and select Properties.

4. Select the Access tab.

5. At the bottom of the Access property page, click the Relay button.

6. Select All Except The List Below and click the Add button.

7. Type in the IP address of the internal mail server and click OK twice to return to the Access property page.

8. Click the Delivery tab.

9. At the bottom of the Delivery property page, click the Advanced button.

10. In the Smart Host input box, type the FQDN of the internal mail server. The SMTP Virtual Server will then send all SMTP requests it receives to the internal mail server.

11. Click OK to return to the Delivery property page and click OK again to return to the IIS snap-in.

12. Close the IIS snap-in.

Configuring the SMTP Filter Property Pages

Once the SMTP Filter is enabled and the necessary settings are configured, many other settings must be configured to customize your use of the filter. As shown in Figure 14.1, in addition to the options on the General page, the SMTP Filter property pages allow you to configure how SMTP handles attachments, users/domains, keywords, and SMTP commands.

If you select the Attachments property page, you can configure the SMTP Filter to look for and handle some attachments differently than others. Figure 14.2 shows the Mail Attachment Rule dialog box, which allows you to set attachment rules. You access this dialog box by clicking the Add button on the Attachments property page. In this dialog box, you can specify the name, file extension, or size of attachment that SMTP should look for when filtering attachments to mail messages. The filter checks each attachment to see whether it fits any of the rule requirements. Once an attachment fulfills the requirements, the filter performs the action specified by the rule. For example, if you decide not to accept any mail messages with an .exe extension, you can add a rule specifying that all mail attachments with the .exe extension be discarded by choosing Delete Message as the action. Rules are automatically assigned an order of priority in case an attachment meets more than one rule's criteria. You can change the priority order on the Attachments property page of the SMTP Filter.

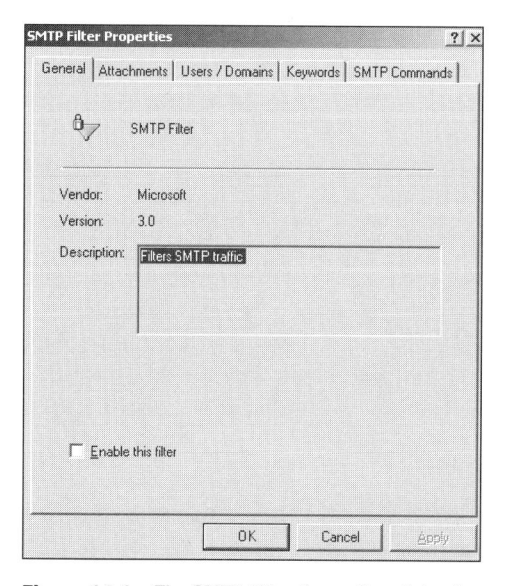

Figure 14.1 The SMTP Filter Properties dialog box.

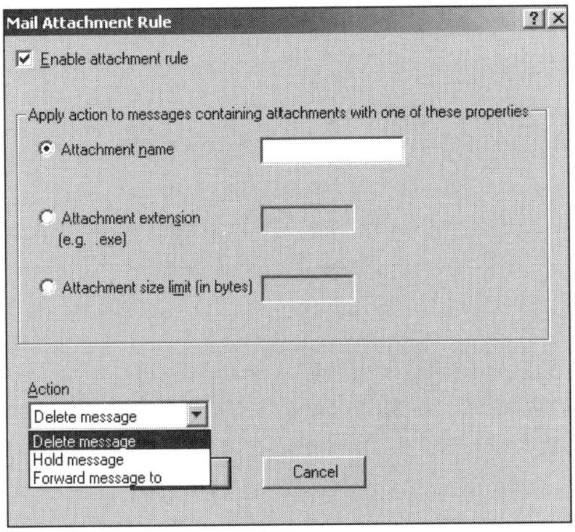

Figure 14.2 The SMTP Filter Mail Attachment Rule dialog box appears when you click the Add button on the Attachments property page.

The Users/Domains property page allows you to specify if messages from specific individuals or from a specific domain should be rejected and not allowed through the ISA server. If you are receiving a lot of junk mail from the WeAreJunkMail.com domain, you can specify that all mail from that domain be rejected. The Users/Domains property page is shown in Figure 14.3 with the WeAreJunkMail.com domain name listed under Rejected Domains. Because each user from that domain will be listed as *someone@WeAreJunkMail.com*, all messages from users in that domain will be rejected.

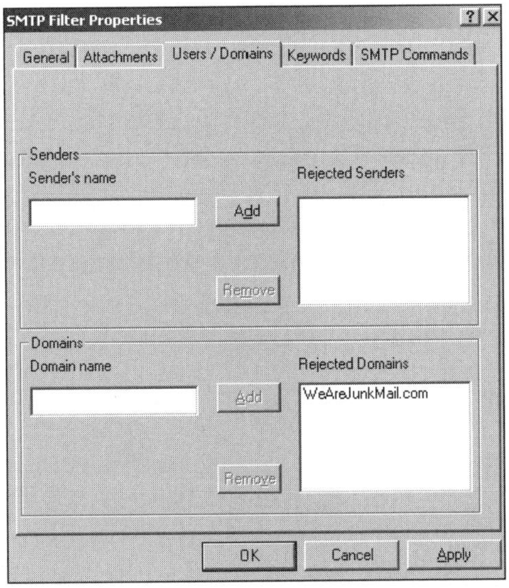

Figure 14.3 The SMTP Filter's Users/Domains property page with a rejected domain listed.

The Keywords property page works similarly to the Attachments property page. You can add Mail Keyword rules that will cause the SMTP Filter to search the header or contents of a mail message, or both, for certain keywords. You can use this feature to look for inappropriate types of content that company policy does not allow. Make sure that any rules that you configure match company email policy. Also, even though legally in a business all email is the property of the company and no privacy laws for users exist, it is best to let users know that their email will be filtered for certain types of attachments and words if you are going to set up these rules.

The SMTP Commands property page allows you to guard against attacks that try to overburden the mail server buffers. Such an attack gives the mail server so much information to process that it cannot keep up with regular mail service. You can make the SMTP Filter check for messages that are larger than a certain size by specifying that size in the SMTP Commands dialog box. If a message using one of the commands exceeds the specified size, you can configure how ISA Server should handle the message. Several commands are listed by default in this property page, and each has its own specified size. Figure 14.4 shows some of the SMTP commands defined by default in the SMTP Filter. You can edit these commands by selecting one and clicking the Edit button, and you can add more to the list by clicking the Add button.

The RPC Filter

The Remote Procedure Call (RPC) protocol passes messages between remote computers and has an important role in Windows 2000 and earlier versions of Windows operating systems. A majority of services, including Exchange Server,

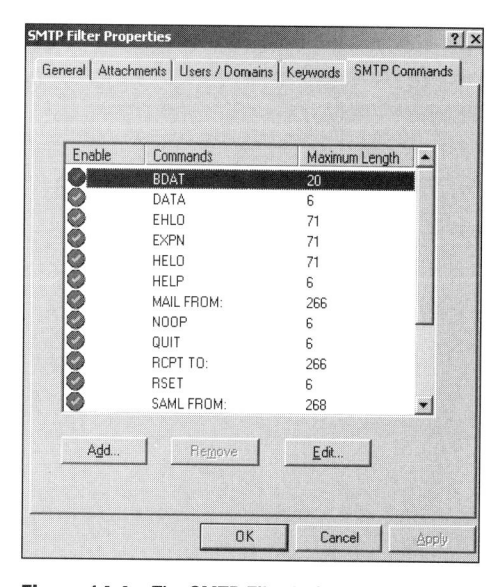

Figure 14.4 The SMTP Filter's SMTP Commands property page.

use RPCs to send messages between computers using its services. Exchange Servers version 5.5 and below send messages to and from each other using RPCs. Also, some clients to Exchange use RPCs to send messages to the Exchange server. Because ISA Server rejects and stops all traffic except that traffic that is specifically allowed, those servers and clients that are using RPCs to pass their messages will not get through ISA Server unless specifically allowed.

By default, the RPC filter is enabled and working on an ISA server. Figure 14.5 shows that there are no other property pages other than the General page and no other configuration is necessary for the RPC Filter. If you are using Exchange Server 2000, SMTP is the default protocol used to send messages between servers instead of RPCs. All but the most recent Microsoft mail clients use RPCs to communicate with the Exchange server, however, so you may still need this service. The RPC Filter handles RPC traffic, but a server publishing rule is required if you need server-to-server or client-to-server RPC traffic for your mail traffic. A protocol definition for RPC is already created by default when ISA Server is installed.

DNS Setup

You will have to configure a DNS server differently when the mail server is located behind an ISA server. External users need a DNS server that contains a record for the mail server. This record must contain the external IP address of the ISA server. DNS records for use with SMTP and MAPI clients will require additional configuration. SMTP clients will request an MX record. This record should contain the name of the Exchange server and the IP address of the ISA server's external interface.

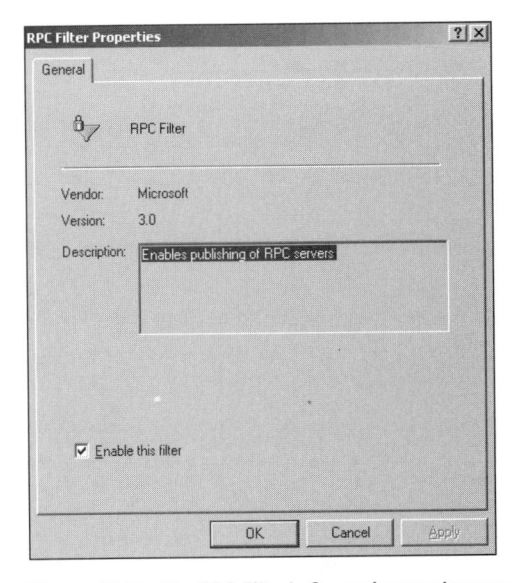

Figure 14.5 The RPC Filter's General property page.

You should also configure the Exchange server with the IP address of an external DNS server for outbound mail. You will need to enter the IP address of either your ISP or your own external DNS server if you are not using an ISP in the DNS tab in the properties of the Exchange server.

Exchange and ISA on the Same Server

If you load Exchange Server on the same server as ISA Server, you cannot use server publishing rules to protect Exchange's services. Instead, you use packet filters to protect the services provided by the Exchange server. A nice feature of the Mail Server Security Wizard is that it will recognize that the IP address input for the mail server matches the IP address of the ISA server. It will then automatically create packet filters instead of server publishing rules or protocol rules. The packet filters will assume that the default port numbers will be used for each protocol that you specify is needed. You will need to edit the properties of the packet filters created by the Mail Server Security Wizard if you are using other port numbers.

ISA Server and NLB

Network Load Balancing (NLB) is a part of Microsoft's Cluster Server. Although it was first introduced as a part of Windows NT 4 Enterprise Edition, Cluster Server is now a part of the Windows 2000 operating system in certain versions. Although you can install ISA Server on any version of Windows 2000 Server, you must install it on Windows 2000 Advanced Server or Datacenter Server if you want to run NLB with ISA Server.

Microsoft Cluster Server

Microsoft Cluster Server is designed to create a fault-tolerant environment for the services on your network. Fault tolerance comes in many forms, but Microsoft's Cluster Server is designed to allow a client to continue to receive responses to service requests even if a server that it is connecting to fails or is disconnected from the network. Included in this fault tolerance is a way to evenly distribute client requests among available servers. This distribution of requests includes redirecting requests when one of the servers providing the service fails. Duplicating every service on your network can provide fault tolerance, but you also need to tell the clients that are connecting that they need to switch over to a different server when the primary one fails. Cluster Server allows the switch to the available server to be automated so that your clients do not notice that a failure has occurred. To do this, you create clusters on your network. These clusters are groups of individual servers that offer a common collection of applications and appear to a client as if they are one server.

Microsoft's Cluster Server actually is two different services: Cluster Service and Network Load Balancing (NLB). Cluster Service is the part that provides fault tolerance to services within a network. NLB is the part that evenly distributes—and redistributes if necessary—requests among available servers. Cluster Server is a

Windows 2000 service that is available for use only on Windows 2000 Advanced Server and Datacenter Server. Cluster Service has the more complicated setup of the two services. Some applications are cluster-aware while others are not. As long as an application or service works with TCP/IP as its protocol suite, Cluster Server can work with it.

NLB does require some extra setup, both on the Windows 2000 server and on the ISA server. The main reason you would want to go through this effort is to achieve fault tolerance for client requests. If you have any reasons why your ISA server simply cannot fail, then NLB can help you. Microsoft suggests you use NLB if you have a standalone ISA server and/or if you have SecureNAT clients. The use of an array provides built-in fault tolerance because it sets up more than one ISA server to act in concert. A standalone ISA server cannot be installed into an array, however. An alternative is to use NLB to provide the fault tolerance that would otherwise be provided by an array. SecureNAT clients also need the fault tolerance provided by NLB. SecureNAT clients are usually configured with the ISA server's IP address as the Default Gateway in their IP address settings. Although arrays work together to provide the same ISA services to a network, they each have an individual IP address on their internal network interfaces. Firewall clients can refer to arrays by name. This allows them to benefit from the fault tolerance that arrays provide. Because a SecureNAT client must be configured with the IP address of one ISA server, if that one ISA server fails, it will not be able to ask for another. The drawback to using NLB for standalone SecureNAT clients instead of an array is that NLB is designed only for use with inbound requests. Arrays can be used to provide fault tolerance for inbound as well as outbound requests.

To set up ISA Server with NLB, you must have at least two servers. You can spread the load across as many ISA servers as you want to use—up to a maximum of 32. All servers that will participate in the load balancing with NLB must be configured identically. This means that Windows 2000 Advanced Server or Datacenter Server and NLB need to be loaded on each server. Then, you must install ISA Server using an identical setup, including the type of installation and mode. Table 14.2 shows the programs you should load on each ISA server to prepare for NLB setup.

Of course, all of this is unnecessary if you have the Enterprise Edition of ISA Server in an Active Directory environment and all of your clients are Firewall

Table 14.2 Setup requirements for ISA servers that are configured with NLB.

Program	Requirement
Windows 2000 Advanced Server or Datacenter Server	NLB requires these versions of Windows 2000.
Microsoft Cluster Service	NLB must be installed on the ISA server.
ISA Server	Install with identical configurations, including type and mode of installation.

clients. If any of these elements are missing, however, NLB can provide some of the benefits of an array even when one is not on the network. It's almost as if you are setting up the ISA servers as an array unofficially, because array members would have the same installation and mode automatically. However, if you have the Standard Edition of ISA Server, you cannot create an array. NLB provides fault tolerance for incoming connections when you don't have the software to create an array. Also, even if you have the Enterprise Edition of ISA Server, if you are not using Active Directory, you cannot set up an array. NLB provides an alternative when you have different setups and SecureNAT clients instead of Firewall clients.

Installing NLB

Installing Microsoft's Cluster Server requires some planning and possible network configurations. During the installation, you will be asked to enter an IP address for the cluster that you are creating. This IP address is published to the clients as a single IP address for the cluster. Cluster Server maps this IP address to the IP addresses of the servers that are designated as part of the cluster. In the event of a failure of the one of the servers in a cluster, the client will attempt to reconnect to the cluster's published IP address. Microsoft's Cluster Server will respond to the failure by remapping the published IP address to the IP address of another of the servers in the cluster. The client is reconnected to another machine that can provide the service it was using. The client computer will reconnect without user intervention, and the user is able to continue unaffected by the failure. For more information about Microsoft's Cluster Server, refer to Windows 2000 Advanced Server Help. To install NLB on a Windows 2000 server, complete the following steps:

1. Insert the Windows 2000 Advanced Server or Datacenter Server CD in the CD-ROM drive.

2. Open Control Panel.

3. Double-click Add/Remove Programs.

4. In the Add/Remove Programs dialog box, click the Add/Remove Windows Components button. The Windows Components Wizard will start, giving you a list of optional Windows components.

5. Place a checkmark next to Cluster Service and click Next. Figure 14.6 shows the Windows Components dialog box with the Cluster Service component selected. You will need to have the Windows 2000 Advanced or Datacenter Server CD or connectivity to the installation files.

Note: *If Cluster Service is not listed, you may have Windows 2000 Server installed instead of Windows 2000 Advanced Server or Windows 2000 Datacenter Server.*

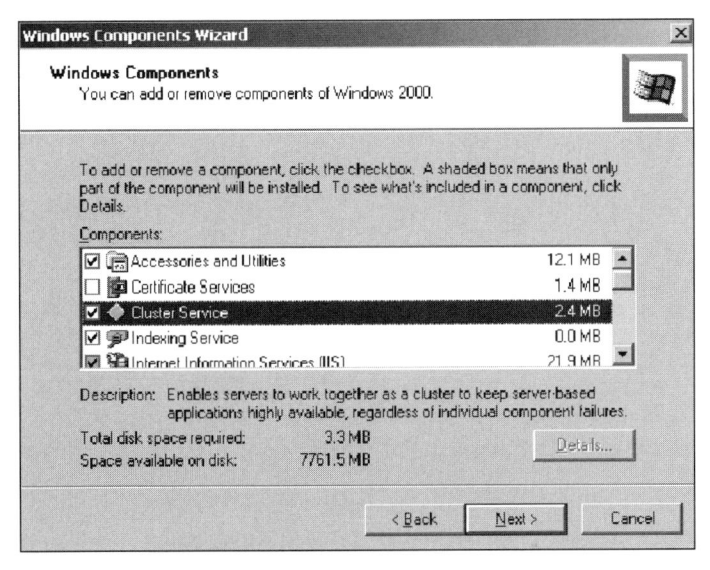

Figure 14.6 The Windows Components dialog box with Cluster Service selected.

6. Whether or not the computer is a member of a domain, a dialog box will appear informing you that all members of a cluster must belong to the same domain. Figure 14.7 shows the information dialog box when the computer is not a member of a domain.

7. Once the Cluster Service components are installed, click Finish.

8. Click OK to close the Add/Remove Programs application.

9. Close Control Panel.

Configuring NLB for Use with ISA Server

Once Network Load Balancing is loaded onto the Windows 2000 server, you must configure it to work with ISA Server. When you create a cluster, you have to configure an IP address for the entire cluster. This IP address is different from the IP addresses for each of the members of the cluster. It is the IP address that users will see when they connect to the cluster. Select a number for each ISA server that

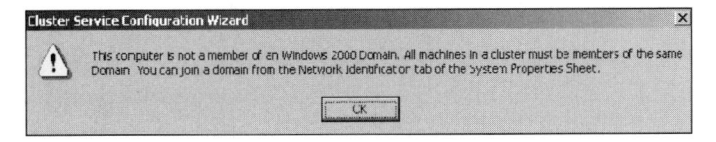

Figure 14.7 A dialog box appears informing you that all members of a cluster must belong to the same domain.

belongs to the cluster. Each priority number will specify which ISA server will take over traffic if another fails. The lower numbers have higher priority. You must configure these settings on the internal network adapter on the ISA server. You can access this dialog box through Network And Dial-Up Connections. To configure NLB for use with ISA Server, complete the following steps:

Note: The settings in this list are specific to the needs of ISA Server. Other applications may need different settings.

1. On the ISA server, click the Start button, point to Settings, and select Network And Dial-Up Connections.

2. Right-click on the internal ISA Adapter and select Properties.

3. Place a checkmark in the Network Load Balancing checkbox and click the Properties button.

4. On the Cluster Parameters page, in the Primary IP Address box, enter the IP address of the Network Load Balancing cluster. This should be the IP address that is referred to in the external DNS host record for the ISA server.

5. Select the Host Parameters tab. Enter the priority number for that particular ISA server.

6. In the Dedicated IP Address box, enter the IP address that identifies this individual ISA server.

7. Click OK to close the Properties dialog box of the ISA server's network adapter.

8. Close Network And Dial-Up Connections.

Repeat these steps on every ISA server that is a part of the NLB cluster.

An Alternative to NLB

If you don't have a great need for fault tolerance and you have more than one ISA server, you might choose a simpler solution than using NLB. For example, if you have two or more standalone ISA servers that are accepting connections from the same network, you might be able to balance the load between them by using the round-robin feature in DNS. This feature does not provide fault tolerance if an ISA server goes down, but it does distribute the requests across available servers.

Round-robin DNS is easy to set up. In the DNS server that clients will use, create a DNS record for each ISA server. The name for each ISA server must be identical, while the IP address should be the IP address of the adapter that users will connect to. The DNS server will recognize that it has records with identical names. When queried about an IP address for that name, the DNS server will evenly rotate which record it will return to the querying client. Although this method is simpler than using NLB, it provides only a load balancing solution.

Because the DNS server will not know when an ISA server fails, it will not be able to provide fault tolerance and redirect clients to a working ISA server. Also as is often the case, the easiest solution does not provide the best results. DNS is not designed to provide load balancing so there is no guarantee that all requests will be evenly balanced.

ISA Server and Terminal Services

You can use Microsoft's Terminal Services to remotely administer ISA Server. Although Terminal Services can have a complicated planning phase and setup for applications, the setup for remote administration is much simpler. To use Terminal Services in this capacity, you will need to load Terminal Server on the ISA server and then enable the client for Terminal Services on the computer that will administer ISA Server. If the remote administration computer is located outside the internal network, you might need to set up a protocol rule allowing Remote Desktop Protocol (RDP) to pass through the ISA server. RDP is used by Terminal Services. ISA Server has a protocol definition for RDP installed by default.

Integrating ISA Server with a Web Server

Most services that ISA Server is supposed to protect should be installed behind it on the local network or on a perimeter network. However, some networks are configured with a Web server installed on the same server as ISA Server. Normally, Web publishing rules would be used to protect a Web server, but when the Web server is installed on the same computer as ISA Server, special configurations have to be made. Two methods are available for handling this situation: One uses Web publishing rules with a bit of extra configuration, and the other uses packet filters.

By default, ISA Server uses TCP port 80 to listen for incoming client requests. Because a Web server, by default, also uses port 80 to listen for incoming client requests, one of these services will need to change its port number. Which one you change depends on whether you want to use a Web publishing rule or packet filters. Use a Web publishing rule to allow ISA Server to continue listening and accepting incoming requests on port 80. Change the Web server to accept incoming requests on a different port. To avoid creating a new port conflict with another service, choose a port number larger than 1023. Create a Web publishing rule that intercepts Web requests and sends them to the port that you configured for the Web server.

As an alternative, you can enable packet filtering for ISA Server and create a packet filter that allows incoming Web requests to connect to port 80. If you want to use ISA Server's Automatic Discovery feature along with this packet filtering solution, configure Automatic Discovery to use port 8080 instead of 80 to listen for client requests. This will avoid another port conflict. If you do not need the Automatic

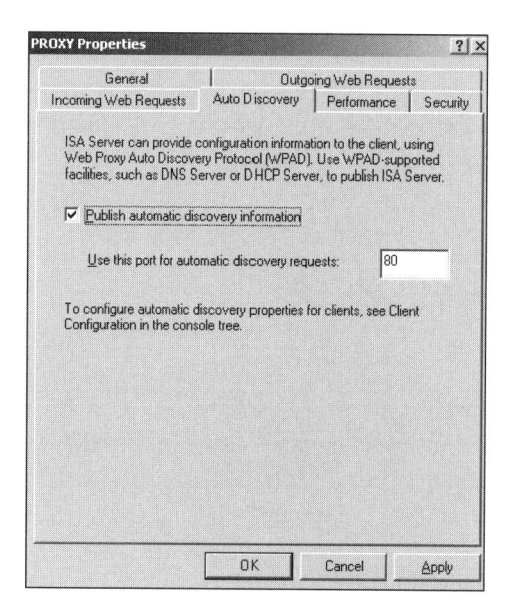

Figure 14.8 To disable the Automatic Discovery feature in ISA Server, go to the propertics of the array or server, select the Auto Discovery tab, and clear the checkmark.

Discovery feature, simply disable it. Figure 14.8 shows the dialog box that disables the Automatic Discovery feature in ISA Server. You can also reconfigure the port number used by AutoDiscovery in this dialog box if you need the feature. To access this dialog box in the ISA Server snap-in, right-click on the server or array, select Properties, and then select the Auto Discovery tab.

Whether you decide to use Web publishing rules or IP packet filters to protect the Web server loaded on the ISA server, you should take additional security precautions as well. When configuring the ISA Server System Security Wizard, make sure you select Secure as the Security level. This setting will provide the most protection for any application installed on the ISA Server, including a Web server.

Chapter Summary

In this chapter, we covered the setup of Web and server publishing rules that allow you to publish services from your internal network out to the Internet. Because some services are more complicated, they require more than one rule or more configurations settings to allow external users to connect to them. ISA Server created wizards and filters to accommodate some of these more complex services so that you can set them up quickly.

With previous versions of Microsoft's Internet security servers, setting up an internal mail server was quite complex. Configurations had to be made in different dialog boxes and on different computers to allow external users to connect to the internal mail server. ISA Server contains a Mail Server Security Wizard and two applications filters that ease this setup and extend its capabilities past that of Proxy Server.

The setup of an email server contains many steps when securing its use through ISA Server. First, you must set up the mail server. Then, you have to configure ISA Server to allow email messages in. ISA Server has a Mail Server Security Wizard that creates server publishing rules for mail servers. You can specify the types of email protocols that you will accept in this wizard. Besides allowing in email, you can also filter the mail and its attachments with the SMTP Filter. The Message Screener add-in to ISA Server must be installed to give ISA Server the ability to filter email and attachments. The SMTP Filter controls how the mail will be filtered and what type of action will be taken on filtered mail and attachments.

Other services that ISA Server and users can benefit from include Cluster Server and Terminal Services. ISA Server can benefit from NLB's load balancing and fault-tolerance services when it cannot be installed into an array. Before installing NLB and integrating it with ISA Server, you need to plan ahead and perform some network configuration. You can use Terminal Services to remotely administer ISA Server. As with NLB and Cluster Server, you must review network design and plan before implementing Terminal Services.

Review Questions

1. What type of rule needs to be set up in ISA Server for it to allow mail services? [Check all correct answers]
   a. Site and content rule
   b. Web publishing rule
   c. Server publishing rule
   d. Protocol rule
   e. Bandwidth rule

2. What component is designed to simplify the setup of an internal mail server on a network with ISA Server?
   a. SMTP Wizard
   b. Mail Server Wizard
   c. RPC Filter
   d. Mail Server Security Wizard

3. What file needs to be configured and placed on an Exchange server when it resides on a network protected by Proxy Server 2.0?

    a. Msiaund.ini

    b. Wspcfg.ini

    c. Mspclnt.ini

    d. Excnfg.ini

4. What is included in the name of a rule created by the wizard used to configure internal mail servers in ISA Server? [Check all correct answers]

    a. The email protocol

    b. The ISA server's IP address

    c. The internal mail server's IP address

    d. Whether the mail server accepts mail from clients or other servers

    e. The schedule used by the rule

    f. The array or server name

5. What port does the SMTP service use by default?

    a. 1755

    b. 25

    c. 80

    d. 8080

    e. 21

6. Email messages using what protocol are allowed through ISA Server by default? [Check all correct answers]

    a. SMTP

    b. POP3

    c. MAPI

    d. None

7. Which email protocols have a predefined packet filter? [Check all correct answers]

    a. SMTP

    b. IMAP4

    c. POP3

    d. MAPI

    e. NNTP

    f. NNTP-S

8. What ISA Server add-in is needed to use the SMTP Filter?
   a. Mail Gatekeeper
   b. POP3 packet filter
   c. Message Screener
   d. H.323 Gatekeeper
   e. None are needed

9. What is the purpose of the SMTP Filter?
   a. Control email connections
   b. Allow email connections
   c. Filter mail content
   d. Allow the administrator to read user's mail

10. When is the SMTPCred.exe tool needed?
    a. Whenever the Message Screener is installed
    b. When the Message Screener is installed locally with ISA Server
    c. When the Message Screener is installed remotely from ISA Server
    d. Only when the Message Screener is installed using an unattended text file

11. What version(s) of Exchange Server use RPCs to communicate? [Check all correct answers]
    a. 5
    b. 5.5
    c. 98
    d. 2000

12. When an SMTP client queries a DNS server for a mail server, what type of record does it ask for?
    a. MAPI
    b. SMTP
    c. A
    d. MX

13. When Exchange is installed on the same computer as ISA Server, what components does ISA Server use to control mail messages?
    a. Mail security rules
    b. Server publishing rules
    c. Packet filters
    d. Protocol rules

14. NLB can be used with what version of Windows 2000? [Check all correct answers]

    a. Professional

    b. Server

    c. Advanced Server

    d. Datacenter Server

15. What service is included in Microsoft Cluster Server? [Check all correct answers]

    a. Cluster Service

    b. Failover service

    c. NLB

    d. Fault Tolerance service

16. What is the prerequisite for an application to work with Microsoft's Cluster Server?

    a. TCP/IP support

    b. RPC support

    c. NetBIOS support

    d. Cluster-awareness

17. Which type of setup for ISA Server benefits the most from NLB? [Check all correct answers]

    a. Standard Edition

    b. Enterprise Edition installed as standalone

    c. Arrays

    d. Cache only

18. What is the maximum number of servers that can be used in a cluster using NLB?

    a. 2

    b. 8

    c. 25

    d. 32

19. What does a user need to do to when connected to an ISA server using NLB if a failure of one of the servers occurs?

    a. Enter the name of the second ISA server.

    b. Enter the IP address of the second ISA server.

    c. Nothing. The connection will fail.

    d. Nothing. The user will automatically be connected to another server.

20. In what application can NLB be configured?

    a. ISA Management

    b. Control Panel

    c. Network And Dial-up Connections

    d. NLB snap-in

21. What can be an alternative to NLB when distributing a load across multiple ISA servers?

    a. The round-robin feature in DNS

    b. A server publishing rule

    c. A packet filter

    d. A protocol rule

22. What is the benefit of implementing the alternative in the previous question?

    a. Automatic failover

    b. Load balancing

    c. Secure publishing

    d. Reverse caching

23. What types of security features in ISA Server can be used when ISA Server and a Web server are installed on the same server? [Check all correct answers]

    a. Web publishing rules

    b. Packet filters

    c. Server publishing rules

    d. Protocol rules

24. What port is used by the AutoDiscovery feature by default?

    a. 1755

    b. 25

    c. 80

    d. 8080

    e. 21

25. What service or protocol uses the port referred to in the previous question by default?

   a. RPC

   b. SMTP

   c. HTTP

   d. FTP

Real-World Projects

Note: This exercise assumes a test Windows 2000 Server with Service Pack 1 as well as Enterprise Edition of ISA Server installed. Read the instructions carefully and do not change the settings on your production machine unless you understand the options presented. If you are unsure about an option, do not make a change and instead read the ISA Server Help files about the option to be installed.

"Joe?" The IT manager stuck her head inside the server room. "We need to talk about an issue."

"What issue?" asked Joe. This did not sound good.

"Well, you know that new feature we just implemented on the Web site?"

"You mean the new feature that allows users to mail comments to the site administrator?" Joe said.

"Yes, that's it. The problem is that some strange individuals are sending…well, let's say questionable…I mean explicit…I mean…" The IT manager trailed off.

"Are you saying the users are sending dirty pictures?" asked Joe.

"Yes, that's it." She looked relieved. "Is there anything we can do about it?"

"Well, there isn't any dirty picture filter, but I believe we can do something about it," said Joe.

"Thanks, Joe," said the IT manager. "This is a bit of an emergency, so could you let me know by lunch what can be done?"

Joe did a little research and decided the best way to tackle the problem was by using the SMTP Filter. However, it did require a substantial amount of setup. He decided to enable and configure the SMTP Filter.

Project 14.1
To enable the SMTP Filter on ISA Server:

1. Open ISA Management.

2. Expand Internet Security And Acceleration Server and then expand Servers And Arrays.

3. Expand the name of the server or array on which you want to enable the SMTP Filter.

4. Expand Extensions and select the Application Filters container.

5. In the details pane, double-click SMTP Filter.

6. In the properties of the SMTP Filter, make sure you have the General tab selected. Click the Enable This Filter checkbox to place a checkmark in it.

7. Click the OK button to close the SMTP Filter Properties sheet.

After Joe enabled the filter, it still had a red arrow icon on it, which indicated it wasn't working.

"It must need to be configured," he thought.

Joe looked in the configuration of the SMTP Filter and discovered that he could filter pictures but that he would need to add specific attachment rules that filtered every graphic type. Just adding all of those would be a pain, and what if he forgot to include a certain graphic type? Then he had what he thought was a rather brilliant idea. He would discard all attachments over one byte in size. This would definitely discard all graphic attachments!

Project 14.2
To configure the SMTP Filter to discard attachments:

1. Open ISA Management.

2. Expand Internet Security And Acceleration Server and then expand Servers And Arrays.

3. Expand the name of the server or array on which you want to configure the SMTP Filter.

4. Expand Extensions and select the Application Filters container.

5. In the details pane, double-click SMTP Filter. The SMTP Filter Properties pages will open.

6. Select the Attachments page.

7. Click the Add button to add a new Attachment rule.

8. In the Mail Attachment Rule dialog box, make sure Enable Attachment Rule is selected.

9. Select Attachment Size Limit (In Bytes).

10. Enter "1" in the input box next to Attachment Size Limit (In Bytes).

11. Select Delete Message as the Action.

12. Click OK.

13. Click OK again to close the SMTP Filter dialog box.

Joe finished configuring the SMTP Filter and saw that the red icon was still on the SMTP Filter. He was missing something. The filter was configured, but for some reason, it still did not work. Because he wanted to filter attachments, the Message Screener was also required. It was an ISA Server add-in that had not yet been installed.

Project 14.3

To install the Message Screener Add-in on ISA Server:

1. Open Control Panel.

2. Double-click Add/Remove Programs.

3. Make sure you are in the Change Or Remove Programs dialog box and select Internet Security And Acceleration Server. Click the Change button.

4. In the Welcome To ISA Server Setup dialog box, click the Add/Remove button.

5. Select Add-In Services and click the Change Option button.

6. Place a checkmark next to Message Screener and click OK.

7. Click the Continue button to install this option. Setup will update ISA Server.

8. A dialog box will appear informing you that ISA Server has been updated successfully. Click OK.

9. Click OK to close the Add/Remove application.

10. Close Control Panel.

After installing the Message Screener, Joe checked the SMTP Filter in ISA Management. Finally, the red icon was gone. He went to tell the IT manager that the questionable attachments should not show up again.

CHAPTER FIFTEEN

Troubleshooting and Reporting

After completing this chapter, you will be able to:

✓ Describe the troubleshooting guidelines

✓ Explain the Windows 2000 basic troubleshooting process

✓ Configure Internet Explorer 5

✓ Use troubleshooting resources

✓ Understand the ISA Server troubleshooting process

✓ Employ ISA Server reporting functions

✓ Create reports

✓ Enable logging

✓ Enable the reporting mechanism

✓ Enable daily and monthly report summaries

✓ Create a scheduled report job

✓ Configure a report job period

✓ Configure a report job schedule

✓ View a report

✓ Specify user credentials for a report job

✓ Configure the location of reports

✓ Save reports as Web pages

✓ Delete a report

✓ Sort report data

As an ISA administrator, you will undoubtedly face situations in which things are not working properly. Perhaps what you've set up just does not work as it is supposed to. Or maybe things have been working properly, but they suddenly stopped working this morning. You are responsible for anything that happens to your network, and you need to have troubleshooting skills to determine what is going on. Furthermore, you may have to report to your boss what you've found through troubleshooting. In this chapter, we will focus on troubleshooting basic problems you are likely to face, and we'll show you how to create reports for your findings.

Troubleshooting Guidelines

Several guidelines exist for troubleshooting issues that may confront you in your environment. Some of them may seem like common sense, but they are the small things that are most easily overlooked. Here is a list of things you should check:

- Was everything working in the first place? If not, what is the new problem? If everything was working, what has changed?

- Is the hardware properly built to support the server role you are trying to assign? Do you have the proper hardware components, such as CPUs, memory, hard disks, SCSI cards, LAN cards, and so on? Does the system have the power source, and is the system powered up?

- Is the physical network connection properly in place? Is the network cable properly connected to your system's network card and the network patch panel? If the activity link light does not show up on the LAN card or the network patch panel, can the network cable be replaced so that the activity link light is solidly lit? Are the routers (default gateways) properly working? (You may need to ask the folks on your network team.)

- Is the system on the network able to communicate with other hosts on the same subnet? Is the system able to communicate with the default gateway? Is the system able to communicate with other hosts on the remote subnet?

- Is the proper name resolution mechanism in place, such as DNS or WINS? Or do you need to specify an IP address to allow access to other hosts?

- If your clients are DHCP clients, is the DHCP server configured correctly, and is it up and running? Are your clients getting correct IP addresses and other information, such as subnet mask, default gateway, and DNS addresses?

- Is everything documented and accessible in case you need that information in the future?

These are things you can look into. However, let's say the server just suddenly stops working. Now what? You should consider the following:

➤ Are there any circumstances that you did not have any control over, such as power outages, network outages, application server outages, and so on? If yes, are they now fixed? (You may need to talk with the appropriate department responsible for these events.)

➤ Has an administrator changed a setting on the system? If so, what is the new setting and has it been documented? If the change caused something not to work, can you roll the change back so that you can return to a stable working environment?

➤ Have any users mistakenly or accidentally changed a setting on the system?

If the above situations do not apply, do you have resources to explore the problem further—such as administrators, books, vendor technical support, and other resources—in a timely manner?

Once everything is fixed, you should also document the possible cause, how to fix it, and how to prevent it in the future. A good administrator does not make the same mistakes twice and keeps excellent documentation explaining what to do in case of problems.

Windows 2000 Basic Troubleshooting

Before we get into ISA Server-specific troubleshooting, we will go through some Windows 2000 basic troubleshooting that administrators must perform before deciding that a problem is an ISA Server-specific issue. This section will be useful for any server, such as a Web server, SQL server, Exchange server, and even a normal Windows 2000 file server.

Windows 2000 provides a native utility called Event Viewer. Event Viewer captures many system activities, such as a system reboot, service failures, and other events, and you can view what has been happening on the system you are trying to troubleshoot. Let's take, for example, a reboot of a system. In many cases, applications running on the system are affected by a reboot. When rebooting a SQL server or Exchange server, you may have to stop SQL or Exchange services on the system before the reboot so that you can make sure all the data transactions are completed and written to the hard disk. Stopping SQL or Exchange services before a reboot will also make the reboot faster because the shutdown process tries to stop these services anyway. But you have a worse scenario if someone reboots the server accidentally or the system hangs for some reason (possibly application errors) and needs to be soft-rebooted. (The soft reboot usually requires somebody to push the reset button on the system, but the hard reboot requires the system to be powered down and back up.) The server comes up fine, it seems, but you do not know if the application services have started correctly. Application owners normally have to log onto the system and make sure their applications are working correctly. At this point, however, you can do some basic troubleshooting, and this is where Event Viewer comes in.

You can see Event Viewer in several different ways, but the easiest is to select Start | Run and enter "eventvwr". Another way to access Event Viewer is to go to Start | Programs | Administrative Tools | Event Viewer, or you can access Event Viewer from the Computer Management MMC snap-in. To access the Computer Management MMC snap-in, right-click on the My Computer icon on the desktop and click Manage. In the Computer Management MMC, expand System Tools in the left pane if it has not been already expanded, and expand Event Viewer.

When you access Event Viewer, you typically have three logs listed: the Application log, the Security log, and the System log. Depending on the service that the system provides, such as a domain controller role or a DNS server role, you may see additional logs, but for the discussion of basic Windows 2000 troubleshooting, the Application log, Security log, and System log are enough. In a nutshell, the Application log keeps track of application-related events. The Security log will log any auditing information if the security log is configured. The System log will log system- and service-related information and errors. If you have errors related to ISA Server, you would probably find most of them in the Application log. If you have auditing turned on for some elements, such as user logon or system reboot, you would find them in the Security log. Figure 15.1 shows Event Viewer.

Select which log you want to see by clicking the appropriate log on the left pane. For instance, you can click on the System log in the left pane, and you will see all the events recorded in the right pane. Often you will see a lot of events recorded in both the Application and System logs, but you will not see any events in the Security log unless you have specifically turned on the auditing feature. If you double-click one of the events on the right pane, you will see something like Figure 15.2.

As you can see in Figure 15.2, you can get a lot of information. You see the date and time of the event recorded. You want to find out exactly when the event you are looking for happened. Another important bit of information here is the Event ID. It is usually a four-digit number that does not make sense if you just look at it. The way to find out what the Event ID is usually involves going to the **http://support.microsoft.com** site or using the Microsoft Knowledge Base CD, which is a part of Microsoft TechNet distribution. If you are lucky, by searching the Event ID, you may be able to find out some information about the event. Unfortunately, in some cases you cannot find the information from the Microsoft site just mentioned. In this case, you should try searches based on key words from the Event

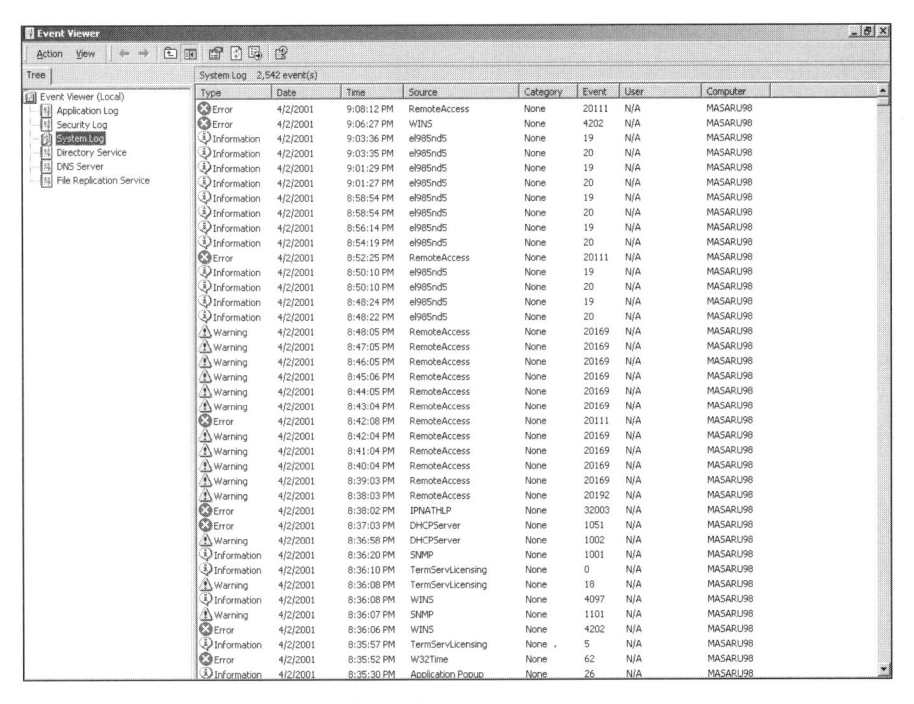

Figure 15.1 The Event Viewer MMC snap-in.

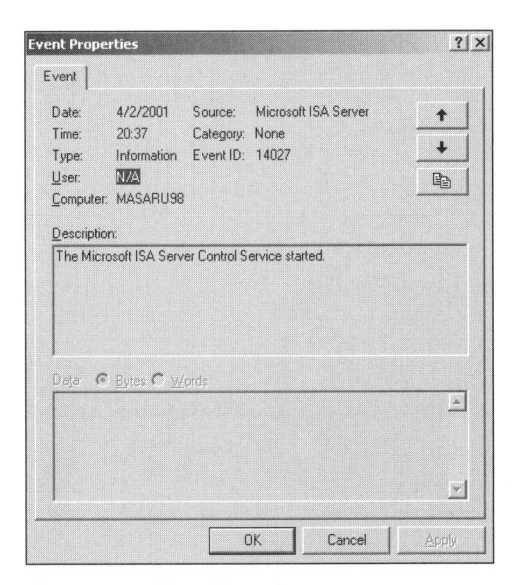

Figure 15.2 Event Properties.

Viewer event, which may help the support search engine find related information. So, before going to the site, take a close look at the description on the event. It usually gives you a pretty good idea of what the event is all about.

Another good thing about Event Viewer is that you can connect to a remote system to see the remote system's events as long as you have proper permissions to it. Although you have to be a member of the Administrators group to see Security log events, you can see both Application log and System log events with minimal permissions. In this way, you do not have to be logged onto a remote system locally all the time. The Windows 2000 Event Viewer snap-in lets you connect not only to Windows 2000 systems but to Windows NT 4 systems as well. Therefore, if you have a single MMC, with several Event Viewer snap-ins, you could possibly be viewing events on many systems physically located in Europe and Asia Pacific countries, right from your workstation that is physically located in the United States! You may have ISA servers in different geographical regions, and if you need to compare events recorded in these systems, being able to load several Event Viewers from different systems can be quite powerful for system administrators. Windows NT 4 Event Viewers lacked the configuration to load multiple Event Viewers on one screen, and it was very hard to see several Event Viewers at once, although you were able to access a remote system's Event Viewer. Figure 15.3 shows how to connect to a remote system.

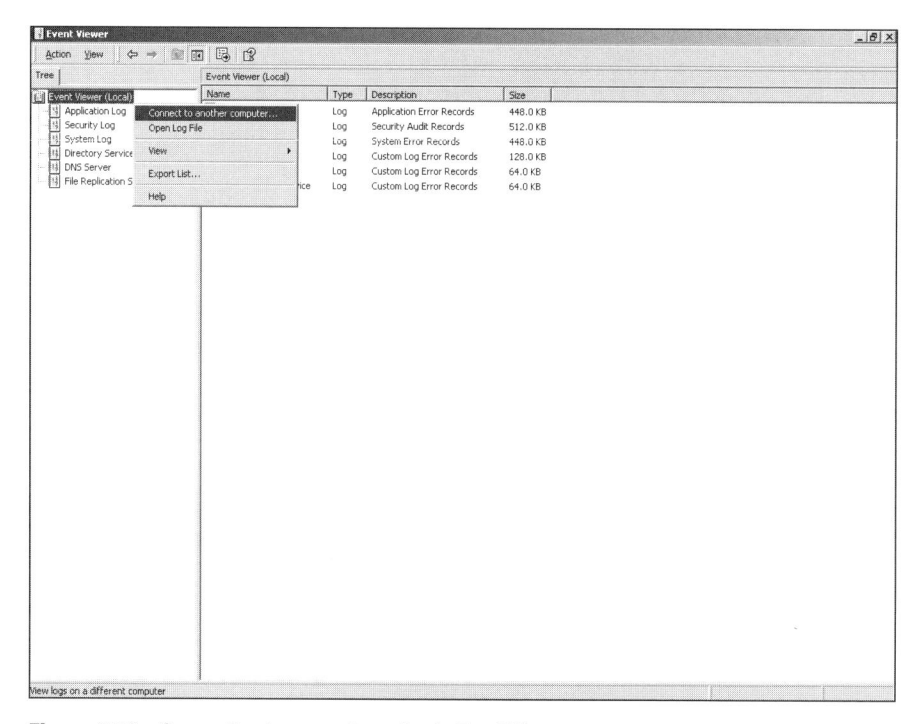

Figure 15.3 Connecting to a remote system's Event Viewer.

To access several Event Viewers in a single MMC snap-in, take the following steps:

1. Go to Start|Run and enter "mmc". Click OK.

2. The command in Step 1 will bring up the blank MMC window. Click the Console menu at the top of the window, which is usually titled Console1, and select the Add/Remove snap-in menu. You can also invoke the same command by pressing Ctrl+M.

3. The Add/Remove window comes up. Click Add.

4. The Add Standalone snap-in window opens. Click on Event Viewer, and then click Add.

5. The Select Computer window comes up. If you are logged on locally to the system for which you are trying see Event Viewer, leave the default selection of Local Computer and click Finish. If you are trying to see Event Viewer for a remote system, select Another Computer and enter the remote system name or its IP address. You can also click Browse to select a remote system. Once you click Finish, the Event Viewer icon with either Local or the system name appears in the Add/Remote snap-in window.

6. Add as many systems as you need by repeating Steps 3 through 5, and click Close on the Add Standalone snap-in window when you are all done.

7. Click OK in the Add/Remove window.

8. In the Console Root window, you will see the Event Viewers you just have added.

You will hear about other problems from your clients. In many cases, the conversation goes something like this: "Hi, this is technical support. What can I do for you?" "Well, I am trying to browse the Web site, but I am not able to. Can you fix it?" Client disconnections from the network can be caused by many different things, including underlying network problems. It is still a good idea to go through the list of things mentioned in the guidelines section to make sure you have the network cable connected to your system and so on, but from the workstation that is having problems, you can do TCP/IP connectivity testing. We will use a command, **PING**, that was introduced in the Chapter 3. The order specified here is not the same as what Microsoft recommends, but it is the order that most technical support people perform to reduce the troubleshooting time. These steps assume that things worked fine the previous day but now the clients are complaining about disconnections. Take the following steps to see if you have TCP/IP connectivity working properly:

1. Go to Start|Run and enter "cmd". This will display a command prompt. You can also select Start|Programs|Accessories|Command Prompt.

2. Enter **ping** *system name*. To access a host named dontpingme, you would enter the command **ping dontpingme**. If the host is on the network, the name-resolution mechanism is functioning, and the host is reachable, you would get replies back from the host.

3. If the host replies, you are in good shape. But if not, you start troubleshooting.

4. Ping the host with its IP address. This will verify that the name-resolution issue isn't preventing your connection. If you get a reply, then look for a name-resolution issue to be fixed, which normally requires the network team to be involved. If you get no replies, go to the next step.

5. Ping the remote host's side of the gateway. This is typically the router IP address. If you know the host name assigned for the other side of the gateway, you can also try it. The basic idea here is that if you can access the remote host side of the gateway, you can determine that the connectivity issue lies between the other side of the router and the remote hosts. Routers usually have at least two IP addresses assigned—one for the subnet your workstation is on, and another for the subnet remote hosts are on. If you don't get ping replies from the other side of the gateway, then go to the next step.

6. Ping your side of the gateway. If you don't get any replies, then the network problem is local. Your subnet has some problems. If you do get replies, then it is possible that the router has not been configured correctly to route packets, or the router is in fact not functioning properly. (Ask the network team nicely to replace it in that case, but you would need to prove that many of your clients on your subnet are experiencing the same problems.)

7. If you can ping your side of the gateway, you should be able to ping your neighbors in your subnet. If you cannot ping your neighbors, then you need to start checking your local system.

8. Ping your IP address and the loopback IP address, 127.0.0.1. In most cases, you will get replies from these IP addresses. If you don't get replies from your IP addresses, check your IP address configuration. If you don't get replies from 127.0.0.1, you will need to make sure the TCP/IP protocol is installed correctly. If not, reinstall the TCP/IP protocol.

IE5 Configuration

When clients are connecting to the ISA server to utilize Web Proxy functionality, one of the things that could cause their browser not to work is the Web Proxy configuration. In Internet Explorer, you can reconfigure the proxy setting by going to Tools|Internet Options, clicking the Connection tab, and then clicking the LAN settings. Figure 15.4 shows Local Area Network (LAN) Settings.

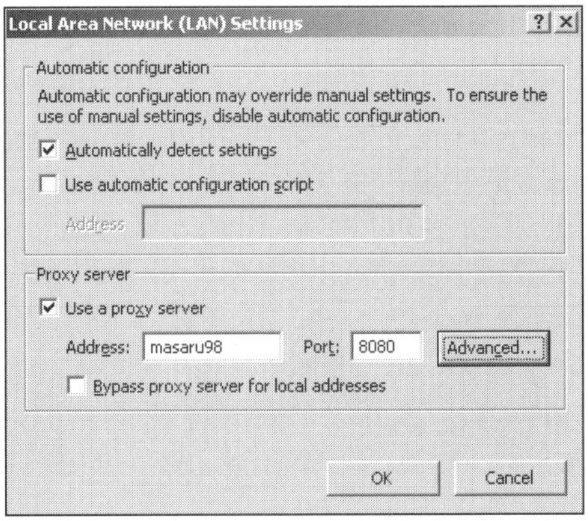

Figure 15.4 LAN Settings.

The bottom half of the figure is the proxy setting you need to provide. Click the Use A Proxy Server checkbox and enter either the proxy server (or the ISA server installed in Cache or Integrated mode) hostname or its IP address. Specify the port number the proxy server uses. ISA Server uses port 8080 as the default. You can also click Bypass Proxy Server For Local Address so that when the internal Web servers or FTP servers are accessed, the proxy server's caching is not in effect. If you click the Advanced button, it will bring up the proxy settings screen, and you can configure which proxy server's IP address to use for various protocols, such as HTTP, Secure, FTP, Gopher, and Socks. Although you can specify individual IP address, in most cases you would be going through the same proxy server address. If you need to access non-default port numbers for these protocols on the remote server, enter them in the proxy settings screen. If the configured port numbers on your system differ from those on the proxy server, you will not be able to successfully communicate with the protocol. An option is available that you can enable to make one proxy server IP address effective for all the protocols except Socks. Also, you can specify IP addresses as exceptions so that when accessing these IP addresses you specify as exceptions, browser will not go through the proxy server. When you are accessing internal Web or FTP servers, this is where you enter their IP addresses. You can use a wildcard (*) to specify multiple IP addresses. For instance, you can use 192.* to include all the servers using IP addresses that start with 192 in the first octet. If you need to add more than one subnet, then you can use a semicolon to separate entries, as in 192.*;10.*.

Troubleshooting Resources

It is nearly impossible to remember all the aspects of Windows 2000—you'd have to absorb too much information. What is more important than memorizing everything about Windows 2000 is where to go for help so that you can fix your problem. The following list shows some of the help you can count on in case you have no idea what is going on:

➤ *Microsoft TechNet*—Microsoft TechNet is a yearly subscription program that Microsoft offers to the public. You pay a yearly membership fee of around $300 as of this writing, and Microsoft will send you CDs that contain service packs, resource kits, evaluation programs, and many other programs. Every month, Microsoft will also send you updated CDs if available. The CDs titled Microsoft Knowledge Base contain the CD version of the support database that you can query, and it provides tons of information. The Web version can be accessed at **http://support.microsoft.com**.

➤ *Windows 2000 and ISA Server Online Help*—Windows 2000 and ISA Server Online Help manuals are readily available by pressing the F1 key on the keyboard. You can search on your problem, and you may be able to find the answers you need.

➤ *Your colleagues*—The colleagues in your office could also help you. You can find experienced administrators out in the field who have seen the exact problem you are facing. Also, try to attend some of the user groups in your area. For example, a user group called the Rocky Mountain Windows Technology User Group (**www.rmwtug.org**) has a monthly meeting both in Denver and Colorado Springs, and this is where many experts on Windows NT and Windows 2000 come in. It is open to public, and many students who are trying to become MCSEs also attend it. The user group usually gives you time to ask people in the group to share issues they are facing in their work environment. In many cases, you can get pretty good advice on what you should do next. You should be able to find a user group in your area.

➤ *Your instructors*—You may have taken an instructor-led training class before, and the instructors are supposed to be familiar with the subject. Many Microsoft Certified Trainers (MCTs) are usually MCSEs or MCSDs who have experience using various Microsoft and other products. You would go to your instructors for help as the last resort because they are typically busy, but they may be able to solve your issues. If not, they will probably be able to find someone who would be able to help. Therefore, when you take instructor-led training classes, make sure you get the instructor's contact information, such as email address and phone number. That could save you some time in the near future.

➤ *Exam Cram and Exam Prep publications*—Coriolis' Exam Cram and Exam Prep publications cover Microsoft and other products extensively. You can refer to them to find answers.

➤ *Other Web sites and newsgroups*—Other Web sites and newsgroups are available that you can search to obtain information about the issues you are facing.

ISA Server Troubleshooting

Now we will go through a bit more specific ISA Server troubleshooting. In general, when deploying ISA servers in your environment, issues you would face seem to be related to access policies, authentication, caching, clieZt connections, dial-up entries, logging, and ISA Server services.

You are probably familiar with troubleshooting in some of these categories. You never know when your clients will notice issues you should be aware of. We will go through some of the main problems you may face. Keep in mind that issues described in each category are the main ones you will likely see in your network environment, and you will need to use your own expertise to solve various issues. Before you do anything that changes the ISA server configuration, take a look at Event Viewer to see if you can get any insights from it.

Resolving Issues with Access Policies

In Chapter 6, we discussed access policies. Access policies consist of site and content rules, protocol rules, and IP packet filters. You use site and content rules to determine if and when users or client address sets can access content on specific destination sets. For example, you could create a site and content rule to deny access to **private.coriolis.com**. Protocol rules are used to determine which protocols clients can use to access the Internet. Finally, IP packet filters allow you to intercept and either allow or block packets destined for specific computers on your corporate network.

In a nutshell, an access policy defines who can access what. Below are some likely scenarios you could face:

➤ When you are initially setting up the ISA server and testing it, one of the issues that you will likely face is that clients cannot access external Web sites with their browser. An example is the 502 proxy error. This could happen any time, but it most likely would occur right after you set up the ISA server on your network. After you notify your clients that they can access the Internet, you get a call from someone saying, "I want to check my stock prices and read newspapers on the Internet, but I can't. What's going on? You told me I could access my sites through the ISA server!" Proxy Server 2.0 allowed all the communication to or from the Internet by default when it is initially set up. ISA Server, however, does not initially allow any communication to or from the Internet; in fact any communication not specifically allowed by the access policy will be denied. Furthermore, you may get calls from clients stating that they cannot use Network News Transfer Protocol (NNTP), Post Office Protocol 3 (POP3), or RealAudio. To fix this issue of not being able to communicate with the outside world, complete the following steps: Create protocol rules that allow specific users to use the protocols. Popular Web protocols are HTTP, HTTPS, and FTP. Then, create site and content rules that allow users access to particular sites, such as **www.coriolis.com**, using the protocols specified by the protocol rules. See Chapter 6 to learn how to create protocol rules. You should also check to make sure packet filtering is not disallowing packets that should be allowed. If connections were working correctly yesterday and they do not work this morning, the client browser settings or an ISA server setting might have changed. Check the browser settings of the client to ensure that the proxy port is specified correctly. The default port for ISA Server is 8080. If you changed the port number for administrative reasons, perhaps you forgot to tell clients to change it, or perhaps the clients simply failed to change it.

➤ Suppose you need to enable a protocol rule and also disable a protocol rule. Then, after you disable the protocol rule, you find that clients are still able to use the protocol allowed by the rule. Why? When you disable a protocol rule, client sessions that have existed before are not closed, although new sessions will not be opened. For example, if a client has been using a Net2Phone protocol with configured rules, the session will be kept even after you disable the protocol rule allowing the access. To fix this issue, you must disconnect the client sessions. This also means that clients will need to reestablish their connections using the protocol that was just reconfigured.

To disconnect a client session, take the following steps:

1. Open the ISA Management MMC by clicking Start|Programs|Microsoft ISA Server|ISA Management.

2. Check the View menu in the ISA Management to make sure that the Advanced option is enabled.

3. Expand Servers And Arrays, the name of the array, and Monitoring.

4. Select the Sessions container.

5. In the details pane, right-click the session you want to disconnect, and then click Stop.

Resolving Issues with Authentication

Before you read this section, you may want to reread Chapter 7 so that you are not missing any small basics about authentication. In any case, you, or perhaps application developers at your company, might want to create Web sites that require some sort of authentication because they contain sensitive information. This capability is not restricted to Web sites but can also be extended to other applications that can use ISA Server's functionalities. Successful authentication requires configuring some settings. (See Chapter 7 for more information.) The main issue you face involves the client-side browser—for example, if the client is using Netscape.

Suppose you set up the NTFS permissions on a Web server so that certain people with proper credentials can access a particular folder of the Web site. In this case, users will be prompted to provide credentials when they access Web objects such as a Web page in the NTFS-protected subfolder. This is where anonymous users can run into problems with not having enough permissions to get access to certain resources on a Web site. Often you will not hear problems from any users of Internet Explorer 3 and above. You can, however, hear complaints from Netscape users stating that they cannot successfully access the Web site. The issue here is that ISA Server may have been configured to accept only Windows Integrated authentication. In this authentication mode, only NT Challenge and Response authentication is accepted. With this authentication, the user ID and password are encrypted in a way that only Windows platform clients (most of them, anyway) can understand. This authentication method is supported under Internet Explorer 3.0 or later, and old Netscape browsers, such as version 3, do not support credentials data through the NT Challenge and Response authentication. The latest version of the Netscape browser (version 5+) seems to support the NT Challenge and Response authentication.

To fix this issue, you can configure ISA Server to require other authentication methods, including Basic or Digest. Basic authentication sends and receives user information—such as the user ID and password—as text characters that are encoded but not encrypted. Digest authentication is similar to Basic authentication, but it protects the authentication credentials through a one-way encryption process called hashing. The result of this process is called a hash or message digest, and you cannot decipher the original text from the hash. The hashing process adds information to the password before hashing so that nobody can capture the password hash and use it to impersonate the true user. When you're experiencing authentication problems, checking the method of authentication and changing to one that all of your browsers can use may solve the problem.

Resolving Issues with Caching

When an ISA server is deployed in your environment in the Cache or Integrated mode, and the caching on the ISA server does not work, you need to troubleshoot the situation. This should not happen often; after all, what is the point of deploying ISA Server if it does not do what it is supposed to? We will look at two cases you want to watch out for.

Clients call you one day complaining that the Web access seems to be extremely slow. Every time they access a Web site, it takes a while. When the same client revisits the same Web site, it takes about the same time to get the Web page. You try it by yourself, and you notice the slowness of accessing Web sites as well. You suspect maybe the Web Proxy service is hung, and you try to restart the service to see if it clears the problem. However, the Web Proxy service won't start because you have a corrupted cache contents file.

Whenever the cache contents file becomes corrupted, the Web Proxy service will not be able to start. You should take a look at Event Viewer to see if you have any useful information, which may give you some ideas of what is going on. If you do not see anything useful in Event Viewer, you can try to delete all the cache contents files in the cache manually to see if that helps you restart the Web Proxy service. You can also reconfigure the drives allocated for caching. For each NTFS drive where you have the cache set up, you'll see a folder called urlcache on the root of the drive. In this folder, you'll see a subfolder called dir1 and the dir1.cdat file. All the cached contents will be stored in the dir1 folder. The dir1.cdat folder is the configuration file that ISA Server maintains so that it can find the cached contents in a timely manner. You probably won't be able to determine whether the cached contents in the dir1 folder are corrupted or the dir1.cdat file is corrupted, so your best bet is to delete all the cache contents in the dir1 folder. If you are lucky, you might be able to restart the Web Proxy service. If not, try deleting the dir1.cdat file. This file is the configuration file for caching, however, and deleting it will cause the configuration to be lost. Therefore, if the first step does not work, you might just try to reconfigure the drives allocated for caching. This process basically clears the cache contents and the cache configuration file, and Internet object caching will start from scratch. When these processes are executed, as the cache clears, users might experience some performance degradation until the cache is filled. It is, however, much better than not being able to provide caching functionality to end users.

Now we'll look at the second scenario. You get calls from clients saying every time they access the secure Web sites starting with HTTPS, the connections seem to be slow, although all other Web sites with HTTP can be accessed faster. Clients ask you to fix this problem. This situation happens because ISA Server caches only items that meet the caching criteria defined. For example, if an Internet site uses Secure Socket Layer (SSL), it is normally a good idea not to cache contents from the site because its data may be sensitive, such as a credit card number or social security number. To solve this issue, you need to decide which contents to cache and configure the contents to cache accordingly. When clients access objects that are cached, network performance improves because the objects are retrieved from the ISA Server cache rather than from the Internet. If your clients are commonly accessing objects that are not cached, however, you might not perceive improved performance.

Resolving Issues with Client Connections

When things are not working well on an ISA server you have deployed, you may get a lot of calls from your clients telling you what's wrong on the ISA server. Client connections are the major issues you will be facing as an ISA server administrator.

Let's suppose you have a server that is functioning as a Web server and FTP server using IIS 5. You decided to install the ISA server in the Caching mode, and when the installation completes, none of the clients are able to access the Web sites on this system, although they are able to access the FTP sites. What could be causing the problem? You remember that you have modified the default settings for the Web server, but you don't recall which settings you have changed. This issue could be very similar to a hardware conflict. Perhaps two different hardware devices are set up to use the same Interrupt Request Queue (IRQ) or memory ranges. When this happens, these devices do not function. The same might be true for a port; perhaps an allocation conflict exists. More than one service on the ISA server might be trying to bind with a specific port on the external interface, which could include the ISA server itself. For example, when the ISA server is installed, it uses port 8080. It is, however, possible that some other service, such as the HTTP service, uses port 8080 (HTTP uses the port 80 by default). Or the FTP service (which uses port 21 by default) has somehow been modified so that it uses port 8080. At this point, you would have two or possibly more services trying to use the same port, and therefore, none of them would function. You could try a couple of things to address the problem. First, bind the other services to the internal interface so that the ISA server listens only to the external interface. The external interface should not have any other services bound because it is visible from the Internet. Second, Microsoft recommends that you do not run additional services on your primary firewall, which could be the ISA server, because the primary firewall could be attacked by hackers. You should install the other servers behind the ISA server computer whenever possible.

In another scenario, you have a Windows 2000 Server that has Internet Connection Sharing (ICS) configured. It has been working wonderfully. You deploy ISA Server on the same system that has ICS, and now ICS does not work. Why? ICS is normally used in a small environment to share public IP addresses. It works well as long as you do not add any other application that provides functions similar to it. In this case, the application is the ISA server. Unfortunately, ICS does not run if ISA Server is installed on the same system. You would probably want to use ISA Server rather than ICS because it will handle more users and provide more services. To fix this issue, you need to disable ICS and configure clients to use ISA Server, or you can uninstall ISA Server and stick with ICS.

Resolving Dial-up Entries Issues

This section covers ISA Server's dial-up functionality issues. If the ISA server is configured to dial up to an ISP to perform scheduled content downloading, you need to ensure dial-up works properly.

Suppose you have an ISA server on which you want to set up the Scheduled Content Download function. You think you have configured everything correctly.

The Scheduled Content Download is supposed to dial out to the Internet at 11 P.M. every night to download Internet objects. Because you don't want to stay at the office until 11 P.M., you configured the ISA server to dial out to the Internet at 11 A.M. instead for testing. Well, 11 A.M. comes and goes, but for some reason, the ISA server does not dial out to the Internet. You manually invoke the dial-out, and it works fine. What could be causing the auto-dial to fail? This situation happens if you have specified credentials correctly for the network dial-up connection but not for the dial-up entry in the ISA Management. If this is the case, only the manual dial-out will work. To fix this issue, you can reconfigure the credentials used by the dial-up entry in ISA Server. Another possible cause is that the ISA server computer does not have proper permissions to use the dial-up connection. In this case, the dial-up connection fails. To fix this issue, you need to reconfigure the dial-up connection and allow everyone to use the connection.

In another scenario, suppose you have an ISA server that is configured to dial out to the Internet when necessary. You have just finished setting up the modem, and automatic dial-out works fine. You have noticed that even though no dialing activity is occurring, the dial-up connection never hangs up, and this is using the phone line unnecessarily. What is causing this problem? This situation happens when a client request is made and ISA Server sends name-resolution requests to both the internal DNS server and an external (Internet) DNS server, even if it is a name-resolution request for a system on the local network. Keep in mind that Microsoft recommends configuring ISA Server to use only internal DNS servers and configuring the internal DNS server to forward unresolved requests to an external DNS. To fix this issue, you need the internal DNS server configured as a client of ISA Server, and you should configure it to forward unresolved requests to an external DNS. Be consistent on this configuration model for all the ISA servers in your network to make it easier for you to troubleshoot similar dial-up problems.

Resolving Issues with Logging

Logging provides a method of keeping track of what is happening on the ISA server. You can refer to the log file to find details, but if the log files do not log the information that you are looking for, they can be totally useless. IIS lets clients access the Web server using the Internet guest user account, IUSR_ComputerName, which is created by default when IIS is installed. This account is used to allow anonymous connections. Anonymous connections can cause problems when logging ISA Server activity.

Let's say you have a Web server that requires authentication. When a user accesses a particular subfolder of the Web server, the user is required to enter his or her credentials. Everything seems to be working fine. A day after you configured the authentication on the Web server, you are trying to find out who accessed the Web site with credentials. Unfortunately, however, the log file is missing critical information about users, such as their username. This situation could happen because client access might be anonymous, which means clients are not actually getting authenticated. In this situation, individual client access information is not logged in the log file. ISA Server does not always require that clients authenticate themselves by default. If anonymous access fails, the ISA server asks for a username and password for authentication of the user. This happens because the Web server does not have the default authentication method configured, and only anonymous access has been enabled. To fix this issue, the incoming and outgoing Web request properties need to be configured. You can make ISA Server always require that Web Proxy clients authenticate themselves using Basic authentication, Windows Integrated authentication, or Digest authentication.

Resolving Issues with Services

When ISA Server services are not running, ISA Server will not function as expected. This needs to be corrected right away. Once the installation of ISA Server is fully completed, you are normally able to stop or start services without problems. You may, however, confront some issues while installing ISA Server.

For example, let's suppose you are trying to install ISA Server. The installation looks like it completed successfully, but you get a message in Event Viewer stating that an ISA Server service did not start. What have you done wrong? You must complete several steps before installing ISA Server—forgetting any of these steps can cause this error. These steps are outlined in Chapter 2. You could also get this error message if the local address table (LAT) is not configured correctly and does not include the internal network adapter IP address that communicates with Windows 2000 Active Directory. In this case, the ISA Server services are not able to start. See Chapter 2 for more information. To add the appropriate entries to the LAT, follow these steps:

1. Stop ISA Server services and packet filtering.

2. Reconfigure the LAT. You are not able to run ISA Management because the ISA Server services have stopped, so you will have to configure the LAT using the ISA Server Administration COM objects. For more information, see "Constructing the Local Address Table" in the ISA Server Software Development Kit.

3. Reboot the computer.

Reporting

Another useful functionality of ISA Server is its reporting capability. ISA Server's report provides a summary and analysis of the communication patterns that ISA Server has been dealing with. Because the reporting functionality is built into ISA Server, you do not need to write Structured Query Language (SQL) queries or custom scripts. For your convenience, you can even schedule ISA Server to create reports every once in a while. If you plan to analyze reports at a later time, you can save them to a folder you specify on the ISA server.

Creating Reports

This section will go through the steps for creating a report. Follow these steps in the order given to create a successful report. To create and view a report:

1. Enable logging for the relevant ISA Server components. Although it is possible to create the report when logging is disabled, the reports will not contain any helpful, current information. To enable logging for a specific service:

   a. Open the ISA Management MMC by clicking Start|Programs |Microsoft ISA Server|ISA Management.

   b. Expand Servers And Arrays, the name of the array, and Monitoring Configuration. Then click Logs.

   c. In the right pane, right-click the applicable service, and then click Properties. By default, you will see three service logs: Packet Filters, ISA Server Firewall Service, and ISA Server Web Proxy Service.

   d. On the Log tab, make sure the Enable Logging For This Service checkbox is selected. It is selected by default.

   e. Click OK.

2. Enable the reporting mechanism. This option must be enabled in order for you to create reports. See the section "Configuring Reports" later in this chapter for more details. To enable reports, take the following steps:

   a. Open the ISA Management MMC by clicking Start|Programs|Microsoft ISA Server|ISA Management.

   b. Expand Servers And Arrays, the name of the array, and Monitoring Configuration.

   c. Right-click on Report Jobs, and then click Properties.

   d. On the General tab, select the Enable Reports checkbox.

   e. Click OK.

3. Specify that reports be created based on daily or monthly data. When you enable the summary process, the daily summary process runs every day at 12:30 A.M., no matter when you have scheduled reports. The monthly summary process combines all the daily databases into a single monthly summary. The process collates all the logs available on all the servers in the array. If a daily summary is missing, then the monthly summary process checks the logs to see if the information is available from the logs. If the information is not available, the monthly summary process generates an error. To enable and configure a report summary, take the following steps:

a. Open the ISA Management MMC by clicking Start | Programs | Microsoft ISA Server | ISA Management.

b. Expand Servers And Arrays, the name of the array, and Monitoring Configuration.

c. Right-click Report Jobs, and then click Properties.

d. On the Log Summaries tab, make sure the Enable Daily And Monthly Summaries checkbox is selected. It is selected by default.

e. Under Number Of Summaries saved, in Daily Summaries enter the number of daily summaries to save. The default value is 35. This means that at least 35 daily summaries need to be saved to create an average daily summary.

f. In Monthly Summaries, enter the number of monthly summaries to save. The default value is 13. This means that at least 13 monthly summaries need to be saved to create an average monthly summary.

g. Click OK.

4. Create a scheduled report job so that the report job is actually created. This step is necessary before you view any of the predefined five reports. See the section "Scheduling Reports" later in this chapter for details. To create a report job, take the following steps:

a. Open the ISA Management MMC by clicking Start | Programs | Microsoft ISA Server | ISA Management.

b. Expand Servers And Arrays, the name of the array, and Monitoring Configuration.

c. Right-click on Report Jobs and select New | Report Job.

d. On the General tab, in the Name field, enter the name of the report job.

e. In the Description box, enter a description of the report job. This step is optional.

f. Click OK. If you are configuring a report job on a remote system or an array, you will need to specify credentials. Click OK.

Note: Enter credentials that include a user account with proper permissions, Windows 2000 domain name, and password. Click OK, and the newly created report job should show up in the right pane.

5. Configure a report job period. To do so, follow these steps:

a. Open the ISA Management MMC by clicking Start | Programs | Microsoft ISA Server | ISA Management.

b. Expand Servers And Arrays, the name of the array, and Monitoring Configuration. Then click Report Jobs.

c. In the right pane, right-click on the applicable report job, then click Properties. For this example, use Report Job 1.

d. On the Period tab:

➤ To create reports that show the previous day's activity, click Daily.

➤ To create reports that show the previous week's activity, click Weekly.

➤ To create reports that show the previous month's activity, click Monthly.

➤ To create reports that show the previous year's activity, click Yearly.

➤ To create reports that show activity for a specified period, click Custom and then enter the desired dates in From and To.

e. Click OK.

6. Configure a report job schedule. To do so, follow these steps:

a. Open the ISA Management MMC by clicking Start | Programs | Microsoft ISA Server | ISA Management.

b. Expand Servers And Arrays, the name of the array, and Monitoring Configuration. Then click Report Jobs.

c. In the right pane, right-click on the applicable report job, and then click Properties.

d. On the Schedule tab, click one of the following:

➤ To create the report immediately, click Immediately.

➤ To create the report at the specified time, click At and enter a date and time.

For this example, confirm that Immediately is checked.

e. Under Recurrence Pattern, select one of the following:

➤ To create a report once, select Create Once.

➤ To create reports every day, click Create Every Day.

➤ To create reports on specific days, click Create On The Following Days and select the appropriate checkboxes for the day of the week.

➤ To create reports once a month, click Create Once A Month and type the day of the month on which to create the reports.

f. Click OK.

7. Finally, you can view the generated reports. To view a report, take the following steps:

a. Open the ISA Management MMC by clicking Start | Programs | Microsoft ISA Server | ISA Management.

b. Expand Servers And Arrays, the name of the array, click Monitoring|Reports, and then click the report type you want to see, such as Summary, Web Usage, Application Usage, Traffic And Utilization, or Security.

c. In the right pane, right-click on the applicable report and then click Open.

Viewing Predefined Reports

In many cases, when you are starting to use the ISA Server's reporting functionality, you don't know where to start. You can have many items on the report. Fortunately, ISA Server includes predefined reports that you can use in the beginning. Once you get used to the reports, you can customize them. The following is a list of predefined reports available on ISA Server. We will take a closer look at each of the predefined reports:

- Summary reports
- Web usage reports
- Application usage reports
- Traffic and utilization reports
- Security reports

Summary Reports

The summary reports combine all the data from the Web Proxy service and Firewall service logs, and are helpful for the network administrator or the person managing or planning a company's Internet connectivity. Summary reports describe network traffic usage, and they are sorted by application.

Web Usage Reports

The Web usage reports are based on the Web Proxy service logs, and are helpful for the network administrator or the person managing or planning a company's Internet connectivity. Web usage reports describe common responses, list the most popular Web browsers and the busiest users, and show you how the Internet is being used in your company.

Application Usage Reports

Application usage reports are based on the Firewall service logs, and are useful for the network administrator or the person managing or planning a company's Internet connectivity. Application usage reports describe Internet application usage in a company, which includes incoming and outgoing traffic, top users, client applications, and destinations.

Traffic and Utilization Reports

Traffic and utilization reports combine data from the Web Proxy and Firewall service logs, and they can help you plan and monitor network capacity and determine bandwidth policies in your network. Traffic and utilization reports provide total Internet usage by application, protocol, and direction; average traffic and peak simultaneous connections; cache hit ratio; errors; and other statistics.

Security Reports

Security reports are based on the Web Proxy service, Firewall service, and packet filter logs, and they can help identify attacks or security violations after they have occurred in your network. Security reports list attempts to breach network security.

Configuring Reports

You can configure ISA Server to produce the following log files to record activity:

- *Packet filter logs*—Packet filter record attempts to pass packets through the ISA server.

- *Firewall service logs*—Firewall service logs record attempts to communicate using the Firewall service.

- *Web Proxy service logs*—Web Proxy service logs record attempts to communicate using the Web Proxy service.

Report Database

The ISA Server reporting mechanism combines the summary logs from the ISA servers into a database on each ISA server. When a report is created, all relevant summary databases are combined into a single report database.

You can view the reports on that ISA server only. This means that you will not be able to view the reports if you run ISA Management on the same array from another ISA server.

Scheduling Reports

The ISA Server reporting mechanism allows you to schedule reports, based on the data collected from the log files. You can schedule reports to be created on a recurring, periodic basis: daily, weekly, monthly, or yearly. The report can include daily, weekly, monthly, or yearly data.

When you schedule a report job, you will need to specify the following:

- The period of activity that the report should cover

- When and how often the report needs to be created

- The username of a user authorized to create the report

Credentials

When you create a scheduled report job, the reports are created on the server from which you configure the job. However, if the server belongs to an array that has multiple ISA servers, the reporting mechanism accesses the logs on each of the servers in the array. As a result, the user who is creating the reports must have appropriate permissions to access and use the reporting mechanism on the servers in the array. You have to configure an appropriate username and pass appropriate credentials to create the reports for all the servers in the array.

By the same token, when you administer ISA Server remotely, you can create reports for the administered server or array. However, you must have appropriate permissions to access and use the reporting mechanism on each ISA server computer in the array. All members of the Domain Admins group can create reports. Furthermore, users who meet the following criteria can create reports:

➤ The user must be a local administrator on every ISA server computer in the array.

➤ The user must be able to access and launch Distributed Component Object Model (DCOM) objects on every ISA server in the array.

Specifying User Credentials for a Report Job

To specify user credentials for a report job, follow these steps:

1. Open the ISA Management MMC by clicking Start|Programs|Microsoft ISA Server|ISA Management.

2. Expand Servers And Arrays, the name of the array, and Monitoring Configuration. Then click Report Jobs.

3. In the right pane, right-click on the applicable report job, and then click Properties.

4. On the Credentials tab, in the Username field, enter the name of a user who has permission to create the report. You can click Browse to select a user account. In this case, the domain name in Step 5 will be filled out automatically.

5. In the Domain field, enter the user's domain, such as "coriolis.com".

6. In the Password field, enter the user's password.

7. Click OK.

Other Functionalities

Next, we will discuss some functions that you don't have to use when you're creating reports but that are good to know about nonetheless. As you become experienced in ISA Server administration, you might want to use these functions to customize your reports.

Configuring the Location of Reports

To configure the location of reports, follow these steps:

1. Open the ISA Management MMC by clicking Start | Programs | Microsoft ISA Server | ISA Management.

2. Expand Servers And Arrays and the name of the array, click Monitoring Configuration, and then click Report Jobs.

3. Right-click on Report Jobs, and then click Properties.

4. On the General tab, make sure that the Enable Reports checkbox is selected.

5. Do one of the following:

    ➤ To save the reports in the ISAReports subfolder of the ISA Server installation folder, click ISAReports Folder.

    ➤ To save the reports in another folder, click Directory, click Browse, and click the folder in which to save the reports.

Saving Reports as Web Pages

You can save report as Web pages so that they can be accessible on the company's intranet or even on the Internet. You can also save reports in Microsoft Excel format. Follow these steps:

1. Open the ISA Management MMC by clicking Start | Programs | Microsoft ISA Server | ISA Management.

2. Expand Servers And Arrays, the name of the array, Monitoring, and click Reports.

3. Click the applicable report type, such as Summary, Web Usage, Application Usage, Traffic And Utilization, or Security.

4. In the right pane, right-click on the applicable report and then click Save As.

5. In the Save As dialog box, enter a name of the report you want to use. In the Save As Type list, choose Web Page (*.htm; .html). If you need to save the report in Excel format, choose Excel Workbook (.xls).

Deleting a Report

To delete a report, use the following steps:

1. Open the ISA Management MMC by clicking Start | Programs | Microsoft ISA Server | ISA Management.

2. Expand Servers And Arrays and the name of the array, click Monitoring, and then click Reports.

3. In the right pane, right-click on the applicable report and then click Delete.

4. Confirm the deletion by clicking OK.

Sorting Report Data

To sort report data, follow these steps:

1. Open the ISA Management MMC by clicking Start|Programs|Microsoft ISA Server|ISA Management.

2. Expand Servers And Arrays and the name of the array, click Monitoring, click Reports, and then click the report type you want to sort, such as Summary, Web Usage, Application Usage, Traffic And Utilization, or Security.

3. Right-click a report type, and then click Properties.

4. Click a tab and then, in the Sort Order field, select the option you want to use to sort the data in the report.

5. Click OK.

Chapter Summary

As an ISA administrator, you will face situations in which your network is not working properly. You are responsible for anything that happens to your network, and you must have some troubleshooting skills to determine what is going on. This chapter introduced several guidelines that you should follow to troubleshoot problems in your network. Many of guidelines are generic and will be useful for environments where different kinds of servers are used.

The Windows 2000 basic troubleshooting process includes using the built-in Event Viewer, using the **PING** command, and ensuring the correct browser configuration.

It is also important to know where to go for help when you have no idea what is causing the problem. Troubleshooting resources include Microsoft Technet, Windows 2000 and ISA Server Online Help, your colleagues, your instructors, and Coriolis publications, among others.

Generally, we can categorize ISA Server troubleshooting as follows: access policies, authentication, caching, client connections, dial-up entries, logging, and services.

ISA Server also has reporting capability. ISA Server's report provides a summary and analysis of the communication patterns that ISA Server has been dealing with. Because the reporting functionality is built into ISA Server, you do not need to write Structured Query Language (SQL) queries or custom scripts that you would normally have to write. You can also schedule ISA Server to create reports every once in a while, which is very nice. If you want to analyze the reports later, you can save them to a folder you specify on the ISA server.

Review Questions

1. Which of the following is a category of ISA Server troubleshooting? [Check all correct answers]
   a. Troubleshooting access policies
   b. Troubleshooting caching
   c. Troubleshooting client connections
   d. Troubleshooting services

2. ISA Server access policies include which of the following? [Check all correct answers]
   a. Site and content rules
   b. Protocol rules
   c. Information rules
   d. IP packet filters

3. After the first deployment of ISA Server, clients are not able to browse external Web sites with their browsers through ISA Server's Web Proxy service. What is the possible cause?
   a. Clients are using the Netscape browser.
   b. External Web sites are down.
   c. ISA Server initially does not allow any communication to or from external Web sites.
   d. ISA Server is down.

4. After you disable a protocol rule, clients can still use the protocol that is allowed by the rule. What is the possible cause?
   a. Clients sessions have not been disconnected.
   b. Something is wrong with the rule configuration.
   c. You did not disable the protocol rule after all.
   d. Clients have administrator permissions in the Windows 2000 domain.

5. ISA Server failed to authenticate a Netscape user. What is the possible cause?
   a. The user is accessing an SSL site.
   b. The user is using Netscape version 3.0.
   c. You have to use Internet Explorer to use ISA Server's functionality.
   d. ISA Server is configured only to accept Windows Integrated authentication.

6. ISA Server caches some data, but not from all traffic. What is the possible cause?
    a. Cache on an NTFS partition is not configured properly.
    b. Not all traffic meets the caching criteria defined.
    c. One hard drive on the cache has failed.
    d. The user's browser is not configured properly.

7. Clients cannot connect to a particular external SSL site. What is the possible cause?
    a. It is using port 80.
    b. It is using port 443.
    c. Your browser is not able to access an SSL site.
    d. It is using a port other than 443, and you are not accessing the correct port.

8. ISA Server's dial-out to the Internet failed, although manual dial-out works. What is the possible cause?
    a. ISA Server does not support automatic dial-out.
    b. The dial-out number has not been specified.
    c. The dial-up entry credentials are incorrectly specified.
    d. When manual dial-out works, automatic dial-out to the Internet never works.

9. You cannot find client authentication information in the log file. What is the possible cause?
    a. The log is not correctly configured.
    b. You are looking at the wrong log file.
    c. Client access was not authenticated properly.
    d. Client access may be anonymous.

10. External clients cannot send email through the system running Exchange Server, which is set up as a firewall client behind the ISA server. What is the possible cause?
    a. A port conflict for the SMTP port
    b. A port conflict for the POP3 port
    c. A port conflict for the IMAP4 port
    d. A port conflict for the SSL port

11. Providing a summary and analysis of the communication patterns that ISA Server has been dealing with is called what?

    a. Summary

    b. Reporting

    c. Analysis

    d. Summary information

12. Predefined reports include which of the following? [Check all correct answers]

    a. Summary reports

    b. Analysis reports

    c. Application usage reports

    d. Communication reports

13. Combining summary logs from the ISA servers into a database on each ISA server is called what?

    a. SQL database

    b. Report database

    c. Access database

    d. Summary database

14. To schedule a report job, which information do you need to provide? [Check all correct answers]

    a. Period of activity the report needs to cover

    b. When and how often the report needs to be created

    c. Username of a user authorized to create the report

    d. One of the Windows 2000 domain administrator's credentials

15. When troubleshooting network connectivity using the **PING** command, which one of the following should you ping first?

    a. Your own IP address

    b. The loopback IP address

    c. Your default gateway IP address

    d. The remote host IP address that you are trying to reach

Real-World Projects

Note: This exercise assumes a test Windows 2000 server or Advanced Server with Service Pack 1 or Windows 2000 Datacenter Server installed. Read the instructions carefully and do not perform this install on your production machine unless you understand the options presented. If you are unsure about an option, cancel the installation and read the help files provided with ISA Server about the option to be installed.

Reia is an ISA Server administrator for a small company in Colorado. She was hired only about a month ago, and she's still learning about ISA Server administration. Keith, an experienced ISA Server administrator, is responsible for training Reia so that she can take care of most of the day-to-day support tasks. Day-to-day tasks normally involve providing support for clients who may have problems using their browser through the ISA servers deployed in their network environment; and creating reports for all the ISA servers so that Keith and Reia can make sure none of them is congested as a result of heavy access from clients. One of the tasks Keith has assigned to Reia is to deploy an ISA Server array in a test lab, and see whether she can create reports. With help from Keith, she has successfully set up an ISA server array with two ISA servers in it, which is joining a test Windows 2000 Active Directory domain. When they are about to start working on creating reports, a phone in the test lab rings.

"Is this Reia? Hi, I'm John in the Human Resources department. I thought we had decided not to use Net2Phone for our long distance. However, I can use Net2Phone to make calls just like before. Did you not disable the function?"

Reia replies, "Yes, we disabled Net2Phone in a protocol rule, and you should not be able to use it any longer. Are you telling us that you're still able to use it?"

John answers, "Yeah, I just used it to talk with my customer in San Diego, and it worked fine. Do you know what is going on?"

Reia says, "Hmm.... I'm not sure."

John says, "Well, what are you going to do?"

Reia looks at Keith to see if he has any ideas. Keith has been getting ready for the ISA Server reporting that they are supposed to perform, and he does not seem to be listening.

Reia asks Keith, "You don't happen to know what's going on, do you?"

Keith smiles. "Of course I do. You are talking to probably one of the best ISA Server admins here in this company."

Reia thinks to herself, "Well, there is only one ISA Server administrator in the company, and who else could I ask?" Aloud Reia asks him, "So what is the problem?"

"The HR department's computers are not shut down, and many HR staff members have been making calls using Net2Phone," Keith explains. "Therefore, when we disabled Net2Phone yesterday, HR people had made connections using Net2Phone. Because the connections were made before we disabled Net2Phone, they are still able to use it. Didn't I tell you there was one thing we would have to do before we went home last night?"

Reia says, "No, you did not tell me anything. I thought we did everything we were supposed to."

Keith replies, "Anyhow, let's take care of it right now. It's not hard to do. Hey, John, can you try to use Net2Phone in 10 minutes and see if it still works? It shouldn't work after 10 minutes, but if it does, call me back again."

"All right." John hangs up the phone.

Keith instructs Reia: "Well, you just need to disconnect clients sessions so that the new protocol rule becomes effective." Reia takes the following steps to disconnect client sessions.

Project 15.1

To disconnect an existing user session:

1. Open the ISA Management MMC by clicking Start | Programs | Microsoft ISA Server | ISA Management.

2. Expand Servers And Arrays and the name of the array, click Monitoring | Sessions, and then click Services.

3. On the View menu, make sure that Advanced has a checkmark next to it. If not, select Advanced. See Figure 15.5.

4. In the details pane, right-click the session that you want to disconnect, and then click Stop. For this example, if you do not see any sessions listed, continue to the next project. If you see a user account that you can possibly disconnect, do so after notifying the user.

Reia sees a lot of users listed in the session, and she disconnects all of them. Now when they try to connect to Net2Phone again, they won't be able to. It has been about 10 minutes, but John does not call back. It looks like things are working now.

"Now, we can get to work," Keith says. He starts explaining what the ISA Server's reporting functionality is all about, and Reia learns four steps must be performed before a successful report can be generated. Keith tells Reia, "The first step to create a report is to enable logging for relevant ISA Server components. Because

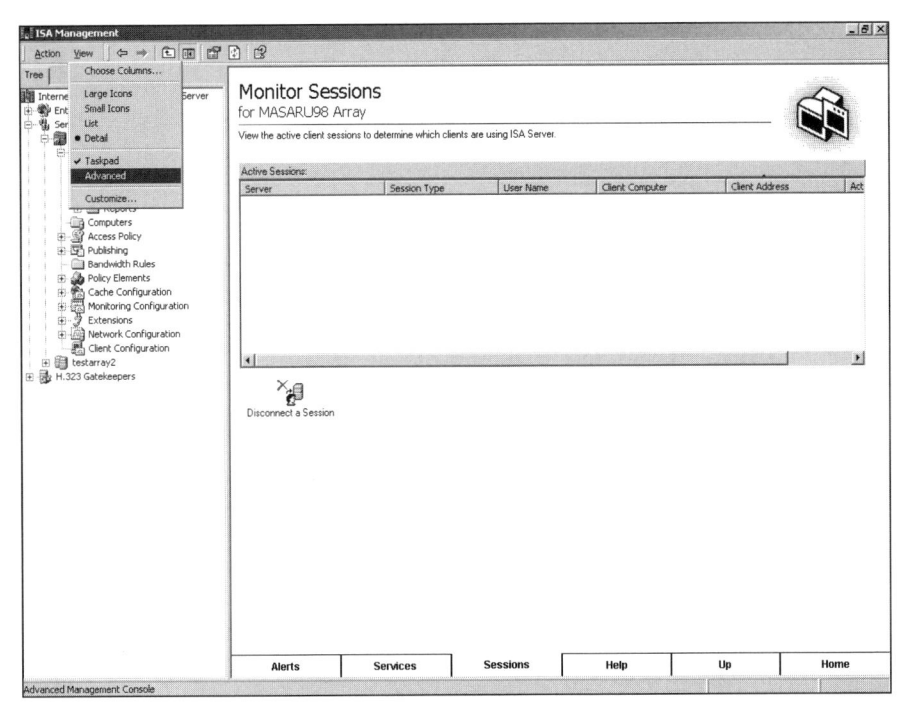

Figure 15.5 The Advanced option on the View menu.

we are interested in all the services, we will enable logging on packet filters, the ISA Server Firewall service, and the ISA Server Web Proxy service. Although logging is enabled by default, let's just make sure." Reia is looking at the console of the ISA server and takes the following steps.

Project 15.2

To enable logging for specific services:

1. Open the ISA Management MMC by clicking Start | Programs | Microsoft ISA Server | ISA Management.

2. Expand Servers And Arrays, and the name of the array, click Monitoring Configuration, and then click Logs.

3. In the right pane, right-click the applicable service, and then click Properties. By default, you see three service logs listed: Packet Filters, ISA Server Firewall Service, and ISA Server Web Proxy Service. See Figure 15.6. For this example, repeat Steps 3 through 5 for all the services listed.

4. On the Log tab, make sure the Enable Logging For This Service checkbox is selected. (This option is selected by default.) See Figure 15.7.

5. Click OK.

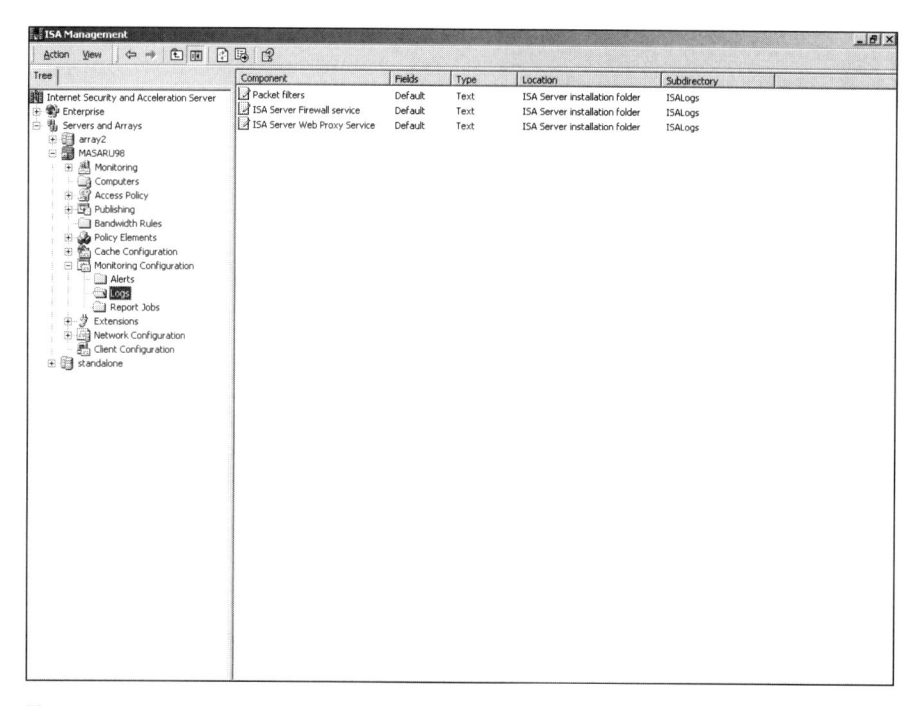

Figure 15.6 The default service logs.

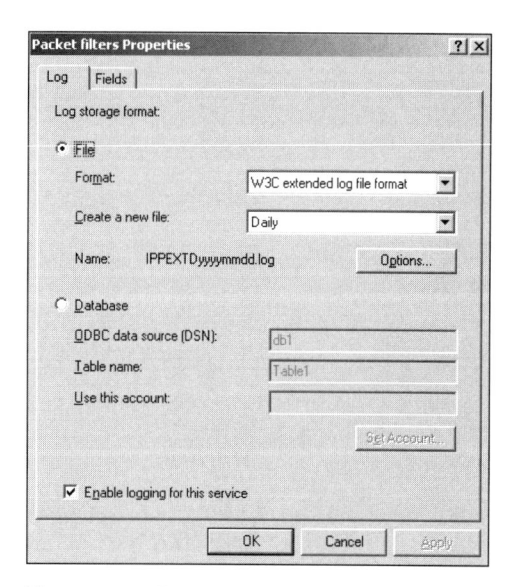

Figure 15.7 Packet filters properties.

Keith continues, "The next step is to enable the reporting mechanism. Again, this is enabled by default, but let's make sure."

Project 15.3
To enable the reporting mechanism:

1. Open the ISA Management MMC by clicking Start | Programs | Microsoft ISA Server | ISA Management.

2. Expand Servers And Arrays, and the name of the array, click Monitoring Configuration, and then click Report Jobs.

3. Right-click on Report Jobs, and then click Properties. See Figure 15.8.

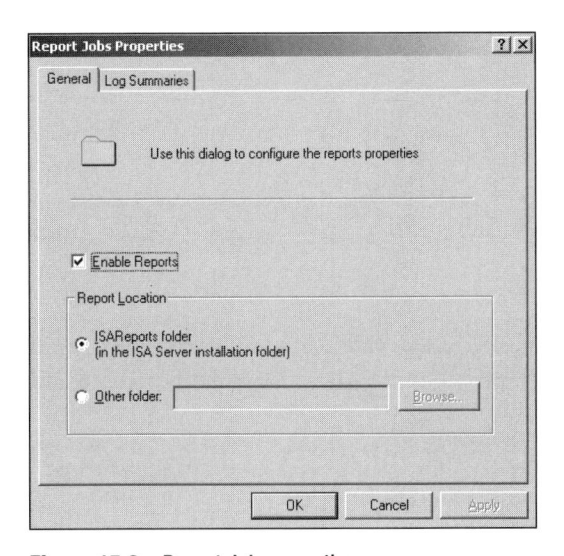

Figure 15.8 Report Job properties.

4. On the General tab, select the Enable Reports checkbox.

5. Click OK.

"The next step is to enable daily and monthly report summaries," explains Keith.

Project 15.4
To enable daily and monthly report summaries:

1. Open the ISA Management MMC by clicking Start | Programs | Microsoft ISA Server | ISA Management.

2. Expand Servers And Arrays and the name of the array, click Monitoring Configuration, and then click Report Jobs.

3. Right-click Report Jobs, and then click Properties.

4. On the Log Summaries tab, make sure the Enable Daily And Monthly Summaries checkbox is selected. (This option is selected by default.) See Figure 15.9.

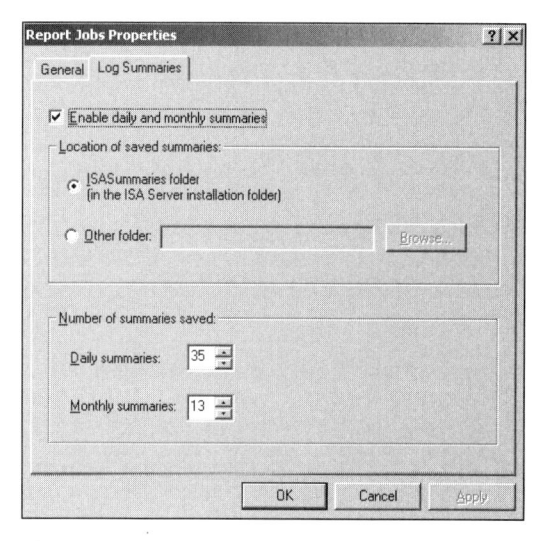

Figure 15.9 The Log Summaries tab.

5. Under Number Of Summaries Saved, in the Daily Summaries field, enter the number of daily summaries to save. The default value is 35. For this example, use 30.

6. In the Monthly Summaries field, enter the number of monthly summaries to save. The default value is 13. For this example, use 12.

7. Click OK.

Keith continues, "Are you having fun yet? Just a little bit more. The next step is to create a scheduled report job. Keep in mind that you need to complete this step before you can view any reports."

Project 15.5

To create a scheduled report job:

1. Open the ISA Management MMC by clicking Start|Programs|Microsoft ISA Server|ISA Management.

2. Expand Servers And Arrays, and the name of the array, and click Monitoring Configuration.

3. Right-click on Report Jobs and select New|Report Job. See Figure 15.10.

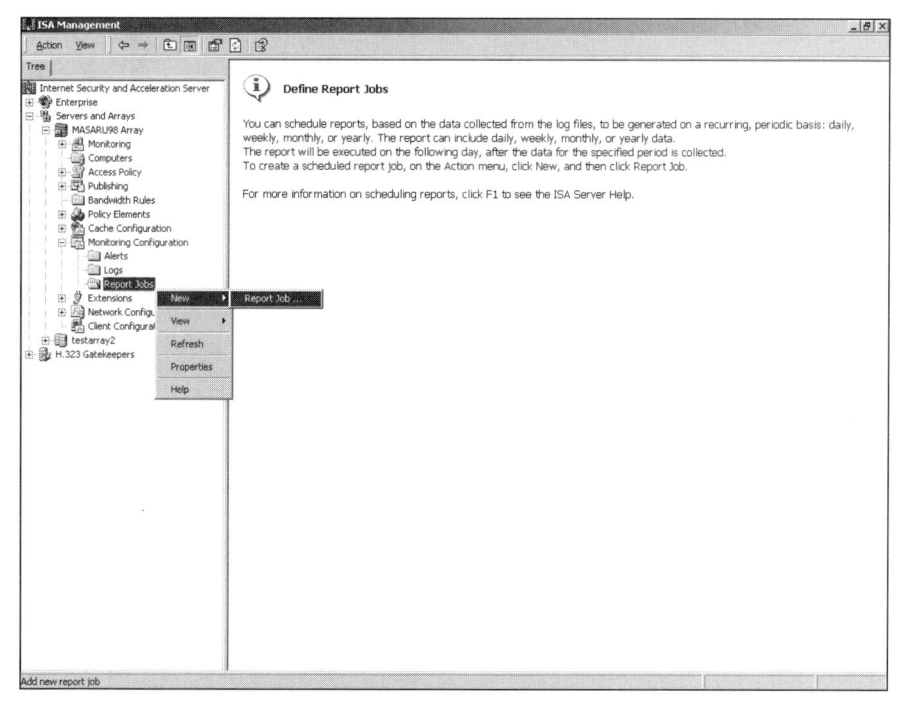

Figure 15.10 The Report Job command.

4. On the General tab, enter the name of the report job in the Name field. For this example, enter "Report Job 1". See Figure 15.11.

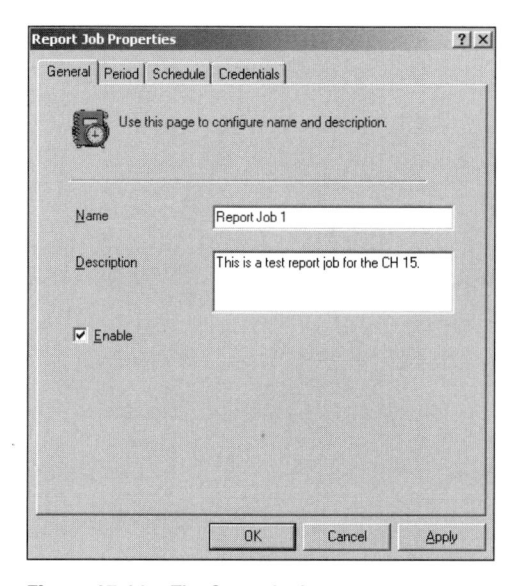

Figure 15.11 The General tab.

5. In the Description field, enter a description of the report job. For this example, enter "This is a test report job 1". (This step is optional.)

6. Click OK. You will see the following pop-up message: If you are configuring a report job on a remote system or an array, you will need to specify credentials. See Figure 15.12. Click OK.

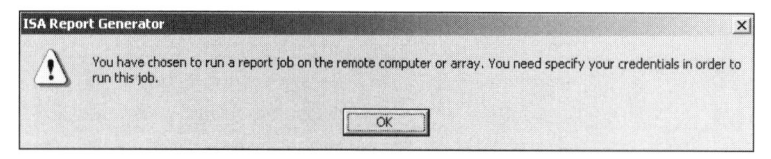

Figure 15.12 The ISA Report Generator message.

7. Enter credentials that have proper permissions. Then, click OK. The report job should show up in the right pane. For this example, enter the administrator account, domain, and password for the Windows 2000 Active Directory domain you are working on. See Figure 15.13.

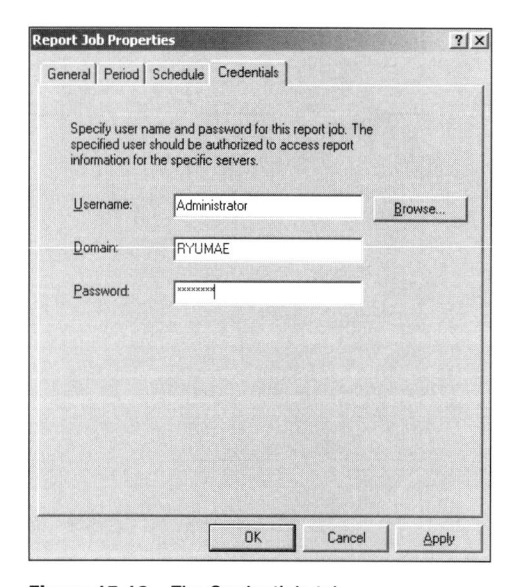

Figure 15.13 The Credentials tab.

Project 15.6

To configure a report job period:

1. Open the ISA Management MMC by clicking Start | Programs | Microsoft ISA Server | ISA Management.

2. Expand Servers And Arrays, and the name of the array, click Monitoring Configuration, and then click Report Jobs.

3. In the right pane, right-click on the applicable report job, and then click Properties. For this example, use report job 1. See Figure 15.14.

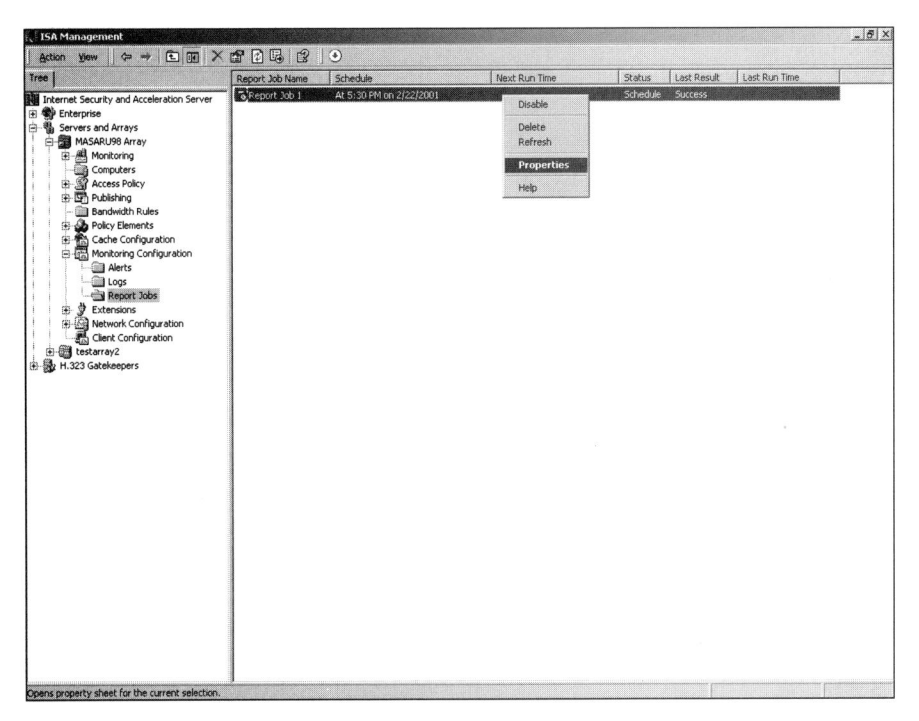

Figure 15.14 The Report Job Properties command.

4. On the Period tab:

   ▶ To create reports that show the previous day's activity, click Daily.

   ▶ To create reports that show the previous week's activity, click Weekly.

   ▶ To create reports that show the previous month's activity, click Monthly.

   ▶ To create reports that show the previous year's activity, click Yearly.

   ▶ To create reports that show activity for a specified period, click Custom and then enter the desired dates in From and To.

   See Figure 15.15. For this example, make sure that Daily is selected.

5. Click OK.

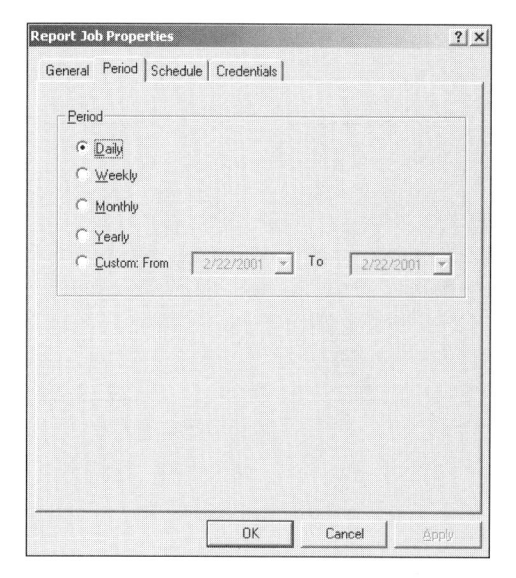

Figure 15.15 The Period tab.

Project 15.7

To configure a report job schedule:

1. Open the ISA Management MMC by clicking Start|Programs|Microsoft ISA Server|ISA Management.

2. Expand Servers And Arrays and the name of the array, click Monitoring Configuration, and then click Report Jobs.

3. In the right pane, right-click on the applicable report job, and then click Properties.

4. On the Schedule tab, click one of the following:

    ➤ To create the report immediately, click Immediately.

    ➤ To create the report at the specified time, click At and enter a date and time.

    See Figure 15.16. For this example, confirm that Immediately is checked.

5. Under Recurrence Pattern, select one of the following:

    ➤ To create a report once, select Generate Once.

    ➤ To create reports every day, click Generate Every Day.

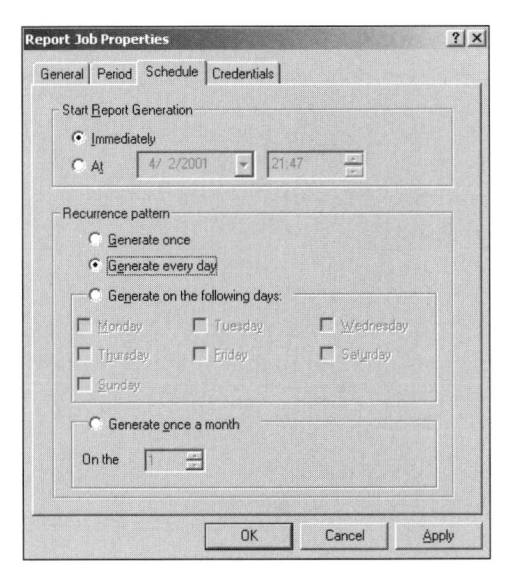

Figure 15.16 The Schedule tab.

- To create reports on specific days, click Generate On The Following Days and select the appropriate checkboxes for the day of the week.

- To create reports once a month, click Generate Once A Month and type the day of the month on which you want to create the reports.

For this example, select Generate Every Day.

6. Click OK.

Keith continues, "Well done. Let's take a look the report. You may actually like it!"

Project 15.8
To view a report:

1. Open the ISA Management MMC by clicking Start | Programs | Microsoft ISA Server | ISA Management.

2. Expand Servers And Arrays and the name of the array, click Monitoring | Reports, and then click the report type you want to see, such as Summary, Web Usage, Application Usage, Traffic And Utilization, or Security.

3. In the right pane, right-click on the applicable report and then click Open. For this example, if you see reports that have already been created, click on each of the reports to see how it looks. If you do not see any reports, that means your logs are empty, and you may need to come back to this exercise later once logs contain some logging information.

Reia is surprised because she did not create any visible reports. "How come I don't see any reports generated?" she asks.

"Well, that's because this is a new ISA server array, and nobody is connected to it," Keith explains. "Therefore, all logs are empty. We need to create an environment where client systems do connect to this ISA server array so that we can get some log files filled with entries. We will do that tomorrow."

CHAPTER SIXTEEN

Setting Up External Client Connections

After completing this chapter, you will be able to:

✓ Configure DUN entries

✓ Configure dial-up entries in ISA Server

✓ Differentiate between the VPN setup wizards in ISA Server

✓ Configure the ISA server to accept VPN connections

✓ Configure clients to access the ISA server externally via VPN

✓ Select the correct VPN configuration based on client needs

✓ Maximize bandwidth use on WAN connections

In this chapter, you will learn how to set up your network to receive connections from clients located outside your main network and how to configure your ISA server when it needs to dial out to the Internet. Although the ability to connect externally has been available for quite some time, configuring and administering access was burdensome in the past and created security risks. Administrators thought they had it bad, but for the user, remote connections were no picnic, either. The simple act of accessing a small text file from an external connection could easily take the better part of an hour. Checking email or running programs across an external connection was virtually impossible using these old, external connection methods.

ISA Server can accept dial-in connections directly or through a virtual private network (VPN) for added security. Also, you can configure ISA Server to dial out to remote networks. ISA Server integrates directly with Windows 2000 dial-up networking settings to create dial-up entries, which ISA Server uses. Also, the ISA Server wizards that create VPNs integrate directly with the Routing And Remote Access Service (RRAS) to create settings in both the RRAS and ISA Server snap-ins. In this chapter, we will discuss setting up external connections to effectively create dial-in solutions on ISA Servers.

Remote Connections and Clients

Although the majority of client computers are connected locally (through some form of physical connection within the confines of the building where the servers are located), some users require the use of client computers that can be connected remotely. A remote client is a computer that is connected to the local area network from somewhere outside the reach of the organization's physical connections. Clients that are connected locally are typically connected to the network using some sort of a network interface card (NIC). These days, most NICs use an RJ-45 connection running 10BaseT or 100BaseT. However, networks are not limited to this type of connection. A variety of other NICs are still in widespread use. Installing and setting up the software for clients to ISA Server is discussed in Chapter 5. If any of these clients are remote, the network might require additional configuration and different hardware.

You can grant external access to servers from remote clients using several methods. Although ISA Server has built-in capabilities to accommodate remote connections, connecting external clients can also be accomplished through the use of third-party software. In the past, the use of third-party products was the method of choice due to its low cost and relatively simple methods of configuration. However, implementing, maintaining, and training users to use these products can be costly and impose their own associated security risks, not to mention the additional burden of administering users' rights and restrictions to these connections.

To provide a secure and inexpensive connection using existing hardware, you can configure ISA Server to permit access by external connections through the use of Windows 2000 dial-up services. All anyone needs to access the network is the phone number of the modem line or Integrated Services Digital Network (ISDN). By using ISA Server's capabilities to connect remote users, you are able to stay within one security model provided by Windows 2000 and ISA Server. You will not have to try to integrate other products, and you will avoid the possibility of creating security holes in the process.

Dial-up Networking and the Routing And Remote Access Service

From the standpoint of hardware, the cheapest method for external clients to connect to the main network is through a dial-up connection and a modem or even ISDN adapter. Of course, the capability to do this predates ISA Server. ISA Server's purpose is to make connections more secure, and this is what ISA Server can do for dial-up connections. Dial-up Networking (DUN) sets up a dial-out connection from a computer running Windows 2000 (and other Windows operating systems), and this is still how a connection should be set up when connecting to an ISA server through a dial-up connection.

The first thing you need to do for an external client is to set up the external client. Entries used by DUN to connect external clients to an ISA server don't need any special configuration when you're first creating the dial-up connection. The clients simply need to configure a phonebook entry to the ISA server. You will need to configure security settings at the ISA server, a process we will cover later in this chapter. To configure a phonebook entry using DUN, complete the following steps:

1. On the client, choose Start | Settings | Network And Dial-up Connections.

2. In the Network And Dial-Up Connections dialog box, double-click Make New Connection to start the Network Connection Wizard.

3. In the Welcome dialog box, click Next.

4. For a direct connection to the ISA server, select Dial-up To Private Network. Figure 16.1 shows the Network Connection Type dialog box and the type of connections available. Click Next.

5. In the Phone Number To Dial dialog box, enter the phone number of the ISA server. Click Next.

6. In the Connection Available dialog box, specify whether you will restrict the use of the phonebook entry to yourself or to all users. Click Next.

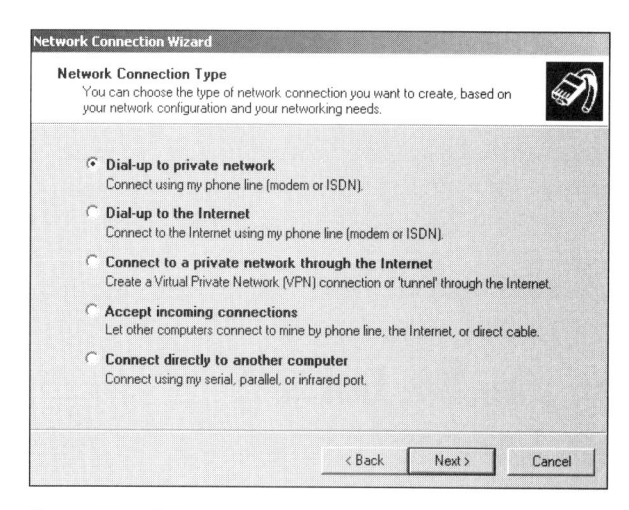

Figure 16.1 Select the type of connection you would like to make in the Network Connection Type dialog box.

7. To complete the entry, type a descriptive name for it. Click Finish.

8. A dialog box will appear that will allow you to dial the connection you just created. Click the Dial button to test the connection.

9. Close Network And Dial-up Connections.

These steps set up a direct modem or ISDN connection to the ISA server. This means security will not be applied to the connection until it hits the ISA server. Because information from your internal network is going out to the client, you might want more security. Also, your users might need to make long-distance telephone calls to reach your ISA server. Later in the chapter, we will cover the implementation of a VPN as an answer to these issues. If a VPN is not configured, no other special configurations need to be made just for remote clients.

The RRAS normally accepts remote connections from external clients. But when ISA Server is loaded on a server, it can accept remote client connections instead of the RRAS service and apply security settings to them. The RRAS service can still be installed and enabled on the ISA server, but ISA Server will accept the connections and the configuration settings should be set on the ISA server instead of the RRAS server.

Dialing Out to the Internet

Not only can an ISA server accept incoming dial-up connections, but also it can dial out to the Internet. The settings that allow an ISA server to dial out to the Internet for internal clients are needed when the ISA server's connection to the Internet is not persistent. Just as with external clients, the cheapest connection available to the Internet even for an ISA server is a connection that dials out to the Internet. ISA Server has several settings that allow you to control this type of connection. These settings can be complicated to configure because they are dependent on settings from other applications on a Windows 2000 server.

Dial-up Entries

Dial-up entries are policy elements. As we discussed earlier, DUN allows a Microsoft operating system to make an outbound dial-up connection. The same is true when you're configuring a dial-up connection on an ISA server. First, you must create a phonebook entry in the Network And Dial-up Connections application. You can then use this entry in ISA Server to control the outbound connection. You must create a DUN phonebook before you can create a Dial-up Entry policy element. Don't let the similarity of the names of these elements confuse you. Dial-up entries in ISA Server are created from existing DUN phonebook entries created ahead of time in the Network And Dial-up Connections application.

Configuring Dial-up Access

Dial-up entries specify how the ISA server will connect to the Internet, using an internal connection such as a modem or ISDN adapter. Follow the directions given earlier to create a DUN phonebook entry in the Networking And Dial-up Connections application. However, in the Connetion Type dialog box, you need to choose Dial-up To The Internet instead of Dial-up To Private Network. After creating the phonebook entry, you can create the Dial-up Entry policy element in the ISA Server snap-in.

Create a Dial-up Entry in ISA Server

To create a dial-up entry:

1. Open ISA Management.

2. Expand Servers And Arrays.

3. Expand the array you would like to configure.

4. In the selected array, expand Policy Elements.

5. Right-click Dial-up Entries, point to New, and then click Dial-up Entry.

6. In the New Dial-up Entry dialog box, type a name for the new dial-up entry.

7. In the Description box, enter a description for the entry.

8. In the Use The Following Network Dial-up Connection box, type the name of an existing Windows 2000 network dial-up connection. If you don't know the name, click Select and choose a network dial-up connection from the list. A list of existing DUN phonebook entries will appear.

9. In the Username box, type the name of a user authorized to use the network dial-up connection. Also, enter the password for the user account.

10. Click OK to close the Dial-up Entry dialog box.

If you have a dial-up connection on members of an array, you must create DUN phonebook entries on each member of the array and then repeat the steps for creating a dial-up entry on each server that is a member of the array. Give the DUN phonebook entries on each member of the array identical names.

One More Necessary Setting

If the dial-up connection is the primary connection to the Internet, you need to adjust one more setting to get the connection to work. Once you have created the dial-up entry on each ISA server that has a dial-up connection, you should configure the ISA server to use the dial-up entry as its primary connection. This configuration setting is not a policy element, but instead is located in the Network Configuration container in the ISA Server snap-in. To configure a dial-up entry as your primary connection, complete the following steps:

1. Open ISA Management.

2. Expand Servers And Arrays.

3. Expand the array you would like to configure.

4. In the selected array, right-click Network Configuration and select Properties. Figure 16.2 shows the Network Configuration Properties dialog box.

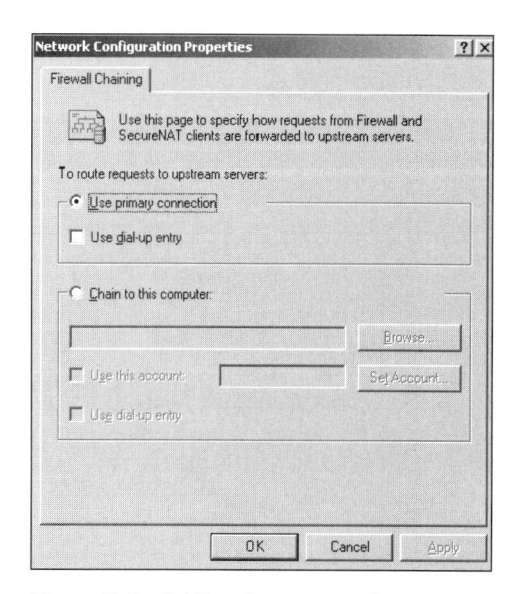

Figure 16.2 Set the primary connection as Dial-up in the Network Configuration Properties dialog box.

5. Under Use Primary Connection, place a checkmark next to Use Dial-up Entry.

6. Click OK to close the Network Configuration Properties dialog box.

7. Close ISA Management.

Don't let the explanation of the setting in the dialog box fool you. Even though this dialog box gives the impression that it is only for routing requests to upstream servers, you must access this dialog box when you are dialing out to any external network, and your ISP qualifies as an external network. For more information on this subject, refer to the Knowledge Base article Q2863635.

Setting Active Dial-up Entries

If you create multiple dial-up entries, ISA Server automatically designates the first one as the active dial-up entry. The active dial-up entry lets ISA Server know which one it should use when it goes to pick from the dial-up entries to dial out. The first dial-up entry created ends up being the active dial-up entry by default so you automatically have one. If no active dial-up entry exists, ISA Server won't know which entry to use and it won't make the dial-up connection. You should keep a few rules in mind when dealing with the active dial-up entry. While a dial-up entry is designated as active, it cannot be deleted. You can change the active dial-up entry, but you can set only one per standalone server and only one per array. Be careful when you set a new active dial-up entry, because when you do, you will immediately disconnect any currently connected users.

To set a new active dial-up entry:

1. Open ISA Management.

2. Expand Servers And Arrays.

3. Expand the array you would like to configure.

4. In the selected array, expand Policy Elements.

5. Select Use Primary Connection, then place a checkmark next to Use Dial-up Entry.

6. In the details pane, select the applicable dial-up entry.

7. Click the Set As Active Entry button in the ISA Server snap-in. A checkmark will appear on the telephone icon that represents a dial-up entry. Figure 16.3 shows the Dial-up Entry detail pane. The Set As Active Entry button is the last button on the toolbar. This button does not appear on the toolbar if the active dial-up entry is selected.

8. Close ISA Management.

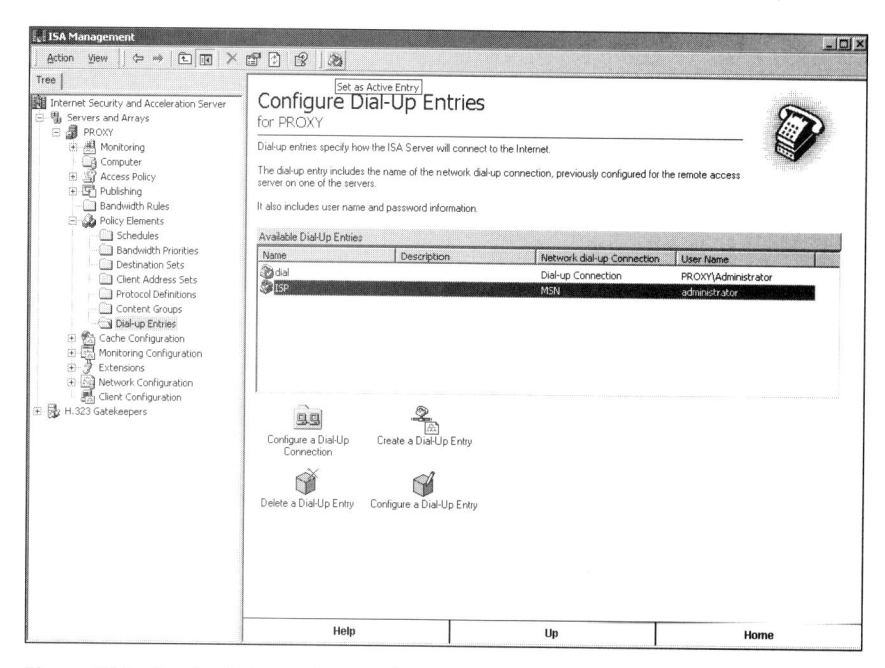

Figure 16.3 To set a dial-up entry as active, use the Set As Active Entry toolbar button in the ISA Server snap-in.

Skipping a Connection to ISA Server

In some cases, you may want certain clients to be able to skip the connection to ISA Server and make their own direct connection to the Internet. Even though this is skipping the security measures that ISA Server could provide to the computer, a situation might occur where this ability would be necessary. If you have only one ISA server providing a connection to the Internet and it were to become unavailable, could you go without it? If a connection to an external network is an overriding need, you might have to set up a direct access route for the computers on your network. Of course, if security is the paramount factor and connectivity at all times is less important, you probably don't want to use direct access. It depends on the needs of your network. Direct access is configured in the Client Configuration container in the ISA Server snap-in. Direct access is available only for Web Proxy clients, and it will require that clients have their own connection to the Internet, such as a modem and a phone line.

To configure direct access for clients, complete the following steps:

1. Open ISA Management.
2. Expand Servers And Arrays.
3. Expand the array you would like to configure.

4. Select Client Configuration.

5. In the details pane, right-click Web Browser and then click Properties.

6. Select the Backup Route tab. This dialog box is shown in Figure 16.4.

7. Place a checkmark next to If ISA Server Is Unavailable, Use This Backup Route To Connect To The Internet.

8. Select Direct Access for clients to connect directly to the Internet when the ISA Server is unavailable.

9. Click OK to accept the changes.

10. Close ISA Management.

This change will propagate down to Web Proxy clients so that they will know to try direct access if the ISA server fails to respond to their requests.

Setting up a direct connection to the Internet in case the ISA server fails is only one way that the term *direct access* is used when configuring an ISA server. In ISA Server, direct access also refers to the internal users' access to specific servers on the internal network or on external networks. If users on your internal network need to use the services being published from your internal network or even from an external network, you probably want them to be able to use these services without going through the ISA server. By default, internal users are able to directly connect to internal servers on your network without having to go through the ISA server, but this is only because

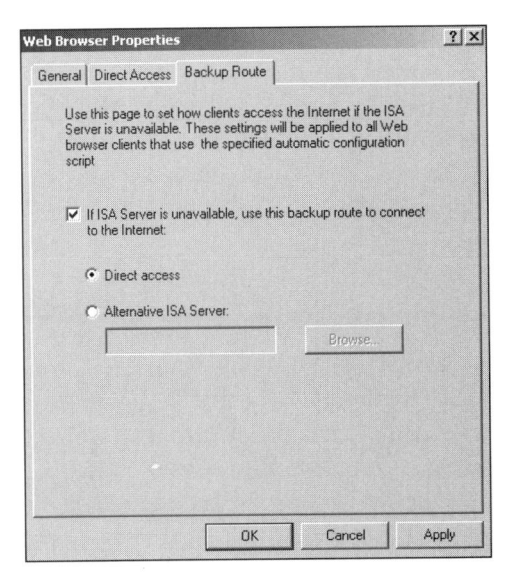

Figure 16.4 Selecting Direct Access on the Backup Route tab in the Web Browser Properties dialog box allows internal users to try their own connection to the Internet if the ISA server fails.

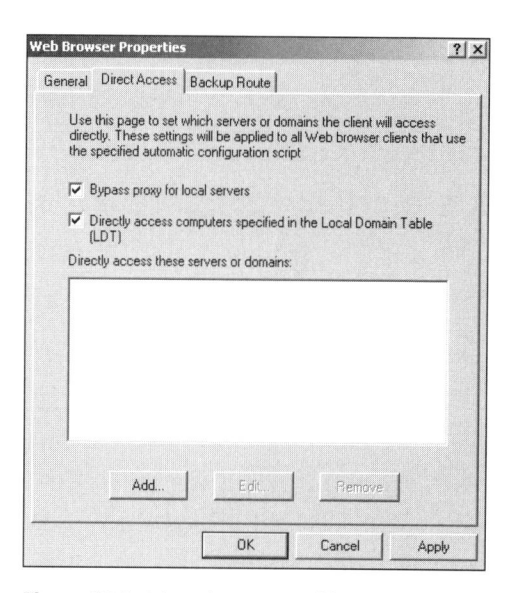

Figure 16.5 Internal users are able to directly connect to internal servers because of the settings in the Direct Access tab of the Web Browser Properties dialog box.

this direct access to these services has already been configured for them. Figure 16.5 shows these default settings in the Web Browser Properties dialog box in the Client Configuration container in the ISA Server snap-in. Enabling the option Bypass Proxy For Local Servers allows the internal computer to directly connect to a computer that does not have a domain suffix in its name. Without a domain suffix, this setting assumes that the computer is being referred to by its host name alone instead of by its Fully Qualified Domain Name (FQDN). In this case, the assumption is that the computer must belong to the same domain as the requesting computer. Enabling the option Directly Access Computers Specified In The Local Domain Table (LDT) ensures that the computer checks the LDT before connecting to ISA Server. Any server that belongs to a domain listed in the LDT is assumed to be local, and the client makes a direct connection to that computer.

These default settings take care of internal connections, but if you want internal users to be able to make a direct connection to any external computers, you will need to add those servers to the list under the checkmarks. In some circumstances, you might need direct access to external computers. For example, if you have another company location that uses a different DNS domain name, you might not feel the need to protect an internal user's connection to this server. Also, if an Internet security server is protecting this external location, your users will have to pass through it before making a connection to the other server anyway. Bypassing your own ISA server may save connection time for users connecting to this other trusted server. To set this up, you can refer to the server by IP address or DNS name. You can enter a whole range of IP addresses or enter the whole domain suffix if your users need to connect to a number of servers at that network.

To configure Web Proxy clients for direct access to external computers, complete the following steps:

1. Open ISA Management.
2. Expand Servers And Arrays.
3. Expand the array you would like to configure.
4. Select Client Configuration.
5. In the details pane, right-click Web Browser and then click Properties.
6. Select the Direct Access tab.
7. Click the Add button. Figure 16.6 shows the Add/Edit Server dialog box that allows you to specify external computers to which your users can connect without going through the local ISA Server.
8. Select IP Addresses Within This Range and enter an IP address or a range of IP addresses, or select Domain Or Computer to specify a computer name. You can specify a range of computer names with the * wildcard.
9. Click OK to accept the changes.
10. Click OK to close the Web Browser Properties dialog box.
11. Close ISA Management.

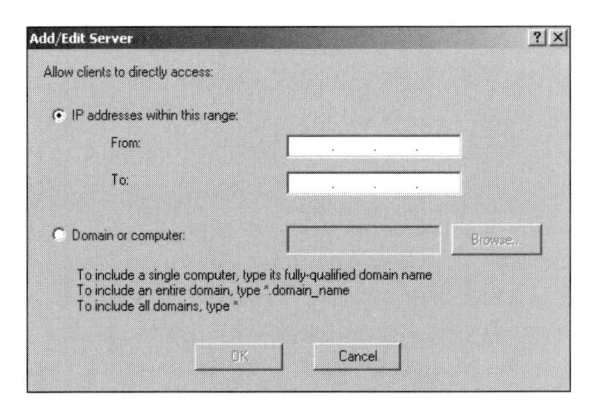

Figure 16.6 The Add/Edit Server dialog box lets you specify servers that internal users can connect to without going through the local ISA server.

Virtual Private Networks

If you have a lot of users using mobile devices, mainly laptops, on the road, your company must provide a connection to them so that these offsite users can access the internal network resources. A downside to dial-up connections is that they can cause roaming users to make long-distance calls to your network. These charges can add up. One solution is for your users to dial in to the Internet and connect to your network that way. If they dial in to a national or global ISP, they can reach your network, regardless of their distance from it, with a local phone call. Of course, network security comes into play here as well. If roaming users can access your network, so can anyone else with an Internet connection. You must be able to authenticate offsite users who are allowed to access the internal network resources. In fact, not only do you need to make sure that only authenticated users access the network, but also you need to ensure that internal company information downloaded to an external user is secure.

The basic idea of a VPN is simple: Use a public network as if it were a private one. Instead of paying tens of thousands of dollars a month for a private dedicated connection between remote locations and your internal network, you use the Internet to make remote connections. The disadvantage of this cheaper alternative is that private company information is out on the Internet and anyone with a connection to the Internet can attempt to break into your network. This is how the idea of a VPN came about. The purpose of a VPN is to secure an inexpensive Internet connection between external users and your internal network. VPNs use authentication and encryption to accomplish this.

VPNs make it easy for users to understand and use remote connections to an internal network. Users don't have to worry whether they are connecting from home or from a hotel while traveling—the connection will seem the same to them. Also, once they are connected to the internal network, users can access folders and files in the way they would if they were on the local network.

A VPN can be integrated directly into a network that uses ISA Server. To do this, you establish and run the VPN connection from the ISA server. The local ISA VPN computer connects to an ISP, creating the connection to the public network. Also, the VPN on the ISA server can accept incoming connections from external clients. Figure 16.7 shows this connection to the internal network through the ISA server. An external client initiates a request for a VPN session. The external client initiates a connection with its ISP. Next, the client's ISP routes the connection to the ISA server's local ISP. When the client's connection is authenticated, the VPN connection is made. Data is then passed through the VPN tunnel created by the virtual point-to-point connection between the two ISPs. The data must also be encrypted to be a true VPN connection.

A VPN is not just for remote or roaming users; it can also be used between fixed locations. In addition, a VPN can be extended into branch office situations, where you have two or more separate branch offices in different geographical locations

Figure 16.7 Connecting an external client using a VPN.

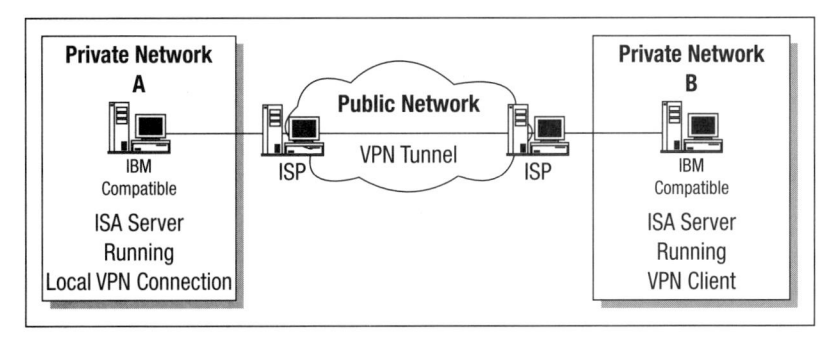

Figure 16.8 Connecting two networks using a VPN.

and you need to use a VPN for their communication. Here, you have an ISA server acting as the VPN gateway in each office, and these VPN gateways are configured to establish VPN communications when necessary. In Figure 16.8, two individual networks are connected using a VPN connection. In this example, Private Network A consists of an ISA server running the local VPN connection.

Integrating a VPN and ISA Server

Normally, a VPN is created in the RRAS snap-in. But ISA Server has a set of wizards that allow you to set up a VPN on an ISA server in just one console. Instead of having to create the VPN in the RRAS console and then configure it for use with ISA Server, you can use the ISA Server snap-in to perform all the steps of creating and configuring the VPN for use with ISA Server.

ISA Server provides three different VPN wizards that you can use to establish VPN connections. We will describe each of these wizards and how you can use them to configure a VPN connection. As we discussed earlier, you would create a VPN and use these wizards in two situations:

➤ When you have one branch office connecting to another branch office and each office has at least one ISA server acting as the VPN ISA server.

➤ When you have offsite users—such as salespeople who are on the road or people working from home—connecting to the local network not by directly dialing into the local network but by using a VPN connection through the Internet.

You will usually need more than one wizard to connect different ends of the connection. Each wizard sets up a different part of the connection. Table 16.1 lists each VPN wizard and describes its purpose.

Local or Remote?

If both the Local and Remote ISA VPN Wizards allow incoming and outgoing connections, how do you know which one you should run on your ISA server? If you have two separate networks that you want to connect through a VPN, which one is the local ISA server and which one is the remote one? The answer to these questions is, of course, it depends. It depends on which network users are trying to reach—in other words, which network is the main network location that contains the resources users need.

The wizards are designed so that the Local ISA VPN Wizard is run on the local network. This side of the VPN connection will be set up to receive connections from a remote network by default. On the remote network that will be initiating the VPN connections, you run the Remote ISA VPN Wizard on the remote ISA server. The remote ISA server connects to its ISP when a computer in the remote network attempts to communicate with a computer in the local network; data is encapsulated and sent in the VPN tunnel. In order to be a VPN connection, all the data that is transferred also has to be encrypted, and therefore, you would need some other data-encryption mechanism that Windows 2000 uses. We will discuss these encryption protocols later in this chapter.

Table 16.1 VPN wizards.

Wizard Type	Purpose
Local ISA VPN Wizard	You use this wizard to set up a VPN that receives or initiates connections. Use it on the ISA server located on your local network.
Remote ISA VPN Wizard	You use this wizard to set up a VPN that receives or initiates connections. When configuring VPNs on geographically separated ISA servers, use the Local ISA VPN Wizard on one and the Remote ISA VPN Wizard on the other.
Set Up Clients To ISA Server VPN	You use this wizard to connect both remote and roaming clients to a main network location.

Changes Made by the VPN Wizards

In a situation with two remote locations being connected by a VPN through the Internet, you need to run the Local ISA VPN Wizard on the local ISA server first. The wizard creates a dial-on-demand connection on the ISA server that will receive incoming connections through the VPN. The connection is labeled dial-on-demand because the ISA server uses the connection only when needed, such as when external clients make requests. The wizard also creates IP packet filters for the incoming connections and configures static routes for the packets. Static routes ensure that the VPN connection goes through a predefined route so that packets do not get lost. All of the configuration settings created by the Local ISA VPN Wizard are saved into a .vpc file on the local hard disk.

You should run the Remote ISA VPN Wizard on the remote ISA server after you run the Local ISA VPN Wizard on the ISA server located at the main network. Before running the Remote ISA VPN Wizard, make sure the connection from the remote ISA server to the local ISA server is working because the Remote ISA VPN Wizard will try to connect to the local ISA server to download the .vpc file created during the Local ISA VPN Wizard. It will use this file to create its own IP packet filters and set up its own static routes to the server designated as the local side of the VPN.

If you are connecting roaming users to a VPN, you will need to run the Clients To ISA Server VPN Wizard. You run this wizard on the local server at the main network. It sets up the ISA server so that it will accept incoming VPN connections from roaming clients. To do this, it creates static IP packet filters that accept incoming connections. Whereas the Local ISA VPN Wizard can be configured to accept incoming connections and can initiate its own connections, the Clients To ISA Server VPN Wizard can be set up to accept incoming connections only.

PPTP or L2TP?

A VPN creates a virtual tunnel through the Internet by encrypting the data and authenticating the user, like making a tunnel through the Internet just for your users. A tunneling protocol such as Point-to-Point Tunneling Protocol (PPTP) or Layer 2 Tunneling Protocol (L2TP) is used to encapsulate the data that is sent between the local network and the remote network. Each of these protocols uses a separate protocol to encrypt the data being sent. Before Windows 2000, PPTP was the only choice for the tunneling of data over a remote connection when you were using Microsoft products. PPTP uses Microsoft Point-to-Point Encryption (MPPE) as its encryption protocol. MPPE is a Microsoft proprietary encryption protocol, which means it is not compatible with non-Microsoft systems. On the other hand, L2TP uses IP Security (IPSec) as its encryption protocol. Because both L2TP and IPSec are open Internet standards, and IPSec is considered to have stronger encryption. In most cases, you should select L2TP/IPSec when creating a VPN.

Configuring the Wizards

Now that we have covered the purpose of each VPN wizard and the changes that each makes, we will now examine the steps for using each of the three wizards.

Local ISA VPN Wizard

When the Local ISA VPN Wizard finishes, it creates a VPN configuration settings file with the file extension .vpc. When setting up the other end of the connection using the Remote ISA VPN Wizard—a process we will explain next—you use the .vpc file so that the remote ISA server knows exactly what to set up.

Although you normally set up the local ISA server to receive a VPN connection, assuming your local network has the resources that others need to access it securely, you can also set up the local ISA server to initiate a VPN connection. This is an optional setting that is included in the steps of the wizard.

A VPN can be configured only on an ISA server that is installed in Firewall or Integrated mode. An ISA server installed in Cache mode cannot be configured as a VPN server.

Because the RRAS service actually creates the VPN, it must be installed and running on the ISA server before you can run the Local ISA VPN Wizard. Figure 16.9 shows the warning dialog box that appears if the RRAS service is not yet installed on the ISA server. Also, if the RRAS service is installed but not started, the wizard will ask if you want to start the RRAS service.

To use the Local ISA VPN Wizard to configure the local ISA server, complete the following steps:

1. Open ISA Management.
2. Expand Servers And Arrays.
3. Expand the array you would like to configure.
4. In the selected array, expand Network Configuration.
5. In the details pane, click on the Configure A Virtual Private Network (VPN) icon. You can also right-click the Network Configuration container and click Set Up Local VPN ISA Server.

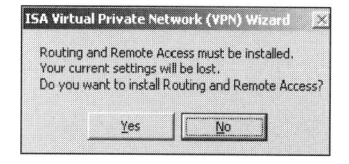

Figure 16.9 You will see this warning if the RRAS service is not installed.

6. The Local ISA VPN Server Wizard starts. Click Next on the Welcome To The Local ISA Server VPN Configuration Wizard screen.

7. On the ISA VPN Identification page, enter a name for the local network and the remote network. This is a name by which you want to refer to each network in the ISA Server snap-in. The wizard automatically creates a unique VPN name based on the local network and remote network name that you provide. For this example, enter "local1" for the local network name and "remote1" for the remote network name. The wizard will then show the VPN connection name as "local1_remote1". Click Next.

8. On the ISA VPN Protocol page, select the protocol to use. The choices are Use L2TP Over IPSec, Use PPTP, or Use L2TP Over IPSec If Available, Otherwise Use PPTP. For this example, leave the default selection, Use L2TP Over IPSec. Click Next.

9. If you want your ISA server to be able to initiate a VPN as well as accept incoming connections, you can use the Two-way Communication page to set this up. If two-way communication is needed where the local ISA VPN server does initiate a VPN connection, place a checkmark next to Both The Local And Remote ISA VPN Computers Can Initiate Communication. By default, the checkbox is not selected, meaning the local ISA Server will be configured only to accept a VPN connection but not to initiate it. If you select the checkbox, then provide the remote ISA VPN server's FQDN—such as isa.coriolis.com or the IP address—and if the remote ISA VPN server is a domain controller, enter the name of the domain.

10. On the Remote VPN page, specify the IP ranges on the remote ISA VPN server that the local ISA VPN Server can contact. Click Add.

11. Enter the IP address ranges. Click OK. If you need to add more IP address ranges, repeat Steps 8 and 9 until you have all the ranges entered. Then, click Next.

Note: *If you are not connected to the external network, the wizard will not be able to continue to the next step.*

12. On the Local Virtual Private Network (VPN) Network page, specify the local ISA VPN IP address that will be used to accept VPN connections from others. This is the IP address of the external network adapter on the ISA server. Also, the lower part of the dialog box lists ranges of IP addresses from the LAT on the local VPN server. Specify the range that includes the internal network adapter of the local ISA server so that a static route can be configured for incoming connections through the VPN. Click Next.

13. On the ISA VPN Computer Configuration File page, specify the file name for the configuration file that will be created on the local ISA server and then used

by the Remote ISA VPN Wizard. You can also encrypt the configuration file by supplying the password that will also be used by the Remote ISA VPN Wizard. If you specify only the file name but not the absolute file path, the file will be saved into windir\security\template by default. If you save it to another location, make sure the appropriate NTFS permission is set so that others cannot mistakenly access the file. The wizard adds the file extension .vpc automatically and you do not have to specify it. Click Next.

14. On the Completing The ISA VPN Wizard page, confirm you have configured all the desired options, and then click Finish. You can click Details to see all the configurations. You can also place checkmarks in the provided list to see other configuration dialog boxes.

15. When the wizard complete, it looks as if nothing happened. This is because the dial-on-demand interface is created and displayed in the Routing And Remote Access Service.

16. To view the connection you just created, expand the server name and open the Routing And Remote Access Server snap-in. Expand the name of the server on which you just created the VPN. Then, click Routing Interfaces. In the right pane, the interface just created, local1_remote1, should show up.

17. Close ISA Management.

Remote ISA VPN Wizard

The Remote ISA VPN Wizard allows you to configure the Remote ISA server so that it can create a VPN connection to a local ISA VPN server. This wizard does the same thing as the Local ISA VPN wizard, but it configures the VPN for the remote network. However, because it uses the VPN configuration settings file (.vpc) created by the Local ISA VPN Wizard when creating the dial-on-demand interfaces, the connection to the local ISA VPN server must be working before you run the Remote ISA VPN Wizard on the remote ISA server.

To use the Remote ISA VPN Wizard to configure the remote ISA Server, complete the following steps:

1. Open ISA Management.

2. Expand Servers And Arrays.

3. Expand the array you would like to configure.

4. In the selected array, expand Network Configuration.

5. In the details pane, click the Configure A Remote Virtual Private Network (VPN) icon. You can also right-click the Network Configuration container and click Set Up Remote VPN ISA Server.

6. The Remote ISA VPN Server Wizard starts. Click Next on the Welcome To The Remote ISA Server VPN Configuration Wizard screen.

7. On the ISA VPN Configuration File page, specify the location of the configuration file that was created when you ran the Local ISA VPN Wizard. Also, provide the password that was used to encrypt the configuration file. Then, click Next. If the passwords don't match, you will get an error message. Reenter the password and click Next again.

8. On the Completing The ISA VPN Wizard page, confirm you have configured all the desired options, and then click Finish. You can click Details to see all the configurations.

9. When the wizard is finished, it looks as if nothing happened. This is because the dial-on-demand interface is created in the Routing And Remote Access Service.

10. In the RRAS snap-in, expand the server name where the dial-on-demand interface was created. Then, click Routing Interfaces. In the right pane, the interface just created should show up.

11. Close the RRAS snap-in and then close ISA Management.

Clients To ISA Server VPN Wizard

The Clients To ISA Server VPN Wizard sets up a VPN server on the ISA server computer in support of external clients. The wizard sets up a local VPN server that supports both PPTP and IPSec/L2TP tunnels, and opens the appropriate ports on the ISA server to allow clients to connect to the VPN service. Remember that when ISA Server is installed, it shuts all the ports by default—a different behavior than that of Proxy Server, which opened all the ports by default when installed. Therefore, the appropriate ports must be opened so that VPN connections from offsite clients can be made.

To use the Clients To ISA Server VPN Wizard to configure the local ISA server, complete the following steps:

1. Open ISA Management.

2. Expand Servers And Arrays.

3. Expand the array you would like to configure.

4. In the selected array, expand Network Configuration.

5. In the details pane, click the Configure A Client Virtual Private Network (VPN) icon. You can also right-click the Network Configuration container and click Allow VPN Connections.

6. The ISA VPN Server Wizard starts. Click Next in the Welcome To The ISA VPN Configuration Wizard pane.

7. On the Completing The ISA VPN Wizard page, confirm that you have configured all the desired options, and then click Finish. You can click Details to see all the configurations.

8. When the wizard is finished, it will look as if nothing happened. However, as clicking Details reveals, the ISA server VPN has been configured to accept VPN connections from offsite users.

9. Close ISA Management.

Making Changes to the VPN

Once any or all of the wizards have been run, you can still modify the settings that have been created by them. However, you will need to create the IP packet filters on your own. Because the wizard makes configurations within the ISA server and the RRAS snap-ins, you might have to make changes in each of them.

Adding L2TP Support After the Wizard

L2TP can be thought of as the next version of PPTP. L2TP works in a fashion similar to PPTP but is a combined development effort with Cisco, the de facto leader of routing products. L2TP combines the technologies of Cisco's Layer 2 Forwarding (L2F) with PPTP. The protocol is currently an RFC draft but is expected to be an industry standard very soon. L2TP works in the Data Link layer of the OSI model, hence the name *Layer 2*. L2TP is used to create the VPN.

If you want to add L2TP as an encapsulating protocol after you have already run the wizard, you must also create two IP packet filters. Configure one of the IP packet filters by completing the following steps:

1. Open ISA Management.

2. Expand Servers And Arrays.

3. Expand the array you would like to configure.

4. In the selected array, expand Access Policies.

5. Right-click IP Packet Filters, point to New, and select Filter.

6. Type a descriptive name for the packet filter and click Next.

7. In the Servers step of the wizard, select Only This Server. Then select the server name from the drop-down list. Click Next.

8. Set the Filter Mode option to Allow Packet Transmission and click Next.

9. Select Custom for the Filter Type option and click Next.

10. In the Filter Settings dialog box, set the IP protocol option to UDP and select the Local Port drop-down arrow. Select Fixed Port and type in 500 in the Port Number box. Click Next.

11. Apply the filter only to the local server by selecting This ISA Server's External IP Address and entering that IP address.

12. In the Remote Computers dialog box, select Only This Remote Computer and enter the IP address of the remote ISA VPN server.

13. Review the settings in the Summary page and click Finish to create the packet filter. You can use the Back button to change any of the settings.

Configure the other required IP packet filter by completing the following steps:

1. Open ISA Management.
2. Expand Servers And Arrays.
3. Expand the array you would like to configure.
4. In the selected array, expand Access Policies.
5. Right-click IP Packet Filters, point to New, and select Filter.
6. Type a descriptive name for the packet filter and click Next.
7. In the Servers step of the wizard, select Only This Server. Then select the server name from the drop-down list. Click Next.
8. Set the Filter Mode option to Allow Packet Transmission and click Next.
9. Select Custom for the Filter Type option and click Next.
10. In the Filter Settings dialog box, set the IP protocol option to UDP and set the Local Port option as Fixed Port. In the Port Number box enter 1701. Click Next.
11. Apply the filter only to the local server by selecting This ISA Server's External IP Address and entering that IP address.
12. In the Remote Computers dialog box, select Only This Remote Computer and enter the IP address of the remote ISA VPN server.
13. Review the settings in the Summary page and click Finish to create the packet filter. You can use the Back button to change any of the settings.

Adding PPTP Support After the Wizard

One way to add more configurations to the VPN is through the RRAS service. If you select L2TP Over IPSec during the initial wizard, you can also add PPTP support through the RRAS snap-in.

Bandwidth Issues

Because of cost and line constraints, you must address the issue of available bandwidth when you have external connections. ISA Server allows bandwidth to be allocated by setting bandwidth priorities and effective bandwidth. Before setting out to work on any bandwidth issues, however, you must have a good understanding of how bandwidth is affected by external connections. Starting at the source of a problem (insufficient bandwidth) might be more beneficial than attempting to treat the symptoms (setting bandwidth priorities).

Identifying Bandwidth Issues

How best to utilize bandwidth is an important issue in any organization. The type and speed of the wide area network (WAN) connection and the connection to the Internet will determine the relevance of this data. Before configuring the bandwidth priorities, you must know the bandwidth available to the remote clients. Just as a chain is only as strong as its weakest link, the speed of a connection will be determined by its slowest connection point in the route. Bandwidth is a measure of data throughput over a connection in a set amount of time. Higher bandwidth means greater throughput of data in a given period of time.

Recent Trends

Fortunately, the availability of bandwidth has increased exponentially over the past few years while the price has decreased. A few years ago, a WAN with moderate traffic would have typically been connected with 56Kbps. High data throughput or real-time application requirements would have necessitated additional bandwidth. Now, even small branches on a WAN can be connected using 512Kbps for roughly the same cost as 56Kbps only a few years ago—and before this book reaches its first revision, this figure is likely to double.

Connection Methods

Users should also know that their method of connection has a direct effect on connection speed. Though standard WAN connections have improved considerably in a short period of time, analog modem connection speeds have essentially topped out at 56Kbps. Achieving 56Kbps throughput is nearly impossible on a standard analog phone line, so connections are generally somewhat below that. If a remote user is connecting from an external client using an analog modem, the fact that you have high-speed connections throughout the organization and connecting the organization to the Internet becomes less relevant for that user. On the other hand, if a user is connecting to the Internet using a high-speed cable modem or DSL, bandwidth on the user's end of the connection should not be a problem.

Bandwidth problems aren't limited to the user's connection. Bandwidth bottlenecks can occur anywhere in the route along which the data travels. Users may question why they experience delays and bandwidth issues when connecting using high-speed connections, such as a DSL or cable adapter. Users, and especially administrators, should know how the remote connection is configured and what bottlenecks may exist along the route.

Identifying the Bottlenecks

Figure 16.10 shows a high-speed network for locally connected users. However, those connections present several bandwidth problems for users connecting externally. The Internet connection from Server A is a T1 connection. The Internet connection from the remote client to the ISP is a DSL line. Both of these connections are reasonably fast. This means that the user's connection to Server A should be fairly fast. If the user requires services somewhere within the Headquarters location, the user should have no problem using the necessary services and should experience little or no delay in retrieving data. In many cases, the remote user may not notice any delay accessing most network services when connected in this manner. However, if the user needs to connect to Branch Office 1 to download data from Server B, the request must first be routed from the Headquarters location to Branch Office 1's location. Now, the external user's request will take a bit longer to process for a few reasons. First, the data needed by the user must be routed further than it had before, making one additional hop in each direction. Next, the

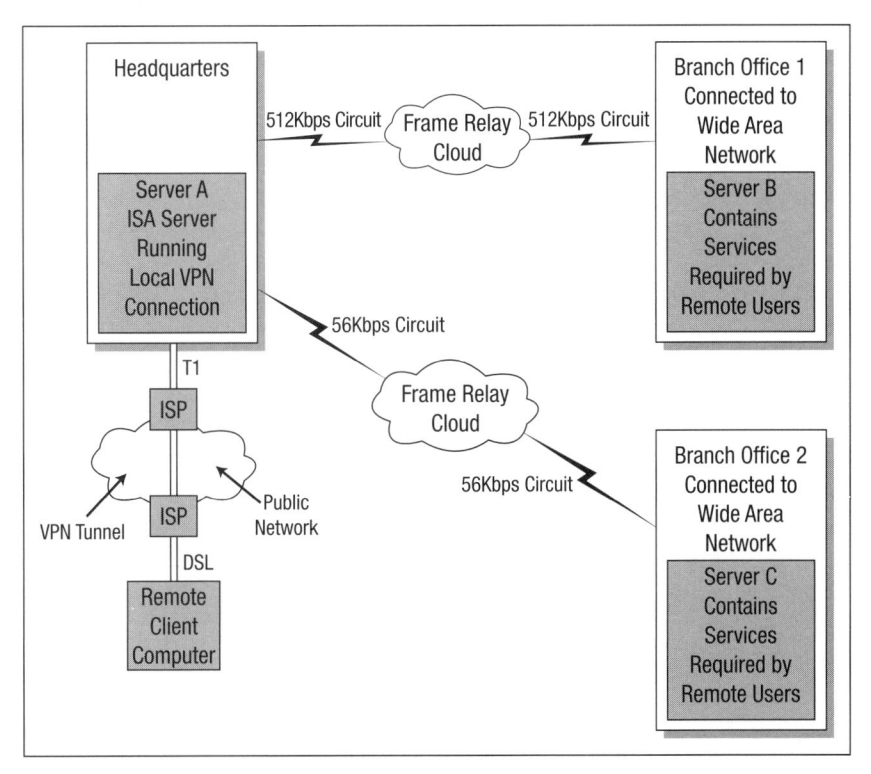

Figure 16.10 Identifying bandwidth bottlenecks.

request has been routed through a circuit that has less bandwidth than the previous request (512Kbps in this case). Third, the external user's request must compete with all the traffic that exists between Server A and Server B. Depending on the nature of the network, this traffic can be significant. Now, if the external user wants to access data on Server C in Branch Office 2 while connected remotely to Server A, the user would experience the same delays as in the first and second examples but would suffer additional delays because the 56Kbps circuit would take much longer to process the request than any other link on this network.

To further illustrate the difference the amount of bandwidth can make, we can use an analogy and compare data on a network to cars on a freeway. In this example, the link from the remote user's client computer to the ISP would be analogous to a toll road: Less traffic is present than on an ordinary highway, so finding an available lane isn't usually an issue. The link between Server A and its ISP could be compared to another freeway. A freeway can have several lanes. During non-peak times, traffic can fly by. However, during peak times, such as rush hour, getting from one place to another can take significantly longer because of all the cars on the freeway at one time. The connection between Server A and Server B can be compared to an ordinary highway. With a few lanes going in each direction, traffic moves along at a decent pace as long as too many cars don't attempt to get on at the same time. The connection between Server A and Server C can be compared to neighborhood surface streets, with one or two lanes in each direction. If a bus or large truck gets in front of you, you just have to wait until it clears out of the way before you can speed up and continue on your journey.

How Traffic Affects Available Bandwidth

To illustrate how bandwidth is affected by network traffic, consider how freeway traffic is affected by vehicular traffic. No matter how many lanes are on a highway, drivers have a preference for how fast they drive. When few or no cars are present, drivers can drive as fast as road conditions permit. When more cars are present, drivers begin to compete for space in each of the lanes until eventually they have to begin to slow down. At some point, when too many cars are on the highway, they start lining up on the on ramps until space is available.

Now that you know how bandwidth works and is affected by traffic, depending on the number of concurrent external connections and the amount of data to be transferred, you might need to set bandwidth priorities. Bandwidth priorities define the level of priority applied to connections that pass through the ISA server. A network connection that has a bandwidth priority assigned will stand a better chance of passing through ISA Server than a connection without a bandwidth priority. A network connection with a higher bandwidth priority will be more likely to pass through ISA Server than a connection with a lower bandwidth priority. In other words, connections without an assigned bandwidth priority will have lower priority than connections with assigned priorities. Returning to the freeway analogy above, assigning priorities would be similar to an ambulance passing on the freeway. When an ambulance is present but doesn't have its siren or lights on, traffic moves normally, but when an ambulance has its lights and siren on, cars move over and let it pass.

Setting Effective Bandwidth

As shown earlier, external connections using dial-up and VPN connections demonstrate how bandwidth can be an issue for users. One of the settings that you can specify for the dial-up entry in the ISA Server snap-in is Effective Bandwidth. The Effective Bandwidth setting helps a modem to use all of its available bandwidth. Figure 16.11 shows the dialog box that allows you to set Effective Bandwidth. It would appear that you need to sum all of your connections to come up with the number that you enter for Effective Bandwidth. However, the number that you enter needs to be the maximum speed of the modem.

To specify the Effective Bandwidth setting for a modem, complete the following steps:

1. Open ISA Management.
2. Expand Servers And Arrays.
3. Expand the array you would like to configure.
4. In the selected array, expand Policy Elements, then expand Dial-Up Entries.
5. Double-click on the dial-up entry that you need to set effective bandwidth on.
6. Select the Bandwidth tab. Figure 16.11 shows the Bandwidth tab in the dial-up entries property sheet.

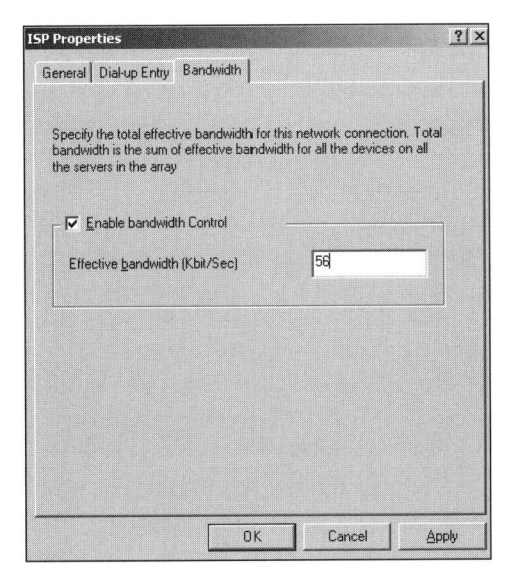

Figure 16.11 The Bandwidth tab allows you to set bandwidth control on a modem connection.

7. Place a checkmark next to Enable Bandwidth Control.

8. In the Effective Bandwidth Kbit/Sec field, enter the speed of the modem that the dial-up connection will be using.

9. Click OK.

10. Close ISA Management.

Chapter Summary

ISA Server's external connections can be dial-up or persistent. If ISA Server has an external dial-up connection, then the setup can be a lot more complicated than if it is a persistent connection. Dial-up connections require support from more than just the ISA Server snap-in.

To configure a connection that allows ISA Server to dial out, you must create a dial-up entry policy element. On a Windows 2000 Server, you create outbound dial-up connections in the Network And Dial-up Connections application. In this application, a DUN phonebook entry is created. When a dial-up entry is created in ISA Server, it must be based on a DUN phonebook entry. You must create this phonebook entry prior to running the Dial-up Entry Wizard in ISA Server.

Dial-up connections made by roaming users or branch offices can create long-distance charges. One solution to this problem is to use the Internet as a connection medium. A VPN allows private information to be transported over a public network by encapsulating and encrypting information. Normally, the RRAS service sets up a VPN on a Windows 2000 Server, but you can set up a VPN on an ISA server through the ISA Server snap-in.

ISA Server has three wizards that configure a VPN for different networking circumstances. These wizards create all of the necessary settings in the RRAS service and in ISA Server. These settings include IP packet filters and static routes as well as encryption and connections settings. The three wizards configure settings for a VPN on an ISA server to provide a VPN connection from remote clients or roaming clients and can also create a VPN between the main network and a branch network location.

Even though dial-up connections are an inexpensive way of connecting remote clients and networks, these types of connections also come with bandwidth issues. Networks connected by VPNs and other types of WAN connections can suffer from bandwidth fluctuations caused by network traffic. One way to help this problem at the ISA server is to specify Effective Bandwidth in the properties of the dial-up entry.

Review Questions

1. ISDN stands for what?
   a. Integrated Digital Services Network
   b. Integrated Services Digital Network
   c. Integrated Diagnostic Servicing Network
   d. Integrated Servicing Diagnostic Network

2. What must you create before creating a dial-up entry in the ISA Server snap-in?
   a. A DUN phonebook entry
   b. A connection to the modem
   c. A protocol definition
   d. A server publishing rule
   e. Nothing

3. DUN is used for what? [Check all correct answers]
   a. Setting up connections that dial out from a Windows NT Server
   b. Setting up connections that dial out from a Windows 2000 Server
   c. Setting up connections that accept dial-in requests from a Windows NT Server
   d. Setting up connections that accept dial-in requests from a Windows 2000 Server

4. In what applications are DUN phonebook entries created?
   a. ISA Server snap-in
   b. Dial-up entries
   c. Dial-Up Networking
   d. Network And Dial-up Connections

5. What kind of connections qualify as dial-up entries in the ISA Server snap-in? [Check all correct answers]
   a. Modem
   b. T1
   c. DSL
   d. ISDN
   e. T3

6. In what container will you find dial-up entries in the ISA Server snap-in?
   a. Access Policy
   b. Publishing
   c. Network Configuration
   d. Client Configuration
   e. Policy Elements

7. What service in Windows 2000 Server normally configures a server to accept multiple dial-in connections?
   a. RAS
   b. RRAS
   c. DUN
   d. Network And Dial-up Connections
   e. ISA Server

8. If modems offer the slowest connection speeds, why are they so often used?
   a. Modems are faster than ISDN connections.
   b. They are the most improved.
   c. They are the cheapest.
   d. ISA Server requires them.

9. Setting up a dial-up entry on an ISA server allows it to do what?
   a. Accept incoming connections
   b. Allow outgoing connections
   c. Apply server publishing rules to outgoing connection
   d. Apply Web publishing rules to outgoing connections

10. What settings in the ISA Server snap-in must be configured to allow client connections to be able to connect through an ISA server to an external network? [Check all correct answers]
    a. Policy Elements—Dial-up Entries
    b. Policy Elements—Destination Sets
    c. Policy Elements—Content Groups
    d. Network Configuration—Allow Dial-up Connections
    e. Network Configuration—Firewall Chaining—Primary Route

11. What significance does the active dial-up entry hold for an ISA server?
    a. It lets the ISA server know where the dial-up entry is located.
    b. It lets the ISA server know which dial-up entry is in use.

c. It lets the ISA server know which dial-up entry to use.

d. None

12. How is the active dial-up entry reset in ISA Server?

    a. In the properties of a dial-up entry

    b. Using a toolbar button

    c. Automatically when it is used

    d. Automatically when it is created

13. What are often-stated reasons for implementing a VPN? [Check all correct answers]

    a. To allow roaming users to connect

    b. To speed up a connection

    c. To save on long-distance telephone charges

    d. To add security

    e. To connect to branch offices inexpensively

14. A VPN is run on which server when used with ISA Server?

    a. On the ISA server

    b. On the internal network behind the ISA server

    c. Only on a DMZ

    d. On the Web server

15. A VPN is normally created using what service on a Windows 2000 Server?

    a. RAS

    b. RRAS

    c. DUN

    d. Network And Dial-up Connections

    e. ISA Server

16. How is direct access defined in ISA Server? [Check all correct answers]

    a. Allowing internal clients to connect to internal servers without going through ISA Server

    b. Allowing internal clients to connect to external servers applying ISA Server rules

    c. Allowing internal clients to connect to external servers without going through ISA Server

    d. Allowing external clients access to internal servers without going through ISA Server

17. Which VPN wizard(s) in ISA Server should be used when connecting the main network to a branch office? [Check all correct answers]
    a. The Local VPN ISA Wizard
    b. The Remote VPN ISA Wizard
    c. The Clients To Server VPN Wizard
    d. All of the wizards are used in this situation.
    e. None of the wizards fits this situation.

18. Which VPN wizard in ISA Server should be used when connecting roaming users to a main network?
    a. The Local VPN ISA Wizard
    b. The Remote VPN ISA Wizard
    c. The Clients To Server VPN Wizard
    d. All of the wizards are used in this situation.
    e. None of the wizards fits this situation.

19. What is MPPE? [Check all correct answers]
    a. An encapsulating protocol
    b. An encryption protocol
    c. An open Internet standard
    d. A proprietary Microsoft protocol
    e. An email protocol

20. Which protocol is used for encrypting packets when creating a VPN with L2TP?
    a. PPP
    b. PPTP
    c. MPPE
    d. IPSec

21. What is the file extension of the file that aids in the creation of VPNs in ISA Server?
    a. .vpn
    b. .vpe
    c. .vpc
    d. .vnn

22. Which VPN wizard creates the .vpc file?
    a. The Local VPN ISA Wizard
    b. The Remote VPN ISA Wizard

    c. The Clients To Server VPN Wizard

    d. None

23. Which VPN wizards use the .vpc file? [Check all correct answers]

    a. The Local VPN ISA Wizard

    b. The Remote VPN ISA Wizard

    c. The Clients To Server VPN Wizard

    d. None

24. Where is the Effective Bandwidth setting configured?

    a. In the properties of the Network Configuration container

    b. In the properties of the Web browser on the Client Configuration tab

    c. In the properties of the appropriate dial-up entry

    d. In the RRAS snap-in

25. What should the Effective Bandwidth setting be set to for modems?

    a. 56Kbps

    b. The speed of the internal network

    c. The speed of the external network

    d. The speed of the modem

    e. The speed you would like the modem to go

Real-World Projects

Note: *This exercise assumes a test Windows 2000 Server with Service Pack 1 and ISA Server installed and an external dial-up connection. Read the instructions carefully and do not change the settings on your production machine unless you understand the options presented. If you are unsure about an option, do not make a change and instead read the ISA Server help files about the option to be installed.*

Jane's company opened a new branch office located in Seattle. The company headquarters is located in Portland, and the Seattle office was the first branch office opened by the company. Jane was responsible for the main office's connection to the Internet, and the task of connecting the new branch office to the main office fell to her. Because cost was an issue, after many meetings and discussions the company chose a VPN as its connection method. The construction on the office was finally completed, and the computers and office furniture were all set up. Now suddenly everyone seemed to think that the connection between the offices was urgent.

An ISA server protects the main location, and Jane knew she needed to integrate the VPN with the ISA server. She had prepared herself by researching the integration of ISA Server and VPNs. She found that the VPN can actually be configured right in the ISA Server snap-in. She needed to install and enable the RRAS service on the ISA server because it would create the VPN, but she could create all the settings she needed through the ISA Server snap-in.

On the local ISA server she would run the Local ISA VPN Wizard and on the remote ISA server she would run the Remote ISA VPN Wizard to configure the VPN between the Seattle and Portland offices.

Project 16.1

To run the Local ISA VPN Wizard, complete the following steps:

1. Open ISA Management.

2. Expand Servers And Arrays.

3. Expand the array you would like to configure.

4. In the selected array, expand Network Configuration.

5. In the details pane, click the Configure A Virtual Private Network (VPN) icon. You can also right-click the Network Configuration container and click Set Up Local VPN ISA Server.

6. The Local ISA VPN Server Wizard starts. Click Next on the Welcome To The Local ISA Server VPN Configuration Wizard.

7. On the ISA VPN Identification page, enter a name for the local network and the remote network. This is just a name by which you want to refer to each network in the ISA Server snap-in. The wizard automatically creates a unique VPN name based on the local network and remote network name that you provide.

8. On the ISA VPN Protocol page, select the protocol to use. The choices are Use L2TP Over IPSec, Use PPTP, or Use L2TP Over IPSec If Available, Otherwise Use PPTP. For this example, leave the default selection, Use L2TP over IPSec. Click Next. Jane selected L2TP/IPSec because it was the most secure encapsulating and encryption protocol combination available.

9. If you want your ISA server to be able to initiate a VPN as well as accept incoming connections, use the Two-way Communication page to set this up. If two-way communication is needed where the local ISA VPN server does initiate a VPN connection, place a checkmark next to Both The Local And Remote ISA VPN Computers Can Initiate Communication. By default, the checkbox is not enabled, meaning the local ISA server will be configured only to accept a VPN connection but not to initiate it. If you select the checkbox,

then provide the remote ISA VPN server's FQDN—such as isa.coriolis.com or the IP address—and if the remote ISA VPN server is a domain controller, enter the name of the domain. Two-way communication might be needed, so Jane clicked the checkbox and provided the needed IP addresses.

10. On the Remote VPN page, specify which IP ranges on the remote ISA VPN server that the local ISA VPN server can contact. Click Add.

11. Enter the IP address ranges. Click OK. If you need to add more IP address ranges, repeat Steps 8 and 9 until you have all the ranges entered. Then, click Next.

Right after Jane clicked the Next button, an error message popped up. Figure 16.12 shows the error message that appeared.

ISA Server

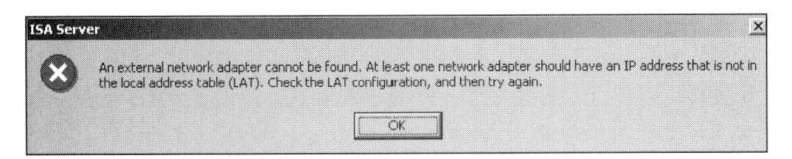

An external network adapter cannot be found. At least one network adapter should have an IP address that is not in the local address table (LAT). Check the LAT configuration, and then try again.

OK

Figure 16.12 An error message can appear when you run the Local ISA VPN Wizard if the external connection is not currently connected.

What could have gone wrong? She read the message. It was complaining about an external adapter. Nothing had been said about needing a live external connection while the wizard was being run, but that seemed to be the problem. She connected to her ISP so she could try the wizard again.

Jane repeated the first 11 steps of the wizard, then clicked the Next button, hoping the error message would not appear this time. It didn't. Now she knew that the external connection needed to be active during the VPN wizards in ISA Server. She continued on with the wizard.

12. On the Local Virtual Private Network (VPN) Network page, specify the local ISA VPN IP address that will be used to accept VPN connections from others. This is the IP address of the external network adapter on the ISA server. Also, the lower part of the dialog box lists ranges of IP addresses from the LAT on the local VPN server. Specify the range that includes the internal network adapter of the local ISA server so that a static route can be configured for incoming connections through the VPN. Click Next.

13. On the ISA VPN Computer Configuration File page, specify the file name for the configuration file that will be created on the local ISA server and then used by the Remote ISA VPN Wizard. You can also encrypt the configuration file by supplying the password that will also be used by the Remote ISA VPN Wizard. If you specify only the file name but not the absolute file path, the file will be

saved into windir\security\template by default. If you save it to another location, make sure the appropriate NTFS permission is set so that others cannot mistakenly access the file. The wizard will add the file extension .vpc automatically—you do not have to specify it. Click Next.

14. On the Completing The ISA VPN Wizard page, confirm that you have configured all the desired options, and then click Finish. You can click Details to see all the configurations. You can also place checkmarks in the provided list to see other configuration dialog boxes.

15. When the wizard is finished, it looks as if nothing happened. This is because the dial-on-demand interface is created and displayed in the Routing And Remote Access Service.

16. To view the connection you just created, expand the server name and open the Routing And Remote Access Server snap-in. Expand the name of the server on which you just created the VPN. Then, click Routing Interfaces. In the right pane, the interface just created should appear.

17. Close ISA Management.

Next, Jane called the Seattle office. She needed to lead the administrator through the steps of the Remote ISA VPN Wizard.

Project 16.2

To run the Remote ISA VPN Wizard:

1. Open ISA Management.

2. Expand Servers And Arrays.

3. Expand the array you would like to configure.

4. In the selected array, expand Network Configuration.

5. In the details pane, click the Configure A Remote Virtual Private Network (VPN) icon. You can also right-click the Network Configuration container and click Set up Remote VPN ISA Server.

6. The Remote ISA VPN Server Wizard starts. Click Next on the Welcome To The Remote ISA Server VPN Configuration Wizard.

7. On the ISA VPN Configuration File page, specify the location of the configuration file that was created by the Local ISA VPN Wizard. Also, provide the password that was used to encrypt the configuration file. Then, click Next. If the passwords don't match, you will get an error message. Reenter the password and click Next again.

8. On the Completing The ISA VPN Wizard page, confirm that you have configured all the desired options, and then click Finish. You can click Details to see all the configurations.

9. When the wizard is finished, it looks as if nothing happened. This is because the dial-on-demand interface is created in the Routing And Remote Access Service.

10. In the RRAS snap-in, expand the server name where the dial-on-demand interface was created. Then, click Routing Interfaces. In the right pane, the interface just created should appear. Close the RRAS snap-in.

11. Close ISA Management.

The VPN and the connection between the offices were now ready for use.

CHAPTER SEVENTEEN

Scenarios

After completing this chapter, you will be able to:

✓ Combine services available in ISA Server

✓ Design and implement an ISA Server setup for a small network

✓ Set up DNS support for SecureNAT clients

✓ Design a remote client solution with ISA Server

✓ Set up a three-homed perimeter network

✓ Design a large network solution with ISA Server

✓ Design a secure mail server using ISA Server

✓ Set up a back-to-back perimeter network

✓ Change a dial-up VPN connection to a persistent one

With so many services introduced and detailed in our book, this chapter details scenarios that show how services can be combined. We have not yet covered some services, such as the configuration of Local Address Tables (LAT) in a perimeter network and some Routing and Remote Access (RRAS) configurations that affect the Virtual Private Network (VPN). We have examined other settings—such as the installation of an ISA server, the configuration of a VPN, and the upgrade of the Standard Edition of ISA Server to the Enterprise Edition—but not all in one chapter.

Small Network Scenario

The Bongo Drum Company, located in Indianapolis, Indiana, makes percussion instruments. Until recently, employees who wanted a connection to the Internet used a modem and a phone line from their desk to get to the Internet. However, demand for Internet access is growing, and department managers are making strong arguments for giving their employees access to the Internet. Although there are 440 employees who work for the company, only 150 need access to the Internet. The remaining employees work in the factory and have no access to a PC during work hours.

Physical Network Description

The company's network spans two buildings—one building is the factory where the percussion instruments are made, and the other houses administrative, engineering, and executive employees. With just a few PCs in the factory building, the whole network is one subnet. The company is connected with a 10BaseT network and uses DHCP for IP addressing. It also has an internal Windows Internet Naming Service (WINS) server for name resolution.

Current Hardware

The company currently has two servers: a Pentium 90 with 128MB of memory and a 300MHz Pentium II with 256MB of memory. All computers are connected with a 10BaseT network.

All employees in the administrative building have a PC; just a few PCs are located in the factory building. These PCs have 486 processors with 16MB of memory each.

Current Software

On each of the 150 employee PCs, the operating system is Windows 95, and Internet Explorer 3.02 is used as the Web browser. One of the servers is a Windows NT 4 Server installed as a domain controller. This server contains all of the user accounts for the company. It also serves as the file and print server. The other server—on which SQL Server is loaded—is a Windows NT 4 domain member that contains employee and customer databases.

Issues

The company wants a way to provide its users with a connection to the Internet without compromising the security of internal company information. The company has never needed to be on the leading edge of technology and does not want to invest a substantial amount of money to set up or maintain a link to the Internet. It is looking for a simple, effective solution.

Solution

The IT department at the Bongo Drum Company is essentially two people. Working together to learn about the capabilities and administrative tasks of ISA Server, they are able to come up with a list of proposals. The first recommendation is to centralize the connection to the Internet and put an end to the individual links through modems. To do this, they must have a new server to load the Internet security server ISA Server. A new server is needed because the two other servers have important tasks that keep them busy. Also, each contains sensitive information that must be protected from the connection to the Internet. The ISA server should provide caching and firewall capabilities. The recommended connection is Integrated Services Digital Network (ISDN) to an Internet Service Provider (ISP).

The proposal also contains recommendations that all employees be able to access all Web sites and that a written policy be created spelling out the proper use of the Internet connection by employees. Support for Internet applications is not necessary, so only the Web Proxy client is needed for the employee PCs.

Server Hardware

The new server specifications meet Microsoft's hardware recommendations. The minimum system requirements for an ISA server are a 300MHz Pentium II processor with 256KB of memory. Two to four gigabytes of hard disk space are needed to provide cache services for up to 500 users. With this in mind, the company chose a new server with a 300MHz Pentium II processor and 256KB of memory. It also has a 10GB hard disk, of which 4GB will be used for forward caching for internal clients.

The server comes with an internal network adapter that connects it to the internal network. An ISDN adapter needs to be installed for the external connection to the ISP, however.

Server Software

Because ISA Server requires Windows 2000, the company must purchase that operating system and apply the latest service pack. The company wants the transition to be simple, so the solution is to purchase the Standard Edition of ISA Server and install it as a standalone server. This way, a Windows 2000 domain environment is not needed and all other servers can keep the same configuration. If growth is necessary at a later time, the company can purchase the Enterprise Edition of ISA Server and upgrade the Standard Edition to the Enterprise Edition.

The ISA Server must be installed in Integrated mode so that the network can benefit from both the caching services and firewall protections provided by it. Also, the administrator will have to create a protocol rule allowing clients to access Web sites. Because the primary connection to the Internet from the ISA server is dial-up, an extra setting is also needed. If you do not let ISA Server know that the dial-up connection is the primary connection to the Internet, it will not be able to proxy internal client requests using that connection.

Steps for Installing the New ISA Server

On the new server, you need to install Windows 2000 Server and the latest service pack. TCP/IP will install as the protocol suite by default. Partition the 10GB drive with one partition and format it with NT File System (NTFS).

Because you are installing the Standard Edition of ISA Server on the new server, it will automatically install as a standalone server. Complete the following steps to install this server according to the Bongo Drum Company's plan:

1. Insert the ISA Server Standard Edition CD into the CD-ROM drive.

2. In the dialog box that welcomes you to the installation, click Continue.

3. A welcome screen appears that introduces the installation of ISA Server. Click Continue to move to the next step.

4. A dialog box will appear asking for the CD key. Enter the key from the back of the ISA Server jewel case and click OK to continue the installation.

5. The next screen will display the Product ID number for this installation of ISA Server. If you ever have to call Microsoft product support, the support person will ask for this number, so you should write it down. Then, click OK to continue.

6. The End User License Agreement (EULA) will appear. Click I Agree to continue the installation.

7. Click the Typical button to install the typical components for the ISA Server.

8. A message will appear letting you know that ISA Server will install as a standalone server.

9. In the next dialog box, select Integrated as the mode of installation.

10. When the cache settings appear, create a cache of 4MB on the C: drive.

11. In the next dialog box, construct the LAT. Make sure all of the IP addresses used on the internal network are included as well as the IP address of the internal network adapter of the ISA server. Ensure that the IP address of the external ISDN adapter is not included on the LAT. Click OK to finish constructing the LAT, and then click OK again to continue the installation.

12. In the Finish dialog box, click the Finish button.

Configuring the New ISA Server

After the new ISA Server is installed, you need to configure some options to set up the access and connections for your internal users. When ISA Server is first installed, no connections are allowed into or out of the internal network. Because you are not publishing any services from your internal network out to users on the Internet, you don't have to configure any publishing rules. You do need to create rules that allow internal users to get out to the Internet. For security reasons, it is best to create rules that allow access to services or objects your users need. The other option is to create rules that allow open access to all services out on the Internet. Because the Bongo Drum Company is not technically sophisticated, access should be allowed to Web and FTP sites only. This means users won't be able to connect to or run Internet applications. Expect that as users become more sophisticated, you might need to relax the rules to allow more access.

Configuring Access

To allow access to Web sites only, you need to configure a rule that will let all internal users access the Internet with HTTP, HTTP-S, and FTP protocols. Gopher support is not needed at this time. By default, an open site and content rule allowing access to all sites is created during the ISA Server installation. However, access is allowed only if both a site and content rule as well as a protocol rule allow access. The protocols that you want to allow already have predefined protocol definitions created during the installation of ISA Server. All that is left is to create the needed protocol rule.

To create a protocol rule for access to Web and FTP sites, complete the following steps:

1. Open the ISA Server snap-in called ISA Management in the Programs menu.

2. Expand Servers And Arrays.

3. Expand Access Policy for a server-level protocol rule.

4. Right-click Protocol Rules.

5. Point to New and select Rule. The New Protocol Rule Wizard will start.

6. In the first dialog box, type "Web-FTP Access" as the name for the new protocol rule. Click Next.

7. In the Rule Action dialog box, select Allow. Click Next.

8. In the Protocols dialog box, select Selected Protocols and place a checkmark next to the protocol definitions for FTP Download Only, HTTP, and HTTPS. Click Next.

9. In the Schedule dialog box, select the Always option. Click Next.

10. In the Client Type dialog box, select Any Request. Click Next.

11. Review the summary of information and click Finish. You can use the Back button to change incorrect information.

The settings in this rule allow all internal users to make HTTP, HTTP-S, or FTP requests to the ISA server at any time of the day.

Configuring Dial-up Connections

The first step in configuring the ISDN dial-up connection is to get an account with an ISP. When you get that account, the company will give you instructions on the configuration of the dial-up networking (DUN) connection on your ISA server. For this scenario, we will name the DUN entry WeDeliverISP because it is the name of the ISP contracted by the Bongo Drum Company. After this connection is created, the next step is to create a dial-up entry in ISA Server so that it can use the DUN connection to dial the ISP.

To create a dial-up entry in ISA Server, complete the following steps:

1. Open ISA Management and expand Servers And Arrays.

2. Click the plus (+) sign next to the name of the server.

3. In the selected server, expand Policy Elements.

4. Right-click Dial-up Entries, point to New, and then click Dial-up Entry.

5. In the New Dial-up Entry dialog box, specify the name of the ISP as the name for the new dial-up entry.

6. In the Description box, enter "Entry that dials the WeDeliver ISP. Signed 1 year contract June 1, 2001, for service" as a description for the entry.

7. In the Use The Following Network Dial-up Connection box, type the name of the Windows 2000 network dial-up connection you just created—in this case, "WeDeliverISP".

8. In the Username box, enter the name of a user authorized to use the network dial-up connection. Also, enter the password for the user account.

9. Click OK to close the Dial-up Entry dialog box.

As a final step, you need to let ISA Server know that its primary connection to the Internet is dial-up. Also set the Primary Connection as a dial-up entry in the Network Configuration properties of ISA Server. To do so, follow these steps:

1. Open ISA Management.

2. Expand Servers And Arrays.

3. Expand the array you would like to configure.

4. In the selected array, right-click Network Configuration and select Properties.

5. Under Use Primary Connection, place a checkmark next to Use Dial-up Entry.

6. Click OK to close the Network Configuration Properties dialog box.

7. Close ISA Management.

Configuring Clients

To keep users from making their own connection to the Internet using the client Web browser, you must configure Internet Explorer to use the ISA server. The client computers just need the Web Proxy client because they are allowed to connect only to Web sites at this time. Because all of the client computers have version 4 of Internet Explorer, several options are available to get these configuration changes to all of the client computers. For example, you can send all employees who have an email account a message that includes a link to the configuration script that ISA Server creates when it is installed. When the employees read and sign the new policy explaining the appropriate use of an Internet connection, they check a box indicating that they have connected to the link and run the script on their computer.

Network with Remote Locations

MarketDirect and Mail2You have been competitors in the direct marketing business for the past five years. Now they are planning to merge their two companies, and some planning is necessary to make the transition a smooth one. Mail2You has been in business for 20 years in the Chicago area, but recently it has been struggling as a result of changes in the direct marketing industry brought on by the Internet and the growing use of technology. MarketDirect, located in Sacramento, California, has been in business for only five years, but in that time, it has built a reputation for being progressive with technology. Because of this reputation, the companies decided to keep the name of the newer company, MarketDirect, after the merge is complete. The companies will each continue to operate at their current locations.

Physical Network Description

MarketDirect has only 50 employees, and its current location is a single subnet with an ISA server protecting an ISDN connection to the Internet. Figure 17.1 shows this network configuration.

Mail2You is not a technologically sophisticated company. Although most of the 75 employees have PCs, the company just has a peer-to-peer network and does not have any connection to the Internet.

Current Hardware

MarketDirect has two servers. Both have 300MHz Pentium II processors with 256MB of memory. All client PCs at MarketDirect have Pentium-based processors with 64MB of memory. Mail2You has a 486DX66 with 64MB of memory that it used for a file and print server. The client PCs at Mail2You are a mixture of client computers and operating systems.

Current Software

The employee PCs at MarketDirect are a mix of operating systems. The company has made three major PC purchases over the last five years, and the PCs came with an operating system already installed on them. The first shipment of 10 PCs shipped with Windows 95. The second shipment of 25 PCs came with Windows NT 4 Workstation, and the last shipment of 15 came with Windows 2000 Professional preinstalled. No changes have been made on the PCs' operating systems. All clients are configured as Web Proxy clients to the ISA server.

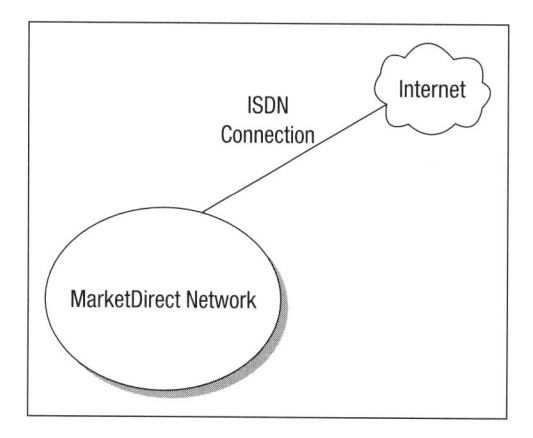

Figure 17.1 MarketDirect's current network configuration is simple.

Both servers at the company have Windows 2000 Server installed as the operating system. One is configured as a domain controller, while the other is a domain member that serves as an ISA server.

Issues

The new, larger MarketDirect wants to maintain its reputation as a technically progressive company. The combined management realizes that a substantial investment is needed to bring the whole company in line with the current technologies available. MarketDirect currently has a dial-up ISDN connection to an ISP that the entire company uses. So far, 128Kbps has been enough bandwidth because the majority of the connection's use came from the 15-person sales team while they researched new clients. All of the new employees acquired from the merge will also need a connection to the Internet.

The company also feels that it is now large enough to solicit business through its own Web site. The company has already created a new Web site and is ready to publish. It needs to include support and security for this Web site.

Web Server Requirements

The company is expecting about 100 hits per second when the Web site opens, but it would also like to plan for growth just in case the Web site takes off. This plan needs to include hardware settings that can support increased activity. Also, the plan needs to include security features because the company is concerned about the security threat the Web site will pose to the internal network.

Solution

First on the list is a recommendation that a separate server be purchased to host the Web site. Also, a perimeter network—also known as a Demilitarized Zone (DMZ)—should be set up to separate the Web server from the internal network. With the current number of employees, a three-homed ISA server can be used to create this perimeter network. The proposal list also includes installing an ISA server at the remote network location and creating a VPN between the two locations.

Hardware

The ISA server that protects the Web server and the internal network needs to have a 300MHz Pentium II processor. The current ISA server already has this. According to Microsoft recommendations, the current memory size of 256MB should support the forward cache requirements of internal users and the reverse cache requirements of the Web site. Web site activity needs to be logged, and the logs should be checked to track any increase in activity. Memory and the rest of the hardware are an issue when publishing a Web server because ISA Server is providing reverse caching services to the Web site. The company plans to purchase another Pentium

II or Pentium III processor if Web site activity grows dramatically. Microsoft recommends the addition of an ISA server with a 550MHz Pentium III processor for every 800 hits per second. This means a Web site with 2,400 hits per second would need a three-ISA-server array to provide the support recommended by Microsoft. ISA Server Standard Edition can work with up to four processors on a server. If more processors are needed, the Enterprise Edition of ISA Server must be used.

The three-homed perimeter network will require more configurations to the MarketDirect ISA server. Another network adapter should be added to the current ISA server that will connect to the Web server. Also, a DSL adapter that will provide the persistent connection to the ISP must replace the ISDN adapter.

The 486 server at the Chicago location must be replaced with a 300MHz Pentium II server with 256MB of memory. This server will provide the remote VPN connection.

Software

All users who do not have a PC will receive one. The company will develop a schedule for updating all the client operating systems to Windows 2000 Professional over the next six months.

The company will set up an internal DHCP server with a scope created for internal clients. This scope will give the IP address of the ISA server as the Default Gateway in the TCP/IP settings. This will allow the internal clients to act as SecureNAT clients to the ISA server.

The domain controller server already has a DNS server installed on it. This DNS server must be configured as a forwarder and a slave to an external DNS server at the ISP. Also, the company must configure a protocol rule on the ISA server that allows the DNS queries through to the external DNS server.

Configuring the Three-Homed Perimeter Network

Once the correct hardware is installed on the Sacramento ISA server, the LAT must be configured. The construction of a LAT must often be changed when perimeter networks are involved. Different types of perimeter networks require adjustments to the LAT configuration. In a three-homed perimeter network, the LAT contains the IP address ranges of the internal network, which is usually the case. However, the LAT cannot contain the IP addresses of the servers connected to the newly created perimeter network. This rule applies only to a three-homed perimeter network. Later in this chapter, we will discuss the configuration of a LAT for a back-to-back perimeter network.

Configuring the ISA Server

Both the Chicago and the Sacramento ISA servers must be configured differently because each is on a different side of the VPN. Both servers are installed as the Standard Edition of ISA Server and in Integrated mode to provide caching as well as firewall capabilities. The VPNs will use L2TP\IPSec as the encapsulating and encryption protocols.

Configuring the Local VPN Server

Even though the Sacramento location has fewer users than the Chicago location, it is still designated as the local VPN server. This is because the Sacramento location is the company headquarters and the location of the Windows 2000 domain. To start the creation of the VPN and designate the Sacramento location as the local location, you must run the Local ISA VPN Wizard on the ISA server at the Sacramento location. You can accomplish this by completing the following steps:

1. Open ISA Management.

2. Expand Servers And Arrays.

3. Expand the server you would like to configure.

4. In the selected array, expand Network Configuration.

5. In the details pane, click on the Configure A Virtual Private Network (VPN) icon. You can also right-click the Network Configuration container and click Set Up Local VPN ISA Server.

6. The Local ISA VPN Server Wizard starts. Click Next on the Welcome To The Local ISA Server VPN Configuration Wizard screen.

7. On the ISA VPN Identification page, enter "Sacramento" as the name of the local network and "Chicago" as the remote network name. The wizard automatically creates a unique VPN name based on the local network and remote network names you provide. For this example, it will be Sacramento_Chicago. Click Next.

8. On the ISA VPN Protocol page, select the protocol you want to use. The choices are Use L2TP Over IPSec, Use PPTP, or Use L2TP Over IPSec If Available, Otherwise Use PPTP. For this example, leave the default selection of L2TP Over IPSec. Click Next.

9. For this example, you will set up a VPN that initiates as well as receives connections. You can set this up on the Two-way Communication page. Place a checkmark next to Both The Local And Remote ISA VPN Computers Can Initiate Communication. By default, the checkbox is not checked, meaning the local ISA server will be configured to accept a VPN connection but not to initiate it.

Once you select the checkbox, provide the remote ISA VPN server's fully qualified domain name (FQDN)—in this case, ChicagoISA.marketdirect.com or the IP address. If the remote ISA VPN server is a domain controller, enter the name of the domain.

10. On the Remote VPN page, you need to specify the IP address ranges on the remote Chicago ISA VPN server the local ISA VPN server can contact. Click Add.

11. Make sure you are connected to the ISP, then enter the IP address ranges. Click OK and then click Next.

12. On the Local Virtual Private Network (VPN) Network page, specify the local ISA VPN IP address that will be used to accept VPN connections from others. This is the IP address of the external network adapter on the ISA server. Also, the lower part of the dialog box lists ranges of IP addresses from the LAT on the local VPN server. Specify the range that includes the internal network adapter of the local ISA server so that a static route can be configured for incoming connections through the VPN. Click Next.

13. On the ISA VPN Computer Configuration File page, specify the file name for the configuration file that will be created on the local ISA server and then used by the Remote ISA VPN Wizard. Encrypt the configuration file by supplying a password, which will also be used by the Remote ISA VPN Wizard. If you specify only the file name but not the absolute file path, the file will be saved into windir\security\template by default. Enter the name "VPN" and click Next. The wizard automatically adds the file extension .vpc to the end of the file name—in this case, the file name will be VPN.vpc.

14. On the Completing The ISA VPN Wizard page, confirm you have configured all the desired options, and then click Finish. Click Details to check all the configurations.

15. When the wizard is complete, no configuration settings appear in the ISA Server snap-in. To view the connection you just created, you will need to open the Routing And Remote Access Service snap-in by selecting Routing And Remote Access in the Administrative Tools menu.

16. In the RRAS Server snap-in, expand the name of the server on which you just created the VPN. Then, click Routing Interfaces. In the right pane, the interface just created appears. Select the Sacramento_Chicago connection to check the connection settings.

17. Close the RRAS snap-in.

18. Switch back to the ISA Server snap-in and close that also.

Configuring the Remote VPN Server

Once you've run the Local ISA VPN Wizard on the local server, you are ready to set up the remote server. To do this, you must run the Remote ISA VPN Wizard on the Chicago ISA server. Before you can do this, you have to set up and establish the remote connection between the Sacramento and Chicago locations. The Chicago ISA server will need to contact the Sacramento ISA server to download the configuration file. In the Local ISA VPN Wizard, this file was named VPN.vpc. Run the Remote ISA VPN Wizard by completing the following steps on the Chicago ISA server:

1. Open the ISA Management and expand Servers And Arrays.
2. Expand the server you would like to configure.
3. In the selected server, expand Network Configuration.
4. In the details pane, click on the Configure A Remote Virtual Private Network (VPN) icon. You can also right-click the Network Configuration container and click Set Up Remote VPN ISA Server.
5. The Remote ISA VPN Server Wizard starts. Click Next on the Welcome To The Remote ISA Server VPN Configuration Wizard screen.
6. On the ISA VPN Configuration File page, specify the location of the configuration file that was created by the Local ISA VPN Wizard. Also, provide the password used to encrypt the configuration file. Then, click Next. If the passwords don't match, you will get an error message. Re-enter the password and click Next again.
7. On the Completing The ISA VPN Wizard page, confirm that you have configured all the desired options, and then click Finish. You can click Details to see all the configurations.
8. When the Wizard completes, it looks as if nothing happened. This is because the dial-on-demand interface is created in the Routing And Remote Access Service.
9. In the RRAS snap-in, expand the server name where the dial-on-demand interface was created. Then, click Routing Interfaces. In the right pane, the interface just created should appear. Close the RRAS snap-in.
10. Close ISA Management.

Configurations for SecureNAT Connections

You must still create a protocol rule that allows the DNS requests from SecureNAT clients to pass through the ISA server. To do this, you'll have to run the New Protocol Rule Wizard again. In the first step, name the new rule "DNSForwarding".

In the next step, click Selected Protocols and place a checkmark next to the DNS Query protocol definition. The rest of the settings are the same as with the AllAccess protocol rule. It may seem redundant to create a DNSQuery protocol rule when the AllAccess protocol rule allows all protocols, including DNS queries. But if the policy of the company changes and the AllAccess protocol rule is replaced by something more restrictive, then SecureNAT clients will no longer be able to resolve Web addresses. ISA Server blocks all requests not specifically allowed, so it is a good idea to make a separate rule for DNS queries just in case.

The clients need to be configured as DHCP clients to receive the correct Default Gateway and DNS settings that will allow them to act as SecureNAT clients.

Upgrade a Network That Has Outgrown Its Settings

Let's say two years have passed since MarketDirect took over Mail2You and gained a second location for the company. Since then, MarketDirect acquired another direct marketing company in the Chicago area, and the corporate headquarters in California has continued to grow. The California and Chicago locations have grown to 325 employees and 500 employees, respectively. It is time for another revamping of the network to accommodate the larger size and increased traffic.

Physical Network Description

The network looks much the way it did two years ago—with a three-homed perimeter network at the California location and a VPN between the two networks. An Exchange server has been added to the perimeter network for email traffic, and the administrators ran the Mail Server Security Wizard to configure the necessary settings on the ISA server. All client computers are running Windows 2000 Professional, and all servers are running Windows 2000 Server with the latest service pack applied.

Issues

Employees are increasing their use of the Internet, and users at each location are complaining of slow connections when they're downloading Web pages. Also, the sales force has just requested the ability to authenticate with client Web sites. Some new clients want the sales force to be able to log on to private intranet Web sites to download information they need. Recent test attempts have failed. MarketDirect's Web site must allow for more customer interaction. Sales department managers are asking for a way to allow prospective customers to fill out a form that states the type of services they would like to see offered.

Solutions

The new, much expanded IT department located at company headquarters in Sacramento has outlined suggestions that will upgrade the present design to one that can handle more traffic and address the other issues that have been raised. The first suggestion is to upgrade from the Standard Edition of ISA Server to the Enterprise Edition. When the company first set up ISA Server, there were only 125 users, but the increase in users and the volume of traffic call for the more scalable Enterprise Edition. The Enterprise Edition of ISA Server will also allow the Chicago location to create an array to better deal with the traffic in that location.

The Enterprise Edition will better handle the addition of servers that is needed to handle the increased usage of the Internet connection. Because each location generates quite a bit of traffic, it is a good idea to give each its own connection to the Internet. An upgrade to the connection to a faster line is also suggested.

The VPN can still be used to communicate between the connections. Another suggested change is to the three-homed perimeter network. Replacing this with the back-to-back perimeter network will allow the handling of more traffic. To accommodate the sales department requests for customer forms on the Web site, the company needs to add a SQL Server to the perimeter network so that the Web site can post the information gathered in the forms to a database on the SQL Server.

The sales department attempts to be authenticated to customer sites have failed because they are SecureNAT clients. The Firewall client is the only client that supports individual user authentication. The Firewall client must be installed on at least the ISA client computers in the sales department.

Decisions

Because MarketDirect has built its reputation and growth on the use of technology in the direct mail business, the management of the company decides to follow the advice of the IT department. The solutions are accepted, and a T1 connection is selected for the upgraded connection between the locations.

Hardware

Three new servers need to be purchased—two for the Sacramento location and one for the Chicago location. One Sacramento server is for the SQL Server, which will reside on the perimeter network. The other server will protect the perimeter network. The Web site is up to 500 hits per second, but until the hits go up to 800 per second, the current hardware—which includes a Pentium II with a 300MHz processor and 256MB of memory—is sufficient.

Software

The company will purchase the Enterprise Edition of ISA Server and upgrade the Standard Edition ISA servers. After the upgrade is complete, the ISA servers will still be standalone. The company can create an array after the upgrade to the Enterprise Edition is complete.

Configuring the Back-to-Back Perimeter Network

At this point, you need to remove the network adapter on the original ISA server that connects to the internal network. Only an adapter to the perimeter network and an adapter to the ISP are necessary. Install the second ISA server and make sure it has two network adapters—one connected to the internal network and one connected to the perimeter network. Figure 17.2 shows the back-to-back perimeter network at the MarketDirect Sacramento headquarters.

Configuring the LAT

Because the ISA servers in a back-to-back perimeter network each protect a different network, each server's LAT needs to be configured differently. One ISA server is protecting the internal network, while a separate ISA server is protecting the perimeter network. In a three-homed network, the LAT contains the IP address ranges of the internal network; however, in a back-to-back perimeter network, only the ISA server that protects the internal network should contain the IP addresses of the internal network. The LAT on the ISA server that protects the

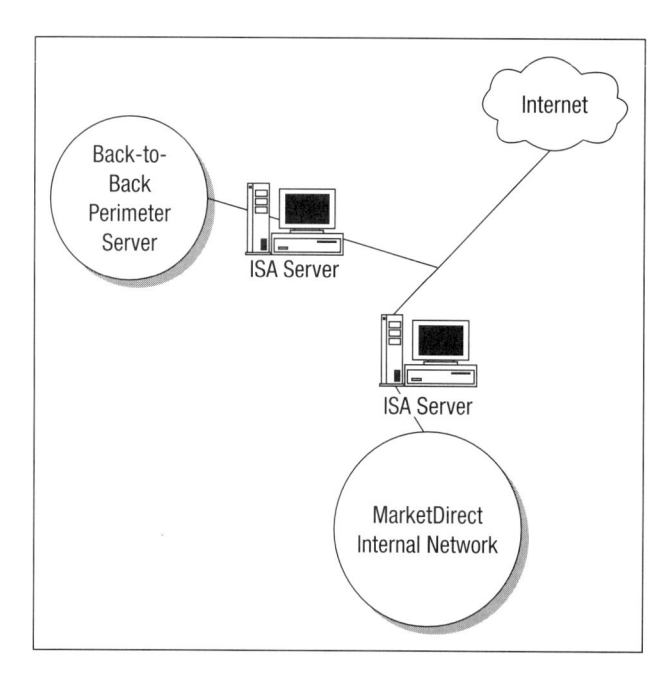

Figure 17.2 The new back-to-back perimeter network at the Sacramento headquarters.

perimeter network should be configured differently. This ISA server's LAT should contain only the IP addresses of the servers on the perimeter network and the IP address of the ISA server that is protecting the internal corporate network.

Upgrading the ISA Server to Enterprise Edition and Creating an Array

The original ISA server must be upgraded to the Enterprise Edition and an array has to be created. Before you begin the process, it is best to back up each ISA server that you will be upgrading just in case something goes wrong. To perform the backup, complete the following steps on each Standard Edition ISA server:

1. In ISA Management, expand Internet Security And Acceleration Server and then expand Servers And Arrays.

2. Right-click the name or the server that you need to upgrade to an array and select Back Up.

3. Type a path and filename in the Store Backup Configuration In This Location text box. You can also enter a description of the purpose and date of the backup in the Comment box.

4. Click OK to create the file that backs up the configuration settings of your ISA server.

You are now prepared to start the upgrade to the Enterprise Edition of ISA Server. In each existing ISA server, insert the Enterprise Edition CD in the CD-ROM drive and run the Enterprise Edition setup program. Setup will detect the Standard Edition of ISA Server and ask if you want to upgrade the settings. Select Yes, and the settings will be upgraded with no more input needed. All policies and rules, cache settings, LAT entries, and the mode of the ISA server will be upgraded. Even if you want to, you will not be able to make any changes to the settings during the upgrade. Also, the server will still be a standalone server at the end of the upgrade. To create an array, you have to upgrade the server in the ISA Server snap-in. To do this, complete the following steps:

1. In ISA Management, expand Internet Security And Acceleration Server and then expand Servers And Arrays.

2. Right-click the name or the server that you need to upgrade to an array and select Properties.

3. Select Promote, and then click Yes.

4. In the Set Global Policy dialog box, you can choose either Use Default Enterprise Policy Settings or Use Custom Enterprise Policy Settings. If you select Use Default Enterprise Policy Settings, then any existing server rules that are in

conflict with the default enterprise policy will be deleted. If you select Use Custom Enterprise Policy Settings, then you must choose between Use Array Policy Only (if you want to create your own array policy) and Use This Enterprise Policy (if you want to select a different enterprise policy rather than the default one). Also, you can select the option Allow Array Level Access Policy Rules That Restrict Enterprise Policy if you want the enterprise policy to allow you to set access policy rules that work within the boundaries of the enterprise policy you selected. For this example, select Use Custom Enterprise Policy Settings and then select Use Array Policy Only. This will allow all settings to be controlled at the array level.

5. Place a checkmark in Allow Publishing Rules if you want to keep the publishing rules you have already created on the server. This will keep the server publishing rules created for the Exchange server and the Web publishing rules created for the Web server that are located in the perimeter network.

6. Select the option Force Packet Filtering On This Array if you want to create packet filters at the array level.

7. Click OK.

Create an array at the Sacramento and Chicago locations. Then, add a new server to the Chicago array to handle the increased traffic in that location. When the T1 connection is set up between the two locations, you must configure the VPN to work with a persistent connection instead of a dial-up one. To do this, complete the following steps:

1. Select Routing And Remote Access in the Administrative Tools menu. The RRAS snap-in will open.

2. In the RRAS snap-in, expand Routing And Remote Access, and then expand the name of the ISA server working as the VPN server.

3. Select Routing Interfaces. In the details pane, right-click the Sacramento_Chicago VPN connection that was created for MarketDirect and click Properties.

4. Select the Options tab. Figure 17.3 shows the choices available on the Options tab.

5. In the Connection Type section, select Persistent Connection.

6. Click OK.

7. Close the RRAS snap-in.

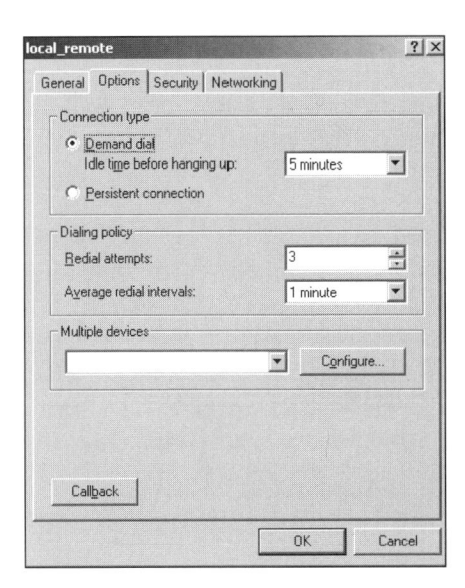

Figure 17.3 The Options tab in the properties of the VPN connection.

Chapter Summary

Different network configurations can require different combinations of services on ISA Server. In this chapter, we presented three scenarios, each requiring different settings.

In a small network scenario that contains one location and just 150 users, the configurations depend on the services needed by the users. In the scenario presented in this chapter, the users were not technologically proficient and just needed Web proxy connections to the Internet. This required very few configurations on the ISA server. An ISA server had to be installed and a protocol rule had to be configured for user access.

In a scenario that required a remote connection between networks, two ISA servers were required and a VPN was established between the two. A Web server was also included in this scenario. This did not require another ISA server, but at the request of the company, a perimeter network was created to protect the internal network from incoming traffic.

In the final scenario, the company from the second scenario had outgrown its configurations. Because of high traffic and strained network connections, the ISA servers were upgraded to the Enterprise Edition. This allowed for the creation of arrays and the addition an array server, for a total of two, at the Chicago location. Also, the three-homed network was changed to a back-to-back perimeter network. This required the addition of an ISA server. The LAT protecting the internal network was configured differently from the LAT protecting the perimeter network.

Review Questions

1. What is the minimum recommended processor for ISA Server?

    a. 100MHz Pentium

    b. 200MHz Pentium

    c. 300MHz Pentium II

    d. 300MHz Pentium III

2. Microsoft recommends that 125 users be supported by what size of hard disk cache for forward caching purposes? [Check all correct answers]

    a. 1GB

    b. 2GB

    c. 3GB

    d. 4GB

    e. 5GB

3. Why would a company choose the Standard Edition of ISA Server over the Enterprise Edition?

    a. The company wants room for growth.

    b. The company needs caching abilities only, not firewall capabilities.

    c. The cost is lower.

    d. The company does not need ISA Server add-ins.

4. If a company's client PCs are 486 machines with 66MHz processors and 16MB of memory, hardware upgrades are necessary in order for the PCs to become any kind of ISA Server client.

    a. True

    b. False

5. The Bongo Drum Company has client PCs that have Windows 95 and Internet Explorer 3.02 installed. What software upgrades on these PCs are needed in order for them to become ISA Server clients?

    a. The operating system must be upgraded.

    b. The browser must be upgraded.

    c. None, unless employees want to access Web pages.

    d. None, unless employees want to connect to Internet applications.

    e. None.

6. The management of the Bongo Drum Company does not want to format the new server's hard disk with NTFS and would like to use FAT32 instead. This server will be the ISA server for the network. What should you tell them?

   a. This will not affect ISA Server's performance.
   b. Proxy services will not be available.
   c. Firewall protections will not be available.
   d. Caching services will not be available.
   e. This is not possible.

7. Why doesn't the Bongo Drum Company configure the Default Gateway for SecureNAT clients?

   a. Because of the current network configuration, the SecureNAT clients can get a connection without it.
   b. Their routers configuration is sufficient for SecureNAT configurations.
   c. The company does not want to use SecureNAT for their clients.
   d. The company has Firewall clients instead.

8. The Bongo Drum Company creates a protocol rule for Web access, but includes a protocol definition for three of the protocols supported by the Web Proxy service. Why?

   a. The services provided by HTTP are not needed at this time.
   b. The services provided by HTTP-S are not needed at this time.
   c. The services provided by FTP are not needed at this time.
   d. The services provided by Gopher are not needed at this time.

9. The Bongo Drum Company sets up a protocol rule, but does not set up a site and content rule. Why?

   a. The company doesn't need to connect to any sites.
   b. A site and content rule allowing all access is configured by default in ISA Server.
   c. A protocol rule allowing all access is configured by default in ISA Server.
   d. The company plans to configure a site and content rule later.

10. When an ISA server is publishing a Web server, Microsoft recommends the addition of another ISA server for every _____ hits per second.

    a. 100
    b. 400
    c. 500
    d. 600
    e. 800
    f. 1,000

11. What service does the ISA server provide that requires it to support the situation described in the previous question?

    a. Forward caching
    b. Reverse caching
    c. Redirection
    d. Protocol rules

12. The Enterprise Edition can work with how many processors in one ISA server?

    a. Up to 32 when installed on Windows 2000 Server
    b. Up to 32 when installed on Windows 2000 Advanced Server
    c. Up to 32 when installed on Windows 2000 Datacenter Server
    d. Always an unlimited number

13. What method is MarketDirect using to configure its SecureNAT clients?

    a. DHCP clients
    b. SSL clients
    c. Client software
    d. No configuration is needed.

14. Why is the Sacramento location configured as the local VPN server when the Chicago location has more users?

    a. The administrators don't know what they are doing.
    b. The Sacramento location has the domain controller.
    c. The Sacramento location thinks it is more important.
    d. The Sacramento location has the Web server.

15. How is a protocol definition for a DNS query created?
    a. In the Policy Element container in the ISA Server snap-in
    b. By running the Protocol Definition Wizard
    c. It is created automatically when ISA Server is installed.
    d. It cannot be created.

16. What kind of processor on the ISA server is needed to support the expected hits of 100 per second on the MarketDirect Web server?
    a. Pentium, 200MHz
    b. Pentium II, 300MHz
    c. Pentium II, 550MHz
    d. Pentium III, 550MHz

17. What kind of processor on the ISA server is needed to support the new expected hits of 500 hits per second on the MarketDirect Web site?
    a. Pentium, 200MHz
    b. Pentium II, 300MHz
    c. Pentium II, 550MHz
    d. Pentium III, 550MHz

18. What IP address ranges need to be included in a LAT for a three-homed perimeter network?
    a. The internal network's computers
    b. The ISA server protecting the perimeter network
    c. The computers on the perimeter network
    d. The remote VPN ISA server

19. What IP address ranges need to be included in a LAT for the ISA server protecting the perimeter network when configuring a back-to-back perimeter network? [Check all correct answers]
    a. The internal network's computers
    b. The ISA server protecting the perimeter network
    c. The computers on the perimeter network
    d. The ISA server protecting the internal network
    e. The remote VPN ISA server

20. When can the IT department of MarketDirect create the new array for the ISA servers?

   a. Never—once it is standalone, it can never belong to an array.

   b. Before the upgrade to the Enterprise Edition

   c. During the upgrade to the Enterprise Edition

   d. After the upgrade to the Enterprise Edition

21. In what snap-in is the VPN connection changed from dial-up to persistent?

   a. RRAS snap-in

   b. Dial-Up Networking snap-in

   c. VPN snap-in

   d. ISA Server snap-in

CHAPTER EIGHTEEN
Sample Test

Question 1

You have a 500MHz Pentium III server with 192MB of memory, a 2GB hard drive with 50MB available on a NTFS partition that is running Windows 2000 Server. What must you change before installing ISA Server 2000? [Check all correct answers]

- ❏ a. Install a faster processor.
- ❏ b. Add memory.
- ❏ c. Add drive space.
- ❏ d. Defragment the drive.
- ❏ e. Load Windows 2000 Service Pack 1.

Question 2

Which reasons are valid for installing ISA Server in an array configuration? [Check all correct answers]

- ❏ a. Combined licensing
- ❏ b. Shared usage policies
- ❏ c. A common Enterprise Policy
- ❏ d. N+1 redundancy

Question 3

You want to deploy ISA Server on your network of Linux and Windows 98, NT, and 2000 machines as a caching and firewall server for all clients with as little workstation configuration as possible. Clients run Web browsers and FTP. Which client will you use to implement this?

❍ a. SecureNAT

❍ b. Web Proxy

❍ c. Firewall client

❍ d. This cannot be accomplished with a single client.

Question 4

You are a member of the Enterprise Administrators group for your domain and are about to install the first ISA Server in your array. What do you need to do? [Check all correct answers]

❑ a. Join the Schema Admins group for your domain.

❑ b. Join the Directory Admins group for your domain.

❑ c. Run the Enterprise Initialization tool.

❑ d. Run the Schema Extension Wizard.

Question 5

Corporate policy has been changed so that regular employees may visit sites only within the **company.com** and **subsidiary.com** domains during business hours. Regular employees may have access to all sites after work hours and during lunch (12-1 P.M.). The company's business hours are 8 A.M.–6 P.M. Administrators continue to be allowed access to all sites at all times. All workstations are running the Firewall client software. How do you achieve this? [Check all correct answers]

- a. Create a protocol rule denying access to the HTTP protocol except during scheduled work hours.

- b. Create a site and content rule denying access to addresses not in the destination set of **company.com** and **subsidiary.com** during work hours. Set it to apply to the Administrators group.

- c. Create a site and content rule denying access to addresses not in the destination set of **company.com** and **subsidiary.com** during work hours. Set it to apply to the Everyone group.

- d. Create a site and content rule denying access to addresses not in the destination set of **company.com** and **subsidiary.com** during work hours. Set it to apply to a group created to include all users except administrators.

- e. Create a site and content rule denying access to addresses not in the destination set of **company.com** and **subsidiary.com** during work hours. Set it to apply to a client address set including all workstation IP addresses except the administrators' workstations.

- f. Define the "work hours" schedule to be 8a–12p and 1p–6p, Monday through Friday.

- g. Define the "work hours" schedule to be 8a–6p, Monday through Friday.

Question 6

You have configured a client address set to include your workstations on the 172.16.2.0/24 subnet. Servers and print servers are located on the 172.16.1.0/24 subnet, and you recently added a subnet because you have expanded the number of clients beyond the prior subnet's capacity. Which ways can you add the new 172.16.3.0/24 subnet to the existing client address set? [Check all correct answers]

❑ a. Open the ISA Management MMC and navigate to Policy Elements|Client Address Sets. Select the existing set and click Configure A Client Set. Select the Addresses tab and edit the existing ending address to 172.16.3.255.

❑ b. Open the ISA Management MMC and navigate to Policy Elements|Client Address Sets. Select the existing set and click Configure A Client Set. Select the Addresses tab and add 172.16.3.1 – 172.16.3.255.

❑ c. Open the ISA Management MMC and navigate to Policy Elements|Client Address Sets. Double-click the existing set and select the Addresses tab. Edit the existing ending address to 172.16.3.255.

❑ d. Open the ISA Management MMC and navigate to Policy Elements|Client Address Sets. Double-click the existing set and select the Addresses tab. Add 172.16.3.1 – 172.16.3.255.

Question 7

You have just added a Linux machine to your network and need it to access the Internet via your ISA server using the standard corporate rules. Currently, Internet access policies are set for users and groups. All other machines are currently using the Firewall client software. How do you best configure this? [Check all correct answers]

❑ a. Load the firewall client for Linux on the machine.

❑ b. Load Services for Unix on the ISA server.

❑ c. Configure a client address set on the server that includes the IP address of the Linux machine and set up rules for access that refer to that client address set to match the existing rules. Set the Linux machine's default gateway to point to the ISA server.

❑ d. Configure a destination address set on the server for the Linux machine and set up rules for access that refer to that destination address set to match the existing rules. Set the Linux machine's default gateway to point to the ISA server.

❑ e. Configure the Linux PC's browser to use the ISA server as a proxy.

Question 8

You have just installed your first ISA server in its own array and loaded the Firewall client on your test network of five workstations. They are running Windows 98, Me, NT, and 2000. None of them can connect to any Internet hosts. What do you need to do?

○ a. Reboot all of the clients.

○ b. Unload the Firewall client and set the default gateway to the ISA server's IP address.

○ c. Reconfigure TCP/IP settings on all of the clients.

○ d. Create a new protocol rule allowing Internet access.

Question 9

You have a WAN between Pittsburgh and Harrisburg, Pennsylvania. The Harrisburg site has a T1 connection to the Internet, and Pittsburgh has a 128K link to Harrisburg. Currently a three-server ISA array is located in Harrisburg, which serves users in both sites. Management in Harrisburg wishes to cut costs companywide and increase the speed between the two sites for Internet and corporate traffic. Which solution would best serve the company's interests?

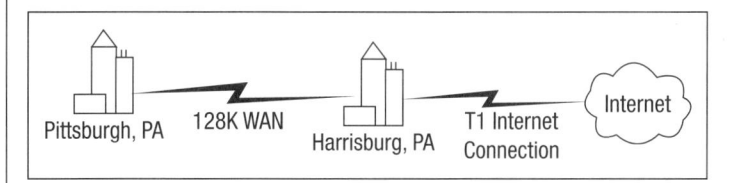

○ a. Install a second array in Pittsburgh and have it prefetch commonly used pages during off-hours.

○ b. Install a second array in Pittsburgh connected to the Internet via T1 and configure a VPN connection between the two sites. Eliminate the 128K WAN link.

○ c. Install additional array servers in Harrisburg to speed response times.

○ d. Replace the 128K WAN link with a T1 link.

Question 10

Your ISA server array has developed a problem. Clients from Unix and Windows environments are now unable to connect to the Internet. No changes have been made to any of the servers in at least a month. Your Internet connection is up. Running Internet Explorer at any ISA server gives you the same failure as the clients. Running the commands **Tracert** and **PING** to external hosts by name from the ISA servers both fail, but you can successfully **PING** external hosts by their IP addresses. What is most likely the problem?

○ a. Your ISP's DNS servers are down.

○ b. Your router to the Internet link has failed.

○ c. Your internal DNS server is down.

○ d. The ISP's router for your Internet connection has failed.

Question 11

You are responsible for a citywide network in Orlando, Florida. Eight sites within the city are connected by WAN links with at least T1 bandwidth. Seven of the sites are connected in a hub-and-spoke configuration with a central location. The central site has an existing Internet connection protected by an aging firewall. You are replacing it with an ISA server array and configure the first computer. When the setup has completed, you allow all users to access the Internet at any time. However, only users in the central location can do so successfully. What must you do to allow users in the other sites to access the Internet? [Check all correct answers]

❑ a. Add their IP addresses to the client address set.

❑ b. Add their IP addresses to the destination set.

❑ c. Add their IP addresses to the Local Address Table.

❑ d. Add their IP addresses to the routing table.

❑ e. Add routes to the remote subnets to the routing table.

Question 12

You have an existing Proxy Server 2.0 running on Windows NT 4, and you've applied Service Pack 4. All hardware is on the HCL for Windows 2000 and meets the necessary requirements for ISA Server. What must you do to upgrade to ISA Server and retain all existing settings? [Check all correct answers]

- ❏ a. Upgrade the server to the latest NT 4 Service Pack.
- ❏ b. Upgrade the server to Windows 2000 with the latest service pack.
- ❏ c. Defragment all drives.
- ❏ d. Load ISA Server.

Question 13

You are responsible for a worldwide network and are adding an ISA server array with a T1 Internet connection to a rapidly growing remote site in Saskatoon, Canada. Clients are a mix of Windows 9x, NT, and Windows 2000. They use DHCP for TCP/IP configuration. To keep client configuration simple, you have chosen to use SecureNAT for client connectivity. You configure SecureNAT on the server to service the existing addresses. However, client requests are still being routed to the corporate ISA Server array. What do you need to do to rectify the situation?

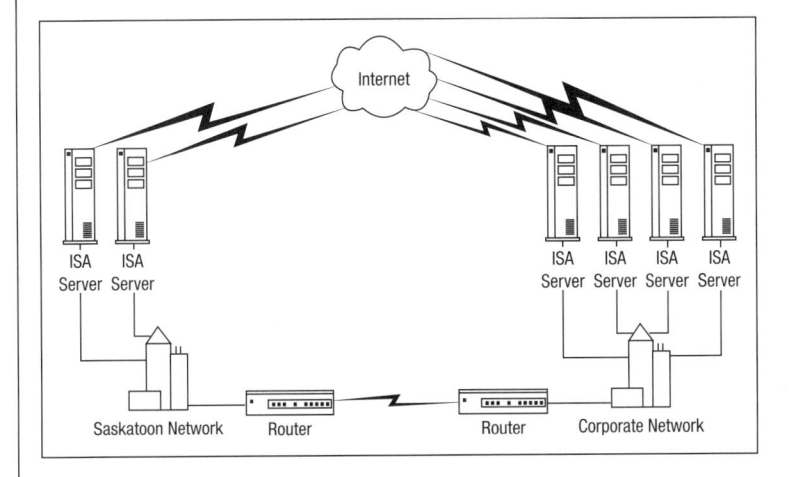

- ○ a. Set the clients' default gateway to point to the local ISA server array.
- ○ b. Set the Saskatoon router to direct any non-corporate traffic to the ISA server array.
- ○ c. Set the corporate router to direct any non-corporate traffic to the ISA server array.
- ○ d. Set the clients to use multiple default gateways.

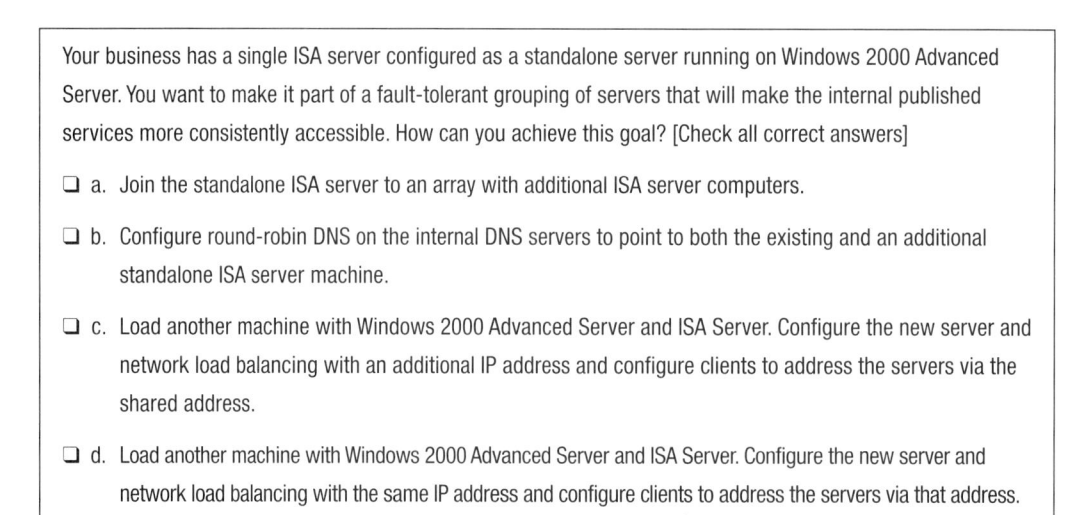

Question 14

Your business has a single ISA server configured as a standalone server running on Windows 2000 Advanced Server. You want to make it part of a fault-tolerant grouping of servers that will make the internal published services more consistently accessible. How can you achieve this goal? [Check all correct answers]

❑ a. Join the standalone ISA server to an array with additional ISA server computers.

❑ b. Configure round-robin DNS on the internal DNS servers to point to both the existing and an additional standalone ISA server machine.

❑ c. Load another machine with Windows 2000 Advanced Server and ISA Server. Configure the new server and network load balancing with an additional IP address and configure clients to address the servers via the shared address.

❑ d. Load another machine with Windows 2000 Advanced Server and ISA Server. Configure the new server and network load balancing with the same IP address and configure clients to address the servers via that address.

Question 15

You have a network configured with a two-server ISA server array. The servers are named ISAServer1 and ISAServer2, and the array is named ISAArray1. You want to publish the internal email server so it can be accessed via the Internet. How can you achieve this? [Check all correct answers]

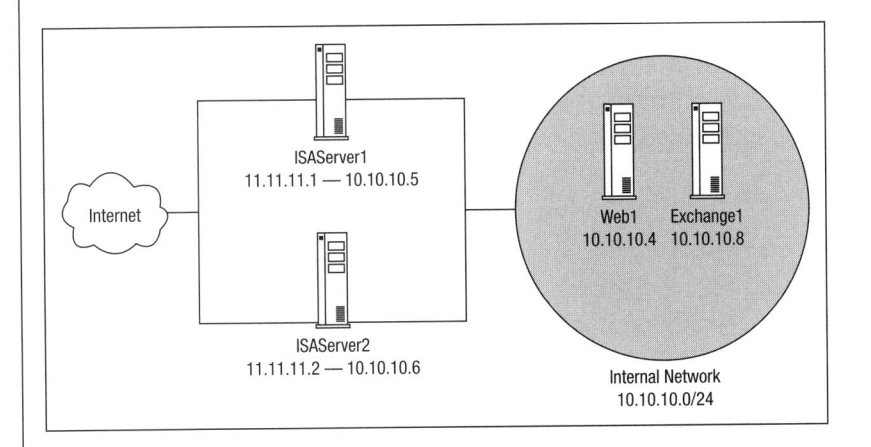

```
                    ISAServer1
                    11.11.11.1 — 10.10.10.5
    Internet                                    Web1      Exchange1
                                                10.10.10.4  10.10.10.8
                    ISAServer2
                    11.11.11.2 — 10.10.10.6
                                                Internal Network
                                                10.10.10.0/24
```

❏ a. Run the Publish A Server Wizard on each of the array members and specify the appropriate external and internal IP addresses.

❏ b. For the array, right-click on Server Publishing Rules and select the Secure A Mail Server Wizard. Specify the appropriate external and internal IP addresses.

❏ c. For each server, right-click on Server Publishing Rules and select the Secure A Mail Server Wizard. Specify the appropriate external and internal IP addresses.

❏ d. Run the Publish A Server Wizard on the array and specify the appropriate external and internal IP addresses.

Question 16

You have a network configured with a two-server ISA server array. The servers are named ISAServer1 and ISAServer2, and the array is named ISAArray1. You want to publish the internal Web server so it can be accessed via the Internet. How can you achieve this? [Check all correct answers]

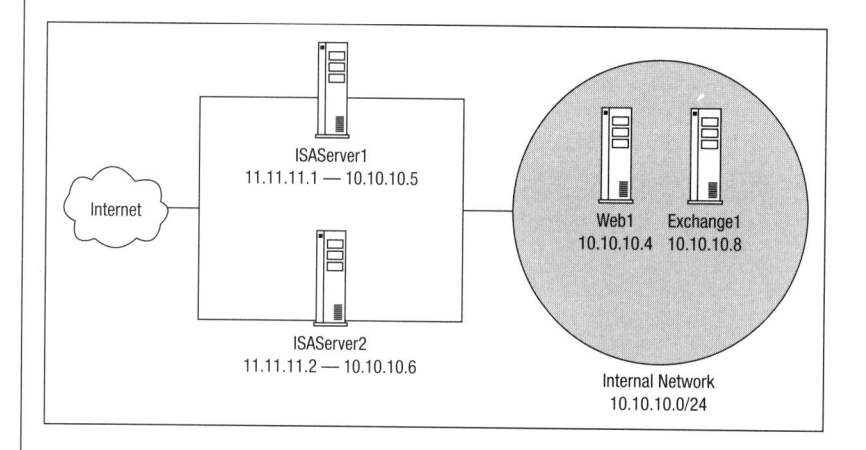

```
        ISAServer1
     11.11.11.1 — 10.10.10.5
Internet                           Web1      Exchange1
                                10.10.10.4   10.10.10.8
        ISAServer2
     11.11.11.2 — 10.10.10.6
                                   Internal Network
                                   10.10.10.0/24
```

- ❏ a. Configure a Web publishing rule that includes a destination set of the internal Web server and a client address set of the Internet machines you want to have access to the internal server.

- ❏ b. Configure a Web publishing rule that includes a client address set of the internal Web server and a destination set of the Internet machines you want to have access to the internal server.

- ❏ c. Configure a static route pointing to the internal Web server.

- ❏ d. Run the Publish A Server Wizard on the array and specify the appropriate external and internal IP addresses.

Question 17

Your ISA server has been up and running for two weeks. You use the ISA Management console to set up a new daily report job. When you go to view the report, you find nothing there. How do you fix this?

- ○ a. Under the Daily Report Job, select Run Now.
- ○ b. Stop and restart the Microsoft ISA Server Control service.
- ○ c. Stop and restart the Microsoft Web Proxy service.
- ○ d. Wait until tomorrow, when the first daily log will be created.

Question 18

You have an ISA server machine named ISA1 running in Integrated mode that runs IIS and an SMTP listserver. Corporate policy requires all firewalls to be secured as much as possible. How do you secure the server? [Check all correct answers]

- ❏ a. Open the ISA Management console and drill down to Servers And Arrays|ISA1|Computers|ISA1. Right-click on the server and select Secure.
- ❏ b. Open the ISA Management console and select the Enterprise Policy for security.
- ❏ c. Open the MMC and load the Security Templates snap-in. Select the ISA Server Security subfolder.
- ❏ d. Use the Dedicated security template.
- ❏ e. Use the Secure security template.
- ❏ f. Use the Limited Services security template.

Question 19

You have an ISA server array that is used solely for caching and firewall duties. It consists of three servers: Larry, Moe, and Curly. The array is named Stooge. You have been asked to harden the servers as much as possible in accordance with your company's stringent security policy. How do you do this?

- ○ a. Configure each server individually with the Secure security template.
- ○ b. Configure the array with the Secure security template.
- ○ c. Configure each server individually with the Dedicated security template.
- ○ d. Configure the array with the Dedicated security template.
- ○ e. Configure each server individually with the Limited Services security template.
- ○ f. Configure the array with the Limited Services security template.

Question 20

You have an ISA server array configured with default settings. You have a client PC that you want to connect to the Internet using Web Proxy. What steps are required for this to occur? [Check all correct answers]

- ❑ a. Configure the array with the Web Proxy security template.
- ❑ b. Configure the client with the Web Proxy client software.
- ❑ c. Confirm the client is using port 8080 to communicate with the ISA array.
- ❑ d. Create a site and content rule allowing access to the Internet for the client address.
- ❑ e. Create a site and content rule allowing access to the Internet for the user.

Question 21

You have an ISA server configured in Cache mode behind an existing hardware firewall. The firewall allows traffic through based on port number instead of checking the state of each packet. Your supervisor sees an article explaining that ISA server is a firewall too, and would like the firewall functionality installed and configured. How do you achieve this without losing existing functionality?

- ○ a. Execute the **setup //modechange /firewall** command.
- ○ b. Execute the **setup //modechange /integrated** command.
- ○ c. Remove and reinstall ISA Server in Firewall mode.
- ○ d. Remove and reinstall ISA Server in Integrated mode.
- ○ e. Enable stateful inspection under the security menu in the ISA Management console.

Question 22

Your users need to access an external Web site that is updated every night. You would like to "preload" the Web site into the ISA server cache before the business opens at 7:00 each weekday morning. How do you do this?

- ○ a. Enable Active Caching. Actively cache the page every Monday – Friday at 11:00 p.m.
- ○ b. Enable Active Caching. Actively cache the page every Sunday – Thursday at 11:00 p.m.
- ○ c. Create a Scheduled Content Download job referencing that site scheduled to run every Sunday – Thursday at 11 p.m.
- ○ d. Create a Scheduled Content Download job referencing that site scheduled to run every Monday – Friday at 11 p.m.

Question 23

Your users need to access a Web site graphic that is updated hourly. Currently, when they access the page it pulls up old information until they click Refresh. The users also want the large graphic to load as fast as possible. How do you fix this? [Check all correct answers]

- ❏ a. Set Caching to Frequently.
- ❏ b. Set caching's TTL to no more than 60 minutes.
- ❏ c. Set Active Caching to Frequently.
- ❏ d. Configure Page Prefetching to occur every 30 minutes.
- ❏ e. Configure Scheduled Content Download to occur every 30 minutes.

Question 24

You have an ISA server array on which you need to change the array policy. Who can do this? [Check all correct answers]

- ❏ a. Enterprise Admins
- ❏ b. Domain Admins
- ❏ c. ISA Admins
- ❏ d. Array Admins

Question 25

You have an ISA server array consisting of four ISA servers configured in Integrated mode. Two of them are in your main site in the Netherlands, and two are in a secondary site in Germany, connected to the main site by a T1 connection. Both locations have direct Internet communications via T1 and are connected together over a WAN with T3 bandwidth. Clients in the Netherlands should access Internet content located in Germany via the German ISA servers and other content via their own ISA servers. A properly configured client in the Netherlands requests a Web page from Germany. Which server(s) respond to this request?

- ○ a. One in the Netherlands, accessing the content directly
- ○ b. One in Germany, accessing the content directly
- ○ c. One in Germany, forwarding the request to the upstream server in the Netherlands
- ○ d. One in the Netherlands, forwarding the request to the upstream server in Germany

Question 26

Your company, located in Perth, Australia, has recently been purchased by a larger corporation based in Sydney. You had a Proxy 2.0 server and a local Internet connection. Your parent company connects to you via WAN and has an ISA server array in Sydney. It configures your Proxy server as a downstream member of its proxy chain. It also removes your local Internet connection. Users can no longer access streaming content, even though your parent company tells you all permissions are properly set. How can this be fixed?

○ a. Implement ISA Server at your location.

○ b. Have corporate headquarters install the H.323 Gateway service.

○ c. Update your Winsock Proxy chain configuration.

○ d. Configure NAT on your workstations.

Question 27

You have a 500-user network and want to lock down your Internet connection to eliminate abuses. Your ISA server is configured in Caching mode. Users access the Internet via Web Proxy. You want to limit users' ability to access all but named Web sites. What do you need to do to achieve this result?

○ a. Load the Firewall client on all PCs.

○ b. Reload ISA Server in Firewall or Integrated mode.

○ c. Set an access policy by user account.

○ d. Set an access policy by IP address.

Question 28

You currently have a network in Hamburg, Germany, at 10.10.0.0/16 and are adding a remote site in Hagerstown, Maryland. The remote site is a new facility and will have an IP address range of 10.11.0.0/16. Both sites have ISA server arrays, and you decide to configure the connection between the sites via VPN due to high transatlantic communications costs. Both arrays connect to local ISP services at T1 speeds. You configure one server in each array as a VPN router. What addresses will be in the LAT in Hagerstown?

○ a. 10.10.0.0 – 10.10.0.255 and 10.11.0.0 – 10.11.0.255

○ b. 10.10.0.0 – 10.10.255.255 and 10.11.0.0 – 10.11.255.255

○ c. 10.11.0.0 – 10.11.0.255

○ d. 10.11.0.0 – 10.11.255.255

Question 29

Your enterprise network based in London is adding a remote site in Munich. Due to connection costs, a VPN will be used for communications between the sites. London already has in place an ISA server array running in Integrated mode. Munich will be a new installation, so the ISA server array there is the primary concern in order to integrate the new site into the corporate Active Directory structure. You configure a server in London to accept VPN connections using the Local ISA VPN Server Wizard. However, once the VPN is established, the downstream ISA array in Munich is not communicating with the main one in London. How can you fix this? [Check all correct answers]

- ❏ a. Use the ISA Management tool to reconfigure the VPN authentication options.
- ❏ b. Run the VPN Array Connector Wizard in Munich.
- ❏ c. Add the address range for the London network to the Munich ISA server array.
- ❏ d. Add the address range for the Munich network to the LAT on London's ISA server array.

Question 30

Your network in Flower Mound, Texas, will be used as a central communications point for a nationwide sales force. You have purchased laptops and nationwide dial-up accounts for all of the sales staff and want them to be able to connect via VPN to the Texas site for database updates and centralized applications. What must you do to configure the VPN at the server and the first laptop? [Check all correct answers]

- ❏ a. Run the Set Up Clients To VPN Server Wizard on the ISA server.
- ❏ b. Run the Set Up Clients To VPN Server application on the laptop.
- ❏ c. Configure a dial-up connection to the ISP on the laptop.
- ❏ d. Configure a PPTP connection on the laptop connecting to the IP address of the Texas router.
- ❏ e. Configure a PPTP connection on the laptop connecting to the IP address of the Texas ISA server.

Question 31

You have users running AOL Instant Messenger to chat with other people outside the company during business hours. Because your company didn't implement an Internet usage policy, and the users work performance is similar to others not using the service, the IT Director has decided that the service will not be blocked. However, he wants to be sure that the AOL Instant Messenger traffic does not interfere with other Internet traffic of a business nature. What do you suggest as a technical solution? Your company is running ISA Server in Integrated mode with all workstations running the Firewall client.

○ a. Create a bandwidth priority of 1. Create a bandwidth rule referencing that priority for all AOL Instant Messenger traffic for all users.

○ b. Create a bandwidth priority of 10. Create a bandwidth rule referencing that priority for all AOL Instant Messenger traffic for all users.

○ c. Create a bandwidth priority of 100. Create a bandwidth rule referencing that priority for all AOL Instant Messenger traffic for all users.

○ d. Create a bandwidth priority of 200. Create a bandwidth rule referencing that priority for all AOL Instant Messenger traffic for all users.

Question 32

You have been requested to configure your ISA server array to notify a group of administrators if any sort of attack on your ISA server array is detected. The group has a group email address, countermeasures@yourcompany.com, which forwards the email to each individual recipient. How do you configure this?

○ a. In the ISA Server snap-in, go to the Monitoring Configuration|Alerts tree and configure the Intrusion Detected alert to send SMTP mail to countermeasures@yourcompany.com.

○ b. In the ISA Server snap-in, go to the Monitoring|Alerts tree and configure the Intrusion Detected alert to send SMTP mail to countermeasures@yourcompany.com.

○ c. In the ISA Server snap-in, go to the Monitoring Configuration|Alerts tree and configure the Attack Detected alert to send SMTP mail to countermeasures@yourcompany.com.

○ d. In the ISA Server snap-in, go to the Monitoring|Alerts tree and configure the Attack Detected alert to send SMTP mail to countermeasures@yourcompany.com.

Question 33

You have a back-to-back configuration of ISA server machines. In your perimeter network, you currently have a Web server and an FTP server. How do you best configure ISA Server A? [Check all correct answers]

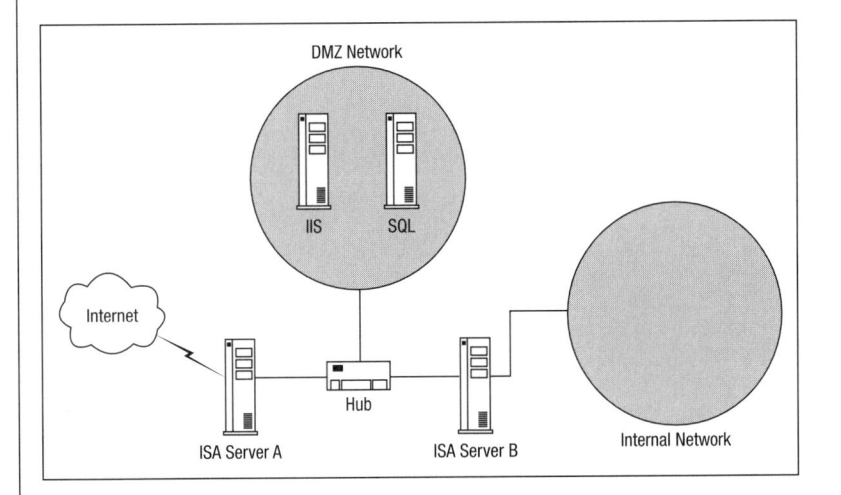

- ○ a. Set up ISA Server A with a LAT including the DMZ only.
- ○ b. Set up ISA Server A with a LAT including the DMZ and the corporate LAN.
- ○ c. Set up ISA Server A in Firewall-only mode.
- ○ d. Apply the Dedicated security template to ISA Server A.
- ○ e. Apply the Secure security template to ISA Server A.

Question 34

You have a single ISA server configured in Caching mode. When you set it up, you had 125 users and the cache was sized at 125MB. Your network has grown, and you now have 257 users who have begun to complain about speed. You decide to resize the cache to the recommended ____.

- ○ a. 229MB
- ○ b. 257MB
- ○ c. 152MB
- ○ d. 521MB

Question 35

You have a number of users who need to use NetMeeting to access other NetMeeting clients outside your network. You have configured the H.323 Gatekeeper on the ISA server, and users can contact other machines if they place calls. However, they do not receive inbound calls. How can you rectify the situation?

○ a. Create a DNS SRV record on your external DNS Server referring to service Q931 on port 1720.

○ b. Create a DNS SRV Record on your internal DNS Server referring to service Q931 on port 443.

○ c. Add the internal machines as destinations on your H.323 Gatekeeper machine.

○ d. Add the H.323 Gatekeeper machine to the routing table on your ISP's router.

Question 36

You want to allow H.323 Gatekeeper to work for a select number of users, who belong to the AD group NetMeeting Users. You want other users to have no access. How do you accomplish this?

○ a. You can run the Permissions Wizard.

○ b. You can right-click on the H.323 Gatekeeper server, select Permissions, remove existing permissions, and add the group there.

○ c. You can add the group to the H.323 global group.

○ d. You can remove existing permissions and add permissions for that group from the array's access policy.

Question 37

You have a small peer-to-peer network that needs to connect to the Internet. Workstations are Windows 98 PCs. Workstations are currently sharing files and printers over an Ethernet TCP/IP network. Your budget is small, but you have received an ISA server computer as part of a grant and would like to use it to make the most of your Internet connection. Because of budget constraints, your organization has not purchased a dedicated line, and inexpensive connections like DSL are not available in your rural area. You want to configure your ISA server to dial a 56Kbps modem to your ISP to receive mail from its POP server and to access Internet content. Each user has a POP3 mailbox on the ISP's system. How do you configure this? [Check all correct answers]

❑ a. Configure the default gateway on all workstations to point to the ISA server's IP address.

❑ b. Reconfigure client browsers and email applications to use the network as the Internet connection.

❑ c. Configure a dial-up connection on the ISA server to connect to the ISP.

❑ d. Create a dial-up entry in your policy elements.

❑ e. Configure ISA Server to allow access to all clients.

Question 38

You have an ISA server configured for RRAS dial-on-demand Internet connectivity. Your ISP has four dial-up access points within your local calling area. Typically, these are busy, so you want to dial the next number if the first you try is busy. All numbers should be usable for dial-up. How can you configure this?

- a. Add a dial-up entry under Policy Elements for each dial-up number.
- b. Add a Connection entry in Policy Elements for each dial-up number.
- c. Enter the additional phone numbers as Alternates in the RRAS dial-up entry.
- d. Enter the additional phone numbers in the Policy Elements for the dial-up connection.

Question 39

Management has determined excessive FTP downloading to be a drain on productivity and on the computer equipment. You are asked to deny FTP download access to all but a group named Web Developers. All workstations are running the Firewall client. How do you do this?

- a. Insert a packet filter to deny FTP access to non-Web Developers.
- b. Create a bandwidth priority for FTP. Assign it to non-Web Developers. Set the priority to 5.
- c. Create a new protocol rule allowing access to Web Developers. Remove or modify existing rules that currently grant access to the FTP protocol.
- d. Create a site and content rule allowing FTP access only to Web sites that Web Developers are working on.

Question 40

Users on your network are sharing music files. Your company sees this as a legal liability and wants access blocked. You download the client software for yourself and find that it uses TCP port 6969. As far as you see, no secondary connections are used. How do you block access to this service?

- a. Create a new protocol definition for connections on TCP port 6969 and create a protocol rule denying access to this protocol.
- b. Create a traffic definition for connections on TCP port 6969 and generate a traffic rule denying access to that traffic.
- c. Create a new packet definition for connections on TCP port 6969 and create a packet filter denying access to these packets.
- d. Create a Denied Protocol entry for connections on TCP port 6969.

Question 41

You have a multisite WAN with Proxy 2.0 in all locations. Currently, Internet connections are serviced through the corporate location only and cached downstream at the remote locations. You have upgraded the network to Windows 2000 and are about to upgrade all of the Proxy servers to ISA servers. All clients currently use Web Proxy but should get full Internet access to all protocols after the upgrade with no loss of connectivity. Which of the following will meet these goals?

○ a. Corporate clients with Firewall client, corporate Proxy Server 2.0 to ISA Server, remote clients to Firewall client, and remote Proxy Server 2.0 to ISA Server.

○ b. Remote clients to Firewall client, remote Proxy Server 2.0 to ISA Server, corporate clients with Firewall client, and corporate Proxy Server 2.0 to ISA Server.

○ c. Corporate Proxy Server 2.0 to ISA server, corporate clients to Firewall client, remote Proxy Server 2.0 to ISA Server, and remote clients to Firewall client.

○ d. Remote Proxy Server 2.0 to ISA Server, remote clients to Firewall client, corporate Proxy Server 2.0 to ISA Server, and corporate clients to Firewall client.

Question 42

You have multiple departments in your organization, each with its own building at the corporate site. Each department has an ISA server that is downstream of the ISA array in your data center, which is connected to the Internet. A user connects to the Internet and requests a Web page. Shortly thereafter, another user from the same department requests the same Web page. Which servers have the page in cache and which server services the second request?

○ a. All servers in the organization have it in cache, and the departmental ISA server services the request.

○ b. One of the array servers has it in cache, and it services the request.

○ c. One if the array servers and the departmental server both have it in cache, and the departmental server services the request.

○ d. The departmental server is the only server to have the page in cache, and it services the request.

Question 43

You have a back-to-back ISA Server configuration. ISA Server A has been hardened and is properly configured. How do you publish the Web server and FTP Server to the Internet?

○ a. Publish FTP via a server publishing rule and HTTP via a Web publishing rule.

○ b. Publish HTTP via a server publishing rule and FTP via a Web publishing rule.

○ c. Publish FTP and HTTP via server publishing rules.

○ d. Publish HTTP and FTP via Web publishing rules.

Question 44

You have a three-homed perimeter network as pictured. What should the LAT be for your ISA server array?

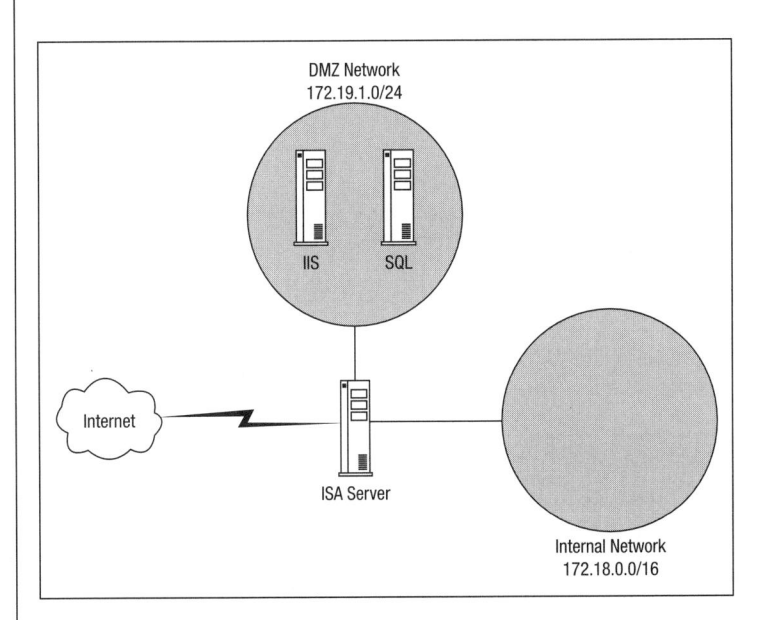

○ a. 172.18.0.0 – 172.18.0.255

○ b. 172.18.0.0 – 172.18.255.255

○ c. 172.18.0.0 – 172.18.0.255 and 172.19.1.0 – 172.19.1.255

○ d. 172.18.0.0 – 172.18.255.255 and 172.19.1.0 – 172.19.1.255

Question 45

Your network is configured as shown in the diagram below. The ISA server is installed in Integrated mode. You need to publish the Web and mail servers to the Internet. The Windows 3.1 client should have fast Internet access to Web and FTP services, and the Unix client should have full Internet access. Place the labels in the correct positions to accomplish these objectives.

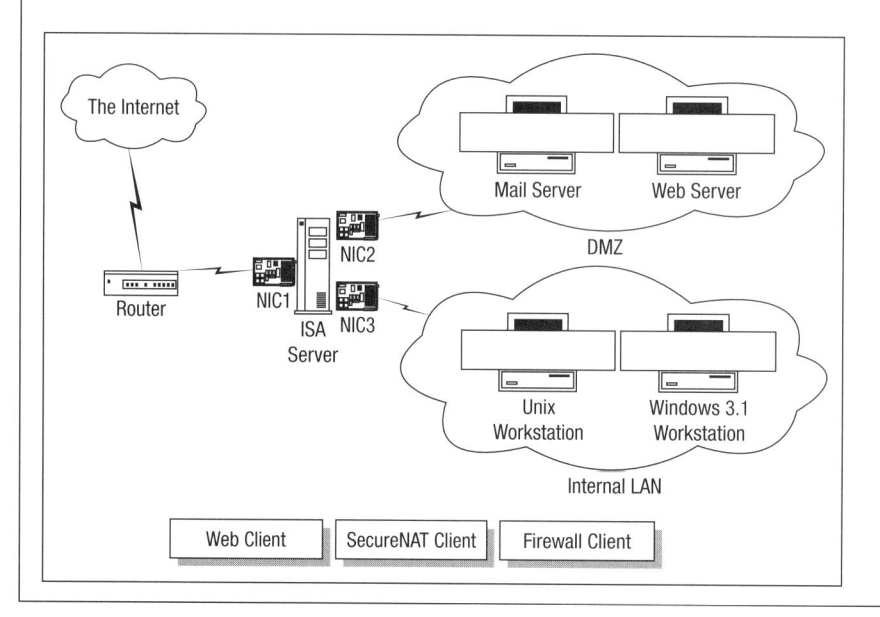

Question 46

To justify a new, faster Internet connection, you have been asked to determine which protocols are used most often and which Web sites are accessed most often. You have an ISA server in Integrated mode running with the default settings. All users are currently allowed to access all Internet resources. How can you get this information? [Check all correct answers]

- ❏ a. Configure a report job to run daily. Check the Web usage report immediately.
- ❏ b. Configure a report job to run daily. After 24 hours have passed, check the Web usage report job for the information.
- ❏ c. Configure a report job to run immediately. Check the Web usage report immediately.
- ❏ d. Configure a report job to run immediately. After 24 hours have passed, check the Web usage report job for the information.

Question 47

You are hearing complaints about the slowness of your Internet connection and want to determine which users are most active on the Internet. In addition, you want to determine which Web pages are being accessed most frequently so you can see how much use is non-business-related. You are looking for ongoing weekly information to present a case of use over time. How do you do this?

○ a. Configure a report job to run immediately. Check the Web usage report immediately.

○ b. Configure a report job to run daily. Check the Web usage report tomorrow.

○ c. Configure a report job to run weekly. Check the Web usage report tomorrow and each week thereafter.

○ d. Configure a report job to run weekly. Check the Web usage report each week, starting a week from today.

Question 48

You have a single ISA server in Cache mode. Prior to the installation of ISA Server, it was successfully hosting VPN connections. Since the install, however, VPN connectivity has been lost. How do you fix this?

○ a. Run the Local ISA VPN Wizard.

○ b. Run the Set Up Clients To ISA Server VPN Wizard.

○ c. Reinstall ISA Server with the same settings.

○ d. Reinstall ISA Server in Integrated mode.

Question 49

You have an ISA server configured in Integrated mode. Users are complaining about slow Internet access. You check traffic and determine that the Internet connection you have is not currently a bottleneck. You check CPU utilization, the network queue, the disk queue, and memory page faults/sec. CPU utilization is averaging about 40 percent, with occasional spikes to 100 percent. The network queue length is averaging 0–1. The disk queue length is averaging at about 3–4. You are getting about 5–10 page faults/sec. What can you do to increase performance of the server?

○ a. Add memory.

○ b. Add another physical disk, and relocate the cache to it.

○ c. Add a network adapter and share the bandwidth with Adapter Fault Tolerance.

○ d. Add another CPU or replace the current one with a faster CPU.

Question 50

Your ISA server running in Integrated mode seems to have lost some of its prior performance. Also, when you're running management tools at the console, they seem more sluggish than before. You check CPU utilization, the network queue, the disk queue, and memory page faults/sec. CPU utilization is averaging about 20 percent, with occasional spikes to 100 percent. The network queue length is averaging 0–1. The disk queue length is averaging at about 3. You are getting about 100–150 page faults/sec. What can you do to increase performance of the server? [Check all correct answers]

❑ a. Configure the cache to take a lower percentage of available memory.

❑ b. Add a second CPU or replace the current one with a faster CPU.

❑ c. Add RAM.

❑ d. Add another physical disk, and relocate the cache to it.

CHAPTER NINETEEN

Answer Key

For asterisked items, please see textual representation of answer on the appropriate page of this chapter.

1. b, e	18. a, e	35. a
2. b, c	19. e	36. b
3. b	20. c, d	37. a, b, c, d, e
4. a, c	21. d	38. c
5. d, f	22. c	39. c
6. a, b, c, d	23. b, c	40. a
7. c, e	24. a, b	41. d
8. d	25. d	42. c
9. b	26. a	43. a
10. a	27. c	44. b
11. c, e	28. b	45. ★
12. b, d	29. c, d	46. b, c, d
13. b	30. a, c, e	47. d
14. b, c	31. a	48. d
15. b	32. a	49. b
16. a	33. b, c, d	50. a, c
17. d	34. a	

Question 1

Answers b and e are correct. The minimum memory requirement is 256MB. You must apply Windows 2000 Service Pack 1 if you're installing ISA on a 2000 Server or Advanced Server. Answer a is incorrect because the minimum processor requirement for ISA Server is a Pentium II, 300MHz. Answer c is incorrect because available drive space required for installation is only 20MB, although you will require additional space if you are caching. Answer e is incorrect because you are not required to defragment a drive before software installation.

Question 2

Answers b and c are correct. Shared usage policies can be set at the array level, whereas the arrays can share a common Enterprise policy. Answer a is incorrect because licensing costs for ISA Server are per CPU, so an array would not change licensing costs. Answer d is incorrect because N+1 redundancy would be valid for a RAID disk system, but not necessarily for an array. In fact, an ISA server array may consist of a single ISA server configured as an array for manageability or for future expansion.

Question 3

Answer b is correct. The Web Proxy client will support FTP, HTTP, and HTTPS. Answer a is incorrect because SecureNAT will not support caching. Answer c is incorrect because the Firewall client will not install on Linux. Answer d is incorrect because the result can be achieved via the Web Proxy client.

Question 4

Answers a and c are correct. You must belong to the Schema Admins group and execute the Enterprise Initialization tool prior to the installation of ISA Server itself. Answer b is incorrect because Directory Admins do not have the authority to modify the schema, which is required for ISA Server. Answer d is incorrect because the Schema Extension Wizard is not a part of the ISA Server product.

Question 5

Answers d and f are correct. A site and content rule allows the administrator to set allowed sites instead of simply turning Web access on or off. Work hours were designed to exclude lunch so that employees could use the Internet unrestricted during that time. Answer a is incorrect because it would allow no Web access during off hours and full access during work hours. Answer b is incorrect because it would restrict the administrators instead of non-administrators. Answer c is incorrect because it would restrict administrators and non-administrators alike. Answer e is incorrect because it is machine-specific instead of user-specific. Administrators may need access from any machine, and the Firewall client allows user-specific restrictions. Answer g is incorrect because the lunch hour is included as part of the workday.

Question 6

All answers are correct (a, b, c, d). Any of these methods may be used successfully to extend the client address set.

Question 7

Answer c and e are correct. You can use either SecureNAT or Web Proxy to achieve the goals. Answer a is incorrect because no firewall client is available for Linux. Answer b is incorrect because Services for Unix would make the ISA server appear to be a Unix server but would not redirect Internet traffic. Answer d is incorrect because destination addresses are the addresses of Internet hosts you want to access or deny access to.

Question 8

Answer d is correct. ISA Server defaults to a secure configuration during installation and blocks all Internet access by default. Answer a is incorrect because the setting is at the ISA server, so a client reboot would have no effect. Answer b is incorrect because the ISA server is secured for all clients, not only Firewall clients. Answer c is incorrect because TCP/IP settings are not specified in the question; thus, it can be assumed that they have no bearing on the answer in this case.

Question 9

Answer b is correct. Configuring a VPN using local Internet connections is generally less expensive than a dedicated line. The VPN will also offer potentially higher bandwidth between the two sites. Answer a is incorrect because it wouldn't speed up network traffic and would affect only selected Internet traffic. Answer c is incorrect because the bottleneck is the WAN connection, not the Harrisburg array. Answer d is incorrect because its cost would be significantly higher than the cost for a local T1 connection.

Question 10

Answer a is correct. The key to this one is that a **Tracert** or **PING** by name fails, but by address succeeds. Therefore, the failure is in name resolution, or name-to-IP mapping, which is handled by DNS. Answer b is incorrect because the **PING** by IP address would also fail in that case. Answer c is incorrect because that would not affect external addressing. Answer d is incorrect because you would not be able to access the IP addresses in such a situation.

Question 11

Answers c and e are correct. Because the clients have not been configured, you might conclude that Web Proxy or SecureNAT is being used. The ISA server did not detect the additional networks, because its only default gateway should be the one to the Internet. Therefore, the addition of those subnets to the LAT and the addition of routes to those subnets will resolve their connectivity problems. Answer a is incorrect because the client address set is not required for full Internet access. Answer b is incorrect because destination sets are Internet addresses and would not include the clients. Answer d is incorrect because routing is done to networks, not individual machines.

Question 12

Answers b and d are correct. Windows 2000 Server with Service Pack 1 is required for ISA Server to install. Answer a is incorrect because ISA Server will not run on Windows NT 4, and the service pack is not required to upgrade the server to Windows 2000 Server. Answer c is incorrect because defragmentation is not necessary, even though it is a good practice.

Question 13

Answer b is correct. The only effective way to achieve your end with multiple client operating systems is to have the local router redirect Internet traffic to the local ISA server array. Answer a is incorrect because it would cause a loss of connectivity with the corporate parent. Answer c is incorrect because it would load up the WAN connection with traffic to the corporate parent and then back to the ISA server array. Answer d is an attractive option but incorrect because it would work only for Windows NT and 2000. Windows 9x is limited to a single default gateway.

Question 14

Answers a and c are correct. You can promote a standalone Enterprise Edition of ISA Server to an array. You can also configure NLB using Windows 2000 Advanced Server. Answer b is incorrect because DNS round-robin provides load balancing, not fault tolerance. If an ISA server fails, DNS will continue to send requests to the unavailable ISA server. Answer d is incorrect because you cannot have multiple devices configured with the same IP address. Network load balancing requires an IP address for each machine, as well as an additional IP address for the load-balancing feature.

Question 15

Answer b is correct. The Secure A Mail Server Wizard is a little difficult to locate the first time. You'll find the option to launch this wizard on the context menu that appears when you right-click on Server Publishing Rules. Once the wizard starts, you specify internal and external IP addresses to make the server secure but available to the outside world. Answer a is incorrect because the Publish A Server Wizard is not used for Exchange servers and would be used only once to configure the entire array. Answer c is incorrect because you need to configure the array only once; you don't have to configure each server in the array. Answer d is incorrect because the Publish A Server Wizard is not used for Exchange servers.

Question 16

Answers a is correct. You want to publish internal content (the destination) to external Internet devices (the clients). Answer b is incorrect because it reverses the client and destination information. Answer c is incorrect because it is not an available option from the ISA server, and because it would defeat any possible benefits of ISA caching or firewalling. Answer d is incorrect because the Publish A Server Wizard does not handle the HTTP protocol.

Question 17

Answer d is correct. Although the server has been up and running for two weeks, the daily report generation has just started and has not finished the first day's report. Answer a is incorrect because you do not have the option to "run now"—the job is already running but has not yet produced its first output. Answers b and c are incorrect because stopping and restarting the services do not affect the daily report.

Question 18

Answers a and e are correct. Security is handled through the ISA Management console, and Secure is the appropriate security configuration for an ISA server with IIS and SMTP services active. Answer b is incorrect because security is handled at each server, not at the Enterprise policy. Answer c is incorrect because the MMC Security templates are Windows 2000 templates. After you secure the server, however, you will see changes here. Answer d is incorrect because the Dedicated template is made specifically for an ISA server that handles no services other than an ISA firewall. Answer f is incorrect because the Limited Services template is designed for an ISA server that is not running any services other than ISA caching and firewall.

Question 19

Answer e is correct. Each server is individually secured. Because ISA is installed in Integrated mode, the Limited Services security template would be the proper one to use. Answers b, d, and f are incorrect because they specify security at the array level, not the server level. Answers a and c are incorrect because they specify the incorrect security template. The Secure template would be used on an ISA server that has additional services, such as IIS or NNTP. The Dedicated template would be used on an ISA server that is a firewall only.

Question 20

Answers c and d are correct. The default port for the array to be addressed with Web Proxy is 8080, and without user authentication, access should be allowed by a site and content rule specifying the client's address. Answer a is incorrect because no Web Proxy security template exists. Answer b is incorrect because you do not have to install client software—it's integrated into the browser. Answer e is incorrect because the user is not authenticated.

Question 21

Answer d is correct. To change the configuration of ISA Server, reinstallation is required. Answers a and b are incorrect because the suggested command will not work. Answer c is incorrect because Firewall-only mode does not allow caching. Answer e is incorrect because the only way to enable firewall features is to reinstall.

Question 22

Answer c is correct. A Scheduled Content Download job should run the night before each business day, so Sunday–Thursday is correct. Answers a and b are incorrect because Active Caching is an ISA feature designed so that page content is current. Answers a and d are incorrect because the schedule is wrong.

Question 23

Answers b and c are correct. Active Caching refreshes the objects in cache before they expire, keeping the current object available to the user instead of an older version. Having the TTL, or Time To Live, set to an hour or less will ensure that Active Caching updates the object in the cache often. Answer a is incorrect because setting Caching to Frequently expires the object in the cache but does not pull a new copy into the cache, so it would take a while to pull the graphic down. Answer d is incorrect because the Page Prefetching option does not exist. Answer e is incorrect because Scheduled Content Download can run only daily.

Question 24

Answers a and b are correct. Both Enterprise Admins and Domain Admins have the authority to change array policy. Answers c and d are incorrect because the ISA Admins and Array Admins group do not exist.

Question 25

Answer d is correct. The local ISA server in the Netherlands will request the page from the upstream server in Germany. Answer a is incorrect because the Netherlands server will check the cache in the upstream server in Germany. Answers b and c are incorrect because the local server will be accessed, not the one in Germany.

Question 26

Answer a is correct. Proxy 2.0 doesn't support upstream firewall chaining (referred to in Proxy 2 as Winsock proxy chaining). Answer b is incorrect because the H.323 Gateway is not required at corporate because packets are not even being sent to the corporate location. Answer c is incorrect because Winsock Proxy in Proxy 2.0 cannot connect to an upstream ISA server. Answer d is incorrect because the client configuration is already connected to the local Proxy server.

Question 27

Answer c is correct. Web Proxy will use user authentication via the browser. Answer a is incorrect because the Firewall client is not required. Answer b is incorrect because the server need not act as a firewall to limit user access. Answer d is incorrect because the Web Proxy service uses username and password authentication.

Question 28

Answer b is correct. With a 16-bit subnet mask, 65,535 addresses are available, so 10.11.0.0–10.11.255.255 is the correct range. Also, addresses on the other end of the VPN connection are considered local. Answer a is incorrect because it is assuming the wrong subnet mask (or a /24 CIDR address). Answer c is incorrect because it has the wrong subnet mask and is missing the local addresses on the corporate network. Answer d is incorrect because it is missing the local addresses on the corporate network.

Question 29

Answers c and d are correct. Both networks need to be part of the LAT in both sites for proper ISA Server functionality. Adding the remote network to the local LAT is not a function of either the Local ISA Server VPN Wizard or the Remote ISA Server VPN Wizard. Answer a is incorrect because the VPN would be configured in the RRAS MMC and because the VPN is already successfully connected. Answer b is incorrect because no VPN Array Connector Wizard exists.

Question 30

Answers a, c, and e are correct. You need to have the ISA server configured to accept VPN connections and the laptop configured to initiate a dial-up to the ISP, followed by a VPN connection to the ISA server. Answer b is incorrect because this is run within the ISA Management application, not from a client. Answer d is incorrect because the router would not accept a PPTP connection—and even if it did, you would be separated from the network by the ISA server.

Answer Key

Question 31

Answer a is correct. The lowest priority is the lowest number, compared to the default priority of 100. You may have other bandwidth rules in place, so using a priority of 1 is safest. Answers b, c, and d are all incorrect because they do not reference the lowest possible priority.

Question 32

Answer a is correct. The default Intrusion Detected alert is found under Monitoring Configuration. With a SMTP server address and email address, it can automatically notify an email address. Answers b and d are incorrect because the Monitoring tree shows monitoring results but does not configure monitoring. Answer d is also incorrect, as is answer c, because no default Attack Detected monitoring job exists.

Question 33

Answers b, c, and d are correct. The outside ISA server is most secure when running as a dedicated firewall, secured with the Dedicated security template, and it requires all internal addresses to be listed in the LAT. Answer a is incorrect because it leaves the corporate LAN out of the LAT, which will cause ISA Server A to see requests from those addresses as external addresses. Answer e is incorrect because it is the most open security template, designed for a server running IIS or email in addition to ISA Server.

Question 34

Answer a is correct; 229MB is 100MB plus .5MB/user, rounded up. All other answers are incorrect because they don't adhere to the correct formula.

Question 35

Answer a is correct. The SRV record advertises the H.323 service as available to look up connection information for inbound calls, so callers can now look up the address of the machine they want to contact. Answer b is incorrect because of the faulty port number. Answer c is incorrect because internal machines need not be configured as destinations for this protocol. Answer d is incorrect because the machine should already be in the routing table on the ISP's site.

Question 36

Answer b is correct. You assign permissions to users and groups separately on the H.323 server's Permissions tab within the ISA Management console. Answer a is incorrect because the Permissions Wizard does not exist. Answer c is incorrect because the H.323 global group is not created by ISA Server installation, so its rights are unknown. Answer d is incorrect because the array's access policy is separate from the H.323 Gateway.

Question 37

All answers are correct (a, b, c, d, and e). These are all necessary steps in configuring an ISA server for dial-on-demand connection to the Internet.

Question 38

Answer c is correct. Because ISA Server runs on top of Windows 2000, it is dependent on some Windows 2000 services. Answer a is incorrect because you would have a dial-up entry. Answer b is incorrect because Policy Elements contains no Connection entry. Answer d is incorrect because you cannot change or add phone numbers in Policy Elements.

Question 39

Answer c is correct. It is easiest to manage your server with as few rules as possible. The default is for all traffic to be blocked until explicitly granted. So rather than creating a new group, removal of all existing permissions for the protocol prior to setting new ones is the cleanest way to achieve your goal. Answer a is incorrect because a packet filter cannot do this by group. Answer b is incorrect because even though traffic would be set to a very low priority, it would still be allowed. Answer d is incorrect because it limits FTP access by site, not by group.

Question 40

Answer a is correct. What you must do to achieve your objective is to define the protocol used and block it. All other answers are incorrect because they are not protocol rules and will not perform the tasks required.

Question 41

Answer d is correct. Because the locations are connected with hierarchical caching, the remote sites must be upgraded first. The Firewall client should be installed from the ISA server it connects to, so servers should be in place before upgrading the client software. If the server name and IP address are the same, existing Web Proxy clients will retain their connectivity. Answers a and c are incorrect because the remote sites should be upgraded first for the proxy chains to work properly. Answer a is also incorrect, as is answer b, because the ISA server needs to be in place before upgrading the clients.

Question 42

Answer c is correct. Array members use Cache Array Routing Protocol (CARP) to determine which one has content so that all members don't duplicate the others' content. When a request passes through a proxy chain, however, a device at each level retains the information in cache. Answer a is incorrect because the other departments do not have the page in cache, and only a single array member does. Answer b is incorrect because the departmental server caches the page and services the request. Answer d is incorrect because the array server that fetched the page from the Internet also retains a copy of the page in cache.

Question 43

Answer a is correct. The FTP service is viewed as a server for publishing purposes, and HTTP content is published via the Web publishing rule. All other answers are incorrect because they reference the wrong rule for each item.

Question 44

Answer b is correct. The LAT for an ISA server in a three-homed configuration should include internal addresses only, not addresses in the DMZ. Answer a is incorrect because it specifies too few addresses. Answer c is incorrect because it specifies too few internal addresses and it specifies the DMZ addresses. Answer d is incorrect because it specifies the DMZ addresses.

Question 45

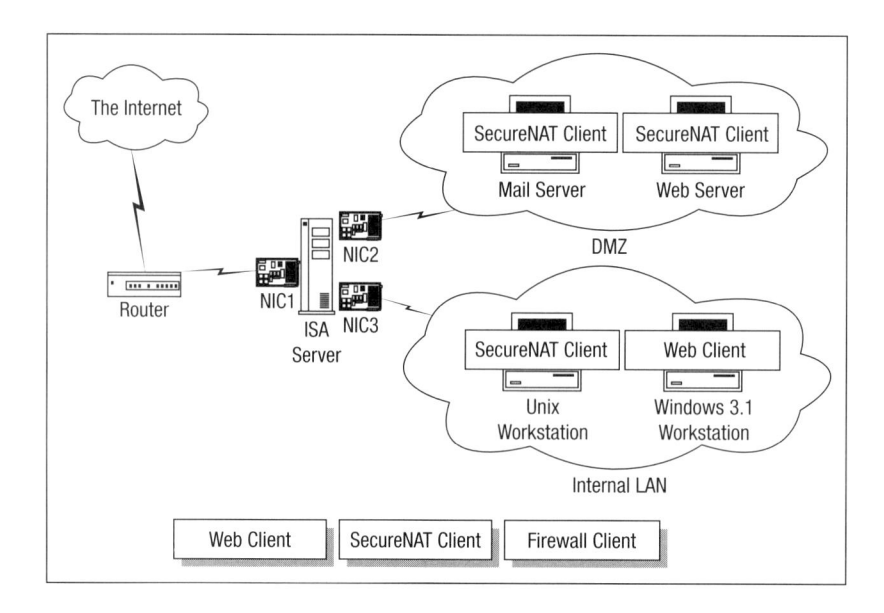

Both the Web server and mail server will be published to the Internet. This requires the SecureNAT client. The Unix client also requires the SecureNAT client for full access to Internet services, because there is no Firewall client for Unix. Because the Windows 3.1 machine also does not have an available Firewall client and only needs Web and FTP access, the firewall client is sufficient.

Question 46

Answers b, c, and d are correct. A daily report job will be accessible one day after it is started, but an immediate report job will be accessible within minutes. Answer a is incorrect because the daily report will not be available immediately.

Question 47

Answer d is correct. A report job, recurring weekly, can be accessed each week and will become available seven days from when it is first scheduled. Answers a and b are incorrect because of the shorter period between job runs. Answer c is incorrect because the report would not be available that soon.

Question 48

Answer d is correct. ISA Server cannot host VPN connections unless loaded in Integrated or Firewall mode. Answer a is incorrect because the Local ISA VPN Wizard would configure the ISA server to accept incoming VPN calls from other networks. Answer b is incorrect because, while it is the correct way to configure an ISA server to accept client VPN calls, it will not function on a caching-only ISA server. Answer c is incorrect because it would not change the cause of the problem, which is the ISA Server installation mode.

Question 49

Answer b is correct. The disk queue length shouldn't average over 2, so the disk is not responding as quickly as it needs to in order to keep up with the operating system. Answer a is incorrect because the low number of page faults indicates sufficient memory. Answer c is incorrect because the network queue is short, indicating that network speed is sufficient. Answer d is incorrect because the CPU use is acceptable at about 40 percent.

Question 50

Answers a and c are correct. You have an issue with available memory, which you can resolve either by limiting the cache's use of RAM or by installing additional RAM. Answer b is incorrect because the CPU use is acceptable at about 20 percent. Answer d is incorrect because the disk queue length is artificially high due to disk activity from the memory page faults.

Appendix A
Answers to Review Questions

Chapter 1 Solutions

1. **c, d.** A firewall client can be installed only on the most recent Microsoft operating systems, including Windows 98 and 2000. The firewall client integrates with Active Directory to allow user-based security. If a network has operating systems other than the most recent ones available from Microsoft, you don't need to load proxy client software. You can use SecureNAT instead.

2. **a, d.** A proxy server protects outbound and not inbound Internet traffic. A firewall protects an internal network from inbound Internet traffic and not outbound.

3. **b, c.** UDP and TCP are Transport-layer protocols in the TCP/IP suite. While both protocols deliver packets, the difference between the two is that TCP guarantees delivery of the packets while UDP does not.

4. **b, e.** Although there are five parts in a full URL, only two of those parts form the socket that is the connection between the client and the server. The two parts that form the socket are the IP address and the port number.

5. **a.** There are over 65,000 ports, but only the first 1,023 have been given the designation of well known. This means you can assign them to a service for default use.

6. **b.** Although Active Directory integration adds many features to ISA Server, it is not required to be on the network when the service is installed.

7. **d.** The H.323 Gatekeeper service allows applications like NetMeeting—which provides real-time connections—to work with ISA Server.

8. **c.** The Internetworking layer is responsible for addressing in the four-layer OSI model. Other layers of the OSI model have responsibilities that do not involve addressing.

9. **a.** Both TCP and UDP are available as options when you're programming a service to use the TCP/IP protocol suite. UDP does not guarantee delivery of a packet, and because it does not take the time to guarantee delivery, it can provide a faster delivery than TCP. Transport-layer protocols are not a part of socket formation.

10. **a, b.** Using SecureNAT as a proxy client option lets you avoid loading client proxy software on client computers. Since there is no software to load it, no client operating system is required. However, the clients will receive only basic proxy services and will not have enhanced features, such as user-based security.

11. **a.** Firewalls protect an internal network from inbound requests.

12. **b.** Proxy servers protect internal clients that are making outbound requests to the Internet.

13. **d.** A router can block packets at the Network layer. This makes it a simple firewall.

14. **c.** A Circuit-level proxy is required when users need access to Internet applications. It makes a connection between the client and the Internet server that allows communication between the two but still provides protection to the client.

15. **b.** A computer or component provides cache when it offers a quicker method of accessing data than going back to the original source. Different services use different cache methods.

16. **d.** Storing Web pages on the hard disk provides a quicker retrieval than does going back out to the Internet. Many caches use memory, but Web pages would take up too much space in memory.

17. **d.** Transparency refers to a client being unaware that a proxy server is interfering in its connection to a server on the Internet. Most proxy servers are not truly transparent in that the client is aware that a proxy server is interfering with the connection to an Internet server.

18. **a.** OSI describes a networking model and is not a protocol.

19. **b.** Cache is a service provided by proxy servers and is for outgoing requests for Web pages.

20. **b.** Often a firewall will reject all incoming requests to a network, but a Web server residing on an internal network must accept incoming connections from the internet. For this reason, incoming connections for the network need to be treated differently and have different protections than incoming connections for the internal Web server.

21. **b.** The .NET platform is a group of services that when used together can aid in the development of applications that work over the Internet. Each service—ISA Server included—can be used separately and in capacities other than in support of .NET's goals.

22. **d.** At the release of ISA Server, Proxy Server had been released for four years.

23. **c.** As part of the BackOffice suite, Proxy Server's strongest feature is its ability to integrate with Windows 2000. Proxy Server can use directory services in Windows operating systems. That way, you avoid holes in security that can result from having a different security structure than the operating system.

24. **d.** Firewall client for ISA Server can be loaded on five operating systems: Windows 95, Windows 98, Millennium, Windows NT 4, and Windows 2000.

25. **d, e.** You can load ISA Server only on Windows 2000 Server. The three versions of Windows 2000 Server on which you can load ISA Server include Server, Advanced Server, and DataCenter Server. Only two of these, Server and Advanced Server, are listed in this question.

26. **a.** ISA Server works only with TCP/IP. Proxy Server supported IPX/SPX on internal adapters only, but ISA Server doesn't offer that support.

27. **d.** Protocol rules, site and content rules, and packet filters are all listed under the Access Policy container in ISA Management.

28. **b.** You can access Internet applications without loading client proxy software on the individual clients. This was not the case with Proxy Server 2.0. Although client proxy software is not required to make a connection, many more administrative options are available if you load the firewall client on the clients.

Chapter 2 Solutions

1. **c.** ISA Server requires the processor of the system to be a Pentium 133MHz or higher processor. However, the recommended processor is Pentium II 300MHz or higher.

2. **e.** ISA Server's minimum memory requirement is 128MB. However, the recommended amount of memory is 256MB.

3. **d.** 20MB of available hard disk space is required.

4. **b.** Although the installation completes with one NIC, you will not be able to do too much, because the purpose of the ISA Server is to route packets between internal and external networks.

5. **c.** The ISA Server requires Windows 2000 Server with Service Pack 1, Windows 2000 Advanced Server with SP1, or Windows 2000 Datacenter Server.

6. **d.** To use ISA Server's caching feature, you will need a Windows 2000 NTFS partition (version 5).

7. **d.** Windows 2000 Active Directory domain is required to use the array feature and advanced policies.

8. **b.** Proxy Server 2.0 configurations can be migrated to the ISA Server.

9. **a, b, d.** ISA Server supports Firewall mode, Cache mode, and Integrated mode.

10. **a, c, d.** Firewall mode supports application filters, packet filtering, and server publishing.

11. **a, d.** Cache mode supports alerts and Web publishing.

12. **b, d.** The ISA Server array is recommended in any situations where you have Active Directory available on your network.

13. **a, c, d.** ISA Server supports SecureNAT clients, Firewall clients, and Web Proxy clients.

14. **d.** Web Proxy clients are recommended for forward caching Web objects.

15. **c.** Firewall clients are recommended to allow access only for authenticated clients.

16. **b.** You configure one NIC for the internal network (LAN) and another for the external network (the Internet).

17. **b. ipconfig /all** shows the MAC address of a NIC.

18. **c. PING** checks to see if you can reach a remote host.

19. **a, b, c.** 224.0.0.0 to 239.255.255.255 are multicast addresses and are not normally used by ISA Server for its clients.

20. **b, c.** These permissions are required to make changes to the Active Directory schema.

Chapter 3 Solutions

1. **c, d.** Windows 2000 Server and Windows 2000 Server Service Pack 1 are required to install ISA Server. An NTFS partition is required only for the setup of cache and not all ISA servers need to provide Web cache.

2. **c.** The minimum recommended cache size is 100MB. The installation wizard will default to this size when configuring cache.

3. **b.** Although the minimum recommended cache size is 100MB, cache can be configured at only 5MB. Of course, it will not be able to hold as many Web pages as a larger cache could.

4. **c.** During a custom installation, you can add or remove options. However, if you remove the checkmark for Administrative Tools, you'll get an error.

5. **b, c.** Only Cache and Integrated modes provide caching services. Firewall mode provides no caching services and therefore requires no cache setup.

6. **d.** Like many services that integrate with Active Directory, ISA Server does not require Active Directory. Instead, integration with Active Directory provides enhanced services. An array is a configuration of ISA Server that is available only when ISA Server is integrated with Active Directory.

7. **a.** The purpose of the LAT is to let ISA Server know which ranges of IP addresses are internal and do not need to go out onto the Internet. Only internal ranges of IP addresses should be included in the LAT.

8. **b.** Setup.exe runs the installation wizard for ISA Server. ISAAutorun.exe offers several options; installing ISA Server is just one.

9. **a, b.** The LAT should contain only internal ranges of IP addresses. If it contains external ranges of IP addresses, ISA Server will believe that they belong to the internal network and not allow them on the Internet. If an IP address range is not included, ISA Server will send a packet bound for that IP address out to the external connection instead of allowing it to reach its actual destination on the internal network.

10. **d.** The unattended installation file for ISA Server must be named msiaund.ini.

11. **a.** The unattended installation file for ISA Server must be located in the root of the installation server.

12. **c.** If a value is not specified in the ISA unattended installation file, the default value for that option is used.

13. **b.** There are five possible sections in the unattended installation file for ISA Server.

14. **a, d.** The path of the installation files for ISA Server and the product ID number from the back of the ISA Server jewel case are required. The **/Q** parameter specifies that an unattended installation is desired, while the **/U** parameter instead specifies that an uninstallation is desired. The name and the path of the unattended installation file for ISA Server cannot be changed, so they are not required.

15. **b.** External IP addresses should not be on the LAT. A persistent external Internet connection could be added to the LAT during the installation of ISA Server.

16. **a, c.** The Getting Started Wizard can be launched at the end of the installation or in the Taskpad from the ISA console.

17. **e.** Once the enterprise has been initialized and the ISA Server schema has been added to Active Directory, you cannot remove that information.

18. **a.** Creating an array occurs during the installation of the first member.

19. **d.** Joining an existing array does not affect the ISA Server installation time. However, it does shorten the configuration time.

20. **a.** Initializing the enterprise places the ISA Server schema into Active Directory. This needs to be done only once and it is not reversible.

Chapter 4 Solutions

1. **b, d.** Proxy Server 2.0 can run on Windows NT 4 and Windows 2000 Server.

2. **b.** False. When you're upgrading to ISA Server, Windows 2000 Service Pack 1 is always required.

3. **e.** Proxy Server runs within the World Wide Web Publishing Service, w3srv.

4. **a.** Proxy Server runs within the main IIS process, called the inetinfo process.

5. **b.** False. The LAT is constructed the same way in ISA Server and Proxy Server.

6. **b.** Proxy Server can be upgraded to ISA Server only from version 2.0.

7. **a.** True. Since IIS and Proxy Server run from within the process and Proxy Server requires IIS, they are administered from the same interface, Internet Services Manager.

8. **a, b.** You can run TCP/IP and IPX/SPX on the internal network when Proxy Server is the Internet security server.

9. **a.** Only TCP/IP can be run on the internal network when ISA Server is the Internet security server.

10. **c.** Proxy Server creates a folder MSP\Config during installation to store server backup files.

11. **b.** The extension for the Proxy Server backup file is .mpc.

12. **a, b.** In ISA Server, you can set site and content rules to block or allow certain domains and IP addresses to which internal users try to connect. In Proxy Server 2.0, you did this with domain filters.

13. **a.** The short name for the Winsock Proxy Service is wspsvc; therefore the command used is **Net Stop wspsvc**.

14. **c.** You can also use the Services application in Control Panel to stop Proxy Server services.

15. **c.** Cache setup has not changed from Proxy Server 2.0 to ISA Server. Cache is configured and used in much the same way in both. ISA Server simply detects and uses the Proxy Server cache settings.

16. **b.** The recommended method of upgrading a Proxy Server array is to first remove all of the members, then upgrade each one individually. The first former member to be upgraded should create a new array. The rest of the former members can join the new array as they are upgraded to ISA Server.

17. **a.** Proxy Server does not have its own administrative interface. Instead, it shares IIS's administrative interface, Internet Services Manager.

18. **b.** Unlike Proxy Server, ISA Server has its own administrative interface, called ISA Administrator.

19. **c.** Proxy Server is upgraded with the same application that performs a new install of ISA Server. This application, called Setup.exe, starts both installations the same way and searches for previous versions once it has begun.

20. **d.** Although you can remove ISA Server after an upgrade from Proxy Server, no option is available that allows the server to be returned to a pre-upgrade state. The best method is to remove ISA Server, reinstall Proxy Server, and then restore Proxy Server settings from backup. Proxy Server 2.0 includes this backup utility.

Chapter 5 Solutions

1. **b, c, d.** The Web Proxy client, the Firewall client, and the SecureNAT client are the three major client types in ISA Server.

2. **b, c.** The Firewall service supports Winsock applications in versions 1.1 and 2.0.

3. **d.** Internal clients can connect to ISA Server on port 8080.

4. **c, d, e, f.** The most recent Windows operating systems are the only operating systems that can be Firewall clients.

5. **e.** The only requirement for Web browsers to be clients of the Web Proxy service is that they be CERN compliant.

6. **a.** ISA Server supports Socks client in version 4.

7. **c.** Only the Firewall client requires the installation of extra software on the client.

8. **b, c, d.** The Web Proxy and the SecureNAT clients both require configuration at the client level. The Firewall service needs to have extra software loaded on the client so this can also be considered client-level configuration.

9. **c, d.** The HTTP redirector filter and the Socks filters are application filters and therefore extensions to ISA Server.

10. **b.** The Firewall client should never be loaded on the ISA server because it will interfere with settings on the ISA server.

11. **c.** The Locallat.txt file should be saved on the client in \Mspclnt folder for its settings to apply.

12. **c, d.** The Firewall client can be configured manually (through configuration files on the ISA server called Mspclnt.ini or Msplat.txt) or locally (by creating a Wspcfg.ini or Locallat.txt file on the client).

13. **b.** The LDT is the Local Domain Table. The LDT is used to allow clients to distinguish between local and remote computer names.

14. **c.** The Firewall client is the only client that uses the LAT.

15. **d.** The Socks client is set up by default because the Socks application filter is loaded by default and Socks clients are SecureNAT clients.

16. **d.** The default gateway on SecureNAT clients will need to be configured. On a complex network, you may also have to configure the routers and DNS servers if SecureNAT is the major ISA server.

17. **a.** WPAD stands for Web Proxy AutoDiscovery when configuring the Automatic Discovery feature.

18. **e.** Only Internet Explorer 5.0 supports AutoDiscovery.

19. **e.** AutoDiscovery can require a lot of configuration, including the ISA server, the individual client, DNS, and DHCP servers.

20. **a, c.** Clients can be configured to use AutoDiscovery either individually or all at once in ISA Administrator.

21. **b, c.** Only Web Proxy and Firewall clients can use AutoDiscovery.

22. **a.** AutoDiscovery is used to configure clients that change locations often and need to have their ISA Server settings changed often.

Chapter 6 Solutions

1. **a.** A policy is a collection of rules and elements. Policies do not control access to ISA Server, but instead let ISA Server know how to handle incoming and outgoing requests.

2. **c, e.** Array and enterprise policies are types of policies available for use with ISA Server.

3. **e.** The rules that deny access in an enterprise policy override the rules in an array policy. Anything denied in an enterprise policy cannot later be allowed in an array policy.

4. **b.** False. ISA Server creates default enterprise and array policies.

5. **b.** False. By default, no access into or out of the internal network is allowed by ISA Server. This includes access to the Internet.

6. **a, c, d.** Before an enterprise policy can be created, a few important preconditions must be met. First, Enterprise Edition of ISA Server must be installed. Also, ISA Server must be installed in a Windows 2000 domain environment, and the ISA Server schema must be installed in Active Directory.

7. **a.** Rules that deny access are applied before rules that allow access. Site and content rules and protocol rules control different types of connections, so their application is not ordered.

8. **a, c.** Only site and content and protocol rules are included in an enterprise-level policy.

9. **c, d.** The protocol definition policy element can be used when defining bandwidth rules and protocol rules.

10. **c.** The bandwidth priority policy element can be used only when defining bandwidth rules.

11. **b, c.** The content group policy element can be used when defining site and content rules as well as bandwidth rules.

12. **b, c.** The destination set policy element can be used when defining site and content rules as well as bandwidth rules.

13. **a, b, c.** When defining a protocol definition, the Transport Layer protocol (either UDP or TCP), the port number, and the direction of the connection (inbound or outbound) are all defined. The protocol that will be allowed or disallowed is not defined in the protocol definition.

14. **c.** Client address sets allow an administrator to group together IP addresses.

15. **a.** Some rules can be applied to a group of users. For an enterprise policy, these groups are defined in the Active Directory Users And Groups console. Computer Management is used to define groups for standalone ISA servers only. Groups of users are not defined in ISA Server snap-in.

16. **c.** Bandwidth priorities can be set between 1 and 200. Higher numbers receive a higher priority.

17. **d.** MIME stands for Multipurpose Internet Media Extensions. The acronym is used to stand for Multipurpose Internet Mail Extensions when applied to email attachments only. Internet browsers and servers have been extended to include support for MIME types.

18. **b.** Bandwidth rules work with the QoS Scheduling service to add priority to Internet connections that pass through ISA Server.

19. **a, c, d.** Internet applications that provide realtime services such as video, audio, and conferencing are at their best quality when they have priority over other types of services, such as file transfers.

20. **a.** Although Proxy Server 2.0 provided dynamic packet filters, only static packet filters are available in ISA Server. This is because rules, which are better at controlling traffic, should be used instead of packet filters.

21. **b.** Packet filters have a less important role in ISA Server than in previous version of Internet security servers because rules and policies allow better control over connections than do packet filters.

22. **d.** Only bandwidth rules can be placed in any kind of order. Other types of rules cannot.

23. **d.** When a backup configuration file is created for policy configuration settings, it has a .bif extension.

24. **c, e.** Both array- and enterprise-level policy configurations can be backed up.

Chapter 7 Solutions

1. **a, b, c, d, e.** Internet Explorer version 5 supports all methods of ISA Server authentication.

2. **a, b, e.** Only Integrated Windows Authentication does not support Netscape as a client browser.

3. **a, c.** Basic Authentication supports all types of clients, and Integrated Windows Authentication using NTLM supports Internet Explorer running on Windows NT or an earlier Windows operating system. Server-side certificates are supported by Internet Explorer version 2, but client-side certificates are not.

4. **b, d.** Digest Authentication and Integrated Windows Authentication using Kerberos as the protocol both require a Windows 2000 environment.

5. **b.** False. Encoding and encryption have great differences between them. Encoding is used for compatibility, and encryption is used for security.

6. **b, d.** Encoding translates characters into ASCII so that they can more easily be read by the receiving computer. It is not a secure method of transmitting information.

7. **a.** Basic Authentication is the only method of authentication that uses encoding.

8. **b.** Basic Authentication is described in the standards for HTTP in version 1.0.

9. **b.** Hashing is only one-way because each side of a connection must perform a calculation to see if the correct data was hashed. It verifies information without sending it over a network.

10. **b, c.** When a hashing function is performed, the result can be called either a message digest or a hash.

11. **b.** Hashing is considered safe because the password is verified without actually sending it over the network.

12. **b.** When Basic Authentication is selected as the authentication choice, a dialog box immediately appears. This message warns you of the lack of security and possible compromise of sensitive user-account password information when using Basic Authentication.

13. **c.** Integrated Windows Authentication and Windows 2000 use version 5 of the Kerberos protocol.

14. **a.** NTLM stands for NT LAN Manager. (Bill Gates has been quoted as saying the NT stands for *New Technology*.)

15. **a, b, d.** The three major elements in the Kerberos process are the client, the server, and the KDC.

16. **b.** When Kerberos is the protocol being used for Integrated Windows Authentication, a Windows 2000 domain must be present on the network.

17. **c.** The KDC controls the allocation of keys in the authentication process set up by the Kerberos protocol.

18. **d.** Certificates are a part of the SSL process and use SSL to complete a connection.

19. **d.** A CA, or certificate authority, is responsible for creating certificates and distributing them when it receives a certificate request.

20. **a.** A client and a server must both trust a certificate authority to use and accept its certificates.

21. **a, b, c.** Although authentication is configured when adding or editing a listener, it is required only by a rule or by selecting Ask Unauthenticated Users For Identification when in the Outgoing Web Requests or Incoming Web Requests property pages.

22. **c.** Pass-through authentication occurs when an ISA server allows a requesting client and a destination server to complete the authentication process directly without interference.

23. **a, b.** When multiple ISA servers or Proxy servers are forwarding requests to one another, then chained authentication is needed. Otherwise, authentication requests will not be forwarded to or from external connections.

24. **d.** Pass-through authentication is automatic and does not need to be set up.

25. **a.** Chained authentication is set up through a routing rule.

Chapter 8 Solutions

1. **a.** Allowing internal clients to access the Internet with caching is called forward caching.

2. **b.** Allowing Internet clients to access the internal Web servers with caching is called reverse caching.

3. **c.** Downloading Internet resources on a scheduled basis is called scheduled caching.

4. **e.** Obtaining Web-related objects from different ISA servers in an ISA array is best described as distributed caching.

5. **d.** The ISA Server configuration in which several ISA servers or ISA server arrays are connected in a cascading manner is best described as hierarchical caching.

6. **c.** To allow both SecureNAT and firewall clients to use the caching features, you will need to use the HTTP redirector filter.

7. **c.** An ISA Server array uses Cache Array Routing Protocol (CARP) to make sure there are no duplicates of the cached information.

8. **d.** To use CARP, you need a Windows 2000 domain.

9. **d.** One of CARP's many features is deterministic request resolution path created by hash-based routing, which does not query other ISA Servers.

10. **b.** You configure CARP in the ISA Management MMC.

11. **b.** An intra-array IP address needs to be an internal IP address.

12. **a, b, d.** A scheduled cache content download can download Web-related information at Single URL, Multiple URLs, and Entire Web site levels.

13. **c.** The scheduled cache content download will fail when client authentication is required to access a Web site.

14. **d.** The behavior of one ISA server taking over the functions of another failed ISA Server is called fault tolerance.

15. **b, c.** CARP is offered by both Proxy Server 2.0 and ISA Server.

16. **a, b, c.** Web proxy routing can use three different options:
    - Client requests will be retrieved directly from the specified destination.
    - Client requests will be sent to an upstream server.
    - Client requests will be redirected to an alternate site.

17. **b.** When you do not want to cache information on an ISA server, you would use cache filtering.

18. **a, b, e.** When you tune the ISA server, your available options are Fewer Than 100, Fewer Than 1,000, and More Than 1,000.

19. **a.** To check the cumulative number of URLs that have been cached, you use Total URLs Cached.

20. **b.** To check the number of times that the Web Proxy Service failed to read from or write to the disk cache, you use Total Disk Failures.

Chapter 9 Solutions

1. **b, c.** The Web Proxy service and the Firewall service are the two main services in ISA Server.

2. **a, b, d, e.** The Web Proxy service handles requests for objects from four protocols: HTTP, HTTP-S, FTP, and Gopher.

3. **d.** The Firewall service handles requests for internal clients that want to connect to Internet applications. It does not retrieve objects. These kinds of requests are passed from the Firewall service to the HTTP Redirector Filter.

4. **a, b, c, d, e, f.** All listed operating systems are possible clients of ISA Server. The reason that so many operating systems can be clients of ISA Server is that the Web browser is actually the client to ISA Server. The only requirement for the Web browser is that it be CERN compliant.

5. **e.** To be clients of the Web Proxy service, Web browsers must be CERN compliant.

6. **c.** Since the HTTP protocol's capabilities have been expanded, its use is eclipsing that of FTP.

7. **d.** Because Gopher is used to display a list of what is available on an Internet server, the use of hyperlinks on the World Wide Web is replacing this protocol.

8. **c.** The HTTP redirector filter is an application filter.

9. **d.** SSL is used to secure Web pages and stands for Secure Sockets Layer.

10. **b.** SSL secures a Web page by encrypting the information in it.

11. **a.** The default port for Web connections using HTTP is TCP port 80.

12. **b.** ISA Server accepts internal client connections using HTTP on port 8080.

13. **c.** Port 443 is the default port used by SSL.

14. **c.** A certificate is used to prove the identity of the computer on which it is installed.

15. **a.** Because both parties are not known before the start of a secure session on the Internet, SSL must establish a session with an asymmetric key pair.

16. **c.** SSL tunneling allows ISA Server to start the establishment of an SSL connection. ISA Server then allows the internal client and the Internet server to begin direct communication for the duration of the secure session.

17. **d.** Unlike SSL tunneling, SSL bridging never allows direct communication between the internal client and the Internet server during a secure session.

18. **e.** Although there is a default port for SSL, when the SSL listener is enabled it does not specify a port number. You need to complete this setting when you're enabling the SSL listener.

19. **a.** Using security requires more packets to establish and maintain a connection between a client and server. This makes a connection with security slower than one without security.

20. **e.** Any port can be set to accept incoming Web requests.

21. **b, c.** The HTTP Redirector Filter redirects requests from the Firewall service to the Web Proxy service so that they can be processed through cache and, if necessary, fulfilled on the Internet. All Firewall and SecureNAT client requests go first to the Firewall service. When the HTTP Redirector Filter is disabled, these requests cannot be redirected and so are unsuccessful.

Chapter 10 Solutions

1. **d.** SSL stands for Secure Socket Layer, and it is mainly used by Web servers such as IIS to encrypt data flowing between the server and the client browser to maintain security on sensitive data, such as credit card and social security number information.

2. **c.** The ISA Server Security Configuration Wizard is based on the Windows 2000 built-in security templates, which allow you to configure your ISA server at several different security levels.

3. **b.** All others except for b are security-level options.

4. **a.** The Dedicated configuration includes Limited Services as well as Secure configurations.

5. **d.** The files securesv.inf and hisecsv.inf do not exist in Windows 2000. Dedicated uses hisecws.inf, which configures the ISA server in the most secure configuration.

6. **a.** You will need to copy security templates from the original Windows 2000 CD and run the Security Configuration Wizard again.

7. **b.** When you're applying the Security Configuration Wizard, it keeps a log file named securwiz.log, which is created in the ISA Server installation directory.

8. **a, b, c, d.** The ISA Server administrator should be aware of all of these.

9. **a, b.** ISA Server's intrusion detection detects both ping-of-death and UDP bomb attacks.

10. **a.** A ping-of-death attack occurs when a server receives ICMP echo requests with a large amount of information added to them so that the receiving side system's kernel buffer overflows.

11. **b.** A UDP bomb attack occurs when you receive illegal UDP packets, causing some older operating systems to crash.

12. **c.** A land attack occurs when you receive a TCP SYN packet with a spoofed source IP address and port number that match those of the destination IP address and port number. The receiving system gets confused, because it seems to be receiving the packet from itself.

13. **d.** An all ports scan attack is an attempt to access more than the preconfigured number of ports.

14. **a, d.** Alerts can do the following: send an email message, run a program, report the event to a Windows 2000 event log, stop selected ISA Server services, and start selected ISA Server services.

15. **b.** You can configure ISA Server Alerts in Monitoring Configuration in the ISA Management MMC snap-in.

Chapter 11 Solutions

1. **d.** Although media actually has different meanings when referring to computers, multimedia does not. Multimedia means multiple file formats presented together.

2. **a, c.** RealPlayer and NetMeeting are the only examples of applications that run different file formats together simultaneously. The other applications run just one type of file format.

3. **b.** PSTN stands for Public Switched Telephone Network. This is the telephone network that is normally used to make telephone calls.

4. **a, b.** H.323 is considered an umbrella standard because it defines standards for a number of different components, but all of the components support multimedia connections.

5. **c.** An H.323 Gateway, like other gateways, translates between different environments. An H.323 Gateway specifically translates between H.323 and non-H.323 file formats and protocols.

6. **a, b, c, e.** All choices except for an H.323 Gateway can be an H.323 endpoint. This includes client PCs running NetMeeting, which also qualifies as a terminal, other terminals, H.323 Gatekeepers, and MCUs.

7. **e.** An MCU is a Multipoint Control Unit designed to connect multiple H.323 terminals so that all can participate in a realtime conferencing connection.

8. **a.** Not only does an H.323 Gatekeeper cause the creation of an H.323 zone, but it also can control and manage that zone.

9. **d.** Though the RAS acronym can stand for Remote Access Server, when it is referring to H.323 standards it stands for Registration, Admission, and Status.

10. **b.** False. Although a gatekeeper manages and controls H.323 zones and connections, this control is not required in the H.323 standards.

11. **b.** If an H.323 gatekeeper is set up, only one is allowed per zone.

12. **a.** True. Even though it is not a required component for H.323 connections, if one is set up on a network, then the terminals must use it to make their connections.

13. **a.** The ITU developed the H.323 standards.

14. **a, d, e.** Call Management, Zone Management, and Call Authorization are all a part of an H.323 Gatekeeper's control and management of a zone.

15. **b, d.** Both Firewall and SecureNAT clients can be used with the H.323 Gatekeeper service. The Web Proxy client cannot because it is not designed to deal with any kind of application including multimedia or conferencing applications.

16. **a.** A DNS SRV record is a service locator record that allows services to find the addresses of servers that have specific services loaded on them.

17. **c.** An H.323 DNS SRV record will resolve H.323 service requests and point them to the H.323 Gatekeeper.

18. **c, e.** The Q931 protocol is part of the H.323 standard and is used for call control and call setup.

19. **c.** The T.120 standard specifies a format for data transmissions as part of a multimedia connection.

20. **a, c.** Windows Media Technologies saves bandwidth over slow connections by using non-realtime connections and a high level of compression to send media presentations.

21. **c.** Six protocol definitions are created for use with the Streaming Media Filter during the installation of ISA Server.

22. **a.** Because the Streaming Media Filter is an application filter, it takes the place of a protocol rule to approve the use of streaming media in a network. No protocol rules are required.

23. **c, d, e.** By default, protocol definitions for streaming media are created for the PNM, MMS, and RSTP protocols.

24. **c, d.** A server running Windows NT 4 with Service Pack 4 is the minimum operating system required for installing Windows Media Server, so it can also be loaded on Windows 2000 Server.

Chapter 12 Solutions

1. **a.** Any service that supports the TCP/IP protocol suite can be published with ISA Server.

2. **c, d.** Only Web publishing rules and server publishing rules are contained in a publishing policy. Although IP packet filters can control incoming requests, they are not a part of a publishing policy.

3. **a, c.** Web publishing rules can be used only for ISA servers installed in Cache and Integrated modes.

4. **b, c.** Server publishing rules can be used only for ISA servers installed in Firewall and Integrated modes.

5. **d.** If a published server's IP is not on the LAT, Internet users will reach the ISA server but the ISA server will be unable to connect them to the published server.

6. **a, b.** The properties sheet of an array (for Enterprise Edition) or an individual ISA server (for Standard Edition) is where you'll find the dialog box that allows you to configure a listener.

7. **c.** By default, a Web publishing rule is created during the installation of ISA Server.

8. **a.** By default, all incoming packets are rejected because of the default publishing policy.

9. **c, e.** Client address sets and destination sets can both be used when creating a Web publishing rule.

10. **b, c.** Discard and redirect are the choices for a rule action in a Web publishing rule.

11. **a, b, c.** A port can be set for HTTP, FTP, and SSL requests when creating a Web publishing rule.

12. **c, d.** Only Integrated and Certificate authentication should be used when publishing through ISA Server. With other authentication methods, the IP address of the internal server may be exposed.

13. **b.** SSL bridging is defined by two separate connections from the ISA server: one from the client and one to the server.

14. **a.** True. SSL bridging allows caching to occur even when using SSL because the ISA server decrypts all packets it receives and checks the cache before sending them back out.

15. **c.** SSL bridging is configured in the properties of an existing Web publishing rule and is not configured in the New Web Publishing Rule Wizard.

16. **a, c.** Protocol definitions and client address sets are the policy elements that can be used in a server publishing rule.

17. **a, c, d.** If you set up your Exchange server and Proxy server according to the Knowledge Base article Q181420 and you are still using Exchange Server 5 or 5.5, you do not have to do any configuration changes once you update your Proxy server to ISA Server. However, if you keep this configuration, you will not be using server publishing rules to protect your internal Exchange Server. Instead, the settings upgraded from Proxy Server will use packet filters.

18. **c.** The Message Screener can be configured to filter the contents of email messages.

19. **b.** False. Allowing only inbound connections would seem to be an obvious setting, but due to the architecture of some services, outbound connections may be necessary also.

20. **c.** Some services by design must establish a separate outbound connection to a client that is establishing an inbound connection. If you want to publish a service through ISA Server that is designed this way, you must allow these outbound connections.

21. **b.** Rules in ISA Server are used in place of dynamic packet filters that were used in Proxy Server 2.0.

22. **b, c.** When referring to DMZs, Microsoft also uses the terms perimeter networks and screened subnets.

23. **b, c.** Packet filters can be used in Firewall and Integrated ISA Server modes only.

24. **d.** The DNS host record for a server being published from an internal network needs to have the IP address of the ISA server's external interface.

Chapter 13 Solutions

1. **a, c.** An array is a logical grouping of more than one ISA server in a parallel fashion where a central configuration is shared among them. Chaining is a logical grouping of more than one ISA server in a cascading fashion where configurations are not shared among them.

2. **c.** Chaining is a logical grouping of more than one ISA server in a cascading fashion (see Question 1). In many cases, the chaining is done using several different geographical regions, such as the main office and branch offices in different locations.

3. **d.** There was no separation between Standard and Enterprise editions in RC1, and there was no way to promote a standalone server to an array member in RC1.

4. **c, e.** The ISA Server final product has both Standard and Enterprise editions.

5. **a.** The more ISA servers you have in an array, the better Internet browsing performance will be. This is because you will have more cache space, and more Internet objects will be stored locally.

6. **d.** Fault tolerance is achieved by configuring multiple ISA servers in an array so that if one system fails, others in the array can take over the workload that the failed system was responsible for.

7. **c, d.** When creating an array, all the member ISA servers in the array must be in the same site and the same Windows 2000 domain to utilize the high-speed connectivity in the site and the Active Directory schema.

8. **b.** Alerts can be configured for all the member ISA servers in an array or for an individual ISA Server in an array.

9. **a, c, d.** The cache configuration properties include HTTP, FTP, and CARP protocol properties.

10. **b, c.** You have to be a member of the Domain Admins group for the domain where the array is created or a member of the Enterprise Admins group.

11. **b.** Chaining is also referred as hierarchical proxying as multiple ISA servers are connected in a cascading (hierarchical) fashion.

12. **d.** ISA Server Enterprise edition installation modifies the Active Directory Schema so that all the ISA Server functions can be supported. Each array member needs to refer to the new Active Directory schema to function properly.

13. **a, b.** You can either create a new configuration or copy a configuration from an existing ISA server array to save some time.

14. **b.** When promoting a standalone server to an array member, if default enterprise settings are configured to use enterprise policy only, ISA Server deletes all of the array policy rules using the policy settings updating rules.

15. **c.** If you need to add an ISA server to an existing array, you have to specify the array name when installing it as the member for the array.

16. **b.** If the ISA server is functioning properly, and if you want to load the backup configuration file, it would be easiest to load it from a local hard disk.

17. **d.** The backup configuration includes enterprise policies and enterprise policy elements.

18. **c.** It is recommended to back up the enterprise configuration first and then back up the array's configuration.

19. **c.** By default, only the member of the Enterprise Admins group can create, configure, and apply enterprise policies.

20. **a, b, c.** Packet filters, alerts, and server publishing rules can be configured on each ISA server.

Chapter 14 Solutions

1. **c.** Even though a wizard creates the rules for mail servers, they are still server publishing rules.

2. **d.** The Mail Server Security Wizard in ISA Server is designed to simplify the integration of a mail server in an internal network that uses ISA Server.

3. **b.** According the Knowledge Base article Q141820, a configuration file called Wspcfg.ini needs to be placed on the Exchange server when it exists on a network with Proxy Server 2.0.

4. **a, c, d.** The Mail Server Security Wizard automatically names the rules it creates and includes as part of the name the email protocol, the IP address of the internal mail server, and whether it is configured for client-to-server or server-to-server communication.

5. **b.** The SMTP service uses port 25 by default.

6. **d.** By default, no email messages are allowed through ISA Server.

7. **b, c, d, e, f.** Protocol definitions are created by default during the installation of ISA Server for IMAP4, POP3, MAPI, NNTP, and NNTP-S.

8. **e.** The SMTP Filter is not dependent on any ISA Server Add-ins. Although you cannot filter keywords or attachments without the Message Screener Add-in, the SMTP Filter does more than just these tasks.

9. **c.** The SMTP Filter is used to filter email messages based on keywords, the origins of domains and/or users, attachments, and SMTP commands.

10. **c.** The SMTPCred.exe tool needs to be run on the computer that the Message Screener is installed on when the Message Screener is installed remotely from ISA Server.

11. **a, b.** Like many Microsoft services, Exchange Server versions 5 and 5.5 use RPCs to communicate with other Exchange servers. This changes in Exchange 2000, which uses SMTP instead.

12. **d.** An SMTP client that queries a DNS server in search of a mail server will ask for the MX record.

13. **c.** Packet filters are used instead of rules when Exchange Server and ISA Server are installed on the same server.

14. **c, d.** Both Windows 2000 Advanced Server and Windows 2000 Datacenter Server support NLB.

15. **a, c.** Microsoft Cluster Server includes the Cluster Service and NLB.

16. **a.** The only requirement for an application to benefit from Cluster Server's services is that it support TCP/IP as its protocol suite.

17. **a, b.** Because the Standard Edition of ISA Server installs as a standalone server only, it and Enterprise Edition when installed as a standalone server can benefit from the services provided by NLB. Arrays have failover abilities built in that standalone servers do not have.

18. **d.** Cluster Server and NLB can create clusters with up to 32 servers.

19. **d.** A user will be reconnected to a new server automatically without any intervention necessary when a failure of an ISA Server using NLB occurs.

20. **c.** Network And Dial-up Connections includes an NLB option once Cluster Server is installed.

21. **a.** The DNS round-robin feature is an alternative to NLB.

22. **b.** Only load balancing is provided when using DNS round robin. If an ISA Server fails, the DNS server will still direct requests to it.

23. **a, b.** Web publishing rules and packet filters can be used when ISA Server and a Web server are installed on the same computer.

24. **c.** By default, the AutoDiscovery feature in ISA Server uses port 80.

25. **c.** HTTP also uses port 80 by default.

Chapter 15 Solutions

1. **a, b, c, d.** All the options are categories of ISA Server troubleshooting.

2. **a, b, d.** Access policies include site and content rules, protocol rules, and IP packet filters. Information rules do not exist on ISA Server.

3. **c.** ISA Server initially does not allow any communication to or from the Internet.

4. **a.** When you disable a protocol rule, client sessions that existed before this action are not closed, and therefore, you need to disconnect those client sessions.

5. **d.** If ISA Server is configured to accept only Windows Integrated authentication, Netscape users will not be authenticated by the ISA server. This is because old versions of Netscape browser, such as version 3.0 do not support NT Challenge and Response authentication.

6. **b.** ISA Server caches only items that meet the caching criteria defined. It is normally not a good idea to cache data from sites that use SSL.

7. **d.** Some sites do use different port numbers to make the sites more secure. The default port number for SSL sites is 443, but it can be changed so that only authorized people know the correct port number.

8. **c.** You have correctly specified credentials for the network dial-up connection, but the dial-up entry credentials have not been specified correctly.

9. **d.** Client access may be anonymous, and anonymous connections are not logged in the log file.

10. **a.** Exchange Server may not be able to bind to SMTP port (port 25) on the ISA Server. Some other services might have bound to port 25 previously.

11. **b.** ISA Server's reporting capability provides a summary and analysis of the communication pattern that ISA Server has dealt with.

12. **a, c.** Predefined reports include Summary reports, Web usage reports, application usage reports, traffic and utilization reports, and security reports.

13. **b.** ISA Server's reporting mechanism that combines the summary logs from the ISA server into a database on each ISA server is called the report database.

14. **a, b, c.** To schedule a report job, you will need to provide the period of activity the report needs to cover, when and how often the report needs to be created, and the username of a user authorized to create the report.

15. **d.** Although Microsoft's recommendation of starting troubleshooting is to ping your loopback IP address (127.0.0.1), in reality, it is not reasonable. You would just ping the remote host you are trying to reach to see if you can get replies from the remote host.

Chapter 16 Solutions

1. **b.** ISDN stands for Integrated Services Digital Network.

2. **a.** Before you can create a dial-up entry in the ISA Server snap-in, you must create a DUN phonebook entry on the same server in the Network And Dial-up Connections application.

3. **a, b.** DUN creates settings that allow a Windows NT and Windows 2000 Server to dial out to make a connection to another computer.

4. **d.** DUN phonebook entries are created in the Network And Dial-up Connections application.

5. **a, d.** Dial-up entries can be created for modem and ISDN connections.

6. **e.** Dial-up entries are a policy element and are located in the Policy Element container in the ISA Server snap-in.

7. **b.** In a Windows 2000 Server, normally the Routing And Remote Access Server is the service that allows multiple incoming dial-in connections.

8. **c.** Modems are popular because they offer the cheapest connection to an external network.

9. **b.** A dial-up entry sets up an outgoing connection from an ISA server. It is not needed to accept incoming connections.

10. **a, e.** If an ISA server has a dial-up connection, you must configure two settings to allow clients to use it. The Dial-up Entry is a policy element that must be configured, but also ISA Server must be told that its primary route is through a dial-up connection. This setting is configured in the Network Configuration properties on the Firewall Chaining tab.

11. **c.** The active dial-up entry lets the ISA server know which dial-up entry it should use when dialing out.

12. **b.** Even though ISA Server Help files state that the active dial-up entry is reset in the properties of a dial-up entry, it is actually set by using a toolbar button.

13. **a, c, d, e.** All of the listed answers except for speeding up a connection are reasons why VPNs are implemented. Added security always slows down a connection.

14. **a.** A VPN should be run on the same server as ISA Server.

15. **b.** A VPN is normally created by the Routing And Remote Access Server on a Windows 2000 Server.

16. **a, c.** The term direct access can be used to describe internal clients accessing internal resources and internal clients accessing external resources without going through the ISA server.

17. **a, b.** When creating a VPN from the main network to a branch office, both the Local VPN ISA Wizard and the Remote VPN ISA Wizard are needed.

18. **c.** Only the Clients to Server VPN Wizard is needed on an ISA server to allow roaming clients to connect through a VPN.

19. **b, d.** MPPE is a Microsoft proprietary protocol used for encryption when using PPTP to create a VPN.

20. **d.** IPSec is the encryption protocol used by L2TP.

21. **c.** The extension of the file used to aid in the creation of VPNs is .vpc.

22. **a.** Only the Local VPN ISA Wizard creates the .vpc file.

23. **a, b.** The .vpc file that the Local VPN ISA Wizard creates is also used by the Remote VPN ISA Wizard.

24. **c.** The Effective Bandwidth setting is configured in the properties of the appropriate dial-up entry in the ISA Server snap-in.

25. **d.** The Effective Bandwidth setting needs to be set at the speed at which the modem is designed to transfer.

Chapter 17 Solutions

1. **c.** The minimum recommended processor for an ISA server is a 300MHz Pentium II.

2. **b, c, d.** The Microsoft recommendation for up to 500 users is two to four GB.

3. **c.** Of the answers listed, only cost would be an issue for a company. The reasons listed in answers b and d apply to both editions, and room for growth is provided by the Enterprise Edition instead of the Standard Edition.

4. **b.** False. Hardware does not determine which computer can become a client to ISA Server. Web Proxy clients need a Web browser only, and the hardware configuration given in this question can support a CERN-compliant Web browser. Also, any operating system can be a SecureNAT client. In addition, Windows 95 can be installed on a 486 processor and it can be a Firewall client.

5. **e.** Internet Explorer 3.02 is CERN-compliant and that is the only requirement for Web Proxy clients.

6. **d.** If the ISA Server has no NTFS-formatted drives, then caching services will not be available.

7. **c.** The Bongo Drum Company does not want a SecureNAT client.

8. **d.** The protocol rule includes protocol definitions for HTTP, HTTP-S, and FTP, but does not include a protocol definition for Gopher because that access is not needed at this time.

9. **b.** A site and content rule allowing access to all sites is created by default in ISA Server, so only a protocol rule must be configured.

10. **e.** Microsoft recommends another ISA server be added for every 800 hits per second to a Web site.

11. **b.** An ISA server provides reverse caching services when publishing a Web site.

12. **c.** The Enterprise Edition of ISA Server is not limited in the number of processors, so the operating system limit is observed. This is up to four for Windows 2000 Server, eight for Windows 2000 Advanced Server, and 32 for Windows 2000 Datacenter Server.

13. **a.** MarketDirect is using DHCP to get the necessary configurations to the SecureNAT clients.

14. **b.** The Sacramento location has the domain controller for the network.

15. **c.** The DNS Query protocol definition is created during the installation of ISA Server.

16. **b.** 100 hits per second on a Web site can be supported by a 300MHz Pentium II on the ISA Server.

17. **b.** Because a 300MHz Pentium II can support up to 800 hits per second on a protected Web site, the current configuration will still work.

18. **a.** The LAT on a three-homed perimeter network needs to be configured with the IP address ranges from the internal network only.

19. **c, d.** For the server that protects the perimeter network in a back-to-back configuration, the LAT needs to include the computers on the perimeter network and the ISA server that protects the internal network.

20. **d.** The new array can be created only after the Standard Edition of ISA Server is upgraded to the Enterprise Edition.

21. **a.** The RRAS snap-in must be used to change a dial-up connection to a persistent connection.

Appendix B
Objectives for Exam [70-227]

Installing ISA Server	Chapter
Preconfigure network interfaces	2
• Verify Internet connectivity before installing ISA Server.	2
• Verify DNS name resolution.	2
Install ISA Server. Installation modes include Integrated, Firewall, and Cache.	3
• Construct and modify the local address table (LAT).	3
• Calculate the size of the cache and configure it.	3
• Install an ISA Server computer as a member of an array.	3
Upgrade a Microsoft Proxy Server 2.0 computer to ISA Server.	4
• Back up the Proxy Server 2.0 configuration.	4
Troubleshoot problems that occur during setup.	3

Configuring and Troubleshooting ISA Server Services	Chapter
Configure and troubleshoot outbound Internet access.	15
Configure ISA Server hosting roles.	15
• Configure ISA Server for Web publishing.	15
• Configure ISA Server for server proxy.	15
• Configure ISA Server for server publishing.	15
Configure H.323 Gatekeeper for audio and video conferencing.	11
• Configure gatekeeper rules. Rules include telephone, email, and Internet Protocol (IP).	11
• Configure gatekeeper destinations by using the Add Destination Wizard.	11
Set up and troubleshoot dial-up connections and Routing And Remote Access dial-on-demand connections.	15
• Set up and verify routing rules for static IP routes in Routing And Remote Access.	15
Configure and troubleshoot virtual private network (VPN) access.	16
• Configure the ISA Server computer as a VPN endpoint without using the VPN Wizard.	16
• Configure the ISA Server computer for VPN pass-through.	16
Configure multiple ISA Server computers for scalability. Configurations include network load balancing (NLB) and Cache Array Routing Protocol (CARP).	8

Configuring, Managing, and Troubleshooting Policies and Rules	Chapter
Configure and secure the firewall in accordance with corporate standards.	10
• Configure the packet filters for different levels of security, including system hardening.	6
Create and configure access control and bandwidth policies.	6
• Create and configure site and content rules to restrict Internet access.	6
• Create and configure protocol rules to manage Internet access.	6
• Create and configure routing rules to restrict Internet access.	13
• Create and configure bandwidth rules to control bandwidth usage.	6

(continued)

Configuring, Managing, and Troubleshooting Policies and Rules *(continued)*	Chapter
Troubleshoot access problems	15
• Troubleshoot user-based access problems.	15
• Troubleshoot packet-based access problems.	15
Create new policy elements. Elements include schedules, bandwidth priorities, destination sets, client address sets, protocol definitions, and content groups.	6
Manage ISA Server arrays in an enterprise	14
• Create an array of proxy servers.	14
• Assign an enterprise policy to an array.	14

Deploying, Configuring, and Troubleshooting the Client Computer	Chapter
Plan the deployment of client computers to use ISA Server services. Considerations include client authentication, client operating system, network topology, cost, complexity, and client function.	15
Configure and troubleshoot the client computer for secure network address translation (SecureNAT).	15
Install the Firewall client software. Considerations include the cost and complexity of deployment.	15
• Troubleshoot AutoDetection.	5
Configure the client computer's Web browser to use ISA Server as an HTTP proxy.	9

Monitoring, Managing, and Analyzing ISA Server Use	Chapter
Monitor security and network usage by using logging and alerting.	15
• Configure intrusion detection.	15
• Configure an alert to send an email message to an administrator.	15
• Automate alert configuration.	15
• Monitor alert status.	15
Troubleshoot problems with security and network usage.	15
• Detect connections by using Netstat.	12
• Test the status of external ports by using Telnet or Network Monitor.	15
Analyze the performance of ISA Server by using reports. Report types include summary, Web usage, application usage, traffic and utilization, and security.	15
Optimize the performance of the ISA Server computer. Considerations include capacity planning, allocation priorities, and trend analysis.	15
• Analyze the performance of the ISA Server computer by using Performance Monitor.	8
• Analyze the performance of the ISA Server computer by using reporting and logging.	15
• Control the total RAM used by ISA Server for caching.	8

Appendix C
TCP and UDP Port Assignments

Protocol	Description	Port	Protocol
AOL	AOL Internet Access Protocol	5190	TCP
AOL Instant Messenger	AOL Instant Messenger Protocol	5190	TCP
Archie	Archie Protocol	1525	UDP
Chargen (TCP)	Character generator Protocol (TCP)	19	TCP
Chargen (UDP)	Character generator Protocol (UDP)	19	UDP
Daytime (TCP)	Daytime Protocol (TCP)	13	TCP
Daytime (UDP)	Daytime Protocol (UDP)	13	UDP
Discard (TCP)	Discard Protocol (TCP)	9	TCP
Discard (UDP)	Discard Protocol (UDP)	9	UDP
DNS	Domain Name System	53	UDP
DNS Server	Domain Name System—Server	53	UDP
DNS Server—Zone Transfer	DNS Zone Transfer—Server	53	TCP
DNS (Zone transfer)	DNS Zone Transfer	53	TCP
Echo (TCP)	Echo Protocol (TCP)	7	TCP
Echo (UDP)	Echo Protocol (UDP)	7	UDP
Finger	Finger Protocol	79	TCP
FTP	File Transfer Protocol	21	TCP
FTP Read-only	File Transfer Protocol—Read-only	21	TCP
FTP Server	File Transfer Protocol—Server	21	TCP
FTP Server—Read-only	File Transfer Protocol—Server—Read-only	21	TCP
Gopher	Gopher Protocol	70	TCP
H.323	H.323 Video-conferencing Protocol	1720	TCP
HTTP	Hypertext Transfer Protocol	80	TCP
HTTPS	Secure Hypertext Transfer Protocol	443	TCP
HTTP Server	Hypertext Transfer Protocol—Server	80	TCP
HTTPS Server	Secure Hypertext Transfer Protocol—Server	443	TCP
ICA	Citrix Intelligent Console Architecture Protocol	1495	TCP
ICQ	ICQ Instant Messenger Protocol (Legacy)	4000	UDP
Ident	Ident Protocol	113	TCP
IKE	Internet Key Exchange	500	UDP
IMAP4	Interactive Mail Access Protocol	143	TCP
IMAPS	Secure Interactive Mail Access Protocol	993	TCP

Protocol	Description	Port	Protocol
IRC	Internet Relay Chat	6667	TCP
Kerberos-IV	Kerberos IV Authentication Protocol	750	UDP
Kerberos-Adm	Kerberos Administration	749	TCP/UDP
Kerberos-Sec	Kerberos V Authentication Protocol	88	TCP/UDP
LDAP	Lightweight Directory Access Protocol	389	TCP
LDAPS	Secure Lightweight Directory Access Protocol	636	TCP
LDAP GC (Global Catalog)	LDAP Global Catalog Protocol	3268	TCP
LDAPS GC (Global Catalog)	Secure LDAP Global Catalog Protocol	3269	TCP
MSN	MSN Internet Access Protocol	569	TCP
MSN Messenger	MSN Messenger Protocol	1863	TCP
Microsoft SQL Server	Microsoft SQL Server Protocol	1433	TCP
Net2Phone	Net2Phone Protocol	6801	UDP
Net2Phone Registration	Net2Phone Registration Protocol	6500	TCP
NetBIOS Datagram	NetBIOS Datagram Protocol	138	UDP
NetBIOS Name Service	NetBIOS Name Service Protocol	137	UDP
NetBIOS Session	NetBIOS Session Protocol	139	TCP
NNTP	Network News Transfer Protocol	119	TCP
NNTPS	Secure Network News Transfer Protocol	563	TCP
NTP (UDP)	Network Time Protocol (UDP)	123	UDP
POP2	Post Office Protocol version 2	109	TCP
POP3	Post Office Protocol version 3	110	TCP
POP3	Secure Post Office Protocol version 3	995	TCP
PPTP	Point-to-Point Tunneling Protocol	1723	TCP
Quote (TCP)	Quote of the Day Protocol (TCP)	17	TCP
Quote (UDP)	Quote of the Day Protocol (UDP)	17	UDP
RADIUS	Remote Authentication Dial-in User Service	1812	UDP
RADIUS Accounting	RADIUS Accounting Protocol	1813	UDP
RDP (Terminal Services)	Remote Desktop Protocol (Terminal Services)	3389	TCP
RealAudio/RealVideo	RealNetworks Streaming Media Protocol (PNM)	7070	TCP
RealAudio/RealVideo Server	RealNetworks Streaming Media Protocol	7070	TCP
RIP	Routing Information Protocol	520	UDP
RPC	Remote Procedure Call Protocol	135	TCP/UDP
RPC Port Mapper	Remote Procedure Call Port Mapper—Server	135	TCP/UDP
RTSP	Real-time Stream Protocol	544	TCP
RTSP Server	Real-time Streaming Protocol—Server	544	TCP
SMTP	Simple Mail Transfer Protocol	25	TCP
SMTPS	Secure Simple Mail Transfer Protocol	465	TCP
SMTP Server	Simple Mail Transfer Protocol—Server	25	TCP
SNMP	Simple Network Management Protocol	161	UDP
SNMP Trap	Simple Network Management Protocol (Trap)	162	TCP
SSH	Secure Shell Protocol	22	TCP

Protocol	Description	Port	Protocol
Telnet	Telnet Protocol	23	TCP
Telnet Server	Telnet Protocol—Server	23	TCP
TFTP	Trivial File Transfer Protocol	69	UDP
Time (UDP)	Time Protocol (UDP)	37	UDP
Time (TCP)	Time Protocol (TCP)	37	TCP
Whois	Nicname/Whois Protocol	43	TCP
Windows Media	Microsoft Streaming Media Protocol	1755	TCP/UDP
Windows Media Server	Microsoft Streaming Media Protocol—Server	1755	TCP

Glossary

.NET
A new platform of servers and business ideas from Microsoft that uses the latest technologies available to create Internet-based solutions.

Access policy
An array-level set of rules and IP packet filters.

Active Directory
The name of the directory services provided by Windows 2000.

Address mapping
A setting in ISA Server that allows external adapters on the ISA Server to direct traffic to separate internal servers.

Alerts
An ISA Server mechanism used primarily to notify you when ISA Server detects an attack on your internal network.

All Ports Scan Attack
One of the intrusions into your network that ISA Server can detect. See Chapter 10 for details.

Application Filter
An extra component you can add to ISA Server that extends its capabilities.

Array
A set of ISA Servers that share cache and rule settings.

Array policy
A set of rules and/or filters that apply to one set of ISA Servers specified as an array.

Authentication
A requirement placed on users that they provide appropriate credentials before being allowed access to resources.

Automatic Discovery
A service in ISA Server that allows roaming clients to reconfigure their ISA Server settings without user intervention.

Autorun
A file that runs automatically when a program is launched or a CD is inserted in the CD-ROM drive.

Bandwidth
The amount of traffic that a connection can transfer. It is measured with a unit of time such as kilobits per second.

Bandwidth priorities
A policy element that assigns a number to a connection that gives it a better chance of getting needed bandwidth.

Basic Authentication
Sending and receiving user information, such as user ID and password, as text characters that are encoded.

Bottlenecks
A situation in which a resource is not able to keep up with the demands placed on it, thus slowing down the overall operations of a computer or network by making other resources wait for it.

Cache Array Routing Protocol (CARP)
Routing protocol that ISA Server uses to provide efficient caching and scaling function.

Cache Filtering
ISA Server configuration that allows or does not allow you to cache certain Internet objects.

Caching
ISA Server Caching is the ability to store Internet objects locally so that clients can be served in the LAN. This would increase the network bandwidth.

CERN (Conseil Européen pour la Recherché Nucléaire)
An international organization headquartered in Switzerland. CERN scientists invented the World Wide Web, the first Web browser, and the first proxy server.

Certificate
A component that proves the identity of a computer over a remote connection.

Certificate authority
An entity that creates certificates for use by others.

Chained authentication
A method used by ISA Server of passing authentication requests up a proxy chain without interfering with the packets.

Chaining
ISA Server configuration in which ISA Server is "chained" hierarchically between individual ISA Servers or arrays of ISA Servers.

Client address sets
A policy element. A collection of IP addresses or computer names grouped for use in a rule.

Cryptography
The process of encrypting and decrypting information.

DDNS (Dynamic Domain Naming Service)
DDNS is based on DNS where all the entries are dynamically updated by both clients and the DHCP server.

Destination set
A group of IP addresses and/or a path that groups computers so that a single rule can be applied to them.

DHCP (Dynamic Host Configuration Protocol)
A protocol and service designed to assign IP addresses and other TCP/IP information over a network automatically.

Dial-up
A network connection that is typically only open when in use. When not in use, the connection is closed. See *persistent*.

Digest authentication
Sending the authentication credentials through a one-way process called hashing.

Distributed Caching
The method used by ISA Server to handle load balance caching activities for ISA Servers in an array.

DMZ (Demilitarized Zone)
See Perimeter network.

DNS (Domain Name System)
A system designed for the translation of host names to IP addresses.

DSL (Digital Subscriber Line)
A digital connection to an external network that can be dial-up or persistent.

DUN (Dial-up Networking)
Microsoft's remote access client that allows you to set up dial-up connections.

Endpoint
A participant in an H.323 connection. Can be a terminal, an H.323 Gatekeeper, or an MCU.

Enterprise Edition
An edition of ISA Server that can scale from small to large networks.

Enterprise policy
A set of rules and/or filters that applies to all arrays in a network configuration.

Enumerated Port Scan Attack
One of the intrusions into your network that ISA Server can detect. See Chapter 10 for details.

EULA (End User License Agreement)
A license agreement from a software vendor that you must agree to accept and follow before you can install software.

Firewall
A component on a network that protects internal clients by checking all incoming requests and applying security settings to them.

Firewall client
A client to the ISA Server that must have ISA Firewall client software installed on it.

Firewall service
A service in ISA Server that processes all requests except those using HTTP, HTTP-S, FTP, or Gopher protocols.

Forward caching
A server providing proxy services can save a copy of the objects that it retrieves from external networks for internal clients. It can then speed up client connections to external networks by checking for requested objects in this local store of objects and fulfilling requests without having to access the external network at all.

FQDN (Fully Qualified Domain Name)
A Domain Name System name that includes the full computer name as well as the full suffix.

FTP (File Transport Protocol)
A protocol used to transfer files between computers with dissimilar configurations.

Gopher
A protocol designed to list resources available on an Internet server.

H.323
A set of standards that provides standardization for the hardware and software used in connections using multimedia.

H.323 Gatekeeper
Provides control over H.323 connections. When added to a network, creates an H.323 zone over which it has control over all incoming and outgoing H.323 connections.

H.323 zone
A collection of H.323 components that are controlled by one H.323 Gatekeeper.

Hash
See Message digest.

HCL (Hardware Compatibility List)
The document maintained by Microsoft that lists all of the hardware supported by each Microsoft operating system.

Hierarchical caching
A method used by ISA Server to send an internal request through a series of ISA servers before sending it out to the Internet

to be fulfilled. The requests are sent upstream through a chain of ISA servers so that internal clients receive the benefit of several ISA server caches instead of just one.

Host header
A field in the header of an HTTP packet that specifies the name of the server the client is attempting to connect to.

HTTP (Hypertext Transfer Protocol)
A protocol designed to download Web pages and other documents types between Web browsers.

HTTP-S (Secure Hypertext Transfer Protocol)
A version of the HTTP protocol used when SSL (Secure Sockets Layer) is used to encrypt Web pages.

IETF (Internet Engineering Task Force)
A standards body that publishes RFCs that propose and define Internet standards.

IIS (Internet Information Services)
Microsoft's Web server.

IIS snap-in
The administrative interface for Microsoft's Web server. In the menu, the IIS snap-in is referred to as Internet Services Manager.

IMAP4 (Internet Messaging Access Protocol) version 4
An email protocol that is a superset of the POP3 email protocol. These protocols deliver email to individual mailboxes.

Internet Cache Protocol (ICP)
Microsoft Proxy Server 1.0 used ICP, which had several proxy servers, and each proxy server had duplicate caches of the most frequently requested Internet objects, such as Web pages.

Internet Control Message Protocol (ICMP)
A message control and error reporting protocol that operates in Layer 3 of the OSI model.

Internet Explorer
Microsoft's Web browser.

IP Half Scan Attack
One of the intrusions into your network that ISA Server can detect. See Chapter 10 for details.

IPSec (Internet Protocol Security)
An open Internet standard encryption protocol that works with L2TP to encrypt data.

IPX/SPX
A proprietary protocol stack created by Novell Corporation.

ISA Server snap-in
The administrative interface of ISA Server. In the menu, the ISA Server snap-in is referred to as ISA Management.

ISDN (Integrated Services Digital Network)
A digital dial-up connection that offers two 64Kbps lines to an external network for data and one 16Kbps for connection control. One or both 64Kbps connections may be used for data connections.

ITU (International Telecommunications Union)
An organization that created many standards, including the H.323 standard.

KDC (Key Distribution Center)
A component of Kerberos authentication that distributes and keeps track of encryption keys.

Kerberos
A protocol that runs a secure authentication encryption system.

L2TP (Layer 2 Tunneling Protocol)
A remote access protocol that is an open Internet standard.

Land Attack
One of the intrusions into your network that ISA Server can detect. See Chapter 10 for details.

LAT (Local Address Table)
A list that identifies all ranges of IP addresses on the internal network.

LDT (Local Domain Table)
A list of domain suffixes used by internal clients on an internal network.

Listener
An IP address on a network adapter configured to respond to client requests.

Local Area Network (LAN)
A network that is usually connected with a high-bandwidth network connection (10Mbps+).

MAC address
A 48-bit hardware address that is normally coded directly on the hardware so that it is most often not programmable.

MCU (Multipoint Control Unit)
A device that coordinates the transfer of data between remote clients participating in an H.323 conference.

Message digest
Used in authentication. Consists of a string of text derived from a calculation performed on the password, a few random numbers, and a timestamp.

Message Screener
A component in ISA Server that analyzes the content of email messages based on settings created by the administrator.

Microsoft Cluster Server
A Microsoft service that allows groups of identically configured servers to provide automatic fault tolerance for services on a network.

MIME (Multipurpose Internet Media Extensions) type
Allows a receiving computer to identify the application that will open attachments to a message.

MMC (Microsoft Management Console)
The administrative interface for the most recent Microsoft operating systems.

MPPE (Microsoft Point-to-Point Encryption)
A proprietary encryption protocol that works with PPTP.

Multihomed system
A computer that has more than one network interface card installed.

Multimedia
A presentation that includes the combination of media types, such as sound and video.

NAT (Network Address Translation)
A service designed for a small network that translates internal IP addresses on the local network to public IP addresses for use on the Internet.

Net2Phone
Protocol you can use for voice-over-IP telephone conversations.

Netscape Communicator
A Web browser created by Netscape Corporation.

Netscape Navigator
A Web browser created by Netscape Corporation.

NIC (Network Interface Card)
An adapter that allows a computer to connect to a network.

NLB (Network Load Balancing)
A service in Microsoft Cluster Server that provides fault tolerance and load balancing for incoming connections to a network.

NNTP (Network News Transfer Protocol)
A protocol that allows you to connect to newsgroups on the Internet.

NNTP-S (Secure Network News Transfer Protocol)
A secure version of the protocol that encrypts a connection to a newsgroup.

Novell NetWare
Novell Corporation's network operating system.

NTFS (NT File System)
A proprietary file system used by recent Microsoft operating systems designed for the business market that allows individual file permissions to be assigned and better performance for large drives.

NTLM (NT LAN Manager)
A proprietary encryption protocol understood only by Microsoft operating systems for authentication.

Packet filter
A feature in ISA Server that allows traffic to be blocked or allowed at the packet level.

PBX (Private Branch Exchange)
A telephone service used internally in companies. A PBX system can contain several internal lines connected to just a few external phone lines.

Perimeter network
A network separated from the internal network by firewalls. Also known as a DMZ or screened subnet.

Persistent
A network connection that is always open. See dial-up.

Ping-of-Death Attack
One of the intrusions into your network that ISA Server can detect. See Chapter 10 for details.

Policy
A set of rules and IP packet filters on an ISA server.

Policy element
Reusable grouping defined in the ISA Server snap-in that can be used in the creation of rules.

POP3 (Post Office Protocol) version 3
An email protocol that allows clients to access individual mailboxes.

PPTP (Point-to-Point Tunneling Protocol)
A protocol used to secure remote connections by encryption to create a VPN.

Private IP address ranges
Ranges of IP addresses where network packets are not routable to communicate with the outside world.

Protocol definition
A policy element. A protocol name or port number defined for use in a rule.

Proxy
A component on a network that protects internal clients from external connections by making requests for them.

Proxy Server
Microsoft's original Internet security server.

PSTN (Public Switched Telephone Network)
The network owned by the telephone company that is used to make telephone calls.

Publishing
The act of providing services to clients outside the internal network.

Publishing Policy
A group of Web publishing and server publishing rules.

Q931
A protocol used for call control and setup that is part of the H.323 standard.

Q931 Address
A format for addressing created by combining the IP address and the port number. Q931 addresses must be unique in the registration database maintained by the H.323 Gatekeeper.

QoS (Quality of Service)
A routing mechanism that allows the prioritization of network connections.

RAS (Registration, Admission, and Status) protocol
A protocol used to create the registration database for the H.323 Gatekeeper service.

RDP (Remote Desktop Protocol)
A protocol used by Terminal Services to allow remote access.

Report database
A database on each ISA server that is produced by combining summary logs from all the ISA servers.

Reverse Caching
Reverse caching allows external clients to benefit from cache while accessing a Web site that is located on the internal network or a perimeter network.

Reverse proxy
A service on a proxy server that accepts incoming Web requests and redirects them to an internal Web server.

RFC (Request For Comment)
A document put out by the IETF that defines Internet standards.

RRAS (Routing And Remote Access Server)
A service in Windows 2000 server that allows the server to route network traffic and host remote connections.

Scheduled Caching
Retrieval of Internet objects to the local cache on a scheduled basis.

Screened Subnet
See Perimeter network.

SecureNAT client
A client to the ISA server that has a transparent connection.

Security Configuration Wizard
ISA Server Wizard used to configure ISA servers in three different security modes to ensure they are securely and correctly set up.

Server publishing
Provides services to clients outside the internal network.

Service pack
A set of patches, bug fixes and, in some cases, enhancements to the original version of software.

Session key
A method of encryption in which each participant in a connection is given an identical—symmetric—key to perform the encryption.

Site
A grouping of servers designated in Active Directory. All servers that belong to the same site must be connected by high-speed connections.

SMTP (Simple Mail Transport Protocol)
Protocol used for sending email messages between mail servers.

Snap-in
A component that connects the MMC to an administrative program in the most recent Microsoft operating systems.

Socket
A combination of IP address and port number that creates a connection between computers.

Socks
A standard for allowing clients to connect through a proxy server to Internet application servers.

SRV
A type of DNS record that allows clients to locate a particular service on a network.

SSL (Secure Sockets Layer)
A method of encapsulating and encrypting connections over a network.

SSL Bridging
An SSL method in which the ISA server interferes with all SSL connections that are incoming or outgoing.

SSL Tunneling
An SSL method in which the ISA server, after an initial check of the connection, allows an internal client and an Internet server to communicate directly with each other.

Standalone
An ISA server that does not share settings with other ISA servers.

Standard Edition
A scaled-down version of ISA Server that can be installed only in a standalone method.

Streaming media
A method of delivering media files that allows a smoother transmission.

T.120
A format for sending data over H.323 connections.

T1
A high-speed digital network connection that includes 24 64Kbps channels, totaling 1.544Mbps.

Terminal Services
A service provided by Microsoft that allows access to services on a remote computer.

Terminals
Client endpoints in an H.323 connection.

Time To Live (TTL)
The amount of time that an object is kept as a valid resource.

Transparent
A type of connection that has a degree of interference not readily apparent to all participants.

UDP Bomb Attack
One of the intrusions into your network that ISA Server can detect. See Chapter 10 for details.

URL (Uniform Resource Locator)
A standard format for specifying an address to a Web page.

VPN (Virtual Private Network)
A connection that secures a remote link to a network and allows private information to travel safely over a public network, such as the Internet.

Web Filter
An extra component you can add to ISA Server that extends the capabilities of the Web Proxy service.

Web Proxy service
A service in ISA Server that processes requests for objects if they are using HTTP, HTTP-S, FTP, or Gopher protocols.

Web publishing
Providing Web pages to clients outside the internal network.

Windows Out-of-Band Attack
One of the intrusions into your network that ISA Server can detect. See Chapter 10 for details.

Winsock
Makes a connection between computers at the Session layer of the OSI model. Designed to work like the socket interface for use on Windows. Short for Windows sockets.

WMT (Windows Media Technology or Server)
A server component that allows a network to host multimedia transmissions.

WPAD (Web Proxy AutoDiscovery)
The name of an alias that needs to be created in a DNS server in support of the Automatic Discovery process. Used to support Web proxy clients.

WSPAD (Winsock Proxy AutoDiscovery)
The name of an alias that needs to be created in a DNS server in support of the Automatic Discovery process. Used to support Firewall clients.

Index

Bold page numbers indicate sample exam questions.

10BaseT, 452
100BaseT, 452
443, port, 249
80, port, 253, 401
8080, port, 113, 114, 253, 401, **522**

A

Acceleration
   and ISA Server, 2, 14
   relationship to caching, 205
Access policies. *See also* Policies.
   array-level, 158
   purpose of, 142, 421, **524, 529**
   and site and content rules, **513**
   troubleshooting, 421–422
ACK packets, 272
Active Cells folder, 299
Active Directory, 18, 30, 88
Active Terminals folder, 298
ActiveMovie, 306
Address mapping, 329
Address sets, client, 150–151, **514**
Administration Tools, 60, 61, 76
Alerts, configuring, 274–275, 368
All ports scan attack, 272
Anonymous user account, 180
Application Center 2000, 4
Application-layer protocols, 5, 6
Application-level connection, 14
Application usage reports, 431
Array
   advantages of using, 354–355, **511**
   allowing publishing rules in, 367
   assigning policies to, 366, 368 (*See also* Array policies)
   backing up/restoring, 364
   and bandwidth, 71, 355
   and cache size, 71, 355
   configuring cache for, 367
   configuring server-specific settings in, 367–368
   contrasted with chaining, 356–357
   contrasted with standalone ISA server, 33
   creating, 73–74, 360–362
   defined, 354
   deleting, 362
   and fault tolerance, 71, 355
   forcing packet filtering for, 367
   guidelines for creating, 356
   illustration of, 355
   installing ISA server in, 357–359, **511, 512**
   promoting standalone ISA server to, 74–75, 359–360
   purpose of, 32–33
   sharing of configuration information among ISA servers in, 355, **511**
   upgrading Proxy Server 2.0, 95–96
Array policies. *See also* Policies.
   combining with enterprise policies, 368
   configuring, 366–368, **523**
   contrasted with enterprise policies, 143, 364–365
   and multilocation networks, 164
   purpose of, 143
Asymmetric cryptography, 247, 253
Attachment rules, SMTP Filter, 335–336, 392–393
Authentication, 179–201
   clients supported by specific types of, 186, **524**
   combining rules and, 191
   and Firewall client, 18, 36, 131
   passing around requests for, 189–191
   pros and cons of using, 180, 185–186
   purpose of, 180
   setting up, 186–189, **524**
   troubleshooting, 422–423
   types of, 180–185
   and Web publishing rules, 326
Automatic Discovery feature, 128–130, 401–402

591

B

Back-to-back perimeter network, 496, 501, 502, **527**
Back Up utility, 167
Backup file
    for array configuration, 364
    for enterprise and array policy settings, 167
    for enterprise configuration, 364
    for Proxy Server 2.0 configuration, 89–90, 100
Bandwidth
    and arrays, 355, 369
    bottlenecks, 472–474
    and external connections, 472–476
    how traffic affects, 474–475
    and multimedia applications, 290, 306
    recent trends in, 472
    setting effective, 475–476
Bandwidth priorities, 161, **526**
Bandwidth rules
    creating, 162–163
    and ISA Server installation, 160–161
    order of application for, 163
    policy elements used in, 145
    purpose of, 142, 159
    and Quality of Service scheduling, 160
Base64 encoding, 181
Basic authentication, 180–181, 186, 326
basicdc.inf file, 267
basicsv.inf file, 267
.bef file, 364
.bif file, 167
BIOS, system, 37, 41, 42
BizTalk Server 2000, 4
Bongo Drum Company scenario, 488–493
Bottlenecks, bandwidth, 472–474
Bridging, SSL, 251–252, 326–328
Browsers. *See* Web browsers.
Bug fixes, 58–59

C

Cache. *See also* Caching.
    and arrays, 355, 356, 366, 369, **530**
    calculating disk space required for, 61–62, **527**
    chaining, 207, 214–216, 222
    filtering, 218
    scheduling download of, 213–214, **523**
    setting up, 66–67
    tuning and monitoring, 219–220, **533, 534**
    and Web Proxy service, 257
Cache Array Routing Protocol. *See* CARP.
Cache chaining, 207, 214–216, 222
Cache content download, scheduling, 213–214, **522**
Cache filtering, 218
Cache mode, 14, 31–32, 66
Cache report, TMF, 204
Caching. *See also* Cache.
    and chaining, 357
    defined, 17, 205
    diagram of process, 208
    hardware requirements for, 29–30
    how it works, 206–210
    purpose of, 221
    relationship to acceleration, 205
    troubleshooting, 423–424
    types of, 206–207
Call routing
    creating rules for, 301–303
    folder, 299
    specifying destination for, 299–300
CARP, 210–213
    benefits of using, 211, 221, **530**
    configuring, 211–213
    and distributed caching, 207
    meaning of acronym, 207
    purpose of, 207, 210–211
CERN
    and Web browsers, 244, 257
    and Web Proxy clients, 35, 114
Certificate authority, 184
Certificates
    clients that support, 186
    companies that make, 248
    and encryption keys, 248
    establishing identity with, 248–249
    installing, 184–185
    loading, 249
    purpose of, 184, 248
    and SSL, 184–185, 248
Certified Trainers, Microsoft, 420
Chained authentication, 190–191
Chaining
    cache, 207, 214–216, 222
    contrasted with array, 356–357
    defined, 356–357
    setting up, 362–363
    and sharing of configuration information among ISA servers, 357
Circuit-level connection, 13–14
Cisco
    Layer 2 Forwarding (L2F), 470
    router, 266

Clean installation, 31
Client address sets, 150–151, **514**
Client requests, services for handling, 112
Clients
   choosing, 36, 118–119, 130–131
   combining, 118
   reconfiguring after upgrading from Proxy Server
     to ISA Server, 97–98
   setting up, 119–130
   types supported by ISA Server, 34, 98, 112
     See also specific types.
   types supported by Proxy Server 2.0, 97–98
Clients To ISA Server VPN Wizard, 464–465,
   469–470, **525**
Cluster Server, 396–399
Commerce Server 2000, 4
Conferencing software, 291. *See also* NetMeeting.
Connections. *See also* Internet connections.
   application-level, 14
   and bandwidth, 472–476
   circuit-level, 13–14
   setting up, 452–471
   troubleshooting, 418–419, 424–426, **533**
   types controlled by ISA Server, 9–10
Content filtering, 334, 336–337. *See also* SMTP Filter.
Content group, 149
convert command, 30
Counters, performance, 220
Credentials, for report jobs, 433
Cryptography, 247, 253
Custom installation, Enterprise Edition, 59–60

D

Daily reports, 430, **520**, **532**
DDNS, 37
Dedicated security option, 267, **527**
Default rule, 339
Demilitarized Zone, 337, 495
Denial of Service attack, 267, 272
Destination sets, 147–148, 218, 323–324
Destinations, call routing, 299–300
DHCP server
   configuring, 129–130
   purpose of, 35
   recommended book on, 35
   and SecureNat clients, 35
   and TCP/IP configurations, 37
Dial-up connection. *See also* DUN.
   hardware required for, 37
   ISDN adapter settings, 39
   modem settings, 39
   troubleshooting, 425–426
   and VPN, 452, 453–458
Dial-up entries
   contrasted with DUN phonebook entries, 455
   creating in ISA Server, 455–457
   setting active, 457–458
Dial-up Networking. *See* DUN.
Digest authentication, 182, 186, 326
Digital envelope, 247
Digital hashing, 182
Digital signature, 247
Direct connection
   configuring, 458–461
   hardware required for, 37
Directory browsing, 326
Directory name, in URL, 7
Disk Failures counter, 220
Disk space
   for cache, 61–62
   for different installation types, 61
Disk URL Retrieve Rate counter, 220
Distributed caching, 207
Distributed proxying, 355
DMZ, 337, 495
DNS
   and computer names, 126
   configuring server, 128–129, 395–396
   and host headers, 325
   and IP address translation, 7
   recommended book on, 35
   round-robin, 355, 357, 400–401, **518**
   SRV record, 304–305, **528**
Domain controller templates, 267
Domain filters, 97, 98
Domain Name System. *See* DNS.
DoS attack, 267, 272
Downstream server, 356–357, 362
DUN
   configuring phonebook entry using, 453–454
   and dial-up access, 455
   purpose of, 453
Dynamic Domain Name Server, 37
Dynamic Host Configuration Protocol server.
   See DHCP server.

E

Effective Bandwidth setting, 475–476
Elements
   policy, 145, 165
   rule, 142
Email filter. *See* SMTP Filter.

Email server. *See* Mail server.
Encoding, 181
Encryption, 181, 247–249, 253, 465
Enterprise Admins group, 40, 360, **512, 523**
Enterprise Edition
   backing up/restoring configurations, 364
   and caching, 66–67
   contrasted with Standard Edition, 56
   installation modes, 65–66
   installation types, 59–62
   installing, 59–69
   and LAT, 67–69
   number of CPUs supported by, 56
   standalone *vs.* array, 62–65
Enterprise Initialization program, 40, **512**
Enterprise policies. *See also* Policies.
   applying to selected arrays, 366
   assigning default, 365
   combining with array policies, 368
   configuring, 365–366
   contrasted with array policies, 143, 364–365
   creating, 166
   and multilocation networks, 164
   purpose of, 143
   software requirements for, 144
   updating settings for, 360
Enumerated port scan attack, 272
Envelope, digital, 247
Ethernet network, 37
Event Viewer, 413–418
Exam Cram/Prep publications, 420
Exchange Server
   as component of .NET platform, 4
   and ISA Server, 387–388, 396
   and Proxy Server 2.0, 387–388
   and RPCs, 394–395
Extensibility, ISA Server, 18

F

Fault tolerance, 214, 355, 357, 369, 397, **518**
File Transfer Protocol. *See* FTP.
Filename, in URL, 8
Filters. *See also* Packet filters.
   cache, 218
   domain, 97, 98
   H.323 Protocol, 295–296
   HTTP Redirector, 244–245, 255–257
   message, 331, 334 (*See also* SMTP Filter)
   packet, 337–339, 367, 368
   relationship to rules, 97

   Socks V4, 117–118
   Streaming Media, 306–308
Firewall
   and application-level connection, 14
   contrasted with proxy server, 12–13
   defined, 10
   hardware requirements, 29
   how it works, 10
   ISA Server as, 15–17
Firewall client
   and Active Directory, 18
   and AutoDiscovery of settings, 128–130
   combining with other clients, 118–119
   configuring files, 123–126
   contrasted with Web Proxy client, 115
   defined, 18
   features supported by, 34–36
   installing, 122–123
   and LAT, 114–115
   operating systems that support, 115
   removing, 123
   and user authentication, 18, 36
   and Winsock applications, 114–115
Firewall mode, 14, 31, 66, **527**
Firewall service
   log, 432
   purpose of, 112
Forward caching, 206
FQDN, 460
FTP
   access policies, **529**
   as application-level protocol, 7
   and server publishing rules, **531**
   and Web Proxy clients, 113
   and Web Proxy service, 244, **512**
Full installation, Enterprise Edition, 59–60
Fully Qualified Domain Name, 460

G

Gatekeepers, 291, 292, 298. *See also* H.323 Gatekeeper service.
Gateways, 291, 292, 293
Getting Started Wizard, 17, 69
Global policies, 360
Gopher, 113, 244

H

H.323-compliant applications, 292–293
H.323 Gatekeeper service, 291–305
   adding server to, 298

and address translation, 293
components of, 291–292
configuring, 303–305
control functions, 294
installing, 297–298
and ITU standards, 291
and NetMeeting software, 17, 291
and permissions, 304, **528**
property pages, 303–304
purpose of, 291
settings, 295–297, 298–305
SRV resource record, 304–305, **528**
troubleshooting connection problems with, 299
H.323 Protocol Definition, 296–297
H.323 Protocol Filter, 295–296
H.323 Protocol Rule, 296–297
Hackers, 17, 18, 272. *See also* Intrusion detection.
Hard disk space. *See* Disk space.
Hardware Compatibility List, Windows 2000, 28
Hardware requirements, ISA Server, 28–30, 36–37, **511**
Hashing, 182
HCL, Windows 2000, 28
Help manuals, Windows 2000/ISA Server, 420
Hierarchical caching, 207, **530**
Hierarchical proxying, 357, 369
hisecdc.inf file, 267
hisecws.inf file, 267
Host headers, 325–326
Host Integration Server 2000, 4
Hot fixes, 58–59
HTTP
  as application-level protocol, 6, 7
  and Web Proxy client, 113
  and Web Proxy service, 243, **512**
  and Web publishing rules, **531**
HTTP Basic authentication, 181
HTTP Redirector Filter, 244–245, 255–257
HTTP-S
  and SSL, 250
  and Web Proxy client, 113
  and Web Proxy service, 243, **512**
Hypertext Transfer Protocol. *See* HTTP.

I

ICMP, 270, 271
ICS, 425
IIS Server, 7, 391
IMAP4, 332, 388, 389
Inbound connections, protecting network from, 10, 15–17. *See also* Firewall, Intrusion detection.

inetinfo process, 98
Installation
  clean install *vs.* upgrade, 31
  of Enterprise Edition, 59–69
  gathering information for, 57–59
  hardware requirements, 28–30, 61–62
  of ISA server for small network, 490–493
  of ISA server in array, 357–359, **511**
  modes, 14, 31–32, 65–66, **522**
    (*See also* specific modes)
  options, 59–62
  software requirements, 15, 30, 37–42
  of Standard Edition, 75
  types, 59–62
  unattended, 69–72, 76
Installation Wizard, 92–95
Integrated mode, 6, 14, 31, **522, 533**
Integrated Services Digital Network. *See* ISDN.
Integrated Windows authentication, 183–184, 186
Internet
  security considerations, 2, 9–10, 88, 163–164, 253
  as vehicle for integrating variety of devices, 3–4
Internet Connection Sharing, 425
Internet connections
  and bandwidth, 472–474
  direct *vs.* dial-up, 39, 204–205, 452, 458–461
  and multimedia applications, 290–291
  and OSI model, 4–5, 13–14
  ports and sockets, 8–9
  TCP/IP protocols, 6
  troubleshooting, 418–419, 424–426, **516**
  types controlled by ISA Server, 9–10
Internet Control Message Protocol. *See* ICMP.
Internet Explorer
  authentication types supported by, 186
  troubleshooting, 418–419
Internet Messaging Access Protocol 4. *See* IMAP4.
Internet Security and Acceleration Server 2000. *See* ISA Server.
Internet security servers. *See also* ISA Server.
  background on Microsoft's, 2–3, 18
  packaging of firewall and proxy services in, 18
  purpose of, 18
Internet Security Systems, 271
Internet Services Manager, 98, 99
Internetwork layer, TCP/IP, 5
Intrusion detection
  configuring, 273–274, **526**
  contrasted with alerts, 274
  and ISS, 271
  types of events handled by, 271–274

IP addresses
    as component of URL, 7
    grouping with client address sets, 150–151, **514**
    private ranges, 40
    purpose of, 7, 8
    spoofing, 272
IP half scan attack, 272
IP protocol, 6
IP Security. *See* IPSec.
ipconfig/all command, 38
IPSec, 465, 469, 471
IPX/SPX protocol, 15, 88
ISA Administration Tools. *See* Administration Tools.
ISA Management
    as administrative console for ISA Server, 98–99
    and client address sets, **514**
    creating/deleting arrays in, 360–362
    and Mail Server Security Wizard, 388
    purpose of, 98
    and server security, **521**
    software requirements, 30
ISA Server
    administration/management of, 15, 30, 98–99
    client software, 33–36, 98
    as component of .NET platform, 4
    deploying more than one, 32–33
    and Exchange Server, 387–388, 396
    extensibility of, 18
    as firewall, 15–17
    hardware requirements, 28–30, 36–37, **511**
    installing (*See* Installation)
    integrating with other services, 386–403, 463–465
    and Internet protocols, 6, 15, 270
    and Microsoft Cluster Server, 396–399
    new features, 14–15
    and NLB, 396–401
    Online Help manuals, 420
    performance-enhancing services, 14
    performance report/information, 204, 220, **533**
    promoting standalone to array, 74–75, 354, 359–360
        (*See also* Array)
    as proxy server, 17–18
    purpose of, 2
    reconfiguring after upgrade from Proxy Server, 96–98
    reporting features, 427–435, **532**
    SDK, 18
    security considerations, 269–273, **521**
    software requirements, 15, 30, 37–42, **511**
    and Terminal Services, 401
    troubleshooting, 412–413, 421–427
    tuning and monitoring, 219–220
    types of connections controlled by, 9–10
    uninstalling, 75, 99–100
    upgrading from Proxy Server 2.0, 31, 88–101, **517**
    versions, 56 (*See also* Enterprise Edition, Standard Edition)
    and VPN, 463–465
    and Web servers, 401–402
    and Windows operating system, 4–5, 15
ISA server array. *See* Array.
ISA Server Control service, 245
ISA Server mode, 65–66
ISA Server Release Candidate 1. *See* RC1.
ISA Server schema, 40
ISA Server Security Configuration Wizard, 266–269
ISAAutorun.exe, 57
ISDN, 39, 453
ISS, 271

K

KDC, 183–184
Kerberos protocol, 183–184
Key Distribution Center, 183–184
Keys, encryption, 247, 248–249, 253
Keywords property page, SMTP Filter, 394
Knowledge Base, Microsoft, 420

L

Land attack, 272
LAT
    adding IP addresses to, 40, 68, 96–97, **516**, **524**, **525**
    and CARP, 213
    configuring for perimeter network, 502, **526**, **530**
    constructing, 67–69
    and Firewall mode, 66
    and Proxy-Server-to-ISA-Server upgrades, 89, 96–97
    and publishing, 321–322
    purpose of, 67
    and Windows 2000 Routing Table, 39–40
Layer 2 Forwarding, 470
Layer 2 Tunneling Protocol. *See* L2TP.
Layers, OSI *vs.* TCP/IP model, 5
LDT, 126, 460
L2F, 470
Limited Services security option, 266, 267, **521**
Listeners, 186, 189, 254–255, 322–323, 368
Load balancing, 354, 357, 369, 396–401, **518**.
    See also NLB.

Local Address Table. *See* LAT.
Local Domain Table. *See* LDT.
Local ISA VPN Wizard, 464–468, 497
Log file
  illustration of, 268
  purpose of, 268, 426, 432
  resolving problems with, 426–427
L2TP, 465, 469, 470–471

M

MAC address, 38
Mail server
  complexity of setting up, 331, 387
  protocols, 332
  publishing, 331–337, **519, 532**
Mail Server Security Wizard, 331, 332, 334, 387–389, 396, **519**
Mail Wizard rules, 332, 389
mailalrt service, 91
Mail2You scenarios, 493–505
MAPI, 332, 389
Mapping, address, 329
MarketDirect scenarios, 493–505
MCTs, 420
MCUs, 291–292, 293
Measurement Factory, The, 204
Media
  contrasted with multimedia, 290–291
  protocol definitions, 307
  streaming, 306
Memory Bytes Retrieved counter, 220
Memory requirements, ISA Server, 29, **511**
Memory Usage Ratio Percent counter, 220
Message digest, 182
Message Screener, 333–334, 390
Messaging Application Programming Interface. *See* MAPI.
Microsoft
  and development of Internet security servers, 2–3
  and .NET platform, 3–4
  troubleshooting resources, 420
Microsoft Certified Trainers, 420
Microsoft Cluster Server, 396–399
Microsoft Internet Explorer. *See* Internet Explorer.
Microsoft Internet Information Server. *See* IIS Server.
Microsoft ISA Server Control service, 245
Microsoft Knowledge Base, 420
Microsoft Management Console. *See* MMC.
Microsoft Point-to-Point Encryption, 465
Microsoft Proxy Server. *See* Proxy Server 2.0.

Microsoft Proxy Server Administration service, 91
Microsoft TechNet, 420
Microsoft Terminal Services. *See* Terminal Services.
Microsoft Windows 2000 Server Administrator's Companion, 268
Microsoft WinSock Proxy Service, 91
MIME, 149–150, 181
MMC, 15, 98, **514**
Mobile Information Server 2000, 4
Modem configuration, 39
Modes, installation, 14, 31–32, 65–66, **522**.
  See also specific modes.
Monthly reports, 430
.mpc file, 89
MPPE, 465
msiaund.ini file, 69, 72
\MSP folder, 89, 90
mspadmin service, 91
MspcInt.ini file, 124–126
Msplat.txt file, 124
Multimedia
  bandwidth considerations, 290
  compatibility considerations, 290
  contrasted with media, 290
  H.323-compliant applications, 292–293
  and H.323 Gatekeeper Service, 291
Multipoint Control Units. *See* MCUs.
Multipurpose Internet Media Extension. *See* MIME.

N

NAT server, 116
.NET platform
  Microsoft's goal for, 3–4
  products included in, 4
NetMeeting, 17, 291, **528**
Netscape Navigator, authentication types supported by, 186
NetShow, 306
Network. *See also* VPN.
  configuring intrusion detection for, 273–274, **526**
  documenting, 270
  formulating policies for, 163–164
  load balancing, 354, 357, 369, **518**
  security considerations, 269–273
  types of intrusions to, 271–273
  upgrading, 500–505
Network Address Translation server, 116
Network installation point, setting up, 57–58
Network Interface Cards. *See* NICs.
Network layer, OSI model, 5

Network Load Balancing. *See* NLB.
Network News Transfer Protocol. *See* NNTP.
New Alert Wizard, 274–275
New Array Wizard, 361–362
New Bandwidth Rule Wizard, 161, 162
New Destination Wizard, 299–300
New Protocol Rule Wizard, 155, 296
New Routing Rule Wizard, 301
New Server Publishing Rule Wizard, 329, 330
New Site And Content Rule Wizard, 150–151, 155–158
New Web Publishing Rule Wizard, 327
Newsgroups, 420
NICs
   configuring, 38
   recommended number of, 37
   types of connections used by, 452
NLB, 396–401
   alternative to, 400–401
   as component of Microsoft Cluster Server, 396–397
   configuring for use with ISA Server, 399–400
   and fault tolerance, 397, **518**
   installing, 398–399
   setup requirements for, 397
NNTP, 7, 332, 389
NNTP-S, 332, 389
NT File System volumes. *See* NTFS volumes.
NT LAN Manager. *See* NTLM.
NTFS volumes, 29, 66–67
NTLM, 183, 186

O

Online Help manuals, Windows 2000/ISA Server, 420
Operating system requirements
   Firewall client, 18
   ISA Server, 15, 30, **517**
OSI model
   connection types, 13–14
   layers, 5
   and L2TP, 470
   purpose of, 4–5
Outbound connections, protecting network from, 10, 17–18. *See also* Proxy server.

P

Packet filter log, 432
Packet filters
   for arrays, 367, 368
   contrasted with domain filters, 97
   contrasted with publishing rules, 337–338
   creating, 338–339
   enabling, 338
   ISA Server *vs.* Proxy Server implementation of, 158–159, 338
   order of application for, 165
   purpose of, 142, 159
Packet-level connection, 13
Packets, accepting unnecessary, 270
Pass-through authentication, 190
PBX-style routing, 299
PBX system, 299
Performance counters, 220
Performance Monitor, Windows NT, 220
Performance report, TMF, 204
Perimeter network, 337–338, 495, 496, **531**
Permissions, H.323 Gatekeeper service, 304, **528**
Persistent connection, 476
Phonebook entry, configuring, 453–454
Physical security, 269–270
PING command, 38–39, 271, 418, **516**
Ping-of-death attack, 271
Point-to-Point Tunneling Protocol. *See* PPTP.
Policies. *See also* Array policies, Enterprise policies, Rules.
   backing up and restoring settings for, 167
   creating, 166
   defined, 143
   determining need for, 144
   enterprise *vs.* array, 143
   and ISA Server installation, 63, 64–65
   planning for network, 163–164
   purpose of, 142, 143
   shared usage, 355, **511**
   updating settings for, 360
Policy elements, 145, 151, 165
POP3, 332, 388, 389
Port 80, 253, 401
Port 443, 249
Port 8080, 113, 114, 253, 401, **522**
Port numbers
   avoiding conflicts among, 401
   and sockets, 8–9
   in URL, 7
   well-known/reserved, 9
Port Scan options, ISA Management, 273
Post Office Protocol 3. *See* POP3.
PPTP, 465, 469, 470, 471, **525**
Private Branch Exchange, 299

Progressive Networks Protocol, 307
Protocol definitions
    creating, 146–147, **529**
    H.323, 296–297
    and ISA Server installation, 145–146
    predefined, 146
    for Streaming Media Filter, 307
Protocol rules
    creating, 153–155, 296–297, **515**
    order of application for, 154–155, 165
    policy elements used in, 145
    purpose of, 142, 153
Protocols, 5–6, 7, 113. *See also* specific protocols.
Proxy Alert Notification Service, 91
Proxy client, 17
Proxy server. *See also* Proxy Server 2.0.
    and application-level connections, 14
    and circuit-level connections, 13–14
    client software, 17–18
    distinguishing from firewall, 12–13
    how it works, 10–12
    ISA Server as, 17–18
    purpose of, 3
    services provided by, 17–18
Proxy Server 2.0
    backing up configuration settings, 89–90, 100
    client software supported by, 97–98, 116–117
    earlier version, 2
    and Exchange Server, 387–388
    integration with other Microsoft products, 2–3, 18
    and IPX/SPX, 15, 88
    stopping services used by, 90–92
    upgrading array, 95–96
    upgrading from Proxy Server 1.0 to, 90
    upgrading to ISA Server from, 31, 88–101, **517**
    and Windows 2000, 95
    and Windows NT 4, 90–95
Proxy services, 10. *See also* Proxy server,
    Web Proxy service.
Public-key cryptography, 247, 253
Publishing
    defined, 10, 320
    and LAT, 321–322
    policies, 320–322
    rules, 320–321, 367 (*See also* Server publishing rules, Web publishing rules)
    security considerations, 320, 326
    using packet filters when, 337–339

Q

Q931 protocol, 305
QoS, 160
Quality of Service Scheduling service, 160
QuickTime, 306, 307

R

RAS protocol, 292–293, 294–295, 298
RC1, 354, 359
RDP, 401
Real Time Streaming Protocol, 307
RealPlayer, 306, 307
Reboot, impact on applications, 413–414
Redirection, 325, 326, **517**
Redirector Filter, HTTP, 244–245, 255–257
Registration, Admission, and Status protocol.
    See RAS protocol.
Release Candidate 1. *See* RC1.
Remote clients, 452–453
Remote connections, 452–453, 493–494
Remote Desktop Protocol, 401
Remote ISA VPN Wizard, 464–465, 468–469, 499
Remote Procedure Call. *See* RPC Filter.
Reports, 427–435. *See also* specific reports.
    configuring, 432
    creating, 428–431
    deleting, 434–435
    saving as Web pages, 434
    scheduling, 429, 430, 432, **520**
    sorting data in, 435
    specifying location of, 434
    specifying user credentials for, 433
    viewing predefined, 431–432
Restore utility, 167
Restoring
    array configuration, 364
    enterprise configuration, 364
    policy settings, 167
Reverse caching, 206, 207, 328
Reverse proxy
    contrasted with firewall and regular proxy, 12, 323
    defined, 10
    purpose of, 320, 323
RJ-45 connection, 452
Roaming charges, 462, 476
Round-robin DNS, 355, 357, 400–401, **518**
Router, 12–13, 266

Routing
    PBX-style, 299
    Web Proxy, 216–218
Routing And Remote Access Service. *See* RRAS.
Routing protocol, 207. *See also* CARP.
Routing rules, 165, 217
Routing table, 39–40, **516**
RPC Filter, 387, 394–395
RRAS, 452, 453–454, 454, 463, **529**
RSA, 248
Rule Action, Web publishing, 324–325
Rules. *See also* Policies, specific types of rules.
    application of, 144–145
    combining authentication and, 191
    creating, 153–154, 155–158, 162–163, 166
    defined, 142
    deleting or disabling, 163
    and ISA Server installation, 63, 64
    list of, 142
    order of application for, 154–155, 163, 165
    policy elements used in, 145
    relationship to filters, 97
    specifying schedules for, 151–152
    testing, 165

S

Scenarios
    network that has outgrown settings, 500–505
    network with remote locations, 493–500
    small network, 488–493
Scheduled caching, 206–207, 213–214, **522**
Scheduled Content Download, 213–214, **521**
Schedules
    for cache content download, 213–214, **522**
    for policy elements/rules, 152–153
    for reports, 429, 430, 432, **520, 532**
Schema Admins group, 40, **512**
Schema installation, ISA Server, 40
Screened subnet, 337–338
SDK, 18
Secure Hypertext Transport Protocol. *See* HTTP-S.
Secure Network Address Translation.
    See SecureNAT client.
Secure Network News Transfer Protocol. *See* NNTP-S.
Secure Sockets Layer. *See* SSL.
securedc.inf file, 267
SecureNAT client
    combining with other clients, 118–119
    contrasted with Firewall client, 116

features supported by, 34–36, **514**
and ISA Server installation, 29
and Network Address Translation, 116
purpose of, 17–18
and server publishing, 330, **532**
setting up, 126–127, 499–500
securews.inf file, 267
Security breaches, 271–273. *See also* Intrusion detection.
Security component, ISA Server, 2, 14, 88
Security Configuration Wizard, 266–269
Security levels, Windows 2000, 266–267, 267
Security reports, 432
Security servers. *See* Internet security servers.
Security templates, 267–268
securwiz.log file, 268
Server publishing rules, 328–337
    and address mapping, 329
    and arrays, 367, 368
    client types, 330
    configuring, 340
    contrasted with Web publishing rules, 320–321, 328–329
    and FTP, **531**
    and mail servers, 331, **519**
    mode requirements for, 321
    protocol settings, 330
Server templates, 267
Servers, .NET platform, 4
Service Pack 1
    checking for installation of, 30
    downloading, 30
    error message, 58
    and ISA Server installation, 30, **511**
    and security updates, 270
Service Pack 2, 270
Services. *See also* specific services.
    combining, 488
    stopping, 90–92
Session key, 183–184
Set Up Clients To ISA Server VPN Wizard, 464–465, 469–470, **525**
Setup Wizard, 57
Shared usage policies, 355, **511**
Signature, digital, 247
Simple Mail Transport Protocol, 331.
    See also SMTP Filter.
Site and content rules
    application of, 155, 165
    creating, 156–159, **513, 522**
    default settings for, 158

policy elements used in, 145
purpose of, 142, 155, **513**
SMTP Commands property page, SMTP Filter, 394
SMTP Filter
complexity of, 332–333
configuring ISA Server and other applications for, 333–334, 390–392
configuring property pages for, 335–337, 392–394
enabling, 333, 389–390
purpose of, 331, 389
SMTPCred.exe tool, 390
Sockets, 8–9, 115, 127
Socks Proxy client
and Proxy Server 2.0, 116–117
purpose of, 34, 97–98
setting up, 127–128
and Socks V4 Filter, 117–118
Socks V4 Filter, 117–118
Software Development Kit, 18
Software requirements, ISA Server, 15, 30, 37–42, **511**
Software updates, 58–59
SP1. *See* Service Pack 1.
Spoofing, 272
SQL Server 2000, 4
SRV record, 304–305, **528**
SSL
and certificates, 184–185, 248
components of, 247–250
and performance, 253
port number for Web pages using, 249
protocol used by, 249–250
and public-key cryptography, 247
setting up secure channel with, 250–252
and Web Proxy service, 246
SSL bridging, 251–252, 326–328
SSL listeners, 255. *See also* Listeners.
SSL tunneling, 250, 251, 326
Standalone ISA server
contrasted with array, 32–33, 62
and policies, 164
promoting to array, 74–75, 354, 359–360
Standard Edition
contrasted with Enterprise Edition, 56
installing, 75
number of CPUs supported by, 56
Stopping services, 90–92
Streaming media
applications, 306
and bandwidth, 306
and ISA Server, 307, **524**

Streaming Media Filter
applications used with, 306
configuring, 308
protocol definitions used with, 307
and WMT server, 306
Summary reports, 431
SYN packet, 272
System BIOS, 37, 41, 42
System Monitor, Windows 2000, 220
systemroot folder, 267

T

T.120 protocol, 295–296
T1/T3 connection, Internet, 39, 204–205
Taskpad, 15, 16
TCP/IP
layers, 5
ports and sockets, 8–9
protocols and services included in, 6
software configuration, 37–42
TechNet, Microsoft, 420
Templates
domain controller, 267
security, 267–268
server, 267
Terminal Services, 30, 401
Terminals, H.323, 291–292, 293, 294
Three-homed perimeter network, 495, 496, **531**
Time to Live counter, 209
TMF cache report, 204
Token Ring network, 37
Total Disk Failures counter, 220
Total Memory Bytes Retrieved counter, 220
Total URLs Cached counter, 220
Traffic reports, 432
Trainers, Microsoft Certified, 420
Training classes, 420
Transparent proxy, 12
Transport-layer protocols, 5, 6
Troubleshooting, 412–435
access-policy issues, 421–422
authentication issues, 422–423
caching issues, 423–424
connection problems, 299, 418–419, 424–426, **516, 533**
general guidelines for, 412–413
H.323 Gatekeeper service, 299
ISA Server, 421–427
logging issues, 426–427

resources, 419–420
services issues, 427
Web Proxy service, 418–419
Windows 2000, 413–419
TTL counter, 209
Tunneling, SSL, 250, 251, 326
Typical installation, Enterprise Edition, 59–60

U

UDP bomb attack, 271–272
UDP protocol, 6
Unattended installation, 69–72, 76
Uniform Resource Locator. *See* URL.
Updates, software, 58–59
Upgrade, Proxy Server 2.0 to ISA Server, 88–101
    advantages of, 88
    contrasted with clean install, 31
    preparing for, 88–90
    Windows considerations, 90, 95
Upstream server, 356–357, 362, 363, **523, 524**
URL
    finding Web page using, 8
    parts of, 6–8
    purpose of, 6
URLs Cached counter, 220
User authentication. *See* Authentication.
User groups, 420
Users/Domains property page, SMTP Filter, 393
Utilization reports, 432

V

VeriSign, 248
Videoconferencing, 292
Virtual private network. *See* VPN.
.vpc file, 466, 468
VPN, 462–471
    advantages of using, 462–463
    configuring ISA Server for, 466–471, 497–499, **515, 525**
    illustrations of, 463
    integrating with ISA Server, 463–465, **533**
    modifying settings for, 470–471
    and roaming users, 462–463
    wizards, 464–471, 476, **525**

W

WAN, 62–63, 290, 307, 472
Web browsers
    authentication types supported by, 186
    CERN-compliant, 244
    configuring, 35
    troubleshooting Internet Explorer, 418–419
Web page
    accessing through Web Proxy service, 246–250
    caching, 17
    effect of ISA Server on secure, 250–252
    saving report as, 434
    using URL to find, 8
Web Proxy AutoDiscovery, 128–129
Web Proxy client
    and AutoDiscovery of settings, 128–130
    and cache, 113–114
    and CERN, 35, 114
    configuring for direct access to external computers, 461, **514, 524**
    features supported by, 34
    planning and deploying, 113–114
    port used by, 113, 114
    setting up, 119–122, **512**
Web Proxy routing, 216–218
Web Proxy service
    accessing secured Web pages through, 246–250
    cache settings, 257
    and CERN, 244, 257
    clients for, 244–245
    configuring, 253–257, 258
    connection settings, 256–257
    extensions to, 246
    how it works, 245–246
    port settings for, 253
    protocols used by, 243–244, 257
    purpose of, 112, 242
    requests handled by, 113–114, 242, 257
    and SSL, 246, 258
    troubleshooting, 418–419
Web Proxy service log, 432
Web publishing rules
    changing port setting in, 325
    client types, 324

configuring, 339–340, **520**
contrasted with server publishing rules, 320–321, 328–329, **531**
destination sets for, 323–324
function of rule action in, 324–325
mode requirements for, 321
relationship to reverse proxying, 323
and reverse caching, 328
security considerations, 326
and SSL bridging, 327
Web server, integrating ISA Server with, 401–402, **532**
Web usage reports, 431, **532, 533**
Weekend schedules, for policy elements/rules, 151–152
Weekly reports, 430, **533**
Wide Area Network. *See* WAN.
Windows 2000
  Active Directory, 18, 30, 88
  Advanced Server, 30
  Data Center Server, 30
  Hardware Compatibility List (HCL), 28
  and .NET platform servers, 4
  Online Help manuals, 420
  and Proxy Server 2.0, 95
  routing table, 39–40
  security levels, 266–267
  Server, 15, 30
  System Monitor, 220
  Terminal Services, 30, 401
  troubleshooting, 413–419
  upgrading from Windows NT 4 to, 90–92
Windows 2000 Service Pack 1
  checking for installation of, 30
  downloading, 30
  error message, 58
  and ISA Server installation, 30, **511**
  and security updates, 270
Windows 2000 Service Pack 2, 270
Windows Internet Naming Service, 488
Windows Media Player, 306
Windows Media Server, 306–307
Windows Media Technologies, 306
Windows NT
  Performance Monitor, 220
  running Proxy Server 2.0 on, 90
  upgrading to Windows 2000, 90–92

Windows out-of-band attack, 272–273
Windows Sockets, 114–115
WINS server, 488
Winsock, 98, 114–115
Winsock Proxy, 33, 97
Wizards
  Getting Started, 17, 69
  Installation, 92–95
  ISA Server Security Configuration, 266–269
  Local ISA VPN, 464–468, 497
  Mail Server Security, 331, 332, 334, 387–389, 396, **519**
  New Alert, 274–275
  New Array, 361–362
  New Bandwidth Rule, 161, 162
  New Destination, 299–300
  New Protocol Rule, 155, 296
  New Routing Rule, 301
  New Server Publishing Rule, 329, 330
  New Site And Content Rule, 150–151, 155–158
  New Web Publishing Rule, 327
  Remote ISA VPN, 464–465, 468–469, 499
  Security Configuration, 266–269
  Set Up Clients To ISA Server VPN, 464–465, 469–470, **525**
  Setup, 57
WMT server, 306–307
Work Hours schedules, for policy elements/rules, 151–152, **513**
World Wide Web Publishing service, 91. *See also* Publishing.
WPAD, 128–129
wspcfg.ini file, 388
wspsrv service, 91
w3svc service, 91

Y

Yearly reports, 430

Coriolis introduces

EXAM CRAM INSIDER™

A FREE ONLINE NEWSLETTER

Stay current with the latest certification information. Just visit **ExamCram.com** and sign up to receive the latest in certification and training news for Microsoft, Java, Novell, A+, and more! Read e-letters from the Publisher of the Exam Cram and Exam Prep series, Keith Weiskamp, and certification experts about future trends in IT training and education. Access valuable insider information on exam updates, new testing procedures, sample chapters, and links to other useful, online sites. Take a look at the featured program of the month, and who's in the news today. We pack all this and more into our *Exam Cram Insider* online newsletter to make sure *you* pass your next test!

To sign up for our twice monthly newsletter, go to **www.ExamCram.com** and click on "Become a Member" and sign up.

EXAM CRAM INSIDER – Another reason Exam Cram and Exam Prep guides are *The Smartest Way To Get Certified*.™ And it's free!

CORIOLIS™
Certification Insider Press

ExamCram.com

The leading resource for IT certification!

This groundbreaking, e-learning Web destination for test preparation and training incorporates an innovative suite of personalized training technologies to help you pass your exams. Besides providing test preparation resources and an array of training products and services, **ExamCram.com** brings together an extensive community of professionals and students who can collaborate online.

ExamCram.com is designed with one overriding philosophy in mind—great access!

Review industry news, study tips, questions and answers, training courses and materials, mentor programs, discussion groups, real-world practice questions, and more.

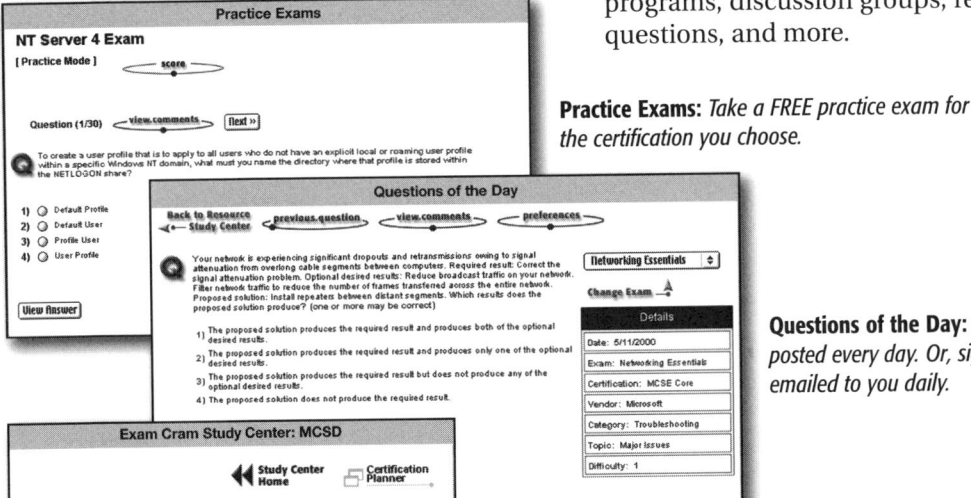

Practice Exams: *Take a FREE practice exam for the certification you choose.*

Questions of the Day: *Study questions are posted every day. Or, sign up to have them emailed to you daily.*

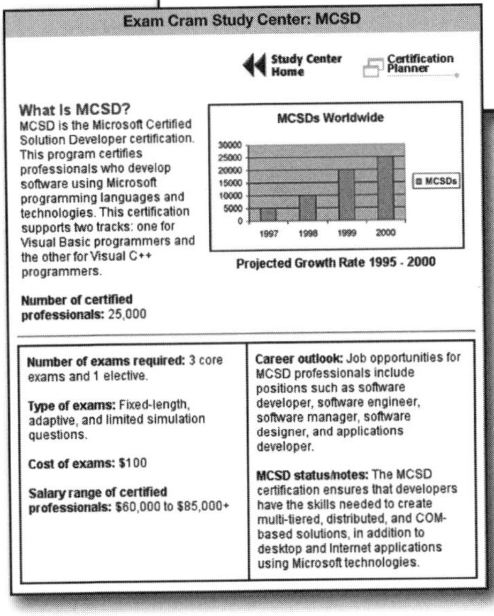

Exam Cram Study Center: *Get the facts on an exam, review study resources, read study tips, and more.*

OTHER HIGHLIGHTS:

Ask the Mentors: Ask questions and search the archives for answers.

Certification Planner: Discover the variety of certification programs offered.

Open Forum: Post your thoughts on weekly topics and see what others think.

Certification Resource Centers: Quickly find out about the newest certification programs.

Join the thousands who have already discovered ExamCram.com. Visit ExamCram.com today!

CORIOLIS
Certification Insider Press

The Smartest Way to Get Certified

What's on the CD-ROM

What's on the CD-ROM

The *MCSE ISA Server 2000 Exam Prep*'s companion CD-ROM contains the testing system for the book, which includes 50 questions. Additional questions are available for free download from **ExamCram.com**; after registering, simply click on the Update button in the testing engine. You can choose from numerous testing formats, including Fixed-Length, Random, Test All, and Review.

Note: the following software (not included on this CD) is required to complete the Real-World Projects:

- Microsoft ISA Server Enterprise Edition
- Microsoft ISA Server Standard Edition
- Microsoft Proxy Server 2.0
- Microsoft Windows 2000 Server
- Microsoft Windows 2000 Server Service Pack (Latest version)
- Microsoft Windows 2000 Professional

System Requirements

Software

- Your operating system must be Windows 98, NT 4, Windows ME, or Windows 2000.
- To view the practice exams, you need Internet Explorer 5.x.

Hardware

- An Intel Pentium, AMD, or comparable 100MHz processor or higher is recommended for best results.
- 32MB of RAM is the minimum memory requirement.
- Available disk storage space of at least 10MB is recommended.

Software developed by Dreamtech Software, India